Classes and Cultures

ENGLAND 1918–1951

Classes and Cultures

ENGLAND 1918–1951

Ross McKibbin

OXFORD
UNIVERSITY PRESS

OXFORD
UNIVERSITY PRESS

Great Clarendon Street, Oxford OX2 6DP

Oxford University Press is a department of the University of Oxford.
It furthers the University's objective of excellence in research, scholarship,
and education by publishing worldwide in

Oxford New York

Auckland Bangkok Buenos Aires Cape Town Chennai
Dar es Salaam Delhi Hong Kong Istanbul Karachi Kolkata
Kuala Lumpur Madrid Melbourne Mexico City Mumbai Nairobi
São Paulo Shanghai Taipei Tokyo Toronto

Oxford is a registered trade mark of Oxford University Press
in the UK and in certain other countries

Published in the United States
by Oxford University Press Inc., New York

First published 1998
Paperback first published 2000

British Library Cataloguing in Publication Data

Data available

Library of Congress Cataloging in Publication Data

McKibbin, Ross.
Classes and cultures: England, 1918–1951: a study of a
democratic society / Ross McKibbin.
p. cm.
Includes bibliographical references.
1. Social classes—England—History—20th century.
2. Social structure—England—History—20th century.
3. Class consciousness—England—History—20th century.
4. England—History—20th century.
5. England—Social conditions—20th century.
6. England—Social life and customs—20th century. I. Title.
HN400S6M39 1998
305.5'0942'0904—dc21 97-33044
ISBN 0-19-820672-0 (hbk.)
ISBN 0-19-820855-3 (pbk.)

3 5 7 9 10 8 6 4

Typeset by Jayvee, Trivandrum, India
Printed in Great Britain by
Biddles Ltd.,
King's Lynn, Norfolk

Preface

This book is about the fundamental mentalities and structures of English society from the end of the First World War until the mid-1950s. These were years when the English came to believe that England was now 'democratic'. Before 1914 England was not conventionally described as a democracy: people thought of it as 'free' or 'constitutional' but not, or not yet, as 'democratic'; and by any serious definition of democracy it was not. Even in the early 1920s use of the word 'democracy' to describe the English polity was not universal. By 1939, however, it was universal. For most of the years which occupy this book, therefore, the English lived in what nearly all agreed was a democracy. They were not, however, necessarily agreed on what democracy meant or should mean.

At the centre of this book is a familiar trinity: class, status, and power, of which here the most important is, for all its imperfections, class. England in this period was a country of social classes into which the English freely categorized themselves. Classes were, of course, not rigid; nor were all their members as one on how they saw the world, but as a categorizing principle class seems to me less flawed than any other. It allows us to generalize while accepting that there are exceptions to every rule. Status, of course, is not the same as class and I have tried to recognize that whenever appropriate. As for power, it would probably be more exact to say that I am concerned with 'authority': that is, something which individuals possess which induces other individuals to respect and obey them. Power is not quite the same as authority; it is what happens when authority is exercised.

I am also concerned with why, on the whole, those who had authority in 1918 still had it, more or less, in 1951, despite the fact that the Second World War significantly recast social relationships. Furthermore, they retained it in a society with a greater potential for conflict than contemporaries were ready to admit. I have attempted to answer these questions by examining England's 'cultures'. I have used this term broadly to mean not only the world of ideas and ideals but also their physical and domestic basis: work, income, family relations, housing, and community. As to the cultures themselves, I have not attempted to write their total history, which would be difficult for any one individual to write. I have, therefore, chosen a number of cultures which I hope to be representative: broad enough in their scope to allow us to reach general conclusions with reasonable confidence.

This means omission. I have excluded two kinds of material. The first is 'formal' politics: high politics, party politics, England's relations with the empire and the rest of the world (except the sporting empire). There is, however, plenty on the United States, because American influence on English civil cultures was much more powerful and problematic. I have excluded formal politics because this is not a book about them. But it is a political book; it is, in fact, probably more a book about the social and ideological foundations of English politics than anything else.

The second exclusion (which is not, in practice, complete) is 'high culture'; a culture contemporaries increasingly called, not always pejoratively, 'highbrow'. I have done this for several reasons: because I am more interested in 'middlebrow' and 'lowbrow' cultures, and historians should be allowed to write on those subjects which engage them; because there is a large and sophisticated literature on 'high culture' which I could not hope to equal nor to which could I add much of interest; and because the great mass of the English people were unmoved, or unmoved directly, by the culture of the country's intellectual élites. Exclusions do imply that certain things will be lost; but this book is about the mass of the English people and high culture was not their culture.

The words 'class' and 'classes' appear here with inevitable frequency. Yet I do not see them as synonymous. Social classes are usually not monolithic; and the occasions when they are may be comparatively few. But there are such occasions and they are often significant; thus in writing about them I have used the word 'class'. In circumstances which imply plurality or difference I have used the word 'classes'. I have tried to be consistent in such usage, though in a book of this size it has been difficult. The reader will, at any rate, know my intention.

This is a history of England and the English people; but their history has often been the history of Britain and the British people. Where it would be absurd to speak of 'English' ideas and institutions which are plainly 'British', I have used the word 'British'. Where they are unambiguously English, or where the words 'England' and the 'English' can be properly used I have done so.

I have prefaced each chapter with a short statement of its content and at the end of each chapter I have written a brief concluding essay summing up its argument. I have summed up the argument of the book itself in a concluding chapter.

Many people, one way or another, have contributed to the book's completion. They are, of course, not responsible for its defects. I would like to thank Lord Briggs, Mr A. E. Cahill, Professor J. Carey, Professor T. C. Cave, Dr M. E. Ceadel, Mr John Cobb, Sir Howard Colvin, Lady Colvin, Mr M. Donnelly, Professor C. Ehrlich, the late Lady Faithfull, Professor C. H. Feinstein, Dr Nina Fishman, Mr P. R. Ghosh, Mrs Helen Ghosh, Dr P. M. S. Hacker, Dr Owen Harries, Dr Jose Harris, Dr B. H. Harrison, Dr A. J. B. Hilton, Mrs Mary Hilton, Mrs Janet Howarth, Professor N. Kurti, Mr G. Lee, Dr Virginia Llewellyn Smith, Dr L. J. Macfarlane, Prof. H. C. G. Matthew, Mrs Sue Matthew, Mrs Helen Messner,

Dr A. Olechnowicz, Professor P. J. Parsons, the late Sir Rudolf Peierls, Mr J. Prest, Professor P. G. J. Pulzer, Professor T. J. Reed, Mr G. B. Richardson, Professor S. T. Robson, Dr J. S. Rowett, Lord Runciman, Professor D. A. Russell, Dr Sarah Street, Sir Keith Thomas, Mr A. F. Thompson, Mrs Mary Thompson, Mr P. J. Waller, Mrs Margaret Wind, Mr R. M. Wood, and the organizers and participants in seminars at the Universities of Cambridge, London, Oxford, Wales, and Warwick, particularly Professor P. F. Clarke, Dr P. A. Johnson, Dr S. Berger, and Dr N. Tiratsoo.

I would like to thank Routledge for permission to quote from M. Young and P. Willmott, *Family and Kinship in East London* (Pelican edn., Harmondsworth, 1970) and P. Willmott and M. Young, *Family and Class in a London Suburb* (London, 1960); and Cameron Books for permission to quote from C. Forman, *Industrial Town: Self-Portrait of St Helens in the 1920s* (London, 1978).

At Oxford University Press I would like to thank Dr J. Roberts for his comments on the book in an earlier draft and Dr T. Morris for his continuing encouragement.

I must also thank the Trustees of the Radcliffe Fund without whose assistance this book almost certainly would never have been finished.

R. I. McK.

Contents

The Upper Class: Honour and Wealth

THE English had no doubt, at least for most of the period 1918–51, that there was an upper class, though they would not necessarily have agreed as to its boundaries. The purpose of this chapter is to define the upper class and to examine how its members behaved towards each other and the wider society. In particular we shall look at the role of the monarchy, its relations with the aristocracy, with the broader upper class, and with the English people more generally; at the aristocracy and its political and social status; at the notion of Society and its function; and finally at wealth, who earned it and how, and the extent to which wealth and the upper class were or were not synonymous.

1 | *The definition of the upper class*

More perhaps than for any other class, formal criteria of membership are lacking. Constitutional or legal terms are confusing: though most would have accepted that the aristocracy was upper class, even by the 1930s the peerage (a constitutionally defined body) included some people who were probably not upper class, and by the 1950s included people who were certainly not upper class. Apart from the acquisition of wealth, however, entry into the peerage was probably the fastest way into the upper class, either for the peer or his heirs. The peerage and the upper class were, therefore, partly synonymous.

Definitions dependent upon wealth are also problematic; a term such as 'plutocracy' (which entered common currency at the turn of the century), though helpful, is both too wide and too narrow. A wealth-criterion, for example, would include the country's richest man in this period, Sir John Ellerman (1862–1933), who neither by birth, education, cultivation, nor inclination was actually a member of the upper class. Yet, while some of the very wealthy would not have been considered upper-class by contemporaries, many of the wealthy were, and of all the attributes of upper-classness wealth was probably the most important. But wealth alone was not sufficient.

In addition, the upper class was partly determined by status, a slippery concept—by how money was spent rather than how it was earned. Moreover, status was double-sided; it was achieved by those who both knew the secret rules of upper classness *and* possessed the characteristics of upper classness imputed to them by others. It was, as a result, in part a class which defined itself, and was defined by others, by its public display. There was also a strong element of self-recognition: 'those men and women members of the Forces in World War II, who in their early days of service, saw and heard this class recognizing its own kind'[1] had no doubt of this.

The tendency of the public and much of the upper class itself to associate upper-classness with social display thus identified it with Society. The image of Society was a very powerful one, in the interwar years particularly, and many of its *habitués* were indeed upper-class. But some of its members would not have been thought upper-class by those who indisputably were. Furthermore, much of the upper class, the 'old' upper class especially, did not choose to 'move in Society': discerning too close an affinity between Society and the upper class is, therefore, hazardous. Even so, Society was not that catholic. Membership required an acceptable mix of breeding, education, wealth, and cultural assumptions, and anyone without that mix was not a member of Society.

However blurred were its margins, however problematic its relations to Society and to wealth, there was undoubtedly an upper class, if only because there were people who could be categorized in no other way: the members of the extended royal family and senior functionaries of the court, the old aristocracy, the political élites attached to the peerage by birth, marriage, or social affiliation, a good part of the gentry, many of the very wealthy and a few who were none of these but who had achieved rapid social ascent one way or another. Numerically this class was small—a tentative guess is that it comprised at most 40,000 people[2]—but in social and political power it was very large indeed: it possessed power utterly disproportionate to its numbers. Moreover, its members had ideological authority; their activities, public demeanour, their hold on much of the popular mind, helped to legitimate the social system on whose summit they perched. The England of this period was to a considerable extent their creation, and to understand it we must understand them.

---

[1] T. H. Pear, *English Social Differences* (London, 1955), 144.

[2] This is a difficult calculation to make. The safest approach is probably to derive a figure which combines wealth and status criteria. If, as one very crude measure, we were to assume that all those who earned £10,000 a year or above in 1919, or its purchasing power equivalent thereafter, together with their dependents, were upper-class, that class would have numbered about 20,000 people. But, of course, many who earned that sum would not have been thought upper-class. Equally, many in the peerage and gentry who could reasonably have been considered upper-class did not earn £10,000 a year. It is unlikely, however, that the latter balances the former, so the total membership of the upper class is almost certainly not 20,000. If we add all those with £10,000 a year, whether peers or not, to all those in the peerage and gentry with less than £10,000 a year—probably the most generous combination of wealth and breeding—we are left with about 30,000 people. This figure partly depends on how many members of a family had the same status as its 'head'. Is the family of a non-titled grandson of an earl upper-class? There is no obvious answer to that. The final figure could, therefore, be closer to 40,000; but could be closer to 20,000. If 40,000, then about 0.1% of the population would be upper-class; if 20,000 then about 0.05%.

2 | The monarchy

At the apex of the upper class, however we define it, was the monarchy and the royal family. The royal family was, of course, not typical of the upper class—it was always in a sense an upper class above the upper class—but it was inextricably connected to it by marriage and culture, and the one could not exist without the other. That in itself makes the monarchy important, even one like the British which was thought to have become politically neutered. But the modern supposedly non-partisan monarchy, partly magical, partly domestic, and very public, was largely, though not entirely, a product of the interwar years and we must see how the product was made.

Although the royal family became increasingly ready after 1918 to move beyond its traditional circle this was accompanied by a real narrowing of its social and intellectual range. Queen Victoria and the Prince Consort, and even more their daughter, the Empress Frederick, could claim a good knowledge of the mental world of the European upper middle classes: they spoke several languages, read widely, and were actively, if somewhat distantly, aware of the main developments in the arts and sciences. This was less true of King Edward VII, yet he was a man of the world with a notoriously wide social acquaintance. It was much less true of his son, George V (1910–36), and his grandsons, Edward VIII (1936), and George VI (1936–52). This was partially due to their almost pitiful formal education: all three were educated by tutors in the least inspiring manner. Their preceptors failed even in the most elementary task of a royal education—the teaching of foreign languages. Neither George V nor his two successors spoke German and all spoke French badly. 'It is really hardly credible', the British consul-general in Berlin wrote of George V, 'that Royal George cannot speak a solitary word of German, and his French is atrocious.' This deficiency was not repaired by the naval training of George V or George VI nor the two years Edward VIII nominally spent at Magdalen College, Oxford—though George V sent Prince Henry, the future duke of Gloucester, to Eton and the result was no more satisfactory. The most striking feature of the royal princes' education was its aimlessness. Queen Victoria was inclined to blame her heir and his wife for this—not without justification—but, apart from ensuring that he was fluent in French and German, she cannot be said to have done much for the future Edward VII. The real problem was that it was no longer clear what was the appropriate education for a member of the royal family. It was thought that the heir should have some idea of the constitutional duties of the crown and various means, including the historian J. R. Tanner and a copy of Bagehot's *English Constitution*, were employed to provide it. Otherwise they learnt not much more than an average officer of the armed forces at the time would have been taught and what they picked up along the way. All three sovereigns, therefore, tended to have the cultural and educational attitudes of landed-gentry-with-military-connections—and that was the milieu in which they usually mixed.

The result was that George V was incurious, tediously concerned with the minutiae of etiquette and dress, relentlessly following the seasons of an English country gentleman. 'The same old round of Sandringham, Ascot, Cowes and Balmoral', wrote the diarist 'Chips' Channon. George V was an excellent shot and was passionately attached to shooting. He was a good, if prudent, horseman and, like George VI, kept a close eye on the royal farms. He preferred Sandringham and Balmoral to anywhere, particularly abroad, which he found 'bloody'. His tastes and style of life were those of any large hereditary English landowner, though without the financial problems which burdened many after 1918. That, with a different education, these tastes might have been something else is suggested by the stupendous royal stamp collection which he began and cosseted all his life.

His wife, Queen Mary (who was to have married his elder brother), better educated and intellectually more *au fait* than he was, might have widened his view of the world, but was too intimidated by him to do so. Unlike his father, however, George was entirely faithful to his wife and, in a way he found difficult to acknowledge, deeply dependent on her. He worried about his children and was anxious to do the best he could for them, but his *ménage*, again unlike his father's, was stifling and loveless. His two elder sons and successors, Edward VIII and George VI, were ineradicably marked by it. Like their father's, their formal education had been wretched and neither did much to make up for it. According to Lady Desborough, a lady of the bedchamber to Queen Mary, on three occasions each separated by several years, the future Edward VIII opened his conversation with the words: 'Lady Desborough, I know you're a bookish sort of person. At the moment, I'm reading such an interesting novel. I think it would appeal to you: it's called *Dracula*.'[3] Both sons resented their father's bullying but reacted to it in different ways. Edward VIII became 'Americanized' and developed a liking for smart company and the Ritz bar. Generational revolt also took the form of affairs with women his father thought utterly unsuitable: all married—like Mrs Freda Dudley Ward—or divorced or about to be divorced, like his two American mistresses, Lady Furness and Mrs Ernest Simpson. But this was a trivial revolt; in hardly any other way did he question the ruling values of his father's court. In so far as he did, it was to replace George V's dourness with a public cheerfulness; but also his dutifulness with restlessness and boredom.

The effect on George VI was less spectacular, though no less obvious: all his life his speech was deformed by a severe stutter which was widely thought to have been induced by persistent paternal ill-humour. Otherwise, he turned

---

[3] O. Sitwell, *Rat Week* (London, 1986), 34.

away wrath by becoming as much like his father as possible. His personal life was blameless. He married safely—in 1923 Lady Elizabeth Bowes-Lyon, the daughter of the earl of Strathmore—and from the point of view of the dynasty's public esteem, very successfully, and produced two daughters adored by the popular press. His interests, habits and circle ('too hemmed in by the territorial aristocracy', Channon noted)[4] were as like his father's as could have been, and were recognized by the father as such. 'You have always been so sensible and easy to work with', George V wrote to him, 'and you have always been ready to listen to any advice and to agree with my opinions about people and things, that I feel we have always got on very well together (very different to dear David [Edward VIII])'.[5]

Although both George V and George VI were punctilious and civil in their personal dealings with ministers of all parties and though their scope for personal intervention was necessarily limited, the politics of the court were thoroughly Tory, though not always party-political Conservative. 'The whole atmosphere', Lloyd George wrote of George V's Balmoral before the First World War 'reeks with Toryism.' In private both George V and George VI, and particularly George V, could be politically indiscreet. Before 1914 George V's indiscretions became known outside his private circle and at one point strained his relations with Asquith, a fact which the king later regretted.[6] George V's own Conservative sympathies were strongly felt and widely known. His role in the formation of the National Government, in persuading Ramsay MacDonald to lead it and thus give it an almost wholly spurious 'national' character, though probably not unconstitutional, was nevertheless hardly prudent. It was not proper of him, for example, to congratulate his ministers for winning the 1931 elections, at the most contentious moment in interwar British history. Yet his actions are not surprising. He had a simple-minded view of patriotism—which in this case was shared by the majority of the electors. But the same event appears differently to different people. Immediately after the 1931 election (a result he deemed 'marvellous') he took his family to see Noel Coward's patriotic revue, *Cavalcade*. 'In a spontaneous demonstration of patriotism,' Kenneth Rose writes, 'the   audience rose at the end of the performance to sing the National Anthem.' Of that occasion, however, Harold Nicolson noted in his diary: 'The King in the evening visits *Cavalcade* and is exposed to a jingo demonstration. This was a grave mistake.'[7] How far the National Government's success in the 1931 elections was due to the king's more or less public association with it must be a matter of speculation; it says much, however, about both the Labour Party's reticence and the extent of its political integration

---

[4] R. Rhodes James (ed.), *Chips: the Diaries of Sir Henry Channon* (London, 1967), 130.
[5] K. Rose, *King George V* (London, 1983), 309.   [6] Ibid. 71.
[7] Ibid. 382; N. Nicolson (ed.), *Harold Nicolson: Diaries and Letters, 1930–39* (London, 1966), 96.

that so little was made of George V's 'private' views, though most Labour leaders knew of them.

Of the first of his successors, Edward VIII, Lady Donaldson writes that he was 'as unthinkingly conservative in outlook as ninety out of every hundred young men born outside the working class'.[8] During the general strike he lent his car and chauffeur to the government and thought the upper and middle classes put on 'a first-class show'. Despite his modernity and genuine sympathy for working-class distress he was entirely a man of his class and time. His modernity, furthermore, seems to have produced an 'up-to-date' and ambitious conservatism which did not recognize the old conventions, and that was one of the reasons why his abdication was accepted without regret by politicians on all sides.

His successor, George VI, was also a man of his time and class, despite some important differences of nuance. Entirely surrounded by the landed classes, intimately connected to them by marriage and style of life, he found the world beyond them difficult to apprehend; there were those within the magic circle, and there were those who were not. This was reinforced by the royal private secretaries, who tended to be recruited from that circle or to seek advice there—even when its constitutional status was uncertain. Thus in 1951, when Attlee's government was on its last legs, George VI's secretary, Sir Alan Lascelles, sought the advice of Sir John Anderson (Viscount Waverley), whose claims to being non-partisan were slight. In any case, Anderson's opinions were 'very much the same as what Bobbety [Lord Salisbury] said to me at Hatfield last week'.[9] And Bobbety was leader of the Conservative Party in the House of Lords whose views were technically irrelevant. The king's relations with Labour leaders were correct, even cordial, but distant; with the older generation of Conservative leaders they were those of intimate acquaintances. It was thus an embarrassment to George VI that so many of those he wished to create Garter knights, when the right to dispose them was made exclusively his in 1946, were either formally or informally Conservatives; and it was a relief when Lord Addison, leader of the Labour Party in the House of Lords, accepted a KG to match the one the king always wanted to give 'Bobbety'.

For all the constitutional niceties of the king's position, therefore, the court was consistently landed and Tory in tone, a result of the slow metamorphosis in political loyalties which in the nineteenth century turned Queen Victoria from a kind of Peelite-Whig into a partisan Conservative; and it was modified only slightly, though discernibly, by Edward VII's eclectic taste in human beings. It is important to remember that the monarchy represented not just a hierarchic status order, but a particular, Tory version of it.

Yet the dynasty had a powerful sense of self-preservation and worked within

---

[8] Frances Donaldson, *Edward VIII* (London, 1986), 121.
[9] J. Wheeler-Bennett, *King George VI* (London, 1958), 795.

constraints of which it was fully aware. This is perhaps best illustrated by George V's role in excluding from Britain the Emperor Nicholas II and his family after the Russian revolution of February 1917. Nicholas was the king's first cousin for whom he professed a close attachment, but from the moment the British government agreed to give the imperial family asylum in this country, the king began a campaign to exclude them which was based almost entirely upon the perceived self-interest of his house. On 6 April 1917, for example, his private secretary, Lord Stamfordham, wrote to the foreign secretary, A. J. Balfour:

Every day, the King is becoming more concerned about the question of the Emperor and Empress coming to this country.

His Majesty receives letters from people in all classes of life, known or unknown to him, saying how much the matter is being discussed, not only in clubs, but by working men, and that Labour members in the House of Commons are expressing adverse opinions to the proposal.

And in case Balfour had not understood the king's intention, that same evening he received an even more pointed letter:

He must beg you to represent to the Prime Minister that from all he hears and reads in the press, the residence of the ex-Emperor and Empress would be strongly resented by the public, and would undoubtedly compromise the position of the King and Queen.[10]

The government, which may have come around to the king's view independently, therefore met all further Russian requests for asylum with obstruction, and Lloyd George apparently agreed to accept perpetual responsibility for the decision. This chilling incident demonstrates how sensitive to possible hostile opinion—probably over-sensitive on this occasion—the crown was and how swiftly it moved when it assumed its interests were endangered; but that was why George V was still on his throne and Nicholas II was not.[11]

Yet the monarchy did more than merely survive in this period: its hold on the popular imagination was much strengthened. It became more public, ceremonial, and glamorous, but also more obviously domestic. After 1918 it had a cultural centrality to British life possessed by hardly any other British political institution. What is the explanation for this? To some extent it must lie in the press, radio, and the cinema; without them the royal family could not have been presented to the British people in the way they were. The extraordinary popularity of the prince of Wales in the 1920s was endlessly reinforced by cinema newsreel accounts of his world tours, and without the radio George V

[10] Rose, *King George V*, 212.

[11] The king's action, or inaction, may in later life have been a burden. 'Chips' Channon, who knew all things, wrote on 30 Oct. 1938: 'Their responsibility in the matter has ever been a millstone to both Queen Mary and King George, and their failure to help their poor Russian relatives in the hour of danger is the one blot on their lives. Of late . . . Queen Mary has been sorely conscience stricken' (Rhodes James, *Chips*, 175).

was unlikely to have become father of his people. The mass-circulation papers reported royal doings in detail and the circulation wars of the 1930s encouraged the press to make the most of them, even when, as with the marriage of the duke of Kent in 1934, public interest did not match press hyperbole. It is also reasonable to argue that a predominantly Conservative press had a political interest in promoting royalty, as did the predominantly Conservative government, which in 1935 decided to celebrate George V's jubilee in the knowledge that 1935 was to be an election year—a fact which gave the king himself some disquiet. That there was an intended manipulation in this, and that the techniques of manipulation developed enormously in interwar Britain, can be taken as given. Yet, as Kingsley Martin argued, no amount of propaganda could have created the sense of loss universally felt on George V's death 'unless the conditions were universally favourable'.[12]

The crown itself was uncertain how far it should encourage royal-family worship. George V was not here a natural. He made no concessions to cameras, disliked the popular press, avoided if he could any but essential duties, and usually looked grim at those he did discharge. Yet he undoubtedly had dignity and it is doubtful if aversion to publicity much diminished his popular impact. During the First World War the Revd Andrew Clark recorded the striking effect of his rather hieratic appearance:

All was now ready for the King's procession ... The hush was now so great that you might have heard the proverbial pin drop. One spectator said that the very birds stopped singing ...
(The solemn silence as the King's procession passed was very impressive—not a word spoken—not a note from any band—no cheering ...) When the King's car passed the officers just put up their hands in salute and the men then stood at attention silently till the officers dropped their hands when the King had passed.
The King looked very ill and sad. Sunken cavities under his eyes and black lines. Directly the King's car ... had passed there was a movement. The villagers went back to their cottages. The soldiers fell in ... and the bands began to play them back.[13]

That the king stopped even the birds singing was not due to craft. His indifference to techniques of persuasion worried even his assistant private secretary, Sir Clive Wigram. 'I have been working very hard', he wrote in 1917, 'to get Their Majesties a good press, and have been to the Press Bureau and other places. I hope that you may have noticed that the movements of the King have been better chronicled lately.' In 1918 he succeeded in having a full-time press secretary appointed at Buckingham Palace; but the office was abandoned in 1931 and not revived until 1944. The king was equally reluctant to use the radio. As early as 1923 John Reith, the general manager of the BBC, had sug-

---

[12] K. Martin, *The Magic of Monarchy* (London, 1937), 14–15.
[13] J. Munson (ed.), *Echoes of the Great War: The Diary of the Reverend Andrew Clark, 1914–1919* (Oxford, 1985), 142–3.

gested that he might give a Christmas or New Year message via the radio; it was not, however, until 1932 that he was induced to deliver such a message: 251 words, written by Kipling, relayed to the empire as well. It was immensely successful and a reluctant king, under pressure from the dominions office as well as the prime minister, agreed to continue the broadcasts, though they were an ordeal for him—the table at which he sat to broadcast was covered with thick cloth to deaden the noise of the text rustled by the king's trembling hands, and an even more terrible ordeal to the still stammering George VI (and thus also to his listeners)[14] who, none the less, in 1939 gave the stateliest message of them all: 'I said to the man who stood at the Gate of the Year, "Give me a light that I may tread safely into the unknown" . . .'. The most famous message, however, and probably the most impressive in its delivery was Edward VIII's abdication speech—also relayed, of course, throughout the United States. This kind of discreet exposure was no doubt amateurish by later standards but that probably did not matter much. George V, for all his recalcitrance, had a sharp eye for occasions which it would be judicious for him to attend; and this in turn was the result of his acute sensitivity to working-class opinion: he repeatedly presided over the FA Cup final, though only rarely went to a major match of the Rugby Union (usually, when he did, to a home international), whose social and geographical constituency was much narrower. Furthermore, his combined qualities of ceremonial aloofness and gruff familiarity were comparatively easy to publicize despite his aversion to publicity.

The career of Edward VIII demonstrates the difficulties of someone who came to rely almost exclusively upon the mass media—indeed, unlike his father or his brother, it sometimes appeared as if he had no existence independent of them. He *was* a press natural. He always had 'boyish charm' and looked young even in middle age. His easygoing ways and cosmopolitan chic made him enormously popular, particularly in the 1920s, and were exhaustively exploited by the international press. He was the man of 'glamour' *par excellence* and inhabited a 'glamorous' world where other 'glamorous' upper-class figures like Lord and Lady Louis Mountbatten, film stars, and, increasingly, sportsmen and women and popular entertainers, had much in common—all of them became fodder, not unwillingly, for gossip columnists. And gossip columnists fed off glamour. Eventually the prince could conceive of no other role. Unlike his brother, the duke of York (George VI), he never treated political or social problems seriously, and began to see the world and his part in it as it was mediated by the press, even though, as he aged, that part became almost infinitely tedious to him. The triumphal world tours, the endless adulation, the cultivated rakishness, the night clubs—all of these nearly

[14] Of which there is a memorable and comic depiction in John Boorman's partly autobiographical film *Hope and Glory* (1987).

incapacitated him as a constitutional sovereign while directing his energies into a restless hedonism. For all the press manipulation, it is hard to believe that his reign would have been anything other than a disaster.

With George VI, the public image of the monarchy self-consciously reverted to that of George V: the duke of York was a more amiable and active version of his father. There was the same domesticity—if anything, more marked—but also the same rather distant dignity. As with his father, the press, the radio and, perhaps above all, the cinema during the Second World War[15] were important in the presentation of this image, but not superordinate; equally, it is unlikely that direct manipulation was any more decisive in his popularity than it was in his father's. Yet if we argue that manipulation was not decisive in evoking this enthusiasm, where do we look?

George V's jubilee (1935), his death and funeral (1936), and George VI's coronation (1937) were all occasions for remarkable popular involvement in royal rituals. We can attempt some explanations for this from contemporary analyses, of which the most substantial was the Mass-Observation study of George VI's coronation day, *May 12*. This was the first of Mass-Observation's published findings about the behaviour of the British people, findings 'exceptional', it said, not simply because they were the first, but because 'as a rule ... Mass-Observation will be dealing with everyday things rather than special occasions'. The Mass-Observation technique was not survey but 'slice-of-life'— observers observing crowds (and, incidentally, each other) and recording their own behaviour and experiences; recording, above all, what they took to be the ordinariness of life. The observers did not always achieve this; ordinariness is all around us and is taken for granted; the temptation is to record the extraordinary—for example, drunkenness, which the observers in this case almost certainly exaggerated.

What emerges from their reports is a kind of inevitable disorder: a day part national festival, part celebration of empire, part typical holiday, part old-fashioned license and misrule—though one of the best examples of this was actually provided by the Southport magistrates during George V's jubilee in 1935, when for the week of the celebrations they allowed children under 14 to attend films classified as for adults only—part working-class carnival and part *bacchanale*. In the High Street area of Glasgow crowds were observed

running about with no apparent aim or purpose. There are a great many drunks. Women in shawls and girls are rubbing their faces with 'make-up' that is used for branding cattle in the market. Streaked with blue or red they look like Maoris, or painted savages in a war-dance. They seem capable of anything.

Small gangs in side streets are lighting fires that may become definitely dangerous in congested areas like these.

---

[15] For this, see J. Richards and D. Sheridan, *Mass-Observation at the Movies* (London, 1987), 162.

The atmosphere is electric. The people seem to feel that to-night the police are powerless. They can do what they like.[16]

At Prestwick on coronation night:

Enthusiasm when the torchlight procession climbs the slope singing *Blaze Away* (two-step) and arrives beneath the bonfire at 10.20. With shouts and cheers the torches are thrown on the pile. Several torches are badly aimed and land in or near crowd but no one is burned. Great flames shoot up from the bonfire. The embankment catches fire but nothing can be done owing to the heat . . . Young boys of 8 or 9 run about near the flames. Several intoxicated youths begin to dance and sing Scotch songs. Torchlight procession-ists sing *God Save the King*. There is a pandemonium of noise, shouts, laughs and songs.[17]

Apparently contradictory aspects of social life were easily combined. Many people sang hymns, popular songs, and 'obscene songs' indiscriminately. 'We walked down the main streets [of Birmingham]—New Street and Corporation Street. They were congested. On a bus some people were singing. They sang in rapid succession *God Save the King, Pennies from Heaven, Daisy*.' And since it was wet in much of the country, people sang *God Save the King* and *It Ain't Gonna Rain No More*. Large numbers of working-class youths, particularly in London, simply larked about, as they did during the jubilee, usually, though not always, in a good-natured way. While the coronation was the occasion for them the celebrations themselves were often not overtly 'royal'. One of the Prestwick observers was surprised at how few specific references there were to London or to the crowning. Prestwick's procession was entirely introverted:

Decorated lorries representing Prestwick's trade and history. Two or three humorous tableaux. Young man on velocipede attracts much attention. Boys' Brigade Band. Model lighthouse on lorry. All the schools represented. There are only a few 'royal' suggestions

---

[16] Mass-Observation, *May 12* (London, 1937), 234–5. The methodology of Mass-Observation has not commanded universal admiration. The sociologist T. H. Marshall in 1937 thought the whole thing was probably 'moonshine' and doubted that without the editorial intervention of social sci-entists it had much interpretative value. (T. H. Marshall, 'Is Mass Observation Moonshine?', *The Highway* (1937).) More recently David Chaney has argued that the study 'effectively directed atten-tion away from the public as the *subject* of everyday experience and substituted the public as *audi-ence* to whom "results" as descriptive profiles, would be reported' (D. Chaney, 'The Symbolic Form of Ritual in Mass Communication', in P. Golding, G. Murdock and P. Schlesinger (eds.), *Communicating Politics* (Leicester, 1986), 131). This is, however, doubtful. It is hard to see how the distinction between the public as subject and the public as audience can be preserved in any social study, and what it loses in structure *May 12* gains in imaginative insight. Furthermore, to have inserted the social scientist would merely have added one more level of mediation and editorial reconstruction. Mass-Observation's general conclusion, that many were enthusiastic participants in the events, some indifferent and a few actively hostile, but that more or less everyone was swept up willy-nilly, seems more than plausible. The unfocused nature of things is normally what constitutes reality. Many of the same issues were raised by Queen Elizabeth's coronation 16 years later. See E. Shils and M. Young, 'The Meaning of the Coronation', *Sociological Review* (1953), 67–76; N. Birnbaum, 'Mon-archs and Sociologists', *Sociological Review*, N.S., 1, 3 (1955), 19; D. Bocock, *Ritual in Industrial Society* (London, 1974), 111.

[17] Ibid. 237.

on lorries. Everything has a strong *local* flavour. An original presentation by Prestwick laundry.[18]

Localism was everywhere: street parties were for insiders only and barricades were often erected to keep outsiders out. Popular enthusiasms, furthermore, could be deflating: in Mass-Observation's view the popularity of the Indian and Australian soldiers, who always received the loudest cheers, was actually due to their hats, the turban in one case, the slouch-hat with emu feather in the other.

To set against these local and private concerns there is much evidence that people willingly participated in an occasion they understood to be national and collective. For one thing, it was difficult to escape; that it was broadcast—and thus on in most pubs[19]—made it ubiquitous. Even those whose concerns were most private of all—like the Mass-Observation correspondent in Leyton who spent coronation eve in bed with his mistress 'G' worrying about 'G''s brother-in-law 'R' who had dreamt of murdering 'G''s sister 'V'—even they were drawn in. While it is true that over-zealous royalism was frowned upon, everywhere patriotic etiquette was spontaneously observed. People rose naturally for *God Save the King*; there was no mocking; those in London who actually saw the royal family went off (apparently) in blissful states; nor were there discernible national or regional differences in degrees of enthusiasm—except perhaps in Scotland where people got drunker. Those music halls, cinemas, and theatres which had special coronation day features were packed.

Mass-Observation itself tried to integrate its findings, even if 'some of them might have been expected anyway'. The celebrations were, as we have seen, inescapable:

People who tried to avoid them found themselves going back to the radio on one ground or another, or showed a sense of guilt, or found themselves interested after all. However, in many ways it was treated as a public holiday and festival like any other, to be enjoyed in the usual ways, carrying the emotional weight natural to the special days of a large society, but no extreme interest in what the function of a King may be or the significance of his Coronation. Even when people find themselves suddenly or powerfully moved by the sight of one of the processions they may not be clear *what* has moved them—the symbolism of a procession and a crowd and a band, in themselves; a patriotic feeling about the country as a whole; or some feeling that refers to this particular Coronation.

It is notable that any break-up of the routine of life is satisfactory to most people . . . And so far as the King himself becomes an object of emotion he is conceived in family or 'Freudian' relations, not as a person who might do anything and hardly as even representing a country or a class. The performance in fact was viewed very largely in an aesthetic way, and this was the way which involved least strain and was for the majority the best social adaptation to the circumstances.[20]

---

[18] Mass-Observation, *May 12*, 195.
[19] As those found who tried to escape it at their usual watering-holes.
[20] Bocock, *Ritual in Industrial Society*, 91–2.

The king is seen primarily as a familial figure and popular feelings about him, though inarticulate, are positive. Nor would it be hard to interpret these feelings as standing for 'moral unity', if by that is meant some collective sense, some notion of shared traditions and history, a general feeling, as a French observer put it at the time, that the crown 'was a national symbol of permanence beyond the reach of contingency'.[21] The legacy of 1914–18 reinforced its symbolic significance; that the king led the national community's mourning on 11 November—then a very solemnly observed occasion throughout the country—associated the crown in a profound way with the nation's disasters and triumphs.

There is little evidence, however, that crown-worship could obliterate social conflicts; and indeed the crown itself always tacitly assumed that there were areas of British life where it could not expect its moral and emotional authority to be effective. Above all, the crown was not prepared to do anything which would seriously risk alienating either working men in general or the Labour movement in particular. We have seen how speedily George V had second thoughts about giving refuge to the Russian emperor; even Edward VIII, whose carelessness about these matters was one of the reasons for his downfall, publicly contributed to the miners' relief fund in 1926 and acutely embarrassed his Austrian hosts in 1934 by insisting on visiting the Karl Marx Hof, heartland of socialist resistance to Dollfuss's coup. George VI as duke of York had 'specialized' in industrial relations—he was known as 'the foreman' by his brothers—and if most of his efforts went into class-collaborative exercises, like boys' camps and industrial welfare, that was still a recognition of the central place of the 'labour question' in British society. The man who sat through every parliamentary debate on the general strike was not the man to engage the crown against the working class. Thus the monarchy was able to achieve its symbolic and morally unifying purpose only by divorcing itself from most of those areas of British life where moral unity was not possible.

In fact, as the Freudian psychoanalyst Ernest Jones argued in February 1936 (trying to explain popular emotions on George V's death), it was difficult for a constitutional monarch to be unpopular. Once government had become 'decomposed' into two persons, 'one untouchable, irremovable and sacrosanct' (the king) and the other 'vulnerable in such a degree that sooner or later he will surely be destroyed' (the prime minister), the king becomes 'above criticism':

A ruler, just as a hero, can strike the imagination of the world in one of two ways. Either he presents some feature, or performs some deed, so far beyond the range of average people as to appear to be a creature belonging to another world ... Or, on the contrary, he may capture the imagination by presenting to us, as it were on a screen, a magnified

---

[21] P. Maillaud, *The English Way* (London, 1945), 89.

and idealised picture of the most homely and familiar attributes. It is here that the child's glorified phantasies of himself and his family find ample satisfaction ... In the august stateliness and ceremonial pomp their secret day-dreams are at last gratified ... When to this is added the innumerable "homely touches" of royalty, the proof that they are of the same flesh as their subjects, together with signs of personal interest and sympathy for their lot, loyalty is infused with affection. And a constitutional monarch, so guarded from adverse criticism, has to have a pretty bad character before it arouses any.[22]

As the direct political influence of the monarchy fell away it was precisely this combination of august stateliness and homely touches which became essential to its social presentation and significance. It is not so much that the monarchy came to represent certain commonly held values—in so far as it did these were often values of the most trite kind—as that it developed a quasi-magical character made more powerful because it was so domestic. In 1937 Kingsley Martin noted a 'recrudescence of sheer superstition' surrounding the monarchy in the last years of George V's reign,[23] and there were indeed a number of widely noticed atavisms: much publicity was given to a crippled Scottish boy who learnt to walk 'after' having met George V; in 1935 there was endless talk of the providential nature of the 'royal weather'; as late as 1939 villagers near Southwold (Suffolk) pressed around George VI to 'touch' him in order to ward off disease. But these were a revival as well as an atavism and the crown itself encouraged such archaisms.[24] George V restored the practice of wearing the state crown at the opening of parliament—abandoned by both Victoria and Edward VII—and, most self-consciously archaic of all, reinstituted the giving of Maundy Money in 1921. George V and George VI were crowned wearing breeches and stockings, whereas Edward VII wore a field-marshal's uniform. Even the successful royal request to restore to the crown the patronage of the Orders of the Garter and the Thistle (1946), which took them out of the sphere of worldly politics, can be interpreted the same way.

That the crown owed its place in British society (as some have argued) to the 'moral unity' it represented is, therefore, probably partly true but that should not be exaggerated.[25] There were simply too many areas of dispute within society which could not be resolved by the intervention of the crown's moral authority. A more cautious statement of this case would be to suggest that the crown was one of those national institutions, and perhaps the most potent,

---

[22] E. Jones, 'The Psychology of Constitutional Monarchy', in *New Statesman*, 1 Feb. 1936. See also Ronald Fairbairn's account of the effect of the king's death on three of his patients in W. R. D. Fairbairn, *Psychoanalytic Studies of the Personality* (London, 1952), 223–9.

[23] Martin, *Magic of Monarchy*, 9.

[24] For a general discussion of this, see D. Cannadine, 'The Context, Performance and Meaning of Ritual: the British Monarchy and the "Invention of Tradition", *c.*1820–1977', in E. Hobsbawm and T. Ranger (eds), *The Invention of Tradition* (Cambridge, 1983).

[25] For the best statement of this view, see Shils and Young, 'The Meaning of the Coronation'. But also Birnbaum, 'Monarchs and Sociologists', and Bocock, *Ritual in Industrial Society*.

which prescribed certain universally accepted boundaries within which disputes took place.

A more likely explanation is to be found in a combination of tradition and technology. The British monarchy, like most European monarchies, had always had a semi-magical character; the less directly active it was politically, the more acceptable its magic became. There is plenty of evidence, for example, that the nineteenth-century monarchy, even when Queen Victoria was at her most retiring, had this character. Furthermore, as life became increasingly dominated at all levels by 'rational' procedures, arguably the magic became yet more acceptable to the public. The members of the royal family themselves, including the rather reluctant George V, were aware of this and became steadily more available for public and ceremonial purposes. Before 1914, however, the audience for these appearances was necessarily limited. After 1918 radio-broadcasting, the cinema, an even more popular popular press and in the late 1930s, a cloud no bigger than a man's hand, television, hugely extended the audience.[26] That this technology was exploited in certain ways by its owners, politicians, civil servants, and the crown itself is unquestionable, but they did not make the monarchy 'magical'—though they described it often enough as such—nor could they have made its magic acceptable had not social conditions been so favourable. Cigarette manufacturers were able to produce cards of the royal family in their millions, but they could not compel children to collect them. Magic and modern technology were immensely powerful: together they permitted the monarchy to survive the crisis of Edward VIII's abdication unruffled.

3 | *The peerage*

To some extent, therefore, the monarchy stood outside the class system but it was also inextricably part of the upper class. Above all, it was the fount of honour: the sovereign created peers and made baronets. Although he did so only on the advice of the prime minister, this was a function the crown treated with utmost seriousness: any attack on the House of Lords (or its members personally) by the Labour Party, any suggestion by its left wing that the House of Lords' powers be infringed—or worse, be abolished—was the subject of anxious reproach from the court. In 1939 three princes of the blood were members of the House of Lords and by status and marriage the royal family was part of that distinct constitutional and legal element of the British upper class, the peerage. The peerage itself, however, while indeed constituting a distinct legal entity, was becoming less homogeneous, though not as heterogeneous as is thought. It

---

[26] The coronation was probably the first public event in the world to be broadcast on domestic television. Cameras were not permitted into the Abbey but the procession was televised. It is thought about 60,000 watched it.

was widely believed that the peerage was debauched in the interwar years; but this was true only if making it more representative of wealth is thought to be debauchery, and it is not true of its numbers. The full membership of the House of Lords (excluding minors not entitled to take their seats) was as follows:

1919	1932	1939	1945	1950
692	731	783	787	840

This was a steady but not spectacular growth; it bears no comparison with some other periods in modern British history—for instance, the late eighteenth century, when the existing peerage was almost swamped. Nor, despite his notoriety, did Lloyd George augment its numbers unusually. In the four post-war years when he was more or less wholly responsible for new peerages, the numbers of creations were:

1919	1920	1921	1922
11	5	12	9

But compared with the average yearly number of creations by decade, 1911–50, they are clearly not extraordinary:

1911–20	1921–30	1931–40	1941–50
10.9	9.3	10.0	12.7

The most profuse decade was in fact 1941–50, when there was an unusual number of political creations, first by Churchill's wartime government and then by the 1945 Labour government which needed quickly to increase Labour membership of the House of Lords. In any case, wars almost inevitably create new needs and throw up men whose sacrifices for the war effort are, as Lord Curzon put it, not 'wholly untinged by the expectation of social preferment to come'.[27] Furthermore, after both the First and Second World Wars large numbers of peerages were bestowed upon the country's military leaders—37 in all.

Despite the scandal of Sir Joseph Robinson, a dubious South African financier who was offered a peerage in 1922 but who, after an outcry, felt obliged to decline it, it was not the peerage but the baronetage which Lloyd George debauched.[28] In 1919 he bestowed 44 baronetcies; in 1920, 19; in 1921, 39; in 1922, 32. But in 1925, for example, the first full year of Baldwin's second government only three were created; and in 1930, the first full year of MacDonald's second government, four. On the whole, the hard-faced men who had done well out of the war were rewarded, if they were rewarded at all, not

---

[27] Quoted in Rose, *King George V*, 247.
[28] For the 'honours scandal', see D. Cannadine, *The Decline and Fall of the British Aristocracy* (London, 1992), 317–18.

with peerages but with baronetcies, a rank which, unlike a peerage, had no direct political status.

What, in fact, underlay much of the criticism of the coalition government's attitude to the peerage was a belief—strongly held in the House of Lords itself—that the government was finding its peers in the wrong circles; was, particularly, breaking the proper relationship between land and honour. The notion that a peerage should be based upon a landed income still had a certain authority. Furthermore, the years after the 1909 budget had not been good for landowners: in the decade 1911–20 only eight 'landed' peers had been created, a deficiency which predominantly Conservative governments in the 1920s consciously tried to correct. Nevertheless, though Lloyd George might have shown poor taste in his peers, he was not in principle doing anything new. In the decade 1901–10 only 12 of 70 creations were landed, and more industrialists than landowners were ennobled. Nor was that a trend which post-1922 governments were actually able to reverse. In the decade 1921–30 only 13 of 93 creations were landed while nearly twice as many industrialists (24) were ennobled. Thereafter the number of new landed peerages fell away to almost nothing: nine in the 1930s, three in the 1940s, one in the 1950s. The last person created whose income derived almost exclusively from land was probably Lord Hesketh in 1935. The Lloyd George government was thus merely confirming a process begun by late-Victorian and Edwardian governments: that was to associate honour with wealth, if not within the lifetime of the money-maker then within that of his heir.

But after the First World War this process was much accelerated. Whereas before 1914 few self-made men were ennobled—unless they also had a political career—it would, for example, have been almost impossible for any interwar government to have denied the Oxford car manufacturer, Willam Morris (Viscount Nuffield), a peerage, if he wanted one—as he did—either because of his great wealth or his huge philanthropic bequests; or Marcus Samuel (Lord Bearsted), founder of Shell Transport, or Weetman Pearson (Lord Cowdray), of 'Shell-Mex', all because they also were very rich and wanted peerages. Wealth was still not automatically rewarded with honour if honour was not sought—neither Sir John Ellerman, richer than any of these, nor any member of the colossally rich Morrison family received peerages—yet it seems clear that if a man were rich enough and determined enough any non-Labour government would give him what he wanted. This was no doubt due to the partial regrouping of property as a single élite after 1918,[29] but also to the increasing reluctance of industrial or commercial wealth to concede a social superiority to land and finance. The social reticence which compelled W. H. Smith to refuse

[29] W. D. Rubinstein, 'Wealth, Elites and the Class Structure of Modern Britain', *Past and Present* (August, 1977), 99.

a peerage in 1886 was noticeably absent in the careers of (say) Lord Beaverbrook (newspapers) or Lord Leverhulme (soap).

We should not, however, exaggerate the significance of this change: the
most common route to the House of Lords was the most traditional—it was via
politics and the law, and these were a faster and more acceptable way to nobility than any other. Of the 320 peers created between 1921 and 1950, 194 had
been MPs, or MPs and ministers, or were 'political' peers. To some extent, of
course, this represented concealed wealth; rich men often become MPs and
many of the new peers did not have long parliamentary careers. But this does
not greatly diminish the importance of politics as a means of mobility. For one
thing, the number of very rich men sitting in parliament was declining: in the
1895 parliament 93 MPs left £500,000 or more; in the 1922 parliament only 36
did so.[30] As politics became more professionalized, honours became part of the
patronage system of the non-Labour parties, while a Labour Party numerically
weak in the House of Lords was obliged to create a number of political peers,
like its national agent, G. R. Shepherd, who could otherwise never have ever
conceived of entering the peerage. Politics, indeed, was very much more likely
than wealth to raise a man from the working classes to the House of Lords: of
the 18 manual workers given peerages between 1918 and 1950 all had been
TUC or trade union officers, Labour MPs or Party officials. A man who wished
promotion to the peerage was, therefore, much better advised to enter politics
than to try to make one million pounds.

But he would have been as well advised to become a lawyer. Between 1911
and 1950 52 judges or barristers were elevated; only industrialists as a category
surpassed them. The law was, of course, a traditional mode of entry into the
House of Lords. In part this was institutional: certain judicial posts carried
with them *ex officio* life peerages (though by convention the holders of these
peerages were active in the House of Lords only on retirement); but it was also
in part a result of the close integration of the country's political and legal
élites: being a lawyer was a good way of entering the House of Lords but the
fastest way to the judicial bench was a seat in the House of Commons. More
than wealth and as much as politics, the law gave a young man of parts opportunities for social ascent. The ascent often began from a reasonably high plane;
many of the most successful lawyers were of upper-middle-class origins before
they started—the young Quintin Hogg, elected MP for Oxford in a famous by-
election in 1938, and a future lord chancellor, was himself the son of a lord
chancellor—but it was the opportunities provided by law and politics which
allowed Rufus Isaacs the most spectacular status advance of this century:
baron (1914), viscount (1916), earl (1917) and marquess (1926). Isaacs had not
been to one of the major public schools (he went to University College School,

---

[30] W. D. Rubinstein, *Men of Property* (London, 1981), 167–8.

London), nor to Oxford or Cambridge; his family, though well-off, was not rich; and, above all, he was Jewish and a central figure in the Marconi scandal. None of these were impediments to his astonishing rise—solicitor-general (1910), attorney-general (1910–13), lord chief justice (1913–21), special envoy, high commissioner and special ambassador to the United States (1917–18), viceroy of India (1921–6) and foreign secretary (1931). What made this ascent possible was the close relationship between the legal profession and political life which has always been characteristic of British society. Eventually, this relationship became suspect; it smacked too much of the old corruption and, more important, the Labour Party was hostile to it. This was so partly because the Labour Party had a long tradition of disliking judges, and partly because many fewer of its members stood to gain by such preferment. After 1940, therefore, the number of new 'legal' peerages fell significantly: only nine were created in the decade 1941–50, compared with 15 in the decade 1911–20, and 16 in 1921–30.

The 'old' aristocracy was dying out. Without creations the peerage was not reproducing itself and even with creations there were some years, as in the 1940s, when there was a net loss. While, however, the aristocracy was being restocked its new members were still coming from a very narrow and largely traditional social range: from the very wealthy (though it now mattered less when or where the money was earned), from former cabinet ministers and from the judiciary, and, not surprising in an era of two world wars, from the country's military chieftains. Above all, new peers continued to be co-opted from the classes in some way directly concerned with politics. Of any two millionaires, any two bankers, or any two landowners, the one with political connections was more likely to want and to be given a peerage. That is why the elevation of the great newspaper proprietors was almost inescapable; indeed, the Harmsworth and Berry families alone produced five peerages: Northcliffe and Rothermere (Harmsworth) and Kemsley, Buckland, and Camrose (Berry). The Berry family were the Barings of the twentieth century and their manifold honours reflected the political needs of the twentieth century's patronage system; newspaper proprietors were richly endowed with peerages because they were the most political class of all.

We should thus not exaggerate the formal political decline of the peerage. The conventional view in the interwar years was that politically it no longer mattered much; but this assumption was based upon the decline of the strictly constitutional powers of the House of Lords and tells us little more. In fact, the peerage continued to be well represented in non-Labour cabinets. Bonar Law's cabinet, for example, contained seven hereditary peers or sons of hereditary peers, Baldwin's first cabinet eight. Both included the duke of Devonshire, the last duke to hold cabinet office. The first cabinet not to include a hereditary peer was MacDonald's 1929 Labour one. But all Conservative or predominantly Conservative governments included hereditary peers or the sons of hereditary peers and the House of Lords was well represented in all cabinets: no less than ten peers served in Chamberlain's.

Furthermore, the peerage retained its traditional interest in the House of Commons. In 1935, the last election of our period to produce a substantial Conservative majority, 30 sons of peers were elected to the Commons including one future prime minister, Lord Dunglass (Lanark), the heir to the earl of Home. All sat as Conservatives or supporters of the National Government; the peerage had thus lost any real political 'mix' and its remaining influence and wealth were thrown overwhelmingly on the side of the Conservative Party. These 30 were the offspring of many of the country's greatest magnates. Five dukes had scions in the Commons (Northumberland, Devonshire, Portland, Hamilton, and Buccleuch), as did the marquesses of Salisbury, Exeter, Bute, and Londonderry and the earls of Crawford and Balcarres, Derby, Selborne, and Ancaster, and earls Beatty and Bathurst. There was still one Irish peer in the House, Earl Winterton (Horsham and Worthing). Two wives of peers also sat in the Commons, Lady Astor (Plymouth Sutton) and the duchess of Atholl (Perth and Kinross), both of whom had directly or indirectly inherited their husbands' seats. But, of course, aristocratic connections went further than that. Thus, for example, the 9th duke of Devonshire had a son in the Commons (Lord Hartington, West Derbyshire), and both his sons-in-law, James Stuart (Moray and Nairn, and indeed son of the earl of Moray) and Harold Macmillan (Stockton-on-Tees). The second Lord Astor of Hever not only had his wife and two of his sons in the House, but also his brother-in-law, H. H. Spender-Clay (Tonbridge). And how do we categorize someone like Henry Channon (Southend), son-in-law of the earl of Iveagh, who inherited the seat from his mother-in-law (who inherited it from her husband) and who was to bequeath it to his son, Paul Channon? In addition, the traditionally 'political' peerage continued to be well represented; the duke of Devonshire, as we have seen, had one way or another three of his heirs in the Commons, and the earl of Derby, the great Stanley of Lancashire, two—Lord Stanley (Fylde) and Oliver Stanley (Westmorland). Territorial influence continued to be marked: Lord Hartington sat for West Derbyshire where the Devonshire seat of Chatsworth was located; Lord Stanley sat for Fylde; Lord Elmley for East Norfolk where his father, Lord Beauchamp, had holdings; Lord Titchfield for Newark in the heart of the great Portland estates in Nottinghamshire; Lord Clydesdale (East Renfrew) where his father, the duke of Hamilton, had traditional authority; Lord William Scott for Roxburgh and Selkirk, which were dominated by the presence of the dukes of Buccleuch; Lord Castlereagh for Co. Down where his father, the marquess of Londonderry, still had much land. The territorial power of the nobility was plainly diminishing, and fewer members of the peerage wished to exercise it; but we should not overrate that. On the contrary, the evidence suggests that, before 1939, where they did wish to exercise their

influence they had little difficulty in doing so. To the extent that the aristocracy disappeared from national politics in the interwar years, it was not so
much expelled as 'simply lost interest'.[31] Nothing, indeed, better illustrates
the political shift of wartime Britain than the defeat of Lord Hartington in the
West Derbyshire by-election (February 1944) by Alderman C. White, an independent Labour candidate, a defeat hardly conceivable in the 1930s.

While, therefore, its constitutional status had changed, the peerage
remained tightly integrated into the political structure of the country, both as
a form of patronage essential to the non-Labour governments and as a con-
tributor to their personnel. Nor was it divorced from the country's economic
structure. In 1923 one hostile critic wrote:

There is no longer any question of the House of Lords representing Norman blood or
generations of titled ancestors. The men who sit on the red benches are great financiers
like Lord Rothschild and Lord Swaythling; captains of industry like Lord Leverhulme
and Lord Pirie; great magnates like Lord Vestey of the meat trust, and Lord Inverchapel
of the P.&O. combine; and finally newspaper proprietors like Lord Beaverbrook and
Lord Rothermere.[32]

That was only a partial truth; Lords Rothschild, etc., did indeed sit on the red
benches, but in the same year there sat on the same benches 242 peers who
were landowners and who between them possessed 7,362,000 acres. What is
true, however, is that the number of peers whose income derived solely or principally from land was declining rapidly. In addition to industrialists or bankers
who were ennobled in their own lifetimes there were in 1923 272 peers who
held directorships in 761 public companies. (In the House of Commons in the
same year MPs held directorships in 713 public companies.) That the tendency
was for peers to be directors of banking or 'commercial' firms reflects only the
bias of the British economy. One hundred and six peers were directors of insurance companies, 66 directors of banks, 79 directors of finance, land and investment companies and 49 of engineering and shipbuilding firms. Sixty-four were
directors of railway companies and 29 of mining concerns, areas of the economy where the peerage had always been well represented. Furthermore, these
directors came from the 'traditional' peerage as much as from more recent
creations and included at least two close to the royal family: King George V's
brother-in-law, Lord Athlone, and his cousin Lord Carisbrooke.[33] It was known
that company promoters were anxious to recruit peers on the grounds that
their names inspired confidence—those recruited were known as 'guinea-
pigs'—and the evidence suggests they had no trouble in recruiting them.

[31] F. M. L. Thompson, 'English Landed Society in the Twentieth Century: I, Property: Collapse and
Survival', *Transactions of the Royal Historical Society* [*TRHS*], 5 series, 40 (1990), 6.
[32] Labour Research Department, *Studies in Labour and Capital*, iii, 'Labour and Capital in Parliament' (London, 1923), 5–6.
[33] Ibid. 18.

Furthermore, it is easy to exaggerate the decline of the aristocracy as a landed interest. Between 1918 and 1921 about eight million acres did indeed change hands, but it was not always penury that drove landed peers to sell. More often, it was simply a desire to diversify income, to be rid of a comparatively low-yielding asset which had lost a good deal of its long-term social and political power. But few were obliged or wanted to sell all their land, and when they did it was mostly for the usual reasons—extravagance, incompetence, or bad luck. The great majority of landed peers, in fact, 'survived'—ensconced in their family seats on the family land, to the immense good fortune of those of their heirs who were similarly ensconced in the 1970s and 1980s. The real 'victims' of the land sales were the gentry: about 1,300 landed gentry sold up in the interwar years and about another 1,000 in the 1940s. The majority of gentry families landed in 1914 were no longer so by 1950.[34] Thus the rather unfashionable conclusion reached by Channon in 1937 that 'it is the aristocracy which still rules England although nobody seems to believe it', has perhaps more to support it than contemporaries thought.

4 | *The upper class as Society*

The sovereign not merely created peerages, he sanctioned much of what was still distinctive about upper-class life. He presided at its most characteristic rite of passage: the presentation at court of débutantes in their 'coming-out,' the high point of a well-born girl's first London season. The fleets of limousines which delivered these girls to the king's feet—fleets which by the 1930s had to be directed by the police—represented an important continuity with pre-1914 upper-class life. The function of the season, part marriage-market, part ordeal, had changed little, even if its events were perhaps less grand. 'Balls' tended to become 'dances'—though the disappearing private ballrooms were in part replaced by Queen Charlotte's Ball (nominally a charity affair) invented by Lady Howard de Walden in 1927 as the climacteric of the season; the débutantes and their escorts were freer to do as they wished; there was more informality. There was also very much more publicity. None the less, it was still recognizably what it had been and its ritual association with the crown helped to ensure that. When Queen Elizabeth II abolished the presentation in 1958 it was a sign both that the old upper class had largely disintegrated and that in any case the crown was no longer willing to be publicly associated with a rite whose social legitimacy had vanished.

The crown also sanctioned some of the more conspicuous features of upper-class leisure. The royal day at Ascot was the most fashionable day—though by no means the most important—in the racing calendar, and George V continued

---

[34] Thompson, 'English Landed Society in the Twentieth Century', *TRHS*, 5 series, 40 (1990), 12; *TRHS*, 6 series, 1 (1991), 11–13.

his father's patronage of Cowes. The construction of the royal box on the centre court at Wimbledon was a deliberate and successful attempt to raise the social status of an event which had hitherto been by no means wholly an upper-class affair. Furthermore, the active participation by all three kings probably shielded field sports from those who were not admirers of country pastimes.

The crown, therefore, as a legal-constitutional and a social institution helped to preserve the solidarity of the upper classes. Its solidarity was also preserved, at least as a public conception, by Society. Since the late nineteenth century the idea of Society had changed but not its political consequences. When Queen Victoria spoke of 'ladies in Society' she meant fashionable members of the ruling class, and Society, though its doings were widely known about, was confined largely to the ruling class—as a way of ordering relationships within that class. Society thus had a clear political function: those in Society could either directly or indirectly expect to rule. After the First World War this was no longer true; while many members of Society could expect to rule, its political function was less overt. Society now presented a picture of metropolitan glamour which none the less still legitimated the existing distribution of wealth and social esteem. Society was able to bring together worlds of fashion, learning, power, and sport which hardly met at all in most of the continental countries.

The representative people at a first night in England would be members of the aristocracy, a few of the better known racecourse owners, the most recent successful airman or better still airwoman; an actor or actress is to be found here and there. In Weimarian Germany, however, it was the artistes and their critics who were the guests of honour, and whose presence was essential if the opening was to be successful.[35]

Nor was there hostility between Society and the political élites, as in France, for example. (There the *beau monde* was dominated by a nobility largely excluded from republican politics.) Finally, Britain had a powerful and technically sophisticated mass press which gave immense publicity to Society and which was in turn exploited by it—in this sense the relationship of Society to the press was like that of the royal family. The *Daily Mail*, the *Daily Sketch*, the *Daily Express*, and the popular weekend papers like the *News of the World* were essential to Society: as we shall see, it could not exist without them.

The fact that the perceived life of Society changed considerably throughout the period did not therefore matter much, even though the great political entertainments of the nineteenth century declined rapidly after 1918. Lady Londonderry kept up Londonderry House, and its eve-of-the-session parties were a fixed point in the parliamentary season—it was there, according to Labour legend, that Ramsay MacDonald lost his loyalties; but Devonshire House,

---

[35] H. Durant, *The Problem of Leisure* (London, 1938), 47.

Dorchester House, Grosvenor House all closed and the old first line of duchesses, Portland, Beaufort, Rutland, Devonshire, Buccleuch, hardly entertained at all in London. Similarly, the former dominant social families like the Cecils, Russells, and Greys became 'mere cliques'. Immensely wealthy Jewish families like the Rothschilds, the Sassoons, and the Monds continued to entertain, but this rather self-consciously exclusive entertaining was quickly replaced by a more 'democratic', though equally public and plutocratic, version. When 'Circe' [Edith], Lady Londonderry issued an invitation like the following,

> YE ARCHAIC ARK ASSOCIATION
> Londonderry House, Park Lane
> Her Arkship Circe the Sorceress
> commands the attendance of
>
> at a feast to be held in the Antediluvian
> Dining-den of the Ark

it was clear that things were not what they used to be.[36] Lady Londonderry complained that Society was becoming 'Americanized'; but she hastened that process, not least by her patronage of American hostesses like Laura Corrigan, as well as by giving parties whose tone is suggested by the above. Significantly, the most energetic and therefore the most publicized hostesses were all but two (Mrs Greville and Lady Colefax) Americans: the duchess of Roxburghe, Lady Astor, Lady Granard, Lady Cunard, Lady Mendl, Mrs James Corrigan.

That so many of the most successful hostesses of the period did not come from the magic circle—were not even English—has several possible explanations. One is that a number of women of unusual drive and native intelligence determined to 'prove' themselves in the most difficult way they could imagine—by the social acquisition of people who would otherwise have cut them dead. Laura Corrigan, for example, was born Laura Mae Whitrock in Wisconsin of very poor parents, and her life before she married the immensely wealthy James Corrigan was deliberately obscured. Mrs Greville, though the heir to William McEwan, the great Scottish brewer, was illegitimate, and her husband, Ronald Greville, an impecunious member of Edward VII's set, seems to have been bought for her by her father. Her famous snobbery, her desperate desire to associate herself with crowned heads in both life and death—she left her jewels to Queen Elizabeth, the Queen Consort, and large sums to Princess Margaret and the queen of Spain—we can, without difficulty, assign to her socially ambiguous origins. Lady Cunard, born Maud Burke in San Francisco, was, in a sense, always reinventing herself. She changed her country, her status and, in the 1920s, her name: the abandonment of the sober 'Maud' for the shimmering 'Emerald' speaks for itself.

---

[36] Patrick Balfour, Lord Kinross, *Society Racket* (London, 1933), 126–7.

Social ambiguity might also explain their relentlessness. Mrs Corrigan succeeded by dint of her husband's money, by approaching the least intellectually demanding members of the upper class and, above all, by *never* admitting defeat. Once Lady Londonderry capitulated—and with her the Londonderry acquaintance—she never looked back. In the case of Lady Colefax, the determination, the 'lion-hunting' as her contemporaries called it, had a frantic character which often unnerved the pursued. The desire to accumulate the most successful, the most fashionable, the most powerful, seemed to dominate her existence. The novelist Mary Borden, later Lady Spears, left a cruel but recognizable portrait of her in a short story, 'To Meet Jesus Christ':

To go from a Pirandello play to a ball in Park Lane, a musical At Home at an Embassy in Portland Place, a reception at the India Office, and a supper in Soho, and to mark down a new quarry in each place, and roll home exhausted at four in the morning with half-a-dozen new intimate friends, who include the great Italian dramatist, a Crowned Head, the French writer of the day [probably a reference to Paul Valéry, whose great English patron Lady Colefax was], and some woman who had snubbed her for years, was something of an achievement, but this was her average nightly bag. (*Four o'clock and Other Stories* (London, 1926), 273)

In the end, 'Lottie' goes mad, as she chatters to the empty chair where, she insists to her guests, sits the Son of God they all have been invited to meet.

The fearsome social ambition that lay behind their activities seems now, and was to many then, alarming and off-putting, but people, often against their better judgement, nevertheless kept coming back. The fact was that these hostesses had a pretty clear idea what their guests actually wanted. Mrs Corrigan's brilliant and inventive parties, planned 'like a military operation',[37] were based upon an informed judgement of the tastes of her chosen circle. Mrs Greville appears to have been a mischief-making reactionary—a 'galumphing, greedy, snobbish old toad' Cecil Beaton called her[38]—but those who attended her knew they would meet very grand people in her very grand house, Polesden Lacy—and that was something that (as she knew) they could not resist. Lady Cunard, for all her tiresomeness, was quick-witted, a sharp conversationalist, and knew how to give good parties. Lady Colefax, the mightiest huntress, was kind-hearted, intelligent, and cultivated. Thus Virginia Woolf, whom she chased unrelentingly and who gave in only at the point of exhaustion, found that she actually liked her, though in smallish doses and preferably not *chez* Colefax. Moreover, she had courage: when she found herself on her uppers after the death of her husband and the loss of much of her American income during the depression, she mobilized her social connections and set about redecorating their houses. The result was the firm of Colefax & Fowler which had the kind of aesthetic influence on furnishing in the 1930s that Laura Ashley was to have in the 1970s and 1980s.

---

[37] B. Masters, *Great Hostesses* (London, 1982), 206–7.   [38] Ibid. 88.

The wish to accumulate 'lions' no doubt did meet certain intensely felt personal needs, but the opportunities the hostesses exploited were sociological ones. They played an important part in integrating the upper class at an important moment of social transition: the point at which the comparatively closed social élite of the nineteenth century—still to a considerable extent based on landed wealth—gave way to a more open and eclectic élite, but before that élite became so eclectic (as it did after the Second World War) as to have no real social unity at all.

Those who might expect admission to an interwar salon were, though diverse, fairly well defined: such members of the aristocracy who wished still to be socially active; much of the parliamentary-political class (and not just Conservative); the most successful figures in literature, the arts and that area of popular entertainment with the widest reach—like Cole Porter, Noel Coward, Charlie Chaplin, and Laurence Olivier and Vivien Leigh; successful sportsmen and women, though not as many as the press liked to believe; and those leading journalists and academics, like J. M. Keynes, who had a public persona. The comparative absence of businessmen is noticeable. Arguably, businessmen were not interested in this kind of world, nor could their routines fit a sociability which was ideally suited to the metropolitan rhythms of politics and the arts. Or their comparative exclusion could support the view that in England business lacked social cachet—hostesses were simply reflecting the prejudices of the élites they entertained. There is probably something to both these explanations; but exclusion of businessmen was not invariable. Lady Colefax, for example, who thought most British businessmen utterly second-rate and uncompetitive, was none the less ready enough to 'take up' those she thought first-rate. She, in fact, 'took up' Israel Sieff of Marks & Spencer, quite consciously using her connections to push him very hard indeed. Nor is there any evidence that he tried to resist her blandishments.

Not all hostesses embraced the whole range. Lady Londonderry was very political, Mrs Greville largely so. The two who aimed most at catholicity were Lady Cunard and Lady Colefax. Since they served more or less the same clientèle they were in ill-concealed competition, which reached its peak during the short reign of Edward VIII, who was successfully 'lion-hunted' by both,[39] as were leading figures in the cultivated arts. Lady Cunard, furthermore, expended much of her private fortune on Thomas Beecham's ventures during her long and troubled liaison with him. Of the two, Lady Colefax is probably the more interesting since she most consciously worked to integrate élites: that was her project. Her acquaintance was colossal and breathtaking in its smartness. 'I would so like to ask someone to meet you', E. M. Forster wrote to her, 'whom you don't know, but whom do I know whom you don't know.

---

[39] Thus, of the abdication, so it was said, 'The Ladies Colefax and Cunard | Took it very, very hard.'

I don't know.'[40] She was thus credited with an influence she almost certainly did not have. Desperate to talk to Churchill in January 1942, the Zionist leader, Chaim Weizmann, told her that 'you alone can help me in these difficulties.'[41] Lady Colefax was also unusual in being politically left-of-centre. She usually voted Labour, including in 1931, though not in 1945 since she really did believe Churchill had won the war, and was hostile to the policies of the National Government. She was always careful to include Labour politicians and their spouses in her capacious circle: of a lunch with Lord Jowitt, she tells Bernard Berenson, the other guests included ' "Flos" Bevin [Ernest's wife] a grand old English housewife and full of fun. I've known her for ages . . . Humorous and very courageous, enjoys life—you would delight in her.'[42] And she was a profound admirer of J. M. Keynes—'We must pray all our prayers for the long life of Keynes.'[43] That they succeeded, at least to some extent, in integrating élites was recognized when the system they created had largely disappeared. Harold Nicolson, who was as integrated by them as any individual, noted of a 'BBC Forum' he shared with Robert Boothby, the Conservative MP, and Kingsley Martin, the editor of the *New Statesman*, that 'we say that the disappearance of Society means that young men have no opportunity of meeting the great men of their age.'[44] And the system worked because there was still some consensus as to who the great men of the age actually were.

Increasingly, the hostesses also saw their role as the integration of Anglo-American élites. 'Society', as it was understood at the time, was in any case a significantly Anglo-American affair, if only because so many of the most active social entrepreneurs were themselves American. But the drive came from both sides. Conquering the English social system was a task several American women set themselves, and it was at the house of one American, Lady Cunard, that another, Mrs Ernest Simpson (herself a go-getting hostess) made the greatest conquest of them all. On the other hand, eliciting American support for a decaying empire, particularly when it became clear that without such support that empire could scarcely survive, might be deemed a patriotic duty. Thus for some, of whom Lady Colefax is again the best example, because the most self-conscious, the introduction of Americans 'into English drawing rooms' was an act of policy. Throughout the Second World War, her 'ordinaries', weekly dinners at the Dorchester for which the guests paid and which were rather hated by her regulars, were designed specifically to bring American and English élites together. Which élites the Americans met or ought to meet was a matter

[40]   E. M. Forster to Sibyl Colefax, 1 May 1934, Colefax MS Eng. c.1362, Bodleian Library, Oxford. For a sympathetic but not uncritical portrait of Lady Colefax, see K. McLeod, *A Passion for Friendship* (London, 1991).

[41]   Weizmann to Colefax, 11 Jan. 1942, Colefax MS Eng. c.3170, Bodleian Library, Oxford.

[42]   Colefax to Bernard Berenson, [?] July 1948, Colefax MS Eng. c.3176, Bodleian Library, Oxford.

[43]   Colefax to Berenson, [?] July 1945 (ibid.).

[44]   H. Nicolson, *Diaries and Letters, 1945–62* (ed. N. Nicolson, London, 1968), 212.

upon which a good deal was thought to hang. At Lady Londonderry's, Mrs Greville's, or even Lady Cunard's, they were more likely to meet conservative
élites; which meant in the 1930s those who favoured appeasement. Why, Sibyl
Colefax asked, did US ambassadors know nothing of England?

They only dine with other ambassadors, with the House of Lords of any kind or sort—
with occasionally members of the Cabinet . . . I'd wager that Houghton [A.B. Houghton,
US ambassador to Britain, 1925–9] had never met Clifford Sharp—Leonard Woolf—May-
nard Keynes or any of the Liberal left either in politics or literature—and Mr Houghton's
pronouncements in the US do beautifully point this moral—I'm quite sure he dined with
the Abercorns—with the Northumberlands probably with half or ¾ of the diehards in
England—because they are all in just that section of London society he frequents—+
there's no doubt that Sara [sic] Wilson—Alice Keppel e tutti quanti have assured him that
England is down and out, because they spend all their time telling this to each other.[45]

Lady Colefax, whose American acquaintance was as vast as her English and
encompassed the same range—from Thomas Lamont, the chairman of J. P. Morgan, to the novelist and playwright Thornton Wilder—deliberately set out to
assimilate Americans to this other England.

Much publicity was given to the hostesses—most of which they sought, however discreetly. Even more publicity was given to their children: not least, Lady
Cunard's daughter, Nancy. Society's cult of youth and the press's willingness
to adhere to it created endless copy. The frantic activities of the Bright Young
Things and their successors, the parties, the sensations, though easily satirized, as Evelyn Waugh memorably did in *Vile Bodies*, were quite consciously
public activities which would not have occurred but for the press. And it was
precisely for this reason that the London season, losing whatever stateliness it
once might have had, became so hectic:

People rush from one party or restaurant to another, to a third and fourth in the course
of one evening, and finish up with an early morning bathing-party, transported at
60 mph to the swimming-pools of Eton through the dawn. On the river, a languid
evening on a punt is not enough. There must be dancing as well, at Datchet or at Bray,
and a breakneck race down the Great West Road afterwards.

The next day there is no question of resting in preparation for the evening's exer-
tions. Appointments all the morning, with hairdressers or commission agents or committees; cocktails at the Ritz before lunch, luncheon parties; tennis afterwards or golf
at Swinley, or bridge; charity rehearsal teas, then cocktail parties, a rush home to
change for an early dinner and the theatre or ballet, after which the whole cycle begins
all over again.

Once the week-ends were a rest from all this feverish activity; but now they are more
strenuous than the week itself—all its pleasures crammed together into a third of the
time, with large, riotous, bright young house parties, a dozen people motoring down for
the day on Sunday, everyone rushing round the countryside in fast cars, and at night

---

⁴⁵ Colefax to Berenson, [?] 1933, Colefax MS Eng. *c*.3176, Bodleian Library, Oxford.

bridge and backgammon and truth games and practical jokes till all hours of the morning.[46]

The way the bright young people chose to present themselves is well demonstrated by the piece one of the better-known among them, Margaret Whigham, wrote in the *Daily Sketch* in March 1932:

"Margaret has gone mad!" My friends really did not conceal their thoughts when I announced, last Autumn, that I was going to Egypt. I mean they have always seen me round Bond Street, in and out of the Ritz, or at Ascot, and they considered the Embassy Club my spiritual home. It is in a way, for I love the gay life of the West End, Ascot, Cannes and all the other fun that comes the way of the modern young woman.

However, I had heard so much about Cairo's gay life that I bade a fond farewell to Jackson—that's the Embassy Club cat—and sallied forth into the big world.

Now Egypt really does come up to expectations—but not from a Ritz-Carlton point of view. I found I had to abandon all that and appreciate it in the light of stepping back into the Bible. The natives are just heavenly in their colourful robes, and especially at Assouan ...

Cairo, you see is only a pretty poor imitation of London, Paris and Cannes, and though I love that kind of life I only love it at its best ...

Actually, the best thing in Cairo is the Ghezira Club where they have polo, racing, tennis, golf, and everyone who is anyone goes there for tea.[47]

Miss Whigham (the future duchess of Argyll) was not as featherheaded as this suggests; she was writing to a formula and the formula was one demanded both by the press and its readership, as well as one acceptable to her.

The publicity given to youth by the press was accentuated by the tendency of Society (as we have seen) to assimilate to itself the cinema and the world of sport. Film stars, so long as they were successful enough, had instant access, and were much sought after: the well-publicized honeymoon visit of an almost stereotypical 'Society' couple, Lord and Lady Louis Mountbatten, to Charlie Chaplin was thought to have benefited all of them. Access at some level was also (almost) guaranteed to successful popular musicians, even black ones; to aviators and speed aces—the Mollisons and Sir Malcolm Campbell were lionized—and unsuccessful attempts were made to lionize Lindbergh when he took refuge in England in 1936. While it was assumed that Hollywood in the early thirties tended to parody London Society, by the late thirties it was thought that London Society resembled a Hollywood film. It is unlikely that this was accidental. When the most potent image of the age was the cinema, a Society which successfully exploited the press was certainly ready to manipulate the pictures. But the media also manipulated Society: the relationship between them and the wider audience for whom these glamorous rituals were intended was never stationary.

---

[46] Balfour, *Society Racket*, 222–3.
[47] *Daily Sketch*, 14 Mar. 1932, quoted in Balfour, *Society Racket*, 225.

Having been colonized by the press and the cinema, and having colonized them, it was inevitable that Society should propagate its own literature. There thus arose the Society novelist and the Society playwright. The Society novelist *par excellence* was Michael Arlen. Arlen was not himself English by birth—he was Romanian—and this gave his style and plots an exaggerated cosmopolitanism which was an essential ingredient in the Society novel. His novels and short stories were not simple fantasy romances of the sort soon to be manufactured in vast numbers by Mills and Boon; they were what Lord Kinross called 'hard-boiled': there was no innocence and no chastity. His hugely successful novel *The Green Hat* (1924) perfected the genre and had numberless imitators. The heroine, Iris Storm, (with 'a pagan body and a Chislehurst mind'), who drives the required Hispano-Suiza, is doomed from the start; the disasters of her life are unexpectedly explicit—her husband has syphilis, she herself has an abortion in Paris, many of her friends are drug addicts, she commits suicide by driving the Hispano-Suiza into the tree which was her favourite refuge as a child. But the abyss into which she descends is one of both luxury and glamour; night clubs and restaurants, Paris and the Riviera; in a sense, Society as both its members and its audience liked to think of it. The novel was also revealingly self-referential.[48] At one point Arlen describes the current fashionable novelist as one who

will go down in history as the originator of Pique as a profitable literary idea. He had hit on the discovery that English library subscribers will wholeheartedly bear with any saucy and illegal relation between the sexes if the same is caused by Pique. He had observed that the whole purpose of a 'best-seller' is to justify a reasonable amount of adultery in the eyes of suburban matrons. He had observed that in no current English novel was there ever mention of any woman having a lover because she wanted a lover: she always took a lover because something had upset her, as in real life she might take an aspirin.

Arlen was easily satirized, as Barry Pain did amusingly in 1926 in *This Charming Green Hat Fair* (the heroine drives a Hispano-Ford and is unable to commit suicide by driving into a tree because the car is incapable of sufficient acceleration), but his readership liked what he wrote and showed no sign of resenting either the life or privileges of his characters; indeed by pandering to popular stereotypes of a decadent Society he made it in some ways even more alluring.

The Society playwright *par excellence* was Noel Coward (the 'Master'). Coward derived his reputation not simply from writing skilful social comedies but from having claims, like Arlen, to a more serious purpose. Thus *The Vortex* (1925) purported to deal with the 'problem' of drug addiction in smart society.

---

[48] As he was in private: 'These are exciting times. I am harried. I am ageing. The pace is terrible. The cost very monstrous. The price of emeralds! Darling, the books I shall have to write—and which you won't read.' (Arlen to Sibyl Colefax, 1 April [?], Colefax MS Eng. *c*.3159, Bodleian Library, Oxford.)

It was a *succès d'estime* as well as a popular success and impressed people by no means philistine. Count Kessler wrote in his diary

Saw Noel Coward's *Vortex* at the Comedy Theatre. He also plays the lead, a young drug addict. A very powerful piece. Coward's performance is superb. With shattering realism yet masterly restraint, and no cheap tricks, he acts the tragedy of the son of a vain, pleasure-seeking, thoroughly depraved and heartless beautiful woman. The ending, though, is inconclusive because there is in fact no way out of the situation.[49]

What is significant about Coward, however, is that he was a hero of Society itself. The later satirical plays, though witty if well acted, had no barbs: they were as popular with the smart society they claimed to satirize as with anyone. Furthermore, Coward was a patriot; he actually saw nothing wrong with Society or with society. The review *Cavalcade* was a sentimental tribute to the social status quo, as was his famous wartime film, *In Which We Serve* (a film made possible by his friendship with that adornment of Society, Lord Louis Mountbatten).

Between 1914 and 1939, Society in part changed both its composition and its practices. Before the First World War it was almost exclusively aristocratic and had a specifically political function; so that social ostracism, or worse, social death, were real sanctions in the life of the ruling classes. This was no longer true. Being taken up by a hostess might help a man on the make in his political ambitions but did not necessarily do so. Nor was appearance in Society obligatory: Baldwin rarely attended and Neville Chamberlain only occasionally—unlike his half-brother Austen. But Society did not lose its political function; that function simply became more indirect. Society, which was the popular idea of the upper class and which for most people represented the upper class, associated itself with glamour, with success, and with wealth; it allowed itself to be satirized in an anodyne way and was not averse to seeing its style of life depicted as decadent as well as dramatic. Above all, it encouraged the notion that it was in some sense 'open' and therefore appropriate to a democratic age. That is why so many of its most successful members, either as party-givers or party-goers, were wealthy Americans and its essential parasites gossip-columnists (of whom the most famous was 'William Hickey'—for a time the future Labour MP Tom Driberg—and who included a large number of impecunious members of the aristocracy) and film stars. Indeed, it should be emphasized, to a considerable extent we are observing an Anglo-American phenomenon. In both countries the evolution of Society, *mutatis mutandis*, was similar. The august and very opulent world of Mrs William Astor gave way after the First World War to New York café society. F. C. Jaher writes:

When actress Marie Dressler told Mrs Fish, "I want to be able to tell my mother that

---

[49] C. Kessler (ed.), *The Diaries of a Cosmopolitan: Count Harry Kessler, 1918–1937* (London, 1971), 257 (19 Mar. 1925).

I have had dinner with Mrs Stuyvesant Fish," she replied, "I shall be proud to tell my children that Marie Dressler has dined with me." This exchange foreshadowed a regrouping of élites that fully materialized after World War I. Society figures, reversing the previous course of relations, began to pursue athletes and entertainers, and the search for sensation replaced that continuity of tradition which held the old guard together.[50]

That an Anglo-American family like the Astors should be at the centre of this evolution was not accidental. And the development of an Anglo-American Society opened its British branch to all sorts of American influences, including, Americans who, unlike the Astors, were not acceptable at home. Lady Louis Mountbatten had to defend herself in the courts—which she did successfully—against the charge that she had had an affair with the black singer Paul Robeson;[51] and the charge could be made because he, like Josephine Baker in France and Germany, had an entrée to Society in Britain which he could not have had in the United States.

To some who observed it from the inside, evolution was in fact degeneration. Patrick Balfour, Lord Kinross, one of the impecunious aristocrats who earned his living writing about it, thought it a kind of historical perversion; the whole of British political and social development since 1832 had, in his view, reached 'its apotheosis in the fashionable middle-class plutocracy of the nineteen-thirties'.[52] Harold Nicolson ascribed to it a still direct but now malevolent political role:

The harm which these silly selfish hostesses do is really immense. They convey to foreign envoys the impression that policy is decided in their own drawing-rooms. People such as Simon and Hore-Belisha (who are middle-class individuals flattered by the adulation of what they suppose—with extreme incorrectitude—to be the aristocracy) are also impressed by the social efficiency of women such as Mrs Greville and Lady Astor. Anybody who really knows the latter understands that she is a kindly but inordinately foolish woman. Yet these people have a subversive influence. They dine and wine our younger politicians and they create an atmosphere of authority and responsibility and grandeur, whereas the whole thing is a mere flatulence of the spirit.[53]

Both are partly right, though Nicolson was probably closer to the truth. Society was unquestionably plutocratic but to call it 'middle-class' is to diminish its scope. Its social reach was much wider than that. For one thing a good part of the aristocracy was still active in it; for another it continued to embrace the court and the territorial nobility which surrounded the court: the prince of Wales was always a member of Society until his abdication as king and departure from the country, as were the duke and duchess of Kent. Moreover the

---

[50] F. C. Jaher, 'Style and Status: High Society in late Nineteenth Century New York', in F. C. Jaher (ed.), *The Rich, the Well Born and the Powerful* (NY, 1973), 274.

[51] P. Ziegler, *Mountbatten* (London, 1985), 114. She certainly did not have an affair with him, but she may have known him.

[52] Balfour, *Society Racket*, 270.   [53] Nicolson, *Diaries and Letters, 1930–1939*, 396.

press tended to treat as Society occasions those ritual events of the Season, like Ascot or Cowes, which were still very much royal and noble affairs, as well as newer additions to the fashionable life, like the All-England tennis championships at Wimbledon, which were conspicuously embraced by Society in the interwar years and even had royal participation—in 1926 the duke of York was induced to play in the men's doubles. Society was closely implicated in club-land and the messes of the smart regiments, however much some of them affected to despise it. Oxford and, to a lesser extent, Cambridge, were assumed by the press to be suburbs of the West End—not altogether inaccurately. Society also reached into the fashionable *demi-monde*: Fitzrovia, that Bohemian province which straddled Oxford Street between Shaftesbury Avenue and Howland Street, was by no means excluded. The pre-1939 volumes of Anthony Powell's *A Dance to the Music of Time* capture this fusion well; the narrator (like the author) combines a slightly down-at-heel career as writer-journalist with marriage to the daughter of an earl.

Certainly, Society was not constituted by a Proustian aristocracy, largely divorced from the political life of the nation, where the noble *faubourg* existed mainly for itself. Its most fashionable hostesses were intensely political and many politicians were very fashionable. But Society, as Nicolson recognized, did not make opinion. Sir John Simon and Leslie Hore-Belisha *were* flattered at the attentions of Mrs Greville and Lady Astor but it is unlikely that they paid much attention to their views. The political role of Society was essentially one of public display. Interwar Society, more fluid and less apparently exclusive than its pre-1914 predecessor, was just as concerned to protect and promote privilege: but the means it deployed were different. An endlessly publicized glamour, an emphasis upon smartness and modernity, and a largely spurious Americanization were powerful weapons in legitimating privilege and making it acceptable to a mass electorate. Insofar as the new system can be personified, it was in the person of King Edward VIII himself—smart, modern, 'democratic', Americanized in speech and dress, but, as we have seen, utterly conservative, indeed (which was more unusual) reactionary in his views.

For whom was all this meant? We learn something from the newspapers which reported it; but there were different ways of reporting it. The papers who wrote for the élites, conspicuously *The Times* but also the *Daily Telegraph* and the *Morning Post*, which were read by the stratum immediately below the élites, still recorded it in a court-circular manner: there were things one needed to know and it was on the court page that one found them. The sensationalizing of Society was confined to what contemporaries called the popular press—the *Daily Express*, the *Daily Mail*, and the *Daily Sketch* particularly—though the *Daily Herald* in a half-disapproving way did so as well in the 1930s—but which were in the broadest sense middle- and lower middle-class papers. But even these papers had very large circulations: in the 1930s both the *Mail* and the *Express* sold over two million copies each.

While, however, weeklies like the *News of the World* with large working-class readerships reported Society scandals, often very lubriciously, it is unlikely that many members of the working class were much exposed to Society news except when a member of the royal family was involved, and not always then. But no reader of the middle-class press, however cursorily he or she in fact read it, could escape Society, and it was not intended that they should. How they reacted, of course, is less knowable. Those who observed it before 1939 were inclined to think that the press and cinema presentation of Society did its work—it inflamed the native snobbery of the middle classes and procured their attachment to a conservative social hierarchy. Patrick Balfour, whose *Society Racket* was the best informed but also the sourest examination of its public face, thought that the whole exercise was indeed a 'racket', designed simply to exploit 'the social narrowness of villadom, its caste-distinctions and general class-consciousness', in which it succeeded. Paul Cohen-Portheim accepted this:

The interest which the whole nation takes in Society is astonishing. In continental countries for all their *snobisme* and reverence for the nobility, the masses know very little about the 'best people', who remain private individuals; in England people in Society are public characters. Every newspaper tells you about their private lives, every illustrated paper is perpetually publishing photographs of them, and they are as much popular figures as cinema-actors are. Their parties and their dresses, their weddings, christenings and funerals, their houses and their travels are all described and depicted. It is difficult to say whether this is due to a conscious effort to make Society popular or whether the great public simply demands it . . . It is above all the vast lower middle classes that are most passionately interested in what sort of dress the Duchess was wearing . . .

The first duty of Society is to be a show for the masses, particularly during the three months of the London Season, when it has not a moment's rest . . . in fact to carry out each day is a spectacular programme quite beyond human powers.[54]

Cohen-Portheim is, of course, simply attributing to Society the role which in the mid-nineteenth century Bagehot attributed to the court: that of suborning the populace by a tremendous display of pomp and glamour. We must not, however, assume too easily that such a strategy worked. There is plenty of evidence that many in the middle classes, particularly those of nonconformist background, rather disapproved of Society and were offended by it. Yet it does seem that, at least in the interwar period, Society, as the public, glamorous (and histrionic) manifestation of the social and political élite, promoted the interests of that élite. To that extent, there is a parallel with Bagehot's view of Queen Victoria's court, though of course the press and cinema played a greater part here.

In so doing, it also promoted a unity within the upper class when it might

---

[54] Balfour, *Society Racket*, 27; P. Cohen-Portheim, *England: the Unknown Isle* (London, 1930), 112–13.

otherwise have dissolved. While association with the crown, as we have seen, helped to preserve the upper class, and while the peerage certainly had more political and social power than many imagined, even before 1939 the cultural unity of the upper class had fragmented. In the field of cultural manners, not only was the line between the upper and the upper middle classes becoming blurred, the upper class was actually losing ground. Those areas of social and economic life which were exclusively upper-class were becoming narrower and their inhabitants fewer. Politics, the Church, the civil service, even the armed forces, where members of the upper class who needed occupation found it, were now dominated by the upper middle class. Apart from Society—eclectic though it in fact it was becoming—it was only in the country, in landed pursuits, that the upper class could still be certain of setting the tone. It was thus that the army in part held off the service middle class. The extreme attachment to the horse of the pre-1939 army had no parallel in the country's other public professions: when he was general officer commanding-in-chief Southern Command, General Sir Alexander Godley hunted with fifteen packs. Riding in the drag hunt was compulsory at the Staff College at Camberley and Lord Gort's popularity as commandant of the college visibly declined when he suggested that officers might fill their leisure hours more profitably than by following the drag. If anything, the atmosphere was even more equine in the Indian Staff College at Quetta. The anachronisms of the army were perpetuated partly by the traditional recruitment of officers from the Irish peerage and from minor landed families and partly from their social isolation, an isolation made worse by prolonged periods of service in India or the Middle East. Yet even this was under attack. Many more officers were being recruited from Wellington, Clifton, or Marlborough than from Eton, and the vestigial gentry life-style which the Staff Colleges still practised was alien to most regiments outside the Brigade of Guards or the Rifle Brigade.[55]

In terms of social behaviour the norms were increasingly those established by the upper middle classes. This was true even in that stronghold of primary socialization, the public school system. By 1918 there were probably only four or five indubitably 'upper-class' schools: Eton, Harrow, Westminster, Winchester, possibly Charterhouse, possibly Ampleforth. Upper-class boys might go to other schools but that did not make these schools upper-class. Even Eton's most striking products, however repellent or alluring they found the place,[56] tended to be Collegers who earned a place by examination and were probably upper- or professional middle-class in origin. Eton, Harrow, and Winchester represented the apogee of the educational system, but the

[55] Brian Bond, *British Military Policy between the Two World Wars* (Oxford, 1980), 44–70; Cannadine, *Decline and Fall of the British Aristocracy*, 273.

[56] The best account of Eton in this period is probably by Cyril Connolly, a Colleger who found it both repellent and alluring. See his *Enemies of Promise* (London, 1949).

education received by an upper-class boy differed hardly at all, if at all after 1918, from one received by an upper-middle-class boy at one of the other major public schools and what he was taught was increasingly determined by the middle-class schools. The difference is to be found in this: that a good school was overwhelmingly important in the social education of the upper middle classes, in the inculcation of the cultural manners appropriate to a ruling élite, whereas it counted less for the old upper classes, for whom birth meant as much as education.

This distinction was best preserved in the way the upper and upper middle classes educated their daughters. There was no 'upper-class' girls' school, though there were some which were understood to be better or smarter than others, and there were convent schools, like St Mary's Ascot, which eventually tried to turn themselves into upper-class schools. Even in the interwar years many well-born girls were educated at home or, after a fashion, abroad. This usually meant they were badly educated. Which was not necessarily a disaster—the creativity of the Mitford sisters, as chronicled by Nancy and Jessica, clearly flourished in the absence of education. But it did mean, even in the case of the Mitfords (or particularly in the case of the Mitfords), that there were large numbers of facts about the world, commonplace to upper-middle-class girls, which were simply unknown to girls from the upper class—which is why for many of them the Second World War was such a revelation. Upper-middle-class girls, however, sent to St Leonards or Wycombe Abbey were being educated very much like their brothers at equivalent boys' schools, even if in later life they did nothing with their education.

The erosion of specifically upper-class cultural manners is perhaps best seen in speech. Although what came to be called Received Standard English—what is understood to be the model for correct English—was once the language of the upper classes, even before 1914 this was ceasing to be the case. H. C. Wyld, the great historian of the English language, noticed the changes within his own lifetime. In pronunciation, he wrote, the upper-middle-class habit of observing the phonetic value of spelling was prevailing. Thus, even in the traditional upper classes, it was becoming common to pronounce 'odious' 'odeeus' rather than 'odjus'; the 'ng' was restored to words like 'hunting and shooting' and not to do so was increasingly thought careless; locutions like 'ain't' were not heard in good company any longer—except when, as in the interwar period, they were taken up as fashionable cockneyisms. The same was true of vocabulary: in areas of contention upper-middle-class usage normally became polite usage. Of words in dispute at the time Wyld was writing—in the first 25 years of the century—only in two cases, 'vest' for 'singlet' and 'napkin' for 'serviette', did polite usage opt for the upper-class variant.[57] 'Looking-glass'

---

[57] H. C. Wyld, 'Standard English and its Varieties', in *Modern Language Teaching* (Dec. 1913); 'Class Dialects and Standard English' in O. Elton (ed.), *A Miscellany Presented to John MacDonald Mackay*

rather than 'mirror' sounded archaic, even though 'mirror' was undoubtedly a vulgarism.

Wyld attributed this change to the upper-middle-class domination of the public school system. The older public boarding schools and the royal military and naval colleges, left to themselves, were very successful in preserving archaic forms. But the newer boarding schools were scarcely able to do this even if they had wanted to. Still less could the great London day schools. The boys who went there had a much wider social range, if only because most of them travelled daily on London transport, and many came from families of lower social status than the average at the schools they attended. These schools were inevitably and constantly importing vulgarisms into the speech of the country's governing élites.[58]

But these élites were largely male and males were overwhelmingly educated away from home. Upper-class forms of speech were, therefore, best preserved by well-born girls who did not go to school. Archaisms of pronunciation—'orff', 'Orstralia', 'goff' (golf) etc., and of accent, survived longest on the female side and can still be heard among, for example, the older women members of the royal family. Yet even in this period such archaisms could excite derision or hostility. Nancy Mitford was asked to leave her London firewatching unit in 1940 because her fellow-watchers found her accent intolerable, and she is herself a good example of the socially isolated upper-class girl. When in the 1950s she tried to rule on matters of linguistic taste, she decreed certain words to be correct (or 'U'), like 'looking-glass', which had not been deployed for a generation by upper-class men of her own age or upper-middle-class girls educated at a public school.

Society was, therefore, important not simply because its glamour and display enchanted a mass electorate but because without it the upper class might have collapsed into the upper middle class almost completely. Culturally and economically this was anyway an almost inexorable development, but Society, both as a fact and as a popular conception, acted to perpetuate the upper classes as a social institution, as an upper *class*, and to hinder the decay of their political authority.

5 | Riches

Although the inhabitants of Society were not always themselves rich (and the rich were not always members of Society) the rich in interwar Britain were very

(Liverpool, 1914); *A History of Modern Colloquial English* (London, 1920). There are, of course, other cases of upper-class usage prevailing. 'Pudding', for example, rather than 'sweet' is still 'correct' though it is uncertain how long it will remain so. A more recent case is the word 'loo' for lavatory. It became common in the 1920s and 1930s in the upper classes and spread to the middle classes after the Second World War. It established a new binary divide—between the classes who call the lavatory a 'loo' and those who call it a 'toilet'.

[58] Wyld, 'Standard English', 253.

rich; but, like Society, wealth had to some extent changed its composition, and its proportions: the very rich, if we measure *income*, were not as rich as they were in 1914, nor were there as many of them. This was due not to a dispersal of wealth holdings, but to taxation and inflation. Although the severity of both the supertax and income tax was mitigated after the fall of Lloyd George's coalition, most of the tax changes as they affected the wealthiest were unchanged. Thus in 1914 a single man who earned £10,000 a year retained 92 per cent of it; in 1920 he retained only 57 per cent. In 1935 he would retain 69 per cent—though that was a very much larger proportion than he would have retained after 1940. There is another way of looking at the results of higher taxation. In 1914 there were about 5,000 incomes of £10,000 or above and about 9,200 in 1925. But in 1914, 80 per cent of those incomes were still £10,000 or above after taxation; in 1925, after taxation, only half that number reached £10,000 or above. That calculation, furthermore, does not allow for inflation. The man who in 1914 earned £10,000 after taxation would in 1925 have needed £18,000 a year (at the same rate of taxation) to have preserved the real value of his income against inflation. Because of the change of the incidence of taxation, however, that man would have needed a gross income of £30,000 a year in 1925. Consequently, the number of people who earned in real terms net of tax £10,000 a year had fallen from 4,000 in 1914 to 1,300 in 1925. The really very rich, therefore, were much thinner on the ground in 1925 than they had been in 1914.

There are, however, two important qualifications to this conclusion. The first is that the process by which the rich became poorer was much slowed down after 1925. The restoration of 'normal' economic and social conditions between 1920 and 1925 halted the pauperization of the rich; thereafter, at least until the late 1930s, they may even have recovered some lost ground. The second is that income is not wealth: it is the profits derived from wealth. But taxation does not necessarily diminish *wealth* even if, as in the case of estate duty, it has been designed to do so. We thus find that changes in the degree of wealth-concentration were much less significant than changes in post-tax income. Assuming that the wealthiest 1 per cent of the adult population represent the very rich (though in practice that includes many people who we might best describe as very well off) we find that in 1911–13 they held 69 per cent of the total personal wealth in England and Wales but in 1936–8 still 56 per cent. That undoubtedly represents a significant decline—though much less than the decline in income of the top 1 per cent—but it is probably a misleading decline. The percentage of total personal wealth held by the top 5 per cent of the adult population shows a smaller decline: from 87 per cent to 79 per cent. A likely reason for this is that *inter vivos* gifts designed to avoid death duties (transfers of assets during the lifetime of the giver to his heirs, who are themselves already members of the top 5 per cent) concealed the wealth of the top 1 per cent. Thus the actual concentration of wealth within families was probably greater than the nominal concentration of wealth—which was itself before 1939 still extreme.[59] Furthermore, data which suggest that, though the number of super-rich fell in the period, the number of ordinary rich increased in both real and nominal terms, support the view that there was concealment of wealth, even though it was easier to make £100,000 in the interwar years than to make a million.[60] Moreover, particularly during the Second World War, some members of the aristocracy cultivated a half-comic rhetoric of pauperization which should not be taken too seriously.[61] It is thus likely that some contemporary observers were over-impressed by the decline of the super-rich, real though that decline was.[62]

There was also some redistribution of wealth amongst the rich. How much a rich man or woman lost—and an increasing proportion of the country's wealth was held by women, usually widows[63]—depended on the mix of their assets; thus generalization is difficult. It is clear that those who depended significantly on landed wealth were a good deal worse off than they had been in 1914, which is why so many landowners were anxious to part with at least some of their land. In 1930 Bowley wrote that the

combined effect of the rise of prices, of income-tax, super-tax, and death duties, and the stationariness of income from land, has been to destroy the wealth of many landed proprietors, lead to the closing of some country houses and selling of others, and also to the selling of many farms, so that the former tenants are now owners.[64]

And it is likely that one of the reasons for the withdrawal of a number of landed peers and peeresses from Society was precisely this. If that rich person also held large holdings of railway shares or housing for rent or foreign

---

[59] Jack Revell, 'Changes in the Social Distribution of Property in Britain during the Twentieth Century', *Third International Conference of Economic History* (Paris, 1965), 378–80.

[60] Rubinstein, *Men of Property*, 41–3.

[61] A fine example of the genre, which could come straight from *Put Out More Flags*, is this from the marchioness of Anglesey: 'I am very *tired*. I still have my hotel of between 24 and 30 evacuated persons from Liverpool and gradually *all* assistance is removed from me by Charlie's [Lord Anglesey's] poverty—and problems such as how to heat their part of the house (*and* indeed ours too) with *no* central heating allowed us *at all* this year, [and there] is hardly any coal, + if we have coal, no labour—so it is hard on *me*, who has to find ways and means,—secretly

I have no secretary

no personal maid

" housekeeper

" cook

" handyman

+ I, who love bed + 10 hrs. sleep, never get more than 6. And its not labour of love, I can't dramatise it—as I am *fond* of doing—because there is no time to see it that way!' (Marjorie, Lady Anglesey to Sibyl Colefax, 6 Dec. 1939, Colefax MS Eng. *c*.3168, Bodleian Library, Oxford.)

[62] A. L. Bowley, *Some Economic Consequences of the Great War* (London, 1930), 131–9.

[63] Revell, 'Changes in the Social Distribution of Property', 382–3.

[64] Bowley, *Some Economic Consequences of the Great War*, 139.

bonds he or she was doubly worse off. The disorganization of the international economy after the First World War and the relative decline of London as a centre of international finance also undermined the fortunes of the great City merchant bankers, particularly the Jewish families closely concerned with foreign government issues.

The interwar years saw an undoubted shift in the balance of wealth from land and international finance to commerce, manufacturing, and food processing. While there were about 29 'landed' millionaires and 62 'landed' half-millionaires between 1920 and 1939, there were 153 non-landed millionaires and 349 non-landed half-millionaires. Of the non-landed millionaires 44 were in manufacturing, 40 in food, drink and tobacco, 61 in commerce and finance, and six in publishing. The numbers in food and tobacco processing are, as W. D. Rubinstein notes, striking: 17 in brewing and distilling, 11 in tobacco and 12 in food. The number of millionaire brewers equalled the number of cotton and chemical millionaires combined, while the first earl of Iveagh (Guinness) left at his death in 1927 an estate of £13.5 million, the second largest of the interwar years. There were as many millionaire members of the Wills family (tobacco) as there were of the Rothschild and almost as many millionaires per capita in Burton-on-Trent (so Rubinstein suggests) as there were in the City.[65] Tobacco also provides the only genuine rags-to-riches story of the period. Bernhard Barron, born in the Russian empire, who invented the penny-in-the-slot cigarette machine and founded Carreras cigarettes, was, more remarkably, a large public benefactor of the Labour Party (his son was given a baronetcy by the second Labour government); and at his death in 1930 he left £4 million. There is little doubt that this shift in great wealth anticipated the immense family fortunes that were to be made in the service sector after the Second World War—though in its magnitude the wealth of some of those families, like the Wolfsons and the Sainsburys, dwarfs both in money and real terms anything which preceded it. As does one other huge family fortune which had its origins in the interwar service sector, that of the Moores, whose really immense wealth grew out of the football pools, and who were (and are) better known to the British and Scandinavian public as Littlewoods.

The First World War thus had a significant effect on the distribution of personal income. It was not as significant, however, as many at the time thought or as the complaints from the rich would suggest, since in part it represented a redistribution of wealth *within* the economic élites (as well as redistribution downwards), which permitted many to lead a markedly plutocratic life-style both in Britain and abroad. Furthermore, redistribution of wealth was appreciably less significant than redistribution of income; in so far as it occurred, it was as much from the rich to their heirs as anything else.

---

[65] Rubinstein, *Men of Property*, 60–7.

The Second World War, however, did have for the rich more serious consequences and, at least for the period of this book, they were to be permanent. There were three reasons for this. First, rates of taxation were raised to levels which severely reduced income on all forms of wealth, but particularly on income from investments, where the top marginal rates exceeded 90 per cent. Taxation was at such a point as to force substantial asset sales by the very rich. Second was the destruction or expropriation of assets. These could to some extent be replaced, but the loss of income from overseas assets liquidated during the war was for many never replaced. Third was the immobilization of income due to exchange and expenditure controls. The rich man was not free to do as he wished even with his post-tax income. For much of the period 1940–51 he was unable in law to purchase foreign currency assets; nor was he in law able to convert more than a tiny sum of his sterling into another currency when he went abroad. The result was not simply a relative and absolute loss of income but a clear dispersal of wealth: the proportion of total personal wealth held by the top 1 per cent of the adult population declined from 56 per cent in 1936–8 to 43 per cent in 1954. (But we should notice that the proportion of total personal wealth held by the next 4 per cent continued to *rise*, from 23 per cent to 28 per cent, as it has done throughout the century, which implies that there was, as in the interwar years, considerable deliberate transfer of wealth by gift to heirs.)

The Second World War, however, probably did more to alter the public and social role of wealth than it did to its composition. For one thing it largely eliminated Society as it was known before 1939. Although several of the more famous hostesses like Lady Cunard and Lady Colefax continued to entertain in the smarter, bomb-proof London hotels (even the shelters were smart—that of the Ritz was known as the *Abri du Ritz*), the war necessarily abolished most of the conditions which permitted Society's existence, and that was largely true of the rest of the decade. An opulent occasion after 1945 was something to be noted. 'Lunched with Ann Rothermere at Warwick House overlooking the Green Park,' James Lees-Milne wrote in his diary in March 1947. 'Very pre-war, butler and footmen, wines and desserts.'[66] Paper rationing reduced the amount of space newspapers were prepared to devote to Society news; government action, particularly during the war itself, suspended many of the occasions on which Society was made manifest; foreign currency restrictions largely emptied the continental resorts of the English who had been so conspicuous there before 1939—dollars or Swiss francs, legally or illegally acquired, were highly coveted by the former travelling classes and a few of them, including Noel Coward, appeared before the courts as a result of this. At home the wealthy were certainly able to mitigate the rigours of wartime and

---

[66] J. Lees-Milne, *Caves of Ice* (London, 1984), 141.

post-war austerity through superior access to the black market but, if made public, that simply caused resentment. In addition, Society had lost esteem. The marked redistribution of social esteem which occurred during the Second World War undermined Society's capacity to play a public part and the implication (rightly or wrongly) in a now discredited Chamberlainism of a number of its leading members perhaps further undermined it. Although Society revived a little in the 1950s, it never resumed its full-blown pre-1939 character.

Much of its public role, therefore, devolved upon the royal family. The monarchy had almost entirely escaped the odium which after the outbreak of war surrounded some other sections of the country's élite—indeed, if anything the war enhanced its reputation. Simply by elimination, much of the glamour of the 1940s, such as it was, was provided by the royal family and its ceremonial centrality to the national life was further entrenched. The post-1945 Labour government for its own purposes acquiesced in this. It duly made available extra clothing coupons for Princess Elizabeth when, with great pomp, she married Philip Mountbatten in November 1947—partly to ensure that the wedding dress designed by Norman Hartnell was up to the occasion, partly to enable him and British fashion to compete internationally with the now reopened and spectacularly successful Parisian houses. While it is the case, therefore, that both the rich and Society were as close to abasement in the 1940s as they ever were likely to be, paradoxically, one of the two beneficiaries of this was the monarchy—the other was the Labour Party. And of the two, the principal beneficiary was the monarchy, a tribute to its capacity to detach itself from the fortunes of a class with which it was in almost every way intimately related.

In 1918, even in 1939, the upper class, although difficult to define, undoubtedly meant something. By the early 1950s this was much less certain. At the end of our period, G. D. H. Cole wrote:

In effect, as a social class of really national significance the upper class has nearly ceased to exist though much is left of its snob appeal. For practical purposes, the great majority of those who used to feel they belonged to it, even as mere hangers on, have become merged into the middle classes, and would now think of themselves as 'upper middle class'.[67]

That a large part of the upper class should have collapsed into the upper middle class was probably inevitable. The relative decline of the significance of landed wealth, and the increasing diversity of wealth—the post-1945 businessmen and financiers were 'socially a mixed lot', Cole thought—undermined such economic unity as the upper class had ever possessed. Furthermore, the cultural supremacy of the upper class, even as arbiter of fashion, was already passing. But the Second World War much accelerated this process; the partial

---

[67] G. D. H. Cole, *Studies in Class Structure* (London, 1955), 69.

loss of esteem and of economic power, and the enforced decay of Society, hastened the upper class's dissolution into a number of overlapping coteries which had only a limited notion of themselves as constituting a single class.

Yet several characteristics of the pre-war upper class did survive. Much of its old stamping-ground was simply occupied by the royal family; the tendency of plutocracy to be the dominant element was merely accelerated and the existence of sub-classes whose *raison d'être* was public display continued. The pre-1939 upper class, certainly in its guise as Society, was already heavily influenced by 'glamour', which encouraged a social eclecticism. After 1945 the glamorous did not have to be well born or well bred; but it was not compulsory before 1939 either. The successful sportsmen and women or the film stars who were so prominent in the 1950s were not exactly socially shy in the 1930s. Furthermore, the mutually reinforcing relationship between the media and glamour, immensely powerful in the 1950s and beyond, was already powerful before the Second World War, even though the audience was after 1945 greatly enlarged. These survivals, therefore, ensured that the social status quo was almost as much legitimated by wealth and glamour after the Second World War as before. And, if anything, the legitimating role of the royal family was even larger.

THIS is the first of two chapters on the middle class in these years. In this chapter we will look at its size, wealth, and changing social composition, the emergence from an essentially Edwardian middle class of a 'modern' middle class, to some extent aware of its modernity. What were its relations with the state and other social classes, particularly the working class? To what extent did its members think they were favoured or disfavoured by social movements? In answering these questions the chapter suggests there were three more or less discrete phases in the middle-class life-cycle, each of which had its own history.

1 | *Composition and numbers*

Who were the middle class? There was no definition on which all could agree, and in defining it people might choose different criteria. There were, furthermore, several well-entrenched historical stereotypes of the English middle class: that it had 'large incomes, led a life of comfort and abundance, [and was] served by numerous domestics in luxurious houses';[1] that it was made up of a vast army of clerks and their families, an army which read the 'popular' press, like the *Daily Mail* or *Daily Express*; or that it was a class defined by what it could not have—comprised of people who, however difficult their circumstances, were, unlike the working class, entitled to no assistance from the state:[2] the members thus had in common a powerful grievance—they gave but did not receive.

Aside from such stereotypes, contemporaries could adopt an income criterion. The middle class began and the working class ended at £250 a year. All the major social surveys of the period employed such a criterion, and by doing so they unquestionably excluded the great mass of the manual working class. This figure was also based upon a tacit cultural assumption: that a 'middle-class' style of life was possible only on an income of £250 a year or above. By

---

[1] E. Goblot, *La Barrière et le niveau* (Paris, 2nd ed., 1967), 15 n.

[2] In 1919 the *Daily Mail* lightheartedly suggested that the 'middle classes were those folk who come below the peerage, but who do not have [national] insurance cards' (*Daily Mail*, 25 Nov. 1919).

that criterion about 13 to 15 per cent of the English population in this period were middle-class.[3]

This is much too restrictive a definition, for there were many who did not earn £250 a year who thought of themselves, and were thought by others, to be middle-class. This was especially true of the minor clerical and distributive trades; in 1921 1.3 million people were employed in them; in 1951 2.4 million. Here was the world of the petty clerks and salesmen, insurance agents and shop assistants, the world of H. G. Wells's 'Kipps' which gave English life its particular cast. It was certainly a socially marginal world, often of immediate working-class origin,[4] often deeply alienated from its work—more alienated, perhaps, than any other social group.[5] To deny them middle-class status on these grounds would, however, be wrong. By education (frequently at grammar school), by style of life, salary, dress and deportment, by social aspiration, by what was expected of them from parents, employers, and society, these men and women were middle-class. And by that most crucial of social indicators, fertility, they were the most 'middle-class' of all.

Their middle-class status was further reinforced by how they were seen by the manual working class. In a factory or business they were physically and functionally associated with management, and often the only part of 'management' that working men and women ever dealt with. They had it 'cushy', 'pushed pens', were 'one of them up there'.[6] As a result of this belief the appointment of a working man to a clerical position meant that he was lost to the working class for ever. Equally, it was minor clerks who administered public policy; and if the policy or its administration were unpopular as, for example the dole was in the interwar years, they bore a disproportionate share of the odium.[7] Necessarily, they stood in the front line of the class war and if they frequently held 'middle-class' attitudes more strongly than anyone it is hardly surprising.

The assumption, therefore, that the middle class began at £250 a year has little value. What mattered was occupation and the social aspirations and manners which occupation demanded. On this ground, and one other— their very strong sense of not being working-class—those in clerical work must be regarded as middle-class.[8] If that is so then the proportion of the total

---

[3] In the 1920s, one of the principal organizations of small businessmen, the National Businessmen's Association, described its constituency as follows: 'By "middle class", for the purpose of this Association, is meant that section of the community (men and women) who, through their financial position, would be ineligible to receive state aid or municipal relief during periods of adversity, and whose incomes have been above and including £250 per annum.'

[4] F. D. Klingender, *Clerical Labour in Britain* (London, 1935), 64–5; D. Lockwood, *The Black-Coated Worker* (London, 1958), 109.

[5] H. Durant, *The Problem of Leisure*, 62–3; also R. McKibbin, *The Ideologies of Class* (Oxford, 1990), 158–9.

[6] Lockwood, *Black-Coated Worker*, 131.   [7] McKibbin, *Ideologies of Class*, 246–9.

[8] Even the Marxist Francis Klingender, who argued that clerical workers were becoming a proletariat, admitted this (Klingender, *Clerical Labour in Britain*, pp. xi–xxii).

population which was middle class is much more than 15 per cent. Using occupational classifications derived from the censuses of 1921, 1931, and 1951—there was no census in 1941—we find that the middle-class proportion of the occupied population was 21.71 per cent in 1921, 21.93 per cent in 1931, and 27.81 per cent in 1951—about 9 million people in 1921 and 13 million in 1951. The bulk of this substantial increase in the size of the middle class came in the number of clerical workers, who increased from 6.72 per cent to 10.68 per cent of the occupied population.

The middle class increased not only in size, itself important enough, but, more significantly, drastically changed its composition. This took place primarily in the 1930s and, despite the disruptions of war, in the 1940s. The social structure of the middle class in 1921 was little different from 1911, and in 1931 not much different from 1921, but in 1951 very different indeed. The difference was most marked in three respects: in the huge increase in the membership of the technical and scientific professions; in the overall decline in the number of employers; and in the rapid entry of women into 'minor' middle-class occupations.

In 1911 the great majority of 'higher professionals' had been members of professions which stood outside the industrial economy or were pre-industrial in origin: the church, the law, medicine, or the armed forces. The only profession of any significance which might be called industrial was engineering, a category which included architects, surveyors, and marine architects. In 1931 this had changed, though not remarkably: there were relatively fewer clergymen and lawyers and relatively more in engineering and science-based professions. In the next twenty years, however, the change was remarkable, and in the engineering and scientific professions the increases were spectacular: in 1951 there were five times as many engineers and ten times as many in the scientific professions as in 1911. There were fewer clergymen both absolutely and relatively.[9] In 1911 the higher professional middle class was predominantly composed of clergymen, lawyers, and doctors; in 1951, its bent was predominantly technical, scientific and commercial. In 40 years, therefore, its composition had been transformed.

In the 'lower' professions the same happened; perhaps to even greater an extent. The professions which grew fastest were not even recognized as categories in the 1911 census. In 1921 there were 5,000 laboratory technicians, in 1931, 11,000; in 1951, 69,000 (in 1911 laboratory technicians were treated as 'physicists'). In 1921 there were 38,000 draughtsmen; in 1931 59,000; but in 1951 134,000. Again, both these cases suggest that the real changes came in the 1930s, and were accelerated by the great prestige of science and technology in

---

[9] For these changes, see G. Routh, *Occupation and Pay in Great Britain* (London, 1980), 13; for the 'middle-class' occupations in 1931, see A. M. Carr-Saunders and D. Caradog Jones, *A Survey of the Social Structure of England and Wales* (2nd ed., London, 1937), 52.

the Second World War and by the demands of the economy after it. In 1948 engineering apprenticeships were the largest single destination for male grammar school leavers: something which would have astonished a grammar school headmaster in the 1920s.[10] These were not the only 'lower' professions to grow rapidly—so did a number of public sector ones, like librarians and social workers—but they were the most striking. The 'lower' professions thus tended to follow the same course as the higher: a large increase in total size— from about 560,000 in 1911 to nearly two million in 1951—and a marked shift towards technical and scientific occupations.

The second obvious change in the structure of middle-class employment— and one associated everywhere at the time with modernity—was the extent to which they were becoming salaried employees. This was reflected in the marked fall in the number of employers, 692,000 in 1921 to 457,000 in 1951, and an even more marked increase in the number of managers and administrators—704,000 to 1.246 million. Further, this occurs almost *wholly* in the 1930s and 1940s: in 1931 the numbers were little different from 1921.

This was accompanied, however, by an increase in the numbers of those self-employed until the war and only a slight falling-off thereafter: a seeming paradox. But this is, in fact, a result of a significant increase in the number of proprietor farmers and small shopkeepers. The number of farmers rose after both world wars. The huge land sales of 1919–21 raised it from 73,000 in 1911 to 135,000 in 1921; and, although the agricultural depression of the 1920s forced some off the land, the emphasis on self-sufficiency during the war and post-1945 price support schemes raised the number yet again to 179,000 in 1951.

The rise in the number of small shopkeepers has, however, hardly to do with the middle class at all. Many of the new entrants to the trade were almost certainly unemployed working men or women who opened small shops with negligible capital.[11] If entry was high so was the rate of bankruptcy, but despite this, the number of entrants always exceeded the number of bankrupts. In 1931 there were 362,000 self-employed shopkeepers; in 1911 only 275,000. For those who stayed in business until 1939 the war years were good and that tended to hold people in the trade. Thereafter, full employment and the competition of the multiple stores had their delayed if inevitable effect. By 1951 the number of small shopkeepers had fallen to 312,000.

These two exceptions aside, at all levels and in all occupations the accelerating tendency was for the middle classes to work for others. In 1951, for example, relatively more lawyers, architects, and accountants were salaried

---

[10] F. Campbell, *Eleven Plus and All That* (London, 1956), 123–7; R. V. Clements, *Managers: A Study of their Careers in Industry* (London, 1958), 66.

[11] See H. J. H. Parker, 'The Independent Worker and the Small Family Business', *Journal of the Royal Statistical Society* [*JRSS*], xcv, pt. ii (1932), 355–6.

employees than in 1921. This was due not just to incorporation or the increasing size of practices, but to the growing habit in other industries of recruiting them as house-employees. This led to an immense expansion in the managerial class: a result of industrial amalgamation, the steady elimination of smaller businesses from the market, and the very rapid increase in the number of clerical workers in commercial and service industries.[12]

To the degree that these changes benefited people, they benefited primarily men. Thus the middle class of 1951 differed from that of 1921 in one other important respect: in the extent to which women had come to predominate in low-status, low-pay 'middle-class' occupations while effectively remaining excluded from those of high status and pay. The most telling examples are the changing sex-distribution of clerical workers and teachers. Clerking was an occupation which had been emphatically masculine in the Edwardian period but was by 1950 increasingly dominated by women.[13] The consequence was a degrading of its social status and the creation of intense pressures from men to confine women to its most socially inferior levels.

In 1921 of 287,000 teachers, 210,000 were women; in 1951, while the number of teachers had increased to 440,000, the number of women teachers had actually fallen to 207,000. The explanation is to be found in the expansion of the secondary schools. The number of elementary schools did not much increase; nor the number of those who taught in them. The real growth was in the grammar schools, and their teachers required longer training—usually a university degree. Given the disproportionately small number of women in the universities that inevitably meant the recruitment of a disproportionately large number of men. Furthermore, the 'marriage bar', the requirement that women should retire at marriage or first pregnancy,[14] operated in most education authorities as it did in the higher professions. Male teachers themselves worked to demean the status of their female colleagues: nor did they conceal their purpose.[15] In so far as women gained advancement it was as principals of elementary schools or in schools closed to men—like some of the girls' grammar schools.

In the higher professions, women only slightly improved their relative position: 6 per cent of their membership in 1911, 8 per cent in 1951. Despite the slight increase, women remained doubly disadvantaged. Those professions

---

[12] See below, pp. 73–7.

[13] In 1911 there were 654,000 male clerks and 179,000 female; in 1951 932,000 male and 1,409,000 female.

[14] See below, pp. 82–4.

[15] In 1939 the president of the National Association of Headmasters (which had seceded from the National Union of Teachers in order to oppose equal pay and the appointment of women as head teachers) said that 'only a nation heading for a madhouse would force upon men—many men with families—such a position as service under a spinster headmistress.' (Quoted in J. Lewis, *Women in England: Sexual Divisions and Social Change, 1870–1950* (Brighton, 1974), 198–9.)

where they could expect increasing access, like law or journalism, were those which were growing slowest. In the fastest growing ones, the 'technical' or 'engineering' professions, women remained almost completely excluded: thus in 1951 they constituted 1 per cent of the engineering professions, as they had in 1911 and 1931. In terms of relative access women made no overall advances in the higher professions, either before or after the Second World War.

Where they were found in the higher professions, it was at their lower ends: most female professionals were doctors, and of those the majority were in general practice—there were very few specialists or hospital consultants. Similarly, although women crowded the executive grade of the civil service, in 1939 there were none among the 550 officials whom H. E. Dale thought constituted the *corps d'élite* of the higher civil service.[16] Some sections of it, like the foreign office, excluded them altogether; those few who were appointed to other departments (so long as they were unmarried) were the social equals of their male colleagues or else had 'indefinable' masculine qualities: were 'biggish women' in the ambiguous words of Sir Warren Fisher, head of the home civil service.

Elsewhere, the expansion of 'middle-class' women's employment occurred in those areas always thought proper for women: in nursing and in newer but similar occupations of similar status, like social work or municipal librarianship; as restaurant managers, pub managers, and boarding house keepers—the ogreish landlady of the seaside holiday, so beloved of English folklore was still in evidence. But even she was in decline; only as publicans did women increase their numbers. Otherwise the management of accommodation and catering became increasingly male-dominated.[17] It was the old story: as hotels replaced boarding houses or as better restaurants replaced inferior ones, men replaced women in their management.

These structural changes within the middle class were profound and had major implications. There is nothing here to suggest that England's 'decline' was to be found in a backward-looking and inflexible middle class dominated by a rural nostalgia. It had, on the contrary, and surprisingly quickly, become predominantly a technical–scientific–commercial–managerial class. To the extent that there are explanations for English 'decline' they must, therefore, be found elsewhere. Furthermore, as we shall see, it was on the basis of this hugely expanded managerial middle class that a self-consciously modern and, in a particular way, democratic middle class emerged in the 1930s: one that saw itself, rather than organized labour, as the 'progressive' class. And in 1939 there was little reason to think otherwise.

---

[16] H. E. Dale, *The Higher Civil Service of Great Britain* (Oxford, 1942), 52.

[17] Women made up 20% of all managers in 1911, 17% in 1921, 13% in 1931 and 15% in 1951.

2 | The political life-cycle of the middle class, 1918–1951

The middle class of 1951 was not the same as the middle class of 1918, nor was the social and political experience of each of its members by any means uniform. But the middle class, none the less, began and ended the period, as anti-working class: a quality which perhaps more than any other defined it. How did this happen and how did it relate to the wider experience of the middle class?

The middle-class life-cycle had, broadly speaking, three phases: 1918–23, 1923–38, and 1938–51. Each of these was not, of course, self-contained, but each had strong individual characteristics, of which contemporaries were very conscious, and all were related both to movements in the economy and the way people thought political power was distributed.

(I) 1918–1923

For the middle class as a whole, though not for all its parts, this first phase of its post-war evolution was the worst. For some it was a genuine 'crisis'; but since the crisis was comparatively short and resolved largely in favour of the middle class, it has tended to be expunged from our historical memory. And the evidence we have is often such as to invite scepticism. Yet while it lasted no one could escape it; and even if, as some thought,[18] the crisis was exaggerated, it is impossible not to be struck now by the precariousness of life as much of the middle class saw it at the end of the First World War; by the sense of helplessness with which many contemplated their future. Impossible because this sense was expressed by both the political right and left. The Middle Class Union, founded in 1919, with its calls for the 'hapless middle class' to 'mobilize' as the war of labour and capital tore society apart,[19] might appear as yet another in the long line of organizations of middle-class defence; but its rhetoric was also to be found on the left. Only a year later, for instance, the trade unionist and future Labour MP J. Holford Knight described the average day of the new proletariat, the clerical middle class, in almost exactly similar terms.[20] This distressed world was best evoked by the former Liberal cabinet minister, C. F. G. Masterman, whose *England After War* is perhaps the most revealing description of the English middle classes as they saw themselves at this fraught moment.[21]

Though much of the middle class—and others as well—believed this distress to be common to them all, it is clear on any closer analysis that the experience of the middle classes—here the plural is appropriate—was more complicated.

[18] See, for example, A. L. Bowley and R. G. Hawtrey in *JRSS*, lxxxiii, pt. i (1920), 116–24. Bowley was the country's leading statistician and Hawtrey the senior treasury economist.

[19] Sir H. Brittain, 'Middle Classes, Mobilise!' in *Review of Reviews* (May 1919), 316–18.

[20] J. Holford Knight, 'The Black-Coated Poor', *Contemporary Review* (May, 1920), 690–1.

[21] C. F. G. Masterman, *England After War* (London, 1922), 69–70.

To begin with, the First World War affected middle-class holders of property in different ways. A number of forms of property that were characteristically theirs lost much of their value. The war and government action more or less eliminated the small landlord, the owner of accommodation rented mostly to working-class tenants. In many cases such property became almost worthless: it could not be sold but the yield from rents was insufficient to provide an income. At the same time, inflation was transferring wealth from nearly all lenders to borrowers, with the result that the real income earned by mortgage-holders probably declined by a quarter.

Equally, those securities thought in 1914 'safe' and typical of the portfolio of the small rentier had significantly depreciated; again, largely from inflation. Holders of stock in railway, gas, and tramway companies, public utilities, and banks or local authority loans lost up to half their real income from these sources. Foreign and colonial ordinary railway shares, common in such a portfolio, probably lost about a third of their capital value. Someone, therefore, who in 1914 lived moderately well off the yield from a small row of terrace houses and from home and colonial railway companies might in 1919 have become very poor indeed.

But such people were comparatively few and, in any case, their poverty really represented a redistribution of wealth within the middle class: thus middle-class borrowers did well as middle-class lenders did badly. Farmers were also beneficiaries; and the great land sales of 1919–21, since the vendors were often aristocratic or gentry, actually represented a net gain to middle-class wealth. Above all, those who owned property in the commercial or service sectors tended to gain from the war; and this, unlike the temporary prosperity of manufacturers, was to be a permanent addition to their wealth.

Business income and commercial profits had grown enormously during the war and decontrol in 1919 raised them further. All those who earned their living by commerce benefited. Because of the high level of wartime money incomes, shopkeepers were not required to give credit or to seek it; commerce was able to liquidate debts but did not acquire new ones; continuing shortages of goods meant rapid turnover. New forms of middle-class wealth created by the war were thus primarily located in business and commerce, and it was here, if anywhere, that the 'profiteer' flourished.

Most members of the middle class, however, did not earn the bulk of their income from the ownership of property or from commerce. The majority were salaried; but again it is difficult to generalize. In the period 1919–23 as a whole there is little evidence that the middle class as a whole suffered, absolutely or relatively, from post-war circumstances. A comparison between money incomes and the cost of living index in 1923 suggests that among the middle class only the higher professions failed to maintain real income—numerically the least significant element—and even they lost only slightly. Clerical workers (the 'black-coated' professions as contemporaries called them) made modest gains, while managers and administrators, in the private sector particularly, did very well.[22] Despite an almost universally held belief, the middle classes in 1923 had done very much better than the working classes: neither working-class men nor women made real-earnings comparable to the real earnings gain of middle-class men and women.[23] Furthermore, those middle-class occupations which were notoriously pauperized prove to be nothing of the kind: elementary school teachers, whose 'plight' was notorious, had made clear gains in real earnings since 1914.

Why was it so widely believed that much of the middle class had been pauperized after the war? The answer is that 1923 was not representative of the years immediately after the war. In November 1920, for example, the cost of living index reached 276 (1914 = 100), a figure it did not reach again for a generation. In the same month average money salaries were only twice their 1914 money level—significantly lower than the ratio of working-class wages. At the end of 1920, therefore, middle-class real earnings were lower, perhaps significantly lower, than 1914. For some male clerks in the private sector the loss was not recovered until the 1930s. To a commentator writing in 1920 the pauperization of the middle class might indeed have seemed a possibility.

It depended, however, whom in 1920 he chose to observe. Those who earned their living from business profits were facing anything but extinction; and administrators and managers almost certainly maintained their real earnings throughout the period. It was the professional and clerical classes whose real income was so unpredictable; but for some of them decline was measured not against the working class but in terms of narrowed differentials within their own class. The grandees of the old free professions, like law and medicine, were significantly worse off in 1923 than in 1914, while their juniors were significantly better off. Such relative changes are most obvious in the judiciary and the civil service. The opulent Edwardian judge who earned £5,000 a year in 1914 earned £5,000 a year in 1923, as he did in 1939. He never recovered his pre-war standard of life; nor did senior civil servants. The most traditional of all the free professions, the church, was the one which suffered most. The bishops never recovered their real earnings, while the real incomes of the parish clergy did not reach their 1914 levels until the early 1930s. At Christmas 1920 the average clergyman had a real income no higher than it was at Christmas 1820.

The effect of these losses on the professional middle classes was very uneven. Many absorbed them without apparent difficulty: judges and permanent heads of department, many of whom had never lived 'up' to their salaries before 1914, probably just saved less. Herbert Samuel, the former and future Liberal cabinet minister, who was in a position to know, thought the actual style of life of the

---

[22] See Routh, *Occupation and Pay in Great Britain*, 120–1.   [23] Ibid.

upper middle class in 1920 was scarcely different from 1914. There is certainly little evidence that they had difficulty in meeting the traditional charges on an upper-middle-class income; however much they asserted otherwise.[24]

The observer of the middle classes in 1920 or 1921 would, on the contrary, have been struck by the plight of the lower and clerical professions: those who also had traditional charges on their incomes but who, unlike judges, did have difficulty meeting them. The pleas for help by distressed persons published profusely in the middle-class press suggest hardship was acutely felt by those who found they could no longer afford the number and quality of clothes their employers still demanded; by those who had to forgo their already modest holidays; by those, like the retired or widows, who could no longer afford domestic service; and, above all, from those who felt they had to have their children educated privately.

C. F. G. Masterman assumed that the middle-class 'salariat' would wish to have their children educated at public or private schools. Were he writing in 1939 he would not have been so confident; but in 1920 his salariat were those employed in 'traditional' middle-class occupations where social status was known to depend in part upon having children in public or private schools. Thus the *Bank Officer* could write in November 1920—a bad moment for bank clerks—that present circumstances left their children with 'no option but the Council School. We have no complaint against the curriculum of State education, but it does not pay a bank man to send his children there.'[25] In some other occupations, the church or teaching, for example, a sense of what was proper in education, and an eye to their children's advancement, compelled parents to seek a public or private education for their children. For them, the costs of education in 1919–21 must have been severe.

We can conclude, therefore, that for two or three years after the war many middle-class families suffered an appreciable loss of real earnings and the social disappointment which comes with frustrated expectations. By 1923, however, these losses had (as we have seen) for most been more than made up. There were two reasons for this. The first was the rapid deflation of prices which began in December 1920: the cost of living index in January 1923 was one-third lower

[24] Samuel in *JRSS*, lxxxiii, pt. i (1920), 125. It is conceivable they preserved their status in surprising ways. E. M. Delafield's 'provincial lady' (largely a self-portrait) was in the habit, during moments of crisis, of pawning her great-aunt's diamond ring: 'Customary painful situation between Bank and myself necessitates expedient, also customary, of pawning great-aunt's diamond ring, which I do under usual conditions, and am greeted as old friend by Plymouth pawnbroker, who says facetiously "And what name will it be *this* time?" ' (E. M. Delafield, *The Diary of a Provincial Lady* (Virago ed., London, 1984), 29.) Truth or rhetoric? She and her husband none the less maintained throughout the interwar years a household of cook, maid(s), governess, gardener (plus boy), ran a motor-car, and had both their children educated privately, apparently without strain, the odd testy letter from the bank manager apart. And it is hard to believe that many members of the upper middle class resorted to a pawnbroker in such circumstances.

[25] Quoted in Lockwood, *Black-Coated Worker*, 103 n.

than it had been two years earlier. Most money incomes, wages or salaries, fell with it, but salaries (middle-class) fell much less than wages (working-class), since salaries once fixed are apt to stay fixed. Middle-class money incomes, therefore, tended to be much more stable than prices: the result was to force up middle-class real income and restore the pre-war relationship of salaries to wages.

The second reason was the low level of middle-class unemployment. The immediate result of the deflation which began in December 1920 was a rapid rise in working-class unemployment, which, even when it fell back in the mid-twenties, remained historically high. Its consequence was a sharp fall in total working-class income. Deflation, however, had no such consequences for the middle classes—either their jobs or their income. The 'stabilization' of the British economy which began in early 1921, partly as a result of government action, was, in practice, almost wholly to their benefit.

For the middle classes the story thus had a happy ending. Yet no one could confidently have predicted that; and the 'crisis' left long memories. As a result, the 1920s experienced more severe class conflict than at any other time in modern British history; and this produced powerful ideological antagonisms and stereotypes that long survived the decade. Furthermore, these hostilities moved in more than one direction: in these few years, and very unusually, there was much middle-class hostility to certain forms of wealth, especially to wealth held by those thought to have profited illegitimately from the war and its aftermath. The 'profiteers' were one of the most ubiquitous social images of the time, impossible to overlook in the press or popular literature. Their cars, furs, jewels, parties, yachts, and holidays were to those with grievances one of the most distasteful consequences of the war. They appear, moreover, to have been a middle-class preoccupation: there is little evidence of much working-class hostility to the profiteers who were for many working men and women probably indistinguishable from the rich in any case.

Yet while the profiteers figured prominently in the mental landscape of the post-war middle classes it was not clear who they actually were. For J. M. Keynes (not, certainly, a typical member of the middle classes), post-war inflation was caused by 'the megalomania of Lord Leverhulme' and other great industrialists seeking 'superprofits' (a view he later repudiated), and many agreed with him. To others, profiteers were speculators able to amass riches—so it was widely believed—by 'cornering' various markets, and whose life-style differed little from that attributed to the Edwardian plutocrat. The profiteers were the *nouveaux riches* of the 1920s; identified by vulgar display and, above all, by the wearing of furs. M. V. Hughes recollected her son saying of the neighbours they acquired in 1922: 'I think they must be *nouveaux riches*, mother, the wife is wearing a fur coat.'[26]

[26] M. V. Hughes, *A London Family between the Wars* (London, 1940), 44.

For most people, in so far as they had contact with a profiteer, he was the family greengrocer or butcher, the local version of the commodity speculator ('The cost of food continually rises. On all hands the evidence of petty prof-iteering is to be seen.')[27] The over-hasty measures of decontrol created, in effect, a legal black market, and it was usually the butcher or the greengrocer who was reported to the anti-profiteering committees which sprang up in much of the country, particularly in the southern counties or the London suburbs.[28]

For nearly everyone, no doubt, the profiteer as a type had elements of all these. Even if the only profiteering people actually experienced was their butcher's, they could still believe in the existence of the megalomaniac indus-trialist or the fur-swaddled commodity speculator. That they had such a strong sense of the profiteer was greatly to discredit the Lloyd George government, which became irredeemably associated in the middle-class imagination with a rapacious and extravagant plutocracy, and with those who had exploited a national crisis to feather their own nests, while ordinary people suffered. This view had a long life: it was, for instance, successfully exploited by J. B. Priestley in his radio broadcasts during the Second World War.[29] Profiteering, together with the 'sale of honours',[30] did much to destroy Lloyd George's reputation, and in the longer term, by discrediting him, profiteering may have discredited the more unorthodox economic policies which he later espoused. Heterodox alternatives to the policies followed by men of known moral rectitude after 1922, particularly if they involved 'profligate' expenditures, were too easily associated with the apparent debauchery of his government.

The idea of the profiteer had one other more malign consequence: it tended to reinforce a comparatively discreet but almost universal anti-semitism within the English middle class. The public image of the profiteer was all too often someone with 'cosmopolitan' attributes such as gargantuan jewellery and furs. What the post-war profiteer and the Edwardian plutocrat had in com-mon—other than too much money—was that both were thought to be Jewish. The hostility to the profiteers did not create anti-semitism—the history of any

[27] Holford Knight, 'The Black-Coated Poor', 690–1.

[28] Richmal Crompton, an acute observer of the mood of the female southern middle class, in one of her earliest 'William' stories (May 1922), has her hero, for the usual complicated reasons, over-charging for sweets. His irate female customer threatens appropriate action: 'I shall certainly not pay more than twopence . . . And I shall report the shop to the Profiteering Committee. It's scan-dalous.' (*Just William* (London, 1922), 196.) William's village was based loosely on the area around Bromley Common and the social origins of his customer are not difficult to guess.

[29] In a broadcast of July 1940, for example, Priestley said that the country had done nothing for the 'young heroes' after the First World War: 'after a year or two there were a lot of shabby-young oldish men about who did not seem to have been lucky in the scramble for easy jobs and quick profits, and so tried to sell us second-hand cars or office supplies we didn't want, or even trailed around the suburbs asking to be allowed to demonstrate the latest vacuum cleaner.' (Quoted in K. Morgan, *Consensus and Disunity* (London, 1979), 7.)

[30] For the 'sale of honours', see above, p. 16.

golf club would quickly establish that—but, together with Bolshevism, it probably prolonged its natural life. The Lloyd George government played its role in that also. Given its association with the profiteer, it was unsurprisingly associated with Jewish self-advancement and almost certainly suffered for it.[31]

The casual anti-semitism of the interwar years was to be found at all levels of English life: in the detective novels of the 1920s and 1930s, with their 'fat Jewesses' and 'sheenies'; in many of the public schools; in the recruiting habits of the civil service;[32] in the ubiquity of Jewish jokes. The anti-semitism of the First World War tended to legitimate the anti-semitism of the Second, from that shown by some members of the general staff (partly responsible for the fall of the Jewish secretary of state for war, Hore Belisha)[33] to the underground and anecdotal anti-semitism of popular wisdom. 'Jews push ahead in food queues', 'Jews dodge military service': allegations impossible to prove or disprove, but all part of the folklore of wartime Britain.[34] Jews were widely thought to have appropriated the best accommodation in the evacuated cities (or, conversely, in the nicer towns to which people were evacuated). There was even a story, most bizarre of all, that the Germans deliberately refrained from bombing Jewish-owned flats and houses.

Had middle-class hostility to wealth 'illegitimately' acquired been the only outcome of the First World War, its social and political implications could have been much more profound than they were, but it was always inhibited by an even greater hostility to the organized working class. The middle classes in

---

[31] Commenting, for example, on the defeat of the official Conservative candidate (Sir Herbert Jessel, a Jew, who supported the Lloyd George coalition) for the St George's division of Westminster in a by-election in June 1921, the chairman of the Conservative Party, Sir George Younger, wrote that 'far too many Jews have been placed in prominent places by the present government.' (Quoted in Morgan, *Consensus and Disunity*, 245.)

[32] In 1939 H. E. Dale was able to identify in the membership of the higher civil service only one person known to be Jewish, though there were two others (both married to Christians) whose names suggested they might be Jewish. (Dale, *Higher Civil Service of Great Britain*, 52.)

[33] Hore-Belisha 'provoked comments on his racial origins and traits which can only be described as vile' (Bond, *British Military Policy between the Two World Wars*, 70).

[34] The most assiduous student of anecdotal anti-semitism was George Orwell. See in particular S. Orwell and I. Angus (eds.), *The Selected Essays, Journalism and Letters of George Orwell* (London, 1968), iii. 332–41. Although a critical collector of folkloric anti-semitism he was himself oddly credulous. Noting the supposed tactlessness of some of the Jewish refugees, he reports 'a remark by a German Jewess overheard during the Battle of France: "These English police are not nearly so smart [i.e. well-dressed] as our SS men" ' (Orwell, *Selected Essays*, ii. 290–1). But this remark, 'overheard' everywhere in 1940, bears all the signs of and must surely be urban legend. Despite the ubiquity of a social anti-semitism, we should remember that people's experience of it differed. A pupil in the 1930s of St Paul's Girls' School, one of the London day schools where successful Jewish families often sent their children and which were sometimes believed by the Jewish community to practice informal discrimination, thought it comparatively unusual. She writes: 'Two Jewesses at St Pauls were cold-shouldered but one was a "swank" and the other came to school in a Rolls Royce with a liveried footman to open the door; but there were plenty of others who were wholly accepted.' (I am indebted to Lady Colvin for this information.) See, however, an entry in Nella Last's diary for Nov. 1940. She records a conversation with her tax inspector son as they drove to Bowness: 'The

1920 and 1921, wrote C. F. G. Masterman, spend their leisure time 'cursing the working man and cursing the profiteer',[35] and the order in which he placed these objects of anathema is almost certainly right. The intense, but diffuse, dislike of the profiteer was always secondary to an even more intense, but better directed, dislike of the 'working man'. All in the middle class, even those who must themselves have been profiteers, thought they had cause to fear the trade unions, and it was in the early 1920s that the middle class began to identify the working class as a whole with the trade unions and for whose activities the middle class would have to pay.[36] The trade unions in turn were endowed with an almost supernatural power: Masterman thought that the 'salariat' contemplated the programme of the miners 'with something of the emotions' felt by primitive peoples when they gazed at an eclipse of the sun.[37] As the Conservative MP Sir Harry Brittain said when urging the middle classes to mobilize, it was 'Labour, Labour, Manual Labour every time'.[38]

The unions were, in fact, much less successful at defending their members' wages and jobs than many supposed, but in the first two or three years after 1918 to any member of the middle class, capitalist or clerk, it must indeed have seemed 'manual labour every time'. The seemingly endless industrial disputes, the huge increase in union membership before 1920 and the apparent readiness of the Lloyd George government to placate the unions at every opportunity confirmed in the mind of the middle class their helplessness before an aggressive and powerful trade union movement. It was for this reason, and not just the profiteers, that class tension in the early 1920s was higher than at any time in living memory.

This fear of the unions was accompanied by an anti-working-class folklore not dissimilar to the anti-profiteer folklore. Even Masterman, usually sceptical of social folklore, could believe it. 'The municipality', he wrote, 'pays its scavengers and street cleaners substantially higher salaries than it pays its elementary school teachers.'[39] But *no* municipality ever paid its dustmen more than its elementary schoolteachers: even in 1920 the money income of a male elementary schoolteacher was more than twice that of a local authority

---

country roads and the bay at Bowness were thickly scattered by obvious townspeople, and Arthur said in a rather disgusted tone, "The place is stiff with Jews". Rather amused I said, "Well, why not? They are only people". He considered for a while and then said, "I think I have got the Manchester outlook on Jews", and I asked what he meant. He told me that it was that Jews were a parasite people, and lived "on" rather than "with" others … "In Manchester there is a clause in lots of new home deeds that they have not to be let or sold to Jews. I think I am getting quite biassed as you call it." '
(Quoted in R. Broad and S. Fleming (eds.), *Nella Last's War, 1939–1945* (London, 1981), 83.)

[35] Masterman, *England After War*, 69–70.
[36] I have discussed this elsewhere. See McKibbin, *Ideologies of Class*, 270–3; also J. Bonham, *The Middle Class Vote* (London, 1954), 54.
[37] Masterman, *England After War*, 76.
[38] Brittain, 'Middle Classes, Mobilise!', *Review of Reviews*, 316.
[39] Masterman, *England After War*, 71–2.

labourer. Nor were such stereotypes of the overpaid working man confined to men in work. From the moment unemployment became serious (1920–1) and, for many, prolonged, a related social folklore became widespread: tales of whole families living comfortably on the dole; even, most improbably of all, but believed by many, of women alighting from motor cars to collect the dole. That many of these tales were only half-believed or proffered as truths somewhat guiltily did not diminish their political or social force.[40]

It was thus in these years that the middle classes identified themselves as the constitutional classes, the 'public', and the 'public' was increasingly seen as directly opposed to the organized working class—who were definitely not the 'public'. Defence of the middle class, therefore, became defence of the constitution and the rights of the public; and the Conservative Party became the party of the public because it was the party of the constitution. Hence, in 1924, when Churchill announced his return to the Conservative Party he did so as a 'Constitutionalist', and as such was elected MP for Epping. The public also identified itself with 'society': the defence of the middle class then became the defence not just of the constitution but of society itself.

The most striking manifestation of this was the emergence of the middle classes as strike-breakers. The 1920s was the first and last decade in which large numbers of middle-class people were prepared, by breaking strikes, to defend the constitution in person. By 1922 the willingness of motor car owners, undergraduates, or City clerks to drive trams or trains, to carry coal, or to maintain municipal services was widely noticed. The most remarkable demonstration of this was during the general strike in 1926. The readiness of tens of thousands of volunteers to assist in the maintenance of essential services, and the feeling almost universal amongst the 'public' that the strike was an attack upon the constitution was a direct result of their experience in the immediate post-war years. The middle classes were as solid as the working classes and that is why the strike was defeated: as the novelist Arnold Bennett wrote after lunching at the Reform Club—'Most people gloomy, but all uncompromising.' For the strikers the image of the strike-breakers was ineradicably middle-class: that so many of the volunteers wore plus-fours suggested to working men that the golf clubs had disgorged their members *en masse*. As they may indeed have done.[41]

---

[40] For an entertaining compilation of these, see S. Haxey, *Tory MP* (London, 1939), 25–6.

[41] For details, see J. Symons, *The General Strike* (London, 1959), 72–7. Some undergraduates did, of course, support the strikers—among them Hugh Gaitskell, recruited by G. D. H. Cole. Nor did all volunteer. Some were plainly unhappy at acting as strike-breakers, and those who did refuse appear to have encountered no hostility. In retrospect, some of the strike-breakers regretted their actions: J. C. Masterman, then history tutor at Christ Church, Oxford and later provost of Worcester College, Oxford, who organized a party to work on the Southampton docks, told the author that he thought his behaviour was ill-advised. It may also have been unwise. There is a whole alternative folklore of what happened to rugby hearties after a couple of days' hard work on the docks. For an excellent

The extent to which the notion of the 'public' and the 'constitution' served to conceal from people what they were actually doing is well illustrated by a half-comic episode reported by M. V. Hughes. As a result of the strike her local station (in outer London) was closed:

And as there was suspicion that our stationmaster had 'red' leanings, a watch had to be kept on the station. For this purpose Arthur [her son, a pupil at Merchant Taylors' School] was chosen. Merchant Taylors' School had an enforced holiday, so he embraced the job wholeheartedly. Each morning I saw him off (with sandwiches and so on), dressed in his cadet uniform, and carrying concealed in a deep pocket a policeman's truncheon.[42]

Arthur, it seems, succeeded in locking the station master out of his station and vaguely terrorized him with the truncheon. In due course he received a 'handsome letter' from the prime minister 'thanking him for his national service'. It was, Mrs Hughes wrote, 'a never-to-be-forgotten effort that the country made to live through that strike'. Her only comment on it in tranquillity was: 'all was soon forgotten and normal again.' The triumph of her class was merely a daily event.

(II) 1923–1938

The steady fall in prices which began in December 1920, the restoration of the pre-war ratio of salaries to wages, and the development of persistently high working-class unemployment from 1921 on, largely restored the position of the middle class (though income redistribution within the middle class tended to survive) at the expense of both rich and poor. For many of them the years from 1923 to the outbreak of the Second World War appeared a kind of golden age. No doubt it was never as golden as people remembered it; yet in many ways the middle classes were uniquely favoured.

First: the stability of middle-class money income after 1923 is striking. Between 1923 and 1938, apart from small changes in the rate of taxation, there was only a slight variation in money income: while salaries fell somewhat from 1928 they rose again to pre-depression levels by 1936. Prices, however, continued to fall faster than salaries; and when they began to drift up in the 1930s money incomes also tended to drift up. Even with such drift the all-item cost of living index in January 1939 (155) was still significantly lower than it had been in January 1923 (178). For most members of the middle class, therefore, there was a more or less continuous rise in real income throughout the period, while the favourable relationship between salaries and wages established between 1921 and 1923 was maintained until 1938.

study of Oxford during the strike, see R. S. Sephton, *Oxford and the General Strike, 1926* (Oxford, 1993); also D. Archard *et al.*, 'Corpus in the 1926 Strike', *Pelican*, 2, 1 (1972); McKibbin, 'Oxford and the General Strike, 1926', *Oxford Magazine*, 98 (1993).

[42] Hughes, *A London Family*, 101–3.

Second: while it is true that throughout most of the interwar years anyone in continuous employment with a relatively stable money income probably made real income gains, the middle classes were peculiarly advantaged since they were much more likely to be continuously employed than the working classes. In the higher professions unemployment was negligible. Even in those middle-class occupations most sensitive to economic downturn unemployment was nowhere near 'working-class' proportions: in 1931 amongst chemists and metallurgists it was 5.7 per cent, amongst draughtsmen 6.8 per cent; amongst clerks it was 5.7 per cent for men and 4.4 per cent for women. The middle classes were not entirely unscathed: for managers and administrators, particularly in the heavily depressed textile industry, jobs could be difficult to find and promotion slow. Indeed, textiles, notoriously the small family-owned firms, was the only industry where middle-class men experienced in something like pure form the frustration and anxiety of the working-class unemployed.[43] Yet even in 1931 unemployment amongst administrators and managers in the 12 major industrial groups was a mere 1.9 per cent.[44] The only members of the middle class to experience serious unemployment were actors and musicians, both in professions with notoriously irregular patterns of employment. In the case of musicians, unemployment had little to do with the depression as such: it was primarily a result of the talking movies which eliminated the need for cinema musicians.[45]

The 1931 levels of middle-class unemployment can tellingly be compared with those of the working classes. At any one time in that year between one-fifth and one-quarter of the working class was unemployed. The *majority* of working men and women in the interwar years were at some moment in their lives genuinely unemployed; the *majority* of the middle classes never faced such unemployment at all. This distinction not only enhanced the relative real income of the middle classes but was responsible for a genuine fissure in the social experience of the English people in the interwar years.

Such relative gains were, furthermore, reinforced by a system of taxation which markedly favoured the majority of the middle classes. Although obviously distorted by the First World War, the tax régime of interwar Britain was substantially that established by Lloyd George between 1909 and 1914: one that tended to penalize the very wealthy via death duties and a 'supertax' (surtax) on high income, and the poor by regressive consumption duties. Although the middle classes did not, of course, escape altogether many came close to

---

[43] See Clements, *Managers*, 59–60: 'Prospects looked black, pay was poor, they were as exploited as cheap labour, uncles quarreled with cousins, fathers with nephews, firms went bankrupt, employees were sacked. Many grew up in a social milieu that led them to expect something better; their relationship with the firm sometimes involved them personally in problems that wracked top management and proprietors.'

[44] C. Clark, *National Income and Outlay* (London, 1938), 46.   [45] See below, p. 399.

doing so: as a result of 'abatements' allowed for children, in 1929 a married man with two children earning £400 a year paid no tax; a man on £500 a year with two children paid only £8. Middle-class incomes were thus related to family responsibilities in a way working-class incomes were not. Even after 1931, when tax rates were raised in the emergency budget of 1931, they were not at levels which much affected the majority of the middle class, and the increases were abolished in 1934 and 1935 anyway. Despite constant complaints of an overbearing taxation the proportion of middle-class income appropriated by the state in the interwar years was slight and, for many, non-existent.

All these made middle-class consumption a striking aspect of interwar England. With the exception of the year 1930–1 middle-class consumption of durable goods rose without interruption and this was responsible, in turn, for the whole culture of 'shopping' which people remembered so fondly in the 1940s. Real income gains made possible the private housing boom, largely a middle-class phenomenon, which was also, like shopping, one of the most conspicuous features of the period.[46] And they made possible the last occasion when the middle class, via domestic service, stood in a personally superior relationship to the working class. In 1931 about 500,000 households had one or more servants in residence, while the majority of households with an income of £400 or more employed servants either on a residential or daily basis. Though not as cheap as they had been, servants were still comfortably affordable by any moderately well off family. Anecdotal evidence suggests, however, that this relationship was deteriorating. Domestics were now more unwilling employees, and tended to be older. After 1918 working-class girls usually became servants only if all else failed, and were more likely to do the work grudgingly or not at all. There was a high turnover and girls frequently left abruptly amidst much mutual recrimination, often accompanied by accusations of theft. It is possible, furthermore, that as middle-class houses got smaller mistress and servant 'got on top of each other' in ways larger and more spatially segregated houses were designed to obviate. Arguably, in any case, the First World War sufficiently undermined social hierarchies to make domestic service an increasingly unacceptable social relationship. For many families the collapse of domestic service after 1940 might well have been a relief, however difficult the transition, because it re-established the privacy of middle-class life.

We should not, of course, exaggerate the uniformity of middle-class experience. The sociologist Philip Massey found, for example, that middle-class income earners of £350–£400 a year were able to save little. He suggested that within the middle classes there was 'a kind of demarcation' at about £500 a year. Below that figure middle-class families might have some, but by no

---

[46] For the housing boom, see below, pp. 73–7.

means all, of the appurtenances of a middle-class life.[47] For many middle-class families—whose incomes were frequently less than £400 a year—life could still be very straitened; the more galling because the possibility of the comfortable life was so near. None the less, for the 'luckier majority' of the middle classes, the interwar years were a time when 'technology had already yielded many of its benefits while, as yet, few of its snags were apparent.'[48]

(III) 1938–1951

Contemporaries thought the middle-class golden age came to an end in 1940–1 with the full mobilization of the war economy. But it in fact began to peter out in 1938, when income movements started to work against salaries, though not profits. The money level of middle-class incomes tended to get stuck, while between 1938 and 1940 money wages of manual workers rose by a remarkable 30 per cent. This sudden reversal of fortunes, which was probably due to rearmament, came at the beginning of two decades during which the middle class as a whole lost relatively to the working class as a whole.

It was not a steady decline, but had three stages: 1938–44, when there was continuous loss, 1944–6 when there was some recovery; and 1946–51, when there was further decline to levels in some cases lower than 1944. In 1929, for example, the average salary of a clerk was 128 per cent of the wage of an average manual worker. In 1952 it was 110 per cent. Although male clerks thought they were uniquely disfavoured, this erosion was true of the whole 'salariat'. Engineering draughtsmen, members of a rapidly growing technical profession, were even more disfavoured: in 1940 the money income of an engineering draughtsmen was 83 per cent of the manual earnings index—itself low enough; in 1945 it was 78 per cent; in 1950 70 per cent. So with the higher professions: whereas the index of manual earnings rose from 100 in 1937 to 241 in 1949, that of the higher professions rose from 100 to only 188.

There was an income continuum whereby all incomes were redistributed downwards with the greatest relative beneficiary being the unskilled manual worker. The consequence was (as between 1914 and 1920) a redistribution both between and within classes; income differentials within the middle class were, therefore, significantly reduced. The index of civil service pay is a good instance of this effect. At the top of the civil service, the administrative class, the index rose from 100 in 1938 to 128 in 1950; at its bottom, manual-working post office engineers, it rose from 100 to 207. Of the index more generally, two things are most obvious: the striking gains made by manual workers at the expense of everyone else; and the failure of women employees to make any

---

[47] P. Massey, 'The Expenditure of 1,360 British Middle-Class Households in 1938–39', *JRSS*, cv, pt. iii (1942); see also D. Caradog Jones, 'The Cost of Living of a Sample of Middle-Class Families', *JRSS*, xci, pt. iv (1928).

[48] S. Glynn and J. Oxborrow, *Interwar Britain: A Social and Economic History* (London, 1976), 69.

relative gains at all—an experience, with few exceptions, common to women throughout the economy.

Moreover, a higher proportion of earnings was taxed in 1945 than in 1938: marginal rates were raised and abatements reduced. Those on annual incomes of £250–£700 in 1938 paid 2.7 per cent of it in tax; but in 1947 12.7 per cent. For those on annual incomes of £700–£2000 the figures were 9.3 per cent and 22.7 per cent. These rates were a long way from confiscatory and nowhere as high as those levied on the 'rich', but for people who were used to a very favourable tax régime, the prolongation of these changes after the wartime emergency (when they were, on the whole, accepted with relative equanimity) was both unwelcome and resented.

It would, of course, as ever, be wrong to argue that the social history of all members of the middle class was the same. Even Roy Lewis and Angus Maude, whose book *The English Middle Classes* (1948) ventilated most of their grievances, conceded that. They admitted that a man who had bought his house outright by 1939 'is very different from . . . his opposite number who had no house before the war'.[49] Middle-class parents certainly emerged from the war much better off than their children who served in the forces and returned as adults. Self-employed members of the middle class, or those whose incomes derived from a variety of sources, were able to protect themselves better than those who lived solely from their salaries. Shopkeepers, for example, as in the First World War, were notoriously able to sell whatever they had, and were none too deferential when they did. Above all, businessmen and business employees, though they were subject to severe rates of taxation on investments, were able to escape the worst effects of taxation by the addition to their salaries of untaxed or 'tax efficient' increments. In the 1940s British business first began to pay its more senior employees not only in taxed income but in 'perks': 'working-day' holidays, life and medical insurance contributions, pension contributions, assistance with children's education, subsidized mortgages, and the 'company car'. By these means style of life and perhaps morale was in part preserved when it could have become dangerously undermined.

Nor were the middle classes disadvantaged by wartime and post-war social policies. Both the coalition and Labour governments were careful not to means-test much of the social provision introduced in the 1940s. The middle classes were, therefore, as much beneficiaries of family allowances as the working classes; the National Health Service was eventually to relieve many middle-class families of the burden of private health insurance, a real grievance before 1939; and food subsidies represented a partial return for the higher rates of tax. The 1944 Education Act, by abolishing secondary school fees, was to give the middle class, like everyone else, free access to a

---

[49] R. Lewis and A. Maude, *The English Middle Classes* (2nd ed., London, 1948), 206.

quasi-public school education; and the middle class was the principal beneficiary.[50] Indeed, non-means-tested provision of this sort may have over-
favoured the middle class: not that any would have admitted it. Finally, for a
small but influential section of the middle class, the farmers, the 1940s rather
than the 1930s were the golden age; and made even more golden by the policies of the Attlee government.

The Attlee government, indeed, had learnt a lesson from Lloyd George. The
effect of its policies, even if they did not eliminate the bullying shopkeeper or
the black market, was to eliminate the idea of the profiteer from middle-class
politics (and thus perhaps to diminish the force of anti-semitism). The characteristic product of the 1940s was the 'spiv',[51] the usually working-class sharpster
who guided middle-class persons through the wonderlands of the black market: but the public perception of him, half-contemptuous, half-affectionate,
was quite different from its unambiguously hostile perception of the profiteer.

Even compared with the golden age, furthermore, the exceptionally high
levels of economic activity in all sectors of the economy throughout the 1940s
substantially widened prospects of promotion, particularly in industry.
Although middle-class unemployment was very low in the interwar years, promotion was often difficult, and there was always the middle-class equivalent
of the dead-end job. That was a source of class tension. The biggest grievance,
though not the only one, that the ordinary middle classes had against the
upper middle class and the upper class, was that they monopolized the best
positions in industry and finance—a monopoly not, it was often thought,
earned by merit. In the 1940s, on the contrary, promotion was almost too easy;
many men appointed to managerial posts during the war were often unsatisfactory and had to be replaced.

The conditions of life for the middle classes in the 1940s were not, therefore,
as grim as some depicted it; a fact that most members of the middle class were,
from time to time, aware. After 1945, however, people became reluctant to
admit publicly that there were gains as well as losses; for some the Attlee government came to represent only loss. There were two reasons for this: the
effects of wartime austerity on the conventional standards of middle-class life;
and the genuine status decline suffered by many of the middle class throughout the decade.

The greyness of life after 1945, the narrowness of social and cultural choice,
the restrictions upon personal consumption, affected the middle class no
more than the working class but the comparative effects were more harsh.
Many of the attributes of life commonly regarded as essential by the middle
classes either disappeared or became almost impossible to retain. For the first
time in British history the comfortable classes had to run their households

[50] For the effects of the 1944 Education Act, see below, pp. 259–62.
[51] For the spiv, see below, pp. 450–2.

unassisted and for many this particular rite of passage was painful. All the middle class felt keenly the restrictions on clothing. Good clothes were important for status and promotion, and were a subject on which employers could be unyielding. In the 1940s employers had to be less demanding but the noticeable shabbiness of much of the middle class caused both shame and resentment. For the better-off middle classes, as great a deprivation were the restrictions on motoring. By 1939 the majority of households on £500 a year or more owned a car and motoring had become one of the most popular middle-class pastimes. The car had also become an important measure of status. Both account for the extreme unpopularity of petrol rationing after the war and the sense of loss it imposed. It also accounts for the determination of the Conservative Party to abolish rationing as soon as it could. For those who had been used to having a holiday abroad before the war—and in 1939 nearly one and a half million had done so—currency restrictions caused the same kind of loss (though greatly encouraged the package-holiday industry), and, unlike the upper classes, members of the middle class were usually not able to find ways around them. Finally, the deprivations of the British middle class were to complicate its attitudes to the United States; much more so than Britain's post-war policy might suggest. Americans were immediately conspicuous in the commercial centre of any British city in the 1940s by the newness and quality of their clothes; and the middle classes were inevitably more conscious of that than anyone else; as they were of Britain's mendicant status and their own comparative poverty. Those who prided themselves on their standards and modest comfort found American abundance an almost undeserved reproach. The contrast between the austere existence of the English lower middle classes in the late 1940s and the Aladdin's Cave of America's (unearned) wealth was a perpetual grievance, and is well observed in David Lodge's semi-autobiographical novel *Out of the Shelter*.[52]

Such deprivation also conditioned the attitude of most of the middle class to the Labour government and the Labour movement. By the end of the decade that attitude was usually hostile and sometimes very hostile. Despite the gains the 1940s brought to all classes, much of the middle class was acutely aware of the redistribution of social esteem which had undoubtedly occurred throughout the war. Those employed in clerical occupations were particularly conscious of this redistribution. They often suffered the sharpest falls in living standards at the outbreak of the war—especially younger men who had bought

---

[52] The novel (1970) is set at the end of our period and recounts the visit of a 16-year-old boy (Lodge) to his sister (in reality his aunt) who works for the American occupying forces in Germany. The description of the boy's first exposure to American living standards and its painful contrast with what he had been accustomed to in a south London lower-middle-class household is very telling. His 'sister' refuses to return to England on the grounds, amongst other things, that there is no adequate domestic heating, nor disposable paper handkerchiefs. See Lodge's 'Afterword' to the 1985 edition.

houses by mortgage—since they were most likely to be called up: there were not many middle-class 'reserved occupations'. They resented the apparent truculence of the working class and were sensitive to the widely insinuated criticisms that they were less 'useful' to society than manual workers. The relative position of miners and bank clerks before and after 1940 was something of which both were well aware. Even qualifications like a grammar school education, which before the war had seemed so desirable, now appeared only to confirm the uselessness of those who possessed them.

In some cases clerks, especially in the public sector, simply threw in their lot with the industrial working class, but the majority conspicuously did not. The result was a rather aggressive-defensive attitude to manual workers. With many 'black-coated' workers the reaction 'has taken a rather savage form and has been directed in an undisguised manner at the trade union movement'. When asked to define the working class 'black-coated' workers tended to use terms which maximized social distance: working men were 'dustmen', 'roadsweepers', or 'navvies'.[53] They were not defined as skilled workers precisely because skilled workers appeared too close and too threatening.

John Bonham found that this hostility to the working class, and to the Labour Party with which it was exclusively identified, was expressed in remarkably similar terms at all levels of the middle class:

'The Labour Party', said a newsagent and tobacconist, 'condemns anyone or anything with initiative'. A farmer called Labour 'totalitarian socialism', and a barrister's wife asserted 'Nationalization is a better name for it'. So down the income and social scale through employees as well as business owners, we get complaints of 'bossing people about' (this from the wife of a civil servant), 'destruction of individuality' (doctor), 'red tape and restrictions' (farmer's wife), and 'regimentation and controls' (wife of a shop manager).[54]

Stereotypes of working-class profligacy and wealth survived well into the 1950s, even though by then attitudes had softened somewhat:

the lower intellect people are mostly inclined towards Labour aren't they? I think it's because they're the sort of people that won't do things for themselves. They want everything doing for them instead of working hard and saving a bit of money and buying a house. They'd rather live on a council estate.[55]

The people who've made the most money since the war are the lower classes, but they don't seem to know how to spend it wisely. The ordinary sort of person—I suppose you would call them middle class—the sort of people who put their family first, they haven't done too well. I've noticed that the people who've got the money these days don't spend it on their families but on the dogs and such things. (Civil Servant's wife)[56]

53 Lockwood, *Black-Coated Worker*, 127.   54 Bonham, *Middle Class Vote*, 141–2.
55 B. Jackson and D. Marsden, *Education and the Working Class* (London, 1962), 56–7.
56 P. Willmott and M. Young, *Family and Class in a London Suburb* (London, 1960), 117–18.

We should not exaggerate the violence of this hostility to the working class: it could certainly have been worse. The French neo-liberal writer Bertrand de Jouvenel, who was sympathetic to their plight, was none the less struck by the patriotic calm with which the middle classes bore their misfortunes.[57] But the evidence suggests wartime fraternity and egalitarianism did not long survive the war itself. Even during the war it was possible to combine a wholly patriotic commitment to victory without sharing at all its fraternity. The wartime diaries of Mrs Milburn, a decidedly upper-middle-class figure, though utterly patriotic, are unbending in their hostility to the unions, the Labour Party, and any expressions of 'class consciousness'.[58] Nor, as Lewis and Maude pointed out, was there a saviour immediately at hand.[59] Except perhaps the Conservative Party; as in the 1920s, there was in the 1940s a huge expansion in the membership of the Conservative Party: another step on the road to its becoming the party of the resentful ratepayer.

The middle class thus ended the period as it began: anti-working class. And anti-working classness remained one of its defining characteristics. But in 1951 much of it was anti-working class in a different way, partly because it was a different middle class; or, rather, a more complicated one. Despite the intervention of the First World War, the middle class of the early 1920s was primarily Edwardian and continued to reflect the social structure of the Edwardian years. Although as we have seen there was some change in the 1920s, its structure was still then professional–clerical–commercial. Furthermore, though the majority of its members were not rentiers, a significant element were, and it was they who in many ways set the tone. The historian thus has a strong sense that the bitterness of class relations in the years immediately after the war were Edwardian class relations gone wrong. The active fear of the working class in the 1920s; the sense that there was a lower depth which could sweep away property, decorum, the constitution; these were all Edwardian panic-fantasies which the early 1920s, unlike the Edwardian years themselves, contrived to make reality for much of the middle class. It is the reaction of an essentially Edwardian middle class which explains the remarkable popularity of Warwick Deeping's *Sorrell and Son* (1925), an essentially Edwardian novel. This unpalatable concoction of snobbery, fear, and wish-fulfilment can only be understood by the circumstances in which it was written: that it so obviously spoke to so many in middle-class England suggests how powerfully its socially explicit images—of profiteers, of uncouth working men, of a heroic code of virtuous behaviour—were shared by them.[60] Even the images were Edwardian: the

---

[57] B. de Jouvenel, *Problems of a Socialist England* (London, 1949), 206.

[58] P. Donnelly (ed.), *Mrs Milburn's Diaries* (London, 1979), 144, 194.

[59] Lewis and Maude, *English Middle Classes*, 95; also I.-M. Zweiniger-Bargielowska, 'Rationing, Austerity and the Conservative Party Recovery after 1945', *Historical Journal*, 37 (1994), 173–94.

[60] For a further discussion of *Sorrell and Son*, see below, pp. 481–2.

profiteer differs little from the plutocrat; the heroic individual differs little from the masterful empire-builder. The behaviour of those who rallied to the constitution in 1926, who donned their plus-fours to break strikes, was Edwardian behaviour which the circumstances of the early 1920s seemed to render appropriate.

Such behaviour, however, was almost inconceivable in the 1930s: the middle classes of the 1930s were too relaxed and optimistic. Even in the 1940s, when they were not at their most optimistic, there was little of that desperation all too observable in the early 1920s. In part this was due simply to economic and political change. The 1930s, unlike the early 1920s, were economically very favourable to the middle classes; conversely they were unfavourable to the organized working class. And in 1931, the Labour Party, the political arm of the organized working class, itself suffered a major defeat. The social peace of the 1930s was, therefore, procured largely (in one way or another) at the expense of the working class.

But that was also true of the later 1920s. The explanation, therefore, lies in the fact that the middle class of the 1930s was not only larger but much more technical and scientific. Not unreasonably, much of that class came to think of itself as 'modern'; perhaps the most modern of England's social classes. Because it was 'modern', and because an increasing number of its members were employed either by the central or local government, it was less hostile to the state and the working class than the 'old' middle class. Compared with the 'old' middle class it was, for example, much readier to have its children educated by the state. At the moment when the grammar schools were rapidly developing as much sought-after middle-class institutions, the *Bank Officer* was still (1933) warning bank employees, paragons of the 'old' middle class, that the 'council school', however admirable its teaching, was 'an institution of which few bank clerks will avail themselves save under stress and misgiving'. It was also more willing to accept state social security provision: the NHS was probably as popular with the 'modern' middle class as with the working class. The 'productionism' of the 1940s, the emphasis upon industry and technology, both softened middle-class hostility to the Attlee government—productionism was something they both had in common—and propped up the social esteem of a number of middle-class occupations. Finally, many in the 'new' middle class were of working-class origin themselves and, though the evidence suggests they departed the working class without regret,[61] they rarely had that embittered attitude to the working class which characterized the middle class of the 1920s.

The consequence of the recomposition of the middle class was the development by the late 1930s of a confident individualist democracy based upon

---

[61] See below, p. 265.

notions of expertise and public engagement.[62] This optimistic, individualist democracy, however, scarcely survived the Second World War. One effect of the war was to associate democracy with the working class; and the predominant notion of democracy thereby became collective rather than individualist. This tended to unite the middle class, new and old, against 'socialism', 'bureaucracy', and the 'unions', as they had been united in the early 1920s.

Even so, some younger middle-class men and women (if only a minority) remained permanently influenced by wartime definitions of democracy; and for those who were not, their individual experience of the war often contrasted awkwardly with the general experience of their own class. For some young middle-class men, particularly, the war was a personal and emotional apogee. It represented either liberation—as to Brian Aldiss's hero 'Horry', who was emancipated by the sheer proletarian awfulness of the army from the social and sexual constraints of the provincial bourgeoisie[63]—or a feeling that never again would life be so intense. It was partly this sense of anti-climax and disappointment which permitted a second great regrouping of the middle class, which rallied to the Conservative Party in the later 1940s as it had rallied to the Conservatives in the early 1920s.

[62] See below, pp. 482–5.   [63] Brian Aldiss, *A Soldier Erect* (London, 1971).

III   The Middle Class (II)

THE last chapter was a chronological history of the middle class. This chapter is more thematic. It considers patterns of middle-class expenditure, the development of private housing and its social effects, middle-class associationalism and social networks, the differences between the 'traditional' and 'non-traditional' middle class, patterns of marriage and domesticity, and the growth of an 'apolitical' sociability which allowed the various middle classes to regroup in self-defence and to act, in certain circumstances, as a single class.

1 | *Expenditure and housing*

In their 'material' lives the members of the middle class differed both from the classes below them and amongst themselves. Between the middle and working classes the main difference was, of course, income: the 'average' middle-class family earned twice the income of the 'average' working-class family and spent twice as much. In 1938–9 the total family expenditure of the 'average' working-class family was 85s per week, the 'average' middle-class family 172s per week. Thus many of the observable differences between the two classes (particularly in the accumulation of assets) were the result simply of different incomes. But this is not true of all forms of expenditure. For example, not only did working-class families spend a much higher proportion of their income on food, they actually spent *more* per capita on food staples (bread, sugar, potatoes, etc.) than the middle classes.[1]

Only on food, however, did total working-class outlay approximate that of the middle classes and only on fuel and light was it significantly more than half. The middle classes spent, for example, twice as much on clothing as the working classes. Again, this was partly the result of larger income, but it also reflected a different 'order of urgency'. Suitable clothing was necessary both for the job and for social status: it was one of the last things that could be sacrificed. When middle-class incomes were pinched, as in the early 1920s, this

---

[1] Massey, 'Expenditure', 171–4; R. G. D. Allen and A. L. Bowley, *Family Expenditure* (London, 1935), 49–50.

necessary expenditure could become a burden, and for those who were expected to maintain a middle-class standard on less than £250 a year (for whom the surveys make no provision) it was probably always a burden.

Expenditure on insurance, pensions, and health also differed radically between the middle and working classes, a consequence of differences both in income and in the ways the state subvented income. Thus, for instance, while the 'average' working-class family spent nearly as much in 1939 on trade union, Friendly Society, and burial club subscriptions (17.74d per week) as the 'average' middle-class family (19.49d per week), and very much more on un-employment and national health insurance (25.01d per week as against 9.78d per week), the 'average' middle-class family spent more than four times as much on payments to pension funds, on insurance premiums etc—131.06d per week against 31.72d. per week. (These figures represent sterling old pence, averaged.) The total middle-class family expenditure on prudential payments (health, pensions, life insurance, funeral benefits), though more than twice that of a working-class family, was probably less significant than where it was spent. Before the Second World War the bulk of middle-class prudential expenditure was spent privately and this was because the middle classes were, on the whole, ineligible for any kind of state benefit: they could not receive a state pension or unemployment insurance or help with doctors' bills.

Furthermore, throughout this period the middle classes were paid by salary or other type of regular income while the working classes, for the most part, were not. This tended to unite the whole of the middle class in a common way of looking at the world which a regular and calculable income permitted. For the middle classes the 'life-time' income—a known salary stepped by age and promotion and capped by a private (if often inadequate) pension—had become customary. That the scale of income and expenditure varied hugely between one end of the middle class and the other mattered less than that its members increasingly managed their money the same way and in the same spirit. Most members of the middle class had a bank or building society account or both; an ever larger proportion, and by 1951 almost certainly a majority, had a cheque book, and payment by direct debit, particularly for mortgages, was becoming common. This was a form of behaviour from which the working classes, whose incomes were irregular and unpredictable, almost always in cash, and usually not deposited in bank or building society, were largely excluded. This in turn meant that much of the working class, from the middle-class view, 'misman-aged' its finances; it declined to save, and spent extra income on phonographs or radios—things it could not 'afford'. Such apparent fecklessness was central to the construction of middle-class politics both after 1918 and 1945. That the middle and working classes still managed their money in contrary ways had, therefore, a direct political implication.

Within the middle class itself differences in the way people spent their money were increasingly determined by size of income rather than major differences in social priorities. Furthermore, at income levels between £250–£700 the actual sums spent were surprisingly alike: it was only at £700 that the magnitudes became significantly larger.[2] Expenditure per head on food and on type of food appears to have been more or less the same throughout the middle classes, as was outlay on insurance premiums and pension contributions. Equally, money spent on household expenses fell within a narrow band, while outlay on rent and mortgage repayments was fairly similar throughout the lower and middle middle classes: those on £250 a year paid much the same as those on £500. The tendency towards uniformity was increased by the fact that the majority of middle-class incomes fell within the £250–£500 range: of all incomes of £250 or more in 1937, 70 per cent were within that band.[3] The big differences occur in what contemporaries would have thought of as middle-class luxuries. The upper middle classes spent large sums on motoring and the telephone (now necessities to them), which were hardly represented at all in lower-middle-class budgets, and very much more on domestic service. They also spent heavily on the perquisites of upper-middle-class life, particularly travelling; but disproportionately less—perhaps unexpectedly—on entertaining themselves and others.

This suggests that there was a widespread agreement amongst the middle classes about the proper standards of middle-class life. The sociologist Philip Massey, noting the comparative uniformity of rents paid by the middle classes in 1939, commented that 'there exists a sort of minimum middle class rent, below which non-manual workers cannot find the accommodation they feel to be appropriate.'[4] In order to preserve this standard the lower middle classes were prepared to consume a high proportion of their incomes. But there also seem to have been certain assumptions about 'overspending': the middle and upper middle classes could probably have consumed a higher proportion of their incomes than they did. Instead they preferred to save it, either for reasons of prudence or because of a cultural disapproval of conspicuous consumption.

There was, however, one important exception to this. Between the upper and the lower extremes of middle-class income there was a huge difference in the sums spent on the education of children. The majority of upper-middle-class children were educated at public or semi-public schools; the great majority of lower-middle-class children at state schools. This did not always reflect a different social priority: a non-state education was still expected of the children of certain lower- and middle-middle-class occupations and people still struggled to provide it. Most middle-class people were coming to regard a

---

[2] Massey, 'Expenditure', 171–4.
[3] G. Harrison and F. G. Mitchell, *The Home Market* (London, 1939), 93.
[4] Massey, 'Expenditure', 169.

private education as more 'appropriate' for their children but one, however heroic their budgeting, they were quite unable to afford. This was why the expansion of the grammar school system in the interwar years, whose principal beneficiary they were, was so important to them; it gave their children something like a public school education at low costs and by doing so extended to the whole of the middle class the possibility of an 'appropriate' education. Although no one at the time said so, this was an area where the state intervened to support middle-class incomes in a socially significant manner.[5]

It was thus widely assumed that while there was considerable saving amongst the upper income groups of the middle class, there was very little in the lower. But the principal form of middle-class saving was house-purchase. By the outbreak of the Second World War almost 60 per cent of middle-class families either owned or were buying their houses. The bulk of the two million houses built in England in the 1930s without state assistance were built for individual private purchase: they represented overwhelmingly the most important form of middle-class investment and probably the principal aspiration of the English middle classes. Contemporaries were aware of the significance of this; some, indeed, thought that it had created a 'new' middle class, a class whose unity depended solely on the purchase of houses built since 1920.[6]

The belief that house-purchase actually created a 'new' class presumes that interwar house buyers were socially mixed in their origins. There is, however, little evidence for this. Only the very best paid working men could have afforded a house, and then with difficulty. Thus, for example, more than 80 per cent of the country's cheapest houses were rented and this reflects the very low levels of working-class owner-occupation. Industrial working-class towns with relatively high levels of owner-occupation (like Burnley) were the result of pre-1914 circumstances and there most owner-occupied houses were built before the First World War. By the late 1930s less than one-fifth of the working class were owner-occupiers; in fact, the working class owned a smaller proportion of the country's housing stock in 1939 than it had in 1915.[7] The private housing boom of the 1930s had not created a new middle class; rather, it had made the country's private housing stock more middle-class. The rapid fall of construction costs in the early 1930s and the willingness of building societies (often in conjunction with speculative builders) to provide up to 95 per cent mortgages—and to those with occupational pensions, 100 per cent—simply made it possible for much of the middle middle and some of the lower middle class to buy a house for the first time. It was at the time reckoned that a man

---

[5] See below, pp. 259–62.   [6] D. Chapman, *The Home and Social Status* (London, 1955), 26.
[7] M. Swenarton and S. Taylor, 'The Scale and Nature of the Growth of Owner-Occupation in Britain between the Wars', *Economic History Review* [Ec.H.R.], 2, 38 (1985), 392; see also D. L. North, 'Middle-Class Suburban Culture and Lifestyles in England, 1919–1939', unpublished Oxford D.Phil. thesis, 1988, 9–14, 25.

earning £350–£400 a year could afford one with reasonable comfort, though it is likely, so favourable were the circumstances, that a number earning less were also able to do so. Elementary schoolteachers, senior technicians and draughtsmen, senior clerical workers, better-paid shop assistants or buyers, were the kind of middle-class people who could afford houses in the thirties but could not have done so in the twenties. Nevertheless, many who regarded themselves as middle-class could still not do so and remained confined to rented accommodation.

While owner-occupation did not create a 'new' middle class there was, however, a marked geographical bias in the distribution of new housing. Every major northern town had its areas of conspicuously new private housing estates, like Roundhay in Leeds or Levenshulme in Manchester, but the bulk of the new housing was located in the South and parts of the Midlands, particularly in greater London and the home counties, in the southern coastal towns and in those places which were the main beneficiaries of interwar industrial expansion, like greater Birmingham, Oxford, or Bedford–Luton. This made it comparatively easy for middle-class people to move from the North and accentuated their drift south. It also accentuated the growing regional division between North and South and exaggerated the already obvious 'suburban' character of much of southern England, particularly greater London and its home county hinterland.[8] Again, however, it did not create these divisions. New housing was built speculatively to meet an assumed demand and the demand was the result of wider economic and social changes.

None the less, whatever one thought of it, there was no doubt that the huge growth in middle-class home-ownership in the interwar years had great significance. Even though a large minority of middle-class families still rented, home-ownership, in the eyes of contemporaries, more than anything else defined the character of the English middle classes.

The English were always believed to have a peculiar attachment to 'home' (as a building rather than as a community). People were struck, for example, by the number of popular songs which celebrated 'home'.[9] In this sense, therefore, the extension of middle-class owner-occupation merely continued and confirmed a long cultural tradition. There was, however, an accidental element to this which contemporaries were reluctant to acknowledge: British tax laws made owner-occupation an attractive form of investment. Since investment in housing for rent could not be treated for tax purposes as any other capital investment might be (and allowance made for depreciation), it had ceased to be a profitable form of middle-class saving. But the provision of tax relief for interest payments on house-mortgages (originally designed in the

---

[8] For details of the regional distribution of the middle classes, see A. M. Carr-Saunders, D. Caradog Jones, and C. A. Moser, *A Survey of Social Conditions in England and Wales* (Oxford, 1958), 49–50.
[9] Chapman, *The Home and Social Status*, 171.

nineteenth century to encourage working-class house-purchase) made owner-occupation a very desirable saving. Furthermore, financial circumstances after 1929 led to a huge rise in funds put on deposit in the building societies: the Woolwich, whose assets had risen between 1920 and 1925 only from £1.6 million to £2.0 million, saw them rise to £17 million in 1930 and £30.1 million in 1935. It is important to note this, since it is otherwise too easy to assume that the drive for owner-occupation was the result only of cultural tradition.

But contemporaries found it difficult to agree about its consequences (other than that they were profound), or whether they were desirable or not. This was so partly because they were less struck by owner-occupation as such than by what appeared to be its physical manifestation: a vast number of speculatively built semi-detached villas constructed in the 1930s which appeared to have transformed the landscape, particularly in the South of England. In 1936, for example, 3.3 per cent was added to the country's total housing stock, the bulk of it speculative building, a figure never before or since reached. As there were virtually no planning requirements for speculative building and as it reduced costs, the tendency was for 'estates' to be built along existing country roads. This led to the phenomenon of 'ribbon development': long rows of (usually) semi-detached houses strung along the length of arterial roads (of which a classic example is the Kidlington development outside Oxford), distant from shops or services and seemingly devoid of any traditional notion of community. The speed with which this happened, and its omnipresence, took most people by surprise, which is why it occurred largely without restriction. That it did drastically modify the English landscape within a decade is unquestionable.

In the 1930s the virtues or defects of ribbon development were endlessly debated. Nor was it the only form of speculative building for private ownership which people either hated or loved: there was again much unplanned construction of bungalows (particularly in Kent and Sussex and on the south coast)—many as country retreats or as eventual abodes for retirement—and popular with those who bought them but disliked by those who lived nearby or who regarded the countryside as an 'amenity', a word becoming widely used in the 1930s and 1940s. Thus assertions about the 'character' of the English middle classes tended to become inseparable from the character and ownership of their housing. And in turn, what people often had in mind was the 1930s 'spec-built' semi-detached: the physically disaggregated housing most visibly represented by ribbon development—miles and miles of privately built and owned villas and bungalows.

Most of these houses were not designed by architects; they were put up by builders from pattern books and were markedly neo-vernacular in style. Modernism (as the English understood it) was not in fact eschewed; many of the houses had features, like elongated windows and curved outer walls, which were vaguely Bauhaus, but that influence was etiolated and often overwhelmed by vernacular 'touches'. The tendency of the 1920s houses was neo-Georgian; those of the 1930s neo-Tudor rustic. This evolution, as well as that of ribbon development, is almost perfectly illustrated by the houses on either side of the Western Avenue in outer London (the beginnings of the A 40) which combine a rather stately Georgian with an extraordinarily eclectic series of vernacular arrangements: all loosely linked to neo-Tudor or vaguely Georgian shopping centres at major intersections, an immense Odeon cinema and Wallis Gilbert and Partners' great art-deco Hoover factory which rises in glory at the Perivale end. Before 1939 the necessary rurality was preserved: nearly all the land behind the houses was agricultural; indeed, some of it still survives. The Western Avenue 'estates' are good examples of interwar lower-middle-class housing: the road-front quite well detailed; the rest architecturally unfinished. They also express its ideology: low-density, quasi-rural, nostalgic; but irretrievably suburban.

Although the origins of neo-vernacular speculative housing were ultimately in the English 'cottage' tradition, its immediate inspiration was the more expensive and elaborate estates built in Kent, Surrey, and Hertfordshire in the 1920s. These were carefully landscaped, with the houses, often detached villas in substantial grounds, artfully grouped around closes, culs-de-sac or country 'lanes'. They also were speculatively built, but usually by large firms like Costains, Wimpey, Berg, and John Laing, who employed their own architects and who did not need immediate sale. They were not infrequently built near golf courses or else golf courses were built near them; in any case proximity to a course was usually deemed by builders to be essential, and that reflected the importance of golf to the interwar business middle classes.[10] Sales publicity emphasized their rural character, the freshness of the air, the health and calm of the environment, proximity to the metropolis but without metropolitan stress.[11] At a level somewhat lower, the London railway companies, particularly the Metropolitan Railway Company, in order to promote passenger traffic on their new lines, encouraged migration to new estates by evoking the idyllic existence awaiting those who occupied these utopias. The Metropolitan Railway itself was closely associated with the development of estates at Neasden, Wembley Park, Pinner, Rickmansworth, Chorley Wood, Rayners Lane, Eastcote, Ruislip, and Hillingdon. This was 'metroland',[12] celebrated by John Betjeman, personified by Evelyn Waugh's formidable white-slaver, Margot, Lady Metroland, and representing a style of living identifiably and increasingly part of the English social, mental, and physical landscape.

[10] For golf, see below, pp. 359–61.
[11] J. Burnett, *A Social History of Housing, 1815–1970* (London, 1978), 244–70. For excellent illustrations and plans of interwar housing, see D. Calabi (ed.), *Architettura domestica in Gran Bretagna, 1890–1939* (Milan, 1982).
[12] For the origins of the word, see A. A. Jackson, *Semi-Detached London* (London, 1973), 202–3.

The bulk of interwar middle-class housing was derived from these models, the *villages anglais*, and was nearly all a more or less debased version of them. There was, of course, another kind of middle-class ribbon development, like the huge quasi-Webb–Voysey houses erected by the West Midlands' plutocracy along the Kenilworth road outside Coventry, a development several miles in length which turned a country way into a great avenue, or the opulent additions to what people now called stockbroker-belt housing in Surrey. But this was very superior housing indeed; not speculatively built, usually architect-designed by private commission, and having little proximity to the surrounding houses. And they were inhabited by Edmond Goblot's idea of the comfortable English middle classes, cited above, p. 44.

Most of those who moved into spec-built houses in the 1920s and 1930s liked them. There was often much about general provision they disliked—distance from shops, for example, or from elementary schools (which frequently became an 'issue')—but there were few complaints about the houses themselves. Nor was there much evidence (despite contemporary criticism) that they were 'jerry-built'; on the contrary, the general standard, despite a number of well-publicized disasters, was fairly high, particularly of those houses built by large firms. Furthermore, the facilities and general household equipment were nearly always better than the accommodation from which people moved or in which they grew up. Children raised in the new estates usually remembered them with affection, particularly those whose houses still had rural outlooks, whether they were potato fields or dairy farms—although they also remembered the profound silence that fell on the streets when husbands had gone to work and the delivery vans had departed. In terms of domestic amenity the speculatively built middle-class housing of these years was a real gain. Nevertheless, this huge social and demographic change and the form it took was always politically and ideologically problematic.

It was, in the first place, deliberately encouraged by Conservative or Conservative-dominated governments. Although at the end of the First World War it had been concluded that the first task of housing policy was working-class housing, that conclusion was sacrificed to policies which favoured the rehousing of the middle classes: the great majority of houses built in the twenties and thirties were privately built and for sale. Furthermore, one-quarter of these houses were put up with government subsidies.[13] Nor did those responsible conceal the fact that their motives were political: private housing of the villa–garden type was thought to turn people away from 'socialism'. The possession of property, the delights of a garden, and the demands and satisfactions of a small but healthy family provided, it was argued, the best kind of support for an individualist politics. There was thus a clear political

---

[13] North, 'Middle-Class Suburban Culture', 9–14.

dimension to the housing boom which was widely understood. What had probably not been intended was that such a high proportion of new housing would be middle-class.

But there were many who intensely disliked the development of interwar owner-occupation: not merely the housing itself but the patterns of life which it was thought to encourage. Although this dislike was broadly political it was also partly (and, in some cases, exclusively) aesthetic. Some were simply hostile to the architectural and environmental quality of new middle-class housing, particularly those who were younger architects and had been influenced by modernism. They despised what they took to be the spuriousness of the architecture and the emptiness of its human aspect. Others, like Clough Williams Ellis, the creator of the fantasy village of Portmeirion on the Welsh coast, accepted many of the aesthetic assumptions which lay behind interwar private housing, but disliked the apparent cheapness and amateurism of their execution. 'It is held', he wrote in 1928,

to be proper to 'face the road' (the 'face' being the elevation with the front door and the bay window); and this commandment, 'Thou shalt face the road', and its almost universal acceptance, has resulted in the evolution of two utterly different styles of building, one for the front, which is the official public façade to be seen of all men, and the other for the sides and back, which, like dirty linen, are conventionally supposed to be for the family only.[14]

Furthermore, it is clear that Ellis associated this nastiness with a general despoliation of the English landscape (which almost non-existent planning laws permitted) and a casual philistinism at all levels of life—as did the distinguished contributors to the collection of essays, strikingly entitled *Britain and the Beast*, which he edited in 1937. With him an aesthetic critique developed into a political one: he became a strong proponent of state intervention via planning regulation and of council housing. 'Had there been', he wrote, 'no new housing but Council housing since the War [1918] we had been in a far happier case to-day, so far as the look of England is concerned.'[15]

It was, in fact, always difficult to disentangle aesthetics and politics: for some, bad aesthetics implied bad politics. The playwright John Osborne described the new London suburb of Stoneleigh where he spent part of his pre-war childhood as 'bankclerk's tudor', a 'Byzantium of pre-war mediocrity'; however, this ostensibly aesthetic critique was written in the context of a misanthropic autobiography unremittingly hostile to the occupants of the new Byzantium and their way of life ('this fractious, jangling, indomitably Hoovered world was not a welcoming one').[16] Even when comment was more curious than anything else there was often suggested a wider social dis-

---

[14] C. Williams-Ellis, *England and the Octopus* (London, 1928), 28.   [15] Ibid. 121–2.
[16] J. Osborne, *A Better Class of Person* (London, 1981), 38–41.

approval.[17] The reactionary Dean Inge termed the style 'bungaloid', and it was creeping 'bungaloid' the founders of the Council for the Protection of Rural England were determined to resist. The contemporary habit of referring to those who had adopted a middle-class style of life or mannerisms as having a 'bay-window' accent emphasized the extent to which people could associate the pretensions of the house with the pretensions of its inhabitants.

The tendency to elide an aesthetic into a political judgement was notoriously characteristic of George Orwell. His novel *Coming up for Air* (1939) was a sustained attack on most forms of new middle-class housing—the Costain-built, architect-designed estate as well as speculative ribbon development. 'Do you know the road I live in—Ellesmere Road, West Bletchley?' its hero, George Bowling asks.

Even if you don't, you know fifty others exactly like it. You know how these streets fester all over the inner–outer suburbs. Always the same. Long, long rows of little semi-detached houses—the numbers in Ellesmere Road run to 212 and ours is 191—as much alike as council houses and generally uglier. The stucco front, the creosoted gate, the privet hedge, the green front door. The Laurels, the Myrtles, the Hawthorns, Mon Abri, Mon Repos, Belle Vue. At perhaps one house in fifty some anti-social type who'll probably end in the workhouse has painted his front door blue instead of green.

The residents (at least the male residents) lead, according to Orwell, wretched lives, hounded by bosses, wives, and children. They also foolishly imagine they have something to lose. Ellesmere Road, however, 'and the whole quarter surrounding it, until you get to the High Street, is part of a huge racket called the Hesperides Estate, the property of the Cheerful Credit Building Society. Building Societies are probably the cleverest racket of modern times.'

But Orwell's architect-designed estate is no better: a monument to snobbery and cultural fraudulence. Bowling returns to the country of his childhood only to discover that it has been overrun by bijou residences and a desperate rusticity.

Immediately, as though I had asked him, he began telling me all about the Upper Binfield Estate and young Edward Watkin, the architect, who had such a feeling for the Tudor, and was such a wonderful fellow at finding genuine Elizabethan beams in old farmhouses and buying them at ridiculous prices ... He repeated a number of times that they were very exceptional people in Upper Binfield, quite different from Lower Binfield, they were determined to enrich the countryside instead of defiling it ... and there were not any public houses on the estate.

An attack upon stylistic inauthenticity and pretension became, in Orwell's case as in others', an attack upon inauthentic and pretentious values, and upon the society and class which held them.

[17] Mary Ellen Chase, *In England Now* (London, 1937), 38–9. Chase commented on the way the dressing table was placed at the upstairs front window of so many English houses, a strange habit which still strikes nearly all visitors to England.

The extreme domesticity associated with owner-occupation was thought by many, even by those who generally approved of it, to have had other malign effects. The first was on the birth-rate.[18] The fertility of all English social classes had been declining before 1914, but after 1918 the fall was so drastic that only the unskilled working class appeared to be reproducing itself. Middle-class fertility was particularly low; and within the middle classes the fall was most remarkable in the lower middle class, the principal contributors to and beneficiaries of the interwar private housing boom. What people noticed most of all in the private housing estates was the apparent absence of children: England and Wales in 1939 had two million fewer children under the age of 14 than they had had in 1914; 1.5 million fewer than in 1900. The 'only child', something hardly known before 1914, was becoming an interwar phenomenon and nowhere more so than in the new suburbs. Contemporaries (unsurprisingly) thus saw a specific relationship between owner-occupation and middle-class infertility. The sociologists Richard and Kathleen Titmuss, who called it the 'revolt' of the parents, could write in 1942:

It is no exaggeration to say that the clerical class in England and Wales are amongst the most unfertile social groups in the whole of the world. 'O my house, my dear little house, hider of my little failings', runs an Arabian proverb which is not inapplicable to the suburban villas in which this class dwell.[19]

The Titmusses' own book exemplifies this concern, but the most influential, and historically perhaps the most interesting, of these analyses was Guy Chapman's *Culture and Survival* (1940), where the Arnoldian resonances of the title are not unintentional. Chapman, already becoming well known as a historian of France (whose own infertility was a 'problem' that confronted all its historians), and husband of the popular novelist Storm Jameson, argued that as a result of a profound cultural transformation which (he believed) was completed by the 1930s, status was derived largely by the ownership of houses and goods: the dominating social drive of interwar England was competitive consumption. All classes were affected, but most dominated by it was the 'new' middle class, and, in order to consume, 'it retrenches in the one way which will not interfere with the standard of social conduct it has set itself, namely in children.' This literally threatened the survival of the nation.

[Such retrenchment] has been the appropriate remedy of every class in the past which had set itself a standard above that of its necessities. It has been operated by the upper class for more than a century; by the upper middle classes for perhaps sixty years. In neither case was it of particular social consequence, because these two classes have never formed a big proportion of the population, and are renewed by the rise of individuals

----

[18] See also below, pp. 304–14.
[19] R. and K. Titmuss, *Parents Revolt* (London, 1942), 80.

from below. But when the same social philosophy penetrates a large and growing section of the community, the whole social structure may be threatened with dissolution.[20]

In this view, therefore, owner-occupation created a cultural environment where status-order was determined by possessions and possessions achieved by the forgoing of children. While the worst of the demographers' predictions had not been fulfilled by the late 1930s, this view, pessimistic and alarmist, though not implausible, and found on both the political right and left, created the atmosphere in which the Royal Commission on Population was appointed in 1944, an official recognition that infertility was now, as in France, a 'problem' of public policy.

It was also argued that the spatial character of the new forms of owner-occupation destroyed a communitarian solidarity, a sense of place. There was an obvious physical basis to this belief, however much it later became confused with ideological assumptions. The extreme separation of work from home, which in the interwar years became increasingly characteristic of middle-class life and which meant that many spent up to three hours a day travelling, necessarily narrowed the possibilities of social life: sociability became not so much impossible, as confined to circumscribed parts of the week and inevitably almost always 'unspontaneous'. Furthermore, the 'suburbanization' of middle-class England increasingly divorced the home physically from the usual foci of social life—from shops, theatres, cinemas (despite their proliferation), and other places of entertainment, pubs (to the extent that the middle classes went to them), clubs, and associations. This divorce was the consequence of the extreme disproportion between spatial growth and population growth in the 1920s and 1930s: while, for example, the population of Birmingham increased by 25 per cent in the period, its built-up area increased by 68 per cent. In other West Midlands towns spatial expansion was even greater: Wolverhampton and environs grew by 71 per cent; Coventry and environs by 83 per cent. This geographical dispersal was by no means the result only of middle-class housing, but middle-class housing was its prime cause. The social separation of men from work and the physical separation of men and women from collective life or informal sociability became, therefore, a fact of middle-class life—as it was later to become a fact of much working-class life.

It was not unreasonable to think that dispersion and separation might inhibit a wider social existence. When Orwell described the middle classes in the 1930s as sleeping 'the deep, deep sleep of England' he was referring not merely to the silence of the suburbs, but to what he believed to be their social and spiritual slumber. By the 1940s this—as with the apparent infertility of the sleeping suburbs—had become almost an 'official' view. The Royal Commission on the Distribution of the Industrial Population (the Barlow

[20] G. Chapman, *Culture and Survival* (London, 1940), 234–5.

Commission), appointed in 1937 to examine the relationship between industry and labour supply, became in the end a critique of English urban development almost *tout court*, and was partly responsible for the planning as well as the location of industry legislation of the 1940s. Thus when in 1944 the sociologist Kate Liepmann wrote that the polarity between work and home had led generally to a 'social disintegration and civic indifference' due to 'the newness of the dormitories and the thinness of the urban fabric' which such a polarity had produced, she was expressing a wisdom which had by then almost become conventional.[21]

This apparent 'social disintegration', it was argued, had one other consequence: the isolation of the middle-class housewife within a highly routine-bound domesticity, and, to the extent that she had them, within rather barren social relationships. One factor adduced in support of this argument was the near-universal withdrawal of middle-class women from the labour market—willingly or unwillingly—on marriage or at first pregnancy, which meant losing the social relationships of the workplace. Another factor was the expectations of 'modern' housekeeping and child-rearing, which, it was felt, forced upon women a preoccupation with the home, and domestic standards many felt unable to achieve,[22] or, alternatively, fostered an extreme domestic competence, so that the home became a vocation.[23] Critics of such life-styles thought all levels of the middle class equally affected, if in somewhat different ways. In 1928 Lady Rhondda, the energetic, feminist daughter of the great Welsh industrialist D. A. Thomas (whose title she inherited), and the founder of the periodical *Time and Tide*, wrote:

There is a 'Smart Set' or its equivalent in every suburb and in every provincial town in England, a set which spends its time playing bridge in the afternoons, motoring round to see its friends, plays a little tennis, dances a good deal, keeps the most fashionable kind of dog it can afford, spends a large proportion of its time—and more of its husband's or father's money than he can easily spare—at its dressmaker, spends all it can squeeze on jewellery. This public reads a large number of novels. It only glances at the papers; its interest in home politics is, for the most part, confined to thinking how wicked the working-man is to want the money and material comforts it regards itself as all-important; its interest in foreign politics is non-existent. This public is a much larger one than it was sixty years ago and it is a much more serious menace to society.[24]

Lower middle-class women did not have even these diversions. They were supposedly confined to the house, frantically raising an ever-diminishing

[21] K. K. Liepmann, *The Journey to Work* (London, 1944), 83.

[22] See Burnett's comments here: *A Social History of Housing*, 258.

[23] For a good example of this, the British Housewives' League, see E. A. McCarty, 'Attitudes to Women and Domesticity in England, ca.1939–1955', unpublished Oxford D.Phil. thesis (1994), 308–49.

[24] Margaret, Viscountess Rhondda, *Leisured Women* (London, 1928), 29–30.

number of children, dependent not upon an easygoing neighbourliness or a nearby family network, but upon aspirins to see them through the day. It was in this environment that the mental 'problems' of the interwar middle-class housewife, so much a part of the public discourse of the time, apparently flourished. The middle-class wife was

> less the mistress of her household than its drudge. There was no cook to supervise in the kitchen, no maid to answer the door; in a caste-like social system, she would find it difficult to exchange confidences with the 'daily', even if the family had money enough to employ one.
>
> On a newly-settled estate there would be no relatives within hailing distance, to help out in a crisis, or cushion an attack of 'nerves', no callers to leave their visiting cards ... In a life so self-enclosed, a visit to the local shops could count as a major expedition, and the visit of the tradesman's boy the principal day-time event.[25]

It was thus argued by some that the amenity of English middle-class life was purchased at a high cost: politically, by social and civic isolation, if not 'disintegration'; culturally, by the sacrifice of the household to an unprecedented domesticity and the middle-class woman either to a pointless social life or to none at all.

Whether true or not, it was a view held by the predominant strand within contemporary English 'middle-class' feminism, and posed particular problems for them—especially for the feminists associated with *Time and Tide* and bodies like the Six Point Group—Lady Rhondda herself, Cicely Hamilton, Ellen Wilkinson, Winifred Horrabin, Vera Brittain, Rebecca West, Naomi Mitchison, and two of Lady Rhondda's colleagues on the board of *Time and Tide*, Winifred Holtby and Edmée Elizabeth Dashwood ('E. M. Delafield'). Although all of them argued that the aim of any feminism was a woman's independence and her 'equal rights'—which was why their brand is sometimes known as 'equal rights' feminism—they did so within terms which assumed marriage and maternity to be 'normal'. There thus developed a real tension in their feminism between domesticity and independence from which there was no obvious escape.[26] E. M. Delafield's 'provincial lady' (whose life and career were originally written for *Time and Tide*), when she asks herself why she is a feminist, can think of no obvious answer. Her feminism thus took an ironic form, the subversion of those assumptions upon which men defined gender roles, while her existence was otherwise almost wholly domestic.[27] Nor did the working woman necessarily get support from quarters where she might have expected it. Margery Allingham, the detective novelist, who did very well indeed out of her work, could make fun of other working women:

[25] R. Samuel, *New Socialist*, May–June 1983, 29.

[26] For *Time and Tide* feminism and this dilemma, see J. Alberti, 'The Turn of the Tide: Sexuality and Politics', *Women's History Review*, 3, 2 (1994), 169–90.

[27] Delafield, *Diary of a Provincial Lady*, 127, 244.

Ann had rooms in a house in Cheshire Street, the home of two elderly schoolmistresses, and as they entered the large square hall the cold academic atmosphere rose up to meet them. 'Notice the odour of emancipation', murmured Miss Held. 'Come on out of this ice-box'. (*Police at the Funeral*, 1931)

Even an apparent model of female independence like Winifred Holtby personified another of the period's stock domestic types—the unmarried woman chained to the well-being of demanding parents.

2 | *Sociability and social networks*

How far middle-class sociability had, in fact, decayed is difficult to assess. In certain circumstances it does seem to have become very attenuated. The social surveys of the 1940s and early 1950s lend some support to an essentially anecdotal view—formed largely in the 1930s—of the social isolation of the middle-class woman. Many of the middle-middle and lower-middle-class housewives questioned by the social psychologist Elizabeth Bott felt that life was somehow 'against' them, and they did complain of those well-known interwar phenomena, 'isolation, boredom and fatigue'. They wanted more 'entertainment', more contact with friends and, increasingly, to return to work. They were not hostile to child-bearing and rearing, but found little apparent satisfaction in it.[28]

Some concluded that middle-class definitions of friendship had become so exclusive as to shut out the notion of the community altogether.[29] The sociologists Peter Willmott and Michael Young were deeply impressed by the degree to which both husbands and wives in the London suburb of Woodford were preoccupied with their homes. The tendency of husbands to share household duties with their wives as marriages became more consciously 'companionate'[30] drew them more irrevocably into the home. Husbands not only did most of the heavy work, but increasingly much of the washing-up, hoovering, laying of the breakfast table, etc. And, of course, perhaps above all, there was the garden: 'Spent the afternoon in the garden with John. We put in the spring bulbs—daffodils, narcissi and tulips. Then I disbudded the chrysanthemums.' Busy around the home, people often found it difficult to find time to speak to their interviewers. Mr Day, finally tracked down, said 'he had been putting together two sheds at the bottom of his garden so that he could have a larger workshop for his bench. It would be useful when he came to put in the central heating system he was planning for the coming winter.' For Mr Day, as for nearly all owner-occupiers, their houses 'provided almost endless opportunities for work'.[31]

[28] E. Bott, *Family and Social Network* (London, 1957), 83–4.
[29] J. Klein, *Samples from English Cultures*, 2 vols (London, 1965), I, 137–9.
[30] See below, pp. 298–9.   [31] Willmott and Young, *Family and Class*, 21–2, 24.

There is, therefore, some evidence that English middle-class life, partly because of the extent of owner-occupation, had become socially narrow. But this should not be taken entirely at face value. In practice, the patterns of English middle-class life tended to conceal sociability, or else to define it in particular ways, which sometimes misled those who thought of working-class sociability either as the norm or as a bench-mark against which the sociability of other classes could or should be judged. Nor is it necessarily the case that what people observed in the 1950s was true of the 1930s or 1940s.

Willmott and Young argued that there were three reasons for the apparent house-obsession of the English middle classes: pride in ownership; opportunities for craftsmanship; and the notion of the house as a kind of money-making concern. They were struck by the way increasing wealth and modern technology was employed to support 'the new cult of the amateur handyman':

The husbandman of England is back in a new form as horticulturalist rather than agriculturalist, as builder rather than cattleman, as improver not of a strip of arable land but the semi-detached family estate at 33 Ellesmere Road.[32]

It is unlikely, however, that this metamorphosis was typical of the whole of our period. Pride in ownership there certainly was. The middle-class horticulturalist was also omnipresent in the interwar years: those who were not green-fingered or even much interested often found the competitive horticulture of the suburbs distinctly wearing. Visitors to England were always astonished both at the English habit of practising various types of homecraft and the centrality of the house and its furnishings to the self-definition of its inhabitants.[33]

Circumstances permitting, however, this pride in house and garden was also to be found among the working classes. Furthermore, it is improbable that the average owner-occupier of the twenties and thirties was anywhere near the handyman he might have become in the 1950s or later. Repairs and additions to the new estates tended to be done by those who built them, and it would be surprising if many middle-class residents had the skills to undertake extensive homecraft. Labour was cheaper before 1939 and the need to undercut the professionals—so strong a motive after 1945—that much weaker. Finally, the whole technology of do-it-yourself, which makes doing up the house possible for anyone, though developing, was rudimentary before 1939. Although some chain stores like Halfords had made a tentative start before 1939, the sophisticated exploitation of the amateur handyman begins only in

---

[32] Ibid. 27. It is worth noting that, consciously or not, the name Willmott and Young chose for their typical Woodford street, Ellesmere Road, is the same Orwell chose for his highly unflattering depiction of suburbia in *Coming up for Air* (above, p. 79).

[33] Chapman, *The Home and Social Status*, 171–2.

the late 1950s (as Willmott and Young suggest), and even that was modest by the standards of the cavernous DIY superstores of the 1970s and 1980s. What might be thought 'typical' of the home-centredness of the 1950s was probably not 'typical' of the whole period.

Nevertheless, those who had some acquaintance with the 'spontaneous' nature of working-class sociability were struck by its apparent absence in the middle classes. Again, however, this seeming contrast can be misleading. There still existed, for example, a rather self-conscious 'northern' middle class closely concerned with manufacturing production, rather contemptuous of what they called the 'southern' commercial and service middle class and whose definition of work and sociability hardly differed from that of a member of a skilled trade union. They preferred the social world of their workforce rather than that of their wives, from which they tended 'rather belligerently to withdraw'.[34] This produced a rather segmented sociability not unlike that of their workforce.

The 'southern' middle class, wherever they lived, did, furthermore, have informal social relationships, but they were established in different ways. They were usually smaller, but more intimate networks than would have been found in a working-class neighbourhood. Amongst women, friendships were often made through a common interest in the house or (surprisingly often) while walking the dog. The diaries of two married middle-class women in Woodford suggest how the structure of suburban middle-class sociability differed from traditional working-class notions of friendship. 'Mrs Clark' (Woodford):

10.30 Was just finishing off the washing when my friend Phyllis arrived. She lives a few doors away, and we have a great deal in common and enjoy each other's company. This morning she brought in two of her special cakes to sample. She had had company at the week-end—some of her friends whom she described as 'nouveaux riches'—and had made some cakes for their benefit. While I finished the washing and made some coffee, we discussed the party we had both been to on Saturday, and also the possibility of going to an Auction together.

11.45 Phyllis was just about to go when my friend Peggy called. She lives across the road and has three children much the same age as my own. She had promised to come over this afternoon but her elder son was not well, so she came over to invite me to go over there instead for half an hour. She and Phyllis started a discussion about refrigerators.

'Mrs Matthews' (Woodford):

8.45 Got Susan ready for school and took her round there. Then went on to the shops. On the way back saw Mrs Rayburn who has been ill with 'flu and stopped to ask her how she was feeling.

---

[34] Jackson and Marsden, *Education and the Working Class*, 19–20.

10.00 My friend Joyce called. She wanted to know whether I would go over to her house for tea that afternoon instead of the next day as previously arranged. I agreed. We started discussion about washing machines.

10.45 Joyce having gone, I took Dennis (the dog) out for his morning walk in the forest. We have made a lot of friends on these walks—dog-owners seem to find it easier [to make friends].[35]

The contrasts between Woodford and, for instance, a working-class district like Bethnal Green are immediately obvious.[36] The diaries confirm the comparative intimacy of the Woodford friendships; the thickly crowded landscape of Bethnal Green is replaced by a sparsely populated scene. But the individuals depicted here stand much more closely to each other than they do in Bethnal Green. Whereas in Bethnal Green there were acquaintances in every direction, little discrimination was made between degrees of social intimacy. In Woodford friends were few but comparatively close. In Woodford informality was more organized: 'dropping in' was the prelude to a formal meeting, usually afternoon tea. Conversations had less of the random quality of Bethnal Green street-talk. Both abide by clear verbal and social conventions, but the conventions are very different.

We should not, therefore, underrate the importance of informal sociability among the middle classes: in many ways informal sociability was characteristic. Much less common was *casual* sociability; and it is that which really typified the Bethnal Green social landscape.[37] What principally distinguishes the middle classes was formal associationalism: their obvious propensity to join clubs and associations by way of formal membership and direct subscription. In Woodford, 57 per cent of all inhabitants belonged to some kind of club or association, a much higher figure than in any working-class community of the time. In Banbury in the late 1940s there were no less than 110 formal associations, nearly all of them—except those connected to the trade unions or the co-operative movement—dominated by the middle classes. Just as to many working-class men and women 'neighbours' were synonymous with 'friends', so to many middle-class people membership of a club was synonymous with 'friendship'. The act of joining, it is true, meant more for some than for others: membership was frequently passive, as in the case of the huge Conservative associations where people only attended if there were a good speaker or at times of local controversy (the occasion of which was frequently the proposed construction of a council housing estate). Active members were often also middle-aged members. Child-rearing and home-making tended to confine younger families to associations where they had a direct

[35] Willmott and Young, *Family and Class*, 101–5.
[36] See M. Young and P. Willmott, *Family and Kinship in East London* (Pelican ed., Harmondsworth, 1970), 106–7; and below, pp. 182–3.
[37] See below, p. 183.

interest—parent–teacher associations, for example, which in the suburbs had large memberships, usually composed of middle-class parents who could not afford to send their children to independent schools and for whom success in the eleven-plus was crucial for their children.

Everywhere, the pattern increasingly was for husbands and wives to join associations together, but in both newer and traditional middle-class communities social life still had clear gender demarcations. The pervasive importance of male clubbability in business and finance, universities and public schools, the law, the armed forces and, *ex hypothesi*, clubland itself, suggests how highly the upper middle classes still rated the possession of collegial social skills: there circulate in Oxford, for instance, innumerable tales about the failure of distinguished persons to be appointed to posts because of real or supposed social deficiencies—some of which are almost certainly true.[38] Any upper- and middle-middle-class community of the time was marked by a series of overlapping masculine associations of which membership was thought to be—and thus was—obligatory. In the City of London there was unconcealed pressure on ambitious lawyers, accountants, or employees of banks and finance houses to seek membership of a City livery company (preferably a 'better' one if possible) and the Freemasons. Members of a livery company or City lodge (often of both) were also likely to be members of the Territorial Army and to seek membership of socially significant sporting bodies like the MCC and the Rugby Football Union. One obvious characteristic of these bodies was their aggressive masculinity: women were normally forbidden from attending and their attendance was permitted, if permitted at all, only on exceptional occasions (usually a 'Ladies' Night') where the ordinary rituals were suspended.

The same appears to have held true of the provincial middle classes. In Banbury, of 773 members of 'secular' associations, 644 were men but only 129 women. All sporting, political, occupational, and 'hobby' associations were overwhelmingly male. The only secular associations with a significant female membership were charitable organizations and this emphasizes the extent to which women were confined to 'social service'. The only associations which were exclusively for women or where women predominated were religious—like church fellowships or the Mothers' Union—and closely resembled secular charitable societies. Even those strongholds of women's associationalism, the Women's Institutes and the Townswomen's Guilds, had a decidedly 'social service' role. In rural areas and smaller provincial towns the Women's Institutes were important and a high proportion of middle-class women were members. The Townswomen's Guilds had less significance and almost certainly enrolled a smaller proportion of urban middle-class women. In both organizations the

---

[38] In my own institution, St John's College, Oxford, folklore remembers only one thing about the night Einstein dined in 1933: that he committed a grave social solecism by placing his coat underneath his dining chair.

notion of woman as citizen was prominent, and in that sense both united their members to a wider gender-free conception of society. None the less, their existence—like the Masonic lodges—was to reinforce gender distinctions in middle-class sociability and the social roles both sexes were thought to play. But there was a difference: however much some men might have disliked the segregation of their wives' activities, few resented their exclusion. Many women, however, did resent their exclusion from the segregated activities of their husbands.

The Freemasons (or more obviously small-town organizations such as Rotary) probably operated in the suburbs or provincial towns much as they did in the City of London or in the armed forces. Margaret Stacey concluded of Banbury that 'many' of its leading citizens were Masons,[39] and it seems to have been understood in most places that advancement in certain kinds of business and certain occupations (like the police, the civil service and some of the professions) was assisted by lodge membership. Furthermore, the kind of people most obviously recruited by the lodges—the commercial, professional, and service middle classes—represented that element of society whose expansion had been most notable in the interwar years.[40] The music critic Paul Vaughan noted that when his father became chief clerk in the counting house of the Greenwich Linoleum Company he became a Mason, and 'masonics' began to 'crowd out' hitherto important social activities. The interwar years provided a very favourable environment for the Masonic Order and there was an unprecedented growth in the number of lodges. Three thousand new ones were established between 1919 and 1950, by which time there were probably about 450,000 Masons—perhaps 20 per cent of all males of the middle and upper levels of the middle classes were members. There developed a whole resentful folklore about the relationship between the lodges and professional or business promotion, partly generated by those who failed to gain promotion. There probably was some sort of connection between lodge-membership and promotion in certain comparatively closed communities or occupations. At least so some thought: 'A central tenet in my father's view of life,' Paul Vaughan wrote, 'was a belief in the useful connection, the friend, or preferably, relative in the know, who could be relied on to do you a good turn. I suspect this way of thinking figured in his decision to become a Freemason'.[41] Even so, it is uncertain whether men were promoted because they were lodge members and had acquired a 'useful connection' or because membership was itself thought to demonstrate fitness for promotion. Men, indeed, may have joined because the

[39] M. Stacey, *Tradition and Change: A Study of Banbury* (Oxford, 1960), 78–9.

[40] There is little reliable evidence about Freemasonry in this period, but S. Knight, *The Brotherhood* (London, 1984) and M. Short, *Inside the Brotherhood* (London, 1989) contain a good deal of useful information. Knight's conclusion that Masonry was recruited primarily from the 'not directly productive middle and professional classes' (p. 37), a conclusion supported by Short (p. 173, pp. 169–82 more generally), seems wholly reasonable.

[41] P. Vaughan, *Something in Linoleum: A Thirties Education* (London, 1994), 49–50.

lodges were a kind of welfare agency, known to treat widows and children of members generously, or because they stood for an extreme—because deliberately arcane—form of male sociability.[42] Whatever the truth, however, except for the one night of the year, the annual dance, the lodges were one of the most effective ways by which a man's wife could be excluded from the sociability that most mattered to him.

There is little doubt, however, that (as everywhere) contacts did matter. Among the large group of managers studied by R. V. Clements, all of whom grew up in this period, the influence of fathers or relatives was used to find them places in management trainee schemes or in firms run by family members, particularly those without a strong sense of vocation or those who came from families where it was customary for one son to enter business. Most were 'fixed up' by fathers, family friends, or golfing companions.[43] Given the importance of these kinds of contacts it would not be surprising if men came to regard membership of the Masons or similar organizations as a prudent act designed to benefit their offspring.

Within middle-class life, therefore, two powerful social forces were working against each other. On the one hand, while so many married women were excluded from the labour market, a work-based sociability was likely to be overwhelmingly masculine; and a sociability based upon the home and domesticity overwhelmingly feminine. Furthermore, at least in the 1930s, such a segregated sociability actually intensified. In any circumstances some married women were likely to resent this—the aggrieved 'Masonic widow' had long been a middle-class 'type'—but in conditions of a new middle-class ideal, the 'companionate marriage', grievance became more widespread. The gender exclusivity of much middle-class associationalism (particularly men's), however socially legitimated, thus cut across a second, equally powerful social development: the growing expectation that in marriage husbands and wives would 'do' things together and would share the same interests and friends. Such exclusivity also worked against the assumption that the social success of the middle-class family was coming to depend ever more on the social skills of the wife. The tension created by such conflicting forms of sociability was eventually to have major consequences both for the social and gender attitudes of middle-class women and for the structure of middle-class marriage.

3 | *The middle classes: 'traditional' and 'non-traditional'*

The 'public' sociability of the middle classes was shaped by forces which increasingly tended to unite them. Nevertheless, throughout the period

---

[42] Vaughan, *Something in Linoleum*, 55–6.
[43] Clements, *Managers*, 58.

religion remained a significant, if declining, source of division, in part, because it overlapped with other differences—occupational, regional, and cultural. Those, for example, who identified with manufacturing industry and the 'North', who had mild contempt for the 'southern' commercial middle class, were disproportionately nonconformist in origin. Residual nonconformist–Anglican animosities also overlapped with a distinction commonly drawn between the 'traditional' (nonconformist) and 'non-traditional' (Anglican or nothing, or both) middle classes, which in these years often implied a further distinction between the 'immobile' and 'mobile' middle classes.

Before 1914 the Anglican and nonconformist divide had profound social and political importance; in much of the country, other than in the chambers of commerce and professional societies (and not always even in them), it was unusual for individual Anglicans and nonconformists to meet socially. This social distance underlay the popular foundations of the Conservative and Liberal Parties—and in the case of the Liberal Party almost alone guaranteed its long-term viability. By the 1920s the division was closing, but, especially in the provincial towns and the countryside, still comparatively wide. In Banbury, for instance, even in the early 1950s, there were two reasonably self-contained social networks based upon different Protestant allegiances. Thus 'Mr Shaw' and 'Mr Gray' were both prosperous tradesmen with leading positions in the town and many attitudes in common. But Mr Shaw was an Anglican and Mr Gray a Methodist. They moved, therefore, in entirely different social worlds. The Anglican network was closely involved in Banbury sporting associations and had a fairly active club life. The Free Churches, however, had no club of their own, little to do with sport, and depended for sociability on the fellowships, sisterhoods, and brotherhoods attached to the chapels.[44] Furthermore, although organizations like Rotary increasingly provided a social forum for both Anglicans and nonconformists, there remained an important obstacle to full assimilation. Most chapels were still teetotal, as were those still active in them. The Masons, Rotarians, and Lions, however, were nothing if not convivial, and a teetotal member could feel 'out of things' at social occasions as well as being thought rather a wet blanket by non-teetotallers. Although temperance as a widespread social commitment was almost to collapse in the 1950s and 1960s, it was still common enough in the interwar years and the 1940s to impede the complete integration of middle-class élites.

---

[44] Stacey, *Tradition and Change*, 114. In Banbury the Roman Catholic middle class was tiny, but it also tended to lead a closed social existence. The middle classes generally were disproportionately Protestant, just as the working classes were disproportionately Catholic, but it is likely that religion underpinned Catholic middle-class social networks in Lancashire—particularly for those of Irish origin.

The Jewish middle classes, of course, had to cope with social anti-semitism. This was a form of exclusion differing in type and intensity from the exclusions which affected Christians, whatever their religion—even Catholics. On anti-semitism, see above, pp. 55–6.

The second, and in some ways perhaps the most fundamental social division within the middle classes, was between those who were geographically mobile and those who were not. This was a polarity of which people were very conscious: the distinction was repeatedly made between 'natives' and 'immigrants', 'traditional' and 'non-traditional' or, less pejoratively, 'newcomer' and 'host'. They were, however, uncertain whether the distinction was geographical or social. In part, they were thinking of the 'new' commercial and technical middle class of the 1930s and 1940s; in part, of the rehoused and deracinated middle class (often, of course, the same thing), the effect of whose geographical mobility was by 1939 everywhere apparent. It was the process of transplantation, either through suburban development or the growth of new industries in existing communities, which tended to juxtapose 'traditional' and 'non-traditional' middle classes within a single community—a juxtaposition not always harmonious.

The non-traditional middle classes, particularly if they expected to move fairly frequently, were often not much interested in their host community or its institutions. Nor did they necessarily share its values. The same indifference to traditional institutions could extend to the public sphere. In so far as newcomers participated in public life they inclined to be hostile to the 'inefficiency' of native middle-class élites and did not share their traditional loyalty to the community. This frequently led to conflicts over local government expenditure and the recruitment of its professional officers. Newcomers were, above all, concerned to keep down the rates; but they also objected to the way local government seemed to be casually administered by long-established local firms of lawyers, accountants, and surveyors. Attacks on 'inefficiency' were often attacks by outsiders on the closed nature of this administration, but were often interpreted by natives as attempts by outsiders to appropriate local government for their own interest.[45] Nor were newcomers always willing to respect existing commercial arrangements, and this alienated local shopkeepers like the 'first-class' drapers and grocers who were so prominent among native élites. Although they were individualist and deeply 'anti-socialist', these élites were usually not competitive in practice and disliked competition.[46] Immigrants tended to ignore them; they would, for example, shop elsewhere (even in London if they lived near enough) or patronize department stores. The manager of a new Boots or a branch of a London-based firm of surveyors and estate agents might wait a long time before he was invited to join Rotary.

    [45] E. R. Roper Power, 'The Social Structure of an English County Town', *Sociological Review*, 29 (1937), 410–12. In Hertford one firm of solicitors held the majority of appointments, such as clerk to the County Council, clerk to several district councils, coronerships, clerkships to various committees and commissioners of taxes etc. The office of county land agent and county accountant were both held by people in private practice.
    [46] Stacey, *Tradition and Change*, 29–30. An old-established chemist was said to have refused to serve any of his customers who were seen entering the new branch of Boots.

The newcomers were often thought by natives to be stand-offish (some probably were). Men and women who moved frequently before and after marriage, or who were not living in the neighbourhood where they were raised, seemed reluctant to approach neighbours. That was thought to be risky; you could be pestered by people you might not wish to know.[47] Stand-offishness, as we might expect, was not all one-way. There was everywhere the issue of who the children could play with. Native parents were often fearful of their children picking up bad habits, either of speech or manners, or sometimes 'germs' (an obsession of the period), and might forbid contact with immigrant children even of the same social class.[48]

Furthermore, for one important reason, mobility made it difficult for natives to place newcomers within a familiar social hierarchy: it was almost impossible to know the social status of a newcomer's family. Nor was it easy to discover, since newcomers were often socially as well as physically distant from their families, and were increasingly likely to maintain a close affinity only with parents. Cousins, uncles and aunts and, surprisingly often, siblings, became only 'Christmas-card' relations, if even that. While the mother–daughter relation was strong, it was not as strong as in a working-class community—or, at least, strong in different ways—and the primacy of job-promotion (which implied a willingness to move) meant that there was none of that generational propinquity still characteristic of the working class and much of the traditional middle class. That newcomers' parents were rarely seen, and other members of the family usually never, made strangers of people who by most objective criteria belonged to the same social class.

Associational life in almost wholly new communities—like the suburbs of outer London or the larger midland towns—had to be built from scratch. It was here that 'clubs' and 'friendship' could be synonymous; here that associations brought together people who had much in common but who would otherwise probably not have met; here that wives made their profession out of sociability; and here that without their social skills isolation was a real possibility: 'We're too independent, I know that. You've got to be prepared to go out and *make* friends.' The wife of a commercial traveller, a socially marginal occupation anyway, told Willmott and Young that 'unless you're in the swing, like being an active Conservative, suburbia is *hell*.'[49] Nevertheless, most people seemed to have made the effort and the complicated associational life of the suburbs was the consequence.

In 'traditional' communities where there was already an established middle class newcomers were as likely to compete with or disrupt associational life

[47] Bott, *Family and Social Network*, 75.

[48] And these fears could develop rapidly, even in places where natives were, in fact, themselves so new as to be scarcely native. See Vaughan, *Something in Linoleum*, 59.

[49] Willmott and Young, *Family and Class*, 108.

than be assimilated to it. Thus in 1930s Hertford, where the 'new' middle class was largely a dormitory population, and in late 1940s and early 1950s Banbury, where the 'new' middle class was a result of economic growth within the town itself, the effects were almost identical. Hertford became 'no longer the fairly defined social entity' it once was. 'A generation ago . . . the majority of its daily social processes were effected within its boundaries . . . Its social structure as a whole was highly integrated and stable. Each group within it was in some sense a function of the whole . . . Prestige attached to individuals who were known personally and imitated directly.' By the mid-1930s this was no longer true. There had been a partial breakdown in hitherto well-defined relationships like kindred, age-groups, and neighbourhood. This breakdown was manifested 'in the pregnant contrast between natives and newcomers, a contrast which in certain middle-class groups comes near to conflict'.[50]

In Banbury, the 'years around 1930 [when the construction of the aluminium rolling mill brought in large numbers of middle- and working-class newcomers] represent a divide.' Before then, people who said they knew everybody meant

that in the old days they could 'place' anybody they did not literally 'know' in a well-developed social structure which had a recognized status system. This system they can describe; families of similar economic standing, respectability, and length of residence forming 'sets' who visited each other's houses and whose children were allowed to play together.[51]

Older Banburians of all classes thought the immigrants 'foreign' (and, of course, the most foreign was the new working class) because they had different values and customs. The immigrant professional class, often graduates in engineering and metallurgy, were not easily 'placed'. They did not come from Oxford or Cambridge, their families were unknown, and they were not doctors or ministers of religion. And in a sporting club they might prefer standard of play to social comfort. As in Hertford, therefore, one of the immediate consequences of migration was to divide the middle classes by intruding into an existing social structure individuals, occupations, and values it could not easily absorb.

Some of these differences were doubtless irreconcilable. Others would probably have disappeared with the passing of time. But there were more active ways by which people attempted to reconcile them. The first was to avoid them simply by avoiding those with whom you might differ—by mixing only with 'your own kind'. This was the 'traditional' way. In Banbury, for example, the Anglican–Conservative–Bowling connection, though almost entirely 'middle-class', was itself divided by status. There was an 'upper association' centred

[50] Roper Power, 'The Social Structure of an English County Town', 397–8.
[51] Stacey, *Tradition and Change*, 11–14.

upon the Chestnuts Bowling Club and the parish church, and a 'lower' one centred upon the Borough Bowls, the Conservative Club, and the British Legion. The upper association comprised men prominent in the town: members of the Chestnut Bowling Club were at least 90 per cent Conservative and the committee contained three past Conservative mayors and two Conservative borough councillors. The Chestnut Club was, via a common membership, closely allied with the Freemasons and Rotary.

The lower association was clearly of inferior status: there were even a couple of wage-earners, but its members were mostly assistant managers of shops, clerical workers, and owner-managers of small shops and businesses. Except the latter, there were no self-employed men or bank managers. As we might expect the lower association was allied with organizations like the Buffaloes rather than the Masons or Rotary.

These two networks were almost exactly replicated in Banbury's sporting associations. 'Sports I' included rugby, tennis, cricket, and hunting, and a high proportion of committee members came from outside the borough, because these were the kinds of clubs which attracted the neighbouring farmers. They also had high occupational status—bigger farmers, bigger businessmen, self-employed professionals. Again, many were Masons. The overwhelming majority of committee members were Anglican and Conservative, but few were active Conservatives.

'Sports II' was composed of a cricket club, table tennis league, the Post Office Sports Club and the Comrades' Club. It shared some games with 'Sports I', but not many: squash was replaced by table tennis; games with a distinct class character like rugby were not played, nor ones which required expensive equipment. Many committee members were Conservatives and, because of the close connection between 'Sports II' and the Conservative Club, many of them, unlike their opposite numbers in 'Sports I', were active Conservatives.

The overwhelming importance within the sporting clubs both of sociability and sociability with your own kind had obvious consequences. Apart from the case of rugby, no one sport in Banbury was represented by a single club; and excessive competitiveness was deprecated. The dominant consideration was the 'right atmosphere' in the company of the 'right sort'. Social ease decreed which club you joined and social ease was promoted if the club were socially homogeneous.[52] Competition was not the main reason why Banburians played sport: it was disruptive and therefore discouraged. As one competitor remarked of a tennis tournament: 'these do's are 75 per cent social and 25 per cent tennis.' The primacy of social ease had one other, indirect, result: that was to render uncompetitive much English sport, particularly those games like tennis which were principally occasions for middle-class sociability.[53]

[52] Ibid. 86.   [53] See below, pp. 380–3.

As a way of reconciling differences, this worked so long as everyone recognized its conventions and the social hierarchy which underpinned it remained stable. That everyone would, however, recognize the conventions could not always be assumed—the 'new' middle class frequently did not recognize either them or the social hierarchy. Nor did it cater for people of different religious affiliations, even though they might be of similar class. The middle classes were, therefore, increasingly brought together by the development of an 'apolitical' sociability based upon 'depoliticized' social relationships, the elimination of divisive or 'embarrassing' behaviour, and an emphasis upon personal qualities such as niceness and humour. The remarkable growth of the Masonic lodges, together with more open organizations, many of American origin, like Rotary, the Lions, the Elks, the Kiwanis and, of course, the Chambers of Commerce, was partly a result of this development. They became (however exclusive they once might have been) 'neutral' territory where local élites could meet socially unencumbered by other ties like religion. In smaller towns and even in newer suburbs this, in effect, meant bringing together Anglican and nonconformist social traditions into a nonsectarian environment. There was usually a careful balancing of religious interests and a ban on any kind of contentious or potentially divisive discussion. This was territory where individualist businessmen and professionals could unite in political hostility to local trade union and co-operative societies—though it would never have been put like that. Male sociability of this sort represented an 'apolitical' set of silent assumptions which were, in practice, deeply political. The way middle-class businessmen or managers of nonconformist and Liberal background retreated into an 'apolitical' reluctance to discuss politics was actually the way they retreated into the Conservative Party. The associations themselves were also ineluctably drawn into the wider network of the Conservative Party. In the rapidly growing London suburb of Edgware, for example, the Rotary Club was founded by the district's principal developer, the builder A. W. Curton, who was not only its chairman, but active in the Ratepayers' Association and an 'independent' Anti-Socialist councillor.[54]

Thus the Conservative Party was able to appropriate many of the nonconformist connections which had hitherto formed the base of the Liberal Party. To make itself acceptable to these connections the Conservative Party had to refashion itself significantly. Many of its older, rhetorically aggressive traditions were abandoned in favour of a more reticent and sanctimonious style—a style personified by Stanley Baldwin (though also, alas, by Sir William Joynson-Hicks).[55] Around this refashioned Party a broad 'anti-socialist'

---

[54] Jackson, *Semi-Detached London*, 269.

[55] For Joynson-Hicks, see below, p. 277. For an important study of the relationship of the Conservative Party to middle-class associational life in the interwar years, see J. W. B. Bates, 'The Conservative Party in the Constituencies, 1918–1939', unpublished Oxford D.Phil. thesis (1994), 212–34.

coalition was created in the 1930s, one in which people did not 'talk about politics much'.

The depoliticization of personal relations, however, went further. A mode of sociability was devised whose aspiration was the elimination of tension and anxiety from personal relations by the elimination of anything which seemed aggressive or caused 'embarrassment'. The fear of embarrassment and the complexity of the strategies adopted to avoid it increasingly struck outsiders. To be effective such strategies demanded not only a ban on language and behaviour liable to give offence, but techniques by which social situations inherently liable to give offence could be managed. Of these, the most powerful was humour. More than ever, humour was deployed to make social situations 'safe' and the possession of a 'good sense of humour' became central to the middle-class repertoire of social manners.

Out of this repertoire developed a managerial style, particularly important in smaller firms, which emphasized social confidence over expertise. What was sought was 'maturity, ease of conversation and ability to deal with highly placed people'. Successful management consisted in 'getting on with people', and taking the broad view. Technically qualified men were thus rarely appointed to the board: their social skills were too narrow and that was thought to incapacitate them for management. Such a style came fluently to men who had been to public schools; and the smarter the school the more fluent the style. In such an environment men of working-class origins with only technical qualifications could become acutely conscious of their lack of social skills. They had 'difficulties with English', became stuck for words, or lacked the wider education which would remove 'many of the terrors of social and business intercourse'.[56] The result was that within smaller firms social origin—and hence education—largely determined the extent to which men were promoted. It is hard to imagine, for example, Harry McGowan, the moving force behind ICI, a man of little education, notoriously lacking in social skills and good humour, having much success in a smallish family-owned firm in England. But more 'modern' firms were not impervious to the attractions of the sociable style. There were plenty of instances where even they employed public school boys for their presumed social skills—which might even include being good at rugby or cricket.

The outcome of such a social style was inevitably mixed. In its extreme form it led to a host of bans and taboos—particularly sexual and religious—which constantly surprised and bemused visitors to England. It also promoted a lack of seriousness in personal relations: never to talk about politics or religion is, after all, never to talk about two of the most interesting subjects in human history. By encouraging the belief that all relationships, however intrinsically

---

[56] Clements, *Managers*, 42–87.

political, could be depoliticized, this social style became crucial to the development of an 'apolitical' anti-socialist vocabulary: it was the Labour Party
which dragged 'politics' into everything, which took everything so 'seriously',
which politicized human relationships by emphasizing conflict instead of
good humour.

Yet it was also a civilizing discourse in both public and private life. An apolitical sociability preserved personal and family relationships which might otherwise have collapsed and, not uncommon in the 1940s especially, allowed
people to laugh away or treat as a subject of banter the politics of those black
sheep who strayed into the Labour fold. In the hierarchies of work it softened
relations between different ranks and permitted management to manage
without over-aggression.[57] Even as the social distance between the middle and
working classes was becoming perceptibly wider, this code prescribed certain
forms of behaviour which helped to maintain considerable tranquillity in
class relations. The fact that the code was more or less acceptable to all classes
and most political persuasions, and that it provided a 'non-political' discourse
to which people could retreat if offence were likely to be given, stood in the
way of that disastrous politicization of all relationships which did so much
damage to European society as a whole in the interwar years.

4 | The middle classes and the working class

The union of differing middle-class traditions was much quickened after 1918
by the growth of a trade-unionized and apparently politicized working class.
Other differences lost much of their significance in face of this new, common
threat. It had an almost immediate effect on middle-class sociability. Although
middle- and working-class sociability rarely intersected anyway, middle-class
sociability usually kept them firmly apart. Not only did it in practice exclude
the working class, it was often intended to. And this intention was powerful,
particularly amongst people themselves of recent middle-class status. Willmott and Young, for example, when trying to determine pub attendance figures in Woodford, found that many of their respondents denied that they had
been into a pub, but conceded that they might have entered a 'hotel-bar'. On
reformulating their question they discovered that middle-class pub attendance was actually higher than working-class—a fact not unrelated to the ambience of Woodford's pubs:

They are not cosy bars of the Bethnal Green-type . . . They are, quite often, much larger
places with carpeted lounges furnished in pseudo-Jacobean where the landlords wear
crested blazers and call their customers 'old boy', and where drinks are much more

---

[57] For an interesting French view of this, see Jean-Louis Barsoux, 'The Entertainment Industry',
Times Higher Education Supplement, 17 March 1995. 'Humour', Barsoux writes, 'is a vital *point de repère*
in Britain. It is how Britons situate people.'

often pink gins or whiskies and sodas than pints of mild and bitter. The public bars are very much pushed off at the side.[58]

Though they made up about one-third of Woodford's population, the working classes were conspicuously absent from its associational life. A common way of ensuring their absence was the requirement that applications for club membership should be accompanied by references from two existing members. The one organization that working men and women could join, the Darby and Joan clubs, was the one organization the middle classes would not. In Woodford, proximity to the East End of London and native resentment at migration from the East End gave an edge to these exclusions—even more as a number of migrants were Jewish.[59] Manual workers were well aware of this:

They try to be what they can't around here. They've never had it and they're just jumped up and they think they're just it.

The middle class people here are snobs. They put on airs and graces. They are all out for show—nothing in their stomachs but nice suits on.[60]

Such social closure is not surprising: everyone, and not just the middle classes, wants to be amongst those with whom they feel at ease. What added extra bite was the fact of owner-occupation. For most members of the middle class the houses they bought, or wished to buy, were the major social and capital investments of their lives. They were thus exceptionally sensitive to anything that depreciated—or might be thought to depreciate—the value of their houses; and the preservation of their value became a dynamic element in middle-class politics. People feared that any breach in the middle-classness of a community—by the construction of council housing, for example—could lower the 'tone' and disrupt accepted patterns of sociability, and, thereby, simultaneously lower the value of the house. There is a clear relationship between owner-occupation and the intensity of the desire to live 'among one's own kind'.[61] Equally important, owner-occupation turned people into ratepayers and anything that raised the level of rates was resented. This was particularly true of those areas where authorities were building council estates: not only did the estates introduce a social mix, they put demands on local authorities for new provision which could only be met by rate increases. Many public enquiries were enlivened by bitter exchanges between residents and officials, like the following between the improbably named Mrs Bastard and a ministry of health inspector:

---

[58] Willmott and Young, *Family and Class*, 95–6.
[59] There was an attempt by some Woodford residents to change its postal code number, which was East London.
[60] Willmott and Young, *Family and Class*, 119.
[61] D. Chapman, *A Social Survey of Middlesbrough*, NS 50, pts ii–iii (Jan. 1946), 2; pts iv–viii (Sept. 1945), 3–5.

Mrs Bastard: You have ruined my home! (*turning to LCC officials*) Do any of you gentlemen live near an LCC estate? No, I don't suppose you do, (*addressing the Ministry's Inspector*): Do you live near an estate?
The Inspector: They have just bought some land near my house.
Mrs Bastard: Do you like it?
The Inspector: No.[62]

The result of this was the proliferation of ratepayers' associations which became active pressure groups in the newer suburbs.

The development of this form of middle-class consciousness is discreetly noted by M. V. Hughes in her memoirs of interwar London. What Mrs Hughes calls London is actually Hertfordshire (the village of Cuffley) where she and her family moved in the early twenties. Cuffley was then largely rural, but was steadily engulfed by new housing, at first mostly private. In the 1930s, however, the LCC contemplated the construction of several so-called 'out-county' estates in Hertfordshire, and that alarmed owner-occupiers. 'In early days at Cuffley', Mrs Hughes wrote,

the main social affair for all was a meeting of the Conservative Association in the iron [*sic*] school-room. The member would appear breathless from 'some important work in the House', to say a few stirring words, punctuated by thumps from umbrellas when the Prime Minister was mentioned. We used to cull much fun from these. But a still livelier function nowadays is a meeting of our Rate-payers' Association, where real feelings run high, and real words are used.[63]

The development of real feelings had parallels in social life:

Behind our nondescript shop, some distance from the road, was a one-time barn, entitled the Cabin, where teas were served to hikers, school-parties, and mothers on their annual outings. This served as a hall for a dance. There was no distinction of class and a good deal of fun, I gathered. In later years the barn was turned into a brand new hall, still called the Cabin, still used for meetings, and dances, but not quite so unconscious of class distinctions.[64]

There was, in these circumstances, an attempt to create social, even physical, barriers between the middle and working classes. Social exclusion was practised with determination, if often covertly, and the 'affluent workers' of the 1950s and 1960s were to be made aware of it. The most spectacular example of physical exclusion was the 'Cutteslowe Walls', erected in 1934 by the Urban Housing Company in the Summertown district of Oxford to deny inhabitants of council housing access to the nearby private estate. Re-erected in 1939, after the Oxford Council had them pulled down in 1938, the walls were not finally dismantled until 1959—though, in a curious expression of wartime democracy, one was demolished by a rampant tank in 1943.

---

[62] Quoted in Jackson, *Semi-Detached London*, 160–2.
[63] Hughes, *A London Family*, 176.   [64] Ibid. 34–5.

The geographical separation of the classes had, of course, its origins in the nineteenth century and was a remorseless process, but the huge expansion of middle-class owner occupation rapidly accelerated two probably inevitable developments. The first was to turn the Conservative Party into a ratepayers' party. Conservative and ratepayer associations became increasingly difficult to disentangle, and that gave the Party a more homogeneous character. The second was to hasten in local politics the process by which political differences based upon religion or community were replaced by those based upon class. And class differences to a considerable degree meant differences of housing tenure. As the country became increasingly divided between those who lived in housing they owned or were paying for and those who lived in public housing they rented, local government polarized about groups (usually Conservative, but often 'independent' or Liberal) who were thought to represent owner-occupiers, and the Labour Party which was thought to represent council tenants. This, in turn, diminished cross-class sociability and rendered relationships between the middle and working classes even more exiguous.

There are obvious reasons why we might speak of the 'middle classes' rather than the 'middle class'. There were inevitably big differences in style of life between the upper middle class, whose education and social and cultural expectations were often very similar to those of the upper class, and the lower middle class, the inhabitants of the 'little villas' which seemed to face every bypass in the country. Furthermore, while the extent of owner-occupation unquestionably distinguished the English middle classes, a large minority of them were still not owner-occupiers, and that minority began, if anything, to grow in 1938 (not a development they wished). Nor did all owner-occupiers live in the dormitory suburbs or speculative 'estates', even though contemporaries often assumed that they did.

There were also important differences in outlook and social status between the 'traditional' and 'non-traditional' or urban and provincial middle classes, and such differences were not simply 'regional'. The traditional middle class had social reaches both narrower and wider than the non-traditional. The former was more likely to have been born in or near the place where its members would spend their lives, and so be physically close to their families. They were less occupationally mobile and often had, almost inevitably, a 'traditional' view of the social hierarchy. Furthermore, as we have seen in the case of Banbury and Hertford, the traditional middle class could regard with suspicion and indeed hostility the newer 'suburban' middle classes, whose origins were unknown, who were more mobile, and who were often 'better' educated, or, at least, educated in ways and places difficult for the traditional middle class to comprehend. The suburbanization of a country town was in practice as likely to disrupt the middle classes as afforce them. Within this traditional social hierarchy, however, the social reach of a member of the traditional middle class could be more extensive than that of the non-traditional: a doctor in a country town, for example, who treated the landed classes when they were at home, might have the kind of professional and quasi-social acquaintance with the gentry which in London only the most fashionable consultant would have.

Religion was another traditional distinction which continued to divide, especially, the provincial middle classes. Although of declining and, after the Second World War, rapidly declining significance, Anglicanism and noncon-formity still provided almost mutually exclusive social networks, even for those whose class position was identical. What was beginning to unite the mid-dle classes was a secular hostility to the organized working class which was accompanied by the evolution of a secular, 'apolitical' sociability. In the new suburbs of London and the other larger cities religious distinctions were less obvious, in part because the locations for such division—churches, chapels, and their offshoots—often were not conveniently at hand; in part because their more footloose inhabitants tended to have a secularized sociability forced upon them.

Despite these distinctions, however, there was considerable agreement amongst the middle classes as to cultural and social priorities, if only because a large proportion of middle-class households fell within a comparatively nar-row income band. Most members of the middle class believed that there were certain standards in dress, housing, and diet from which they could deviate only with loss of status. Middle-class families, for instance, who were not buy-ing their own homes, tried to rent housing whose quality was equivalent to that of an owner-occupier, and some at least were regretfully conscious of not being owner-occupiers. Perhaps the real difference between the upper and lower reaches of the middle class was how they educated their children. But this tended to be a difference determined not by choice but by income. In any case, the growth of the grammar schools, which were inclined, in both syllabus and tone, to ape the major independent London day schools, put much of the middle class within reach of the right education, if not necessarily of the 'right' people.

What then can we conclude about the middle class as a whole? The first is that it had become (or was becoming) a national class. The most obvious ex-ample of this was growing occupational and residential mobility. It was increasingly accepted that promotion and 'prospects' were more important than proximity to family and this both encouraged and sanctioned mobility. As a result, one's neighbours were not necessarily one's friends. Some social relationships were preserved, but often at a distance; others simply lapsed. The ability, however, of the middle classes to afford or manipulate the technology of modern life could, equally, preserve friendships and family relationships, even at a distance. The middle class was not yet as national as the upper class, which scarcely had 'neighbours' at all, but the fact that, as in Banbury, the newer middle class felt no particular tie to the town or to its traditional networks suggests that middle-class social horizons were coming to approximate those of the upper class.

The second is that the worst predictions about middle-class fertility proved to be greatly exaggerated. Although there was never any return to the fertility rates of the nineteenth century, the secular decline in fertility halted in about 1943–4 and fertility rates then rose sharply. There was thus no evidence that owner-occupation *caused* infertility. The private housing boom of the late twenties and thirties was as much a result of a decision to limit fertility as a cause of it; but in turn it assisted in the steady increase in the marriage-rate which permitted the 'baby boom' of the 1940s.[65]

Third, the belief that owner-occupation had deleterious effects on middle-class associational and family life, and on the position of middle-class women, was probably also exaggerated, though not without truth. In many cases middle-class social resources were greatly stretched, particularly within highly mobile families, and wives or single women were lonely, subject to persistent depressions and vague illnesses, but there is little evidence that this was the rule. Furthermore, the increasing tendency to 'companionate marriage'—for all its imperfections—almost certainly diminished the isolation of middle-class women. Nor does it appear that middle-class families broke apart or were fundamentally disrupted. It is true that middle-class children when adult were increasingly likely to live at a distance from parents and that the middle-class 'extended' family was indeed disappearing, but immediate families were prone to reunite if the mother was widowed, by the mother either moving in with her children or moving nearby.

There was, however, little spontaneity in middle-class social life. Things necessarily had to be organized. This inevitably put much of the weight of sociability on the shoulders of the wife: social life and the associational success of the middle-class *family* was thus increasingly reliant on her social capacities. By the early 1950s, indeed, it was almost possible to argue that there were two definitions of the middle class. The first, the more usual, was based upon the occupation of the husband, upon its prestige, the income it generated, and the lines of masculine sociability—Masonic lodges, clubs, old-boys' networks— which flowed from it. The second was a definition based upon the social success of the middle-class family and such success was largely dependent upon the wife.

At the beginning of the 1950s the middle-class picture of English society was based upon an apparent paradox: that England was becoming more 'middle-class' (which numerically it was), but that the working class had more money.

---

[65] Burnett, *A Social History of Housing*, 257.

Although increasing in size, the middle class, it was often thought, could no longer 'afford' a middle-class style of life, while those who could, the working class, did not wish to. Such a view was widely held in the early 1950s. Within a few years, however, some were prepared to argue that the reverse was, or was becoming, true. The election of a Conservative government in 1951—even one which was not always over-solicitous of the middle classes—was partial consolation. And middle-class attitudes had themselves somewhat softened. Although the Second World War represented in many ways a defeat for a middle-class definition of democracy, many admitted that post-war levelling had not altogether been a bad thing. Some conceded that, to some degree, it benefited them: those of working-class or 'provincial' origins were grateful that it no longer mattered, or at any rate mattered less, whether you had an 'accent' or not.[66] As further consolation it was argued that working-class culture was being destroyed by a remorseless process of *embourgeoisement*.

Such a picture represents the complicated history of the middle classes in this period. Despite what many believed, the economic foundations of middle-class life, though shaken in the early 1920s and in the 1940s, were never seriously damaged. The upper middle class, certainly, lost comparatively and never regained the position it held in 1914; nor after the Second World War did the middle class as a whole regain the comparative position it held in the 1930s. But these were comparative, not (usually) real losses. Furthermore, the collapse of domestic service after the outbreak of the Second World War freed considerable amounts of middle-class income. The ever-lengthening waiting lists for independent schools suggests that middle-class discretionary income had been substantially protected against expropriating governments.

In any case, the post-war Labour government was very cautious in its relations with the middle classes. They were not excluded, as we have seen, from the welfare state, and that government was also very reluctant to attack anything which lay outside its rather austere definition of 'politics'. Thus two of the institutions most central to middle-class life, the public and grammar schools, emerged unscathed, despite their doubtful democratic status and the unquestioned, and growing, advantage they gave to the non-working classes.[67]

Had this actual experience, where gains tended to cancel, or almost to cancel, losses, been acknowledged, or had the middle class employed by the state been as large as it was to become, the middle-class interpretation of its recent history might have been more nuanced. As it was, that interpretation was shaped largely by an ideological hostility to the organized working class, which forged a strong sense both of middle-class unity and loss, and exaggerated the cultural differences between the middle-class and working-class way of life. Such hostility was ideological because its origin was ideological: an

---

[66] Bott, *Family and Social Network*, 173.   [67] For this, see below, pp. 260–2.

intense fear of loss of social esteem and relative status. But this fear was usually expressed in non-ideological, matter-of-fact terms: loss of income, an inability to maintain a 'middle-class' existence, the unfitness of the newly wealthy to spend their wealth wisely. The paradox which lay beneath the middle-class interpretation of its own experience—a growing, but poorer middle class and a shrinking, but richer working class—can be resolved only when this is understood.

ENGLAND was one of the most working-class countries in the world, and this, the first of the two chapters on the working class, is concerned with occupation, wages, and work. It looks at the structure of employment and unemployment, at the changing pattern of working-class earnings over the period, at the ways in which working men and women sought work, and how far they were ready to go to find it. It also considers the culture of work and the degree to which it differed between men and women, industrial relations and the role of trade unions, and how far industrial relations determined a working-class view of history. The chapter, finally, examines the lives of the unemployed and how people coped—or did not—with unemployment.

1 | Employment

Throughout this period the working classes were a large, though slowly declining majority of the English people: they made up 78.29 per cent of the whole population in 1921, 78.07 per cent in 1931 and 72.19 per cent in 1951.[1] This represented about 30.2 million people in 1921 and nearly 32 million in both 1931 and 1951. These overall figures, however, conceal important changes within the composition of the working classes. Not only were they declining as a proportion of the whole population, their skilled component was declining faster than the semi-skilled and unskilled. Overall figures, however, conceal major redistributions within each of these three sub-categories. For male skilled occupations the most significant changes were in coal, textiles, and the metal trades. In the first two there was an uninterrupted decline in total employment: in 1951 they barely employed one-third the number of men they had thirty years earlier. The metal trades, on the other hand, employed about 60 per cent more men than they had in 1921. In the skilled women's occupations, the most significant change was the heavy fall in employment in the

---

[1] These figures, which are based on the registrar-general's classifications and are for Britain as a whole, are taken from Routh, *Occupation and Pay in Great Britain*, 8. Unless otherwise stated all figures in this section are from Routh, 26–39, 137–58.

textile and textile-related industries. The number of skilled women they employed in 1951 was half the 1911 figure.

These remarkable changes in the pattern of employment were a result of profound movements in the economy. Coal and textiles, two of the great 'staple' industries of pre-1914 England, were, with shipbuilding and parts of heavy engineering, the leading casualties both of the interwar depression and structural changes in the economy which began immediately after the First World War and continued, often at an accelerated pace, after 1951. All three industries shed labour virtually without cease in the interwar years—at such a rate, indeed, that they could not meet demand when it returned after the outbreak of war in 1939. Throughout the 1940s, for example, there was a shortage of labour in the mines (met during the war itself by drafting in conscripted civilians, the 'Bevin boys') which became critical in 1947, the coldest winter in living memory, when the country's coal-based electricity and domestic heating suppliers came close to collapse.

For skilled men, however, there was the possibility of alternative employment in the expanding metal trades. As 'heavy' engineering declined in the North-East, Scotland and Wales, 'light' metal industries—automobiles, aircraft, electrical and household consumption goods—grew rapidly in the South—around the London circumference in particular[2]—and the Midlands. There was thus a net gain to employment in the metal trades of 450,000 men. Many of these were fitters, mechanics, or millwrights, whose flexibility allowed them to exploit mechanization. In 1921 there were 429,000 fitters; in 1951 511,000. The growth in the number of machine-tool setters was even more striking: there were only 12,000 in 1931 (when the census distinguished them for the first time), but 112,000 in 1951. Fitters and setters were crucial to maintaining production lines in good repair (in particular in the automobile factories) and were able to move easily from firm to firm and within different departments of the same firm. The expansion of the metal trades, therefore, meant that the skilled proportion of the male workforce fell less fast than its equivalent in the female workforce. Even so, there is evidence that a 'skills-deficit' developed in the 1920s and 1930s: the diminishing number of apprenticeships allocated in engineering and shipbuilding before 1939 almost certainly impeded rearmament by denying industry sufficient skilled labour.

The decline of the skilled female workforce was socially paradoxical. At a time when the enlargement of women's formal political and social rights was almost constant, their relative status within the workforce steadily deteriorated. The number of women who worked on a more or less equal basis with men in 1951 was lower than in 1918; and this was largely due to the decline of one industry—Lancashire weaving. Here men and women (often husband and

---

[2] A. L. Bowley, 'Occupational Changes in Great Britain, 1911–1921', *London and Cambridge Economic Service* (May, 1926).

wife, in fact) worked in similar occupations at almost similar rates of pay, and the majority of women workers were trade unionists—the only industry where that was so. Equality at work, furthermore, was responsible for comparative equality at home; so that the destruction of employment in weaving, the one working-class occupation which guaranteed women some form of job-equality, tended to accentuate the role-segregation which had become characteristic of most working-class families.[3] Nor were there many expanding skilled occupations for women. The one exception, hairdressing and manicuring, employed too few to compensate—although an occupation which was overwhelmingly masculine in 1911 was predominantly female in 1951.[4]

The total number of the semi-skilled rose somewhat in the period, from about 6.6 million to 7.4 million, but declined a little as a proportion of the total workforce. Amongst men, the most important redirections of semi-skilled employment were in agriculture and the metal and distributive trades. Although agriculture was one of the country's smallest major industries—in 1931 only 6.2 per cent of the workforce earned their living from it—there were in the 1920s nearly 700,000 agricultural workers. Those numbers declined throughout the period, as they had since the late nineteenth century; in 1951 there were only two-thirds the number of agricultural workers, foresters, and fishermen that there had been in 1918. In addition, those leaving the land were disproportionately young. The consequence was that the agricultural workforce was becoming not only smaller, but older. The number of skilled workers employed in agriculture, mostly those servicing and driving agricultural machinery, on the other hand, continued to rise in both age groups.[5]

In the metal trades the number of semi-skilled male workers employed increased throughout—as it did with skilled male workers, and for the same reason: the rapid expansion of light metal manufacturing in the interwar years. Thus by 1951 about 250,000 more men were working as semi-skilled workers in the metal trades than in 1921.

The number of men employed in the distributive trades, principally as shop assistants, followed a different pattern. It rose throughout the 1920s, but began to fall in the early 1930s and fell continuously until 1951: from 660,000 in 1931 to 459,000 in 1951. The fall was probably due to the fact that men who once would have become shop assistants later became teachers or draughtsmen, a more unambiguous move into the lower ranks of the middle classes.[6]

---

[3] See below, pp. 166–70.

[4] In 1921 there were 34,000 male hairdressers and 6,000 female; in 1951, 35,000 men and 48,000 women.

[5] Royal Commission on the Distribution of the Industrial Population, *Report* (Jan. 1940), 96–7. This is usually known as the Barlow Report. In 1925 there were 662,000 employed in agriculture; in 1937, 568,000.

[6] Routh, *Occupation and Pay in Great Britain*, 34.

The registrar-general classified shop assistants as semi-skilled—a not unreasonable assessment—but shop-assisting was notoriously a grey area, where young working-class men and women often acquired some of the characteristics (but rarely the income) of the middle classes.[7] That their children, or the bright children of working-class parents more generally, should become teachers rather than shop assistants was, therefore, a logical social progression.

Technical change also influenced the composition of the semi-skilled workforce. While, for example, the total of men employed in transportation was largely stable, drivers of horse-drawn vehicles almost disappeared, to be replaced by a slightly larger number of drivers of commercial motor-vehicles: the decline in the number of men driving horse-drawn vehicles is almost exactly matched by the rise in the number of those driving motor vehicles.[8]

The history of semi-skilled women's work, unlike that of men, was dominated by the effects of the Second World War. Until 1939 the single most important of women's semi-skilled occupations was domestic service. Between 1939 and 1941, however, the number of private domestic servants declined by nearly two-thirds and was never to recover.[9] The war not only denuded middle-class households of their domestics, it denuded the countryside of young women. The disappearance of service eliminated the most important local occupation for country girls, the only one that could offer most of them employment. That in turn hastened the flight from the land and transformed the rural districts, uniquely, into predominantly male enclaves.[10]

For most working women the passing of domestic service was a liberation. Each new generation of women disliked it more than the previous one, and it was increasingly regarded as second-best. Where did these liberated women go? Many who otherwise would have gone into service in the 1930s went into light industry as semi-skilled or unskilled 'operatives'. Women were, indeed, even before the Second World War displacing male labour in the new industries—throughout the interwar years the number of insured women workers increased at a faster rate than the number of men. During the war itself many were employed in factory production, either voluntarily or, after 1941, compulsorily when women were required to register for war service at the age of 16. Others went into 'women's' occupations—hotel service, catering, or personal service: a form of domestic service without the stress of an often demanding individual employer. Many became shop assistants, replacing those men who had migrated to socially and financially more rewarding occupations,

[7] See above, pp. 44–6.

[8] In 1911 there were 404,000 drivers of horse-drawn vehicles; in 1951, 15,000. In 1911 there were 50,000 drivers of motor vehicles; in 1951, 547,000.

[9] In 1931 there were still 1,262,000 private domestic servants; in 1951 only 343,000. The great majority of the latter did not live in.

[10] J. Saville, *Rural Depopulation in England and Wales, 1851–1951* (London, 1957), 122–4.

and thus confirming the inferiority of shop-assisting by establishing it (like elementary teaching) as a 'woman's' job.

By its nature unskilled manual labour is difficult to classify occupationally. Unskilled workers are highly mobile and can move with demand: their numbers are thus largely dependent on the overall demand for labour. There are, nevertheless, certain discernible tendencies. The number of unskilled labourers in the building and ancillary trades nearly doubled, and more than doubled in the metal and engineering trades.[11] Mechanization, however, diminished employment in traditional unskilled occupations, even those, like dock-labouring, famous for overmanning. The number of dock labourers, for example, decreased from 120,000 in 1931 to 81,000 in 1951; the number of messengers from 186,000 to 47,000—here the telephone was largely responsible.

The number of women who worked in unskilled manual occupations was comparatively small. It was generally believed that strength was crucial in manual labouring and that necessarily excluded women, although the experiences of the two world wars, when many women did undertake heavy labour, particularly in agriculture, suggest this belief was as much folk myth as truth. Furthermore, some of those many women who were drafted into manual labour during the war stayed on: in 1951 there were still 1,000 women builders' labourers and 2,000 railway porters. None the less, other than in wartime, most unskilled manual occupations had an intensely masculine culture which very effectively excluded women. The only unskilled occupation where women predominated (and that overwhelmingly) was the one with the lowest social prestige and poorest rewards, charring and cleaning.

The evolving structure of working-class employment shared one important feature with that of the middle class: the decline in the number of those self-employed. In 1911 there were 329,000 self-employed skilled artisans, but in 1951 only 251,000. Many of these were independent blacksmiths, watchmakers, shoemakers, and bakers whose occupations either disappeared or were absorbed by larger units. Unlike the decline of middle-class self-employment, however, the decline of artisanal self-employment was a transitory phenomenon: from the late 1950s on there was a huge increase in 'new' artisanal occupations. If horses no longer needed to be shod, cars had to be repaired. Above all, the building trades had to be serviced by plumbers, electricians, carpenters, and painters and decorators. The decline in working-class self-employment, which contemporaries attributed to structural changes in the economy, was, therefore, more due to the proscription of private house and office building during the 1940s than anything else.

Within the working classes, as within the middle classes, the sex-specific

---

[11] In 1921 there were 252,000 unskilled labourers employed in building and civil engineering; in 1951, 493,000. In metal and engineering, the figures were 238,000 and 529,000 respectively.

levels of participation in the workforce differed widely. It was assumed that all men should work and that, other things being equal, all would work. There was no such assumption about women. Although a much larger proportion of working than middle-class women were employed, amongst the working class, as amongst the middle, paid work was thought both inferior to and preparatory to marriage. The result was that the female proportion of the total workforce scarcely changed at all in the first half of the twentieth century—in 1911 29.7 per cent of the whole workforce was female; in 1951, 30.8 per cent—and never reached the levels of the mid-nineteenth century. Furthermore, before 1939 the great majority of employed working-class women were single; only in the 1940s was that pattern modified.

Of the 1.3 million women who entered the industrial workforce during the First World War, hardly any remained after 1921. Many never thought of themselves other than as temporary workers and were anxious to return to home life. Even if they had wished otherwise, the hostility of the trade unions to women working, particularly in skilled and semi-skilled trades, and the right the unions had procured from the government in 1915 to 'restore pre-war practices' in 1919, would have ejected many women from employment. In any case, the drastic deflation of the economy in 1920–1, which devastated especially the labour market in those industries women had entered in such large numbers during the war—textiles and 'old' engineering and metal manufacture—would have done the same, however favourable other circumstances had been.

To the degree that women wanted jobs the economic environment after 1945 was more benign. In June 1943 7.75 million women were working or in the armed forces; by 1947 that figure had fallen to 6 million. Between those two years younger women left the workforce at a higher rate than married women; the average age of the workforce was consequently higher than in 1939. A large part of the women's workforce had been married before 1939 and 22 per cent had children. Married or widowed women (that is, older women) were more likely to be unskilled operatives than single girls—a reflection of lower expectations and a poorer education. In the later 1940s the government encouraged women to return to work, principally by appeals to their patriotism, but with only limited success. What was achieved was a large increase in the number of women who worked part-time, something new to the twentieth century. By 1949 women working part-time constituted perhaps 9 per cent of the labour force.[12]

2 | *Unemployment*

The working classes are, by definition, those who work; working at particular jobs is what has traditionally distinguished them. But what distinguished many of them in the interwar years was that they did not work. Many

---

[12] G. Thomas, *Women and Industry*, Social Survey, NS 104 (May 1949), 4.

upper-class persons, of course, also did not work, but they could hardly be called unemployed. Amongst the middle classes, even at the worst of the depression, unemployment was very low. But for working men and women unemployment in some form was a familiar experience. The nature of this experience, however, differed widely by occupation, location, age, sex, and duration. England's rate of unemployment was somewhat higher in the 1920s than in comparable countries, but significantly lower in the 'depression' itself, 1929–33, which did not see the dramatic collapses of the labour market which occurred in the United States, Germany, Sweden, Canada, or Australia; there was rather a sharp cyclical accentuation of existing conditions. Within England (as within the whole of the United Kingdom) there were two phases of severe unemployment, 1921–2 and 1929–33, both followed by a significant but only partial recovery.

Had levels of unemployment been evenly distributed throughout the country, its immediate social effects might have been less desolating and its register upon the national memory less powerful. But unemployment was heavily concentrated by industry and region.[13] It was comparatively high in 'old' industries, like coalmining, heavy engineering, shipbuilding, and textiles, and comparatively low in 'new' industries like chemicals, electricals, and automobiles. Since the 'old' and the 'new' industries were largely located in different parts of England—the 'old' in the North-East, the North, and the North-West (and, of course, South Wales and the West of Scotland)—so unemployment was strongly biased by region.[14] Unemployment was at its highest, and its social and demographic consequences most severe in the North-East and North-West (and South Wales), regions particularly dependent upon that fatal nexus: coal for export, iron and steel, shipbuilding and heavy engineering. The greater the dependence on any one or a 'mix' of these industries the higher the unemployment. Jarrow on Tyneside, 'the town that was murdered' as its MP, Ellen Wilkinson, called it,[15] wholly dependent on shipbuilding, thus had 68 per cent of its insured workforce unemployed in 1933. The figure was even higher in some of the smaller pit towns or villages of the North-East or South Wales where, in effect, every insured worker was unemployed. In consequence, the North-East had virtually no net population increase at all in the 1930s, while Glamorgan and Monmouth was the only administrative division of England and Wales with a net population loss.[16]

---

[13] Establishing who exactly was unemployed and where in interwar England is something of a minefield. For careful calculations, see C. H. Feinstein, *Statistical Tables of National Income, Expenditure and Output of the United Kingdom* (Cambridge, 1972), table 58; W. R. Garside, *British Unemployment, 1919–1939* (Cambridge, 1990), 5–6.

[14] Garside, *British Unemployment*, 13.

[15] The title she gave her well-known Left Book Club study of Jarrow: *The Town that Was Murdered* (London, 1939).

[16] Barlow Report, 264–5.

Unemployment, however, was not confined to men; but it is difficult to calculate the number of women unemployed. Many of them did not work in insured trades and were not, therefore, included in the usual measure of unemployment. Furthermore, widespread hostility to married women remaining within the labour force made it difficult for them to claim unemployment benefit. If a married woman left work, for whatever reason, it was often assumed that she had done so willingly. The Anomalies Act (1931), introduced by a Labour government and a woman minister of labour (Margaret Bondfield), incorporated this assumption into legislation. By its provisions women had to convince a court of referees that they had not left work because of marriage and that they could reasonably have expected to find work locally in order to claim benefit. The courts were not easily convinced: between October and December 1931 48 per cent of women's claims were disallowed and benefit stopped, compared with only 4 per cent of men's.[17] The Act particularly affected women textile workers in Lancashire where there was a long tradition of women working and a factory culture of which, almost uniquely, women were members. None the less, given that women were increasingly employed in the 'newer' industries where unemployment was low, the incidence of unemployment amongst women was almost certainly lower than amongst men—perhaps two-thirds the rate.

The duration of unemployment varied widely. The popular stereotype of interwar unemployment—large numbers of men out of work for years at a time eking out a living in decaying communities—though not without an element of truth—is misleading. More typically, men and women experienced comparatively short bouts of unemployment between one job and another: 'unemployment in the interwar period must be seen as a moving stream with the majority of people unemployed for relatively short periods'.[18] Stereotypical long-term unemployment was largely a phenomenon of the 1930s. In 1929 only 11 per cent of unemployed insured workers had been out of work for more than twelve months. After 1932, however, as the total number of unemployed declined, the proportion of the unemployed out of work for twelve months or more rose steadily and remained at high levels until 1937.[19] The persistence of long-term unemployment after 1933 was due to differential rates of recovery. As the Midlands and the South recovered from the cyclical depression of 1929–33 the levels of overall unemployment fell. There was, however, a much more fitful recovery in the North where the 'old' industries (with the partial exception of textiles) largely stagnated until shortly before the

[17] Lewis, *Women in England*, 190.
[18] Glynn and Oxborrow, *Social and Economic History of Interwar Britain*, 154.
[19] Garside, *British Unemployment*, 16. See also A. D. K. Owen, *A Report on Unemployment in Sheffield*, Survey Pamphlet No. 4, 58–9.

outbreak of war. Much of their workforce as a result remained unemployed throughout the decade.

The incidence of unemployment was also biased by skill and age. Unskilled manual workers were more likely to be unemployed and unemployed for a longer time than skilled workers, as skilled workers were more likely to be unemployed than clerical workers.[20] Older men were more likely to be unemployed than younger, not because they were more liable to lose their jobs but because it was more difficult for them to find new ones; their spells of unemployment tended to become longer with age. Younger men and adolescents, widely thought at the time to be as prone to unemployment as older men, were, in fact, more accustomed to shorter but more frequent periods of unemployment as they moved comparatively rapidly (and often restlessly) from one job to another. The juvenile labour market was unstable, characterized by high turnover and low-skill, 'blind-alley' or 'dead-end' jobs, but not usually by prolonged unemployment.[21]

3 | *Wages and benefits*

(1) 1918–1923

The three phases into which we previously divided the history of salaries, 1918–23, 1923–38 and 1938–51, are almost equally useful for the history of wages.[22] Between 1914 and 1920 there was a rapid increase in money wages with unskilled workers doing better than skilled. Thus in 1920 a bricklayer's rate was 235 per cent that of 1914, but his labourer's was 300 per cent; an engineering craftsman's rate was 231 per cent of 1914, the engineering labourer's 309 per cent. As a whole, these money wage gains, particularly for unskilled workers, brought improvements in real wages, though usually not as great as contemporaries thought. It was widely believed, for example, that the strongly-unionized skilled workers had secured large real wage gains either by exploiting their scarcity during the war or by industrial action after it. What skilled workers succeeded in winning, however, was not so much overall real wage gains as marked reductions in hours worked. By the beginning of 1920 average hours worked in the skilled trades was about 13 per cent lower than in 1914: thus their real gains were in wages per hour worked rather than in total wages.[23]

From the end of 1920 to the beginning of 1923 there was a heavy fall in money wages, heavier than the fall in money salaries, a consequence of the drastic deflation of the economy which began in early 1920. The average

[20] C. Clark, *Conditions of Economic Progress* (London, 1951), 470.

[21] Garside, *British Unemployment*, 94–108; also below, pp. 121–2.

[22] See above, pp. 50–67.

[23] S. N. Broadberry, *The British Economy between the Wars* (London, 1986), 81–3.

weekly fall in money wages (excluding coalminers' wages) was 17s 6d in 1921 and 11s in 1922. For miners, the falls were more severe: their average money wages fell by £2 in 1921 and another 10s in 1922. Almost alone among the working classes the miners suffered real-wage losses between 1920 and 1923, which is why industrial relations in the coalfields were so bitter and sympathy for the miners so widespread. For most other workers, however, money wages never fell as fast as prices. Only in the second half of 1922 did money wages fall faster than prices; for the man or woman *who remained in continuous work* throughout 1921 and 1922 there was a significant increase in real wages.[24]

(II) 1923–1938

The stabilization of earnings in 1923 at levels from which they did not much depart until the mid- to late 1930s preserved the mild redistribution of working-class income downwards which had occurred during the First World War. The striking feature of the second phase in the history of wages, which began in 1923, is the stability of money wages compared with prices. Unlike the period 1921–2, when, even if they did not fall as fast as prices, money wages fell significantly, the huge fall in prices between 1929 and 1934 was unmatched by anything like an equivalent fall in money wages. Once again, men and women *who remained in continuous work* registered marked gains in their real incomes.

But pervasive unemployment eliminated many of the comparative income gains the working class as a whole had made during and immediately after the First World War. The unemployed, however, did receive a 'wage'. From 1919, when the government introduced the 'out-of-work' donation to assist temporarily unemployed returned servicemen, the state was committed, either by unemployment insurance or a 'dole', to paying the unemployed a benefit in lieu of wages. The scale of these benefits was not constant; indeed, they were governed by no less than fourteen régimes between the end of the First World War and the beginning of the second. From November 1920, when payment was substantially increased, to 1939, the rate paid to an unemployed adult man ranged between 15s and £1 per week, hovering mostly about 17s per week.[25] For adult women the range was 12s to 16s per week, with an average of around 15s. The 1927 Unemployment Insurance Act distinguished for the first time 'young men' and 'young women' from both adults and boys and girls. For them the unwelcome distinction meant a sharp fall in benefit: from the adult rates of

---

[24] Between Jan. 1921 and Dec. 1922 the index of weekly money wage rates fell from 100 to 62; the cost of living index from 101 to 49.

[25] This excludes agricultural workers who came within the system in Oct. 1936. Their benefit entitlement was lower: 14s for men and 12s 6d for women until March 1939, and 15s and 13s thereafter. Benefit schedules are in E. M. Burns, *British Unemployment Programs, 1920–1938* (Washington, 1941), 368.

17s (men) and 15s (women) to 14s and 12s, and, except from October, 1931 to July, 1934, this was the usual rate. Between 1920 and 1930 boys aged 16 and 17, apart from one extraordinary period when they were awarded 10s per week, received 7s 6d and then 6s per week, and girls 6s and 5s. In 1930, 17-year-olds were given separate and higher payment, usually 9s for boys and 7s 6d for girls. Unemployment benefit, unlike a wage, was in part calculated upon a 'needs' basis: from November 1921 onwards, families received separate payment for each dependent adult, 5s to 10s, and each dependent child, 2s or 3s.

Thus unemployed men and women were entitled to a 'wage' which was paid partly on the basis of insurance premiums they contributed when in work or, if insurance entitlement was exhausted, wholly by the government. As with all such systems, the relationship of benefits to wages was politically controversial. Those who determined the size of benefit were anxious to operate the rule of 'lesser eligibility'—a rule that benefit should not be of such size compared with wages that people would prefer to remain idle on benefit than to work for a wage. In practice, the attempt to enforce 'lesser eligibility', though probably successful, was not easy. One way was simply to exclude from benefit those whose own behaviour or resources justified their exclusion. Until 1930 applicants had to meet the conditions of the so-called 'genuinely seeking work' clause—a provision of the 1921 unemployment insurance legislation which required recipients of benefit to demonstrate that they were 'genuinely' (and continuously) seeking work. Since the onus of proof was put upon the applicant, the local employment committees were not obliged to show that work was actually available. Between January 1925 and April 1928 a total of 1.715 million people were denied benefit, the majority because they were deemed not to be 'genuinely' seeking work.[26]

The immediate result of the abolition of the 'genuinely seeking work' clause was a significant increase in the number of those who successfully claimed benefit. In 1931 an attempt was made to check this growth via the 'Anomalies Regulations' which excluded from benefit many married women and seasonal and part-time workers.[27] In October 1931 the National Government made conditions more stringent by means-testing transitional payments—benefits paid to those no longer covered by insurance. The Unemployment Act of 1934 further elaborated means-testing: the test on individual income was replaced by a test on the total income of the applicant's household. The household means-test was hated by those subjected to it; but though ungenerous it was not necessarily unreasonable. Many working-class households relied on the earnings of several of their members and the notion of a total family income was familiar both to observers and working-class men and women themselves. But the

[26] A. Deacon, *In Search of the Scrounger* (London, 1976), 21–2, 57.

[27] Many of those excluded from unemployment benefit then sought relief from the Public Assistance (i.e. Poor Law) authorities, so the saving was largely an accounting one.

intrusiveness of the Act's administration, with the immemorial hostility it caused, was never worth the comparatively small savings which were made.

What then was the relationship of benefit to wages? Both had at least one thing in common: they tended to be inflexible. Benefit, indeed, was more inflexible than wages. Although the number of legislative régimes under which benefit scales were set multiplied, the scales themselves were largely invariant. Like money wages, the real value of benefits rose: even after the reductions of October 1931, their real value was higher than in 1929. For those on transitional benefit, it is true, the scale of payments could vary by locality. Until 1934 local authorities were able to set the level of income below which it was thought destitution would follow, and these levels frequently differed, even between adjacent towns. The 1934 regulations were designed to elim-inate these inequities, but were so badly received by those who stood to lose that the government was compelled to restore some of the differentials, which remained in place until 1938.[28] Aside from these local variations, however, the ratio of the real value of benefits to the real value of wages was more or less constant.

Nevertheless, for most unemployed benefit was significantly lower than their working wages. In 1937, for example, 97.7 per cent of men receiving insurance benefits and 93.8 per cent of men receiving assistance were entitled to a maximum payment at least 4s less than their earnings in full-time work.[29] These figures suggest not just that the great majority of the unemployed received (in 1937) at least 4s less than full-time earnings, but that the average workless man or woman received in benefit only half the money value of a nor-mal wage, which is why so many unemployed lived at or near the line of poverty.

There were four categories of people whose benefit might, in certain cir-cumstances, have exceeded their working wage. The first was those whose 'normal' work was part-time and whose normal wages, therefore, were prob-ably substantially lower than average full-time earnings. The second was unskilled labourers with three or more (or if on assistance, four or more) dependent children whose ordinary wage was 40s–50s per week. The third was young men and women and juveniles whose working wage was less than

[28] The 1934 Unemployment Act proposed that all households should be paid at uniform rates. The regulations under the Act, issued on 21 Dec. 1934, imposed increases or decreases in benefit where rents were relatively high or low. The result was that many families paying relatively low rents had their allowances cut. The regulations caused unexpected hostility and anger from a wide range of opinion, and not only the unemployed. The government felt compelled to abandon the regulations as they stood and by the Unemployed Assistance (Temporary Provisions) Act (15 Feb. 1935), the so-called 'standstill Act', effectively restored the cuts and thus the inequities the Act was supposed to abolish. (For the 'standstill crisis', see Garside, *British Unemployment*, 74–81, Burns, *British Unemployment Programs*, 214–19; W. G. Runciman, *Relative Deprivation and Social Justice* (Penguin ed., Harmondsworth, 1972), 78–80.)

[29] Burns, *British Unemployment Programs*, 257.

20s per week and the fourth, unskilled women workers whose normal wage was less than 15s per week. How many people came within these four categories is unknown, but almost certainly they were only a small minority of those receiving benefit. Since all benefit was calculated on some sort of needs basis, it is hard to see how benefit could have been further reduced in the pursuit of 'lesser eligibility' without utterly pauperizing most of the long-term unemployed, whose subsistence needs were only just met by the existing scales. As a result of this relationship between benefit and wages, contemporaries were increasingly struck *not* so much by the overabundance of benefit as by the inadequacy of an unskilled labourer's wage—a wage which established such a relationship in the first place. It was this which made proposals for wage supplements, like family allowances, so attractive.

(III) 1938–1951

For most of the interwar period, therefore, the pattern of working-class earnings was distorted by persistent high unemployment in many parts of the country. The third phase in the history of working-class income is notable for the virtual disappearance of unemployment and for a redistribution of national income which much favoured the working class. Together these factors produced a remarkable rise not merely in the earnings of individuals, but in the earnings of the working class as a whole, within which the principal beneficiaries were male semi-skilled and unskilled workers and female skilled workers.[30]

The only category of salary-earners whose income rose in the same proportion as male wage-earners were managers in the private sector. Female skilled workers outperformed any other category of women, though the earnings of women clerks and forewomen rose faster than those of female semi-skilled and unskilled workers. An index of manual workers' earnings in 1937 and 1949 set against those of the higher professions shows how disproportionately well the manual working class did. In 1949 the average earnings of a manual worker were 241 per cent of their 1937 level; those of a member of the higher professions 188 per cent.

Although working-class income rose fastest after 1938, the year in which middle-class earnings commenced a long relative decline, it seems as if wages had begun to rise after 1935: in 1935 they stood at 99.2 per cent of their 1928 level, in October, 1938 at 107.3 per cent. From 1938 to 1944 their relative rise accelerated. Earnings rose 30 per cent between 1938 and 1940, thereafter increasing at an average 9 per cent per annum until 1944, falling back slightly in 1944–5, but resuming their advance in 1946. These gains can be explained

---

[30] In 1955–6 the average earnings of a male skilled worker were 319% of the 1935–6 level; semi-skilled workers 350%; unskilled workers 337%. The equivalent figures for women were 369%; 270%; 280%.

partly by the effects of full employment after 1941 and the shortage of manual labour in a number of industries, but the rise in wages had begun before then, at a time when unemployment among manual workers was still about 12 per cent. And those who did best were unskilled male workers, amongst whom the rate of unemployment was highest—a good example either of the extent to which wages moved independently of employment or of the lack of movement between one segment of the labour market and another. At any event, wartime and post-war full employment simply confirmed a trend in wages which began around 1935.

Working-class women did much less well than working-class men and less well than middle-class women. No manual working woman gained as much as women managers, administrators, or clerks, and amongst semi-skilled women workers there was a huge relative loss. This was due largely to the 'de-skilling' of women's work within the textile industry—particularly in weaving. After 1945 women textile workers were in effect being paid the wages of unskilled workers. Since their numbers were still so large and their compara-tive loss so great, the relative earnings of working-class women as a whole (unlike those of middle-class women) declined against men's. They were con-fined, even more than in 1914, to comparatively inferior jobs of low prestige and low reward; but this, *mutatis mutandis*, they did have in common with their middle-class sisters. These differentials caused great bitterness, particularly among unmarried working-class women. Very much more than men, they found it difficult to find jobs as they got older, and were much less well paid if they did. Recourse to the Poor Law was a fate many dreaded but all too often experienced. The National Spinsters' Association, founded in 1935, sought the payment of old-age pensions to women at age 55 as a way of alleviating these conditions and secured one million signatures to a petition requesting such a change.[31] It did not come, however, and the ruling assumptions about women's work—that it was in some sense out-of-the-ordinary and met fewer demands than men's work—imposed material deprivations on those unlucky enough not to marry in a society which believed that only through marriage could the spinster discharge her true womanly obligations.

4 | Finding jobs

Despite the increasingly elaborate state provision for job-finding and the expressed hope of legislation from 1908 onwards that the labour market could be 'organized' via the labour exchanges, it is clear that most people found their

---

[31] Lewis, *Women in England*, 155. For the campaigns to improve women's pay and pensions, see H. L. Smith, 'Gender and the Welfare State: The 1940 Old Age and Widows' Pensions Act', *History* (forthcoming) and 'British Feminism and the Equal Pay Issue in the 1930s', *Women's History Review* (forthcoming). I am grateful to Professor Smith for allowing me to read these articles in typescript.

first and usually their subsequent jobs informally—through friends, relatives, or directly personal approaches to possible employers.

In places dependent upon a single or only a small number of industries, jobs and the way they were procured almost chose themselves. Boys followed their fathers or their mates, and it was understood that they would do so. One Sutton (St Helens) miner recalled:

Where we lived there were just two trades—the railways and the mines. It was a question of getting a job as quickly as you possibly could after leaving school. There wasn't much of a choice. Boys who went down the pit would generally go to the same colliery . . . where their mates were. They were determined to be members of the union, simply and solely because their fathers were members.[32]

This man's first job was as a 'drawer' to his father. An engineer, also from St Helens, said that 'when I left school, my father said "what do you want to do?" and I said, "Work in the engine house [of a mine]". My father was an overseer; he got on well with the manager. He just had a word with him and I got in.'[33]

This technique, to get a friend or relative to 'speak for' you with a potential employer, was not confined to the smaller industrial towns. In Sheffield in the early 1930s it was concluded that the juvenile employment exchanges appeared 'to have been responsible for securing comparatively few of the jobs obtained by the boys and girls immediately on leaving school'. A significant number of school-leavers were actually employed by their own parents, and it seems probable that a larger number were employed by relatives and friends. Exploitation of traditional relationships was thus the most important means by which Sheffield adolescents found their jobs:

Intimacy with foremen, shopkeepers, warehouse managers and the like is also very useful when jobs are being sought for sons and daughters . . . The influence of friends was even more important in the case of girls than that of parents and relatives, and it was very little less important in the case of boys. 'I got it through a pal' or 'I got it through a girl I know that worked there' were frequent answers to questions put on this point.[34]

Even as late as 1949 in as unintimate a locale as an 'outer London borough' nearly half of a sample of boys who had registered for national service found their first job either through the intervention or in the footsteps of a 'significant male relative', usually a father, but sometimes an uncle or brother.[35]

---

[32] C. Forman, *Industrial Town: Self-Portrait of St Helens in the 1920s* (London, 1978), 34.

[33] Ibid.

[34] A. D. K. Owen, *A Survey of Juvenile Employment and Welfare in Sheffield* (Sheffield Social Survey Pamphlet No. 6, April 1933), 17–18.

[35] R. F. L. Logan and E. M. Goldberg, 'Rising Eighteen in a London Suburb: A Study of Some Aspects of the Life and Health of Young Men', *British Journal of Sociology*, 4 (1953), 328. Although most evidence does point to the importance of the family in job-search, for a more sceptical view see T. Griffiths, 'Work, Class, Community: The Structure and Values of Working-Class Life in Coal and Cotton Lancashire, with Particular Reference to Bolton and Wigan c.1880–1930', unpublished Oxford

Many young men got jobs simply by 'hanging about' the gates of a factory or workshop until they were noticed by a foreman or manager. The clustering of men around gates wherever it was thought a job might be found was a common sight in interwar England. Nor was it ineffective as an approach. A retired bricklayer, who had been found a job at Pilkington's glassworks by his father (who worked there) remembered how he then found his own job:

I was taken to where there was this broken glass tube, and I said, 'Hey! This is where that boy was cut. Thank you very much. I'm not having that.' I picked up my jacket and walked out ... I walked up the road and stood at the gate of the brickworks. The manager called me and asked what I wanted. I said I wanted a job. There was a boy wheeling barrows of slack up a gantry to the top of the kiln. He said 'Can you do that?' I said I could do it with the boy in it. 'You seem to think a lot of yourself,' he said. 'Let's see you do it.' So I took a barrow of slack up the gantry. It was easy. When I came down, I said, 'I hope I'm getting paid for this. I'm not doing trials for nothing.' He said, 'Don't worry, you'll get paid. When do you want to start?' I said, 'Now.' That was because I didn't want to go home saying I'd walked out of the job at Pilkington's, as the old chap would have beaten me about the place. So I started work at the brickworks at 17s 1d a week. And I didn't tell the old chap.[36]

Girls found employment in more or less the same way. In many cases Mum or an auntie 'spoke for' them and in 'women's' occupations, like textiles, tailoring, or millinery, where families traditionally 'spoke for' each other, employers regarded this as the best means of recruiting a reliable workforce.[37] The writer and social observer Pearl Jephcott thought that while teachers and care committees had perhaps some influence in the search for a girl's first job, the juvenile exchanges had virtually none. Her friends, however, were 'alarmingly influential'. Few girls, she wrote, 'seem to look on [the juvenile exchange] as the place where an enterprising person would be likely to find any particular help in getting the right kind of work. Certain of them regard it as the last resort of the lazy.'[38] Girls went to the 'Labour' only when they had 'no-one to speak for them.'[39]

The job-finding and job-changing habits of adolescent workers had long been perceived as a social 'problem'. It was held that disproportionate numbers of adolescent school-leavers entered 'blind-alley' or 'dead-end' occupations: jobs which paid comparatively well at 14, but for which employers would not pay adult rates at 16. Large numbers of boys and girls, it was

---

D.Phil. thesis (1994), 138–204. Dr Griffiths's work does suggest that there might have been important regional or occupational differences.

[36] Forman, *Industrial Town*, 86.   [37] F. Zweig, *Women's Life and Labour* (London, 1952), 33.

[38] A. P. Jephcott, *Rising Twenty* (London, 1953), 120. Jephcott was active in the girls' club movement in London and her conclusions are based upon survey work done there in the late 1930s and early 1940s.

[39] A. P. Jephcott, *Girls Growing Up* (London, 1942), 75.

thought, were thereby thrown unskilled upon the adult labour market. The education system or the cupidity or poverty of parents was usually blamed for this. The statisticians Carr-Saunders and Caradog Jones argued that elementary education in England prepared boys and girls for only a few occupations in which there was a likelihood of both retention and promotion. The result was that both boys and girls found their way into the distributive trades where jobs for unskilled adolescents were abundant. Whether the education system was or was not to blame the result was the same: the distributive trades were by far the most popular sector for school-leavers to find their first jobs.[40]

The distributive trades by their nature encouraged informal job-searching and a high labour turnover. Here the influence of friends was particularly important, as was the personal approach: 'Alice had a row with the boss, so "we [Alice and her friend] walked out at lunchtime, went into Woolworth's and got taken on there, went back to the boss and gave in our notice." '[41] People were struck by the speed with which adolescents, especially girls, found and changed jobs. Whether or not these jobs were quite the dead ends contemporaries thought,[42] they did constitute a casual labour market dominated by example and word-of-mouth.

The adult labour market, however, was not much more organized. Indeed, the great migration of labour from the North and Wales to the Midlands and the South in the 1920s and 1930s was also largely arranged by word-of-mouth. This migration had all the historic characteristics of earlier migrations. People tended to move in groups, either as friends or families, or, if singly, with the intention of encouraging others to follow. This was particularly true of the migration from Wales. Seventy-two per cent of Welsh migrants to Oxford came under their own steam: those who could not afford transport hitched or caught football trains. Once (or if) established, like all migrants, they acted as agents for the further migration of friends or relatives. One-sixth of all Welsh migrants to Oxford, for example, came from one Welsh mining village, Pontycymmer.[43] The same held for Welsh migration to Slough ('not dead but gone to Slough') and Hayes and Southall. Nor was it confined to Welsh migration. The streets around the new aluminium rolling mill in Banbury were known as 'Little Rochdale' since the men and their families who moved into them originated from the same few streets in Rochdale—a small community was simply transplanted.[44] A traditional pattern of migration gave migrants what they needed most: social support in an unfamiliar and sometimes hostile milieu.

Even by the late 1940s, despite the experience of a rigorously organized and directed labour market during the Second World War, this traditional pattern

---

[40] Carr-Saunders and Caradog Jones, *A Survey of the Social Structure of England and Wales*, 126–7.
[41] Jephcott, *Girls Growing Up*, 89. See also 69–74.   [42] See below, pp. 128–9.
[43] R. C. Whiting, *The View from Cowley* (Oxford, 1983), 70–1.
[44] See below, p. 183.

was not much modified. Men still changed jobs and even occupations casually; amongst unskilled workers a change of occupation 'was a chance product of change of employer'. As before the war, only a minority of men who changed jobs did so through the labour exchanges. Most found them by friends or by 'other means'.[45]

Why were men and women apparently so reluctant to utilize the labour exchanges? First: most of them did not have to. The English labour market was still largely based upon many local economies—some of them very small— whose potential workforce did not need the intervention of the state to find it employment. These local economies were in turn still dependent on networks of intimate social relationships which permitted people to 'speak for' each other and converted the networks themselves into informal labour exchanges. Outsiders were surprised at how far English skilled workers regarded their jobs as 'personal property' which could be passed on to their heirs, and how far employers acquiesced in this.[46] There were some casual occupations—notoriously dock-labouring, for example—where sons and relatives were openly favoured for employment as a way of closing such occupations against a mass of unskilled workers. But employers were also members of these networks; in effect, by allowing one generation of craftsmen to recruit another, they were, like employers in women's occupations, attempting to secure a guarantee of the competence of their workforce.

Nor did adolescents need the juvenile exchanges. During the interwar years, despite persistently high adult employment, it was not difficult for school-leavers to find jobs; often not good jobs, but jobs none the less. After 1945 it was even easier. The demand for labour was such that the traditional techniques for finding jobs could hardly not succeed.

This does not mean, however, that people would necessarily have gone to the exchanges had the old system failed. Working men and women of all ages were suspicious of the exchanges and usually regarded them as only a last hope. For this there is one overwhelming reason which was to have profound implications for British social policy: the labour exchanges were associated in the working-class mind not with jobs but with the dole. Thus there was between the wars an increasing tendency to speak of the exchanges as 'the dole' or the 'dole house', and the juvenile instruction centres to which unemployed adolescents were supposed to go as the 'dole school'. People believed they had a right to the dole but they hated the humiliations they underwent, particularly after means-testing was introduced in the 1930s, in order to get it. By combining dole-payment and job-search in one institution, by encouraging people to think that those who were supposed to help you find a job were also those who

---

[45] G. Thomas, *Labour Mobility in Great Britain, 1945–1949*, Social Survey SS 134 (1951), 64.
[46] W. Williams, *Full Up and Fed Up* (London, 1921), 44.

tried (as was thought) to deny you the dole, successive British governments almost fatally undermined the exchange's employment functions.[47]

It is possible, furthermore, that the surprisingly emphatic contempt girls showed for the exchanges and for the well-meant advice the exchanges purveyed was related to their vague contempt for the unmarried women who usually taught them and who also attempted to purvey well-meant advice. To a working-class girl an adult woman with no man attached to her was, it has been argued, 'an abnormality':

In the girls' eyes the teacher has failed in a marriage market in which practically every older woman has drawn *something*, if not a prize. If she has not actually failed she has anyhow been so eccentric a type of person that she has not thought it fundamentally important to get married.[48]

The exchanges, like teachers and care committees which were also charged with helping them get a job, represented a world which was culturally alien to working-class girls, and so avoided.

Although perhaps only one-fifth of adults found jobs through the exchanges, many men and women, certainly early in their working lives, changed jobs frequently. Between 1935 and 1939, 34 per cent of men changed their jobs at least once, and that figure rose to 41 per cent between 1945 and 1949. In the same periods 23 per cent and 34 per cent even changed the industries in which they worked. In the late 1940s about one-third of all working men and women between the ages of 16 and 24 (a higher proportion of women workers than men) had changed jobs at least once—about 1.6 million men and about 800,000 women. It was not, however, overall a very mobile workforce. Although 1 million people (about 4 per cent of the workforce) moved from the North and Wales to the Midlands and the South-East in the interwar years, for the majority of those who migrated mobility was limited to a move from one town to another within the same region. Nearly one-half of the population never worked in more than one town and three-quarters in never more than one region. Job-changes occurred, therefore, 'among a geographically immobile population likely to be acquainted with local opportunities for employment only'[49]—and this was in part a result of the informal ways in which most people still looked for jobs. Yet throughout this period unemployment was in certain regions persistently high and in some communities almost universal. The apparent immobility of the unemployed was puzzling.

There were several social impediments to mobility. For many skilled men, particularly coalminers and those who worked in ancillary industries, a decision to migrate often implied a decision to accept unskilled labour, and this

---

[47] See below, pp. 157–9 and D. King, *Actively Seeking Work? The Politics of Unemployment and Welfare in the United States and Great Britain* (Chicago and London, 1995), 203–14 particularly.

[48] Jephcott, *Rising Twenty*, 101.   [49] Thomas, *Labour Mobility in Great Britain*, 7.

many were not prepared to do. They preferred to stay where they were, in the hope that skilled work would become available, rather than move to 'inferior' jobs with 'inferior' wages. Nor was it necessarily desirable that they should. The associational life, both lay and religious, of much of the North and Wales was partly dependent upon skilled working men. Where they migrated *en bloc* many social institutions simply collapsed, and it was only the reluctance of men to move that kept many of them in being. It was, indeed, the social as much as the economic consequences to the 'depressed areas' of migration which were responsible for the industrial location policy followed after 1944— that of moving industry to men rather than men to industry.

For older men there were even fewer incentives to migrate. For them the inevitable period of readjustment after migration was longer than for younger men. They were usually less socially adaptable, and their interests often different from their younger fellow-migrants. They were also more likely to lose an established social status by migration—like the Welsh county councillor whose wife had died and whose children had moved to Oxford. Under strong pressure both from them and the labour exchange he migrated to Oxford. He stayed two months. By then the 'insignificance of his position proved too much for him, and he returned to be unemployed but socially recognized in Wales.'[50]

To migrate from the North to the South or from Wales to the Midlands was also to migrate to a different social environment; from a religious culture (to the extent that migrants shared it) which tended to be nonconformist to one which tended to be Anglican; from a political culture sympathetic to the Labour Party and trade unions to one then not sympathetic to them. Migrants, like tenants on the new council estates (and sometimes they were the same), often faced hostile natives who felt they undercut wages and took jobs. The host towns were not 'working-class' in the sense that migrants understood the term 'working-class'. In Oxford (admittedly an extreme antithesis) migrants were astonished at the dress and behaviour of the undergraduates, while the Welsh were sometimes taunted by local youths who tried, *inter alia*, to compel them to sing *God Save the King*.[51]

Men were not surprisingly reluctant to leave parents or dependants or to abandon such domesticity as the dole allowed for the loneliness of a single man's lodgings. Social disorientation and a sense of loss drove many back: of the 90,000 men the ministry of labour transferred from the 'depressed areas' to the South between 1930 and 1937, more than half returned home.

There were also financial obstacles to mobility. Almost everywhere migrants were likely to go was more expensive than where they lived. In particular, rents were usually higher, often much higher. Being unknown, men found it

---

[50] G. H. Daniel, 'Some Factors Affecting the Movement of Labour', *Oxford Economic Papers*, 3 (March 1946), 164–5.

[51] For individual reactions to Oxford, see the interesting personal studies in ibid. 173–9.

difficult to get credit in a new community; and before 1939, working-class life without access to credit was almost impossible. Miners, or others like them, who often had gardens or allotments at home were, at least initially, unable to supplement wages by produce in kind—like vegetables—which made an important contribution to the household of many working men and women. Not only did migrants suffer from this; so did the families they left behind. Men worried about the malnutrition of their children who were frequently and perhaps rightly thought to be victims of their fathers' mobility.

It has been argued that the major impediment to migration was the dole itself: by providing an alternative 'wage' it permitted men and (to a lesser extent) women to stay put—in effect, to queue for 'rationed' jobs—rather than to seek work elsewhere. The dole, it is suggested, indefinitely prolonged job-search and was, therefore, itself partly responsible for the persistence of high unemployment in several well-defined parts of the country.[52] This argument—much debated—is difficult to prove or disprove. It certainly exaggerates the extent to which the dole was an alternative 'wage' for most of the unemployed. As we have seen, the average benefit received by the single unemployed man or woman was only half an average wage. It was enough to keep people alive, but usually in or near poverty. As a financial incentive to immobility it was weak. Furthermore, it is unlikely that the unemployed would be denied *any* support, and even charitable payments could not have been much lower than the single person's benefit. This also holds true for married men with one or two children. For married men with three or more children, however, the financial dis-incentive to migration was stronger. Given that the dole, unlike a wage, was calculated upon a 'needs' basis,[53] and given the higher cost of living in the South and Midlands and the likely absence of wage-supplements in kind, the temptation for a family of five or more to stay put was probably powerful. Thus while married men inclined to change jobs more often than single men, they were much less ready to migrate to another part of the country. The majority of those who did 'go to Slough' were single.

It is therefore possible that the dole did bind men to their communities. But it was probably not the only or most important economic restraint. In order to move, men had to be reasonably certain that there was a job when they arrived. But the labour market in the South or Midlands simply could not have absorbed all 'surplus' labour from the North or Wales. And 'long-distance'

---

[52] For the 'strong' statement of this view, see D. K. Benjamin and L. Kochin, 'Searching for an Explanation of Unemployment in Interwar Britain', *Journal of Political Economy*, 87, 3 (June 1979), and replies in the same, 90, 2 (April 1982). For the 'weak' version, see Glynn and Oxborrow, *Interwar Britain*, 155. See also M. Thomas, 'Institutional Rigidity in the British Labour Market, 1870–1939: A Comparative Perspective', in S. N. Broadberry and N. F. R. Crafts (eds.), *Britain in the International Economy, 1870–1939* (Cambridge, 1992), 301–9; N. Whiteside and J. A. Gillespie, 'Deconstructing Unemployment: Developments in Britain in the Interwar Years', *Ec.H.R.*, xliv, 4 (1991), 668–77.

[53] See above, pp. 117–18.

mobility was undoubtedly sensitive to the trade cycle: in the interwar years mobility was highest in the years 1927–30 and 1933–6, and lowest during the slump of 1930–3.[54] This suggests that geographical mobility was at least partly determined by the perceived demand for labour; the more dynamic sectors of the economy, that is, did not create jobs as fast as the declining sectors lost them, and that is one of the reasons why men did not move.

5 | At work

It was commonly assumed that working-class 'work', particularly the most mechanized, was monotonous and unfulfilling. In a sense, Marx's belief that the capitalist division of labour alienated man from the essence of his being, his labour, was uncontroversial. Many people, for example, who would otherwise have deplored working-class betting condoned it on the grounds that it provided relief from the ineffable tedium of industrial work. It would be surprising, however, if this assumption were always true: the conditions, nature and place of working-class work were markedly heterogeneous; men's attitudes often differed from women's, skilled workers' from unskilled and adolescents' from adults'. The satisfactions which work could provide were often invisible to outsiders, while the 'culture of work', of which work as such was only a part, was equally concealed from those not familiar with it.

Men, it has been argued, may have overstated their satisfaction in work. To have done anything else would have been to question their sense of self-worth.[55] But the evidence that men did find satisfaction in work is so strong as to suggest that there was little undeclared discontent, and that where there was people made little attempt to hide it. Even before the First World War the extent to which men clung to apparently rebarbative workplaces surprised some. Alfred Williams, writing of the Great Western Railway works at Swindon at the turn of the century, noted that the smithies were 'in love' with their jobs; they 'cling to the shed as long as they possibly can; they have an unnatural fondness for the stench and the smoke'.[56] For many men pride in work was a powerful source of satisfaction. Coal-face miners, for example, denied that work was monotonous. Rather they boasted of strength and skill, of the amount of coal they could 'tick off'.[57] The American sociologist Whiting Williams observed with surprise a dispute between two miners as to who could drill a powderhole faster. ' "Swanking", both of them, I suppose, but they were

[54] H. Makower, J. Marschak, and H. W. Robinson, 'Studies in Mobility of Labour: Analysis for Great Britain', Part I, *Oxford Economic Papers*, 2 (May 1939), 94.

[55] J. H. Goldthorpe, David Lockwood, F. Bechhofer, and J. Platt, *The Affluent Worker: Industrial Attitudes and Behaviour* (Cambridge 1968), 11.

[56] A. Williams, *Life in a Railway Factory* (London, 1915), 292–3. See also McKibbin, *Ideologies of Class*, 152–9.

[57] N. Dennis, F. Henriques, and C. Slaughter, *Coal is our Life* (London, 1956), 28–9.

certainly taking pleasure in their workmanship, even though they tell me here that the best workers are the last to boast of it in public because of the tradition against manifest conceit.'[58]

Many men, and not simply craftsmen, took pleasure in machinery and its manipulation, even on assembly lines where the work was entirely repetitive.[59] Skilled men could be deeply absorbed in their work, often to the exclusion of all else. Boys with apprenticeships were notoriously 'steadier' and more enthusiastic about their work than unskilled adolescents.[60] But the dissatisfactions of the unskilled can be exaggerated. Distinctions between 'skilled' and 'unskilled' were often based on convention rather than fact, and were frequently designed to justify otherwise dubious wage differentials. Such distinctions did not, therefore, mean that 'skilled' work was more skilled or intrinsically more interesting than 'unskilled' work. The brickmaker who refused to work at Pilkington's Glass, for example, said he 'loved his work', and stayed at it for 47 years. He hated only his employers, who gave him on retirement a bottle of 'coronation cream sherry' which he could have 'smashed over their heads'. It was the disproportion between the gift and his love of the job which outraged him.[61] Most agricultural labourers were usually classed as 'unskilled'; yet measured job-satisfaction among agricultural workers was higher than in any other category of work, including the skilled. To the extent that men were driven from the land, the reason was not the monotony of work but the social deficiencies of rural life.

A significant proportion of 'mechanical operatives' said they were dissatisfied with their first jobs.[62] Some, no doubt, remained dissatisfied throughout their working lives; it would be surprising if that were not so. But for most the first job was experimental and people clearly made mistakes. Job-satisfaction rose with age, which suggests that men found jobs that suited them best (or bored them least) by trial and error. Thus during the Second World War 90 per cent of all men said they were 'satisfied' with their jobs.[63] The evidence, as we might expect, is rather conflicting. Contemporaries were impressed by the 'restlessness' of male adolescents, the constant job-changing. Yet there was, in fact, a high degree of job stability among boys; the more striking given the nature of most jobs open to them and the speed with which boys took them on leaving school.[64] In 1950, when asked, only 22 per cent of young men said they were dissatisfied with their first jobs.[65] Nor did boys resign their jobs as lightly

---

[58] Williams, *Full Up and Fed Up*, 97.   [59] McKibbin, *Ideologies of Class*, 152–9.

[60] Logan and Goldberg, 'Rising Eighteen in a London Suburb', 330.

[61] Forman, *Industrial Town*, 86.

[62] L. T. Wilkins, *The Adolescent in Britain*, Social Survey 148(P), July 1955, 35. All the data relate to 1950.

[63] B. Hutchinson, *Willesden and the New Towns*, Social Survey, NS (Dec. 1947), 3.

[64] Owen, *Survey of Juvenile Employment and Welfare in Sheffield*, 15.

[65] Wilkins, *Adolescent in Britain*, 35.

as was thought: they were as likely to be dismissed for illness or cycling accidents as to resign.[66] The absence of any statutory protection for young workers against dismissal made the labour market significantly more volatile than it otherwise would have been.

Nor should the degree to which boys ended up in 'blind alley' jobs be exaggerated. Most boys left school at 14 but usually could not secure apprenticeships until they were 16. Two years had to be filled in somehow and 'blind-alley' jobs were a good way to do so. There was a stratum of restless, job-changing, vaguely dissatisfied adolescent boys, but it is doubtful if their restlessness had much to do with the jobs as such. More probably it was the result of upbringing and education.[67]

Few adult men seem to have changed jobs specifically to find more interesting ones. In the late 1940s, of those who did change jobs, 24 per cent left because they were dismissed or made redundant, 39 per cent because of better pay or conditions elsewhere, 35 per cent for personal reasons. The importance of pay meant that married men with children were more likely to change jobs than single men. Most described their new jobs as preferable to the old, though pay and conditions were thought more important than job-satisfaction.

A man's working life involved not merely work itself; surrounding work was the workplace and its 'culture', its particular rituals and relationships. For many men this culture was inextricable from work proper, and it was the culture which gave working life its meaning and satisfaction. For others, workplace culture and its diversions made tolerable the boredom and stress of work. Although the size of a factory or workshop varied widely, the way men behaved at work probably did not. 'Horseplay' or 'larking about' was common everywhere and involved a physical contact which anywhere else, outside sport, was unacceptable:

Outwardly all was friendly and intensely physical in an uninhibited way. Men touched each other very readily: all over there were mock fights and practical jokes ... In quiet conversations the urge was to touch, draw aside by an elbow, rest a hand on a shoulder or simply to lean close. There was an absent-minded quality in the way men worked, waiting for distractions.[68]

Even when distraction was difficult, as on an assembly line, men took whatever opportunities they could. 'You've got to lark around with the mates a bit just to break the monotony.'[69] Men liked to talk and gossip, and talking was an important part of factory culture. This was often done in lavatories, and is one

---

[66] Caradog Jones, *Merseyside*, ii. 208–14. Many employers doubtless sought reasons to dismiss their boy labourers at 16 rather than pay them adult rates.

[67] Wilkins, *Adolescent in Britain*, 4.

[68] B. Jackson, *Working Class Community* (Pelican ed., Harmondsworth, 1972), 77, describing a textile mill in Huddersfield.

[69] Goldthorpe *et al.*, *Affluent Worker: Industrial Attitudes*, 49.

of the reasons why lavatory-time was endlessly disputed with employers. In shops where smoking was prohibited and there was no provision for smoking-breaks, lavatories became 'unofficial smoking rooms' as well as places to talk—and, of course, to bet:

One [lavatory] inside the shed was a hub and centre of social life with up to twenty men there at unofficially 'recognized' break times. It was a long, high narrow room with a row of ten WCs down each side . . . Those WCs not actually in use formed seats for some men who propped the doors open so that they could talk to friends squatting against tiled walls . . . Floor and guttering were always littered with cigarette butts and matchsticks. The once-white tiles were thickly stained with dark brown nicotine from tobacco smoke.[70]

Employers adopted different strategies towards smoking and talking. In places where there was little danger of fire employers permitted men to smoke while they worked. Others formally recognized smoking-breaks, usually by permitting morning and afternoon tea-breaks. During the Second World War all employers were under pressure to do this and many agreed. Others, however, refused and attempted to police (or forbid) trips to the lavatory during working time, or else made the lavatories so disagreeable that men would be deterred from using them.[71] These bans rarely achieved their purpose, so employers devised their own distractions, of which the most successful was 'Music While You Work'—dance music piped throughout the establishment.

A significant element of this culture, and immediately apparent, was sexual play, talk, and swearing. Mock-kissing and mock-embracing, together with obvious sexual gestures, often accompanied 'larking-about', while sexual swearing was relentless. Sex was one thing most men could talk about and this acted as a social tie. It was, furthermore, an inexhaustible source of humour. Sexual swearing also acted as a tie. Like sexual talk it was something most could do, and in some groups it was essential for admittance: 'outsiders' (foreigners, ex-grammar school boys) were known to become full-blooded swearers. For many, particularly for those who had served in the armed forces, where sexual swearing was even more *de rigueur*, it was an inevitable, scarcely noticed part of working life. But, almost as much as sexual play, it had its boundaries: swearing at home or elsewhere was usually not socially acceptable.[72] Distance from or proximity to work defined the extent to which it was acceptable. One observer wrote of Yorkshire miners: 'And yet already as the cage is descending one notices the growing tendency for every adjective and pronoun to become a violent swear-word, and the shift is only a hour or two old before the tendency gains dominance.'[73]

---

[70] Jackson, *Working Class Community*, 71.

[71] F. Zweig, *The British Worker* (Pelican ed., Harmondsworth, 1952), 111.

[72] See below, pp. 166–7.

[73] Dennis *et al.*, *Coal is our Life*, 214–15; see also Jackson, *Working Class Community*, 79–80.

Occupational culture was both demanding and competitive; it required a certain style, widely admired and sought by many. Amongst shipyard workers

the possession of a wide range of knowledge and the ability to handle well the style of conversation with its emphasis on quick wit, quick verbal reactions and rapid changes of tack, carry a social reward. To be regarded as a 'character' or a 'patter merchant' with a witty, caustic and self-mocking style and a wide variety of interests and stories is to have a welcome, and an acknowledgement, in all parts of the yard and often outside it as well.[74]

In those industries where the occupational culture was still comparatively rich, and even in those newer industries where it was much poorer, social relationships themselves were an important part of self-satisfaction.[75] That was why, for example, such a large number of men spent their dinner-hours in shipyards. In one case, despite the very close proximity of their homes to the yards, 71 per cent of workers had their dinner at work.[76]

But the competitiveness of factory culture was only social: though it encouraged men to shine as jack-the-lads, it did not encourage them to shine as workers. In those industries where there were strong ties between workmates, of which shipbuilding is indeed a good example, collective opinion prohibited any behaviour likely to divorce the individual from the group, or weaken its cohesion or which went beyond a tacitly agreed 'fair average'. Working-class people, Richard Hoggart wrote, 'number several vices among their occupational attitudes, but not those of the "go-getter" or the "livewire." '[77] Apart from that needed for the patter-merchant, cleverness or shrewdness was deprecated. The group imposed powerful norms and punished by derision anything which broke them. A 'fair-day's' work meant that a man should do his stint and not shirk; but no more. And he should do nothing which might threaten a mate's job. Nor, therefore, should he ever compete with his mate.[78]

This, it was argued, produced not only an introverted and defensive working class, but a culture which was defeatist and fatalistic. Outsiders were struck by the fatalism of the catch-phrases of working-class speech: 'take life as it comes', 'take the rough with the smooth', 'nothing is worth worrying about', 'worry can kill even a cat', 'take life day by day', 'day come, day go', 'what's the sense of worrying', 'tomorrow never comes' etc.[79] This was the 'traditional' working

---

[74] R. Brown, P. Brannen, J. Cousins, and M. Samphier, 'Leisure in Work: the "Occupational Culture" of Shipbuilding Workers' in M. A. Smith, S. Parker, and C. S. Smith (eds.), *Leisure and Society in Britain* (London, 1973), 107.

[75] Ibid.   [76] Ibid. 107–8.

[77] R. Hoggart, *The Uses of Literacy* (Pelican ed., Harmondsworth, 1966), 82–3.

[78] Zweig, *British Worker*, 91–2. '[Competition] is not encouraged by the group. It is rather an offence against the code of accepted morality [to] do anything to show up the weaker or less efficient or less able mate ...'.

[79] Ibid. 221.

class—much attached to the workplace, but ruled by group opinion, seemingly without ambition and deeply suspicious of and often hostile to management and the technological changes management was always thought to be promoting.

After the Second World War it was argued that a new kind of working man had emerged, one who deliberately chose higher pay over job-satisfaction. This was the 'affluent' worker, employed particularly in those automotive and ancillary industries which had developed rapidly in the 1930s and even more rapidly after the Second World War. Affluent workers did not seek monotonous work but were prepared to endure it in return for high pay. And this they explicitly admitted:

I liked the hat trade all right—it was interesting. But it hadn't picked up after the [Second World] war. I was older and I wanted a job with good pay and security.

When I came out of the R.A.F. the wife wanted income rather than an interesting job for me. I was pushed into the highest-paid work—which in Luton means Vauxhall.

I preferred being in service [as a footman]. It was a clean life and you were mixing with a much better class of people—they were brought up better. But the money wasn't so good.[80]

Despite the good money, both skilled and assembly line workers expressed dissatisfaction and restlessness. Most assembly line men disliked their work and wished to go elsewhere. There was, however, no clear relation between the nature of the job and a wish to move: indeed, craftsmen and setters were even more likely to want to leave than the unskilled workers. Among affluent workers, it was suggested, the monotony and speed of work were all 'apparent sources of deprivation', the cause of psychological and physical stress.[81] Affluent workers' attitudes to work were sharply distinguished from those of workers in coal or steel. The latter were deeply involved in work and the workplace while the former were emotionally and socially detached from the workplace. There was, in part, a structural reason for this. The organization of work in, for example, an automobile factory was highly individuated: a single person usually completed a single process while the nature and speed of work precluded contact with work-mates. The collective nature of work typical of the older industries, with men working in gangs, was largely eliminated. Affluent workers thus rarely associated with work-mates ('Mates are not friends'), had little group sense, and were largely unaffected by group opinion or norms.[82]

This distinction between affluent and other workers is probably overdrawn, since it underestimates how ambivalent all working men were in their attitude to work. Most were undecided as to whether they worked merely for a

---

[80] Goldthorpe et al., *Affluent Worker: Industrial Attitudes*, 34–5.   [81] Ibid. 19–20.

[82] Ibid. 54–61. One informant said of workmates 'it's like the Army. You're best friends but as soon as you're away from work, you forget them. It's the best way.' (p. 59.)

living 'or whether [a man] works because work itself fulfils a deep urge in him': 'when you ask a man satisfied with his job whether he likes it, you are likely to get one or both of two answers: 'I am used to it' and 'There is good money in it.' A man not satisfied with his job will tell you first of all: 'There is no money in the job.' Strong feelings for or against work were 'less common than the combination of liking and disliking at the same time'.[83] Married men, irrespective of where they worked, were ready to change jobs if 'the money' was better. Assembly line or process workers had always been (at best) mixed in their attitude to work, which they had always found stressful. On the other hand, there were apprentice craftsmen working in 'new' industries in London—where the affluent worker proliferated—who were prepared to forgo higher wages for the interest of the job.[84] Rather than seeing the affluent worker as a new and distinct type, we should see him at the extreme end of a continuum where some men emphasized wages, some job-interest, some saw no conflict between the two, but where all weighed one against the other.

Women were thought to have, and to some extent did have, a different attitude to work. The dominating fact of a working-class woman's life when she began work was the prospect of marriage:

the vital factor which affects the girls' as distinct from the boys' attitude towards work is not merely that the girls have marriage at the back of their minds but that the girl from the working-class home is expecting to get married *soon*.[85]

Many girls did not marry 'soon' (or even marry at all); many indeed might wait ten years before marrying, but the expectation of marriage made work for many girls seem merely a temporary condition. Marriage, furthermore, and not first pregnancy, was thought by most to be the proper moment for departure, even if many were compelled for financial reasons to stay in work until pregnancy.[86] The majority of women believed that they should not work after marriage or were doubtful as to its propriety,[87] a view usually reinforced by their husbands.[88] This dogged belief in the primacy of home and family was an obstacle to the recruitment of women during the Second World War and one of the reasons why compulsion was introduced. The reluctance of childless wives of skilled working men in reserved occupations either to work themselves or join the services was considered one of the more shameful manifestations of civilian selfishness. 'This', it was reluctantly recognized, 'is a home-loving population ... Our girls love their homes.'[89]

---

[83] Zweig, *British Worker*, 98–105.
[84] Logan and Goldberg, 'Rising Eighteen in a London Suburb', 330.
[85] Jephcott, *Rising Twenty*, 137.
[86] G. Thomas, *Women and Industry*, Social Survey, NS 104 (May 1949), 6.   [87] Ibid. 17.
[88] Although women themselves did not necessarily regard their husbands' views as decisive as to whether they worked or not.
[89] Social Survey, A.T.S. (Oct. 1941), 45–6.

The result was that young single women had highly unstable working lives. Girls drifted from one unskilled job to another, often every few months,[90] and usually for a variety of reasons. Of 288 women operatives who left their jobs in a factory in 'a slummy area' in one year, 82 left for medical reasons or pregnancy, 44 for home duties, 43 because they were dissatisfied with regulations or forewomen, 64 because they found the work unsuitable, 30 because they found better prospects, 14 because they found jobs nearer home, 7 got married. Ninety-six were sacked: 51 for absenteeism, 31 were thought unsuitable, and, amongst other reasons, 4 were sacked for misconduct, including 'a married woman of thirty making love to a boy, actually caught *in flagrante* in a stockroom, most unusual'.[91] The large number who were still domestic servants were increasingly inclined to stay in a position for only short periods, partly because pay and conditions were poor, partly because service was becoming an unacceptable social relationship. Many girls alternated domestic service with jobs in catering, distribution, or light manufacturing. As they got older, they got less footloose—particularly if they found a job with reasonable pay—but it was not expected that they would develop an 'interest' in it.

It was thought that girls were indifferent or hostile to their work. When asked, for example, what a visitor to Middlesbrough should see, the men almost invariably included the Dorman Long works—and skilled workers were especially insistent—while no woman did, or any other place of work.[92] The social worker and educationalist Margaret Phillips, writing of young women in the early 1920s, said that all of them 'loathed' their work.[93] Henry Durant, who introduced the Gallup Polls to England, wrote of factory girls 'stupefied with boredom':

Hence the emphasized erotic attitude of the factory girls, their display of finery, their love of dancing and cinemas, their loud shrieks of laughter in the streets which serve to draw attention to themselves, their competitive boasting of wild adventures on Monday morning.[94]

The low morale of factory girls, their apparent indifference to work, like their attitude to marriage and the home, became a 'problem' of wartime production. Mass-Observation noted of one munitions factory that the only 'interest' the girls had in work was the passing of time, and how it might be made to pass faster. This 'passive waiting for the day to be over' implied not just indifference to the job, but also 'a profound and very significant reluctance to accept the twelve hours spent in the factory as part of real life at all; it is simply a blank patch between one brief evening and the next.' While this remained true,

[90] Jephcott, *Girls Growing Up*, 69–75.
[91] F. Zweig, *Women's Life and Labour* (London, 1952), 114–15.
[92] Chapman, *Social Survey of Middlesbrough*, NS 50, pts. ii–iii (Jan. 1946), 5.
[93] M. Phillips, *The Young Industrial Worker* (London, 1922), 19.
[94] Durant, *Problem of Leisure*, 91.

Mass-Observation concluded, 'appeals to patriotism as an incentive to increased production are almost valueless'.[95] Working-class women, if only because of their seeming indifference to work, were thought especially fitted to highly mechanized production: they were more content to do 'boring' and repetitive work than men, and their fingers more supple. Docility and dexterity were thus what women brought to the labour market.[96]

Many young working-class women were undoubtedly hostile or indifferent to their work, and while they thought of their earnings as pocket-money (which was all it was, after they had given most to their mothers), or of work as a diversion before marriage, this was inevitable. But the work itself encouraged indifference. The jobs which most girls were permitted to do were increasingly 'boring' and 'repetitive', particularly in the rapidly expanding light manufacturing industry which disproportionately employed women and to which they were drawn in ever larger numbers. Young women, or their parents, had always favoured 'clean' and 'respectable' work, and that is how the light manufacturers always presented the jobs they offered. As a result, they had no difficulty in recruiting. The woman's personnel officer at Beechams could get the 'cream' of schoolgirls because the firm was thought to be 'respectable'—and to have 'taste'. One woman thought the 'new' (post-war) management lacked 'taste'—whereas before the war, 'We used to have a piece of sculpture of two girls sitting by the seaside. One of them has cupped her ear to hear what the other is saying, 'What are the wild waves saying?' The other answers, 'Take Beechams pills'. It was splendid.' Pilkingtons was liked 'because it was a family atmosphere and a family firm'.[97] Women's choice of job or service during the war was often decided for the same reasons: the work was clean, the people respectable, the uniforms nice.[98]

However clean the factory was, however family-like the atmosphere, that the work was monotonous and the chances of promotion negligible could not be hidden. Nor could the fact that the discipline was usually severe. The Peek Frean factory, for example, which pioneered many of the interwar assembly line techniques—it was the first to introduce 'Music While You Work'—permitted no talking or larking-about and stringently enforced its rules, including the ban on trade unionism. At Mullards, owned by the Dutch firm Philips, where discipline was also very severe, the supervisors 'had to be very strict to keep their jobs' ('The chargehand, Mr Collins, was injured in the First World War and had a steel plate in his chest. If he wanted to upset anybody he'd walk down the belt and bang on his tin plate with his screwdriver').[99]

---

[95] Mass-Observation, *War Factory: A Report* (London, 1943), 48.

[96] Zweig (*Women's Life and Labour*, 35) believed that women were happy enough with monotonous work so long as they were allowed to talk while doing it.

[97] Forman, *Industrial Town*, 81–3.   [98] Social Survey, A.T.S., 10.

[99] M. Glucksmann, *Women Assemble: Women Workers and the New Industries in Inter-war Britain* (London, 1950), 178. For Peek Frean's, see 97–9.

These firms also believed in getting the most out of their labour force, usually via the so-called 'Bedaux system' whose effect was to set the assembly lines at an optimally fast pace. The Bedaux system was deeply unpopular—so unpopular that J. Lyons and Co., a well-known practitioner of the fast assembly line, renamed the Bedaux engineers 'time and motion men'—and was the cause of the only serious industrial disputes involving women workers between the wars.[100] Not all firms were so severe. Some, like Morphy Richards, deliberately adopted a more relaxed policy; but, punitive or not, none had difficulty in recruiting. They were 'clean', the conditions 'superior', and most of the obvious alternatives, like domestic service, even worse. It was not until the Second World War, when these firms faced competition from the munitions factories, where traditions were more easygoing, that they had to concede less remorseless routines, like making provision for tea-breaks.

Nevertheless, the extent to which women did passively accept monotony should not be overrated. Any interruption to work routines (usually the loss of electric power) was, Mass-Observation noted, 'acclaimed with unrestrained delight . . . One morning the electricity which drives the machines kept on suddenly going off for a few minutes; and every time this happened a spontaneous shout of "Hooray!" went up all over the room.'[101] Sabotage of the moving belts, like fusing them, was, it has been suggested, one of the few ways open to women to relieve the intensity of work.[102]

Where customs were different and discipline looser the occupational culture of women workers appears in practice to have been rather like men's. In factories and shops where the labour force was mixed there was a good deal of sexual badinage in which women freely joined. 'People are continually passing backwards and forwards: which gives endless opportunity for backchat and occasional horseplay.' The girls said they liked the horseplay: 'Two of the men got hold of Annie Bailey to-day . . . by the arms and jumped her up and down in the dough. We didn't half laugh.' When they could, women, like men, smoked and gossiped in the lavatories (also with their employers' disapproval).[103] For unmarried women work was important for sociability. They liked the gossip and 'many observers of factory life' noted the practice of passing around gifts and sentimental objects which had to be admired.[104] Although the tendency was for women to be employed in highly sex-segregated occupations, they did not necessarily prefer that. The wartime Social Survey found that, of those who had a preference, more wanted to work with men than women; the majority did not care.

In fact, women were probably less hostile to their work than was supposed. When asked during the Second World War, the great majority said they 'liked'

[100] M. Glucksmann, *Women Assemble: Women Workers and the New Industries in Inter-war Britain*, 191; K. G. J. C. Knowles, *Strikes* (Oxford, 1954), 23, 184, 231.

[101] Mass-Observation, *War Factory*, 48.   [102] Glucksmann, *Women Assemble*, 181.

[103] Jephcott, *Girls Growing Up*, 85–6.   [104] Zweig, *Women's Life and Labour*, 68.

their work, and they almost unanimously agreed that women should do war-work, even if many were in practice reluctant.[105] The attitudes of married women or those who had given up hope of marriage almost certainly differed from that of adolescent girls. Many working women thought that housewives spun out their housework to fill in time, and exaggerated its importance.[106] Nor were they unaware of the significance of their work. One married weaver said 'Whenever I hear on the wireless news about the export drive in the cotton industry, I say to myself: "That's me." '[107]

In some parts of the country there was little difference between working men and women in where they made their friends—in Middlesbrough it was suggested that both working men and women made more 'close friends' at work than anywhere else. There was a big difference, though, between both these groups and housewives. In light of the obvious importance to both sexes of workmates as a source of friendship, the authors of this survey commented that 'too great a divorce between place of work and place of residence may have a disintegrating effect'.[108] It seems likely, therefore, that when circum-stances permitted, which, of course, they often did not, men and women approached their work and the workplace in similar ways. What women lost at work, to the degree that they had ever had it, was, as with men, not interest but autonomy. That, however, was a different loss, not confined to the working classes.

6 | *Workplace politics*

How men and women responded to their workplace and its culture was condi-tioned as much by those who employed and supervised them as by their work itself. Working people, however, were often uncertain about workplace hier-archies and thus uncertain about who actually managed them. In small firms or workshops employers and managers were recognizable: people usually knew who made decisions and where. It was here that labour relations (as it was coming to be called) were relatively untroubled and where trade unions were discouraged, as much by the workforce as its employers. But the small employer was slowly becoming less characteristic of industry; more charac-teristic was a bureaucratic management, itself highly stratified and physically divorced from the workshop. Increasingly, therefore, working people had little to do with their employers. Their contacts with the 'office' tended to be with junior clerical staff who stood proxy for employers: it was the clerks rather than employers who became 'them', the enemy. In most firms relations between the shopfloor and the 'office' were notoriously bad, made worse by

---

[105] Social Survey, A.T.S., 12–13.   [106] Zweig, *Women's Life and Labour*, 11.
[107] Ibid. 18.   [108] Chapman, *Social Survey of Middlesbrough*, NS 50, pts iv–viii (Sept. 1945), 8.

the fact that much of the office staff was itself of working-class origin and thus thought jumped-up as well as snooty. Even schoolgirl friendships could not survive this breach, which was widened by the conspicuous distinctions in status and appearance between clerical staff and shopfloor workers. Employers were aware of these distinctions but made little attempt to efface them. In 1947, W. C. Puckey, general manager of Hoover's, said:

The girl of 16 in the general office is probably eligible immediately for the company's pension scheme and other amenities. The office worker has decent cloakrooms—the factory worker usually has no doors or only half-doors because he can't be trusted not to 'mike' [take illicit breaks]. He is still called a 'hand' by many who ought to know better. Many other examples could be shown, but they all add up to the lack of status of the manual worker.[109]

The reluctance of employers to remedy this 'lack of status' was partly because many of them refused to take labour relations seriously, even though to do so was increasingly thought necessary for good management. Few firms had labour relations officers; in most they were a duty of the personnel officer, if anybody, and almost none had any form of consultation with the workforce. Unlike the United States, 'industrial psychology' was not yet thought to be essential to 'scientific management' (though it was to become so after 1945 when so-called 'frictional' strikes became more frequent). In England, scientific management tended to be confined to production processes, to 'time and motion', and so identified with Taylorism[110] or the Bedaux system, both of which in practice worsened labour relations. Nor was much done to soften the peremptory tone which management so often adopted towards the shopfloor. 'An enormous improvement in the manners of management', Sidney Webb wrote, 'would be effected . . . if it were made an invariable rule . . . that every workman were addressed as Mr Blank, and every workwoman as Miss or Mrs Blank, instead of the surname only.'[111] But employers were themselves under pressure from their clerical staffs. Distinctions of status and amenity were for them (and their parents) the first steps on the route out of the working class and not lightly abandoned. They were, furthermore, often compensations for low income: many clerks were less well paid than craftsmen (a fact known to both) and without superiority of status and amenity junior clerical occupations might have been even more dispiriting than they already were.

The fact that for many working men and women the clerical staff was 'management' was due also to the traditions of English manufacture. The

---

[109] Quoted in Knowles, *Strikes*, 215.

[110] 'Taylorism' was a system of 'scientific management' developed by an American engineer, F. W. Taylor, before 1914. Its purpose was to simplify a workman's job as much as possible—ideally to one task—and to eliminate all forms of workplace autonomy by concentrating the entire control of production in the firm's planning department.

[111] S. Webb, *The Works Manager To-Day* (London, 1917), 109 n.

nineteenth-century system of sub-contracting, of working through gangs and of ceding to craftsmen a number of managerial functions tended to diffuse management. This established a tradition of comparative autonomy which survived well into the twentieth century. In shipbuilding, for example, craftsmen were largely responsible for quality control, and it is possible that payment by piecework and bonus had the same effect.[112] To many workmen, therefore, the best management was the most invisible. Asked why they liked the 'good atmosphere' at a steel mill, workmen frequently replied, 'nobody bothers us.'[113] Even where managerial control was more direct, as it increasingly became, the workforce saw little of those who had real executive authority; they were represented by foremen, forewomen, and chargehands, with whom relations were often bad. Hostility to junior clerical staff and shopfloor supervisors meant that grievances were frequently misdirected, particularly when the workforce was un-unionized. Union officials at least knew where power lay.

We should not, of course, exaggerate the degree of hostility to management or employers. In many smaller firms it scarcely existed; in larger ones it varied. None the less, there was, especially in heavy industry, a pervasive suspicion of 'them' and the economic system 'they' operated. Even the commendation 'nobody bothers us' was a negative one. Many working men and women held to a kind of folk-Marxism quite independent of actual party-political allegiances. They believed their own work was the source of all value; the only work that mattered. Without it society would not exist. Clerical workers 'did nothing', nor did that legion of minor officials who battened on the working classes.[114]

The identification of management with 'them', together with this elementary Marxism did much to define working-class notions of criminality and history. Thus pilfering at work from a depersonalized management (or other anonymous agencies belonging to 'them') was almost always thought legitimate. 'Quite respectable men', one commentator wrote,

who would not themselves steal, take a light view of pilfering. They seem to think that because the men have grievances they are justified in such conduct. 'We are robbed all the time, therefore we are justified in robbing'; or 'The employers exploit us, and so why shouldn't we get a bit of our own back?' or 'It isn't poor people who will lose by it', are common trains of thought and argument.[115]

---

[112] E. Lorenz and F. Wilkinson, 'The Shipbuilding Industry, 1860–1965', in B. Elbaum and W. Lazonick (eds.), *The Decline of the British Economy* (Oxford, 1987), 125. W. Lewchuk, 'The Motor Vehicle Industry' in ibid. 140–1. See also Williams, *Full Up and Fed Up*, 55. Williams wrote of a visit to a Welsh tin plate mill: 'It is amazing to think of spending from noon till after eight o'clock thus talking with the workers without a word from the authorities.'

[113] O. Banks, *The Attitudes of Steelworkers to Technical Change* (Liverpool, 1960), 27.

[114] Jackson, *Working Class Community*, 82.

[115] John Hilton (ed.), *The Other War* (London, 1918), 82–3.

Petty criminality was intrinsic to factory culture. The 'fiddling' of time books where piece-rates were paid was very common, to an extent which some working people themselves found distasteful: 'The men aren't greedy here, they just want a fucking lot.'[116] Adolescent girls spoke casually of 'lifting' from their works. They regarded it as 'perfectly legitimate . . . They swap stories on their exploits such as do anglers, possibly with the same amount of veracity.'[117] But clear distinctions were drawn between acceptable 'thieving' and unacceptable 'robbing':

It is always wrong to steal money. Violence is always wrong. Thefts from workmates or landladies is vicious. Thefts from corner shops is utterly wrong. Breaking into the gas meter isn't so much wrong as stupid. But 'nicking a bit' from Woolworth's is all right. So is stealing small useful articles from all large employers.[118]

Many working men and women did steal money and many, men at least, were violent, but in both cases they knew they were departing from a recognized moral code. Even stealing from a small employer was usually 'robbing' because him you were likely to know; theft from him involved an identifiable personal loss. One Manchester boy, if he wanted to steal, went to Cheadle or Didsbury—'no way did you rob a working-class guy'.[119] The idea of right and wrong within the political economy of the working class was thus fairly well defined: stealing from one's own—family, friends, neighbourhood—was wrong; stealing from 'them', from people or institutions you did not know and 'who would not miss it', was not.[120] This was, however, a code which did not survive the communities who created it. Within a generation the principal victims of working-class crime were the working classes.

A willingness to regard employers' property as ripe for expropriation suggests a grievance-ridden view of working-class history. In many industries it is clear that working men (probably more than working women) had indeed long memories of real or imagined grievances. The strength of such grievances, even in industries with powerful unionized and comparatively privileged workforces, surprised outsiders. 'I asked them', one American wrote in 1921 of

---

[116] Jackson, *Working Class Community*, 102.   [117] Jephcott, *Rising Twenty*, 127–8.

[118] Jackson, *Working Class Community*, 84.

[119] D. Robins, 'Sport and Youth Culture', in J. Hargreaves (ed.), *Sport, Culture and Ideology* (London, 1982), 149.

[120] See the story recounted by J. B. Mays, the Liverpool sociologist and popular broadcaster. 'One afternoon a wagon tipped a quantity of coke on the pavement of one of the largest institutions in the district. While the driver and his mate were inside the building, an old lady appeared on the scene and commenced picking up pieces of coke and stowing them away in a large shopping-bag . . . Two small boys observed her activity and took compassion on her age. They immediately offered their assistance and soon all three were busily engaged on the same task. The small boys would no doubt have been astonished if they had been told that they were breaking the law or doing wrong. It was no more than a gesture of juvenile altruism, a deed worthy of Baden Powell himself.' (J. B. Mays, *Growing Up in the City* (Liverpool, 1956), 119.)

workers at a tin-plate mill, 'why, with all the advantages of security from the foremen's firing, their short hours and high wages, health and unemployment insurance etc., they still cared to call themselves Sinn Feiners and Bolshevists. "We '*ave* ter be ter get 'em [all the advantages]." '[121] Remembered wrongs dogged industrial relations. The sociologist Ferdynand Zweig recalled a conversation with a union official in Lancashire:

'But that [memory of wrongs] can be a great nuisance, especially where organized labour is concerned'.
'I agree. Do you know what happens when we propose some adjustments in our union policy, saying that the employers have become co-operative and industrial relations have improved? Someone gets up and recites:
'The Devil was sick,
the Devil a monk would be;
The Devil was well,
the Devil a monk he'd be'.[122]

This hostility was sometimes attributed to an ideological anti-capitalism.[123] It is true, as we have seen, many working people had a strong sense of being 'robbed' and this was obviously associated with a vague feeling that the rewards of capitalism were ill-distributed. But they were probably just as hostile to workplace authority as such: labour relations, for instance, in those industries nationalized by the Attlee government were no better under public than private ownership:

Scores of examples [from the nationalized coal industry] could be given of the prevailing idea among workers that any suggestion emanating from management, since it is designed for greater profit, is likely to be some underhand attack. It will benefit one side or the other; coincidence of interests is unthinkable and they cannot conceive of the boss being philanthropic.[124]

How extensive or intense this feeling was is difficult to gauge accurately. Those who had been among the long-term unemployed were thought the most suspicious: 'they' had 'robbed' the unemployed of their only significant property-right, their jobs, and, therefore, 'they' could never be trusted. Suspicion was also strong in industries like coal, where there had been long traditions of conflict between men and management—though in coal the tradition was uniquely bitter—and in industries with well-entrenched craftsmen who saw most proposals from management as attempts to modify or eliminate their privileges. Contemporaries also thought it characteristic of heavy rather than light and unionized rather than non-unionized industry; of men rather than women. These categories, however, partly overlapped. Heavy industry was more highly unionized than light, and employed more men than women.

---

[121] Williams, *Full Up and Fed Up*, 56.   [122] Zweig, *British Worker*, 85.
[123] Ibid. 190–1.   [124] Dennis *et al.*, *Coal is our Life*, 33.

It also had a more stratified workforce and thus employed more craftsmen. Trade union members, furthermore, had more effective ways of airing grievances than non-unionists. Yet there were exceptions. In iron and steel labour relations had been traditionally good, with apparently little hostility to management or its right to manage.[125] But in a new industry like motor cars, which was largely un-unionized until the 1940s and where employers practised a form of 'welfare capitalism' in order to attach the workforce to the firm, industrial relations were never good: the lavish sporting and social facilities provided by employers were under-used and levels of identification with the firm low. The attitudes of women workers were equally complicated. For those who intended to leave work at marriage the degree of engagement was so low that they were simply indifferent to their employers. Those, however, whose engagement was deeper, or who worked in the relatively few industries where women were unionized probably differed little in their attitudes from men.

There clearly was a relationship—though not necessarily causal—between trade union membership and attitudes to employers. Furthermore, the size and power of the English trade unions was thought to be characteristic of the English working class, as the 'typical' English working man was thought to be a trade unionist. English union membership was indeed comparatively high, but the 'typical' (that is, average) English working man was a trade union member for less than half this period, and the 'typical' English working woman, never.[126] The fact that, at best, only 55 per cent of working men belonged to a union, and the consistently low level of union membership amongst women meant that at no time was a majority of 'potential' trade union members actual members: the highest figure was 45.2 per cent reached in 1920 and 1948. In 1951 the figure was slightly lower—45.0 per cent.

There is an obvious relationship between overall union membership and degrees of economic activity. Membership rose rapidly at the end of the First World War and the first two years of the peace: a period of full employment and inflationary pressure on wages. Between 1920 and 1922 union membership then declined by almost 40 per cent, a fall caused by the severe deflation of the economy and the rapid rise in unemployment. After seeming to stabilize in 1923, union membership fell steadily until 1933. The reason why membership did not recover in the 1920s was due to the continuing depression in the heavily unionized 'staple' industries and the growth of 'new' industries in the Midlands and the South, industries which either had never been unionized or where unions were weak. There was, in effect, a redistribution of the workforce from unionized to non-unionized occupations. The growth of membership after 1933 was due in part to cyclical economic recovery, in part to the

---

[125] Banks, *Attitudes of Steelworkers*, 27.
[126] For figures of trade union membership, see Halsey, *Trends in British Society*, 123–4.

success of some unions, like the Transport and General Workers' Union, in organizing some of the new industries. After 1937 the rearmament programmes accelerated the recovery of the 'staple' industries, particularly shipbuilding and heavy engineering whose workforces were traditionally almost wholly unionized. There was thus a more symmetrical relationship between levels of union membership and overall economic activity in the late 1930s than in the 1920s. From 1941 on there was, except for seasonal interruptions, like the winter of 1947, almost negligible unemployment and this accounts for the consistently high levels of union membership.

But at best (1944) only a little more than one-quarter of 'eligible' women joined a trade union. Why was this? Contemporaries argued that women workers—particularly adolescents—were largely indifferent or hostile to unions.[127] The primacy of marriage, the consequent lack of involvement in their work, and the rapidity with which they changed jobs, discouraged in women the emotional or long-term interest in work which trade union membership was thought to demand. Industry itself, and thus trade unions, were, it was also suggested, too masculine and collective in their ambience to be attractive to women. These were all true but they do not alone explain the seeming reluctance of women to join unions. The industries in which women typically worked were themselves difficult to organize. Characterized by unskilled and repetitive work, often part-time, with a high labour turnover, and a large reserve army of women willing to work in them, they were exactly those industries where trade unionism was weak and easily broken, or simply non-existent. Employers, furthermore, adopted quite different strategies to their women employees. At Hoover's, for example, in the departments where men only were employed, as in the engineering section, management conceded the closed-shop to the AEU (Amalgamated Engineering Union), still predominantly a craft union, while refusing even to recognize unions in the assembly departments (where women were predominant) and dismissing anyone who sought union recognition. Nor were the unions, especially the craft unions, much more encouraging. The AEU, for instance, was famous for its hostility to women, but it was not alone. The Vehicle Workers refused to support the striking women trim-fitters at Rover's (1937) who turned instead, with mixed success, to the TGWU (Transport and General Workers' Union). The unions feared 'dilution'—the employment of women in jobs hitherto confined to male craftsmen, something which even in wartime they accepted only with reluctance—and argued in the interwar years that women were 'taking' men's jobs, whereas, in fact, women were being employed on jobs which would not have been offered to men at all—or if they had been, would have been refused.

How far women disliked the 'masculine' disputation of trade union tactics

---

[127] See, for example, Jephcott, *Rising Twenty*, 122.

is probably also exaggerated. Many women did disapprove of the aggressive preambles to wage negotiations, and disapproved even more of strikes; many doubtless associated them with the aggressive, often violent, masculine behaviour they tried to extirpate at home. These attitudes were, however, not universal. When women belonged to 'men's' unions and did 'men's' jobs they tended to act as men. In the First World War, for example, of the 1.66 million women drafted into industrial work, 750,000 joined unions, including craft unions, and were as ready to strike as the men they replaced.[128] Nor were the accepted stereotypes of women workers always passive ones: the great popularity of the post-war television comedy, *The Rag Trade*, with its formidable female shop steward (played by Miriam Karlin) perpetually shrieking 'Everybody Out' (which itself became a popular catchphrase) suggests there were other, equally powerful stereotypes of the woman at work.

Although employers and employees in much of industry were deeply suspicious of each other, and in a few industries, like coalmining, there was an undeclared war in which the whole country eventually became participants, industrial relations were not the jungle many thought. The majority of workers were not union members and, with the exception of 1926, the year of the general strike, in no year did the number of days lost through strikes even exceed days lost by one public holiday.[129] That statistic would probably have surprised contemporaries; but industries most prone to strikes were those most highly unionized, and unionization was not spread evenly throughout the country. The strikes which after the First World War did much to fashion the interwar view of the labour movement in practice involved a comparatively small number of people in a comparatively small number of industries.

Like trade union membership, the number and distribution of strikes was closely related to changes in the economy. The years between 1919 and 1923 were a period of unprecedented industrial stoppages (and with the exception of 1926 was to have no equal thereafter) as unions attempted first to protect the real value of wages and then to resist cuts in money wages. From 1923 (1926 apart), the number of days lost through strikes declined erratically until 1935, when the effect of falling unemployment was to strengthen the unions' bargaining position, and thus their willingness to strike. There was a sharp increase in both strikes and days lost in 1937 (the most economically buoyant of the decade); and throughout the 1940s, when there was constant full employment, the number of strikes and days lost stabilized at about the 1937 level.

This survey, however, takes no account of how far the total number of days lost in any one year was influenced by strikes in one industry—coal.[130] In seven

[128] Knowles, *Strikes*, 183.
[129] For the statistics of industrial disputes, see *British Labour Statistics: Historical Abstract, 1886–1968* (Dept. of Employment, HMSO, 1971), 396.
[130] For the relative 'strike-proneness' of major industries, see Knowles, *Strikes*, 203.

years of this period, days lost by miners' strikes represented more than half the total number of days lost: in 1926, of the 162 million working days lost no less than 146.5 million were lost by the miners, and of the remainder nearly all were lost by those who struck in sympathy with them. Although the fortunes of mining were partly related to economic movements more generally, many of its problems were unique and remained unresolved—even after national-ization in 1947. Thus when full employment returned to the industry in 1940–1 it proved impossible to establish, even in wartime, anything like indus-trial peace. The workforce was older, embittered and not over-impressed by its patriotic obligations. Had industrial relations in coal been different the over-all record of industrial relations in England would also have been different.

Since both mining and textiles (the second most 'strike-prone' industry) were geographically concentrated, the effect of their relative 'strike prone-ness' was to establish a clear regional bias in the propensity to strike.[131] No Eng-lish region approaches the 'strike proneness' of South Wales, whose miners harboured longer memories and more bitter grievances even than the English coalfields. English regions most prone to strike were those with a mix of min-ing and textiles: the West Riding of Yorkshire, and Lancashire and Cheshire. Noticeable is the propensity *not* to strike of those areas where industry was growing fastest: London and the South East and the West Midlands.

Overall, throughout the period strikes declined in number and composi-tion. The proportion which were 'basic' or 'solidaristic' fell continuously; the proportion which were 'frictional' rose correspondingly.[132] The marked decline in the number of 'wage' strikes was partly due to the more successful management of fiscal and monetary policy in the 1940s—particularly in the smoothing out of fluctuations in wage levels—than in the First World War and its aftermath, but due more to the development of national wage bargaining between employers and unions. This, in turn, was due to the greater readiness of employers to recognize unions as bargaining agents. And it was union pol-icy, wherever possible, to settle wage disputes without strikes: a prudent tactic adopted in face of evidence that increasingly 'wage' strikes were settled in favour of employers.[133]

'Solidaristic' strikes were designed principally to secure union recognition. The unions had been weakened in the interwar years not only by large-scale unemployment in those industries which had traditionally been heavily unionized, but by the rapid growth of industry in areas with little or no trade union history. Of these 'new' industries the most important from the union

[131] Ibid. 197.
[132] This classification is based on ibid. 234. 'Basic' strikes cover all questions of wages and hours; 'frictional', employment practices and working arrangements, including discipline; 'solidaristic', questions of union principle, like recognition, and sympathetic strikes.
[133] Ibid. 235, 243.

point of view was the motor-car industry.[134] The car firms dominated the communities in which they were located; they were large employers and they established the norms for the numerous ancillary firms which depended on them; they created a 'car-culture' which was akin to and as powerful as the work-cultures of the North. Throughout the interwar years the principal companies, Austin (Birmingham), Ford (Trafford Park, Manchester, and then Dagenham in Essex), Morris (Oxford and Coventry), Vauxhall (Luton), and Rover (Coventry) refused to recognize unions or to join the Engineering and Allied Employers' Federation, since recognition of unions was a condition of membership. They usually dismissed anyone thought to be a union 'activist'. They also followed American practice—though it came naturally to the rather autocratic leadership of the industry—by ensuring that wages and social provision were superior to equivalent, union-recognizing engineering firms. Despite persistent attempts at unionization and a number of strikes, none of the car plants had recognized unions by the outbreak of the Second World War. This failure was due—aside from the attitude of the management—to the nature of the workforce. Often recruited from surrounding villages and the rural hinterland, as in Oxford and Luton, it was a workforce habituated to compliance. It was not until the migration of workman from South Wales and the North of England (and of 'cockneys', as all those thought to be from London were called) had significantly diluted the workforce that it became more 'union-minded'. The influence of the Welsh in the only successful strike for recognition before the war—that at the Pressed Steel Works at Oxford (which made car-bodies for Morris) in 1934, where a majority of the strike committee was Welsh—was so obvious that Morris enquired of the ministry of labour whether it might not be possible to halt the future migration of Welsh to Oxford.

It was not until the Second World War that the industry recognized the unions. The withdrawal from effective control of the founding fathers like Morris (now Lord Nuffield) made the firms less rigid. More important, however, was the war itself. Full employment and the willingness of the ministry of labour to intervene greatly strengthened the unions' position, as did managements' fear of anything which interrupted production. Managements' autonomy was further circumscribed by the Essential Works Order of 1941. Originally issued to stop skilled workers moving to those employers who

---

[134] For industrial relations in the motor industry see S. Tolliday and J. Zeitlin (eds.), *The Automobile Industry and its Workers* (Oxford, 1986), 34–52; Lewchuk, 'The Motor Vehicle Industry', in Elbaum and Lazonick, *Decline of British Economy*; Whiting, *View from Cowley*, 53–73, 178–86; N. Fishman, 'Reflections on the Command Structure and Strategy of the Trade Union Movement in the Ford's War at Dagenham, 1931–1946', Paper for the Eighth British–Dutch Conference on Labour History (Sept. 1992). I am grateful to Dr Fishman for a copy of her paper. The reminiscences of Arthur Exell (a Welshman who migrated to Oxford) are very evocative: A. Exell, 'Morris Motors in the 1930s', pts i and ii, *History Workshop*, 6, 7 (1978, 1979), and 'Morris Motors in the 1940s', ibid. (1980).

offered them most, it was disliked by craftsmen; but it also made it difficult for employers to dismiss workmen for trade union activity—their principal weapon before 1939. By 1945 all firms except Ford had recognized the unions and Ford did so in 1946.

This was by no means the case with every employer, but those who refused to recognize unions tended to be smaller or those whose workforce was pre-dominantly female. Thereafter 'solidaristic' strikes were as often intended to secure the closed shop as recognition. But that was not their only function. Before 1927, when the Trades Disputes Act outlawed them, 'sympathetic' strikes—strikes by one union in support of the demands of another—were a per-missible form of 'solidaristic' strike. The greatest of the sympathetic strikes was, of course, the general strike (3–12 May 1926), a strike by the railwaymen, dockers, road transport workers, the printing trades, iron and steel, 'heavy' chemicals, the construction trades, and gas workers in support of the striking coalminers (who had technically been locked out by the coal-owners). In addi-tion to the miners, with a solidarity which surprised both the government and themselves, 1.55 million men came out and remained out until the TUC capitulated to the government. Despite the almost heroic solidarity of those who did come out, the strike could never have succeeded—as the union leader-ship was aware. Not only was the government determined not to accede to the strikers' demands, it had the full support of the 'constitutional classes'.[135] Fur-thermore, the majority of working men did not strike; hardly any women struck, since their trades were largely un-unionized. The general strike was, in fact, a strike of the highly unionized, predominantly male industrial trades in or dependent upon the 'staple' industries, whose decline by the mid-1920s seemed irreversible. The failure of the general strike suggested that as a tactic the sympathetic strike, particularly if it were quasi-political, had only limited utility.

Strikes were not the only form of industrial stoppage. There were other more spontaneous actions of which the most effective—because the most dam-aging—was absenteeism. Absenteeism had many causes. Often it was a result of illness; in many cases, however, it was an unorganized protest against working conditions. There appears, indeed, to have been an inverse relationship between strikes and absenteeism: when the latter was higher, the former was lower and vice versa.[136] Often absenteeism, like casual strikes, was simply a form of holiday. This was particularly so during the Second World War when the workforce was under severe pressure and men and women frequently admitted to physical exhaustion. In 1940, in a well-publicized dispute over the dismissal of a shop steward, 450 workers at De Havilland's 'took an extended holiday' and formed a 'holiday committee' to conduct it.[137] During the war

---

[135] See above, p. 58. [136] Knowles, *Strikes*, 225–6. [137] Ibid. 218.

absenteeism as an option was more attractive than a strike: it did not incur the unpatriotic odium of a strike and it was almost without penalty since firms, after 1941 at least, were largely prohibited from dismissing the absentee. In factories with a large female workforce—women being usually more dutiful than men—absenteeism (though it certainly existed) was probably less significant than high labour turnover. In non-unionized shops women protested informally not by strikes but by leaving.

Many employers resisted unionization on the grounds that the unions encouraged strikes and created grievances where none existed. Much public opinion—working class included—agreed. There is, however, little evidence that this was so. Union leaders rarely initiated strikes and did their best to avoid them. They always disapproved of 'lightning strikes', which became increasingly common after 1945 as their possible cost to workers became decreasingly punitive. Amongst their members, indeed, the most frequent criticism of the unions was that they were not radical enough. Even working men who thought the unions were the 'only allies we've got' could doubt whether 'they really stood up for them'. This view was particularly strongly felt in the interwar years: a St Helens glassworker said his union, the General and Municipal Workers', did 'nothing' for glassworkers; he left it after a year because it was 'useless'. One railwayman said that 'the feeling of most of our chaps was that the union could have done more. No one seemed to have much interest. We had to fight for every rise we got. There were too many grades on the railway; there were umpteen of them.'[138]

There was a widespread belief that union leaders and employers worked hand-in-glove—'they piss in the same pot' Ferdynand Zweig was told—at the expense of the working man and woman. This sense of distance between member and union was exploited—often successfully—by the Communist Party. One Communist, a miner, spoke of the union leadership with a contempt that had a wide resonance:

The local union leaders, there was none of them any good. They were all for themselves. We used to hunt these people. Every boozer they went into to, we should say, what about this, what about that? These miners' leaders could spend more money on beer and treating people than what they made in the pit ... Tinker [J.J. Tinker, Agent of the Lancashire and Cheshire Miners and Labour MP for Leigh, 1923–45] never did any good—he was a figurehead that's all.[139]

This resonance explains the popularity of a figure like Abe Lazarus, a Communist Party organizer, who had been active in the Firestone Rubber plant strike and who was sent to Oxford in 1934 to help organize the Pressed Steel strike. There he attained a status unusual for a Communist in a town like Oxford precisely because he played a role left unfilled by a hesitant union leadership.

---

[138] Forman, *Industrial Town*, 65, 92.   [139] Ibid. 53.

A willingness to play that role also explains the disproportionately large number of Communists who were elected as shop stewards in the motor-car industry.

The authority of shop stewards in many cases depended upon this feeling that the union leadership was untrustworthy. The stewards themselves believed—often rightly—that they were more authentic representatives of shop floor opinion than the union branch secretaries. Everywhere a much higher proportion of union membership voted for shop stewards than for branch secretaries, usually because they thought the stewards the more important.[140] Employers themselves knew this. In 1938, for example, during a dispute over the dismissal of one of the chief shop stewards at Pressed Steel, the representative of the Engineering and Allied Employers' Federation told the union:

You yourself took the matter in hand and told them [the stewards] . . . exactly where they got off, and instructed them that they must keep within the arrangement of the agreement.

I could repeat to you comments of [the sacked steward] . . . which refer quite clearly to his intentions in these works not only with regard to these works but with regard to the Executive of the Union, and the sum total of [his] attitude was that nobody was going to tell him what he could and could not do.

The union representative, in reply to him and to complaints from Pressed Steel about the union membership, said that he knew 'the Pressed Steel people' . . . 'I have met these people in the early days. I had a few damn good dressings down. I knew what it was to try to handle this crowd. I have had as many dressings down as the employers, and probably more.'[141]

Employers who did not recognize unions did not have to deal with stewards, and many must have thought the cost was worth it. But there was a cost: absenteeism, high labour turnover, casual strikes and walkouts—'we used to have plenty of walkouts. Quick walkouts were pinpricks, but they kept people on their toes'[142]—and the emergence of informally elected shop stewards even more truculent (though more easily dismissed) than those elected by agreement with a union. Employers often exaggerated losses due to strikes and underestimated losses due to 'non-union' factors. In fact, production, even in such a strike-prone industry as coal, was little affected by union action. How little can be seen by estimating notional coal 'losses' due to strikes as against other factors.[143] Losses due to strikes are trivial as compared with, for example,

---

[140] Goldthorpe *et al.*, *Affluent Worker: Industrial Attitudes*, i. 99–103. Goldthorpe and his colleagues almost certainly exaggerate the difference in attitude towards the unions between 'affluent' and other kinds of workers. All workers had a markedly instrumental view of their unions—although it was not always their only view.

[141] Whiting, *View from Cowley*, 79.

[142] This was said of Pilkington's (Forman, *Industrial Town*, 105).

[143] For 'coal losses', see Knowles, *Strikes*, 280.

losses due to absenteeism. The extent of such losses in a wholly unionized industry like coal, and during wartime, when the unions did everything they could to eliminate it, suggests how far some working practices were beyond the reach of the unions.

Were the unions successful in protecting the wages and jobs of their members? Wages were subject to influences over which unions had little or no control, and it is unlikely that the movement of wage levels was much affected by union activity: wage gains accrued by strikes were only a small part of total wage increases, nor does it seem that strikers were much more successful than non-strikers in procuring wage increases. Nor did strikes, for example those in the early twenties or the various miners' strikes, do much to prevent money wage cuts[144]—though Keynes's assumption that unions would resist money wage cuts even when real wages were rising more fiercely than they would demand money wage increases when real wages were falling seems to have been correct. To the extent that unions protected wages it was more indirect: by defending improvements in conditions at work and in hours worked. They were, that is, more successful in defending the wage per hour than the wage per working week. Most of the reductions in the working day, the case of the miners notwithstanding, were preserved throughout the interwar years.

Whether the unions protected their members' jobs and whether in doing so they put other people out of work or, in the long term, destroyed the jobs they were supposed to preserve, is hard to know. The evidence is difficult to quantify and usually anecdotal. The only serious examination of the question in the 1930s, that by John Hilton (professor of industrial relations at Cambridge) and his colleagues, concluded that 'the obstructions to industrial efficiency and improvement set up by trade unions are nothing like so serious as is commonly alleged, or taken for granted, in places where industrial small-talk is exchanged'.[145] Ferdynand Zweig, however, thought the problem was not so much the unions themselves as the attitude of their members: the unions 'do not create or foster it, they simply give it a formal expression'. Managers were 'the adaptive class'; the working classes were 'intent on keeping things as they are'.[146]

Certain industries had become notorious either for overmanning or for demarcation disputes between skilled and unskilled unions—or for both. Of these, the most notorious was heavy engineering and shipbuilding, shipbuilding especially. The skilled unions there obdurately resisted attempts by employers to create a specialist semi-skilled category of workman who could best utilize new welding techniques. They insisted their own members could

---

[144] Knowles, *Strikes*, 165–6.

[145] J. Hilton, J. J. Mallon, S. Mavor, B. S. Rowntree, A. Salter, and F. D. Stuart (eds.), *Are Trade Unions Obstructive?* (London, 1935), 334–5.

[146] Zweig, *British Worker*, 81.

'spread' skills to incorporate this and other advances while simultaneously excluding unskilled workers from tasks they could easily have performed.[147] The result in the shipyards was a very inflexible workforce which forced up labour costs. It also became very immobile; one reason why so many unemployed shipwrights or boilermakers stayed put in the 1930s. But shipbuilding was not alone; in much of engineering the craft unions 'captured' new technology, eliminating many of the gains it might otherwise have brought. In cotton textiles the unions objected to increasing the number of looms per worker; in building construction there were disputes between skilled and unskilled workers over the new technique of using wooden moulds for concrete; in the furnishing trades, unions were hostile to mass production techniques on grounds that de-skilling must produce shoddy material, etc. Some of the demarcation restrictions were so tight, John Hilton and his associates wrote, 'it was a wonder that employers have tolerated such terms.'[148]

More difficult to judge is how far this behaviour was that of the unions alone, and how far part of a wider industrial culture in which the more indefensible union practices were complicit with ineffective management. The priorities of the skilled unions in shipbuilding, for instance, in fact coincided with those of the owners: the preservation of skill in order to build ships on individual specification, as a bespoke tailor made suits. The same is true of textiles and the docks: a feeble management tolerated short-sighted trade unions. Furthermore, restrictions and stipulations seem to have been as severe (or as lax) in industries where unions were either weak or non-existent as where they were strong. If so, this suggests that they were the result of a work-culture rather than the institutional 'fault' of the unions as such.

7 | Out of work

Nearly all working-class men and women experienced some period of unemployment in the interwar years. For most, most of the time, it was comparatively short—the hiatus between one job and the next. There were, however, many for whom this was not true: those who were unemployed for comparatively long periods during the depression proper (1929–33), and those who remained unemployed despite the economic recovery of the 1930s. These last, as we have seen, had been largely employed in the 'staple' industries and were, as a result, geographically concentrated in the North-East, the North-West, the West of Scotland and South Wales. As the number of unemployed fell, the proportion of the total who had been out of work for a year or more rose. For most of them, the incidence of long-term unemployment was almost uniquely savage: it struck at communities where the culture of work and the workplace

---

[147] Lorenz and Wilkinson, 'The Shipbuilding Industry', 126.
[148] Hilton *et al.*, *Are Trade Unions Obstructive?*, 334–5.

was peculiarly intense and where anguish at exclusion from this culture was, therefore, equally intense. These were the 'unemployed', for whom unemployment became a way of life.

Interwar unemployment was a public phenomenon. Worklessness drove men (but not normally women) out of doors. As much as bookies or dockers, the unemployed had their stands. They gathered in public libraries, labour exchanges, outside football matches, idled on street corners and leant against lamp-posts.[149] The street-life of the unemployed suggested apathy and self-absorption. An 'outstanding feature' of the unemployed on the streets, one observer wrote, was the silence:

Men stood alone more often than in groups. The young men were more sociable; so were the older men who, I suppose, were pensioners. The middle-aged men were perfectly willing to talk, when I approached them, but more often than not, I found them alone.[150]

'Some men stand aimlessly on the market square or the street corners', another wrote, 'content apparently with a passive animal existence, or with the hour-long observation of passers-by, varied by an occasional whiff at a cigarette'.[151] Among juveniles 'conversation is desultory and usually concerned with local events or with racing and football news'.[152] That the unemployed seemed to outsiders 'listless and apathetic', men who led an existence without routine or purpose, is not surprising: that is how many felt, and that is undoubtedly how many must have looked to those who were not unemployed.

Much of the life of the workless was, however, invisible. Outsiders saw them *only* when they lolled at street corners or propped up lamp-posts. But unemployed life had its own structure and routines which were for many as rigid as anything they knew in work. 'Signing-on' at the labour exchange once or twice a week was obligatory; so, even in places where it was almost pointless, was the business of finding a job. As the American sociologist E. W. Bakke noted, 'hunting a job is the "job" of the unemployed worker'.[153] He calculated that the average unemployed man in South London spent 4–5 hours a day looking for one.[154] This seems to have been an inflexible routine: skilled men went as far afield as a cheap tram might take them; unskilled as far as they could walk. Skilled workers had further advantages. They had greater support from their unions, often had better contacts and were more adept at using pen and paper. Unskilled men usually followed the same rounds as they had when

---

[149] L. Beales and R. S. Lambert (eds.), *Memoirs of the Unemployed* (London, 1934), 191.

[150] E. W. Bakke, *The Unemployed Man* (London, 1933), 183–9.

[151] H. Jennings, *Brynmawr: A Study of a Depressed Area* (London, 1934), 138–41.

[152] G. Meara, *Juvenile Unemployment in Wales* (Cardiff, 1934), 99.

[153] Bakke, *Unemployed Man*, 129.

[154] A consequence was that those appointed by the Carnegie Trust to examine the nature of juvenile unemployment often had difficulty in locating their sample, which was out looking for a job. (Carnegie U.K. Trust, *Disinherited Youth: A Survey, 1936–1939* Edinburgh, 1943, 67.)

work was available; they would hang round factory gates (as they always had) on the off-chance a job would appear and that they would be recognized by the foreman or personnel officer, and move to the next gate if they were unlucky—as they usually were. Since the unemployed never thought there was a 'right way' to find jobs there was obviously a certain randomness in the way they went about it. And that, to outsiders, implied aimlessness. This rather desperate, trudging kind of job-search also made men very tired and tiredness was easily mistaken for apathy.[155] Furthermore, the reluctance of people to use the labour exchanges except for receipt of the dole—precisely because that was where they did receive the dole—eliminated them as places where a more rational and less exhausting form of job-search might have been learnt.[156]

The search for a job, though it imposed a routine, could not occupy the whole day. People had to give structure to those hours not spent job-seeking. Here success was mixed, since it partly depended on the resources the unemployed man had when in work. Skilled workers and (perhaps above all) those who had access to gardens and allotments were most successful. Skilled men could do small paid jobs—undeclared to the labour exchange—or jobs around the house. A 'skilled millwright' said that 'though there is nothing I can do to keep myself efficient', he liked to do 'odd jobs, like mending boots, chopping up boxes for firewood and repairing things'.[157] Workless miners might work 'on allotment or garden, tend fowls or pigs, or do carpentry in their backyard or kitchen, make sideboards out of orange boxes'.[158]

For those who could acquire them, allotments and gardens came closest to being a substitute for work. They had, of course, always been important in working-class life; their importance as sources of creative satisfaction and of food was simply heightened. Walter Brierley's unemployed miner 'Jack', for example, hated winter, and even spring, since he could

do nothing but walk around the garden; everything was in but nothing yet ready for coming out . . . He would be glad when the potatoes would be ready so that he could stay in the garden for whole mornings or whole afternoons . . . When he worked at the pit he could finish the garden in a month and only work in it in the evenings and on the occasional holidays . . . gardening had then never been a delight in itself . . . But for the last two springs he had been too slow, too careful.[159]

Among the unemployed, allotments were popular everywhere. In the North, Sir Francis Dyke Acland wrote, they 'use the hideous huts they put up almost as country cottages'.[160] The Durham miner, it was argued, 'had not a perpetual

[155] I have discussed this elsewhere: McKibbin, 'The "Social Psychology" of Unemployment', in *Ideologies of Class*, 236–7.

[156] See below, pp. 122–4.   [157] Beales and Lambert, *Memoirs of the Unemployed*, 104.

[158] Jennings, *Brynmawr*, 138–41.   [159] W. Brierley, *Means Test Man* (London, 1935), 11.

[160] Quoted in S. P. B. Mais, *S.O.S. Talks on the Unemployed* (London–NY, 1935), 87–8. See also T. Young, *Becontree and Dagenham* (London, 1934), 162.

sense of grievance, but ... rather a determination to make the best of things; to make his allotment or his poultry holding a life for himself'. In the depressed areas they 'are to a large extent providing a fairly full "alternative life" for younger men'.[161] Their role was well understood by voluntary associations, particularly by the Quakers, whose Allotments for the Unemployed scheme provided seeds, fertilizers, and tools on a large scale.

Allotments and gardens, or intensifications of hobby interests amongst those who had them, certainly provided a partial alternative to ordinary work, but are unlikely to have been an adequate substitute, particularly for those who had had a long history of continuous skilled or semi-skilled work. One unemployed man, who had a wide range of hobby interests, wrote that 'sports and pastimes banish depression whilst they are taking place but when I get to bed at night, I lay and imagine every silly possible thing that may happen'.[162] The problem with such alternatives was that they were largely individual activities. They rarely brought men into contact with each other; there were few of those long-term work-based relationships which were such a conspicuous part of the work culture of those areas where unemployment was highest.[163] Nevertheless, they were better than nothing, as the unemployed admitted.

They were, however, not available to all the unemployed. Many men, especially younger ones living in larger towns or cities, once they had gone through the routine of job-finding or signing-on, found the day empty. It was they who confessed to disorientation and a sense of defeat. One young casual labourer said that he and his friends usually 'play draughts or dominoes. We are just about able to play games like those, which don't require much thought. You stop and talk in the middle, and in any case the games never last very long. Card games want too much patience and attention.'[164] Even when routines of a sort had been established people were conscious of a slippery slope. 'I was one of a gang', a young unemployed man from Lancashire said:

We used to stay in bed late in the mornings so as not to need breakfast. I used to have a cup of tea, and then we would all go down to the library and read the papers. Then we went home for a bit of lunch, and then we met again at the billiard hall where you could watch the play for nothing. Then back for tea and to watch billiards again. In the evening we used to go to the pictures. That was how we spent the dole money. In the end I thought I'd go mad if I went on like that.[165]

---

[161] Pilgrim Trust, *Men without Work* (Cambridge, 1938), 75, 216.

[162] Beales and Lambert, *Memoirs of the Unemployed*, 201.

[163] P. Kelvin, 'Work as a Source of Identity: the Implications of Unemployment', *British Journal of Guidance and Counselling*, 9, 1 (Jan. 1981), 8.

[164] Beales and Lambert, *Memoirs of the Unemployed*, 227.

[165] Pilgrim Trust, *Men without Work*, 149. See also K. Nicholas, *The Social Effects of Unemployment on Teesside, 1919–1939* (Manchester, 1986), 103.

These were the young men who were the public face of unemployment, who loafed in the streets and apparently thronged the public libraries and the cinema. The public libraries were certainly attractive to the unemployed, for whom they provided a number of services, apart from being both warm and free. The scene in a big Liverpool public library (where it was 'usual to find the reading-rooms full all day of unemployed men') was typical of much of urban England: 'Some [unemployed] come to look for vacancies in the newspapers; others read trade and technical magazines. Three of those reading rooms have a special arrangement by which urgent vacancies for workers are reported to them from the Employment Exchange and are posted up'.[166] Where interfering librarians had not removed them, the newspapers also had the racing results—important for the unemployed as for most working-class men. For many the libraries were simply places of comfort for passing the time, as for the engineer who went to 'warm sheltered places like the library, where I like to read revolutionary novels'. For others it was a place where a deficient education could be repaired.

The cinema played a similar, though easily exaggerated role. In the public mind the unemployed were always associated with the cinema—as with street corners. The most hostile stereotype had the unemployed repairing to the cinema immediately after collecting their dole. The cinema, like the library, was warm, though not free. But it was even better than the library for escapist time-passing. 'It was the most important feature of the spare time activity of the employed and unemployed alike.'[167] At nights 'there were the pictures, and the long queues outside the "Picture Palace" probably account for more of the "pocket-money" of the unemployed than do the public-houses.'[168] Yet it seems improbable that the unemployed went to the pictures any more often than when in work; and more likely went less.[169] Men were doubtless prepared to sacrifice much before they sacrificed the cinema, but spending on it, like all other discretionary spending, could not, however hard men tried, be maintained on the dole. The unemployed, in fact, drank less, smoked less, bet less, went to football matches and the cinema less. Poverty marginalized them. To the unemployed, it always seemed they were on the edge of things; always on the outside looking in; everything was second-hand, even football results. It was this, as much as unemployment itself, which men found so distressing.

We know much less about how individual women reacted to unemployment, partly because of the widely held assumption that unemployment for women was 'less serious' than for men. How women coped with unemployment seems to have depended on their status within the family and the cultural conventions of the communities in which they lived. If they were married, domestic duties expanded to fill the day; if unmarried and living at

---

[166] Caradog Jones, *Merseyside*, ii. 300.   [167] Bakke, *Unemployed Man*, 178.
[168] Jennings, *Brynmawr*, 138–41.   [169] Pilgrim Trust, *Men without Work*, 275–6.

home much the same happened. If an unemployed husband was prepared to help with home duties—though most were not—a married woman got at least something from her husband's misfortune.[170] Single unemployed women had fewer resources to support them than unemployed men: they were usually unskilled and un-unionized, and few had allotments to dig, hobbies to practise, or 'artistic pursuits' to follow.[171] They were, however, thought to be more gregarious than men: the remarkable success of the 'keep fit' movement had no male equivalent. But for a single, not very sociable unemployed woman living in lodgings unemployment could have been a calvary.

Long-term unemployment put the working-class family under severe pressure. Idleness and disappointment often made husbands bad-tempered and sometimes violent. Many working-class children had fearful memories of their unemployed fathers and this partly accounts for the hostility or contempt with which some later remembered them. The ill-effects of unemployment were, however, usually indirect, caused by the poverty which almost invariably accompanied it (something contemporaries frequently overlooked).[172] Only a small proportion of working-class men were better off unemployed than in work, and even they were little above the poverty line. There were in consequence many disputes between husbands and wives about money, particularly about money spent by husbands on drinking and betting. Husbands by their own lights were rarely profligate; rather they were slow (or declined) to modify their behaviour in changed circumstances. But a one-shilling bet which could be accommodated within a weekly wage could not so easily be accommodated within the dole.[173] It was the obdurate refusal of some husbands to recognize this which so embittered wives, since it was they who then had to make the sacrifices. The relentless attacks which unemployment made on a family's living standards and then, via poverty, on its unity and morale, was a common theme of contemporary literature. The travails of the Hardcastle family, the subject of the most celebrated of the unemployment novels, Walter Greenwood's *Love on the Dole* (1933, dramatized 1934, filmed 1941) were directly a result of their poverty. Nor was it an accident that Greenwood has the daughter, Sally, end up in the clutches of the local bookie. Yet, for all the bitterness, most families seemed somehow to remain intact, and for the unemployed they were a support and solace.[174] Single men, even those who

---

[170] Orwell thought that working-class women acquiesced in this. 'I believe that they, as well as the men, feel that a man would lose his manhood if, merely because he was out of work, he developed into a "Mary Anne".' (G. Orwell, *The Road to Wigan Pier* (Penguin ed., Harmondsworth, 1962), 73.)

[171] Caradog Jones, *Merseyside*, ii. 276.

[172] P. Kelvin and J. Jarrett, *Unemployment* (Cambridge, 1985), 127–8.

[173] For the unemployed and betting, see McKibbin, *Ideologies of Class*, 244. I now think I there underestimated the effect of betting on the finances of an unemployed household.

[174] See Brierley, *Means Test Man*. In this instance consolation came from the son and not from the wife.

thought it wrong to love or marry on the dole, admitted they missed such consolation. So, almost certainly, did single women.

Increasingly, apart from immediate family and acquaintances, the only contact the unemployed had with a wider society was, via the labour exchanges, with the state—not usually a harmonious encounter. This was partly due to the exchanges' grim and shabby appearance: 'We are not at all proud of the premises we are in', the ministry of labour confessed; '. . . some are certainly not a credit to us.'[175] Like prisons, they seemed designed to dehumanize. Though men and women usually adjusted to being on the dole, to the horrors of the exchanges they hardly ever adjusted:

Well, it's the way they treat you, somehow. It's the way the chairs are arranged. You go in and you sit down on a chair and you can't move it. And when you come up to the counter, if you want to speak to the guy you've got to sit forward on the edge of your chair, and he's behind a little window, and he says 'Speak Up'...I don't mind them messing me about, but the trouble is there are some genu-ine [sic] claimants up there and they get messed around as well.[176]

The clerks at the exchanges were in a difficult position, under constant pressure to detect abuse. Before the abolition of the 'genuinely seeking work clause' in 1930 (and often after) claimants were subject to 'a futile and sometimes brutal ritual' about job-searches in which few believed.[177] After 1931 new discriminations, including the hated means test were introduced. The result was that, however helpful or willing the overworked clerks, they were all thought servants of 'them'. Unemployed men tended to regard the exchanges as hostile from the outset, even if for the great majority most of the time the collection of benefit was automatic:

If he has been out of work for some time, each Friday he will have a short period of sickening anxiety lest the clerk should single him out and tell him he is to be sent to the 'Court of Referees'; then will follow a few days consequent dread lest his benefit should be stopped and he be cast on the Poor Law, have to do 'task work' for his maintenance, and take home less to his family in return for it.[178]

The clerks' reputation for insolence may not have been well founded, but 'pleasantness soon wears off when forty to fifty men step up to [the desk] every fifteen minutes'. A permanently interrogative and vaguely accusing air accounted for their unpopularity:

And the bloody blokes wouldn't have their jobs if it wasn't for us men out of a job either. That's what gets me about them holding their noses up.

[175] Report of the Unemployment Insurance Committee [Blanesburgh], ii (1927), *Minutes of Evidence*, Q.270.
[176] Quoted in D. Marsden, *Workless* (London, 1982), 88.
[177] Deacon, *In Search of the Scrounger*, 61.   [178] Jennings, *Brynmawr*, 138.

They treat you like a lump of dirt they do. I see a navvy reach across the counter and shake one of them by the collar the other day. The rest of us felt like cheering.[179]

Dislike of the interviewing officers (who investigated claims of dubious eligibility) and the courts of referees was perhaps more justified. The interviewing officers really were on the hunt for scroungers, since success on the job was measured by disallowed claims. Furthermore, those unemployed who were earning a bit on the quiet could be summoned before an officer if this were discovered or if, as sometimes happened, they were denounced anonymously.[180] Thus when an unemployed man was summoned before an interviewing officer he knew what to expect.[181]

The unemployed man was most likely to come before a court of referees when he went on to so-called 'transitional benefit'; when he had exhausted the benefit to which he was entitled by his insurance contributions. The court was supposed to ensure that the claimant was actually seeking work. Neither court nor claimant knew what was meant by that: whether, for example, a skilled worker *should* accept unskilled work. The courts were also overburdened, ill-informed about the claimant, and composed of local worthies (often of military provenance) whose acquaintance with the life of the unemployed was at best second-hand. The unemployed were thus as hostile to the courts as to the interviewing officers.

To the means test officers, as representatives of a system that intruded humiliatingly into working-class privacy, hostility was altogether more fierce. Given that their function entailed discovering who was actually in work, if necessary by unannounced visits, they could hardly have expected otherwise, however polite and helpful they may have been individually. The diabolical character of the means test, like that of the 'means test man' and the insolence of the clerks, was almost certainly exaggerated in working-class memory; but the means test undeniably had the potential to destroy working-class family life, in that it encouraged sons and daughters who had jobs to leave home (the amount of benefit being dependent on total family income). Yet there is little evidence of widespread family disintegration as a consequence of the means test. This may have been because the system was liberally administered, or because working-class families were successful in evading it. Both, indeed, are likely. The test's place in working-class memory, whether exaggerated or not,

---

[179] Bakke, *Unemployed Man*, 79, 80.

[180] The extent to which the unemployed accepted paid work which was undeclared to the exchanges is unclear. For some, the fear of denunciation may have been such that people would not even do small jobs acceptable to the exchanges. Others, however, thought the chances of denunciation were small. The Carnegie Trust suggested that, in certain areas at least, 'side-lines' were so common 'that betrayal by the neighbours to the Unemployment Assistance officer would have involved every other household. It seemed that the more widespread the subterfuges, the more they were accepted as a normal means of augmenting unemployment allowances'. (*Disinherited Youth*, 70–1.)

[181] Bakke, *Unemployed Man*, 97.

is none the less unsurprising: it symbolized a system of bureaucratic interference by a clerical class which was (rightly or wrongly) always disliked by working-class men and women wherever they found it—in the armed forces, the private sector, or government offices.

Everyone, the unemployed included, thought the comparatively closed social existence of the unemployed unsatisfactory, but there was little agreement as to how it could be reopened. The response of the government was utterly inadequate. Its training programmes for adults were almost non-existent and never seriously considered. Those for unemployed juveniles were equally exiguous and informed more by a notion that juveniles were potential delinquents rather than potential workers.[182] In these circumstances the government was happy to leave the problem to voluntary associations. Throughout the twenties and early thirties about 400 clubs for the unemployed were founded by charitable and religious associations. The 'club movement' (as it was called) was given a countrywide basis when in 1932 the National Council of Social Service became, with some government financial assistance, the coordinating authority. The council, through its affiliates, encouraged the practice of 'adoption': Surrey adopted Jarrow, Bath Redruth, the BBC staff a club in Gateshead, etc.[183] By the end of 1937 there were about 1,550 clubs or centres with a total membership of 150,000 at any one time.[184]

The National Council occupied a space left by a passive government. Its conception of citizenship and its attempt to depoliticize unemployment were very influential in the 1930s, and the study of unemployment it commissioned, *Men without Work* (1938), the most widely read.[185] But the clubs had at best a limited success.[186] They did something to relieve 'the drabness of the lives of the unemployed', but they never earned their affection or even the membership of more than a small minority. This was partly an ideological failure. The council's idea of citizenship was usually not that of the unemployed, nor were they attracted by depoliticized solutions, as Hilda Jennings, whose study of Brynmawr was written very much from the council's perspective, admitted:

For the mass of the unemployed local politics in South Wales only concentrates their thoughts more firmly on the material problems of their existence. 'Vote Labour, and put

---

[182] Marian Bartlett, 'Education for Industry: Attitudes and Policies Affecting the Provision of Technical Education in Britain, 1916–1929', unpublished Oxford D.Phil. thesis (1995), 340.

[183] C. L. Mowat, *Britain between the Wars* (London, 1956), 488–9.

[184] Burns, *British Unemployment Programs*, 276.

[185] For the National Council see A. Olechnowicz, 'The Economic and Social Development of Inter-War Out-County Municipal Housing Estates, with Special Reference to the London County Council's Becontree and Dagenham Estates', Oxford D.Phil. thesis (1991), 184–229; A. D. Lindsay, 'Unemployment: the "Meanwhile" Problem', *Contemporary Review* (June 1933), 687–95; see also Archbishop Temple's intro. to *Men without Work*, ix–xii.

[186] For the clubs at work, see *Men without Work*, 272–347; J. B. Priestley, *English Journey* (London, 1934), 282–4, 325–6.

an end to poverty, misery, and Courts of Referees', is the popular slogan, not 'Stand together and assert the value of man and his right and duty to express himself by work.'[187]

But the failure was also social. The council conceded that the 'public opinion' of the unemployed was not necessarily favourable to the clubs,[188] while the unemployed, even when they realized that those who ran the clubs were well-intended, regarded them as a better-natured variant of those who staffed the labour exchanges: that is, people who patronized the working classes and offered them everything except work—the one thing they really wanted.

   When war broke out in 1939 the long-term unemployed, other than those who had effectively retired from the labour market through age, were re-absorbed into work and the ordinary routines of social life with surprising ease. This was so because the unemployed, for all the bitterness, never thought of themselves as a class distinct from the working class. Nor is there much evidence to support the then fashionable social-psychological theories which suggested that the unemployed progressed in stages to a state of personal and social disintegration. What is remarkable, on the contrary, is how little this happened.[189] Men and women preserved important continuities with their working lives and this was made possible in part—though they would have denied it—by the dole. The most important determinant, therefore, of the life of the unemployed was not unemployment itself but the kind of life they had led before. How much the unemployed read, went to the pictures, were politically active, or joined clubs largely depended on the extent that they did those things when in work. The Pilgrim Trust were struck by this. A place like Rhondda (a 'hotbed of associations') gave much associational support to the unemployed because it always had an intense collective life. Liverpool was exactly the reverse: 'the real obstacle in the way of building up a good club in a large city is not the competition of commercialized amusements but the lack of any social foundations on which to begin.'[190]

Although the manual working class had declined a little proportionately, in 1951 it still constituted nearly three-quarters of the whole population: as it had been in 1918, England was emphatically a working-class country. But the composition of that working class had changed; if not as significantly as the middle class, significantly enough. Many fewer men worked in the staple industries in the 1950s than in 1918; many more in the newer metal trades, in motorized transport, in building and engineering. There were fewer skilled

---

[187] Jennings, *Brynmawr*, 141. For examples of hostility to the clubs, see E. Wilkinson, *The Town that was Murdered*, 233–4; A. Hutt, *The Condition of the Working Class in Britain* (London, 1933), 45–6.
[188] Pilgrim Trust, *Men without Work*, 161.   [189] McKibbin, *Ideologies of Class*, 253–8.
[190] Pilgrim Trust, *Men without Work*, 275–6.

workers; more semi-skilled and unskilled. Migration of labour in the interwar years meant that a considerably larger part of the industrial working class lived and worked in the Midlands and the South-East and a correspondingly smaller part in the North. The working class had also done comparatively well out of the Second World War. It had gained in wealth, in social esteem and political power; it had gained by a mild redistribution of income (which operated within the working class as well) and by the abolition of large-scale unemployment. In terms of standard of living, the second was probably the more important.

The effects of such changes were paradoxical. Contemporaries were inclined to think that the 'traditional' working class reached its apogee in the 1930s and 1940s. In fact, the interwar years had forced major changes on the working class and, through depression and unemployment, greatly weakened its 'traditional' element. Furthermore, the working class of the 1940s in its prosperity and political influence had no historic precedent, while that 'traditional' element was also considerably smaller. The 'traditional' working class of the 1940s was traditional only in the sense that economic circumstances permitted it to behave for the first time in the way people—not least working men and women—assumed the 'traditional' working class should behave.

Interwar unemployment deeply marked the working class. It was a social experience shared by no other class which increasingly isolated one group, the long-term unemployed, within the working class itself. It pauperized many working-class communities and came close to destroying the integrity of the working culture of the North of England as a whole. Despite what contemporaries feared, however, the unemployed taken together were not socially marginalized because they never ceased to think of themselves as primarily working class: they were not the 'unemployed' but working men and women out of work. How they coped with unemployment, therefore, was largely determined by the working culture in which they were raised; not by the consequences of unemployment itself.

Unemployment was, some thought, a result of the immobility of the unemployed. But there is no reason to think that the working class was particularly immobile. Throughout the interwar years large numbers did migrate and though many returned because of loneliness or nostalgia, they usually returned because they could not find a job. In any case, wholescale departure would have utterly impoverished many working-class communities in the North, both culturally and economically, while imposing colossal social costs on the unwilling host communities. Many Northern communities survived precisely because some young men either stayed or returned.

There is no serious historical evidence that the dole acted as a major impediment to labour mobility. The labour market, however, did remain surprisingly informal and local. Throughout this period, except during the war years, the majority of men and women found their jobs not through the labour exchanges but through family, friends, or the grapevine. On average only about one-fifth of jobs were found via a labour exchange. To many, and not only those who had been unemployed long-term, the labour exchange was irredeemably tainted by its association with the dole and those who administered it. The decision to house within one institution job-search and dole payment was thus a fundamental error of social policy.

The culture of the English working man was profoundly work-centred. For many, probably most, work was life. Even if men disliked work itself, though few confessed to that, the workplace and its social relationships were irreplaceable, which is why unemployment was such a trial. But the politics produced by this working culture was shot through with ambiguities. On the one hand attitudes to employers were often dominated by a powerful sense of historic grievance, a conviction that the employer stood for 'them', the whole universe which conspired against working men, a grievance which, for example, underpinned the Labour Party in much of the country and whose workplace expression was the trade union. On the other, it was a very defensive culture which, rather than being always aggressive, tended to withdraw, and demanded only to be left alone. Attitudes to the state and society were shaped by such ambiguities; and no more so than the attitudes of the unemployed or ex-unemployed. They expected the state to find them work and to pay them if it could not; but they bitterly resented its agents—who were analogous to the clerical servitors of management with whom they dealt when they did find work. All were 'them'. As sometimes was the leadership of the unions. Men could be deeply cynical about the motives and actions of trade union leaders, which is why in the larger industries the shop steward was thought a better representative of grievances than permanent trade union officials. But, again, attitudes were complicated. Men combined a purely instrumental attitude to unions with a sense that union membership was an act of working-class solidarity. We should not see them as necessarily holding one view exclusively.

But it is easy to overrate the importance of the unions. For much of the period the majority of working men did not belong to them, and the majority of working women never did. Nor did the unions provoke strikes. The tendency was for the number of strikes to decline. Nor were unions particularly successful at defending the wages and conditions of their members. More significantly, industrial disputes were increasingly about work practices: a mark of the significance men attached to work and to what control of the process of work they still had.

Many of these conclusions, however, do not hold for working-class women. They did less well from the war; worked for lower wages in unskilled jobs men were reluctant to take; were largely un-unionized; and invested much less of their lives in the workplaces and its relationships. There were three, largely self-fulfilling reasons for this: the assumption that women were more docile and more suited to unskilled assembly line jobs; the fact that they were mostly excluded from male-dominated trade unions on the ground that they under-cut men in the labour market; and, most important, the belief that women's destiny was marriage and motherhood, not work. Since most women accepted these, or were obliged to accept them, the result was that their working culture was mostly different from men's. Yet the difference was not inevitable: when women continued to work after marriage, or because they did not marry, work relationships were as important for them as for men. When their work was of the same status as men's—as it often was during the war or in some of the newer industries—they behaved in the same way as men, strikes and all.

v   The Working Class (II)

THE focus of this chapter is working-class domesticity and sociability. It considers relationships within the family, the extent to which they were characterized by 'role-segregation'—the wife's purely domestic, the husband's purely external—and the consequences of segregated roles. It examines working-class 'matrilocality', the relations between mother and daughter, the status of the husband in the home and how the family income was managed. The chapter also assesses working-class definitions of friendliness, the nature of neighbourliness, and the sources of conflict within working-class communities.

1 | Families

An ever-increasing number of working-class men and women married, and did so significantly younger than the rest of the population. When they married, what did they want of each other? Although they unhesitatingly believed in romantic marriages, they were wise enough not to ground marriage upon romance. Wives wanted men who were 'good providers', 'steady' in their work, and quiet and considerate at home. Men wanted wives who were good home-makers and not extravagant, who did not nag or gossip, and who fell in with their husbands' habits. The happiest wives were those whose husbands earned a few shillings above the average, but who were otherwise like all other husbands in the neighbourhood; the happiest husbands were those whose wives accepted that a man must have his freedom and who recognized that marriage was a matter of 'give and take'. Both agreed on the indispensability of children, although they often did not agree on an optimum number.[1] On the basis of these apparently matter-of-fact and homely aspirations many marriages, despite unpromising beginnings, were remarkably stable.[2]

But these aspirations concealed important details which varied between men and women, family and family, region and region. Men and women often

[1] J. M. Mogey, *Family and Neighbourhood: Two Studies of Oxford* (London, 1956), 64–5; Zweig, *Women's Life and Labour*, 53.

[2] Hoggart, *Uses of Literacy*, 43, 58; L. A. Shaw, 'Impressions of Family Life in a London Suburb', *Sociological Review* (1954), 186; G. Gorer, *Exploring English Character* (London, 1955), 125–9.

judged the success of a marriage by different criteria. Men, for example, frequently judged it in terms of possession and sexual power, emphasizing the importance of their wives' chastity and docility. When asked, they would repeatedly say: 'she's true', 'she's a good girl, I can trust her', 'I know I can trust her absolutely', 'she came to me a virgin'. This emphasis upon their sexual rights was a recurrent theme, and during the Second World War, obsessive. The fact that married life was necessarily ruptured during the war, together with the publicity given by the popular press to wifely infidelity, heightened this preoccupation while making doubt about the paternity of children 'an unendurable burden'.[3] In contrast, however, to masculine sexual angst, women sought the domestic virtues: a husband 'who helps in the house', 'who loves the kids', who was not drunk or violent. To the extent that women claimed sexual rights they were usually negative ones: the right to a 'thoughtful' husband, one who respected her by not over-exercising his claims to sexual possession.

Some argued that marital expectations and behaviour differed between various levels of the working class.[4] But a more important determinant of marital attitudes was the geography of working-class households. A comparison of a 'traditional' working-class area of Oxford, St Ebbe's, and a 'non-traditional' council estate, Barton, provides an example of this.[5] Between the two there was of course much in common. All wives wanted considerate husbands who earned steady wages, were punctual, did not drink too much and did not burden their families with their own worries. But they had some obvious differences. St Ebbe's preferences suggest households where husbands and wives had strongly segregated roles and where wives were happiest with husbands who, when at home, were docile and unintrusive. In Barton, however, the household was clearly thought by the wife to be more of a co-operative; overall, marital roles were much more loosely defined. Thus the physical translation of working-class families from an environment in which the majority lived throughout this period to housing which approximated the newer middle-class estates was to modify significantly relations between husband and wife, as it did working-class social relationships more generally.

Until this translation occurred, it is likely that most working-class husbands and wives, particularly in the North but also in all the large conurbations, lived very segregated lives indeed. Women knew little or nothing about their husbands' work. Miners' wives, for instance, were aware that their husbands were miners, but were usually ignorant of what they actually did at or down the mine. Nor were they much interested in finding out.[6] This was not confined to

[3] E. Slater and M. Woodside, *Patterns of Marriage: A Study of Marriage Relationships in the Urban Working Classes* (London, 1951), 146.
[4] Gorer, *Exploring English Character*, 130.   [5] Mogey, *Family and Neighbourhood*, 62–3.
[6] Dennis *et al.*, *Coal is our Life*, 177–84.

miners: an Oxford woman when asked what her husband did, replied—'He makes all kinds of steel . . . (long pause for the right word) things.'[7] To wives of Liverpool merchant sailors, their husbands were at work when they were away, and not at work when they were at home. In this case, the husband's work was apprehended only through his absence.[8]

It was not simply wifely inertia which accounted for this. Husbands were themselves very reluctant to talk about work at home. Indeed, as we have seen, one of the criteria of a good husband was that he did not bring home the problems of his working life, and men were evasive or laconic when questioned about it by outsiders. Husbands—even those who spent least time at home— were also anxious to draw a sharp distinction between home and work. It was noticed how quickly when men came home they dispensed with the impedimenta of work—boots, collar, braces, sometimes tie—and how unwilling they were to put them on again even for visitors.[9]

The idea of 'home' as a place of refuge was protected not only by divorcing 'home' from work, but by other codes which hedged it from the public sphere. One was to adopt a casual attitude to time. At work most men were bound by increasingly tight routines; at home, however, routines could be very lax. In Oxford, most houses visited by one team of observers had alarm clocks which were hardly ever set at the correct time or else clocks which had long since stopped. 'In the light of this', they noted, 'the absence of calendars in the houses is more significant than it would otherwise have been.'[10]

A second was the ban (or attempted ban) on swearing within the home. Swearing, often aggressive and obscene, was an important part of working life, a vehicle for social relationships within a factory or workshop. It was characteristically a phenomenon of the masculine, public world, the antithesis of home. Although women often swore, it was thought unwomanly, even by those who did it, and permissible really only in a crisis. Both men and women attempted to prohibit swearing, their own and their children's. Unless drunk, men tried not to swear in front of their families and especially not at home. There, men who were utterly foul-mouthed in the workplace would speak with the voice of lambs, according to a convention learnt as soon as they began work.[11] But it was a difficult convention to operate in practice, and there were

---

[7] Mogey, *Family and Neighbourhood*, 130. This almost complete divorce of a wife from her husband's work had long been recognized. At the turn of the century Lady Bell wrote of the wives of Middlesbrough iron and steel labourers 'that they were quite detached in interest [from their husband's job]'. Many of them did not know when asked 'what the man's "job" is at the works; some know what the actual name of the calling is but do not know what it implies.' (Florence, Lady Bell, *At the Works* (London, 1911), 324–5.)

[8] M. Kerr, *The People of Ship Street* (London, 1958), *passim*. J. Klein, *Samples from English Cultures* (2 vols., London, 1965), i. 171–2.

[9] Mogey, *Family and Neighbourhood*, 60–1.   [10] Ibid. 129–30.

[11] Dennis *et al.*, *Coal is our Life*, 214–15.

certain places, like workingmen's clubs, where it was unclear whether it should or should not operate. Swearing in the club thus tended to be half-hearted and rather frowned upon. And since much swearing was sexual, this added to the tensions which surrounded it.[12]

But men observed this demarcation as much to protect the sphere of work as to protect home. For many men home was undoubtedly a 'refuge', but for others merely a station on the way. In the North particularly, where a 'traditional' heavy industry bred a 'traditional' working class, the very jealous peer groups of both married and unmarried men further segregated them from their families while relegating women to a well-defined domesticity.[13]

This tendency to exclude home from the public sphere was reinforced by another convention that politics or religion should not be discussed there. Men talked about politics to each other—often at length—and women amongst themselves sometimes;[14] but men and women together, hardly ever. Phrases like 'We're not very interested in politics though we do vote' were common, while wives thought it prudent to avoid the subject ('Well, as a matter of fact I don't discuss things like politics or religion with him; we don't agree and I think it's best not to talk about those things you disagree on, don't you? And men know best about those things, I expect, don't you?').[15] The ejection of the public and the general from domestic life greatly narrowed domesticity and compelled wives on marriage to abandon social activities, like dancing, which had once been important to them.

Such role-segregation had several consequences. It meant that women's emotional energies were almost entirely expended on home and family. The domestic sphere was hers and she no more discussed it with her husband—unless he complained—than he discussed his work with her. The domestic included the children; thus—unlike her sister in a middle-class family—she was decisive in the children's education; or, at least, she was the one who was most ambitious for them. The sociologists Brian Jackson and Dennis Marsden left a telling description of the differences in comportment and manner between husbands and wives who were interviewed at home about their children's education:

---

[12] Objecting to children swearing was the general rule. One mother told Madeline Kerr that her two sons ' "call me b——. You know, not bugger but the other one." I suggested "bastard" and she said, "Yes, that one. I don't mind being called a bugger, but I do object to being called a bastard because I am not one" ' (Kerr, *Ship Street*, 62). Maternal proscriptions were, of course, often ineffective.

[13] See below, pp. 183–5.

[14] It is clear from Mrs Last's diaries that working-class women would on occasion talk politics with each other. See the entry for 26 July 1945: 'At the WVS Centre, we kept wondering how the Election results were going. We got a real shock when we heard our Conservative member had been beaten by *12,000* . . . Then, as more women came into sew, it was like a "jam session", everyone talked at once . . .' (*Nella Last's War*, 297). Not all women at the WVS were working-class, but many were.

[15] Mogey, *Family and Neighbourhood*, 148–9, 61.

Many of the men sat through the interview in pullover and a blue-striped flannel shirt held at the top with a gold stud. Working boots and shoes were replaced by slippers, and collar and tie lay on one side as they took their ease. The wives always seemed much larger . . . Their hair was frequently frizzy from home perms . . . A flowery dress with a flowery pinafore was common. Again, the more prosperous were distinguished by the wife's superior hair-do, and interest in face powder.

Similarly in speech the woman took more care over their accent and grammar. Few of the men troubled at all and 'tha' and 'thee' might replace 'you' as the interview relaxed and suspicion disappeared.[16]

This was the wife's domain, as husbands often recognized by their awkward-ness and initially inarticulate response to outsiders. But it was also his refuge: he wore his slippers and left off his collar and tie. He was 'at ease'.

Wives, when asked to recollect the upbringing of their children, could remember in great detail, not simply how they raised their children, but par-ticular events, like picnics or holidays, in their children's early lives. In con-trast, those comparatively few women who continued working after marriage in jobs which differed little from their husbands (like weavers) were often com-ically vague about their children's upbringing. The less the woman's role was segregated from her husband's, the less she identified herself with home and family.[17]

Role-segregation, however much women dominated the household, tied them to their husbands' lives. A man might be ineffective or withdrawn at home, but he did expect the household to meet his needs, and that was his wife's responsibility. Her failure to do so could lead to explosions, the 'rows' that punctuated working-class life. The hurling of food 'in t' fire', if it were, in the husband's view, inadequately prepared or not ready for him, was a well-known vignette. 'Rows' were important in this life. Although most people tried to keep them within the family, they were inevitably heard by a wide circle of the neighbours. Rows rarely led to anything more serious, although in an en-vironment where violence, both physical and rhetorical, was almost endemic, they could do so.[18] More often their function was 'to clear the air' in conditions where anger was easily created but not easily dispersed. Most husbands and wives were, in fact, reluctant to criticize each other in public; men preferred not to talk about their families at all, while women, all too readily, felt obliged to be loyal to their husbands—however they behaved:

Q. Would your husband help out with the housework?
A. No he wouldn't—he wasn't that way gifted, no he always wanted to be out. It does make life a bit hard work like.

---

[16] Jackson and Marsden, *Education and the Working Class*, 50.

[17] There are illuminating examples of this in D. Gittins, *Fair Sex: Family Size and Structure 1900–1939* (London, 1983).

[18] Kerr, *Ship Street*, 62–3; M. Paneth, *Branch Street* (London, 1944), *passim*.

Q. Did you go out much with him after you were married?

A. No, no, no—well, I—no—I went to whist. He used to like to go for a drink . . . through t'week I didn't go out like on me own, no, well, you can always find sommat to do, can't you.[19]

It is possible that when children had grown up, or when women returned to some kind of work, or, if as happened in the Second World War, voluntary war work took a woman 'out of herself', a wife learnt to resist her husband's routines and his 'moods'. But such transformations were probably rare. More usual was the atmosphere of 'undeclared warfare' when a husband isolated himself completely from his family, as the following exchange suggests:

Q. Did he ever help out with the housework . . .?

A. No.

Q. The children?

A. No. Hopeless.

Q. What about when you were ill?

A. Just had to get on with it.

Q. Did you ever go out together much?

A. No. Never.

Q. Did he go out?

A. Oh yes, drink, drink, drink.

Q. Did you ever go out on your own?

A. No. I was at home . . . On one occasion he brought a girl home. He did. Yeah . . .

Q. Why did you stick it out?

A. Left him twice . . .

Q. You left the kids here?

A. Yes—there'd be no fun in taking the kids with me, that'd be what he wanted.[20]

This was doubtless an extreme case, but the inability of husband and wife to talk about matters that affected both of them, except implicitly, meant that problems were not raised or left to the husband 'on trust'. Of these, the most common was family size: many things were kept silent between husband and wife, but sexuality was the most silent. Husbands and wives did not have the language to articulate it or, if they had, the kinds of relationships which would have allowed them to articulate it. Thus the exceptionally high fertility of the miners was almost certainly in part a result of the extreme role-segregation of their marriages and the consequent inability of miners and their wives to take decisions jointly.[21]

The tendency to a relatively strict demarcation of roles, however much it might have subordinated the wife in a wider sense, gave her none the less great authority within the family. Above all, since the domestic sphere was hers, she, much more than her husband, decided where the family should live, and that

---

[19] Gittins, *Fair Sex*, 133.   [20] Ibid. 140–1.   [21] See below, pp. 304–8.

frequently meant with or close to her own mother. The centrality of the mother, of 'Mum', to the working-class family had long been known anecdotally or as a theme in working-class autobiography or fiction—a fixed point in working-class life that scarcely needed demonstrating. The sociologist Brian Jackson took it 'as read' that kinship patterns were determined by where mothers and daughters lived rather than by the wishes of husbands or sons-in-law. Matrilocality was 'basic to all discussions of community'.[22]

The mother–daughter (or grandmother–mother–daughter) relationship was almost certainly the axis of the working-class family throughout much of England, even if there were exceptions. Where mobility was high or where communities were newly established, matrilocality was inevitably weak. Thus in Oxford, a characteristic interwar 'boom' town, where, like Bedford, Luton, Banbury, or Slough, there was a large migrant population, daughters frequently could not live near their mothers and either a culture of male dominance was imported from the mining and steel towns of the North or Wales, where many of the migrants originated, or else power within the family was more evenly distributed.[23] But among the 'traditional' working classes of the bigger towns and cities of the North and the Midlands (particularly where there were large Irish populations), and in London, the relationship between mother and daughter was intense.

How intense can be seen from the diaries of young wives in Bethnal Green, an almost stereotypically 'traditional' working-class community. 'Mrs Cole', who lived in the same street as her mother, recorded of 'an ordinary day':

After breakfast I bath the baby and sweep the kitchen, and wash up. Then I go up the road shopping with Mum, Greta [a married sister] and the three children. After dinner I clean up and then round about 2 o'clock I go out for a walk with Mum and Greta and the children. I come back at about quarter to four to be in time for Janice when she gets back from school. She calls in at Mum's on her way home just to see if I'm there ... If anything goes wrong and I'm in any trouble I always go running round to Mum's.[24]

Mum was, she wrote, 'always popping in here—twelve times a day I should say'. Mrs Cole's ordinary day was not unusual among the younger women of Bethnal Green.

Nor was Bethnal Green unrepresentative of the 'traditional' working class generally. 'In adult life', the sociologist Madeline Kerr wrote of working class Liverpool, 'the general pattern seems to be for a woman to take her husband

---

[22] Gorer, *Exploring English Character*, 45–6. In his sample, 28% of all men lived with their in-laws; but only 19% of women. Also Jackson, *Working Class Community*, 166.

[23] Mogey, *Family and Neighbourhood*, 80–3. These conclusions are for the post-1945 council estate at Barton. In St Ebbe's, a 'traditional' working-class community in central Oxford, the majority of the wives were born in the locality and one of the reasons for staying there was a wish to live near their mothers (p. 18).

[24] Young and Willmott, *Family and Kinship*, 47.

home to live with her mother' and she gives striking examples of the way in which husbands acquiesced. When Mrs R., for example, married she asked her mother whether she could bring her husband back. 'You can please yourself,' her mother replied, 'but I don't want him.' Within a fortnight Mrs R. had returned home with her husband and there they had remained, even after 25 years of marriage and the birth of several children. When Mrs B. married she immediately went home with her husband. Asked what would have happened had her husband insisted on their living apart from her mother, she said 'in amazement': 'My husband loved my mother. He said I couldn't have a better mother in the world.'

Husbands occasionally did attempt to rupture the relationship, though with apparently little success:

When Billy and Maureen first married, Billy got her a lovely home. One day he returned from work to find a removal van driving from what looked like his house. He stopped his van and asked the man whose things they were moving. He learnt from them they were moving his own. His wife had ordered the van and given instructions. Billy went in and questioned his wife. She said, 'I'm going back to me mother. You can please yourself'. Billy returned with her. It's been like this throughout his married life.

Billy had a number of times tried to force his wife to leave her mother's. On each occasion he failed. Eventually he accepted failure and remained with wife, son, and mother-in-law in mother-in-law's house.[25]

The influence of the wife's mother almost inevitably continued to the third generation. For many children, living in their grandmother's house or close to it, the dominating personality was neither mother nor father, but maternal grandmother, and this was particularly so if the daughter worked (as, for instance, in the textile industry) and left her children with her mother during the working day. In much of the country Mum's Mum was called 'Nan' and Dad's Mum, 'Gran'; but 'Nan' was the crucial granny, and between Nan and grandchildren peculiarly close relationships could develop, freely accepted for the most part by her daughter. These relationships were, indeed, often encouraged by daughters who, anxious to shield mothers who lived apart against loneliness, commonly allowed them to 'borrow' their grandchildren for weeks at a time simply to keep them company. Only at the very end of the period was demographic change weakening the hold of 'Nan'.[26]

Men were obliged to accept the supremacy of Nan. They were, however, very attached to their own mothers, to 'Gran', and in cases of conflict between wives and Grans many supported Gran. Phyllis Wilmott, recalling her own

---

[25] All these examples are from Kerr, *Ship Street*, 40–2.

[26] Bott, *Family and Social Network*, 72. Shaw, 'Impressions of Family Life', 184; Gittins, *Fair Sex*, 137–8. For the nature of this change, which involved the return of mothers to the labour force throughout the period when their grandchildren were being born, see M. Anderson, 'The Emergence of the Modern Life Cycle in Britain', *Social History*, 10 (1985), 75.

upbringing in working-class London, thought there was a kind of guerrilla warfare between her mother and her father's mother:

Mum always implied that Gran's great feat was the way in which she managed throughout her life to pull the wool over her sons' eyes. Certainly, these six-foot-tall, heavy-drinking, hard-working men treated Gran with an unbroken gentleness and deference which their own wives were never granted.[27]

It is possible, in fact, that the significance of working-class matrilocality can be exaggerated: what is perhaps as important is the moral and emotional authority that Mum had over all her children. Equally, a mother's response was expansive rather than restrictive: she widened her embrace so as to include son-in-law or daughter-in-law within her own family.[28] If anyone suffered in this arrangement it was the father. Even in mining communities, where expressions of affection were socially constrained, men seem to have felt deep attachments to their mothers. If asked to compare, a miner might, for example, say of his wife that she was a 'grand woman', but he is 'always prepared to give unstinted and uninhibited praise' to his mother.[29] Such sentiments were rarely felt about fathers. Featherstone miners, despite being markedly favoured by their fathers, often thought them selfish and irresponsible. Nor was this confined to miners. In the 1940s, working-class Londoners could describe their fathers with great bitterness.[30] The historian John Prest, on entering the RAF in 1947, was struck by how often his fellow servicemen would speak of their mothers with intense warmth but almost with contempt of 'wastrel' fathers.[31] Though perhaps less actively hostile, many daughters were probably equally indifferent to their fathers: Pearl Jephcott was struck by the casualness with which girls she knew spoke of their fathers—if they spoke of them at all.[32]

This was not the Freudian hostility boys are thought to bear their fathers. It was the result in many cases of growing up in poverty in unskilled working-class households with an ill-tempered and apparently neglectful father whose behaviour contrasted unforgettably with the stoicism and self-sacrifice of Mum. For boys raised during the 1920s and 1930s, when their fathers had to cope with pressures their sons could not understand—and frequently coped badly—this contrast was uniquely memorable.

They at least knew their fathers in their early years. Many of those raised during the war, however, had no formative memories of their fathers at all; and absence had some of the same consequences as neglect. The war greatly strengthened female domination of the home while simultaneously strength-

---

[27] P. Willmott, *Growing Up in a London Village* (London, 1979), 45.
[28] Hoggart, *Uses of Literacy*, 36–7. Hoggart thought it a natural part of working-class domesticity that *both* son and daughter found it difficult to leave Mum, even after marriage.
[29] Dennis *et al.*, *Coal is our Life*, 142.   [30] Slater and Woodside, *Patterns of Marriage*, 37–8.
[31] I am grateful to Mr J. M. Prest for this information.   [32] Jephcott, *Rising Twenty*, 48.

ening the hold of the wife's mother on her daughter. Wartime marriages were often strangely casual and abrupt affairs—quite unlike the customary peacetime marriage, which usually followed a rather stately courting. With accommodation increasingly difficult to find as both bombing and wartime exigency eliminated much of the available housing stock, newly-wed couples often lived in wretched conditions. As a result, particularly if the husband were in the services, the sensible thing was to return to Mum, where accommodation was provided and rations could be pooled (which meant Mum got control of her daughter's as well as her own ration-book). It followed that boys were raised in households dominated by Mum or Nan in a wartime environment, which normally required from mother and grandmother as much stoicism and self-sacrifice as the depression.

It was also in the nature of working-class households, particularly those with several children, that girls became 'apprentice Mums'[33] at an early age. The larger the family the more likely it was that older girls—and 'older' could mean aged 6—would dress, feed, wash, mind, or take to the cinema their younger siblings, often with great care: 'In the middle of their play they will stop and remember their task and lift their "little Johnny" out of his chair and say "I must take him to the lav." '[34] The deep affection most had for brothers and sisters,[35] together with their intimacy with their own mothers, tended to reinforce both mother–daughter bonds and the widespread notion that a daughter was 'a daughter all her life'. And sometimes even before her life began. One unhappily married young woman told Madeline Kerr:

I knew in the first week my marriage was a mistake so when I was pregnant I prayed the child would be a daughter. All the time I was carrying her I kept saying to myself, 'Please, dear God, let it be a girl, please dear God, let it be a girl. She'll be my companion, she'll be my companion. I'll never be lonely any more.'[36]

The comparative matrilocality of English working-class life, and the predominance within the family of Mum, whether grandmother or wife, had a number of positive and negative results. Positively, it gave the family an institutional centre, a focus for sentiment and sociability at a time when poverty and insecurity might otherwise have torn it apart. Also, Mum frequently

---

[33] Klein, *Samples from English Cultures*, i. 55.

[34] Paneth, *Branch Street*, 38–9. 'Branch Street' was a lower working-class street in Paddington 'on the border of one of the big prostitute quarters.' Care of younger siblings was not, of course, confined to girls; boys often had to do it also. Dr Paneth argues that the exceptionally unpredictable and violent behaviour of the children she worked with—usually directed at adults—was a result of their having to assume adult responsibilities so young. Their resentment at this could not be taken out on their younger siblings, to whom they were, if anything, over-loving, but only on the adults who had imposed those responsibilities upon them.

[35] Some women in later life did in fact resent the extent to which in their youth they had to look after their siblings, though how many we cannot know. (Private information to the author.)

[36] Kerr, *Ship Street*, 48.

guaranteed the family's physical unity. She possessed the rent-book, as she possessed the ration-book, and through the long-cultivated rent collector had privileged access to landlords. If she could not find room in her own home she was often able to find accommodation nearby on the strength of the goodwill she had accumulated with both collector and landlord. One of her most important tasks was thus to 'speak for' her family with the collector, and, if necessary, to pay something on the side: 'We got [the house] through my mother's agent. We had to agree to do it up though and we had to give him a bit of dropsy [a bribe].'[37]

The centrality of mothering to the working-class family arguably encouraged women to triumph over circumstances which otherwise might have destroyed them. Such was the case of Mrs G., the mother of nine children, who at 42 found herself pregnant again. She attempted to induce miscarriage and failed. But when she returned from hospital after the birth of twins, this is what observers saw:

We saw a procession. It consisted of Mrs G. carrying one twin, of Margaret aged 16, carrying the other, of Robert aged 10, carrying his brother John, aged 1, of Maureen aged 12, leading her sisters, Sylvia, aged 4, and Eileen, aged 3, by the hand. The twins were sleeping, everybody else was grinning. Mother was coming home . . . Mrs G. was returning to her husband, eleven children and three rooms . . . Today she was happy, she was hurrying, she was going home.[38]

Mum was also the centre of those 'survival networks' by which extended families looked out for each other and it was she who negotiated mutual assistance with other matriarchs in those larger networks which tied together neighbouring extended families.[39] The existence of a last resort—or, perhaps too often, a first resort—provided both an emotional coherence to many working-class families and the security of someone who could be counted on if the worst happened, as it frequently did.

There were, however, undoubtedly disadvantages to maternal dominance. Mum's role was not always supportive. There were many examples of the way she used her power to manipulate rather than to assist her family, usually in a manner designed to increase their dependence on her. 'Her main goal in life', an observer said of one formidable, interfering mother, 'appears to be to keep all her relatives tied to herself. Any attempts they make to find other relationships even among themselves are foiled with considerable skill.' The effect of this was to disrupt an already delicately balanced marriage. When her son's

---

[37] Young and Willmott, *Family and Kinship*, 40; also Kerr, *Ship Street*, 22.

[38] Kerr, *Ship Street*, 53.

[39] 'Survival networks' is Ellen Ross's phrase. See E. Ross, 'Survival Networks: Women's Neighbourhood Sharing in London before the First World War', *History Workshop*, 15 (Spring 1983), 4–27. The conditions she describes here were still true of the interwar working class. Compare with Young and Willmott, *Family and Kinship*, 50–6.

marriage collapsed—as it did repeatedly—'he has always then homed to his Mum.'[40]

A mother did not need to be directly manipulative: the almost inevitable consequence of her institutional role in the family was to promote her children's sense of dependence on her, and in her daughters even a certain helplessness. 'I couldn't get on without me mother. I could get on without me husband. I don't notice him.' This 'surprising statement' was made by a married woman of 39 with five children. For many wives the glamour of marriage and independence hardly survived the first pregnancy. Then it was back to Mum. Managers of council housing estates soon discovered that a wish to return home underlay many of the hasty removals that disrupted housing policy.[41] The notion of Mum's indispensability was (as we have seen) part of the early training of working-class girls and that established a kind of lineal matriarchy, passed from generation to generation.

The dominance of Mum or Nan, however, in a child's upbringing, and persistent motherly overprotection, tended to freeze social values, perpetuate folk wisdom, and subvert the sense of social reality. This was no doubt often harmless enough, but not always. The clinging to rites like churching, because it pleased Mum, could irritate husbands as an unnecessary maternal intrusion:

When his wife said of churching 'It's your religion, isn't it? I mean you've got to do it', Mr Jeffreys added 'Your Mum's done it—you do it. They're all the same'. When Mrs Robbins, explaining the custom, said 'It's after you've had the baby. You go and give thanks to God that you're safe and all that. It's just a matter of form really', her husband broke in to remark 'Because your mother done it, you mean'.[42]

Mum's influence also transmitted medical folk ways—frequently to do with childbirth (or abortion and miscarriage) where she was usually a powerful presence. The aversion to the professional apparatus of the welfare state—doctors, midwives, nurses, pharmacists—and the preference for 'providence dispensaries' might be seen as a healthy scepticism towards the claims of this apparatus, but represented, more often, a dogged and sometimes harmful adherence to therapeutic superstitions.[43]

Overprotection too had its consequences, particularly in the lower reaches of the unskilled working class. The notorious refusal of mothers to admit that their sons might have indeed broken the law, or to recognize that in the eyes of the police and wider community locally accepted distinctions between good and bad crime had no meaning, resulted in borstal for many boys and a semi-criminal life thereafter.

[40] Kerr, *Ship Street*, 21.   [41] R. Jevons and C. Madge, *Housing Estates* (Bristol, 1946), 71.

[42] Young and Willmott, *Family and Kinship*, 57. Of the 45 married women in their sample, an astonishing 41 had been churched by the time their family was complete.

[43] For abortion and miscarriage, see below, pp. 307–8.

The stability of matrilocal families often depended on how far the husband/son-in-law was prepared to efface himself. If he did so the family could be highly integrated and follow norms which were well understood. But he had to accept a great deal, even if this were the implied bargain of role-segregation. His sexual life was often unsatisfactory;[44] the strength of the mother–daughter bond marginalized him; domestic decisions tended to be taken in the wider family in ways which excluded him. Indeed, if the wife returned to her mother, the husband could find himself acting as surrogate uncle or older brother to her younger siblings.[45] In a culture which formally expected a man to be master of his own household the effect of exclusion was to cause resentment and sometimes rebellion. It is possible that the well-remembered outbursts of violence and drunkenness were, in part, a result of this tension between what a husband expected of himself and what he was in practice obliged to accept.

2 | *Managing money*

For much of the working class for much of the time 'making ends meet' was a central problem of existence. The person who usually had the task of solving this problem was the wife. In their electoral propaganda the political parties consistently appealed to the working-class wife—as to the middle-class wife—as the family's 'chancellor of the exchequer' who, because she had to keep the family afloat, was peculiarly sensible and informed. When the Wartime Social Survey undertook its large-scale enquiry into credit buying it chose women as the whole of its sample, on the probably correct assumption that men simply would not know the answers.[46]

But in making ends meet, in being the 'good manager' husbands wanted, wives had to manage with often very defective knowledge of what their husbands earned. Contemporaries thought there was a certain regional basis to what wives knew. In Lancashire, particularly in the textile towns, many men were thought to hand over the whole of their wages and to conceal none. This was so partly because Lancashire towns

have a definite matriarchal strain often linked with the fact that in depressions, especially in the last Great [interwar] Depression, women spinners and weavers supported their husbands: miners and engineers and many cotton operatives referred to those days, when the women were the only breadwinners.[47]

In London, on the other hand (because 'Cockneys are not as stupid as the Cloggies are'), the man controlled the purse, giving his wife only those sums he thought appropriate. It is in practice, however, difficult to detect obvious

---

[44] See below, pp. 304–5.   [45] Klein, *Samples from English Cultures*, i. 71–2.
[46] Wartime Social Survey, *Credit Buying* (NS 23, Aug. 1942).
[47] Zweig, *Women's Life and Labour*, 49.

regional patterns and much probably depended on individual families and local traditions. The moving letters written by members of the Women's Co-operative Guild (1915) suggested that many wives—regardless of where they lived—were entirely ignorant of their husbands' earnings.[48] Yorkshire miners had a bad reputation and there were many depression stories of wives accompanying husbands to the labour exchange to appropriate the dole before it went elsewhere. Ferdynand Zweig, on the strength of what he admitted to be a very flawed sample, concluded that most wives probably did not know what their husbands earned and prudently did not attempt to find out. But in the majority of cases the arrangement was at least 'satisfactory': husbands gave their wives enough,[49] and in the event of a fall in wages many kept back less for themselves.[50] Nevertheless, it is hard to dispute Charles Madge's conclusion that the working-class housewife was 'the lowest paid, most exploited worker in the country, given a mere subsistence wage, with no limit on hours worked'.[51] And, even in 'satisfactory' households there were inevitably many disputes over money. For many couples who married in the depression such disputes were, in a sense, never settled, even after 1940. What survived was an enduring bitterness or, at best, a 'lack of sweetness' in marital relations.[52]

The Second World War marked a real change in working-class finances which had some effect—but could have had more—on working-class budgeting. By 1941 the war economy had eliminated the long-term unemployment which had blighted the finances of many working-class households and had significantly increased working-class money wages—while, however, restricting the range of goods on which it could be spent. This had substantially reduced the number of those whose lives depended on pawning and the acquisition of debts they could not repay: that great and desperate cycle of working-class debt and credit still common in the interwar years.[53] During the war itself only servicemen's wives, who were not thought good risks, remained in this cycle, that is, wholly reliant on the pawn-shop. But the structure of budgeting and the sums spent were largely unchanged. Most families, for example, could have spent more after 1941 than they did, but there was a 'conventional upper limit on expenditure' which people felt reluctant to exceed.[54] Some, though, could probably have saved more: yet saving depended less on current income than on past experience—especially regularity or irregularity of employment—and background. There thus tended to be a conventional upper limit to saving as well as to spending.

[48] M. Llewellyn Davies (ed.), *Maternity: Letters from Working Women* (London, 1915).
[49] Zweig, *Women's Life and Labour*, 44–52.
[50] C. Madge, *War-Time Pattern of Saving and Spending* (National Institute of Economic and Social Research, Cambridge, 1943), 59.
[51] Ibid. 55.   [52] Dennis et al., *Coal is our Life*, 192–4.
[53] For this, see particularly P. A. Johnson, *Saving and Spending: The Working-Class Economy in Britain, 1870–1939* (Oxford, 1985).
[54] Madge, *War-Time Pattern of Saving and Spending*, 73.

Also unchanged was the weekly collection—the habit by which people paid into 'savings-clubs' fixed sums weekly for a specific, usually short-term, purpose: holiday clubs, Christmas or 'goose clubs', 'chocolate clubs, perm clubs, boot clubs, coal clubs, mail-order clubs', and so on. [55] These, typically, were local clubs, often pub-based, where a well-known and trusted individual acted as treasurer. But the most important of the weekly collections was for the 'death club', burial insurance policies (sometimes with a life insurance component), held with societies like the Prudential or the Royal Liver which were anything but local or amateur in their organization.[56] Burial insurance had long been an important part of the working-class economy and was conceived by most working men and women as indispensable.[57]

The war did change budgeting behaviour in one important way: it increased the level of working-class savings through banks and other institutions. Working-class saving, particularly through the Post Office Savings Bank, had always been underestimated by contemporaries;[58] nevertheless, only a minority of working-class families saved regularly through a savings institution. By the middle of 1941 a clear majority did so.[59] Such increased saving was the result not only of increased money wages but, almost certainly, also a fear of post-war depression; saving 'for a rainy day' as it might have been put.[60]

By mid-1942 at any one time a little over one-third of working-class families appear to have been buying goods (other than food) on credit. Apart from income, the level of indebtedness was dependent upon two closely related variables: age and size of family. Only one-quarter of people over 50 were buying goods on credit, whereas 43 per cent of those under 50 were. Sixty-two per cent of families with three or more children under 14 were buying on credit compared with 27.2 per cent of families without children under 14.[61] As with living standards more generally, the number of children living at home and not working was crucial. The fewer, the higher the standard of living and the lower the levels of borrowing; the more, the lower the standard of living and the higher the level of borrowing.

Goods most commonly bought on credit were (in order) clothes and shoes, hard furniture, household linen, soft furnishings. Were credit to be withdrawn, most thought purchase of clothes would suffer: a sign of the import-

[55] Madge, *War-Time Pattern of Saving and Spending*, 42.

[56] Johnson, *Saving and Spending*, 11–47.

[57] For the extent of life-insurance ownership, see Madge, *War-Time Pattern of Saving and Spending*, 45.

[58] For important correctives to this view, see John Hilton, *Rich Man, Poor Man* (London, 1938), 45–74; Johnson, *Saving and Spending*, 87–125.

[59] Madge, *War-Time Pattern of Saving and Spending*, 49. In some Northern towns the proportion of working-class families holding savings through groups, certificates, and banks doubled between 1939 and 1941.

[60] For an interesting list of sayings by which people justified savings, see ibid. 102. There is no doubt an equally long list which justified not saving.

[61] Wartime Social Survey, *Credit Buying*, 1–3.

ance decent clothing was coming to have. People used several forms of credit: the misnamed 'providence cheques' (which were anything but provident, a kind of hire purchase whereby shops allowed customers to take goods, well above cash price on credit), clubs, straight credit, and hire purchase. What all these schemes had in common was a small down-payment and (usually) high interest rates. Different schemes were associated with different kinds of purchase—clothes and general drapery with providence cheques, furniture overwhelmingly with hire-purchase.

There was a rational and irrational element to the use of credit. People did, in fact, recognize that they were paying rates of interest over the odds; but they had trouble accumulating the cash necessary for outright purchase or larger down-payments. In this way they at least had the use of goods and credit did impose a form of compulsory saving when otherwise people might not save at all. As with so much of working-class budgeting, however, there was a conventional side to buying on credit: that was the way things were always done. 'Immediately children leave school', Madeline Kerr wrote, 'they follow Mum's example':

they fall into the habit of 'taking out cheques' and buying clothes at an exorbitant price 'from the Jew man' because they can pay in instalments and are not asked to pay cash down. Jane, aged 16, had on a grey costume which she got from 'the Jew man' and for which she has to pay £7 12s. and which she is paying off in weekly instalments. She herself told me she knows the costume would cost about £4 from C.& A.'s 'but C. + A. don't let you take a cheque, and where am I going to get £4'. It was quite useless trying to explain to her that if she can eventually find £7 12s., she could save £4 and it would be better to wait till she had £4 before she buys her costume. All three children shouted together that they would never have any clothes to wear that way.[62]

This is poorer working-class budgeting in a nutshell.

3 | Friends and neighbours: the 'traditional' working class

The structure of family life in the traditional working class suggests that its sociability would be more or less strictly demarcated, and this was largely the case. Social relations tended to be sharply divided between men and women, husbands and wives, kin and neighbours, and home and the outside world. Working-class men and women still had social networks which scarcely overlapped; it was thus very unusual for husbands and wives to entertain as a couple. In part this was due to the obvious physical inconvenience of most working-class housing, but more the result of a received culture. Most socially accepted institutions of entertainment were outside the home and most were largely or exclusively masculine in tone and membership. Men and women,

---

[62] Kerr, *Ship Street*, 92.

furthermore, defined friendship differently. Many thought that only men had 'friends'; women had neighbours or relations. Indeed, one man looked 'rather shocked' when the social psychologist Elizabeth Bott asked him whether he saw much of the neighbours.[63] A man would acknowledge having 'friends', who could be close, but would not bring them home; nor did his wife much want to meet them. His wife's 'friends' were her family and sometimes, but more rarely, the neighbours. But the fact that she might not have considered the neighbours friends did not preclude a relationship with them which, to an outsider, had all the characteristics of 'friendship'.[64] Women, for example, who never met in each other's homes and who probably did not think of themselves as 'friends' could nevertheless meet every night in the pub for a beer.[65]

After marriage, if not before, women's most intense relationships were usually with close kin—above all, of course, with their mothers. The energy and emotional commitment which middle-class women might have invested in friendship or association most working-class women devoted to their families. In a real crisis it was to them, rather than the neighbours, that they usually turned. 'Relations did their best for relations, often at considerable personal expense, and at the heart of the kinship system were the women.'[66] This willingness to distinguish between kin and neighbours was made possible by the propinquity of the family: relatives often were neighbours. Outsiders could be startled by the interrelatedness of a traditional working-class community.[67] One observer, noting the strikingly similar appearance of two boys, asked them if they were related. 'Sort of', they replied. They were, in fact, half-brothers, children of the same father who was simultaneously raising two families from two different mothers in the same street.[68] Such propinquity could almost entirely exclude the neighbourhood. Of one mining family, for example, it was written:

This family lives only four doors from the household of the wife's mother and retired father. With this father and mother live another daughter (Mary aged 21), her 27-year-old husband and two very small children . . . Thus the sister, Mary, makes at least three visits a day with one or both children. Her father visits S.T.'s household at least once daily . . . Jean makes the bed each night for her mother who is a cripple. Her two children, Stephen and Joan, obviously regard Mary and their grandmother as very close to them. Anything cooked for a meal by Jean and not eaten is taken to the mother's house to be finished. Jean says, 'We never have any letters or have to write to anybody, all our people

[63] Bott, *Family and Social Network*, 69.

[64] It was argued by J. M. Mogey that the working classes as a whole had a different definition of friendship from the middle classes. He suggested that the middle-class definition was exclusive—it shut out the rest of the community. If this is so, then there was, as Klein points out, no distinction in working-class usage between 'we're all friends' and 'we've no friends' (Klein, *Samples from English Cultures*, i. 137–9).

[65] Kerr, *Ship Street*, 34.   [66] Roberts, *A Woman's Place*, 183.

[67] Shaw, 'Impressions of Family Life', 183. Two-thirds of Shaw's sample, for example, had kin living within easy walking distance of each other.

[68] Paneth, *Branch Street*, 66–7.

are here'. On a Sunday her husband Stanley is always two hours late for his dinner, giving the excuse that he has been visiting his mother and sister at the other end of town. Jean and Mary will either go to the shops together and leave their mother in charge of the children, or take turns to look after them while the other goes out. Both Jean and Mary joke about having four children instead of two. Their brother Ralph has gone to live with his wife some five miles distant in Burley, but each week-end the two of them come home and alternatively sleep in the two households. On Saturday night two or three of these couples will go out together.[69]

In these circumstances, anything, like radio or the pools, which further reduced spare time made non-kin sociability even slighter.[70]

Relationships with neighbours were more complicated, and the common belief that there was much 'popping in and out', though not exactly untrue, is largely romantic. People had to know each other very well in order to 'pop in'. In those places, like a mining village, where the opportunities for female sociability outside the family were few, wives would visit each other and gossip over cups of tea—'taking five' it was called in Featherstone; elsewhere, however, sociability usually stopped at the front door. Unless people had known each other for many years, relations with neighbours tended to be superficial, and women rarely kept up with neighbours if either of them moved. There is much evidence that people were suspicious of their neighbours and large numbers thought them untrustworthy.[71] The shunning of neighbours was the result of a general desire to protect the privacy of the home and, more particularly, to escape neighbourly prying and gossip.[72] The extent to which women accused neighbours of 'betraying confidences' suggests one good reason why people felt they should withdraw. Accusations of gossiping in areas of mixed social status often accompanied an unbalanced mutuality. Some, for instance, were obliged to borrow more than others, while others thought themselves to be constantly giving. A failure of reciprocity therefore often led to further accusations of dishonesty and scrounging.

But being gossiped about is the inevitable risk of membership of any social network. To withdraw for fear of it involves an even greater risk—membership of no network at all, with consequent loss of social support. In practice, therefore, working-class communities, particularly those where all were in the same boat, were characterized by a wary mutuality. In a neighbourhood with few social or economic stratifications, the essence of a successful mutuality was that people were normally neither net debtors nor creditors. They looked out for each other's children, rallied to each other in emergencies and comforted each other in their troubles. The consequence, of course, was that people soon learnt much about each other, whether they liked it or not.[73]

---

[69] Dennis *et al.*, *Coal is our Life*, 205.   [70] Shaw, 'Impressions of Family Life', 192.
[71] Gorer, *Exploring English Character*, 52–5.   [72] Klein, *Samples from English Cultures*, i. 135.
[73] Chapman, *Home and Social Status*, 69.

'Neighbouring', unlike kin-relationships, was normally conducted outside the home and often casually. Women met on the street, in the shops or at their childrens' school. Within the neighbourhood they developed relationships which, if not intensive, were certainly extensive, involving, perhaps, most people in the street and many in those adjacent. 'In my own part of Leeds', Richard Hoggart wrote:

I knew at ten years old, as did all my contemporaries, both the relative status of all the streets around us and where one part shaded into another. Our gang fights were tribal fights between streets or groups of streets.

Similarly, one knows practically everybody, with an intimacy of detail—that these people have a son who 'got on' or emigrated; that those have a daughter who went wrong or one who married away and is doing well . . .[74]

The nature of these networks, their curious mixture of intimacy and detachment, was illuminatingly captured by the sociologist Phyllis Willmott who accompanied 'Mrs Landon' on a half-hour's shopping walk in Bethnal Green—an account which should be compared with the daily round of a middle-class housewife in Woodford (see pp. 86–7).

As she went along the street, nodding and chatting to this person and that, Mrs Landon commented on the people whom she saw.
(1) MARY COLLINS. 'She's a sister of Sally who I worked with at the button place before I got married. My Mum knew her Mum, but I sort of lost touch until one day I found myself sitting next to her in Meath Gardens. We both had the babies with us and so we got talking again. I see quite a lot of Mary now.'
(2) ARTHUR JENSEN. 'Yes, I knew him before I was married. He worked at our place with his sister and mother. He's married now.'
(3) MAVIS BOOT. 'That lady there, I know her. She lives down our turning . . . She's the daughter of one of Mum's old friends. When she died Mum promised to keep an eye on Mavis. She pops in at Mum's every day.'
(4) JOAN BATES is serving behind the counter at the baker's. 'She used to be a Simpson. She lives in the same street as my sister. My Mum knows her better than me.'
(5) SYBIL COOK. 'That's a girl I knew at school called Sybil.'
(6) KATIE SIMMONS. 'She's from the turning. Mum nursed her Mum when she was having Katie.'
(7) BETTY SALMON AND HER MOTHER. 'They live in the next turning to ours. Betty says she's had nothing but trouble with her daughter since she went to school.'
(8) RICHARD FIENBURGH. 'That man over there at the corner. He's a sort of relative. He's a brother of my sister's husband. He lives near them.'
(9) PATRICK COLLIS. This was a man in an old car parked by the shops. 'His mother lives in the turning.'
(10) AMY JACOBS is an old and bent woman who turns out to be Mrs Landon's godmother. 'Usually it's only when I'm with Mum that we talk.'

[74] Hoggart, *Uses of Literacy*, 60.

(11) SADIE LITTLE. This time there was not even a nod. The two women walked straight past each other. 'She's quarrelled with my sister so we don't talk to each other.'

(12) ALFRED CROSLAND. He is the father of the Katie seen a few minutes before.

(13) VIOLET BELCHER ... is an 'acquaintance of Mum's. She's got trouble with her inside.'

(14) EMMA FRANCE. This was an elderly, very jolly woman ... She engaged Mrs Landon in conversation ... Afterwards Mrs Landon explained that Mrs France had been her land-lady in the first rooms her Mum had got for her.[75]

The haphazard nature of this kind of sociability, the confinement of 'friend-ship' to kin and the extent to which women's social experience was grounded within the neighbourhood seemed to foreshorten their intellectual and social horizons. To outsiders, women could seem 'dim', showing incomprehension at questions—as whether they had hobbies or were interested in politics—which invited answers that lay outside this experience.[76] Whether women were, in fact, so 'dim' is difficult to know, particularly as the observer and the observed spoke, in effect, different languages. None the less, the inclination of women from the 'traditional' working classes to see the world largely in local and personal rather than in general or structural terms, and to direct their social energies into family and neighbourhood could undoubtedly make them seem 'dim' to those who saw the world differently.

The sociability of the 'traditional' male working class took place outside the home and away from the family, being, as we have seen, largely work-based. Its effect was almost wholly to exclude women. Men, particularly in the North of England combined themselves into rather jealous peer groups—into a 'secret society' of adult males.[77] In towns or mining villages these groups often formed when men were young, fragmented when they married and then, if its members had not emigrated, re-formed when their children were older—unlike the often equally tightly bound sets of teenage girls which do not nor-mally seem to have re-formed after marriage.[78] Even when they emigrated to the South or the Midlands they took their sociability with them: as in the case of 'Little Rochdale' in Banbury.[79]

The most common institutions of male sociability were the pub and the workingmen's club. Of the two, the pub was the least hostile to women but the extent of their exclusion appears to have differed between North and South. In the North, the vault and the taproom or public bar were barred to women by a convention which had the force of law. They were confined to the best room or the parlour. The public bar was as masculine in spirit as a club: people talked about work, betting, sport, drinking, the weather, and politics. They also bet in

---

[75] Young and Willmott, *Family and Kinship*, 105–6.

[76] Slater and Woodside, *Patterns of Marriage*, 92.

[77] The phrase is from Dennis *et al.*, *Coal is our Life*, 211.

[78] See Jephcott's discussion of 'Hilda's set', *Rising Twenty*, 160.

[79] Stacey, *Tradition and Change*, 109.

the public bar, and most pubs had a bookie's agent on hand. In London, however, women were admitted to and were to be found in all bars and this was
probably so in much of the South and the Midlands. Nevertheless, women
never represented more than a small proportion of pub drinkers: in the late
1930s Mass-Observation calculated that at any one time no more than about
16 per cent of pub-drinkers were women.[80] Of the remainder, the regulars,
those who drank in the same pub on most nights, were mostly older men who
lived nearby. Younger men were more infrequent drinkers and probably less
loyal to any one pub.[81]

The organized heart of male sociability was the workingmen's club, of
which there were huge numbers—Bolton had 65 at the beginning of the Second
World War, while Huddersfield had 70 in the early 1950s. Even a comparatively
small mining town like Featherstone had six. They enrolled a high proportion
of the male population, which in 1950 was 4,800.[82] Most of the clubs were affiliated to the Club and Institute Union and all had to be conducted in a manner
acceptable to the Registrar of Friendly Societies. Their declared aim was to promote mutuality, improvement, and rational recreation; in practice they promoted only mutuality, and by the 1940s they were used almost exclusively for
drinking, betting, and talking. The bar was, as Charles Booth wrote of the London clubs even before 1914, the 'pole of the tent'.[83] Clubs nominally forbade
betting but in most, as in pubs, there was a bookie's agent, and in most betting
was active. The great majority of the clubs refused women membership or did
their best—by keeping, for example, the premises as shabby as possible—to discourage it. Women were often permitted to attend on Saturday evenings or
Sundays when the clubs might have concerts or 'shows' (and these occasions
were to become more frequent in the 1950s), but it was understood that they
were somehow exceptional.

The administration of the clubs, the keeping of accounts, etc., seems to have
been rudimentary; the holding of office was not thought onerous and posts cir-
culated fairly widely among the members. This kept the atmosphere democratic and ensured that a pedantic adherence to rules did not obstruct the real
business of the clubs—drinking and talking. Talk, as in pubs, was overwhelmingly about work and sport:

The topic which [in Featherstone] surpassed all others in frequency is work—the difficulties which have been encountered in the course of the day's shift, the way in which a
particular task has been accomplished, and so on . . . It is said that more coal is 'filled off'
in the clubs than is ever filled off down below and that the men come back exhausted

---

[80] Mass-Observation, *The Pub and the People* (London, 1970 ed.), 134.

[81] Mogey, *Family and Neighbourhood*, 103–4.

[82] Table in Dennis et al., *Coal is our Life*, 144. In 1950 the clubs in Featherstone had a total membership of 6632—implying considerable multiple membership.

[83] C. Booth, *Life and Labour of the People in London*, first series, i (London, 1902), 96.

from a hard shift at the club . . . The only other subject which is regularly discussed is sport, especially Rugby League football.[84]

Politics was discussed—heatedly on occasion—but often in a personalized way. Clubs had other rooms where the conversation was more general and the horizon wider. Here the officials of the unions or the co-ops, or local councillors, drank; here political talk was both better informed and more self-interested.

The social culture of the 'traditional' working class as a whole was probably not as strictly segregated as in the 'classic slums' or mining villages. Both post-1940 prosperity and extensive rehousing were to modify it significantly. Nor were working men as indifferent to associationalism as outsiders thought; large numbers of associations—bowls, angling and picnic clubs, trade union branches, Oddfellows or Buffaloes—were attached to pubs or clubs.[85] But many working men could not afford subscriptions to such associations and those to which they did contribute, like 'Christmas Clubs', were, in their nature, short-lived.[86]

The neighbourhood itself was comprised not only of neighbours, persons to be helped but treated with circumspection; it was a physical entity—streets, shops, cinemas, dance halls, swimming-baths, tow-paths—all close by and all endowed with functions which elsewhere might belong to the home or a society. Even adult men, for whom work was a powerful competitor, were deeply attached to the neighbourhood, while for children and youths, as for women, it was the complement to the house, and central to their lives.

Of those things which defined a neighbourhood the streets were perhaps the most important. The street was not merely a thoroughfare; it was a crowded array of institutions designed for entertainment, sociability, and courting. It might be better, therefore, to think of the 'urban villages' of working-class England as constituted by streets, sub-communities, rather than as communities possessing a unifying focus.[87] Street-life in an 'urban village' was known for its colour and incident, its capacity to divert and fascinate. It was always remembered with affection by men and women; in the early 1920s, a young working-class woman when asked to describe 'Our Street', wrote:

At the back of our house is Belfast Street, and, oh it is a lovely street. Before the war we had no need to go to the Theatre to see a play, because of men and their wives fighting. I can remember once watching a man and his wife fight and the wife pulled her clogs off and threw them at the husband, one cutting his head and the other knocking his teeth out . . .[88]

Outsiders recognized the street as a place of endless, if random, possibilities. In 1925 the psychologist Cyril Burt wrote:

[84] Dennis et al., *Coal is our Life*, 144.   [85] Mass-Observation, *Pub and the People*, 20.
[86] Klein, *Samples from English Cultures*, i. 207–10.   [87] Roberts, *A Woman's Place*, 184.
[88] M. Phillips, *The Young Industrial Worker* (London, 1922), 23.

far more enthralling than any organized game of strenuous sport is the crowded succession of inconsequent episodes which a day in a London thoroughfare unfailingly
affords—a man knocked over, a woman in a fit, a horse bolting . . . a drunkard dragged
along to the police station by a couple of constables . . . Life for the street arab is full of
such random excitations, and becomes an affair of wits and windfalls, not an opportunity for steady, well-planned exercise.[89]

Almost a generation later another observer described a working-class boy
walking along one of his home streets: 'he taps on a window, rings a bicycle
bell, picks up an orange at the grocers, throws it in the air and puts it back.'[90]
The street was a place of diversion, and also the playground of the poor. Children played football, sometimes cricket, and most other games on the streets,
as they had always done, if at growing risk to themselves. Street-life was
equally important for adolescents and young men and women. Groups of adolescent boys would always meet—at the same spot in the same street, much as
a gang would claim a street as its inalienable territory.[91] For unemployed men
in the interwar years the street was as much their domain as that of children
or young men. Furthermore, for large numbers of adult men, employed or
unemployed, the street was where they bet. In the late 1940s B. S. Rowntree
wrote of a drive in a police car through a working-class suburb in London. 'As
the police came in sight, knots of men in street after street broke up and ran,
like sparrows scattering at the approach of a cat. They were the street book-
makers.'[92] The street was also a recognized place of assignation, where young
men and women met and courted. On Friday and Saturday evenings particularly, boys, often smartly and even gaudily dressed, would parade before passing girls—'peacocking' it was sometimes called—or simply picked up girls more
casually. One man recalled that he met his wife on the high street while out
with a friend, as was she. He said, 'there's a couple of nice-looking girls'; they
started talking, and for a while went out as a foursome, then as a pair. 'I grew
to like her because she could ride pillion so well. I fell in love with her.'[93] This
informality and directness contrasts with the formality and indirectness of
middle-class courting: young men and women of the middle class met much
more frequently through third parties and usually on formal occasions—at a
club (like a tennis club), a society, or at work.

The street was also the home of the cinema. From the moment that it
appeared in large numbers just before 1914, the cinema became an indispens-

---

[89] C. Burt, *The Young Delinquent* (London, 1925), 158. But Evelyn Sharp thought it was the life of the
street which was responsible for much 'of the vitality and the wit that are found animating every
grown-up London crowd, whether it gathers to look at a street accident, or a Royal Procession'
(*The London Child* (London, 1927), 87).

[90] Jackson, *Working Class Community*, 168.

[91] S. Humphries, *Hooligans and Rebels* (Oxford, 1981), 174–208.

[92] B. S. Rowntree and G. R. Lavers, *English Life and Leisure* (London, 1951), 128.

[93] Slater and Woodside, *Patterns of Marriage*, 94.

able part of working-class life, partly as a place of entertainment, partly, like the street itself, as a place where young men and women could meet. The extent to which 'going to the pictures' was an occasion for sexual encounters often surprised and sometimes dismayed people. In 1922 one teacher wrote of Sheffield:

Overcrowding at home, the promiscuous company of older workers, the intense and unescapable 'suggestion' of the life of the streets and the cinema, and, above all, the lack of 'higher' interests have produced [in the young worker] a sophistication and precocity which are none the less real for being, in many cases, cleverly concealed ...

They go to the Sheldon Picture Palace three or four times a week, and it is always to see the same picture, and if you say, 'Well, how did you like the picture?' they say, 'Eh, I didn't go for that'. They go parading at the back of the hall, and I think it must be meant for that ...

So much for the young wage-earner's personal interests.[94]

In addition to the cinema, the café became popular as an adjunct of the street in the 1920s. After the First World War, cafés, often owned by Italian or Greek families, rapidly replaced coffee-shops and were established in their hundreds in the working-class quarters of all reasonably large towns.[95] They were warmer than street corners, cups of tea and a 'slab' (a piece of cheap cake or pie) could be made to go a long way, and they were known to have the same function as the cinema and the street, as did their later rivals—the 'milk bar', introduced from Australia in the late 1930s, and the 'coffee bar', loosely modelled on the Italian original, which was to play such an important part in the popular culture of the late 1940s and early 1950s.

The neighbourhood provided both a life of heightened variety and a comforting familiarity. In 1939 the child psychologist Susan Isaacs asked a number of boys and girls from Tottenham (North London) who had been evacuated to Cambridge what they most missed there. All, of course, missed parents and family, but all expressed a real sense of loss, partly for the superior amenity of the metropolis, partly for the rhythms of the neighbourhood. Thus one 13-year-old wrote:

The things I miss most in Cambridge is my Father and Mother and family. I miss my dog and cat and I miss going to the Pictures on a Friday Saturday and Monday. I miss going errans here and I miss the People who live near me my friends. I miss going to see Ice Hockey Played at Harringay Areama [sic]. I miss playing on my skates with a hockey stick. I miss my sister saying 'Come for a ride on your bike'. I also miss playing football in the Playground at school. I miss going swimming at Tottenham Baths.[96]

---

[94] Phillips, *Young Industrial Worker*, 18–19. For the cinema, see below, Chapter XI.
[95] S. F. Hatton, *London's Bad Boys* (London, 1931), 39–40.
[96] This and the following quotations are from S. Isaacs (ed.), *The Cambridge Evacuation Survey* (London, 1941), 66–87.

Another 13-year-old (reported to be 'sullen, hostile and obstructive' at school) wrote:

Most of all I miss my parents and brothers. I also miss the facilities for carrying on my hobbies: Radio (Short Wave) Technical Drawing and Model Aeroplanes. I also miss Sunday marches with the Communist Party and will miss the May-day celebrations in Hyde Park next year. I miss the fellowship and good spirit of my comrades in the Communist Party . . . I miss the safety of London in leaving your bike about without having a post-mortem on it by Cambridge boys who fool about with your brakes and my dynamo has been mucked about with lots of time already. I miss a decent and regular bus service. I miss films that have any resemblance of being new.

'I miss the buses and the heavy lorries which go passed [*sic*] my house at home' was the typical comment of one 13-year-old boy, and a 14-year-old missed 'the thunder of the tube in the underground railway'. The belief that Tottenham was more secure, a place where people did not muck about with your bike, was also widely held, and sometimes written in terms which would have surprised those who knew only London: 'I miss the careful driving of the buses and cars in London, they are reckless and dangerous here. I have had accidents already in Cambridge which I didn't have in London.'

There were many things evacuees liked in Cambridge—though often what they liked was liked because it was familiar ('I like [Cambridge] because there are plenty of Marks and Spencers, Woolworths and all the other shops')—and what they disliked was the absence of things not to be found in most provincial towns, like new films and fish and chip shops every 100 yards. But the feeling that you were 'safer' at home, that your way of life was much less constrained, that you were kept busy with 'errans', and that home was more diverting, represented an intense notion of neighbourhood which people found difficult to feel elsewhere.

4 | Friends and neighbours: the 'new' working class

The majority of the working classes throughout this period lived in privately rented accommodation located within the pre-1914 boundaries of towns and cities. In the interwar years, however, and to some extent in the 1940s, large numbers of working-class families migrated to publicly built and publicly owned housing, mostly on the outskirts of these towns or even beyond their boundaries altogether. While a proportion of new public housing was in the form of flats ('block dwellings'), 90 per cent of the 1.1 million houses built by local authorities between 1919 and 1939 were on suburban estates, and about 4.5 million people lived in them. From all the major English towns people were decanted into outlying or 'out-county' estates which were unique in Europe. Their chief characteristic—like that of contemporary middle-class housing—

was their low density.[97] None of them had more than 12 houses to the acre, and some had densities lower even than this. Most houses were, therefore, either semi-detached, with lines broken occasionally by small terrace rows, or 'grouped' in detached terraces. Virtually all had comparatively large gardens. These estates were the public equivalent of speculatively built middle-class housing and they made almost as much impact on the contemporary mind. Many quickly came to be identified, not always favourably, with their cities of origin: King's Standing with Birmingham, Norris Green with Liverpool, Weybourne with Sheffield, Knowle and Bedminster with Bristol or, largest of them all, the colossal LCC out-county estate at Becontree and Dagenham, which had 120,000 inhabitants by 1939.

All the local authority estates, like so much else in modern English housing, were derived from the garden-city movement. The difficulty for publicly financed housing was that the typical garden-city house—gabled, dormer-windowed, and eccentrically detailed—was too expensive. This was understood by several garden-city architects, most prominently Raymond Unwin (who disliked gables and dormers anyway), who suggested that, by a combination of two aesthetic principles, low density and simplicity of design, public housing could be cheap and still conform to the tenets of the garden-city.[98] What was to become the basis of post-1918 public housing was proposed by Unwin and his followers in *The Garden City* (1906) and in Unwin's own *Town Planning in Practice* (1909). The ideology of the garden-city movement was then incorporated into state housing policy, first, by the Tudor Walters Report (1918) and second, by Christopher Addison at the Local Government Board and later the ministry of health. Tudor Walters, Liberal MP for Sheffield Brightside and an authority on London housing, was asked by Lloyd George to examine the structure of working-class housing. Both Walters and the Lloyd George government were sensitive, indeed over-sensitive, to the possibility of working-class unrest (or worse) in the last stages of the First World War and saw in relatively lavish housing provision an antidote to it. The Tudor Walters Report, which was drawn largely from Unwin's *Town Planning in Practice*, recommended that public housing be of 'middle-class' standard in amenity and equipment, and concluded that this could be achieved by abandoning costly individuality of design in favour of the neo-Georgian austerity promoted by Unwin.[99] The Report was accepted and the money provided by Christopher Addison as minister of health in 1919. The housing department of the ministry, Addison's creation, was dominated by the 'Tudor Walters group', and particularly by Unwin as chief architect.[100]

---

[97] Olechnowicz, 'Out-County Estates', 295. For middle-class housing, see above, pp. 73–9.
[98] M. Swenarton, *Homes Fit for Heroes* (London, 1981), 104–5.
[99] For details of the Report, see ibid. 96–100, 110–11.
[100] For Addison as minister in charge of housing, see Morgan, *Consensus and Disunity*, 89–93.

For all the financial and political vicissitudes of local authority housing over the following thirty years it was the Tudor Walters Report which determined the general pattern of public housing until the 1950s: suburban estates of low density—in effect, dormitory suburbs—composed largely of two- or three-bedroom houses, many without a parlour, set in their own gardens and usually of a plain Georgian style. How plain depended upon the legislation under which they were built. The 1919 (Addison) and 1923 (Chamberlain) Acts were the most generous, and the houses built under them most popular with tenants and local authorities since they most approximated the proper vernacular style; the 1924 (Wheatley) Act, somewhat less generous (though more effective in getting houses built); and, finally, the legislation of 1930, 1936, and 1938, where the emphasis was on economy and slum-clearance, whose houses were plainest of all. Madge and Jevons noticed how the big Knowle and Bedminster estate in Bristol, for example, reflected the evolution of interwar public housing. At Knowle Park were the relatively expensive 1919 and 1923 Act houses (many of them leased) and the more prosperous tenants; next came a band of Wheatley Act houses at somewhat lower rents; Filwood Park, at the western end, contained many 'clearance' houses built under the 1930 Act; and, at the extreme end, were houses provided for families who had been living in condemned accommodation and who were moved under the 1936 and 1938 legislation.[101] Nevertheless, however much tenants differed from each other and their houses differed in cost and decoration, they all came to live in conditions almost wholly different from those in which they were born and raised. That this could perhaps have had profound social implications was understood by contemporaries. Of the Weybourne estate in Sheffield, A. D. K. Owen wrote:

For [the tenants'] closely congested courts they have in exchange a windy hillside, sparsely spread houses and the old social intimacy of the doorstep broken by the unwonted garden. It is clear that a revolution has taken place in the condition of these people, physical and social, and it is a question of very great interest and importance to know what has been the outcome.[102]

By the 1940s it had become 'part of folklore' that the estates had been responsible for marked losses of working-class sociability;[103] that they had produced a family-centred in place of a neighbourhood-centred society.[104] To what extent was this so? and why should the estates have been responsible for it?

Their location and layout made at least some loss of sociability inevitable, and the first to suffer was kin-relationships. In a traditional working-class community propinquity and a tight urban structure was an essential condition for

---

[101] Jevons and Madge, *Housing Estates*, 19.

[102] A. D. K. Owen, *A Report on the Housing Problem in Sheffield* (Sheffield Survey Pamphlet, No. 2, Oct. 1931), 38–9.

[103] Bott, *Family and Social Network*, 184–6.   [104] Mogey, *Family and Neighbourhood*, 152.

kin relationships generally and mother–daughter relationships particularly. Unless extended families moved more or less *en bloc*—and some did[105]—these ties were inexorably weakened or broken altogether. Even where the distance moved was not great and transport easily available, as in towns like Oxford, kin relations decayed. Whereas 60 per cent of the St Ebbe's households had regular kin contacts, at Barton, only three miles away, half that number did so.[106] When people moved to out-county estates, where distance really was a problem, the effect on kin relations was even more severe, as happened when Bethnal Greeners moved to the out-county estate of 'Greenleigh'.[107]

Had kin relationships been replaced by an active 'neighbouring', women (especially) might have been less distressed by family disintegration. Neighbouring, however, was not more active. Except for the pioneers, when people were often forced together in sheer self-defence,[108] there is abundant evidence that neighbours were regarded with the same wariness and sometimes hostility as they had always been. Mutual visiting was rare and few sought each other's company. It was reported of one woman resident of the LCC estate at Watling that she 'had lived four years in the same cottage and is on very good terms with her neighbour [but] has, nevertheless, not been in her house. The boys play together, but each in his own garden, the fence separating them.'[109] People would probably know their neighbours on either side and, indeed, many felt that they should. They could even be on borrowing and lending terms, but everywhere they 'kept their distance', convinced (often with reason) that anything closer would lead to intrusion, gossip, 'rows'. Even more than in traditional working-class communities, there was the fear (as everywhere at the time) that children would pick up 'germs' or bad language if they associated with the neighbours. Thus, of the Barton estate in Oxford, it was noted that, apart from workmates, 'the normal person sees only other members of his family, occasionally a neighbour, less frequently a kinsman, rarely a friend. There is a tendency to reduce relations to a casual, take-it-or-leave-it sort of level'.[110]

Attempts to give the new estates some kind of collective existence via residents' associations all appear to have been unsuccessful. An initial enthusiasm, when the rawness and lack of amenity of the estates, or the hostility of the host communities, seemed to demand a collective response, was soon followed

---

[105] One-third of the residents of 'Greenleigh' had kin living on the estate. (Young and Willmott, *Family and Kinship*, 125.)

[106] Mogey, *Family and Neighbourhood*, 81.   [107] Young and Willmott, *Family and Kinship*, 131.

[108] The sociologist Ruth Durant wrote of the LCC estate at Watling, near Hendon, that 'for the newcomers the two most important factors were the strangeness and newness of the place, bare of all urban traditions and facilities and the antagonism of the inhabitants of the district, which was manifested all over Hendon.' This encouraged in the newcomers a certain defensive solidarity. (R. Durant, *Watling: A Social Survey* (London, 1939), 21.)

[109] Ibid. 88.   [110] Mogey, *Family and Neighbourhood*, 96–7.

by increasing indifference. In Watling, for example, the Residents' Association had 400 members in May 1928, but only 94 a year later. Subsections disaffiliated acrimoniously: the horticultural society in March 1929, and the loan club in September 1931. In July 1931 the *Resident*, the news-sheet of the Association, wrote:

Watling's Horticultural Society has a membership of 800 or thereabouts . . . will it be believed that for some inscrutable reason the Watling Horticultural Society and the Watling Association regard each other with suspicion and (it must be said) with jealousy? Yet such is the case, and so we have the spectacle of the Community Association and the most successful Watling Society keeping up, as a religious observance, this absurd kind of blood feud.[111]

The Watling experience was repeated on the other estates—sometimes with even more acrimony.[112]

What emerged was a new structure of sociability based upon formal organizations meeting specific needs and often attached to traditional institutions. In most places the churches took on new life, not as places of worship, but as associational foci. In Becontree and Dagenham over half the estates' 590 organizations were affiliated to the churches or other religious bodies:

Four of the seven [Anglican] churches have a men's organization attached and one has two. In four cases they are purely social functions. Each church has a Woman's Fellowship, whose activities vary from being mainly religious to being mainly social. In addition there are five branches of the Mothers' Union.

For young people there are seven Cub packs, seven Scout troops, one Rover crew, seven Brownie companies, eight Guide companies and one Ranger company. There is also one branch of the Church Lads' Brigade. In practically every case the organization has a membership restricted to Sunday school members, in some instances solely because of the size of the waiting list. There are ten other organizations for young people, usually boys' and girls' clubs for mainly recreational purposes.[113]

On all estates there were large numbers of sporting associations—often founded by teachers—and everywhere gardening clubs grew rapidly. The Labour Party, which quickly came to dominate most estates politically, nearly always had large and active women's sections, although their function, if not without political significance, was again largely social. We should, however, not underrate the effectiveness of these associations: the Dagenham Girl Pipers and the Luton Girls' Choir both achieved a national status in the 1930s, while the organizers of the Peace Ballot in Watling were able to mobilize 50 per cent of all local government voters compared with 32.4 per cent who voted in the municipal elections, and 40.4 per cent of all parliamentary voters voted in

---

[111] Quoted in Durant, *Watling*, 41–2.
[112] Mogey, *Family and Neighbourhood*, 115–23; Olechnowicz, 'Out-County Estates', 249.
[113] Young, *Becontree*, 184.

Watling compared with 29.2 per cent for London as a whole.[114] Nevertheless, most of the organizations on the estates grew at the expense of those which, like the residents' associations, emphasized collectivity and tended if anything to increase social segregation.

Thus, while a higher proportion of a new estate did belong to formal associations than in the older working-class communities, and while husbands and wives (as we have seen) were more likely to do things together, sociability was a tepid and inadequate substitute for what went before. This was especially so for women. For a woman a move to a dormitory estate was a change in the whole of her life. In these new circumstances women often felt isolated and lonely; they missed Mum and kin and the sociability of the old neighbourhood—which they almost inevitably exaggerated. In Oxford, the department of social services was obliged to organize reunions in St Ebbe's for women who had migrated to the new estates and who wished to 'keep in touch' with a former way of life.[115] Of 'Mrs Harper' who moved to 'Greenleigh' from Bethnal Green, Willmott and Young wrote:

Mrs Harper herself seldom sees her relatives any more. She goes to Bethnal Green only five or six times a year, when one of her elder sisters organizes a family party 'for Dad'. 'It costs so much to travel up there', she said, 'that I don't recognize some of the children, they're growing so fast'. Tired of mooching around an empty house all day, waiting for her husband and children to return, with no-one to talk to and with the neighbours 'snobbish' and 'spiteful', Mrs Harper had taken a part-time job. 'If I didn't go to work, I'd get melancholic'. Her verdict on Greenleigh—It's like being in a box to die out here'.[116]

Many working-class women appear to have developed a version of the 'suburban neuroses', lethargy and depression, which seemingly afflicted middle-class women.

In practice, it is doubtful whether for men the situation was much different. Although they may have kept their workmates and through work a social basis outside the home, men's sociability, for reasons we shall see, was almost as stretched as women's. What spare time men had appears to have been increasingly given to home and family—partly by choice and partly by necessity.[117]

Why was sociability on the estates so restricted? To some extent the answer lies in the way they were conceived and constructed. The bulk of the houses had two and three bedrooms and were designed for families with young or

---

[114] Durant, *Watling*, 95.

[115] I am grateful to the late Baroness Faithfull for this information.

[116] Young and Willmott, *Family and Kinship*, 133.

[117] For post-war analyses of the sociability of the 'affluent worker', who as a type was to some extent anticipated by the skilled workers in the pre-1939 council estates, see J. H. Goldthorpe, D. Lockwood, F. Bechhofer, and J. Platt, *The Affluent Worker in the Class Structure* (Cambridge, 1969), 99–108; also F. Zweig, *The Worker in an Affluent Society* (London, 1961), 205–10.

teenage children. There was little accommodation for single people or older married couples. The result was that the estates, certainly in their early years, had heavily biased age structures. In the 1930s half of Becontree's population was under 18+ and the average age was 23.7. The Bristol estates in the 1930s were likened to a colony: 'The people settling down are young families; the population resembles that of the white population of Northern Rhodesia or of New Zealand in the early years of the twentieth century. This age composition colours all the activities and needs of the community.'[118] But these were precisely those families who had least time, energy and money to give to sociability, and, in so far as they did, sociability was usually related to their children. The sociability of the working class was fragile enough at best; to create a community which excluded those (grandparents, single people, parents with children at work) who could best hold it together was to pauperize it socially.

The physical conception of the estates had the same effect. The social provision which permitted the casual but frequent neighbourliness of the inner cities and towns—pubs, corner shops, cafés, fish and chip shops, barrows and stalls—was almost wholly absent. Some local authorities, like Liverpool, forbade pubs entirely on their estates and all others severely restricted them. When pubs were built they tended to be of the large 1930s 'roadhouse' type with big bars and other facilities, like dance halls, tennis courts, and semi-restaurants appended. These facilities were, in themselves, important, but the size and tone of the pubs did not encourage social intimacy and for many residents they were too far from home anyway. The paucity or non-existence of pubs made the estates rather desolate, and desolate in a general sense. The Pilgrim Trust noted the differences between the new estates in Liverpool and 'the sordid but easygoing and social atmosphere of the old districts':

where the unemployed man has his corner, his friends, his library, and his bookmaker, where he speaks freely when you call on him, where he calls his friends in to tell you all about it . . . Such an atmosphere is utterly different from that in the housing estates, where the unemployed man takes an anxious look round when you mention unemployment and rapidly tells you to come in.[119]

Shopping was also a different affair. The geography of shopping on the estates was strictly controlled. There were no 'parlour shops' or corner shops, nor any of those shopping opportunities which town dwellers knew. Although many denied it (and poor shopping was often given as a reason for leaving the estates), most had adequate shopping, but it was inconvenient and unappealing. Shopping precincts were normally located at the intersections of major thoroughfares and often at a distance from home, to be reached only by bus or long walk. Thus in the smaller estates 'life gravitates to the nearest main road off the estate, where a better shopping centre and perhaps other amenities—

---

[118] Jevons and Madge, *Housing Estates*, 26.   [119] Pilgrim Trust, *Men without Work*, 92.

such as public houses and cinemas—can be found'.[120] There was, it is true, some effort to recapture the spirit of the old urban villages. There was initially a good deal of street trading by costers, but local authorities often disapproved and by the late 1930s it was dying out. On the Becontree estate

pathetic attempts are made on Saturdays at some of the shopping centres . . . to regain the atmosphere of this noisy and crowded shopping. Shop assistants selling butchers' meat, eggs, bacon etc., shout 'Buy', 'buy', 'buy', and bargain with groups of onlookers. On the kerb there are sellers offering flowers, fruit, vegetables and toys to passers by, but the whole scale, both of noise and crowd, is too small for it to be really effective.[121]

The result was that shopping tended to be solitary with few, if any, of the casual encounters that crowded 'Mrs Landon's' half-hour of shopping in Bethnal Green.[122]

In the interwar years it was often assumed that the new estates were transplanted slums—cheap housing where slummies were deposited when their old accommodation became uninhabitable. This was, however, rarely true. By conventional working-class standards the new estates were expensive. As the historian of the Becontree estate wrote:

the people of the Becontree estate are not on the whole what is generally termed 'slum people' . . . most slum dwellers could not afford the rents and travelling expenses and their problems are being dealt with quite separately by slum clearance and rehousing schemes. The enquiries which casual visitors to the Estate sometimes make as to whether the tenants store their coals in the bath, and whether slum habits are changed by the new surroundings . . . are therefore rather purposeless.[123]

From the beginning, the new estates were supposed to charge 'economic' rents upon a calculation of long-term cost, and this was done to preserve the competitiveness of private rental housing. Rents on the estates were thus considerably higher than people were used to or, in many cases, could afford. In Sheffield, for example, rents in the early 1930s were 10s 6d a week for three-bedroom and 9s 1d for two-bedroom houses. In cleared slums, however, 60 per cent of tenants had been paying less than 7s weekly and nearly 30 per cent less than 6s. Since in 1931 40 per cent of heads of households were unemployed in Sheffield the higher rents could put a severe and often unacceptable strain on family finances.[124] Although some authorities lowered rents in the later thirties or, like Leeds, introduced rebate schemes, rents before 1939 were such that only skilled workers who remained in more or less continuous employment were likely to pay them regularly.

It was not only rents which were high on the estates. A new house had to be equipped—furniture, curtains, linoleum—and at a higher level than people

---

[120] Jevons and Madge, *Housing Estates*, 23.   [121] Young, *Becontree*, 100–3.
[122] See above, pp. 182–3.   [123] Young, *Becontree*, 25.
[124] Owen, *Report on the Housing Problem in Sheffield*, 41–3.

were used to. They were conscious of this expense and often worried about it, but were reluctant to lower standards, partly because the estates introduced an element of competitive consumption, partly because many had a strong sense that a new house was a new beginning. For most men transport costs were also higher, which is why as many who could rode bicycles to work.

Sociability inevitably suffered from these additional expenses. High rents meant defaults, which eventually meant ejection. Before 1940, when full employment made default less common, there was in consequence a continuous population turnover. In Sheffield, by 1931 nearly one-fifth of the original inhabitants of 1920s estates had left; most other estates had removal rates of at least 10 per cent a year. In such circumstances, when there was a good chance that neighbours might be neighbours only briefly, anything but the most superficial relationship was unlikely.

Sociability, like the new houses, was also expensive, particularly as attitudes to sociability changed. Women on the Watling estate confessed that they were reluctant to 'visit' because they were ashamed of shabby clothing, something which would probably have worried them less in the East End. The inclination in Watling, therefore, was to retreat into 'domestic isolation'.[125] Sociability was not thought obligatory: when expenses on the home, both necessary and optional, took an increasing share of family income, sociability was a luxury that could be foregone. Husbands were obviously prepared to abandon conviviality if economy required it. On the new estates, even if pubs had been more plentiful, many men would not have frequented them: the informal male sociability of the pub and club was one of the first victims of the dormitory estates and their demands.

Nor was it just money. In the 1930s the 'problem of leisure' and to what creative use it could be put was thought by contemporaries to be a pressing issue of the day. But for many the problem was solved by travelling to and from work. The dormitory suburbs—unlike the satellite towns of the 1950s and 1960s—were purely residential: none presupposed any organic relationship between home and work. The disaggregation of local government and planning, and the reluctance of central government to interfere with the business decisions of particular firms, ensured no co-ordination between those building homes and those building factories. The most notorious example of this was the construction of the Becontree and Dagenham estate at the extreme east of Greater London while most of the new factories were built at the extreme west.[126] The erection of the Ford and Briggs Body plants in Dagenham in the late 1930s was entirely fortuitous and they did not, initially, employ any Dagenham residents. The result was that many men had to travel the width of London to the Great West Road for their work—a daily round trip of about

---

[125] Durant, *Watling*, 89.   [126] Liepmann, *The Journey to Work*, 9.

three hours. This experience was to some degree repeated throughout the country. Except for Sunday and perhaps Saturday afternoon, dwellers on the estates had in practice little leisure time, and were too tired at night to do much else than listen to the wireless and then go to bed.

In these conditions, that families should retreat into an intense privacy is not surprising. The siting and design of the estates did not encourage the old sociability but they did encourage domesticity. To the extent that men had spare time they devoted it to home-centred activities, 'chores' and 'odd jobs' and, above all, to gardening. There is no doubt as to the popularity of gardening, even among the pioneers who had had no experience of it. Unwin's original defence of relatively large gardens for public housing had been a rather absurd commercial one—that people could supplement their wages from the sale of their produce. They were eventually justified as a therapeutic amenity and that is how most people saw them. In the interwar years four million new gardens were established and by 1949 about 70 per cent of gardeners were manual workers—almost exactly their proportion of the population as a whole, and a remarkable change over a generation. Horticultural and gardening clubs were always amongst the largest societies in the new estates and time expended on gardens tended to increase rather than diminish. By the early 1950s it was noted that at least half the families on the Barton estate in Oxford were actually 'in love' with their gardens.[127]

The wireless was the second principal agent of domesticity. By 1939 a majority of residents had radios and by 1950 ownership was almost universal. 'Listening-in' was, of course, common to all classes and had much the same effect everywhere. But it was ideal for people, like those on the new estates, whose spare time and finances were necessarily circumscribed. 'Everything suggests', one historian has commented, 'that the wireless was at the centre of the inter-war council house home; all the family derived satisfaction from broadcasts and of all the alternatives for spending spare time in the evenings, it was the easiest.'[128]

The restricted sociability of the new estates was, above all, inherent in the culture of the old communities: except in one important sphere—relations between man and wife—there is no evidence that people's attitudes much changed. Why, it was asked, should the mere absence of nearby shops, pubs or cinemas make people feel so isolated?

Did they not have each other for company and comfort? However, they carried with them no interests, no objectives, no institutions, only their strong inhibition against

---

[127] Mogey, *Family and Neighbourhood*, 29; Olechnowicz, 'Out-County Estates', 277. More generally, S. Constantine, 'Amateur Gardening and Popular Recreation in the 19th and 20th Centuries', *Journal of Social History* (Spring 1981).

[128] Olechnowicz, 'Out-County Estates', 287; see also Goldthorpe *et al.*, *The Affluent Worker in the Class Structure*, 100–3, where it is pointed out that the main activity of working men living in new estates in Luton in the early 1960s was gardening, doing odd-jobs, and watching television.

mixing freely with their neighbours; it weakened under the great strain of migration, but only temporarily. All wished Watling to be furnished with amenities, yet the majority desired merely those they had known before. Soon, with working, shopping, cinemagoing and perhaps whist playing, they reverted to 'keeping themselves to themselves'.[129]

This account of Watling probably exaggerates the acquired inhibitions on social life, but it emphasizes how dependent working-class sociability was on physical contiguities—people simply living near or with each other. Contiguity permitted a complicated, but casual sociability; when that contiguity disappeared there was nothing to replace it. The intense domesticity of the estates was also less surprising than contemporaries thought. Working-class families had always been, given the opportunity, 'homely' (in Hoggart's sense of 'attached to the home'), and 'homeliness' had always been counted a virtue—thus the popularity of 'homely' BBC radio programmes like *Mrs Dale's Diary* or *The Archers*, even though their settings were often middle-class.[130] It was, indeed, frequently argued that the home-centredness of the estates represented a form of 'middle-classness'; but it was actually much more introverted than middle-class domesticity. Had it, in fact, represented 'middle-classness' we might have expected 'appreciably higher levels of social participation of both a formal and informal kind'.[131] The sociability of the estates—the caution, the suspicion, the domesticity, and the feeling that social withdrawal was safest—was simply a traditional sociability adapted to new physical circumstances.

5 | *Conflict and status*

Although working-class communities were capable of great mutuality, they were also places where people feared social conflict and deployed various techniques to avoid it. In this they were only partially successful; as a result the working class was almost certainly more socially riven than any other class. Conflicts were usually of three kinds: the age-old one between 'rough' and 'respectable'; ones inherent in a situation where people were obliged to 'live on top of each other'; and antagonisms which were familiar to most communities—complaints, for instance, about the neighbours' children or their noise. In practice, these distinctions were probably not so clear; there were discernible patterns to conflict, but they varied according to time and locality.

This was true even of the distinction between 'unrespectable' (a capacious term) and 'respectable'. Much behaviour was, of course, thought 'unrespectable' everywhere: in both 'traditional' (St Ebbe's) and 'non-traditional'

---

[129] Durant, *Watling*, 118.   [130] Hoggart, *Uses of Literacy*, 121.
[131] Goldthorpe *et al.*, *The Affluent Worker in the Class Structure*, 103.

(Barton) Oxford, for example, people disliked pushing neighbours, dirty houses, unkempt gardens, those with too few or too many children, the over-religious and the 'hoity-toity' and those who had quarrels 'noticeable to an out-sider'. Some unrespectable actions—like 'visits at home from soldiers' or 'going out with the lodgers'—have only local and temporary significance, though the implications are plain enough. Yet within both communities there were actions which could be thought by some respectable, by others not respectable. In St Ebbe's itself there were those who thought it respectable and those who thought it not respectable to live there. It was not respectable to have the neighbours in to gossip, but respectable to talk on the doorstep. It was not respectable to go to a psychologist or psychiatrist, but respectable to go to a doctor or hypnotist. In Barton it was both respectable and not respectable to be connected to the Community Centre (about which there had been many rows). While it was respectable to attend church it was held by some not to be respectable 'to go to the wooden church hut' on the estate. A widespread con-fusion as to what constituted the not respectable (or, as it could be called, 'rough') and what the 'respectable' suggests there were probably three kinds of people, 'rough', 'respectable' and those (the largest number) who were a little of both. The 'rough' tended to be expelled from neighbourly relations, the 'respectable' withdrew into extreme privacy, while the middling group had reasonably friendly relations with each other.[132]

In both traditional and new communities there were certain recurrent points of conflict: gossip, noise, and the behaviour of children especially. It has been suggested that these involved 'class judgements' and were the result of developing social stratification within the working class. There is some truth in this. Fear of gossip and accusations of gossiping were also endemic in tradi-tional communities and inescapable. They were a consequence here, not of stratification, but of an enforced physical intimacy where 'private' life was all too public and gossip intrinsic to sociability. Hostility to gossip, and to gossips, represented an attempt to defend privacy in conditions where that was almost impossible.

Accusations of noisiness were almost as common. In new estates these poss-ibly did have a 'class' character; in the older communities, however, they were the complement to the fear of gossiping. People disliked the neighbours hear-ing their rows, but they also disliked having to listen to the neighbours' rows, however much gossip-fodder they provided. On the new estates hostility to noise-makers was even more overt, and 'noisy neighbours' one of the reasons most often given for wishing to move.[133]

The most persistent source of conflict was children. In both St Ebbe's and Barton, for instance, children were central to unrespectable behaviour.

---

[132] Mogey, *Family and Neighbourhood*, 143–4; Stacey, *Tradition and Change*, 105–6.
[133] Figures given in Chapman, *Home and Social Status*, 157.

Children were such a 'problem' because they subsumed all other 'problems'—particularly noise and gossip. The well-known reluctance to allow the children to mix too freely with the neighbours' children was often due to a fear that the neighbours would 'pump' the children for information about their parents. This both breached privacy and could lead to gossip.[134]

They also worried that their children would pick up 'bad language' from other children in the street.[135] It was partly the 'dirty' nature of the swearing that worried people. In a society where sexual acts were surrounded by guilt and anxiety, anything which represented them in language was also likely to cause anxiety—even, or especially, amongst working-class men whose work-time language depended heavily upon sexual swearing. In this situation the very ubiquity of sexual swearing seems to have increased rather than eliminated the taboos which surrounded it. Children were themselves aware of the taboo-nature of swearing and as ambiguous in their attitudes to it as adults. Marie Paneth recalled a conversation between 'Don' and 'George', two of her Paddington charges:

'Going swimming with us, George', I shouted.
'Not in this f——g cold weather', was the reply.
'You shouldn't have said that', Don corrected him.
'Said what?' came from George's astonished lips.
'You shouldn't say f——g when Miss is here. You mustn't swear', Don explained.
This made me very happy.[136]

The extent of neighbourhood conflict seems to have been governed by two variables. The first was living standards or general sense of well-being. Despite the widely expressed affection for the old neighbourhoods, people were not greatly anxious to stay there. When asked in the 1940s, more housewives from the old neighbourhoods said they wished to move than did women from any other community.[137] A desire to move closely correlated with the quality of housing, which is usually a reasonable proxy for living standards as a whole. The worse the housing the more people wanted to depart; the better the housing the more acceptable the neighbours.

The second variable was social status. Conflict was clearly more acute in the socially mixed areas, as many of the new estates were. People here were significantly more intolerant of the neighbours' children, noise, pets, and general behaviour. Here also expectations of respectability were higher and more stringently policed by public opinion. It was, for example, noted of one Bristol

---

[134] Gorer, *Exploring English Character*, 203. Gorer was surprised at how common this fear was.

[135] Hutchison, *Willesden and the New Towns*, 39–42.   [136] Paneth, *Branch Street*, 112.

[137] Forty-eight per cent of wives living in traditional working-class neighbourhoods said they wished to remain where they were; 53% of wives on the new estates; and 77% of those in privately built housing. This survey was done in Middlesbrough, but similar surveys conducted elsewhere at the same time came to similar conclusions. (Chapman, *Home and Social Status*, 156–9.)

estate where a woman took to heart the local authority's advice to turn the front parlour into a bedroom that 'the remarks and curiosity of her neighbours quickly drove the bed back upstairs again. The strong feeling against having beds in the parlour is based on social prestige. As one of the tenants put it—"It's like the lodging-houses you used to see in St Judes, with the bedstead in the front room." '[138]

Social conflicts were most obvious in the mid and late 1930s when people were re-housed under slum-clearance schemes on existing estates where the established tone was 'respectable'. A number of the slum-clearance estates, rightly or wrongly, became notorious—the Bristol Corporation felt obliged to rename one of the most notorious, the Knowle West estate, as a cosmetic gesture. The result was a substantial migration from the estates of upper-working-class families. In the late 1930s the most important single reason why people left the Bristol estates was dislike of the neighbours:

The mixing of classes in very close proximity is resented for many reasons which were openly stated at the interviews.

One objection was the difficulty of bringing up children decently when those of neighbours often have quite different and unmentionable standards of behaviour and language. Noise, quarrelling of adults, dirt, breakages, gossiping and prying were among other complaints. A sense of isolation also results from living among people whose habits differ from one's own.[139]

The extent to which things complained of were expressed in a rather formulaic vocabulary suggests that complaints were partly phrased according to a received tradition. But, however phrased, they were real enough to the complainants: as two students of the Bristol estates commented, the complaints 'cannot be altered by moralizing'. Apart from a 'general improvement in standards', such conflict could 'only be avoided by grouping houses for tenants in small, though coherent, sub-units'.[140]

But the reverse, axiomatically, was also true. Just as natives on the estates were more sensitive to their new neighbours' shortcomings, so the new neighbours were more sensitive to the natives' 'snobbishness' and 'stand-offishness':

'It's like a strange land in your own country [one woman said]. People are jealous [mistrustful] out here. They're made to be much quieter in a high-class way, if you know what I mean. They get snobbish, and when you get snobbish you're not sociable any more.'[141]

Again, these complaints were rather formulaic and unreflective—only others were 'snobbish', as only others were noisy—but the physical structure of the estates, particularly their low-density housing, as well as a traditionally wary

---

[138] Jevons and Madge, *Housing Estates*, 51–2.   [139] Ibid. 69.
[140] Ibid.   [141] Young and Willmott, *Family and Kinship*, 154.

sociability, encouraged the feeling that neighbours were 'snobbish' rather than that they were merely reserved.

The establishment of 'single-status' areas as a matter of housing policy was not easy, since judgements as to whether people lived in 'mixed' streets or not were often highly subjective. It was noted, for instance, that when people defined a street as 'mixed' they usually considered themselves a cut above its other inhabitants. If asked to choose, they thus chose the class or status to which they thought they rightly belonged. 'Respectable' people wished to move from a 'rough' neighbourhood and 'middle-class' people from a 'working-class' neighbourhood.[142] But finding a large enough group of people whose views of each other and themselves exactly coincided defeated most local authorities.

Despite its obvious potential for conflict there is little evidence that party-politics as such caused it. Throughout the interwar years working-class voters were divided fairly evenly between Labour and non-Labour. Except, therefore, in places like the mining constituencies, where non-Labour voters were now heavily outnumbered, neither Labour nor non-Labour voters were or felt outnumbered, an equilibrium that promoted a sense of political balance. After 1940, and especially after the 1945 general election confirmed the extent to which working-class Conservatism had declined, working-class Conservatives could feel isolated and defensive, though understandably tended to keep quiet about it.

The taboo on talking politics at home reduced conflict, and where politics was discussed, it was usually in places like pubs or clubs according to well-understood conventions. Furthermore, the intensity of political allegiance was normally not strong enough to override these taboos: in both St Ebbe's and Barton it was not respectable even to *belong* to a political party. Though many Labour voters thought Tory voters 'snobbish', the more if they appeared to become Tories on moving to the new estates, their own loyalties to the Labour Party were mostly too tepid for them to worry over-much about other people's political affiliations.

There was, however, one exception to this general rule. In the early 1940s and 1950s there was widespread resentment of those who were understood to have done too well out of the wartime economy or the post-war black market. Whether they were neighbours or relatives, they were disliked, though usually for 'working-class' reasons. After the war at least, middle-class resentment of black marketeers was part of its wider resentment of a cumbersome bureaucratic system thought to be unnecessary and self-defeating. To the working class, the black marketeer or (more often) those who exploited their own scarcity value in the labour market were objectionable because they infringed

---

[142] See the discussion of this in Chapman, *Home and Social Status*, 159–60. There is no evidence of regional variations in these attitudes.

a notion of 'fair shares' to which most still adhered. The 'spiv' was a working-class character, and often half-admired, but his customers were not from the working class—and the working class knew it. In the 1940s people willingly avowed their dislike of those who made money quickly and were inclined to regard them all as spivs. The social psychologist Elizabeth Bott recorded a striking example of this. 'Mrs Jerrold', the wife of an optical instrument repairer, an active member of the Labour Party who was 'in spirit' poor middle-class but 'in practice' poor working-class, said of the 'rich working class':

'Those are the people who have TV, fur coats, rocking horses and cars.' Mrs Jerrold said all this very emphatically. Mr Jerrold looked surprised and said, 'Darling, I didn't know you felt like this', and she said, 'Well I do', and went on with rather a tirade about Covent Garden porters earning £20 a week.[143]

Yet these resentments rarely went beyond verbal emphasis. The comparative fragility of working-class sociability, its caution, homeliness, its tendency to look inwards, served to diminish conflict by personalizing it. Disputes originated in personal and familial rather than in wider social relationships. The strict segregation of 'traditional' working-class family life into men's and women's spheres, though it confined women to a role they could hate, further reinforced taboos against potentially divisive behaviour both within and outside the family.

That working-class sociability had in practice so many limitations caused real difficulties for those who were asked to recall it. People were well aware that the received view of sociability was one of warmth and mutuality and struggled to 'remember' it in those terms. The memories they struggled with could be very intractable:

The fact that no one had much made people more friendly and neighbourly in those days . . . They concerned themselves with each other. Everybody knew everybody else. I had enough of friends with six children, the wife and the garden. Plenty of fun with them. People were more satisfied with simple things then. In the evening we had enough to do looking after the kids and getting them to bed—never had any money to go out with anyway. (Canal maintenance worker, born ca. 1901.)

But what this man is actually recalling is the fact he did *not* see much of the neighbours. And there was always someone prepared to tell home truths.

I lived in Central Street. Don't let them fool you with all this stuff about what a great community it was. You'd have eight or ten families in a street, and they'd all be related somehow, but there might be another family just as big. There's a lot of feuding going on. You'd have friendly neighbours so long as you were in with the family. Otherwise things could be pretty rough.[144]

*

---

[143] Bott, *Family and Social Network*, 181–2, and see also 151.
[144] Forman, *Industrial Town*, 141, 142.

Throughout this period the working-class family was characterized by a strong, sometimes extreme, though slowly weakening, role-segregation. Although both men and women were very domestic, in the sense of homely, men, on the whole, occupied a public world centred upon work, women a private world centred upon the home. They found it very difficult to bring these worlds together. The tension between the two was increased by a man's involvement with work-based peer groups and his wife's with kin, and above all, with her mother. It is possible that the matrilocality of the 'traditional' working class, like so many of its other 'age-old' traditions, was a product of a particular moment—the high marriage rates by young working-class adults in the 1930s and 1940s, at a time of extreme housing shortage, obliged them to live with or near Mum[145]—but none the less these two worlds were almost incompatible. Such role-segregation meant that the working class as a whole had a very fragmented, gender-determined social experience; much more fragmented than (say) the contemporary middle class. Strong role-segregation also had political implications: the domesticated, money-conscious, family-managing working-class wife was much closer to the Conservative Party's ideal of the good citizen than was her husband. Equally, no doubt, the Conservative Party was closer to many working-class wives' ideal of good politics than were its opponents.[146] Furthermore, although the Second World War much changed their material circumstances and for a moment took many working-class men and women 'out of themselves', the conventions of the working-class family continued largely unmodified.

Fragmented social experience was reinforced by the tendency of working-class adults, even of men who worked in industries with powerful 'public' occupational cultures, to personalize political and social relationships, to explain the workings of the world in personal terms; and that was so partly because their own conflicts were seen largely in domestic, that is, in personal terms. They were much less likely than members of the middle class to give structural or universal explanations for social phenomena. This was to have real significance in the development of working-class politics.

Between the sociability of the 'traditional' and 'new' working class there was, in fact, little difference. Sociability always depended upon physical proximity, either of kin, who were all around you, or of a neighbourhood with its immediate amenities and chance relationships. If you lived near kin and on top of everybody else you were likely to be sociable; if not, you were unlikely to be sociable. Working-class sociability actually tended to be thin, driven by a search for privacy which in turn led to social withdrawal.

---

[145] M. Anderson, 'The Social Implications of Demographic Change', in F. M. L. Thompson (ed.), *The Cambridge Social History of Britain, 1750–1950*, 3 vols. (paperback ed., Cambridge, 1993), ii. 59.

[146] D. Jarvis, 'Mrs Maggs and Betty: The Conservative Appeal to Women Voters in the 1920s', *Twentieth Century British History*, v. 2 (1994).

Withdrawal was also a result of conflict. Conflict, sometimes violent, was inherent both to working-class families and neighbourhoods; and, since the origin of these conflicts was usually social or economic, they could not easily be eliminated. Social withdrawal, therefore, was one way of avoiding, if not eliminating them. Another was to ban subjects like politics in circumstances where they were likely to cause conflict. The middle classes, of course, did the same thing, but for a different purpose. The increasingly apolitical nature of middle-class sociability was designed to permit a middle-class regrouping whose purpose was fundamentally political and public. Amongst the working classes an apolitical sociability was designed simply to make life worth living. This difference, however, was one of the reasons why the middle classes practised politics with more aggression and conviction, and a stronger sense of class unity, than the working classes.

Education and Mobility

THERE were few things in England less class-neutral than its educational system, or more problematic than social mobility. This chapter examines the development of 'state' education until the early 1950s, the nature and standing of the public schools, the growth of the universities and their relationship to wider society. It looks at the comparative failure of technical education, the function of intelligence testing, and the beginnings of the movement for comprehensive schooling. It also assesses the degree to which, if at all, education promoted social mobility.

1 | Educating democracy

The great majority of the English were educated by the state, if we can speak of a system which was carefully designed to be neither as centralized nor as uniform as 'state education'. The state decreed at what age children could leave school, and it gave financial assistance directly to some secondary schools and indirectly to both elementary and maintained secondary schools, but the structure of education was the responsibility of the local education authorities. The consequence was that both provision and organization differed widely from one authority to another. Aside from these variations, the educational system was marked by a fundamental cleavage between the 'voluntary' and 'maintained' schools. This was a result of the awkward compromise reached in the nineteenth century whereby those schools controlled by the Church of England (and later the Roman Catholic church) retained their independence and, in the case, of the Anglican schools, a monopoly of the elementary education in the areas they served. They received local authority assistance, but always less than the maintained schools; such comparative lack of provision was particularly marked in the rural areas, where a majority of elementary schools were voluntary. Britain thus had no 'national' system of state education and the history of this period is the history of a failed attempt to create one.

The first legislative modification of the pre-1914 system, the 1918 Education Act (the so-called 'Fisher Act', named after its author, the Liberal president of the Board of Education, H. A. L. Fisher), declared that its aim was indeed a 'national system of public education' which was to be achieved by compulsion. Before 1914 the Board of Education had few powers to enforce legislation; it could in practice only advise local authorities on what they were supposed to do. The Fisher Act, and this was its main long-term significance, imposed duties on authorities which the board (if it wished) could enforce. It had two main provisions: the raising of the school leaving age and the establishment of compulsory 'continuing' education. Although in 1918 the nominal school leaving age was 14, the existence of 'exemptions', the right of a boy or girl to leave school before 14 if appropriate work could be found meant that for nearly half England's schoolchildren the leaving age was actually 13 and often 12. The effect of abolishing exemptions (done in 1921) was to convert the nominal leaving age into an actual one. Fisher was also aware that for many children the last two years in school were effectively wasted: nothing of significance was taught to pupils who were anxious only to leave. The Act, therefore, obliged local authorities to devise instruction fitted to the 'ages, abilities, and requirements' of children in their last two years at school.

The most innovative of Fisher's proposals was for compulsory continuation schooling. Local authorities were required to provide 'a sufficient supply of continuation schools' which were to teach 'suitable courses of study, instruction and physical training' to all children between 14 and 16 for (eventually) 320 hours per year. It envisaged making continuation schooling compulsory to the age of 18 by 1925. These proposals were the result of a number of influences. The most powerful was the First World War itself. It seemed to confirm pre-war fears that England was producing an under-educated workforce unable to compete with its rivals, and the enactment of continuing education was seen as a response to the 'problem' of technical education. In addition, the provisions of the Act were influenced by the developing psychological notion of 'adolescence' as a difficult transitional phase between childhood and adulthood when children needed special guidance and discipline. But the proposals were also evasive. Fisher refused to redefine secondary education (as the Labour Party wanted) and hoped that the continuation schools, and the new central schools and special classes, would somehow expand secondary schooling within an unreformed school system. The result of this was that until 1944 'secondary' education meant, in effect, grammar-school education and was necessarily confined to a relatively small number of children.

Apart from the abolition of exemptions and an assertion of the Board of Education's potential authority, none of Fisher's school reforms survived.[1] It was

[1] A related reform, the establishment in 1920 of the Burnham Committee (named after its first chairman, Lord Burnham) which negotiated teachers' salary scales did, however, survive. Another, less openly acknowledged reform also survived. Fisher recommended that mentally or physically handicapped children should receive separate instruction. The result of this regulation was to

known that many employers, particularly in the staple industries, were hostile to compulsory continuation schooling—those whom Arthur Henderson, a former president of the board himself, called 'certain sinister industrial interests'—and they were not mollified by the compromises reached before the bill was enacted. It seems unlikely that they would ever have complied except under the strongest compulsion.[2] In any case, the costs of the Act far exceeded what government was prepared to pay. The budget of the Board of Education was under constant attack throughout 1921 and the 'Geddes Axe' (1922), which further reduced funding for education, finally destroyed it.

The Fisher Act failed almost completely to establish a 'national system of public education'; the pre-1914 system, therefore, remained largely intact. Its basis was the 'all-in' elementary school (what contemporaries called 'board' or 'council' schools) in which 75 per cent of England's children had the whole of their education. The physical and intellectual quality of the elementary schools varied widely. In prosperous areas provision was usually adequate and class sizes 30–40; in poorer areas the elementary schools were inadequate in almost every way.

They are gaunt, bleak buildings . . . It is difficult to conceive anything less like the place in which a normal child would choose to spend his time than the waterless, treeless waste of most school playgrounds. The exteriors of the building are oddly lacking in character, and the interiors are horribly restless to the eye. Walls are broken by wooden partitions fretted by small panes of glass, by cupboards, radiators, blackboards, teachers' overalls, government posters, sewing machines, and unhappy specimens of the animate world, caged in jam jars and fancy vases.[3]

The rural schools were doubly disadvantaged: they drew their pupils from relatively poor agricultural districts where local authority income and expenditure was nearly always lower than in the towns, and a disproportionate number were 'voluntary' schools whose level of provision was invariably lower than in maintained schools. The rural schools also reflected the living conditions of their surroundings: they often lacked running water or proper sanitation, heat or light. With their crumbling asphalt playgrounds, the buildings frequently in an off-putting gothic, the schoolrooms decorated with a somewhat desperate cheerfulness,[4] they formed a large proportion of the notorious

'greatly increase the readiness of middle-class parents to send their children to elementary schools to receive an "efficient" education rather than an "inefficient one" at a private school'. (G. A. N. Lowndes, *The Silent Social Revolution* (London, 1937), 164–5.)

[2] There was also a good deal of parental opposition. For the case of the LCC, where the battle for continuation schools was 'won and lost', see G. Bernbaum, *Social Change and the Schools* (London, 1967), 30–2. By the mid-1920s only Rugby authority was operating continuation schools as required by the Act.

[3] Jephcott, *Girls Growing Up*, 43.

[4] See the description of a village elementary school in H. M. Burton, *The Education of the Countryman* (London, 1943), 24–8: 'Various devotional and patriotic pictures, dating from the days when

'black-list', those schools whose conditions were officially admitted to be unacceptable. The comparatively inferior provision of so many of the elementary schools was inevitable. The 'elementary code' prescribed lower levels of spending for them than for the grammar schools and so ensured that their class sizes would be bigger, their facilities worse and their teachers less well paid and well qualified.

Despite the general failure of the 1918 Act a system whose core was the unreformed council school might have limped on had it not been for the unexpected demand for 'secondary' (i.e. grammar-school) education immediately after the First World War. Although this demand slackened in the early 1920s, it made inescapable the question which Fisher had avoided—the secondary schools and their apparent paucity. The 1918 Act left England with two kinds of 'secondary' education, which ran in parallel. Most children received such secondary education as they had in the all-age elementary schools. In smaller ones there was no distinction between primary and secondary education: pupils worked their way, standard by standard, often hating every minute of it, until they felt it was time to leave.[5] In large elementary schools, upper or senior classes (often called 'higher tops') were organized where children from 12 to 14 received schooling which was meant to differ from conventional elementary education. In those elementary schools which took in children from other schools at age 12, higher tops were usually called 'senior classes'. Many authorities had established 'central schools' (as Fisher had recommended)—in effect, middle schools—where children remained three or four years. Some were selective and admitted children at an eleven-plus examination; others, beginning at about standard v, simply admitted all children from a number of neighbouring schools. In some cases the central schools were departments appended to existing elementary schools.

There was no uniformity about this 'advanced instruction': in one large administrative area most or all of these methods could be found. Authorities differed widely in the way they organized secondary education. In 1925 the Consultative Committee to the Board of Education found nine different types—from highly selective systems like London and Bradford, to Durham which provided only 'higher tops', to Leicester which built a large number of central schools for 'more gifted' children not going to grammar school, and separate senior classes for the rest. Overall provision of advanced instruction was both thin and patchy. In 1923–4 only 5.4 per cent of all children at elementary school were in the senior classes or their equivalent, but this average concealed significant variations. The figure was 8.5 per cent for London and

both church and Empire were more readily accepted as ruling principles in the lives of the young are met with in school after school, but of late years they have grown a little pale beside the excellent posters of the Empire Marketing Board and the Post Office.'

[5] For this dislike of school, see Slater and Woodside, *Patterns of Marriage*, 65.

the larger towns, 7.4 per cent in county boroughs, but only 2.7 per cent in the predominantly rural authorities.[6]

'Secondary' education stood apart from elementary education, even where advanced instruction was taught. Children might go from elementary school to secondary school at 11-plus, but once the great sorting-out had been done there was almost no movement from one type of school to another. Contemporaries understood by secondary education the grammar schools (or County or County High Schools as they were sometimes known) and, where they existed, the junior technical schools. Both were prized, but for different reasons. A grammar school education was becoming essential for admission to 'middle-class' occupations, while the junior technical schools gave a superior vocational education popular with working-class parents. The scarcity of the technical schools[7] and the reluctance of the grammar schools to teach specifically vocational subjects resulted in a large semi-state, semi-private system of vocational schools as an adjunct to both elementary and secondary schools. These were the technical colleges, trade schools, and night schools established by the local authorities and the privately owned commercial colleges, like the ubiquitous Pitman's, which taught basic 'commerce' and accounting, and shorthand and typing.

Local authorities were under almost constant parental pressure to increase the number of places at secondary schools and demand usually exceeded supply. This demand (and the political consequences of not meeting it) would in itself have probably compelled the board to fill the vacuum left by the failure of the 1918 Act to redefine and expand secondary education, but the growing importance of the Labour Party forced its hand. The Labour movement had always favoured wider access to the secondary schools and the abolition of those constraints which it believed excluded large numbers of working-class children from them. The Labour Party had been critical of the 1918 Act for the over-modesty of its ambitions; it also disliked the central schools as attempts to procure a grammar school education on the cheap. In 1922 the Party published *Secondary Education for All* (largely written by R. H. Tawney), a widely read and forceful statement of what was to be Labour's official position on secondary education. Tawney argued for the elimination of the existing parallel system of schooling ('educationally unsound and socially obnoxious') and its supersession by one in which all children proceeded from primary to secondary school. Primary schooling would end at 11 or 12; secondary at 16 or 18. No more central schools were to be built and secondary school fees gradually

---

[6] There is a comprehensive analysis of the structure of English advanced and secondary education in the *Report of the Consultative Committee on the Education of the Adolescent* [Sir W. H. Hadow chmn.] (HMSO, 1927), 47–64. Hereafter cited as Hadow Report.

[7] In 1936 there were only 134 technical schools, of which 37 were trade schools. Of the trade schools, only ten were outside London. (O. Banks, *Parity and Prestige in English Education* (London, 1955), 105.)

abolished. Tawney did not envisage the same secondary schooling for all. 'There is no question', he wrote, '. . . of imposing on all children the kinds of secondary education which are most common to-day.'[8] What he wanted was for all children to have an equal chance of finding the secondary education most 'suited' to them. *Secondary Education for All* was not, in fact, a particularly original document, and it represented predominant opinion within education itself.[9] It also stood for preponderant opinion within the Labour Party, but not all opinion. By proposing a secondary system organized around the existing grammar and technical schools Tawney, by implication, adhered to selection and, so, exclusion. For those in the Labour Party who saw secondary education as a 'broad highway', where all advanced together, this was unacceptable.

The president of the Board of Education in the first Labour Government (1924), C. P. Trevelyan, had only a limited opportunity to implement Labour's policies. He increased the number of free places at grammar schools, encouraged local authorities to raise the school leaving age to 15 (though did not require them to do so) and reversed the expenditure cuts imposed in 1922, the Geddes Axe. More important, he remitted to the chairman of the Consultative Committee of the Board of Education, Sir Henry Hadow, his predecessor's proposal that it 'consider and report upon the organization, objective and curriculum of courses of study suitable for children who will remain in full-time attendance at schools, other than Secondary Schools, up to the age of 15 . . .';[10] to do, in effect, what Fisher felt unable to do in 1918.

The Hadow Report, on which Tawney and Percy Nunn were the dominating influences,[11] recommended the abolition of the all-age elementary schools, and their replacement by two distinct forms of public education, 'primary' and 'post-primary', the one to end and the other to begin at 11-plus.[12] The Report suggested five possible types of post-primary education: the existing secondary grammar schools which followed 'a predominantly literary or scientific curriculum'; existing central schools which gave at least four years teaching from 11-plus 'with a realistic or practical trend in the last two years'; existing non-selective central schools, senior classes, central departments, higher tops, etc., where local conditions precluded any other form of post-primary education; junior technical and trade schools. Above all, it wanted all children leaving primary school to attend 'another institution with a

---

[8] Quoted in R. Barker, *Education and Politics, 1900–1951* (Oxford, 1972), 54.

[9] Ibid. 43–4.

[10] The remit was referred to the Committee on 1 Feb. 1924 by Trevelyan, but the original decision to commission the Report was taken by his predecessor as president, Edward Wood (later Lord Irwin, later still Lord Halifax).

[11] Nunn had been professor of education at the University of London since 1913 and was later director of the Institute of Education, London.

[12] Hadow Report, 71–2.

distinctive staff, and organized definitely for post-primary education'.[13] To encourage movement between schools the Committee recommended that they should all have a common curriculum until the last two years, and that there should be a supplementary examination at 13-plus. They concluded that it was the age at which children typically left that should determine the school's organization and curriculum. Thus they proposed an expansion of the central schools (where children normally left at 15) rather than the secondary schools (where they normally left at 16), since children leaving at 15 mostly required a less academic curriculum. Many of them

feel ill at ease in an atmosphere of books and lessons, and are eager to turn to some form of practicable and constructive work ... [Education] must recognize that there are many minds, and minds by no means of an inferior order, for which the most powerful stimulus for development is some form of practicable or constructive activity. The work of the school must not seem, as sometimes perhaps it still does, the antithesis of 'real life' but the complement of it.[14]

The leaving examination in post-primary schools should, therefore, be less rigid than in secondary schools and their curricula tailored to fit local conditions.[15] The Report also recommended changes in nomenclature: all secondary schools (other than technical schools) should be known as grammar schools, a name which 'links the newer developments of secondary education to an ancient and dignified tradition of culture', central schools be known as 'modern schools' (which was as close as the Committee could get to the German word *Realschulen*), and other post-primary departments known as 'senior classes'. Elementary schools, it suggested, should be called primary schools and the elementary code be revised to exclude post-primary schools, which would henceforth come under the secondary code.

The Report, though generally thought to be innovative, made heavy weather of its reforms. A post-primary education with five variations was overcomplicated and, in any case, merely formalized a rather messy status quo. The Committee could have proposed a secondary education based upon grammar, technical, and modern schools, but it was anxious not to 'obscure distinctions'[16] between the grammar schools and other forms of post-primary teaching. Nothing should be done, the Report said, to hinder the development of 'secondary' education whose growth 'in the last twenty years has been one of the most remarkable movements of our day'.[17] Nor, it continued, should there be competition between the secondary schools and the new post-primary education. In this recommendation lay the embryo of the doctrine of 'parity of

[13] Hadow Report, 79–80.   [14] Ibid. 84.
[15] This was also the Board of Education's view. See Board of Education, *Suggestions for the Consideration of Teachers and Others Concerned in the Work of the Public Elementary Schools* (HMSO, 1923), 41.
[16] Banks, *Parity and Prestige*, 122.   [17] Hadow Report, 80–1.

esteem' which underpinned the 1944 Education Act. Hadow devised proposals which preserved the unique status of the grammar schools while recognizing that the all-age elementary schools were no longer defensible.

The extent to which the grammar school was to be protected (though not altogether intentionally) can be seen in the legislation of the second Labour government (1929). The Hadow Report had recommended that the school leaving age be raised to 15 by 1932. The then Conservative government declined either to enforce or finance the change and on that Labour 'took its stand'.[18] Trevelyan's 1930 bill was primarily concerned with the school leaving age and hardly at all with the organization of the school system. In fact, the bill foundered not on the issue of secondary education, which might have been expected, but on a much older and equally fraught issue—the position of the voluntary, and particularly, the Roman Catholic schools. The raising of the school leaving age would inevitably have imposed new costs on the already straitened voluntary sector. Further state assistance to the voluntary schools, however, without a corresponding increase in local authority control was unacceptable to nonconformists and those who aspired to a wholly secular system. Long negotiations between the board, the churches, and the local authorities were fruitless and the government decided to introduce legislation confined to raising the age of school-leaving and the provision of maintenance grants.[19] On 21 January 1931, however, an amendment moved by John Scurr, Labour MP for Mile End and spokesman for the Catholic Church in the House of Commons, which would have delayed the bill until the voluntary schools were guaranteed what they thought to be adequate funding, was carried. The following month the bill in its entirety was defeated in the House of Lords. Trevelyan felt obliged to resign and his successor, H. B. Lees Smith, was unable to use the Parliament Act to secure legislation of any sort before the government fell in August 1931.

The Trevelyan bill was defeated by two interests: the voluntary schools, and those afraid that the bill would compromise the grammar schools (as the Conservatives did). It was these interests which made the attainment of a 'national system of public education' so difficult. They were also the reason why the 1936 Education Act introduced by the National Government was so limited in its scope. This Act would have raised the school leaving age to 15 on 1 September 1939, except where children could be 'exempted'. But the scale of exemptions was so huge—*The Times* calculated that 86 per cent of children would be eligible—that the Act was, as the Labour MP James Chuter Ede argued, 'not really a Bill for raising the school leaving age [so much as] a Bill for regulating

---

[18] Barker, *Education and Politics*, 58.

[19] For details of Trevelyan's bill and its travails, see D. W. Dean, 'Difficulties of a Labour Educational Policy: The Failure of the Trevelyan Bill, 1929–1931', *British Journal of Educational Studies*, 17 (1969), 293–8.

the entry of children into employment'.[20] The day on which the Act was to come into force Germany invaded Poland; it was suspended when Britain declared war, and its provisions, such as they were, were overtaken by the war and the 1944 Education Act.

With the failure of the 1930 and 1936 education bills the Hadow system was thus the régime which operated until the outbreak of war. As a statement of educational good practice, the Report was generally welcomed. It was supported by the Conservative president of the board at the time of its publication, Lord Eustace Percy, by his civil servants, and by educational opinion.[21] But it never had sufficient funding. The result was that by 1934 only a bare majority of 11-plus children were attending reorganized schools and, as always, there were marked regional variations. In the County of London, for instance, 80 per cent of children went to reorganized schools, but in the rural authorities the great majority of schools remained un-reorganized. Furthermore, the senior classes and central schools continued within the elementary code and all its comparative disadvantages. In the 1930s the average annual cost of buildings in the elementary schools was £35 14s per pupil; in the secondary schools it was £103. There was almost the same disproportion in teacher–pupil ratios and teachers' salaries. That alone, as contemporaries were aware, made the grammar schools very much more desirable than other post-primary education.[22]

Furthermore, the Report, by insisting on such a visible distinction between the grammar schools and the rest, fixed in place the eleven-plus examination, and in the minds of parents the belief that its purpose was not, as Hadow hoped, allocation but competition, where many were called but few chosen. For families the eleven-plus (then often termed the 'scholarship examination') was frequently an ordeal, as distressing to parents as to their children. The habit, common in many elementary schools, of reading out in assembly the names of the successful made failure even more painful and unforgettable. Working-class girls, for whom elementary school was often otherwise a blur, had clear memories of the scholarship examination 'and *exactly* why they failed'.[23] For elementary schools, particularly those without academic traditions, success was a public triumph. When in 1935 a boy at the Popham Road LCC elementary school (Islington) won a junior county scholarship (the first since the early 1920s), the whole school was gathered to hear his achievement lauded by a school governor, who gave him half-a-crown and the school a half-holiday.[24]

[20] *House of Commons Debates [HCD]*, 308, 5.s. 1231 (13 Feb. 1936).
[21] G. A. N. Lowndes, for example, a good representative of moderately progressive educational opinion, was strongly pro-Hadow. (Lowndes, *Silent Social Revolution*, 118.)
[22] G. R. Leybourne and K. White, *Education and the Birth-Rate* (London, 1940), 101.
[23] Jephcott, *Rising Twenty*, 98.
[24] Private information to the author. See Young and Willmott, *Family and Kinship*, 175. See also Mrs Last's comment: 'I saw in the *Sunday Express* that, after the war, *all* children will have a chance of a secondary school education. I sincerely hope it is so. When I look back on the struggle to get the

The eleven-plus had its inevitable consequences. Curricula in those schools which could expect at least some success in the examination became increasingly dominated by its requirements, and that often led to the streaming of the larger elementary schools, with the top stream becoming an informal preparatory school for the scholarship examination. Parents who could afford it sensibly resorted to coaching. The atmosphere in the schools could thus become very competitive: 'We didn't have friends, we only had rivals' one girl recalled.[25] This was all a long way from the non-competitive, meritocratic procedure envisaged by the Hadow Committee. In 1940, after contemplating the record of its (and his) handiwork, Tawney wrote that the country was 'witnessing . . . the nemesis of a plutocratic educational system'.[26]

Hadow's emphasis upon the academic nature of the grammar school (which in part represented the force of the public schools as a model) tended to freeze their curricula, while in practice depreciating the value of the more flexible curricula in the other post-primary schools. A comparison of the timetables of boys' grammar schools between the 1890s and early 1950s shows surprisingly little change.[27] The effect of this emphasis upon the girls' grammar schools, however, was more benign. They had always been reluctant to adopt curricula which significantly differed from those of the boys' schools, or to work on the assumption that their pupils' life-chances differed much from boys'. The schools resisted (often ingeniously) attempts to compel them to teach for marriage or motherhood, and were usually more interested in the university than in the marital successes of their pupils. When they were forced to teach domestic science, it was usually made clear to girls that it was not a serious subject. 'It was regarded', one girl recalled, 'as a bit of a play . . . It was a sort of afternoon when we weren't at School as it were.'[28] Furthermore, the Board of Education itself was reluctant to promote gender-distinctions within secondary schools. Differentiation

must not be such as to impede the Secondary School in its task of giving a good general education both to girls and to boys. To say this is not to pre-judge the question whether the most suitable medium of such an education may not differ in some respects for the two sexes. It means merely that the primary aim ought not to be sacrificed to the desire to provide for what are thought to be the special interests of girls, though use should be made of those special interests in arranging the curriculum.[29]

two boys into the Grammar School and recall how so many of my friends' cleverer children failed the exam, I think again how poor the "scholarship" system was.' (*Nella Last's War*, 248.)

[25] Jackson and Marsden, *Education and the Working Class*, 87.

[26] Introduction to Leybourne and White, *Education and the Birth-Rate*, 12.

[27] Campbell, *Eleven Plus*, 136–48. The Comparisons are based upon the timetables of a number of boys' and girls' grammar schools in London.

[28] P. Summerfield, 'Cultural Reproduction in the Education of Girls: A Study of Girls' Secondary Schooling in Two Lancashire Towns, 1900–1950', in F. Hunt (ed.), *Lessons for Life: The Schooling of Girls and Women, 1850–1950* (Oxford, 1987), 155–8.

[29] Board of Education, *Report of the Consultative Committee on Differentiation of the Curriculum for Boys and Girls Respectively in Secondary Schools* (HMSO, 1923), 130–2.

The curriculum, it thought, might be made sufficiently open not only to allow girls to learn womanly things but to encourage boys to study more 'aesthetic subjects', like music. The result was much less sexual stereotyping in the girls' grammar schools than in the central or other post-primary schools where, if anything, it increased under Hadow.

Despite this, the value of the academic curricula of both boys' and girls' grammar schools was by the mid-1930s widely doubted. Apart from their inflexibility, they were thought to be too much dominated by an examination, the 'matric', which was useless for most pupils though good for the schools' reputation, and they led (it was argued) to persistent overworking of school-children, particularly girls.[30] In February 1936, during debates on the 1936 education bill, the House of Commons (remarkably) carried without a division a resolution moved by E. A. Radford, Conservative MP for Rusholme, that grammar school children were overburdened by homework 'at the expense of rest and recreation'. The former Labour president of the board, H. B. Lees Smith, said that it was 'undoubtedly the case that overpressure is the curse of secondary education'. No pupil could escape it once the school certificate and the matriculation examination had been made 'one and the same':

That development has been a disaster. As a result of it schools are judged by the number of matriculation successes that they can put before the public . . . Therefore, the whole system of secondary education is dominated by this pressing of children between 16 and 17 into passing a university entrance examination the standard age of which is 18.[31]

Furthermore, the apparent rigidity of the grammar school syllabus seemed to violate developments in pedagogical theory while in practice preparing girls and boys who were not going on to university only for minor clerical posts—and even those, since the schools did not teach typing or shorthand, badly.[32] The increasing popularity of child-centred education—much of it borrowed from American educational psychology—the notion of 'learning by doing' rather than learning by dictation, had much influenced the elementary schools[33] and the Board of Education, which actively encouraged it. In the important statement *The Teaching of English in England* (1921), it argued that education 'proceeds not by the presentation of lifeless facts but by teaching the student to follow the different lines on which life may be explored and pro-

---

[30] See G. A. Morrison MP in the House of Commons, HCD, 308, 5.s. 1018–19 (12 Feb. 1936). See also the Board of Education's comment on girls' secondary schools: 'The special danger of girls' schools is that they may become excellently organised and conscientiously loyal groups composed of mediocre and uniform units. Conscientiousness is a virtue; but in the world of education it may also be a vice, alike in the teacher and taught.' (*Committee on Differentiation of the Curriculum*, xv.)

[31] HCD, 308, 5.s. 1066 (12 Feb. 1936).

[32] M. Anderson, *The Missing Stratum: Technical School Education in England, 1900–1990s* (London, 1994), 68.

[33] Lowndes, *Silent Social Revolution*, 170–1.

ficiency in living may be obtained'.[34] In taking this view, however, the board was probably less impressed by American theory than by the widespread, home-grown reaction to the dreary rote-learning which had characterized the policy of 'payment by results'.

It was in this context (1938) that the Consultative Committee under a new chairman, Will Spens, master of Corpus Christi College, Cambridge, completed an examination of the Hadow system. The Spens Report was a significant advance on Hadow and in many ways anticipated the 1944 Education Act. The Report, which concluded that reforms had to be more 'radical' than hitherto, had three main recommendations, and one non-recommendation which is in retrospect the most interesting. The Committee accepted that the curricula of the grammar schools were over-dominated by university entrance. Courses for the 85 per cent of pupils who left at 16 should be complete in themselves; there should be more emphasis on English composition and comprehension and recent history; there should be less emphasis on maths and more on general science and the acquisition of a reading knowledge of at least one foreign language. It accepted the view that the secondary schools had been uncoupled from their communities and argued that, particularly in rural areas, courses should be adjusted to the economic and social nature of these communities.

The Report (secondly) recommended the simplification of post-primary education. It suggested the establishment of a tripartite secondary education organized around grammar schools, technical high schools, and modern schools. The first two were to be selective, but the technical high schools would not normally have a sixth form and would be attached as departments to local technical colleges.

It recommended (thirdly) that all three types of secondary school should come under the secondary code, with similar standards in class size, school buildings, and salary scales. 'Parity of esteem' was thus now formally urged as an aim of educational policy: the technical high schools should be 'in every respect equal in status to grammar schools', and everything should be done 'to secure parity of status' between all three schools.[35]

The notion of parity had been implicit in Hadow but could scarcely be explicit, given the scale of difference between its proposed types of post-primary education. It was explicit in Spens because the Committee had at length and with some reluctance rejected the idea of 'multilateral schools'.[36] The Spens Committee was the first official body to consider multilateralism and recognize the social and educational arguments which favoured it.

[34] Quoted in Bernbaum, *Social Change and the Schools*, 87–90.
[35] *Report of the Consultative Committee on Secondary Education with Special Reference to Grammar Schools and Technical High Schools* (London, HMSO, 1938) (hereafter Spens Report), xxvii, xxxvi.
[36] Spens Report, xix–xxii.

Having rejected it, however, the Committee was obliged to provide an alternative in which parity of status could be presented convincingly; an alternative where the 'multilateral idea' could be 'inherent' in the educational system as a whole.

By the outbreak of the Second World War, though certain 'systemic' elements had been introduced into English state education, it remained fragmented and, at least at the level of the elementary school, without central direction. 'The only uniformity of practice', the Board of Education wrote

that [the Board] desire[s] to see in the teaching of Public Elementary Schools is that each teacher shall think for himself and work out for himself, such methods of teaching as may use his powers to the best advantage and be best suited to the particular needs and conditions of the school. Uniformity in details of practice . . . is not desirable even if it were attainable.[37]

Nor did the board see the purpose of elementary education other than in the most general way:

The purpose of the Public Elementary School is to form and strengthen the character and to develop the intelligence of the children entrusted to it, and to make the best use of the school years available, in assisting both girls and boys, according to their different needs, to fit themselves, practically as well as intellectually, for the work of life.[38]

To the extent that elementary education had a purpose it was to inculcate 'some knowledge of the growth of free institutions at home and overseas, and some idea of the place of the British story in the story of the world'.[39] Indeed, within this otherwise loose régime, political prescriptions of a generally 'democratic' kind were the most specific. The board was opposed to any form of history teaching which could appear xenophobic or 'Empire-minded', while it was 'scarcely necessary to warn teachers against the misuse of the term "Colonies" as applied to the great Self-Governing Dominions'.[40] The board was especially anxious that teachers should instruct their pupils in the origins and functions of the League of Nations, including a teaching manual on the League in the interwar *Handbooks of Suggestions*. Otherwise the board would only advise: when the 'classics' of English literature might be taught and how; what sort of books should be read by younger students; how far teaching should be vocational; how far history or geography should be taught within a local or neighbourhood context.

Although this was a liberal and well-intended régime, more or less designed to fit the majority of pupils for the life they were likely to lead, it gave them a rather sketchy and uncoordinated education:

---

[37] Spens Report, xxxvi.

[38] Board of Education, *Handbook of Suggestions for the Consideration of Teachers and Others concerned in the Work of Public Elementary Schools* (HMSO, 1927), 3, 8.

[39] Ibid. 122–3.   [40] Board of Education, *Suggestions for the Consideration of Teachers* (1923), 85 n.

They have half an hour's Scripture, when they read the parable of the Good Samaritan, learn a verse by heart, and discuss with the teacher which is the more important of the two great commandments. Then they have an arithmetic lesson with the same teacher, and work at written problems connected with percentages. They go on to a lesson on Christopher Columbus when they follow a coloured wall map but use no text-book. The class is dismissed, drinks its bottles of milk, and goes out to the playground for ten minutes. The girls come back to the same room, with the same teacher, for a debate on President Roosevelt. Various people are called out to address the class and make halting and unhappy speeches. [After an hour and a half's break] the girls come back to a lesson on letter writing when they are shown how to write an application for a post. Literature, singing and netball, the latter taken in the playground by another teacher, comprise the rest of the day's lessons.[41]

The day was further broken up by 'endless distractions'—the dinner money, the nurse, the milk money collector and entertainments.

In its guidance for the elementary schools the board was much more willing to see a gender-differentiated syllabus than it was for the secondary schools. Its ruling assumptions were that working-class girls had different aptitudes from working-class boys as well as different life-roles. Girls, for example, preferred the 'descriptive' rather than the 'scientific'. Thus, when instructing girls, the teacher of geography should eschew science and emphasize food supply, clothing, dress, ornaments, etc.[42] Gender-differentiation demanded not only that girls should be taught 'useful' subjects, like cooking, but be taught generally in a 'female' manner. There was, of course, a fundamental class dimension to such differentiation: the higher the social class the more the board thought it necessary for boys and girls to have a similar education.

The state, however, had a clearer conception of what the middle classes should learn. The code prescribed the teaching of English language and literature, history, geography, at least one other language than English, maths and science (both 'theoretical' and 'practical'), drawing, housewifery for girls, and for both boys and girls manual work and physical education. To the degree that this prescription was modified it was, if anything, to make the schools even more 'academic'. Housewifery was, as we have seen, either absent or treated unseriously; the sciences emphasized theory rather than practice; and the syllabus, while more flexible and 'modern' than that of the independent schools, like them accorded prestige to the teaching of classics. They inclined, even the newer and self-consciously innovative secondary schools like Raynes Park in outer London, to follow the independent schools in organization and ethos: 'houses', 'house colours', prefects, uniforms, teachers in gowns.[43]

[41] Jephcott, *Girls Growing Up*, 44–5.

[42] Board of Education, *Suggestions for the Consideration of Teachers* (1923), 41, 83–4.

[43] For Raynes Park, see Vaughan, *Something in Linoleum*, 95–185. The school also played rugby rather than football, but had a school song whose words were composed by the left-wing poet W. H. Auden.

The Spens Report was the bridge upon which educational policy proceeded from Hadow to the Butler Act of 1944. Its recommendations went far beyond the timid provisions of the 1936 Act, but like that Act, the Report was swept away by the Second World War. Unlike many other parts of English society, state education was immediately affected by the war; indeed for many people the closing of the schools was one of the few ways the war had at first much impact. As two observers of the evacuation noted, 'It is entirely in keeping with the character of modern war that before the enemy had achieved any success on the field he had effected a complete dislocation of the English educational system.' Under the government's evacuation arrangements schools in 'evacuating districts' (principally London and the major conurbations) were closed and transferred, teachers and pupils, to 'receiving districts', located usually in the country or in provincial towns. The result was at best muddle and at worst disaster. About one million children were not evacuated, and they were left to their own devices: 'In the towns the children played in the streets—innocently or mischievously accordingly to bent—or stayed in bed till noon and toured the dance-halls, cinemas, and pin tables by night.'[44] In some districts, particularly in London, where 'education suddenly disintegrated', there developed a kind of semi-criminal juvenile *bacchanale*. To the public, the extent to which the state schools had hitherto acted as agents of law and order came as a 'revelation'. In rural areas, children 'rambled in the lanes and fields while the authorities searched desperately for any sort of accommodation in which to house them',[45] and their teachers attempted, without much success, to establish relations with the country schools to which they had been allocated. By November 1939 much of the state educational system had collapsed. The interwar years thus ended as they had begun, with the schools closed. In 1919 they closed to halt the spread of influenza; in 1939, to save children from an aerial bombardment which did not come until the majority of them had returned home.

In November 1939, as an alternative to compulsory evacuation, something the government could scarcely have contemplated, schools in the evacuating districts were reopened. Even so there were still some half-million children at large in January 1940, and the following month the president of the board was obliged to restore compulsory schooling. The 1939 evacuation did much to discredit not simply England's social organization, but also its predominant political and administrative institutions, and the board was no more exempt than the ministry of health or the home office. Its civil servants and its president, Herwald Ramsbotham (Conservative MP for Lancaster), were criticized not only for ignorance and incompetence (so were all the 'home-front' ministers), but faced a charge to which they were very sensitive: that they did not

[44] R. Padley and M. Cole, *Evacuation Survey* (London, 1940), 111, 200.
[45] H. C. Dent, *Education in Transition* (London, 1944), 29.

understand what had happened to state education because they educated their own children elsewhere. This probably helps to explain the speed with which they contemplated major reforms of the system. Furthermore, the evacuation and its aftermath undermined both the principles on which education had been previously governed and the board's confidence in defending them. It was this decisive shift in opinion which produced in 1942–3 the extraordinary attack on the system of state schooling by the senior officials of the board—the same men who had had responsibility for public education throughout the interwar years and who had received the Spens Report with so little enthusiasm. The full-time schooling, they wrote, of most of the country's children was in many ways 'seriously defective', and for 90 per cent ended far too soon:

It is conducted in many cases in premises which are scandalously bad. It is imparted in the case of some schools by persons who need have no qualifications to teach anybody anything. It is conducted under statutes and regulations which emphasise social distinctions and which in general make the educational future of the child more dependent on his place of residence and the financial circumstances of his parents than his capacity and promise.[46]

The board's officials and 'informed opinion' began to draft reform proposals within a few months of the war's outbreak. Geoffrey Vickers's supplement to the *Christian News-Letter* (31 January 1940), 'Educating for a Free Society' was widely discussed[47] and prompted the board—which had itself been evacuated to Bournemouth—to draft its own proposals. In the summer of 1941, with the approval of Ramsbotham, these proposals were despatched to interested parties in the so-called *Green Book* which, although intended to be confidential was 'distributed in such a blaze of secrecy that it achieved an unusual degree of publicity'.[48] Ramsbotham (who was moving too fast for Churchill) was replaced in July 1941 by R. A. Butler, on the assumption that he would slow the pace. In fact, Butler, who well understood (rather better than Churchill) the social consequences of the war, was as determined as his predecessor to see legislation passed.[49]

The delay, however, permitted nearly two years of public discussion during which broad agreement developed on the nature of the reforms, most of which, indeed, had been anticipated by Spens. It was accepted that the 'elementary school' should be abolished and replaced by a primary school, though there was no unanimity as to the age at which primary schooling should end.

---

[46] Bernbaum, *Social Change and the Schools*, 105.   [47] Dent, *Education in Transition*, 169–88.

[48] K. Jeffereys, 'R. A. Butler, the Board of Education and the 1944 Education Act', *History* (1984), 417–18. For the response to the *Green Book*, see Dent, *Education in Transition*, 204–15. The list of organizations to which the *Green Book* was sent is in ibid. 204 n.

[49] For Butler, see J. F. Harris, 'Political Ideas and the Debate on State Welfare', in H. L. Smith (ed.), *War and Social Change* (Manchester, 1986), 239–46.

It was also accepted that all forms of post-primary education should be known as 'secondary', should come under the same code and have equality of status and facilities. The 'scholarship' or 'special place' examination, it was agreed, should disappear, though there was less agreement as to whether secondary school fees should be abolished entirely and whether there should be a single secondary school for all children. There was no disagreement that the leaving age should be raised to 15 without exemptions and then to 16 as soon as practicable.

The most contentious issue was, as ever, religion. The churches were as suspicious of the 1944 Act as they had been of the 1930 bill. Any reform would almost certainly impose new costs on the voluntary system, while any further state assistance to the voluntary schools could be unacceptable to the nonconformists. These were real problems for any government; the attitude of the nonconformists had not ruined the 1902 Education Act, but it had contributed to the ruin of the government (Balfour's) which had introduced it. The Roman Catholics, via the 'Scurr Amendment', had effectively derailed Trevelyan's legislation in 1930–1. And a large minority of the country's children—in the rural areas still a majority—were educated in the voluntary schools.

From the end of 1940, the churches had signalled their determination that Christianity was not to be excluded from the legislation they knew to be in train. In December 1940 they argued that 'no permanent peace is possible in Europe unless the principles of the Christian religion are made the foundation of national policy and all social life',[50] a comment which intimated things to come. On 12 February 1941 the archbishops of Canterbury, York, and Wales issued 'Five Points' in which they proposed that a 'Christian education' in practice be made compulsory in all maintained schools. The 'Five Points', and even more the manner of their presentation, were widely criticized ('no intervention', the editor of the *Times Education Supplement* wrote, 'could indeed have been more ill-conceived or ill-timed'). Nevertheless, nearly all of them found their way into legislation. Both Butler and his deputy, Chuter Ede, assured the churches early in negotiations that religion would have a statutory place in any new legislation, and the continuing centrality of religion to public life was demonstrated both during the bill's drafting and its passage through parliament. Butler had been under constant pressure from his Christian colleagues, and almost every speaker in the debates on the bill adverted to religion; indeed, for many, particularly in the House of Lords, religion was clearly its most important component. Butler and Chuter Ede recognized this and carefully adjusted their own speeches to prevailing sentiment. What distinguished the 1944 debates from their predecessors was the relative absence of denom-

[50] *The Times*, 21 Dec. 1940. For the negotiations between the government and the churches before the 1944 Act was passed, see C. Cannon, 'The Influence of Religion on Educational Policy, 1902–1944', *British Journal of Educational Studies*, xii, 2 (May 1964), 144–58.

inational passion. MPs and peers were less anxious to protect denominational rights than to ensure that the 'Christian religion' was inserted into the maintained sector.

The churches and their political agents thus achieved what had previously been impossible. A form of religious instruction was made compulsory in all maintained schools; the 'time-table' clause was abolished, so permitting religion to be taught at any time in the school day; training colleges were required to make teachers competent in the teaching of religion; and the local authorities were obliged to 'contribute to the spiritual development' of schoolchildren. The objections of the Roman Catholics to the bill were largely met by the introduction of a new category of school, 'controlled status', which permitted them to decide the form of religious instruction, even though their schools would now effectively come under local authority supervision.

The success of the churches reflected both the strengths and weaknesses of English Christianity in the 1940s. An ecumenical Christianity was acceptable in 1944 precisely because belief (and therefore an active religious politics) had been replaced by benevolent indifference. But it was also acceptable because of the now ill-defined but still powerful conviction that England was fundamentally a 'Christian' country,[51] a fact which its educational system should recognize. Many among the political élites, furthermore, thought the 1944 Act peculiarly democratic and, not for the first nor the last time, resorted to Christianity to temper what they feared might otherwise have been a dangerous and unpredictable curriculum.

The secular provisions of the bill represented little advance on Spens's proposals. The school leaving age was to be raised unconditionally to 15 within two years; all post-primary schools were to come under the secondary code; and all secondary school fees were to be abolished. The Act, however, said nothing about the organization of the schools. The public schools were excluded from its provisions to await the findings of the Fleming Committee,[52] in order not to provoke Conservative backbenchers ('a stupid lot', Butler called them) and the Act did not prescribe what sort of secondary school the authorities should adopt. Butler was himself not unsympathetic to the so-called 'multilateral school',[53] but the majority of his Party were as anxious to protect the grammar as the public schools, and again their fears had to be appeased.

This awkward lacuna was filled by the Report of the Norwood Committee (1943) which was published ten days after Butler's white paper, *Educational Reconstruction*. Norwood's Committee was a sub-committee of the Secondary Schools' Examination Council (of which Cyril Norwood was chairman) and had been appointed by the Council to consider a possible reform of secondary school examinations. Norwood elected himself chairman of this

[51] See below, pp. 290–1.   [52] For the Fleming Report, see below, pp. 240–1.
[53] For the multilateral school, see below, pp. 231–5.

sub-committee and, also it appears, elected most of its members. The Report was, consequently, very much a product of his own inclinations. He was then president of St John's College, Oxford, had been headmaster of Bristol Grammar School, Marlborough, and Harrow, and a schoolboy at Merchant Taylors'. Though in many ways a generous and liberal-minded educationalist,[54] he was deeply committed to the grammar school and an academically differentiated secondary education.

Norwood's Committee, like Spens's, recommended a tripartite secondary school system and called upon 'general educational experience' to support the recommendation. There were, it argued, three types of children: those who were 'interested in learning for its own sake, who can grasp an argument or follow a piece of connected reasoning'; those whose 'interests lie markedly in the fields of applied science or applied art [and who] often [have] an uncanny insight into the intricacies of mechanism whereas the subtleties of language construction are too delicate for [them]'; and, finally, others who 'deal more easily with concrete things than with ideas . . . abstractions mean little to [them]'. Each of these types needed its own school: grammar, technical, and modern. The Committee thought individual aptitudes sufficiently developed at age 10-plus or 11-plus for children to be allocated then to the appropriate school, though it conceded that there might be a second allocation at age 13-plus. It hoped that movement between schools would be easy and it suggested that for the first two years of their secondary education all children might follow a broadly similar curriculum. It rejected, however, criticisms of the existing grammar school curriculum, insinuating that the 'problem' lay not with the curriculum but with the 'suitability' of children admitted to the over-expanded secondary schools.

In the absence of any direction from the ministry of education (as the board became known after the 1944 Act), the Norwood Report tended to be the unofficial guide to local authorities.[55] It gave a meaning to a selection process which was familiar and it permitted the natural development of an already existing school structure. Both Spens and Norwood emphasized the importance of the secondary technical schools, which were popular with parents and many employers. Yet their number remained consistently small. The grammar schools convinced themselves and the local authorities that they could teach advanced technical subjects within their own curricula; as a result of this, and a genuine doubt as to what exactly constituted technical educa-

---

[54] For a good statement of his views, see Norwood's *The English Tradition of Education* (London, 1929).

[55] Bernbaum argues that the Norwood proposals 'became the officially accepted form of secondary school organisation' (*Social Change and the Schools*, 113). But they were never 'officially' supported by the ministry or parliament. Local authorities followed them either as a *pis aller* or because the proposals happened to suit them. A few did not wish to follow them at all.

tion, the authorities built comparatively few technical high schools. In 1944, what already existed, therefore, was a quasi-bilateral system: grammar schools on one side, all-age schools, senior classes, and higher tops on the other. It was this system which Norwood legitimated. Under this régime the secondary grammar schools were preserved, while the all-age and other schools evolved into the secondary modern schools characteristic of English education between 1944 and 1965. The technical schools did not disappear but their numbers fell and they educated a decreasing proportion of schoolchildren. The failure to expand the technical schools severely weakened the Norwood system, above all, by making 'parity of esteem' impossible. A differentiated secondary education could 'work' only so long as each type of school had equality both of provision *and* status. Spens and Norwood believed that such equality could be achieved, particularly if the technical schools acted as intermediaries between the grammar and modern schools. Without them, however, the huge academic and social gap between the grammar and modern schools became unbridgeable.

What happened to the technical schools? They were obviously marooned even before the Second World War. Hadow estimated that only 0.3 per cent of children aged between 11 and 16 were in junior technical schools, while in the 1930s only 2.6 per cent of boys leaving elementary schools and 1.4 per cent of girls went to the junior technical schools.[56] Given their apparent popularity, these figures ought to surprise. In practice there were many obstacles to their development, or the development of any form of separate technical school.

They were expensive to build and equip, and since they had to be re-equipped regularly, their recurrent costs were high. Furthermore, staff–pupil ratios were, and had to be, lower than in other state schools. In consequence they were small—in the 1930s 54 per cent of them had fewer than 100 pupils— and that made them even more expensive. The fact that they admitted pupils at age 13 and not 11, which put them out of phase with the usual age of selection, though a problem, was less of a problem than their cost. Nor did they have the unanimous support of employers. They were very popular in engineering and construction, but less so in other industries which were content with their own trade schools, apprenticeships, other forms of part-time learning, or no technical learning at all.

They also had their opponents. The defenders of both the grammar schools and the 'senior' elementary schools feared their competition. The political left disliked them because their pupils were confined to the working class and their syllabuses openly vocational. They were thus presumed to be inferior to the grammar schools. This view was held by Chuter Ede, himself a former teacher. For him, the only way to protect the status of the secondary modern

---

[56] For the technical schools, see Anderson, *Missing Stratum*, 38–127.

school—given that selection was to continue—was to allow it to teach technical subjects at a reasonably sophisticated level. Ede was not against technical education; just against separate schools teaching it. It was Ede who struck from the 1944 Act specific reference to technical schools in favour of a clause obliging local educational authorities to offer secondary education of 'sufficient variety'. This was, as Michael Sanderson points out, a fateful step.[57] Though understandable, Ede's view was short-sighted. Working-class boys and girls did not, in fact, get an appropriate education at many of the modern schools. Indeed, they had the worst of both worlds: they went to schools which were even more working-class ghettos than the technical schools but which did not give them the kind of superior vocational grounding they would have had from the old junior technical schools.

The Butler Act, unlike all its interwar predecessors, was introduced according to plan. On 1 April 1945 all post-primary schools came under the secondary code, to the intense satisfaction of their teachers.[58] Exactly two years later, in almost the worst possible circumstances, the school leaving age was raised to 15. The government also permitted higher expenditure on secondary school building—even in the austere 1940s. These were real gains and must not be denied. But the keystone of the 1944 secondary school structure—'parity of esteem'—collapsed immediately. No one—not teachers, parents, local authorities, the press, nor the schools themselves—thought the modern and grammar schools shared equality of status. Parents correctly saw that the modern schools were the offspring of the old elementary schools and if they were ambitious for their children were determined to escape them.[59] The abolition of fees and the opening of all grammar school places to competition made the eleven-plus examination even more significant. The consequences were not unsurprising: middle-class parents employed techniques, like coaching, which in the decade after 1945 actually *increased* the relative number of middle-class children who entered grammar school.

Local authorities, particularly in areas with a large and articulate middle class, consistently spent more on grammar than on modern schools—there was thus not even equality of provision—and were under constant pressure to increase the number of available grammar school places. The ministry of education shared Norwood's view that too many children went to grammar school—they suggested a figure of 15 per cent—but in practice the national figure was closer to one-quarter. This figure itself concealed wide regional and

[57] Anderson, *Missing Stratum*, 125–6.

[58] See Dent's comment: '[For] a great host of ex-secondary school teachers, 1st April, 1945, meant a tremendous spiritual uplift. Only those who have known the English elementary school system from the inside can fully understand what that day meant to those men and women.' (H. C. Dent, *Growth in English Education, 1946–1952* (London, 1954), 69.)

[59] See Brian Simon's comment on the modern schools in his, *Intelligence Testing and the Comprehensive School* (London, 1953), 22–3.

class variations. There was no geographical parity and children's educational chances increasingly came to depend on where they lived: in Gateshead and Sunderland, for example, less than 10 per cent of children gained grammar school places; but in Westmorland over 40 per cent did.[60]

Although standards within the secondary moderns varied—many were able to use the relative flexibility of their curricula with success—and few were quite the physical and intellectual slums people imagined, none the less they were in provision, morale, and quality of teaching inferior to the grammar schools. This ensured that their relative decay was dynamic, which even sentimental depictions of them, like E. R. Braithwaite's *To Sir with Love*, were unable to hide.[61]

The 1944 Act had sidestepped the issue of social differentiation. It had allowed the Norwood Committee and local authorities to impose a comparatively rigid bilateral system on English state education whose deficiencies were soon apparent. Furthermore, as an attempt to encourage social mobility (one of its aims), the Act had, by entrenching the grammar schools at the expense of the modern schools, arguably increased the 'wastage' of ability for which the pre-1939 system had been so criticized. Nor was there even agreement about the grammar schools. The sociologists Brian Jackson and Dennis Marsden, themselves grammar school products, concluded that

despite all the formal talk about 'individuals' and 'character', grammar schools are so socially imprisoned that they are most remarkable for the conformity of the minds they train . . . Schools born out of class needs; schools based on social selection, further refined with each year after 11; schools offering a complex training in approved images of dominance and deference—are these the bases for general 'individualism', for 'democratic living'?[62]

This was almost certainly not the view of the majority of grammar school alumni.[63] Nevertheless, few would have denied that the 1944 Act had failed to free the country from the educational impasse it faced before 1939.[64] There were, it was argued, two alternative ways of escaping it. One was to accept frankly an élitist system, but one genuinely open to all the talents; to confine the grammar schools 'to that intellectual élite who, irrespective of their home circumstances, are required by a modern democracy to recruit its universities, its professions, and its municipal and civil services'[65] and to derive that élite

---

[60] Campbell, *Eleven Plus*, 39.

[61] For the secondary schools in post-1945 literature, see L. Spolton, 'The Secondary School in Post-War Fiction', *British Journal of Educational Studies*, xi (Nov. 1962–May 1963), 125–41.

[62] Jackson and Marsden, *Education and the Working Class*, 219–20.

[63] For a sympathetic study of the grammar school's ethos, see F. Stevens, *The Living Tradition: The Social and Educational Assumptions of the Grammar Schools* (2nd ed., London, 1972), 89–112, 221–39.

[64] See D. Thom, 'The 1944 Education Act: the "art of the possible" ', in Smith, *War and Social Change*, 115–24.

[65] Lowndes, *Silent Social Revolution*, 118.

from 'objective' tests which would eliminate acquired advantages. The other was more drastic and controversial: to obliterate entirely the distinction between grammar and modern schools by combining them into 'multilateral' or 'comprehensive' schools.

The attempt to procure 'objective' judgements by tests of certain intellectual and mental qualities had its origins in pre-1914 Europe. Binet's development of standardized 'intelligence tests' and the notion of 'mental age', together with Stern's invention in 1911 of an Intelligence Quotient (IQ), provided the conceptual basis for English mental testing. Its early English practitioners, however, were (unlike Binet) much influenced by the eugenics movement, and came to emphasize the inherited quality of intelligence (the 'g' factor), a mental characteristic largely independent of cultural training. Cyril Burt, the most important figure in mental testing throughout the period, defined intelligence 'by a threefold distinction':

it is to be distinguished from attainments—which are acquired, and not inborn, from special abilities which are limited, and not general, and from temperament and character—which are, in their essence, emotional rather than intellectual . . .[66]

Burt was himself a protégé of C. E. Spearman, appointed Grote professor of the philosophy of mind at University College, London in 1911, a eugenist and dogmatic proponent of the view that intelligence was both inherited and measurable.[67] With Spearman's strong support he was appointed psychologist to the London County Council in 1913, and it was Spearman's chair to which he succeeded in 1933. From these posts Burt popularized the notion of mental testing and achieved an unequalled prominence in the field. As a historian of mental testing has commented:

It was just too easy to treat the child's IQ as his share of 'g', precisely quantified. In the years after the First World War, the combination of the tests pioneered by Binet and Simon, a battery of items both carefully varied and carefully balanced, and adjusted for age, with theories of general intelligence and the associated sophisticated mathematical apparatus, was to be a potent one.[68]

The use of standardized intelligence tests had been popularized by the American army in 1917–18. The first British education authority to use them at 11-plus was Bradford in 1919, with tests devised by Burt which he published

---

[66] C. Burt, *The Young Delinquent* (London, 1925), 293. Burt's work has been much criticized since his death, but he was not 'conservative' in educational policy. At the time he was regarded as a moderate progressive (as his friendship with Tawney suggests). There is a careful assessment of Burt's career in L. S. Hearnshaw, *Cyril Burt: Psychologist* (London, 1979) and a sharper critique in L. J. Kamin, *The Science and Politics of IQ* (Harmondsworth, 1974), 55. For a recent and balanced consideration of Burt, see N. J. Mackintosh (ed.), *Cyril Burt: Fraud or Framed?* (Oxford, 1995).

[67] For Spearman's odd career, see G. Sutherland, *Ability, Merit and Measurement* (Oxford, 1984), 121.

[68] Ibid. 127.

two years later as *Mental and Scholastic Tests*. At the same time Godfrey Thomson in Newcastle constructed similar tests for the so-called 'Northumberland Scheme'. Although Thomson was himself sceptical about the 'g' factor, considering it descriptive rather than explanatory, the assumptions that lay behind his tests were the same. In 1925 Thomson moved to Moray House, the teachers' training college in Edinburgh, and there began publishing the famous Moray House tests, the most widely used of all mental tests, based upon English and arithmetic attainment scales.[69]

Throughout the 1920s an increasing number of local authorities and individual schools began to employ the tests for the eleven-plus 'scholarship examination'. In 1928 the Board of Education gave restrained support for mental testing. Once the selective character of the secondary system had been confirmed (which Hadow had done) the board needed a defensible means of selection. The tests, by their claims to apparent objectivity, provided such a means. In 1936 it took the plunge and recommended that properly standardized intelligence tests be used in every eleven-plus examination.

The Hadow Committee itself was obviously influenced by notions of a measurable general intelligence, but it was the Spens Committee which explicitly embraced the idea. '*Intellectual development during childhood*', it wrote,

appears as if it were governed by a single central factor, usually known as 'general intelligence', which may be broadly described as innate all-round intellectual ability. It appears to enter into everything the child attempts to think, or say, or do, and seems on the whole to be the most important factor in determining his work in the classroom.

Furthermore, the Committee's 'psychological witnesses' assured it that

with few exceptions, it is possible at a very early age to predict with some degree of accuracy the ultimate level of a child's intellectual powers, but this is true only of general intelligence and does not hold good in respect of specific aptitudes or interests.[70]

The Committee's confidence was Burt's doing. He was the most important of the 'psychological witnesses' and it was his memorandum on intelligence and testing which convinced it.

Thereafter mental testing became intrinsic to selection for secondary schools in many English authorities, while the 1944 Act, by opening all grammar places to competition, made the utility of 'objective' tests even more apparent. Yet mental testing never established itself in the way Burt and others hoped, and never succeeded in placing secondary school selection beyond dispute. Why was this so?

---

[69] In the study and measurement of individual differences the importance of the Scottish universities and training colleges should be noted. (Ibid. 129; Bernbaum, *Social Change and the Schools*, 80–1.)

[70] Spens Report, 123–4, italics in original.

First, we should not exaggerate the influence of Burt and his followers on the development of educational policy. There were many institutional reasons why English schools developed as they did after 1918. Although obviously influenced by Burt, the Hadow and Spens Committees would in all likelihood have proposed what they did without his intervention. Burt, furthermore, had real doubts as to whether 'accurate' selection at 11-plus was possible. Their recommendations, in fact, followed more or less naturally from the social contexts in which they were written. What Burt apparently provided was an acceptable theoretical justification for a policy—selection—which was already in place.

Second, there was no agreement that general intelligence as understood by Spearman and Burt actually existed. Binet himself doubted it; Godfrey Thomson thought the Moray House tests powerful tools in the assessment of children but not in themselves infallible. Nor could the proponents of general intelligence as an independent phenomenon ever defeat the argument that the *only* way 'g' could be measured was by media (like language) which were undoubtedly influenced by a child's social and cultural training. As one critic noted of a verbal test for 11-year-olds:

in order to have the necessary data to answer some of the questions at all, the testee must know the following things . . . the meaning of such words as 'spurious', 'antique', 'external', 'irregular', 'inexpensive', 'affectionate', 'moist'; that a sovereign is made of gold while a florin is made of silver; that pearls, emeralds, sapphires, diamonds and rubies are precious stones, while gold is not; the relative functions of telephone and telegraph; the use of thermometers, the reasons for saving money; . . . and finally, that a parlourmaid is not expected to do the sewing in a house.[71]

It could be argued, therefore, that the tests measured not intelligence, but literacy or verbal skill. Since mental test scores could, indeed, be improved by coaching that further depreciated their value as objective measurement of the thing, 'g'.[72]

Finally, there were wide variations in the extent to which the tests were used. The view that they were universally employed in the scholarship examination or the eleven-plus is plainly wrong. In Wales they seem not to have been used at all, nor in 64 English education authorities. In any case, the local authorities notoriously did not need mental testing to discriminate between those who should or should not go to grammar schools. There were other, more conventional means by which this could be done; not least by local patronage. 'Upward mobility', it has been argued

was not only gradual but also controlled and structured in very precise ways. The constitution of county and county borough councils as education authorities, together

---

[71] Simon, *Intelligence Testing and the Comprehensive School*, 43.
[72] Dent, *Growth in English Education*, 71–2.

with rate and grant aid for secondary schools, greatly extended the power and patronage at the disposal of local elite groups, not only those substantial landowners, business and professional men who served as councillors and aldermen, but also the secondary school teachers. The involvement of the latter in interviews and oral examinations and the relish and idiosyncrasy with which many of them conducted their inquisition, underlines the extent to which selection for secondary education entailed a very direct exercise of patronage.[73]

The consequence of this was that the number of children who entered selective secondary schools was not proportionate to a putative distribution of 'intelligence' even as measured by mental tests, but was determined by tradition, prejudice, sex,[74] and social and political circumstances, as well as by testing. These ensured that the relative rate of entry into selective schools was very uneven throughout the country.

The alternative to this attempt at perfecting selection procedures was either not to select at all or to do so within very different educational structures. The highly differentiated nature of English education had always had its critics. Their criticisms were partly educational, partly social, and partly political. Some argued that selective education maximized 'wastage' of talent by confining so many to inferior schools; others that it was socially divisive and seemingly unfair; still others that it flouted the basic assumptions of a democratic society. Many, of course, argued on all three grounds. The alternative, it was suggested, was a form of 'common' school—before the late 1940s usually called a 'multilateral' or 'multibias' school, thereafter a 'comprehensive' school. These terms were not, however, synonymous. The multilateral or multibias schools (as their names imply) were to be internally streamed, but having under one roof both the 'grammar' and the 'modern' sides. Increasingly, however, when people spoke of comprehensive schools they meant local non-selective secondary schools with only weak streaming, or none.

By the mid-1920s the Assistant Masters' Association and the NUT supported the idea of multilateral schools—though both did so as much on occupational as educational grounds—and there was some sympathy for it in the Headmasters' and Headmistresses' Associations. The *Times Educational Supplement*, an influential journal, argued for multilateralism throughout the 1930s.

---

[73] Sutherland, *Ability, Merit and Measurement*, 284–5. See Dr Sutherland's conclusion in 'The Magic of Measurement: Mental Testing and English Education 1900–40', *TRHS*, 5.s., 27 (1977): 'An examination of the uses of mental testing in the education system proves to be yet another way of confronting the extent of the impact of the inter-war depression, its contribution to an educational process characterized by intensive selection and the forces which put control of this lock, stock and barrel, into the hands of individual local authorities' (p. 153).

[74] It is possible that girls were under-represented in the grammar schools. Although the proportion of girls in grammar schools was higher than the proportion of boys, given their tendency to do significantly better than boys in mental tests (particularly verbal attainment tests) at 11-plus, the difference should perhaps have been greater.

A number of prominent psychologists and educationalists, like Godfrey Thomson,[75] who were familiar with the American school system, became converted to common schools partly because of their American experience. Thereafter support for multilateralism grew steadily, if patchily. This was true particularly of the Labour movement. In 1930 the National Association of Labour Teachers declared its support for 'common' schools, unstreamed but with a 'highly variegated' syllabus. In 1939 the Labour Party's own education advisory committee urged multilateral schools as 'an immediate practical policy'. Labour representatives on the larger local education committees tended to favour multilaterals, though often tepidly. Here the LCC, as in so many other spheres, gave a lead. Its education committee (whose chairman, Barbara Drake, was Beatrice Webb's niece) had, from the moment Labour gained control in 1933, favoured multilaterals, though on an 'experimental' basis. The TUC, having argued for multilateral schools before the Spens Committee, announced in 1939 that it 'strongly adheres to the policy of multilateral schools without which they do not believe that real parity in education or equality of opportunity in after life can be achieved'.[76]

The Spens Committee thought the idea of the multilateral school sufficiently 'attractive' to consider it 'carefully' and only with reluctance came to conclude that it could not advocate them as 'general policy'. It could not do so because it thought schools would have to be too big, that sixth forms would be relatively too small 'to play their traditional role', that no one head could 'inspire' both grammar and modern sides, that the prestige of the grammar schools might 'swamp' the modern side, and, finally, that special technical courses in multilateral schools would be an unsatisfactory substitute for the proposed technical high schools. The Committee did, however, allow for some experimentation in areas like rural districts which could not support both a modern and a grammar school.[77]

By the outbreak of the Second World War there were three views of the multilateral school: those who opposed them entirely, and whose main concern was to protect the grammar schools; those who were ready to accept them for 'experimental' purposes; and those who wanted them to replace all other forms of post-primary education. To wish the last, however, was not necessarily to wish also for a common curriculum. Although it was understood that 'progressive' opinion favoured multilateralism, it was not yet—as it was later to become—a partisan issue. During the debate on the Spens Report, for example, A. A. Somerville, Conservative MP for Windsor and a former master at

---

[75] Thomson did so largely on sociopolitical grounds. In 1929 he wrote: 'The social solidarity of the whole nation is more important than any of the defects to which a comprehensive high school may be subject.' (Quoted in D. Rubinstein and B. Simon, *The Evolution of the Comprehensive School, 1926–1972* (London, 1973), 16.)

[76] Quoted in Bernbaum, *Social Change and the Schools*, 65.   [77] Spens Report, xix–xxii.

Wellington and Eton, argued strongly for the multilateral school, technical side and all: then 'by degrees you can bring about real parity between all schools and all teachers'.[78]

The Butler Act, as we have seen, made no attempt to prescribe a form of secondary education and there is no evidence that Chuter Ede, Butler's parliamentary secretary, thought it should. The Norwood Report none the less deeply divided the Labour Party. The Party leadership showed little interest in multilateral or comprehensive schools. Both ministers of education in the Attlee government, Ellen Wilkinson (1945–7) and George Tomlinson (1947–51), supported the tripartite system, and in 1946 Wilkinson bravely defended selection before the Labour Party conference:

After all, coal has to be mined and fields ploughed, and it is a fantastic idea that we have allowed, so to speak, to be cemented into our body politic, [the idea] that you are in a higher social class if you add up figures in a book than if you plough the fields and scatter the good seed on the land.

In 1949 Tomlinson rejected the Middlesex County Council's plan to transform its system into a fully comprehensive one. 'All children', he said, 'are not alike, either in their aptitudes or in their standards of ability.'[79] There was also the argument, associated with W. G. Cove, the MP for Aberavon and former president of the NUT, that the abolition of the grammar schools would drive middle-class children into the independent schools. Cove's solution was simple: all children should attend grammar schools, though ones presumably highly streamed, since a common curriculum would leave them indistinguishable from comprehensives.

Outside London and a few other large towns Labour local authorities made little attempt to introduce comprehensives. Both Wilkinson and Tomlinson, and many members of local authorities, came from a generation which were not hostile to grammar schools as such, but hostile to a system which seemed to discriminate against working-class children. They also represented a powerful strand within the Labour movement which saw admission to grammar schools as a reward for striving, and striving itself as worthwhile. Comprehensive schools eliminated the need to strive and thus depreciated the quality of working-class culture. Furthermore, the curricula of the grammar schools, they argued, imparted the kind of knowledge, and self-confidence in the use of knowledge, that working-class men and women needed to possess if they were to join the political élites on equal terms. The conquest of the grammar school, not its abolition, was thus their aspiration.

Pressure for a reorganization of secondary education came not from the government, but increasingly from the membership of local Labour Parties as well as from the National Association of Labour Teachers, and those local authorities

---

[78] *HCD*, 343, 5.s. 1762–4 (15 Feb. 1939).   [79] Quoted in Barker, *Education and Politics*, 38–9.

and trade unions which had always favoured it. Their argument was reinforced by changes in educational theory. The Labour Party had hitherto supported multilateralism largely on social grounds; but the work of educational
psychologists, particularly at the University of London's Institute of Education, suggested that selection, by so lowering the expectations and, consequently, the performance of the majority of children relegated to modern
schools, was educationally indefensible. Such evidence (whether true or not)
greatly strengthened the hand of those opposed to secondary selection. It was
a combination of these interests which eventually committed the Labour Party
at least to multilaterals, and probably comprehensives as well, in its statement
A Policy for Secondary Education. But the Party went out of office in the year it was
issued (1951), and it was to be fourteen years before the Department of Education's circular 10/65 publicly affirmed a Labour government's willingness to
abolish secondary selection.

One consequence of the Labour Party's slow conversion to common schools
was a falling-away by many of those who had once supported them. H. C. Dent
identified 19 July 1944, the day when the LCC first proposed 'a system of Comprehensive High Schools' each of over 2,000 children or more, as the moment
when opinion began to turn against multilateral schools.[80] Until then most
had assumed that the common schools would be smaller, each having about
800 pupils. That they would be much larger was apparently confirmed when in
March 1947 the LCC published its plan to establish 103 multilateral schools, of
which 67 were to be fully comprehensive. It is certainly the case that from then
on bipartisan support for multilateralism eroded. The Assistant Masters and
Mistresses, once sympathetic, now rejected multilaterals, as did (from 1947)
the *Times Educational Supplement*. Even the NUT declined to give them open support, though many individual members continued to do so. In part this change
was a result of the 1944 Act. The inclusion of the modern schools, whatever
they once had been, within the secondary code satisfied many of the hopes of
their teachers. Conversely, by readjusting secondary teachers' salary scales to
the relative disadvantage of grammar school teachers, the Act rather alienated
the former from further educational reform. No doubt, also, diminished
enthusiasm was simply cold feet on the part of some who had painlessly supported ending secondary selection when there seemed little chance it would
happen. But the falling-away was really one manifestation of a much wider
reaction by much of the professional middle class against the policies of the
Attlee government or anything associated with the Labour Party, even though
that government had not itself supported multilateralism. Thus policies
which had been contemplated with relative detachment in the 1930s—as the
Spens Committee contemplated multilaterals—became almost unthinkable in
the very different social and political circumstances of the late 1940s. The atti-

---

[80] Dent, *Growth in English Education*, 78–9. Dent was himself one of those who fell away.

tude of the Conservative Party is an index of this. During the war and the two years after it, the Party was not particularly opposed to common schools. By 1951, sensing the mood of one of the most important elements in its constituency, it was definitely opposed. Thereafter it was almost inevitable that the Conservative Party would attempt to maintain secondary selection, while the Labour Party would attempt to eliminate it.

The 1944 Act had brought important changes, particularly to the conditions and status of teachers. By abolishing secondary school fees it had also taken one step towards opening the system to all ability. But by refusing to define specifically the structure of secondary schools (as the Fisher Act had also refused), or even giving an adequate intellectual or political argument for continuing selection (as it might have done), it left the bipartite system subject to persistent controversy, and the grammar school dangerously exposed, for all the excellence of the education it gave those who could exploit it. Further, by refusing to incorporate the public schools within its remit, it came not much closer to creating a national system of education than Fisher had.

2 | Educating élites: the independent schools

The majority of England's élites were not educated by the state: they were educated in a complicated network of 'public' and 'private' schools. For many people, public schools simply meant Eton and Harrow, as universities meant Oxford and Cambridge. For others, a public school was one of the 'Clarendon' nine[81]—Eton, Harrow, Rugby, Westminster, Shrewsbury, Charterhouse, Winchester, St Paul's, and Merchant Taylors'. Since the last two were predominantly day schools, for those whose conception of a public school was a boarding school it was only the first seven that counted. The middle classes, however, would probably have been aware of at least some of the nineteenth-century foundations—Marlborough, Wellington, Cheltenham, Malvern, Clifton, Lancing, etc.—all of which were 'major' public schools and were thought generally to be the equal of several of the Clarendon nine. The only major public schools which, in fact, clearly stood at the top of the hierarchy were Eton, Harrow, Winchester, Westminster, and perhaps Charterhouse, and Ampleforth among the Catholic schools.[82] Below the major schools, although as like them in organization and spirit as they could be, were the so-called 'minor' public schools; some like the 'Woodard' schools, nineteenth-century foundations intended for the middling middle classes; others, in effect, local public schools which drew heavily on the local middle classes.

---

[81] So-called because they were the nine schools examined by the royal commission on the public schools (1861–4), whose chairman was the earl of Clarendon.

[82] Probably the best way of establishing the hierarchy of schools is by finding out which schools played which at games. For details, see I. Weinberg, *The English Public Schools* (New York, 1967), 69.

Girls' public schools were even more difficult to define. Several, even those modelled on major boys' public schools, were still technically 'private' schools. They had no Common Entrance examination; there was much more mobility of staff; above all, it was known that girls received less 'push' from attendance at a public school than boys did. There was undoubtedly a hierarchy of girls' schools, with Wycombe Abbey, Cheltenham Ladies' College, St Leonards, Sherborne, and Roedean at the top, but their foundation was too recent to give them an undisputed superiority—two of the smartest schools, Benenden and Westonbirt, were actually both interwar foundations. And a much higher proportion of girls' public schools received state support than did the equivalent boys' schools.

In law, the public schools were charities: they could not be run for profit. But there were in addition to them a large number of non-state schools run for profit, the so-called 'private' or 'proprietary' schools. Most of them were elementary schools, private preparatory schools, although there were still a number of secondary schools which drew their clientèle from middle-class parents who could not afford public school fees but still wanted a genteel education for their children.

The private schools varied hugely in quality and provision. Many of the small ones really were poor and beginning to succumb to the competition of the new state primary schools. Others approximated the better preparatory schools. Several of the girls' private secondary schools had good records of getting girls to university (particularly before the First World War)[83] and some people, like the playwright John Osborne, who recognized that their private schools were in many ways appalling, thought they had, none the less, received a defensible education. The private schools could also be relied on to give polish or to eliminate tell-tale signs of a local 'accent'. 'The parent', two sociologists wrote in 1940, 'who would have his child climb highest cannot escape the fear of defeating his own end if he entrusted the early years of education to a public elementary school. To do that might leave a mark [i.e. a local 'accent'] which no subsequent education, however excellent, could easily eradicate.[84]

Yet the boys' private schools were often associated with failure: staffed by teachers who could not find posts in 'better' schools; used by parents who could not pay public school fees; attended by boys who could not win places at grammar schools. It was this image of the private school which Evelyn Waugh fixed indelibly in the public mind via his first comic novel, *Decline and Fall* (1928), where 'Llanabba Castle' with its shady proprietor-headmaster and disreputable staff stood for all the defects and none of the virtues of a private schooling.

    [83] J. Howarth, 'Public Schools, Safety-nets and Educational Ladders; the Classification of Girls' Secondary Schools, 1880–1914', *Oxford Review of Education*, 11, 1 (1985), 70–1.
    [84] Leybourne and White, *Education and the Birth-Rate*, 187.

A little more than half of the public schools received state assistance.[85] These were the 'direct-grant' schools; self-governing institutions which were partly supported by the state in return for their offering 25 per cent of their places free to holders of local authority scholarships. Closely resembling the great public day schools like St Paul's, Merchant Taylors', or Dulwich, many were among the country's most academically distinguished schools. They included (for boys) Manchester Grammar School, King Edward VI School, Birmingham, Bradford Grammar School, Bristol Grammar School, Royal Grammar School, Newcastle, etc.; and for girls, North London Collegiate, South Hampstead, Mary Datchelor's School, King Edward VI, Birmingham, Bedford High School, Blackheath High School, etc.

The non-maintained sector of English education was, therefore, a highly structured one. The schools which comprised it differed enormously in success, prestige, provision, and independence. Before 1944 it is not even certain how many there were and how many they enrolled. The Board of Education estimated that in 1932 there were about 350,000 children between 5 and 14 in both preparatory and private schools, though this was probably a declining number.[86] In 1939–40 there were about 40,000 places at public boarding schools, and about 80,000 attended direct-grant schools.

The important division, however, was not between independent and state-assisted public schools, but between public day and public boarding schools. This division was not so much educational, since the curricula of most of the public schools tended to be broadly similar, as social and political. When contemporaries spoke of 'public schools' they usually meant public boarding schools. When they argued (as many did) that England was dominated by élites educated at public schools, again they usually meant public boarding schools. Much evidence supported them. In 1927, R. H. Tawney calculated that 52 of 56 bishops; 19 of 24 deans; 17 of 25 lords of appeal, justices of the Court of Appeal and the High Court; 122 of 156 county court judges, recorders, metropolitan magistrates and stipendiary magistrates; 152 of 210 civil servants earning £1,000 or more; 33 of 41 English members of the Indian Civil Service; 30 of 47 dominion governors; 62 of 82 directors of the five principal banks; 37 of 50 railway company directors had been to public schools, most of them boarding.[87]

---

[85] In 1942 there were 89 independent schools and 99 direct-grant schools represented in the official organizations of the boys' and girls' public schools.

[86] J. L. Gray and P. Moshinsky, 'Ability and Opportunity in English Education', in L. Hogben (ed.), *Political Arithmetic: A Symposium of Population Studies* (London, 1938), 348. In 1936–7, there were 271 government inspected preparatory schools. (Leybourne and White, *Education and the Birth-Rate*, 184.) Since there were twice as many preparatory schools in 1961 as in 1936 and they educated 55,000 pupils, the proportion of the 350,000 who went to preparatory schools in 1932 must have been comparatively small. Lowndes thought that in 1937 there were about 10,000 private schools educating about 300,000 children (Lowndes, *Silent Social Revolution*, 164–5). If these figures are right, some of the private schools must have been very small indeed.

[87] R. H. Tawney, *Equality* (London, 1931), 94–5.

These proportions were almost the same in 1939: of 830 bishops, deans, judges and stipendiary magistrates, senior civil servants, Indian civil servants, dominion governors, directors of banks and railway companies, 76 per cent were public school products and of these nearly two-thirds had been to twelve of the 'more important' public schools, nearly all of them boarding schools.[88] The domination of the Conservative Party by men educated at boarding schools was well known: in 1955 20 per cent of backbench Conservative MPs came from Eton alone.[89] As late as 1961, 36 per cent of the entries in Who's Who had been to schools represented in the Head Masters' Conference (the body which represented most boys' public schools); one-sixth of those had been to Eton. If allowance is made for size, schools represented by entries in Who's Who were in the order: Eton, Winchester, Wellington, Rugby, Harrow, Westminster, Haileybury, etc.[90] Of these, all with the partial exception of Westminster were boarding schools. Striking in this list is the absence of the great day schools—St Paul's, Merchant Taylors', or Manchester Grammar School—whose record of formal intellectual achievement was nearly always superior to the boarding schools. The tendency of the élites to be educated at boarding schools had particular implications for educational policy; in this period almost every man who held one of the three senior ranks at the Board of Education had been to one of the 'better known' public boarding schools.[91]

Despite the commonly held view that the public schools were hostile to business, their products were as strongly represented there as in politics or law. In one sample of 130 leading businessmen educated in the interwar years, 81 went to public schools, and 15 of those to Eton.[92] It was understood that a public school, though not necessarily a university education, was often a *sine qua non* for promotion to senior management, particularly in smaller family-owned businesses, if only because public schools provided the social, sporting, and linguistic skills thought necessary.[93] The same relationship holds between wealth and the public schools: in 1954 65 per cent of those earning £1,000 or more had been to public school, and of those earning £1,000 or more with sons of school age, 95 per cent were sending them to public schools.[94]

The inevitable result of these relationships was that, as H. C. Dent wrote in 1944, there existed 'a group of schools having for social rather than for educational reasons, an implicit lien on most of the key points of our national

[88] Board of Education, *The Public Schools and the General Educational System* [Fleming Report] (1944), 54.

[89] W. L. Guttsman, The *British Political Elite* (London, 1965), 292–4.

[90] T. W. Bamford, *Rise of the Public Schools* (London, 1967), 320.

[91] G. Savage, 'Social Class and Social Policy: the Civil Service and Secondary Education in England during the Interwar Period', *Journal of Contemporary History*, 18, 2 (1983), 262, 264–5.

[92] J. Fidler, *The British Business Elite* (London, 1981), 84.

[93] Clements, *Managers*, 32. And for the minor public schools, attendance at which 'indicates a certain level of means and pretension', see pp. 56–7.

[94] J. Wakeford, *The Cloistered Elite* (London, 1969), 27.

life'.[95] Within the élites this created powerful school-based but lifelong solidarities, amusingly expressed by Stanley Baldwin in 1923. On becoming prime
minister, he told the Harrow Association, his first thought had been to make a
government of which Harrow would not be ashamed:

I remembered how in previous governments there had been four or, perhaps, five Harrovians, and I determined to have six. To make a Cabinet is like making a jig-saw puzzle
fit and I managed to make my mix fit by keeping the post of Chancellor of the Exchequer
for myself.[96]

These solidarities were easily mobilized: when Sir Arnold Lunn, son of the
founder of the travel firm Lunn Poly, wrote *The Harrovians* (1913), a serious but
not severe criticism of the public schools, he was obliged to resign from his five
London clubs.

For most of this period the public school system expanded, though not continuously. Immediately after the First World War the schools enjoyed
'unprecedented popularity', and, despite the so-called 'inflation of fees' in the
early twenties, this growth continued throughout the decade. Four new boarding schools were founded—Rendcomb (1920), Stowe and Canford (1923), and
Bryanston (1928)—and a large number of private schools appear to have converted themselves into public schools.[97]

In the 1930s, however, this expansion halted. Although the total numbers
enrolled at public schools increased from 27,262 in 1927–8 to 36,510 in 1937–8
and one new boarding school was established, Gordonstoun, by Kurt Hahn on
the model of Salem in Germany, the state secondary schools grew much faster.
It was apparent that the smaller private and public schools were losing pupils
to 'good' grammar schools and public boarding schools losing pupils to public
day schools. Thus several of the major boarding schools contracted significantly: Harrow, for example, from 661 boys to 552 and Cheltenham from
710 to 548.

The competition of the grammar schools was not alone responsible for this
contraction. The schools were affected by the steady fall in the birth-rate
throughout the interwar years. Having expanded in the early twenties to meet
rising demand, they found themselves over-provided in the 1930s when
demand fell away, and excess capacity was expensive to maintain.

Possibly some of their potential clientèle simply found them too expensive.
The public and private schools were dismayed when the Burnham scales were
introduced into the maintained schools in 1919–20. These scales both raised
teachers' salaries and introduced an adequate superannuation scheme. To
retain their own staff the independent schools were forced to raise their own

[95] Dent, *Education in Transition*, 214.
[96] E. C. Mack, *Public Schools and British Opinion* (New York, 1973 ed.), 385.
[97] J. Gathorne-Hardy, *The Public School Phenomenon* (London, 1977), 394–5.

salary and pension scales. Some of them found difficulty in doing this, and a number proposed becoming, in effect, direct-grant schools, a proposal which the Board of Education declined. It was this, together with the cost-inflation of the war and the immediate post-war period, which led to the 'inflation of fees' in the 1920s[98] and to the remarkable para. 502 in the May Report (1931): not the only, but certainly the most overt example of class grievance in that document.[99]

Changes in the social and economic structure of major towns badly affected a number of the schools, particularly in London where so many of the great day schools were located. The removal of many of their potential fee-paying pupils to the new suburbs and the industrial and commercial redevelopment of city centres both weakened their financial base and made them physically less attractive. By 1940 most London day schools—though not the most famous, Westminster, which remained in its cramped site by the Abbey—had migrated to outer London. Schools without large and diversified endowments and which could not migrate, like some of the Girls Public Day School Trust schools, got into real difficulties. In 1937 they wrote to the London County Council asking for assistance. The falling-off in the number of fee-payers, they wrote,

is due to a combination of circumstances, namely (1) the decreasing birth-rate; (2) the growing tendency of parents whose business is in London to remove their homes from London to the outer suburbs and even further afield; (3) changes in the neighbourhood resulting in an influx of residents who cannot afford the fees of the Trust schools (for instance, at Clapham); growing competition from your Council's secondary schools (for instance at Blackheath).[100]

It was partly as a result of this 'crisis' in public school finances, and the conviction reached in the early years of the Second World War that there was almost certain to be an education act which could be ideologically unsympathetic to them, that the public schools asked the president of the Board of Education, R. A. Butler, to appoint a committee (July 1942) under the chairmanship of Lord Fleming to consider the relations of the public schools to the general educational system. The Fleming Committee's terms of reference were deliberately narrowed to exclude the question of whether the public schools should

[98] For details of fees and costs, see Leybourne and White, *Education and the Birth-Rate*, 192–4; Hogben, *Political Arithmetic*, 424.

[99] 'Since the standard of education, elementary and secondary, that is being given to the child of poor parents is already in very many cases superior to that which the middle class parent is providing for his own child, we feel that it is time to pause in this policy of expansion, to consolidate the ground gained, and to reorganize the existing machine before making a fresh general advance'. (*Committee on National Expenditure* [May Report], 1931, 191.)

[100] Quoted in Campbell, *Eleven Plus*, 61–3. For the headmasters' 'touting' at prep schools in order to keep up numbers, see P. H. J. H. Gosden, *Education in the Second World War: A Study in Policy and Administration* (London, 1976), 333.

exist at all—though that did not prevent some witnesses like the TUC and the London County Council arguing for their abolition.

The Committee, which reported two years later, dismissed abolition as a breach of freedom and 'impracticable', but it conceded that the 'trend of social development is leaving the Public Schools out of alignment with the world in which they exist' and that to leave them unchanged would make it impossible 'to close in the world of schools a social breach that ... aggravates, if it does not actually cause, the much more serious divisions in society at large'.[101] It therefore proposed a rather clumsy and bureaucratic scheme whereby public schools which entered it would allocate no less than 25 per cent of their places to boys and girls who held local authority bursaries.[102]

The Fleming Report was not particularly well received. Most local authorities were unenthusiastic on the ground that the scheme was an expensive way of educating a small number of children. Most of the public schools were unenthusiastic since the conditions which led them to seek the Committee's appointment in 1942 were fast disappearing. The 1944 Education Act did not, as they feared, 'collectivize' the schools and they were by the end of the war much more prosperous. With prosperity the need to 'align' the schools with the 'world in which they exist' no longer seemed pressing.

There were several reasons for their new prosperity. The first—though its effects were felt most strongly outside this period—was the change in the birth-rate. The sharp increase in the birth-rate after 1943 allowed the schools to exploit their 1920s physical expansion. In the second, the exceptionally high levels of economic activity after 1940, though also accompanied by high levels of taxation on middle- and upper-class income, permitted people who had always wished to send their children to public school to do so, even those who had been so reluctant in the 1930s.

Many contemporaries, however, thought the reason for the survival (and more) of the public schools was, rather, the changing social character of the secondary grammar schools. Each new infusion of free place holders, it was argued, drove another levy of middle-class children to public or private schools. In 1929, Sir Cyril Norwood, who was not unsympathetic to the state schools, suggested that the introduction of free places in 1907 and their extension in the 1920s had inexorably driven fee-payers from the secondary grammar schools. The parents of these fee-payers were not snobs, 'but they were determined that their children should not "pick up an accent" '. The 1907 legislation had, therefore, 'created a "boom" in public schools'.[103]

Others believed that the 1944 Education Act, by abolishing fees at most state secondary schools, had had the same effect. To turn a grammar school into a state secondary school

[101] Fleming Report, 3–4, 30.   [102] Ibid. 100–4.
[103] Norwood, *English Tradition of Education*, 104–5.

is to make just that change which will prevent the middle classes from sending their sons there: for they send them to school not that they may teach refinement to the children of working-class parents but to acquire the culture of their peers and social superiors.[104]

Until the 1944 Act many middle-class parents thought the local grammar school a cheap alternative to a public school. After 1944 they had to compete to enter the grammar with relegation to a secondary modern school as the price of failure: 'Time will *not* soften that blow.'

Even those sympathetic in principle to the 1944 Act were uneasy about its social consequences. Some of those who now entered grammar schools, one teacher wrote, came from homes which were barely literate. Others

have very low standards of cleanliness and appearance; some seem to have had little training in social behaviour . . . Children like these have very little to give to the social and cultural life of the school; the school itself has to provide much which, before the war, would have been regarded as the normal contribution of the home.[105]

In the 1920s and 1930s it was known that many of the grant-aided schools which were legally obliged to give a minimum of 25 per cent free places did not do so. In 1933–4, of 74 grant-aided schools which received the full government grant, only 31 gave as many as 25 per cent; 28 gave only 10 per cent. The Board of Education was remarkably complaisant in face of this obvious violation of the 1907 legislation. It argued that the shortfall was not due primarily to the 'social objection' (to free places) but to the schools' financial difficulties. It did, however, admit that many schools 'dreaded' the 'incursion' of free place holders. 'The urbanity of the Board's reference to the financial difficulties of Public Schools [i.e. direct-grant schools]', the demographer David Glass wrote, 'does not disguise the truth that social objections were paramount in producing this anomalous situation.'[106]

After 1945, furthermore, with Labour in power and committed, some thought, to radically egalitarian policies, there was an observable tendency, as part of a process of social distancing, for middle-class parents to leave the state sector if they could, as there was a tendency for public or direct-grant schools to distance themselves from activities too closely associated with the working classes—notoriously, for example, by playing rugby instead of football.

There is undoubtedly evidence that the public schools prospered as the state or state-assisted schools became socially mixed. The evidence that many parents would tolerate severe financial constraints in order to send their children

---

[104] Lewis and Maude, *The English Middle Classes*, 237–40.

[105] H. Davies, 'The Social Effect of the 1944 Act on the Grammar School', *The Bulletin of Education*, 23 (Nov. 1950), 5.

[106] D. V. Glass and J. L. Gray, 'Opportunity and the Older Universities: A Study of the Oxford and Cambridge Scholarship System', in Hogben, *Political Arithmetic*, 427. See also J. E. Floud, A. H. Halsey, and F. M. Martin, *Social Class and Educational Opportunity* (London, 1956), 11–13.

to public schools, the intense anxieties that many felt about the future social tone of the grammar schools, the awareness that the public schools system constituted an 'invisible empire'[107] of which it was prudent to be a part, the fears of the direct-grant schools that abolition of fees might alienate much of their potential clientèle, all of these are too well attested to be denied. Nevertheless, the evidence should not be exaggerated. It was, for instance, thought that the free-place system would lead to a 'wave' of new public schools, but it was 'a flood which never came'.[108] Numbers attending state secondary schools always grew faster than those attending public schools and the majority of the middle classes in any case did not send their children to public or private schools. Furthermore, despite the fears that the 1944 Act might socially degrade the grammar schools, the middle classes did not suffer from working-class competition nearly as much as was expected.[109] And of the minority of middle-class children who went to public schools less than half the boys and an even smaller proportion of girls attended boarding schools.

It was, however, the boarding schools which were the keystone of the system, as the Fleming Committee recognized. It was their curricula, their 'tone' which at various removes set the curricula and tone of the public day schools and the grammar schools more generally. The boarding schools changed their character somewhat in the interwar years. There was less emphasis upon games than there had been in 1914, but this was the area where they had been most criticized. Even when the 'tyranny of games' was at its most ferocious the athleticism of the schools was under fire; most notoriously in Alec Waugh's autobiographical novel *The Loom of Youth* (1917).[110] Norwood, perhaps the most representative boarding school headmaster of the period, admitted the obsession with games and blamed the prep schools, who despatched their ill-taught products to the public schools 'with their values wrong'.[111] He tried to diminish the importance of games at both Marlborough and Harrow but with only limited success. It was not until a new generation of headmasters, like Robert Birley at Eton and Robert Longden at Wellington, was appointed in the late 1930s and 1940s that the tyranny was at least partially modified.

The result of this and of modest changes in the curricula was to make the boys' boarding schools more like the girls', where the influence of games, though strong, was never as pervasive and where modern languages, history,

[107] Lewis and Maude, *The English Middle Classes*, 22, 230–44. Lewis and Maude are very shrewd on the attitudes of the upper middle class to education but they exaggerate the extent to which these attitudes were representative of the middle classes as a whole.
[108] Bamford, *Rise of the Public Schools*, 275.   [109] See below, pp. 261–2.
[110] *The Loom of Youth* was written by the 17-year-old Waugh in the summer after he left Sherborne. It was a popular as well as a scandalous success and suited the national mood in that grim year.
[111] Norwood, *Traditions of English Education*, 140–2. For a comic example of the tyranny of games, see T. C. Worsley's account of his first conversation with the formidable J. C. Squire, editor of the *London Mercury*, in T. C. Worsley, *Flannelled Fool: A Slice of Life in the Thirties* (London, 1967), 115–16.

and 'applied' sciences were always more prominent. Before 1914 the curriculum of the major boys' public schools was usually dominated by classics, though most schools also taught mathematics and the 'pure' sciences. In the interwar years classics ceded some ground to mathematics, science and, particularly, modern languages. Those schools, however, which like Oundle significantly reshaped the curriculum by the introduction of applied science and 'practical' subjects were known to be exceptional. This is not entirely as the schools wished it; but as long as the 'ancient universities' (Oxford and Cambridge), to whom some of the boarding schools were almost umbilically tied, continued to offer disproportionate numbers of scholarships in classics (Oxford) or mathematics and classics (Cambridge) the schools had little choice but to continue teaching them. The creeping pace of academic change in the major public schools before 1939 can be seen from the subject-distribution of masters at Eton. As late as 1936 there were 39 classics masters, compared with nine in science and four in history.[112]

Changes in curriculum were much more marked after 1945; partly due to the 'modernizing' experience of war, partly to the enhanced prestige of scientific and technological subjects and, perhaps most important, partly to pressure from business. Business had always recruited heavily from the public schools, but after 1945 firms began both to encourage their senior staff to send their children to public schools (and to provide them with tax-free incentives to do so) while increasingly influencing the curricula of the schools (often through the 'careers master', an ever-more important post-war innovation), a process which culminated in 1956 with the establishment of the Industrial Fund for the Advancement of Scientific Education. The Fund assisted the schools, often lavishly, in the construction of laboratories and workshops, and though it was hoped to extend such assistance to the state secondary schools that, in fact, did not happen.

One of the chief characteristics of the major boarding schools—and here they differed both from the public day schools and the state secondary schools—was the extent to which they were integral to the country's armed forces and its military traditions. For several of the schools, particularly Wellington, Cheltenham (which in the 1930s was still advertising itself as 'the training place beyond compare for defenders of the Empire') and Clifton, the nurturing of future army officers was almost their principal function. Clifton sent 3,100 boys to the First World War, of whom 578 lost their lives, and most other major boarding schools sent at least 2,000. No less than 26 public schools could claim two or more VCs. Their contributions in the Second World War were broadly similar.[113]

---

[112] Mack, *Public Schools and British Opinion*, 366.
[113] Bamford, *Rise of the Public Schools*, 285; C. B. Otley, 'Militarism and Militarization in the Public Schools', *British Journal of Sociology*, 29 (1978), 332.

In 1936, 28 per cent of the schools had special admissions procedures for sons of officers—compared with 4 per cent in 1900. Wellington in 1932 had between 80 and 90 'foundationers' (orphan sons of officers paying nominal fees), 100 sons of officers paying reduced fees, and 200 sons of officers paying full fees. But all the major boarding schools (with the notable exceptions of Winchester, Shrewsbury, and Westminster) trained future officers.[114] Those wishing to be officer cadets usually trained on the 'modern' or 'army' side of the school curriculum, and some schools, like Eton, Harrow, and Clifton, provided both 'army' and 'navy' sides. These sides emphasized science, modern languages, and various forms of 'applied' mathematics and were important as alternatives to a curriculum which would otherwise have been largely classical in content. It was usually on the bases of the 'modern' or 'army' sides that the schools diversified their traditional curricula in the interwar years and, even more, after 1945.

Military–imperial traditions weighed heavily on the schools. One historian of Harrow, for example, described the school chapel as 'virtually a mausoleum':

an aisle remembers the Crimean dead, transepts and porches the South African war dead, a crypt chapel and an organ the Great War dead. Almost every modern furnishing in the chapel is a memento of a dead army or navy Harrovian: windows, stalls, candlesticks, sacred books. In addition the Old Boys of the 1914–1918 War are further commemorated in the 'War Memorial Building', completed in 1926, and containing *inter alia*, a Roll of Honour, a shrine to the dead and portraits of distinguished officers. To complete the picture there are banners of eighteen holders of the Victoria Cross above and around the main platform in the school 'Speech Room'.[115]

The many military ceremonials, the return visits of senior military old boys and the ever-present iconography of English wars and triumphs gave the schools a particular atmosphere.

Their most obvious characteristic, however, was their social isolation: something even their headmasters admitted to be a 'problem'.[116] Isolation was an inevitable consequence of the way the boarding schools had developed. They were mostly in the country or in small towns (unlike the public day schools),

[114] In 1928, for example, Wellington sent 43 cadet entrants to the military colleges, Eton 32, Harrow 23, Marlborough and Cheltenham 17 each, etc. (Figures taken from the 1929 *Public Schools Year Book*). The effect of this relationship was to draw into the higher ranks of the army a larger proportion of boys educated at major boarding schools than any other part of the English élite. In 1939 70% of officers with the rank of lieutenant-general and above went to one of these schools. Even after the outbreak of the Second World War and the discrediting of much of the army's interwar leadership, this domination was not significantly weakened. C. B. Otley describes the army's refusal to increase opportunities for promotion from the ranks as a 'long-standing scandal'. (Otley, 'The Educational Background of British Army Officers', *Sociology*, 7 (1973), 200–1.)
[115] Quoted in Otley, 'Militarism and Militarization', 333.
[116] Weinberg, *English Public Schools*, 108.

and both boys' and girls' boarding schools rigidly controlled the daily routines of their pupils. The schools' goals were detached from wider social goals and this tended to make the 'reality' of school more powerful than the 'reality' of the outside world.[117]

The schools aggravated this by a battery of prohibitions with an obvious class bias. Some schools forbade boys to read newspapers which supported the Labour Party; others would not permit them to meet girls from secondary modern schools or council estates.[118] Many had strict rules as to where boys and girls could and could not go: they usually could not go on public transport or into pubs, cinemas, libraries, dance halls, fish and chip shops, cafés, other schools, industrial works and garages, sometimes not even private homes other than those of masters.[119] They were excluded not only from the world of the urban working class, but from modern life altogether. The result was that those at boarding schools had few contacts outside their own social circle. They tended to see the working class only in their subordinate role—as people who carried your baggage or from whom you might buy a railway ticket. Even the lower middle class was largely unknown to them.

The introversion of the larger boarding schools led to the development of a public school argot which further acted to exclude outsiders; and the more the school differentiated itself from the external world the more highly developed was its argot. Thus Ampleforth, Oundle, Malvern, Charterhouse, and Winchester had elaborate argots whereas day schools and smaller boarding schools had few argot words except nicknames for masters.[120]

The effects of these various forms of social exclusion were undoubtedly felt by those comparatively few boys, and even fewer girls, who were sent to boarding schools by that handful of counties which accepted the Fleming Committee's proposals. These children had not been to prep schools and were made to feel it; they could be treated contemptuously by the tradesmen or barbers who served the schools; they might be called 'oiks' if they were unfortunate enough not to have expunged their 'accents' before they arrived. For some it created severe social tensions—parental visits could cause deep anxiety and embarrassment, and were sometimes not encouraged.[121] A number of the schools did not persist with the scheme. St Edward's School, Oxford, interviewed two boys nominated by the London County Council: one did not want to come and the

---

[117] G. Kalton, *The Public Schools: A Factual Survey* (London, 1966), xx.   [118] Ibid., p. xxiv.

[119] Wakeford, *Cloistered Elite*, 71.   [120] Ibid. 67–8.

[121] Private information to the author. The Boulting Brothers' film, *The Guinea Pig* (1948), attempts, as its name suggests, to treat the scheme positively. The hero, a cockney called 'Jack Read', after some early bad moments, is triumphantly assimilated, which includes losing his accent: 'Gosh sir, jolly good show' he says on being told he has won a scholarship to Cambridge. The company which made it, Charter Films, was named after Charterhouse, the brothers' own school. For a discussion of this interesting film, see R. Durgnat, *A Mirror for England* (London, 1970), 33–4; J. Richards and A. Aldgate, *Best of British: Cinema and Society, 1930–1970* (Oxford, 1983), 90.

other kept running away. 'The experiment', the school's historian notes, 'was terminated with mutual relief.' For those who lasted the course, however, the schools provided the kind of education which, as they recognized, they probably could not have got elsewhere.

The social isolation of the schools had one other result. Within public school argot, of the 58 most commonly used words, 17 were sexual—'none of them', it was noted, 'heterosexual'.[122] Homosexuality in the boys' boarding schools was widely acknowledged in private (and possibly exaggerated) but rarely mentioned officially. Since they could not suppress the activity, the schools sought to censor discussion of it on the grounds that discussion merely gave encouragement to the enemy. *The Loom of Youth* caused dismay as much because it referred almost as explicitly to homosexuality ('the usual stuff') as it did to the tyranny of games. Schools attempted various régimes, some of them very punitive, but in the end seemed to have opted for a policy of looking the other way combined with the occasional exemplary expulsion. The real 'problem', of course, was not sex but the extreme social seclusion of which a normally transient homosexuality was an inevitable manifestation. For many boys the homosexual argot was simply a *façon de parler*, a form of verbal sociability: as boys at day schools talked about girls, or adults the weather, boarding school boys talked about other boarding school boys.

Girls' boarding schools, like, it should be said, girls' secondary day schools, were equally reluctant to face the consequences of adolescent sexuality.[123] There were rigid rules about contact with boys and some schools even attempted to proscribe casual friendships. Girls were chaperoned on almost all occasions and schools often devised almost ludicrous routines in order that their pupils should not meet boys, even accidentally. The consequence was that many boarding school boys and girls were ill-prepared for marriage and the social relationships that usually precede it.[124] After the Second World War, the reluctance of the boarding schools to change their social and sexual values as fast as their pupils caused even more personal distress.[125]

Within the independent sector, it was the so-called 'progressive' schools which attempted to break out of the apparent social and sexual impasse of the traditional public schools. Some, like Bedales, which was co-educational, or Bryanston, which adopted the extremely informal 'Dalton method' of teaching, or even Dartington ('whose only tradition was smoking') after it had been rescued by W. B. Curry, were none the less recognizable as English public schools. Others were not. The two schools which Rudolf Steiner founded or the

---

[122] Weinberg, *English Public Schools*, 168.

[123] Summerfield, 'Cultural Reproduction in the Education of Girls', in Hunt (ed.), *Lessons for Life* 164. One woman who had been at Blackburn High School in the 1930s, asked whether girls then had boyfriends, replied: 'they were naughty girls if they did.'

[124] Wakeford, *Cloistered Elite*, 74.   [125] Kalton, *The Public Schools*, p. xxiv.

one Bertrand and Dora Russell (after 1932 Dora alone) ran at Beacon Hill from 1927 to 1943 consciously broke with most aspects of conventional education.[126] Most celebrated of all, and certainly the public's idea of a progressive school, was A. S. Neill's at Summerhill. Neill, who had been much influenced by Freud and Wilhelm Stekel, departed dramatically from the canons of orthodox pedagogy. He was sometimes successful, sometimes not:

Terrifying [one parent said]. Doors ripped off their hinges and replaced by blankets. Furniture destroyed ... A horde of psychopaths—they stole everything ... We went there on November 5th. There was a huge bonfire. No staff. We rescued little kids from the flames. When I learnt they were going to build a swimming pool I pounced and took the children away.[127]

By 1939 the 26 'recommended' progressive schools had 3,500 pupils; several of them, however, did not survive the Second World War and as a system they did not much disturb the traditional public schools. Their influence, by giving further encouragement and publicity to the 'pupil-centred' and informal philosophies of education becoming popular in both state and independent sectors, was wider and more indirect.

3 | *Educating élites: the universities*

England's universities were its most exclusive educational institutions. Throughout the interwar years England had proportionately fewer students at university than any other country in Europe. Within Great Britain itself, it had (as with secondary school students) proportionately fewer university students than Wales and Scotland.[128] Although there was some growth in student numbers between the First and Second World Wars, it was hardly significant. Total numbers rose from about 40,000 full-time students in 1919 to about 50,000 in 1939, but the proportion of the 'age-group' entering university only rose from 1.5 to 1.7 per cent.[129] What had developed by 1939 was a university structure with four more or less distinct components: Oxford and Cambridge; London; major 'redbrick'; and minor 'redbrick'. Oxford and Cambridge stood at the pinnacle, both in social prestige (unquestionably) and intellectual distinction (more dubiously). They were also (excluding the University of London, a federal

---

[126] See Anthony Quinton's comment on Beacon Hill: 'It was not of the utmost progressiveness; although Russell would not have children forced to do academic work, he required them to show a measure of consideration for others.' (Entry on Russell in *Dictionary of National Biography*, 1961–1970, 905.1.)

[127] Quoted in Gathorne-Hardy, *The Public School Phenomenon*, 328–33.

[128] In 1931 England had 0.9 per thousand at university, compared with 1.11 in Wales and 2.3 in Scotland.

[129] These figures are for Great Britain as a whole. For details and the method of calculating the 'age-group', see Halsey, *Trends in British Society*, 194 n and 206.

body) the two largest universities: in 1937–8 Cambridge had 5,838 undergraduates and Oxford 4,940. Their social exclusivity was based upon the exclusivity of the major boarding schools from which they drew such a large proportion of their students. Most Oxford and Cambridge colleges awarded scholarships by examination and without means-testing. The result was that in 1939 Oxford awarded 77.6 per cent of its scholarships to candidates from public schools; Cambridge 73.4 per cent. About one-third of all these scholarships were offered in classics, and of these 70 per cent went to boys and girls from public schools. The 'closed' scholarships—awards tied by trust to one or more specified schools, nearly all of them, in one way or another, public—favoured public schools by a ratio of 16 to one. In total, Oxford and Cambridge scholarships favoured the public schools by 10 to one. Since the number of these scholarships failed to keep up with the increase in the secondary school population, their effect was to make the 'ancient' universities even more exclusive, as did the Board of Education's decision in 1936 to open the small number of state scholarships, hitherto confined to 'maintained' schools, to all 'recognized' secondary schools. Within two years, 749 of 1,065 state awards were held at Oxford and Cambridge, mostly by undergraduates from public schools.[130]

The two 'ancient' universities also had among their teaching body a disproportionate number of fellows of the Royal Society (FRSs) and fellows of the British Academy (FBAs).[131] None the less, despite this apparent scholarly preeminence, the American student of British universities Abraham Flexner thought Oxford and Cambridge in the 1930s little more than 'advanced secondary schools'.[132] They concentrated overwhelmingly on an intensive teaching of undergraduates via tutorials which were revealingly called in the Oxford women's colleges 'coachings'; college life, single-sex and subject to innumerable quasi-monastic, quasi-conventual regulations, represented little advance on the habits of the boarding schools; graduate education was embryonic. Flexner's description, however, is probably truer of Oxford than Cambridge. Although usually paired, as a kind of academic shorthand, the two universities were not academically identical. By 1939, for example, many fewer Cambridge undergraduates read the humane subjects: 57.9 per cent in Cambridge compared with 81.9 per cent in Oxford (and no other university in the country even approached the Oxford figure). Conversely, many more in Cambridge than in Oxford read science or technical subjects: 31.7 per cent in Cambridge compared with 12.1 per cent in Oxford. Furthermore, the immense international standing of Cambridge in physics (particularly when Lord Rutherford and Sir James Chadwick were directors of the Cavendish

[130] Hogben, *Political Arithmetic*, 430–59; Leybourne and White, *Education and the Birth-Rate*, 246–55.
[131] A. H. Halsey and M. A. Trow, *The British Academics* (London, 1971), 217–18.
[132] A. Flexner, *Universities* (New York, 1968 ed.), 265.

Laboratory), economics, and philosophy, depended on an active, if rather ill-organized, graduate school. The success with which Cambridge assimilated itself to the 'scientific spirit' led the refugee-scholar Adolf Loewe to write that 'during the last generation, Cambridge has acquired a symbolic significance for the English university system corresponding to that which Oxford had during the second half of the nineteenth century.'[133]

Even in Oxford the balance of the humane subjects had changed noticeably. The introduction of the degree in Politics, Philosophy and Economics ('PPE') in the early 1920s was deliberately intended to promote contemporary studies, to do for the modern world what the Faculty of Literae Humaniores did for the ancient, and to meet the common criticism that English degrees were too narrow and inflexible.[134] The construction of new laboratories in the late 1930s provided the base for the rapid growth of Oxford science after 1945.

The two universities were, however, very alike in their teaching methods and the construction of degree courses. Moreover, such was their prestige, they tended to provide a model—as the boarding schools did for secondary education—for nearly all the universities, even those which were originally founded in conscious reaction to them. That model was of a largely residential university, increasingly drawing from all over the country students who read for comparatively specialized degrees in a comparatively short time.

The University of London, the second component of the structure, was *sui generis*. Nominally the largest university in Europe, it was in fact until the 1930s largely an examining body, which united federally autonomous colleges, like University College, King's College, or Imperial College (themselves as large and as academically distinguished as the civic universities), diverse institutions (like the College of Household Science) and a dozen teaching hospitals, all of which grew rapidly after the First World War.[135]

Although the University did possess a central authority it had no real physical existence until 1927 when, with lavish assistance from the Rockefeller Foundation, the 11-acre site at Bloomsbury was purchased from the duke of Bedford. Then it did acquire a physical presence: nothing could be more corporeal than Edward Holden's immense, lowering Senate House ('melancholy as a beached whale'),[136] opened just before the Second World War, which dominated Bloomsbury and the new University buildings that gradually rose around it.

---

[133] A. Loewe, *The Universities in Transition* (London, 1940), 14.

[134] Thus it was for some time known as 'Modern Greats', as the classics degree was known as 'Greats'. For the establishment of 'PPE', see B. Harrison (ed.), *The History of the University of Oxford*, vii (Oxford, 1994), 111–13.

[135] N. Harte, *The University of London, 1836–1986* (London, 1986), 197.

[136] The phrase is J. Mordaunt Crook's in F. M. L. Thompson (ed.), *The University of London and the World of Learning, 1836–1986* (London, 1990), 27. It should be noted, in fairness to Holden, that his original conception was never completed.

London was also singular in that nearly half (45.0 per cent in 1938) its student body were medical students. The University incorporated a dozen teaching hospitals, and it was by far the largest institute of medical teaching in the country. The quality of the education imparted was, however, at best mixed and by American or continental standards often defective. Flexner, who was himself a medic by training and a forceful administrator of medical education, thought only University College Hospital up to standard: the rest were 'amateurish and so, with individual exceptions ... are the clinicians.'[137] There were actually a number of distinguished clinicians (like Sir Alexander Fleming, the discoverer of penicillin, at St Mary's, Paddington, E. C. Dodds, the synthesizer of steroids and the great immunologist Peter Medawar), but the atmosphere at the hospitals tended to be anti-intellectual and hearty-masculine. Women were admitted as students to only one teaching college before 1945 and the others had to be compelled to admit them after the war.[138]

Nevertheless, despite this, London was the only one of the English universities before 1939 to provide any sort of institutional basis for graduate research in the American or German manner. In 1921 the Institute of Historical Research was founded with the constitutional historian A. F. Pollard as its first director, and in 1937 the Institute of Archaeology was established, partly in recognition of the precocity of British archaeological techniques, partly for (and by) its first director, the flamboyant Mortimer Wheeler, then curator of the London Museum.

The institutes, together with the affiliated colleges and societies, gave London a framework for post-graduate research which none of the other English universities possessed, although all were in principle committed to promoting it. In 1917 they had agreed to the introduction of the Ph.D. as an English degree; hitherto those who wanted one, particularly if they were in the physical sciences, medicine, classics, or history, had usually been obliged to go to Germany or Austria. The purpose of the English Ph.D. was, however, not only to provide an alternative for those to whom Germany was now closed, but to encourage foreign students to do their doctoral research in England rather than in Germany. As such, the new Ph.D. was to be part of England's wider struggle against Germany. Once Germany had been defeated, the drive for organized graduate teaching rather flagged. Nevertheless, even though the research institutes did not work entirely as intended, London produced many more graduates with research degrees than any other university and the number increased rapidly: in 1920–1 the University conferred 82 doctorates, and 10 years later, 271.

London was, finally, unique in the number of external students it enrolled.

---

[137] Flexner, *Universities*, 242.

[138] For the London teaching hospitals, see L. P. Le Quesne, 'Medicine' in Thompson, *University of London*, 138–141.

Many of them were taking degrees part-time and the University acted as a validating as well as a teaching institution. The 'London external' was also an imperial degree: wherever there was formal or informal British authority, people were sitting a London degree as a way of advancement. By 1937 there were 79 overseas centres for London degree and matriculation examinations and nearly 5,000 candidates. The Second World War, by scattering many of those who would otherwise have been full-time students, led to a big increase in the number of external candidates. By the end of 1941 their number exceeded that of internal students, and remained so until 1957. In 1950–1, of the University's 51,000 students, nearly 28,000 were external.[139] It was the huge number of external students, and not simply its affiliated colleges and institutions, which made London much the largest of the English universities.

The remaining two components of the university system were the major and minor 'redbricks' (or 'civic' universities as they usually called themselves). These varied greatly in size and status. Several of the Victorian and Edwardian foundations, like Manchester, Liverpool, Leeds, and Birmingham were the size of the major colleges of the University of London, whereas others, particularly the university colleges, had only several hundred students. Most were pre-1914 foundations, though there was some expansion in the interwar years: Reading was chartered a full university in 1926, and university colleges were established at Exeter (1922) and Hull (1927). Most of the civic universities still retained close links with the local economies and societies from which they emerged. These affiliations were often recognized in their government. At Liverpool University 17 categories of people, representing most kinds of Mersey life, were specified for election to its governing body. All MPs elected for the divisions of Liverpool, Birkenhead, Bootle, and Wallasey, the earl of Derby, the lord mayor of Liverpool, the Roman Catholic archbishop, the Liverpool and District rabbi, the chairman of the Mersey Docks and Harbour Board and the secretary of the Liverpool Trades and Labour Council were among them.[140] When University College, Hull, was incorporated, its governing body comprised representatives of the Royal Society, the British Association, the Law Society, the Dental Association, the Royal Institute of British Architects, the Pharmaceutical Society, the Trades Council, the Co-operative Movement, the Free Churches, and urban district and county councils.[141] Several of the universities were associated with locally prominent families. The Wills family were large benefactors of the University of Bristol; University College, Nottingham, was heavily funded by Jesse Boot (Lord Trent), founder of the pharmaceutical chain; Reading by the Palmer family (of the Reading biscuit firm Huntley and Palmer's) and the Sutton family (of Sutton's Seeds); Hull by T. R. Ferens.

[139] Harte, *University of London*, 241. Also Thompson, *University of London*, xxi–xxii.
[140] Halsey and Trow, *British Academics*, 106.
[141] W. H. G. Armytage, *Civic Universities and the State* (London, 1955), 259–60.

Such local ties were reinforced by the student body, two-thirds of whom came from maintained schools, many from within the neighbourhood; here the contrast with Oxford and Cambridge could not have been more obvious. The result was that a number of the civic universities still specialized in courses which reflected the influence of their hinterlands. Leeds, for example, gave diplomas in dyeing, gas engineering, and colour chemistry; Sheffield had degrees in glass technology and metallurgy. Others were associated with particular subjects, like Reading in agriculture or town planning at Liverpool, where the department of civic design under Patrick Abercrombie had no equal.

The civic universities were, however, losing their local character. Although many of their students lived locally, the aspirations of most 'redbricks' were national. They were increasingly drawing their undergraduate body extra-regionally, a development much accelerated after 1945. The model of Oxford and Cambridge was a powerful one, but the intellectual standing alone of many 'redbricks' justified such aspirations. Manchester, for instance, had departments of physics (where W. L. Bragg, who with his father, W. H. Bragg, won the Nobel prize in 1915, was Langworthy professor of physics), history (where T. F. Tout, Maurice Powicke, and Lewis Namier all held chairs in this period), and philosophy of international repute.

For the civic universities there were gains and losses in this development. Their undergraduate bodies became more diverse and perhaps more interesting, and many undergraduates as individuals benefited by breaking with an introverted tradition of local school and local university. The smaller civic universities probably lost some of that negative 'provinciality' which Kingsley Amis memorably satirized in his first (and best) comic novel, *Lucky Jim*.[142] But the hinterlands arguably lost: the slow divorce of the universities from local economic and social concerns of their regions may have impoverished the regions both economically and culturally. And the universities lost a certain social style which had once distinguished them. E. Allison Peers, professor of Spanish at the University of Liverpool, who, under the *nom de plume* 'Bruce Truscot' coined the name 'redbrick' (and wrote an account of the 'redbricks' which was both influential and notorious) noted, for example, that dancing was important to the 'redbricks'—tea-dances, 'hops', 'socials', formal dances and balls—as it was to many aspects of provincial civic life.[143] Such a culture slowly gave way to the more indeterminate campus culture of the post-war period; a change of uncertain value.

[142] Published in 1954. It should be noted that Amis's personal experience was of a Welsh university college, though there is little in the novel to suggest that it could not have been set in an English university.

[143] B. Truscot, *Red Brick University* (London, 1943), 212. For Truscot, see Armytage, *Civic Universities*, 278. More surprisingly, dancing was also central to the student culture of the London School of Economics.

On the eve of the Second World War the English university system was both diverse and comparatively small, still heavily dependent on fee and endowment income. The total money income of the universities had, it is true, more than doubled between 1919 and 1939—£3.02 million to £6.712 million. In 1919, the Lloyd George government had created the University Grants Commission (UGC) under the chairmanship of Sir Walter Moberly, and this body, dominated by academics, advised the government on the distribution of its annual grants. Throughout the interwar years the UGC provided no less than one-third of university income, but hardly more: in 1920–1, 33.6 per cent and in 1938–9, 35.8 per cent.[144] This provision partly compensated for the relative decline in local authority support—many universities were now paying more in rates than they received in support—but only partly, and the financial position of the universities at the outbreak of the war left them little room for manœuvre.

The strengths and weaknesses of the system were well illustrated by its reaction to the most unexpected challenge it was forced to meet—the arrival in England after 1933 of large numbers of German-Jewish scholars, many of the greatest intellectual distinction. As a whole, the German-Jewish migration to England in the 1930s was to enrich profoundly the country's academic life,[145] but the number of refugees the universities were able to house was very limited. The first response was generous: the Academic Assistance Council (AAC) was founded to place refugee scholars in universities or research institutes.[146] England was, furthermore, so long as a sponsor could be found, easier to enter than the United States. But about two-thirds of those who emigrated to England re-emigrated to the United States, including many who would have preferred to remain in England. Increasingly the AAC saw itself as a conduit: arranging for scholars to leave Germany for England and then facilitating their passage and emigration to the United States.

The circumstances which allowed them to be permanently accommodated in England were comparatively few. Individuals of great eminence could be found billets. The most famous refugee of them all, Einstein, had already in 1931 been given a five-year research studentship (i.e. fellowship) at Christ Church, Oxford, which could have probably been made permanent had he wished. Magdalen College, Oxford, elected Schroedinger (who was not Jewish) to a research fellowship on the day his Nobel prize was announced. Even then eminence was not always willingly conceded. When the great Latinist Eduard

---

[144] Halsey and Trow, *British Academics*, 63.

[145] It has been calculated that the Jewish emigration of the 1930s brought to Britain 13 Nobel prizewinners, 63 FRSs, 31 FBAs, two Companions of Honour, two Orders of Merit and four heads of Oxford and Cambridge colleges. (P. G. J. Pulzer in W. E. Mosse (ed.), *Second Chance* (Tübingen, 1991), 8 n.)

[146] For details of the AAC, see Mosse, *Second Chance*, 600–5.

Fraenkel was elected to the Corpus Christi chair of Latin at Oxford in 1934 it took a public intervention from A. E. Housman to put his suitability beyond question.[147] Those who had sponsors with patronage to dispense could also be found places. The most important of these patrons was Frederick Lindemann (later Lord Cherwell), the well-connected Dr Lee's professor of experimental philosophy (i.e. physics) at Oxford, who persuaded the deputy chairman of ICI, Sir Harry (later Lord) McGowan to fund a number of fixed-term research fellowships, some of which were renewed. In this way many refugee scientists, including Francis Simon, Nicholas Kurti, Dennis Gabor, and Kurt Mendelsohn, were able to stay in England.[148] The University of Birmingham, which had elected Rudolf Peierls to its chair of mathematical physics in 1937, was able to find a berth for Otto Frisch, another émigré who had been working with Niels Bohr in Copenhagen but who was in England at the outbreak of the war: a world-historical conjunction, for it was in Birmingham in 1940 that Frisch and Peierls wrote the memorandum which demonstrated that a 'super-bomb' based upon atomic fission was both theoretically and technically possible, and which correctly predicted its consequences.[149]

As for the Warburg Library, one of England's greatest acquisitions from the emigration, it was the determination of its director, Fritz Saxl, to get it out of Germany, and the willingness of the great art collector Samuel Courtauld to pay for its accommodation, which enabled it to be housed in the University of London, where it became an incorporated Institute in 1944.

Prospects for refugees were most promising when they met obvious academic or national needs (like low-temperature physics) or were self-evidently distinguished or had powerful patrons. Where they met these conditions their effect could be transformative. The Warburg Institute, for example, became a refuge for a brilliant generation of German and Austrian scholars—Nikolaus Pevsner, Ernst Gombrich, Rudolf Wittkower, Otto Paecht, Edgar Wind—who completely recast the discipline of art-history in the English-speaking world. In classics, there was a remarkable cohort of refugee scholars—Eduard Fraenkel, Rudolf Pfeiffer (a non-Jewish, anti-Nazi émigré), Paul Maas (who arrived at the eleventh hour in 1939 and eked out a living as an advisor to the Oxford University Press), Stefan Weinstock, Felix Jacoby, Paul Jacobsthal—who professionalized a subject which had hitherto been conducted in a talented

[147] See Housman's letter to the *Sunday Times*, 23 Dec. 1934.
[148] It was Lindemann who was responsible for the election of Einstein to a research studentship at Christ Church and he was also given by that college a fund to be used at his own discretion to assist refugee German physicists. Lindemann, who was particularly anxious to attract German low-temperature physicists, actually went recruiting to Germany in 1933. (Harrison, *History of the University of Oxford*, vii. 160–1.) Christ Church's generosity as well as Lindemann's influence needs to be acknowledged. After Einstein decided to remain in Princeton permanently (1934), he returned the residue of his Christ Church stipend, and the College used the sum to support Eduard Fraenkel and Paul Jacobsthal until both found permanent posts in Oxford.
[149] M. Gowing, *Britain and Atomic Energy, 1939–1945* (London, 1964), 41–7, 389–93.

but often gentlemanly way.[150] In the social sciences the London School of Economics alone gave shelter to an impressive list of émigrés: Hermann Kantorowicz and Hermann Mannheim in law and criminology; Otto Kahn Freund, whose work was to be immensely influential in England, in labour law; Moritz Bonn in political economy; Karl Popper (via New Zealand) in philosophy, probably the most celebrated; R. R. Kuczynski in social statistics; Karl Mannheim whose *Ideology and Utopia*, when published in English translation in 1936, was to make him an outstanding figure in Anglo-Saxon sociology.[151]

Nevertheless, the majority of émigré scholars who arrived here were obliged to go elsewhere, usually the United States; for them England was, as the architect Walther Gropius unkindly said, 'not a country, but a staging post', and England was the poorer for it. It was, for so many, merely a staging post because of the extreme reluctance of the Academic Assistance Council to encourage refugees to apply for posts in English universities where they might compete with English scholars. When the refugee physicist Fritz London thought of applying for a lectureship at University College, Hull, the Council discouraged him. It wrote to his sponsor that 'if German scientists with senior qualifications compete for these junior posts it will be regarded by British graduates and their members of staff as unfair competition ... an abuse of the displaced qualifications and would be an unfair act against younger British competitors.'[152]

There was also the simple paucity of posts. For most refugees English universities could provide short-term assistance but not permanence, being too few in number and too small in size. Outside industry there were few research institutions (and not many in industry either). The United States was able to employ more scholars not only because it was larger and richer, but because it had a more sophisticated university and quasi-university system. The inability of England to absorb more refugees points to the real problem of her universities before 1939: the narrowness of their financial bases, which was, in turn, a consequence of the state's reluctance to fund them more extensively or to encourage more people to attend them.

The state was not entirely passive. There had been a flurry after the First World War; partly because the war itself had seemed to demonstrate the need for greater state involvement; partly because Lloyd George himself had always believed in state-supported technology and research. Immediately after the

---

[150] See the essay 'Eduard Fraenkel' in H. Lloyd-Jones, *Blood for the Ghosts* (London, 1982), 251–60. I am also grateful to Professor P. J. Parsons for his comments on this subject.

[151] Mannheim was also founding editor of the International Library of Sociology and Social Reconstruction, a remarkable series of research monographs published by Routledge & Kegan Paul which was to expand hugely our knowledge of the sociology of modern Britain. For details of LSE and the emigration, see R. Dahrendorf, *LSE: A History of the London School of Economics and Political Science, 1895–1995* (Oxford, 1995), 286–96.

[152] Quoted in Mosse, *Second Chance*, 235–6.

war, the Department of Scientific and Industrial Research, the Agricultural Research Council, and the Medical Research Council were established—all responsible to the Privy Council.[153] But constrictions on government expenditure after 1921 inhibited further state intervention. In the later 1930s, moved again by fear of Germany, the state made half-hearted attempts to expand the tertiary sector: largely by making the technical colleges something like universities and encouraging specific technologies at specific universities.[154] The links were strengthened between the economic needs of particular localities and technical colleges. Mining departments, for example, were established at Wigan, Sunderland, Chesterfield, and Cannock; metallurgy at Rotherham and Sheffield; engineering at Coventry, Birmingham, and Sheffield. But little was done to improve relations between the colleges and the universities which, generally speaking, remained non-existent.

Within the universities, departments of aeronautics were established at Cambridge, London, and Southampton, building construction at London and Manchester, fuel technology at Leeds, London, Sheffield, and Nottingham, naval architecture at Durham and Liverpool, oil technology at Birmingham and London, and technical optics at London. These were important developments but heavily dependent upon private support. Without that, the universities stagnated in the 1930s, even in areas like atomic physics where British science was very advanced. Thus in 1937 the United States had over 30 cyclotrons whereas Britain had none. The reluctance of the state to intervene, however, was not confined to the universities; it was true of the educational system as a whole, and much else within English society.

The universities, like the schools, were badly disrupted by the Second World War. Those in the centres of major cities (particularly in London) often suffered bomb damage, and sometimes even more damage from the military authorities who requisitioned them (Senate House, London, was, for example, Eisenhower's headquarters). Most of the London colleges were evacuated and other universities were reduced to the corners of their premises. They also lost staff and the bulk of their male undergraduates. In 1944 only 68 per cent of full-time university teachers were still in post, and, while the number of women undergraduates actually increased by 13 per cent, the number of men fell by 41 per cent, and in the arts faculties by 76 per cent. Indeed, the National Service Acts deemed arts undergraduates as expendable as members of the clerical occupations and conscripted them in the same way. After 1939 an undergraduate historian stood in the same relation to an undergraduate radio-engineer as a bank clerk did to a miner—'useless' as against 'useful'. By 1945, as a result, there were fewer than 38,000 full-time undergraduates compared with 50,000 in 1939.[155]

---

[153] R. O. Berdahl, *British Universities and the State* (London, 1959), 62.
[154] Armytage, *Civic Universities*, 270–1.   [155] Dent, *Growth in English Education*, 164.

It was assumed throughout the war, however, that the universities would expand rapidly when it was over. This (correct) assumption was in part a consequence of the wider assumption that all forms of social provision would expand, education no less than the rest. It was also a result of the view that the war had demonstrated the usefulness of the universities, particularly university science and technology. The tendency of the universities to take over the kind of basic research hitherto done elsewhere (or not at all) was evident even before 1939; the war only made it more obvious. What were arguably, for example, the two most significant scientific advances of the Second World War anywhere—the demonstration that an atom bomb was feasible, and the synthesis of penicillin—were both made in English universities—the first at Birmingham, the second at Oxford, though none of the scientists principally involved was actually English. Furthermore, as the 'modernization' of the economy became an increasing preoccupation of the political élites, especially in the Labour Party, it was hoped that a university-based science could achieve what private industry had allegedly failed to do before 1939.

The association of the universities with many of the social enquiries of the interwar years—particularly those concerned with the conditions of the working classes—increased the favour with which they were regarded in the 1940s, when the vaguely social-democratic ideology which animated those enquiries was now triumphant. Before 1914 the great social surveys, like those of Charles Booth or Seebohm Rowntree, were privately financed and conducted. After 1918, although the social enquiries were still heavily dependent on private funding from charitable organizations like the Carnegie and Rockefeller Foundations or the Pilgrim Trust, nearly all of them were conducted by the universities. The *New Survey* of London was based at the London School of Economics and the surveys of Merseyside, Sheffield, Southampton, and Bristol, as well as several of the unemployment enquiries, were organized in university departments of social administration.

During the war itself the treasury accepted the UGC's proposals for university expansion, and the civic universities agreed to increase their numbers by 86 per cent. Only Oxford and Cambridge, where there were physical and educational constraints on rapid expansion, were unable to expand as fast. The argument for expansion was supported by the Barlow Report (1946), which recommended large increases in the number of science graduates. By 1947, as a result, the number of science and technology students had doubled, whereas the number of arts students increased by only 50 per cent. The remarkable intellectual achievements of English science in the twenty or so years after 1945, particularly in Cambridge, London, and Oxford (probably in that order), were in part a result of this decision to expand university science, to some degree at the expense of the arts. By 1950 there were nearly 90,000 full-time students compared with 38,000 in 1945 and 50,000 in 1939. The 'redbricks' increased their numbers by nearly 130 per cent—only Leeds, Liverpool, and Reading were less than twice their pre-war size—and it was the expansion of the existing institutions rather than the establishment of new ones which made this growth possible.[156] University College, Nottingham, and University College, Southampton, became full universities in 1948 and 1952, but only one new institution was established, the University College of North Staffordshire at Keele Park, just outside Stoke, which was seen as experimental, a conscious attempt to break with the received model of an English university.[157]

The cost of this expansion was inevitably carried by the state. Total university income rose from £6.7 million in 1939 to £22 million in 1950, and the proportion of that income met by parliamentary grant from 35.8 per cent to 63.9 per cent.[158] It was also assumed that the state should assist in widening access to the universities. It had been argued before the Second World War that one of the reasons why so few English schoolchildren went to university was the expense of a university education on top of a comparatively expensive secondary school education.[159] That argument might have been met by abandoning the notion of a 'residential' university and encouraging students to attend 'local' universities and to live (more cheaply) at home. This was not done; by 1950 nearly one-third of all students were in residence. The Attlee government chose to make awards to those who successfully applied for university entry 'mandatory'—fees were paid for all and maintenance provided on a means-tested basis. That made university education in England expensive both for the state and, although fees were paid, for parents, which was one reason why English universities remained so socially exclusive.

4 | *Educational access and social mobility*

The English educational system was perceived to have a number of functions. One of them, and in the eyes of many the most important, was to encourage social mobility, to ameliorate social divisions, and to minimize educational 'wastage' by opening education to all those who might benefit from it. In accordance with the view that education was the most important variable in a person's life-chances, much of the legislation of the period, particularly the 1944 Act, was consciously designed to do precisely those things. How far, in practice, did it do so?

Contemporaries were well aware that there was an apparent relationship between the kind of job a boy or girl could expect and the kind of education he

---

[156] Ibid. 164–80. For the wartime debate on the future size of the universities, see G. F. Kneller, *Higher Learning in Great Britain* (Berkeley and Los Angeles, 1955), 233–47.

[157] For Keele, see Armytage, *Civic Universities*, 291–2.

[158] Halsey and Trow, *British Academics*, 63.

[159] Particularly by Leybourne and White, *Education and the Birth-Rate*, 221–61. In 1937–8 36.9% of boys and 44.2% of girls were in receipt of some form of assistance while at university.

or she had received. For many 'upper-middle-class' occupations a public school education, or a public school and Oxford or Cambridge education was a *sine qua non*. There was, similarly, a close relationship between varieties of post-primary state education and the occupational prestige which that education could purchase. For example, a boy or girl who went only to a senior school, or a senior school followed by part-time technical school, and left without the school certificate, had usually no chance of finding a clerical occupation 'of better standing', nor a particularly good chance of finding skilled manual work. Those, however, who left a secondary school with the school certificate and went on to 'suitable further training' had an excellent chance of getting either.[160]

If contemporaries were right, social mobility crucially depended upon an ever-widening popular access to the higher levels of the country's educational institutions. Throughout the interwar years, in fact, 'higher' education (i.e. secondary) was closed to the vast majority of English schoolchildren. Of boys born before 1910, a mere 7.0 per cent of those who went to elementary school then went to secondary school; of those born between 1910 and 1929, the proportion had doubled but was still only 14.7 per cent. The numbers of girls who went to secondary school was even lower: 5.4 per cent and 12.2 per cent.[161] In 1932 it was calculated that, of children of equal ability, for every one who received a secondary education by winning a free place, seven fee-payers were able to receive one. As a result, much of the working class before 1939 was excluded from any real formal education except (literally) the most elementary.[162] The 1944 Act, it is true, enrolled more working-class children within secondary education: the number of those who went from elementary school to secondary school increased from 15 per cent in 1938–9 to 22 per cent in 1950–1. There was, furthermore, a much closer correlation between 'measured ability' and entry to grammar school after 1944.[163]

In relative terms, however, the working class as a whole had hardly made any gains. Each new addition to the number of free or special places available for competition—and the 1944 Act made every place in a maintained secondary school competitive—seems slightly to have worsened the position of the working class or to have made no difference. In most parts of the country the proportion of free places won by working-class children was no higher in 1950 than in 1914, and in some places lower; at no point did it equal the proportion won by working-class children in the 1920s.

[160] See the table in Leybourne and White, *Education and the Birth-Rate*, 120–1.

[161] J. Floud, 'The Educational Experience of the Adult Population of England and Wales as at July, 1949', in D. V. Glass (ed.), *Social Mobility in Britain* (London, 1954), 118.

[162] Hogben, *Political Arithmetic*, 374–5.

[163] Floud *et al.* describe the change in south-west Hertfordshire as a 'post-war revolution', but note that in Middlesbrough such a correlation had existed for a generation. (Floud *et al.*, *Social Class and Educational Opportunity*, 51.)

The principal beneficiaries of the partial withdrawal of working-class children from the grammar schools in the 1930s were lower-middle-class children—particularly children of 'black-coated' workers, who in no other decade were so successful in the competition for free places. In south-west Hertfordshire they increased their share by 50 per cent; in Middlesbrough by nearly 200 per cent.[164] This success was in part due to the stability of middle-class employment in the interwar years, in part to the ambition of parents well aware of the grammar schools' position on the 'educational ladder', and in part to the importance of a grammar school education to employers in clerical occupations. Neither before nor since was the relationship between the grammar schools and the 'black-coated' professions more intimate. By 1938, 62 per cent of grammar school leavers were entering 'black-coated' occupations, the lower civil service, commerce and the distributive trades and school teaching, jobs which, as parents knew, more than any others, offered security of employment with modest possibilities for promotion.[165] It was thus in the 1930s that the not wholly inaccurate view of the grammar schools as a 'social factory for turning the sons of clerks and shopkeepers into clerks and shopkeepers'[166] developed, as well as the belief that the apparent overstocking of the clerical professions was a consequence of the overstocking of the grammar schools.

From the late 1930s, however, the number of lower-middle-class children successful in the competition for places was both smaller and socially redistributed. Children of 'black-coated' workers were doubly disadvantaged: they lost to working-class children whose parents were, with the return of prosperity, readier to accept grammar school places for them, and to children from other lower-middle-class occupations, like shopkeeping. The failure of the 'black-coated' middle class to maintain its share of competitive grammar school places had important political and social consequences. It meant that 'black-coated' parents were most inclined to 'frustration' at the working of the eleven-plus examination and to be more distressed at the exclusion of their children from grammar school. This exclusion, together with their obvious loss of social esteem in the 1940s and the discriminatory nature of the National Service Acts during the war itself, was one reason why many 'black-coated' workers and their families were so hostile to the working class and the Labour Party after 1945.

Lower-middle-class loss after the outbreak of war was not simply working-class gain. The proportion of places won by working-class boys and girls in the 1940s was higher than in the 1930s, but that was an untypically 'bad' decade. The relative position of working-class children actually deteriorated after 1944. In south-west Hertfordshire in the early 1950s, for example, the

---

[164] Ibid. 35–6.
[165] Leybourne and White, *Education and the Birth-Rate*, 110.
[166] The comment is by Lord Eustace Percy. Quoted in Banks, *Parity and Prestige*, 124.

proportion of working-class boys winning places at grammar schools actually fell while there was a huge increase in the proportion of middle-class boys who did so.[167] Just as the relative beneficiaries of the 1930s had been the sons of 'black-coated' workers, the relative beneficiaries of the 1944 Act were the sons and daughters of professionals and businessmen. The proportion of their children competitively successful rose everywhere; and often more than doubled. Denied the right to buy places at a grammar school by the 1944 Act, they won them instead by examination, and at no cost.[168] By 1950, about 60 per cent of the children of professionals and businessmen could expect to win grammar school places compared with about 10 per cent of working-class children. Furthermore, the differential proportion of working- and middle-class boys and girls who stayed in secondary school beyond the age of 17-plus was hardly affected by the 1944 Act, and the proportion of working-class boys who left school with the school certificate (or its equivalent) no higher after 1944 than before.

What was true of the grammar schools was *ex hypothesi* true of the universities. Of those boys born between 1910 and 1929 who went to elementary schools, 3 per cent entered university; of those who went to independent primary schools, 15.6 per cent entered university; 11.4 per cent of those from grammar schools but 30.6 per cent of those from independent schools went to university. For girls born in those years, the relationships were the same but worse: 0.7 per cent from public elementary schools; 8.6 per cent from independent primary schools; 6.7 per cent from grammar schools and 12.5 per cent from independent boarding schools. About 8.5 per cent of upper- and middle-class boys and 4 per cent of upper- and middle-class girls went to university compared with only 1.4 per cent of working-class boys and 0.2 per cent of working-class. There was also a marked sex-bias. Whereas the number of boys and girls at grammar school was roughly equal, only one-quarter of full-time and one-fifth of part-time university students were women, figures which were obstinately unchanging. The relative number of women at university was actually lower in 1950 than in 1920.[169] As a system of recruitment, university entrance thus discriminated in two ways: against girls of all social classes and against working-class boys. An upper-middle-class boy who went to a major boarding school had an excellent chance of entering a university; a girl from an unskilled working-class family who went to an elementary school had a negligible one.

Given the widespread assumption that education was the most efficacious agency of social mobility, why did so small a proportion of working-class boys

---

[167] Floud *et al.*, *Social Class and Educational Opportunity*, 43.

[168] That is a further reason to question the view that the educated middle class abandoned the state system after 1944.

[169] Halsey, *Trends in British Society*, 217–18.

and girls go to grammar schools, and an even smaller proportion to university? And why, when they did go, did so many perform below their apparent abilities? In the first place, the most important variable in a child's educational career was parental interest and this was much more common in middle- than in working-class families. Working-class parents frequently knew little about the workings of the educational system in the way middle-class parents learnt to do. They usually did not know which primary school best prepared children for grammar school and tended to choose one 'in a neighbourhood spirit'. Many parents, particularly fathers, were, furthermore, sceptical of the value of a grammar school education, and favoured the 'practical' training they assumed could be got elsewhere. This was reinforced by the experience of the 1930s when half the free places awarded to working-class children were refused, when many parents preferred the central schools, whose courses were shorter and more vocational. And they were right to be sceptical: many employers, except in industries like engineering and shipbuilding, were suspicious of secondary school boys and reluctant to be more flexible in the allocation of apprenticeships, particularly if the unions were opposed to flexibility.[170]

There is also an obvious inverse relationship between family size and grammar school entry. Working-class children who were successful came from smaller than average working-class families, lived in socially mixed areas and went to primary schools where middle-class influence was strong.[171] Since, throughout this period, working-class families were larger than middle-class ones, there was an inherent 'demographic' bias against working-class children in the competition for grammar-school places.[172] This bias was exaggerated by the fact that free and special places were open to all children. As there was an inverse relationship between family size and entry into the secondary system, so there was an inverse one between the poverty of a district and the number of free places it was awarded. Although financial necessity was by no means the only reason why so many working-class children were excluded from grammar school, that middle-class children were disproportionately favoured with free places certainly did not help.[173]

Even if they made it to secondary school, they were less likely to last the distance than middle-class children, and more likely to end up in the school's C-stream: premature leaving and underperformance as much characterized

[170] Banks, *Parity and Prestige*, 184.
[171] Jackson and Marsden, *Education and the Working Class*, 52–3.
[172] Campbell, *Eleven Plus*, 87; Caradog Jones, *Merseyside*, ii. 168–9.
[173] Though this was less true of Roman Catholic children. The unskilled working class was twice as well represented in Catholic grammar schools as it was in state schools. The reason for this is not entirely clear, except that in some way both large families and secondary schools were integrated within Catholic practice. (H. T. Himmelweit, 'Social Status and Secondary Education since the 1944 Act', in Glass, *Social Mobility in Britain*, 145; Floud *et al.*, *Social Class and Educational Opportunity*, 134–8.)

working-class children in grammar schools as non-entry itself. There was, once again, parental hostility to persisting with an 'academic' schooling. In industrial areas, especially after 1940 when employment was full and apprenticeships comparatively abundant, children who 'stayed on' were thought to be those incapable of securing apprenticeships, so that early leaving was associated with bright children and 'staying on' with dull ones. The rhythms of grammar school life, in addition, often disrupted familiar domestic routines. Parents (which usually meant fathers) resented the demands of homework. Homework really was a problem for working-class families whose children went to grammar schools. Frequently without bedrooms of their own, and in families who could not in winter afford to heat a separate room, the majority of working-class grammar school pupils (67 per cent) were forced to do their homework in the bosom of the family, to the frequently intense irritation of father and siblings. That the majority of secondary modern schools gave their students virtually no homework was, therefore, a point in their favour.[174] Middle-class families, on the other hand, usually took it as given that homework subordinated all else.

For children who were not themselves socially ambitious a grammar school could stand for unacceptable and alienating expectations and behaviour. These expectations often involved sport which was, as with public schools, central to grammar school traditions. Boys still attached to their working-class origins often had quite different ideas of 'sport' and 'team', and sometimes expressed these differences passionately:

What about the old team spirit, eh? Ask me about the old team spirit—that's all you get at that school. Team games . . . always team games. Load of crap the whole lot! By jove chaps, the team needs you, by jove chaps, well played . . . The kind of games you can play yourself, Christ, they don't count . . . Christ no! Too tough that snooker doesn't count, cricket counts. Team spirit, by jove chaps![175]

In the northern industrial town of 'Marburton' (Huddersfield) friction was caused when boys wanted to play rugby league instead of football; the school would then suggest playing rugby union, 'a game as remote as lacrosse'. Cricket was an even bigger problem.

Schools sometimes tried to detach students from their origins by discouraging old friendships, membership of youth clubs or customary behaviour: eating fish and chips in public caused almost as much trouble as cricket. For working-class girls these restraints could be very tiresome. Socially more mature than middle-class girls, often regarding themselves as adults rather than children, they resented the compulsory uniforms, the frequent bans on boyfriends, and the sometimes bizarre ways these were enforced. They also

---

[174] Ward, *Children Out of School*, 23.
[175] Jackson and Marsden, *Education and the Working Class*, 106–8.

faced hostility from their friends, who all too often became former friends; and some girls appear to have worn their uniforms as badges of shame.[176]

And there was the question of 'accent'. If children at school chose to speak with a demotic accent, they faced disapproval from both teachers and fellow pupils; some children compromised by trying in class not to speak at all. Others attempted to learn what was by the 1930s usually called 'a BBC accent' but which, if spoken at home, risked paternal hostility.[177] Many adopted the prudent habit of speaking one accent at school and another at home: a policy the Board of Education sensibly encouraged.[178] Choice of one or the other was almost inescapably a statement. The deliberate adherence to a local accent often meant wholescale rejection of the grammar school and its values; cultivation of 'BBC' represented an acceptance of those values and preceded a sometimes heartfelt adieu to class and neighbourhood.

For many working-class children who succeeded in winning places, therefore, the grammar school could not be assimilated into their social assumptions and training: relegation to lower streams and a premature departure were often the inevitable results.

Yet the grammar schools were democratic compared with the universities. For much of this period, after all, probably the majority of middle-class children went to the grammar schools and about 40 per cent of their pupils were working-class. But only a small minority of middle-class and a negligible minority of working-class children went to a university. Before the Second World War 98 per cent of the population was excluded, or excluded itself, from the universities. The majority of employers did not want or expect their employees to have a university degree. To the extent that they sought academic credentials at all these were usually provided by the grammar schools. The school certificate or higher school certificate represented in middle-class occupations the kind of qualification which a university degree was to represent a generation later. The university matriculation, which local employers often foisted on the grammar schools, was the closest to a university qualification most grammar school boys and girls came to. It was the acceptability to employers in 'black-coated' occupations of the school and higher school certificate, even more the 'matric', which explains why such a small proportion of grammar school leavers went to university or university training departments.

In much of business, particularly at its senior levels (those whom R. V. Clements has called the 'crown princes'), a university education was thought

---

[176] Summerfield, 'Cultural Reproduction in the Education of Girls', in Hunt, *Lessons for Life*, 164; Young and Willmott, *Family and Kinship*, 176.

[177] In this, as in other matters, mothers and fathers could be at odds. It seems clear that mothers were usually more sympathetic to polite speech than fathers. (See above, pp. 167–8.)

[178] Board of Education, *Suggestions for the Consideration of Teachers*, 1923, 24; and below, pp. 509–11.

much less essential than a public school one.[179] Furthermore, the habit of people securing qualifications part-time or on the job was very persistent; and it was as common on the technical side as on marketing or accounting. A high proportion of self-made men, either as entrepreneurs or managers, took this route: leaving school at 16 or 17, often with only the school certificate, starting work immediately and then enrolling at local technical colleges part-time.[180]

In these circumstances, many were understandably uninterested in a university education if the university did not, as Oxford and Cambridge did, guarantee certain social premiums which *were* important in the labour market: hence, in the City, if a man had not been to Oxford or Cambridge he was unlikely to have been at university at all.[181] 'Bruce Truscot' noted how limited were the vocational prospects of the graduates of civic universities. Opportunities in business were mediocre since employers, if they wanted any graduates, preferred those from Oxford and Cambridge. What remained?—'For women, secretaryships and librarianships (generally ill-paid), marriage (which a gratifyingly large number of them achieve early) and teaching. For men—teaching only.' During the 1920s and 1930s the arts faculties at the redbrick universities became a kind of 'preparatory school to the Department of Agriculture' (he meant by that the lower reaches of the civil service).[182] A majority of the male honours graduates in arts ended up elementary schoolteachers—that is, with jobs for which a university education was not required at all.

It was, indeed, the teachers' training colleges which partly explain why so few girls went to university. In the interwar years between 13,000 and 18,000 people a year entered teachers' colleges—around 30 to 40 per cent of the numbers at university. The majority of training college entrants were women and for them, much more than for men, the colleges were an acceptable alternative to university. Many girls at training colleges actually refused university places. The grammar school–teachers' college connection was for working-class girls a well-known route into the middle class. Of his own highly mobile family, Graham Lee writes that 'for suitable people, entering the anglican church was a way into the middle class—or teaching for girls.'[183] David Caradog Jones attributed the higher rate of women's mobility on Merseyside to the large number of working-class girls who became teachers.[184] In Huddersfield no less than 46 of a sample of 88 working-class grammar school pupils became teachers: most of them girls and most elementary schoolteachers.[185]

---

[179] Clements, *Managers*, 32.   [180] Ibid. 67–75.   [181] Fidler, *British Business Elite*, 84.
[182] Truscot, *Red Brick University*, 204–5.
[183] I am grateful to Mr G. Lee for this information and for his illuminating comments on the history of his own family.
[184] Caradog Jones, *Merseyside*, ii. 181.
[185] Jackson and Marsden, *Education and the Working Class*, 156.

But many girls simply drifted into teaching. Some were under pressure from their own teachers; Roman Catholic grammar schools were known to push girls into elementary teaching because of the desperate need for qualified teachers in the Catholic primary schools. Many girls convinced themselves that they wanted to be teachers, or that they were saving their parents money (in some cases they probably were), but for many others it was simply a result of ignorance or pessimism. Apart from teaching, they often had no knowledge of jobs available for women graduates, and, of course, there were few jobs for women graduates to know about. For many there was the inevitable, rather hopeless feeling (as for girls in all social spheres) that education for women did not matter, or that a girl was trapped in her milieu whatever she did.[186]

This was a view often shared by working-class parents. Whereas a teachers' training college was something they were usually familiar with, a university was not. A child's expressed desire to go to a university could be received with surprise and dismay:

And then he said, 'But I'll tell you what I'd really like. I'd like to be a maths teacher, and that means I'll have to have a university degree'. Well, I could have fainted! I could honestly! I nearly dropped through the floor!'[187]

Even if the idea of a university were manageable, parents rarely knew about scholarships or bursaries, or which university was appropriate, and were often too diffident to ask.

Parents were frequently at odds over university (as they were over grammar schools), and this did not produce an encouraging atmosphere. Mothers were usually more sympathetic, while fathers took the 'practical' view and favoured a commercial or technical education. Both parents also had often legitimate worries about what would happen to their children at university and how it might disrupt their relations with them. And there were social risks. Those who went to their 'local' university (still very common in the 1950s) and lived at home or came home at weekends, were often very unhappy. They lost contact with neighbourhood and friends while not establishing a new neighbourhood or friendships. Relations with parents could become increasingly tense and distant. For those few who went to Oxford and Cambridge, there could be real disorientation. The tendency for results to 'plummet' after the first year was attributed to 'a lost feeling for source, means, purpose; a loss heightened by the absence of the sustaining powers of social and family relationships'.[188] In more extreme cases, it could lead to a personal collapse: Philip Larkin's novel, *Jill* (1946)—based loosely upon St John's College, Oxford (when Cyril Norwood was president)—is a desolating story of personal misery and social

---

[186] Ibid. 141–2. One girl in their study who had contemplated going to Oxford abandoned the idea when she saw the question 'Father's Occupation' on the application form.

[187] Quoted in ibid. 135.   [188] Ibid. 148–9.

dislocation.[189] That so many boys and girls were discouraged from attending university is not, therefore, surprising, and helps to explain why the proportion of undergraduates of working-class origin at university in 1955 (25 per cent) was little higher than the average for 1927–48 (23 per cent), and for men was, if anything, lower.[190]

Changes in England's educational system did not, therefore, significantly improve the *relative* chances of a working-class boy or girl reaching its socially or academically superior levels. There was *absolute* change—many more working-class children went to grammar school than in their parents' generation—but that was due to increased provision which benefited all classes. The *relative* chances of middle-class children going to grammar school—even more to university—were unaffected; indeed, perhaps improved.

In their 1949 study David Glass and his associates found little evidence of significant intergenerational mobility within England. They conceded, however, that 'if a major change does occur in the future, it is more likely to be found in the first generation whose education profits fully from the provisions of the 1944 Education Act.'[191] As this implies, many of those who went to school in our period reached their occupational maturity outside it. What happened to them? Many were intergenerationally mobile: had, that is, jobs which were 'superior' to their fathers'. But, as Goldthorpe and his associates argue, this was 'objective mobility': a result of the growing size of the middle class generally and the service middle class particularly. Since the middle classes could not meet this expansion from their own numbers, it was met by co-opting working-class boys and girls via the education system. Since, however, downward mobility diminished, the *relative* chances of middle-class boys born to fathers with superior occupations themselves having such occupations improved. A middle-class boy was, in practice, four times more likely to have such an occupation than a working-class boy:

The increasing 'room at the top' [Goldthorpe *et al.* conclude] has in fact been shared out more or less *pro rata* among men of different class origins ... so as to produce no change in their relative chances of access; and, on the other hand, the contraction of the working class has been accompanied by a decline not only in the absolute chances of men of Class I and II origins being found in manual work but in their relative chances also. Over all, therefore, the picture obtained, once the perspective of mobility is adopted, is no longer one of significant change in the direction of greater opportunity for social ascent but rather, of stability or indeed of increasing *inequality* in class mobility chances.[192]

---

[189] The 1964 edition of the novel has a revealing preface by Larkin (pp. 11–19) in which he considers the circumstances in which it was written.

[190] The small rise is due to the significantly increased number of women of working-class origins at university after 1945. (Halsey, *Trends in British Society*, 217–19.)

[191] Glass, *Social Mobility in Britain*, 217.

[192] J. H. Goldthorpe (in collaboration with C. Llewellyn and C. Payne), *Social Mobility and Class Structure in Modern Britain* (Oxford, 1980), 76. We should record here the conclusions of Halsey, Heath, and

Although, revealingly, girls hardly appear in these studies, their experience, to the extent that early marriage did not remove them from work altogether, must be broadly similar to their brothers'.

For the mass of the English people, therefore, the educational system did little to modify a social system which was as closed to them in 1950 as it had been in 1918. It did what was demanded; as it always had. It gave to certain working-class boys and girls the education appropriate to an occupational hierarchy which required some working-class mobility, but nothing more.

The history of English education in these years is a history of failure. Even though the state became steadily more active in the educational system, the hopes which animated the 1918 and 1944 legislation—for a national, democratic, and technically effective system—were none of them achieved. The system was not national, partly because too much lay outside it, partly because there remained indefensible regional differences in the quality of education which the state could offer its children. It was undemocratic, not only because the system could never guarantee 'equality of opportunity' (or anything approaching it), but because it frustrated any commonality of experience. It allowed to develop three educational communities, public school, grammar school, and secondary modern and its antecedents, between whom there were Chinese walls growing ever higher. This represented a fissure in social experience more fundamental than in any comparable country. The civil servants who staffed the board–ministry of education did not wish this; they recognized what was happening but colluded with it through a failure of will and nerve.

Ridge who used the same sample as Goldthorpe. They pose a rather different question but come to a not very different answer. They suggest that the 1944 Act was actually quite good at 'disseminating cultural capital' amongst families who had not previously had it. Eighty per cent of 'first-generation' boys at technical schools and two-thirds at grammar schools had parents who had been to neither. The large majority of boys at university came from families where neither parent was a graduate. In their view, class discrimination in the state system affected completion rates as much as selection—something we have already noted (above, pp. 263–4): working-class boys were much less likely to do A-levels than middle-class boys, and if they did them, less likely to get into university. Furthermore, the increase in the number of working-class boys at grammar schools was matched by a proportionate decline in the number at technical schools—a predictable result of the decay of the technical schools. And the technical schools were the only ones whose own social composition was more or less similar to that of the country as a whole. The grammar schools still grossly over-represented the middle classes while the independent schools remained as exclusive as ever: 'This picture of unequal access to the superior secondary schools has remained depressingly constant over time. For the selective secondary schools as a group, chances of access rose at all levels of the class structure in the middle of our period, but then fell back again to levels very like those of a generation earlier. Thus the likelihood of a working-class boy receiving a selective education in the mid 'fifties and 'sixties, was very little different from his parents' generation thirty years earlier.' (A. H. Halsey, A. F. Heath, and J. M. Ridge, *Origins and Destinations: Family, Class and Education in Modern Britain* (Oxford, 1980), 200. For a summary of their conclusions, 195–219.) See also Caradog Jones, *Merseyside*, ii. 39–42; and M. Ginsberg, *Studies in Sociology* (London, 1932), 169–70.

Nor did the system teach really 'useful' knowledge. The public schools certainly taught the social skills required by members of the English élite: but how useful that was must be a matter of opinion. The grammar schools produced people who were both overqualified and underqualified. They were institutions which were very good at preparing their students for university; that is why so many were dominated by the matriculation. The majority of their students, however, did not go to university, nor did they sit the 'matric'. On the contrary, they entered occupations for which they were academically overqualified and technically underqualified, since the grammar schools would not teach strictly vocational subjects. The higher elementary schools, central schools, and secondary modern schools did teach what purported to be vocationally useful knowledge but which in practice was not. The schools which might have done this, the junior technical schools, were allowed to wither and die—to the cost both of the educational system and the country.

The universities were so exclusive as scarcely to impinge on the system at all. Although they expanded, particularly after the Second World War, and although the state increasingly understood its responsibilities to them, they enrolled so few, and those they did represented such a skewed social profile, that the possibility of their being part of a national or democratic educational system was negligible. The only way they could have broken out would have been via something like the 'GI's Bill', legislation which would have guaranteed more or less all ex-servicemen university entrance. But in the circumstances of the later 1940s that would have put an impossible strain on their resources; though it is in any case unlikely, given popular assumptions, that a majority of ex-servicemen or women would have taken the opportunity. It is characteristic of the universities, at least before the Second World War, that they should have been most affected not by the actions of government or the demands of democratic opinion, but by an entirely unforeseen event: the migration of refugee-scholars from central Europe in the 1930s.

The real impediment to the growth of a national system was the well-entrenched position of the independent and grammar schools. The public schools never lacked critics, and during the Second World War there were many who thought they could not and should not survive. But they had powerful defenders and weak or intermittent opposition. Even the Labour Party (as a whole), though believing the schools socially exclusive, nevertheless thought them educationally excellent, and those members of the Fleming Committee associated with the Labour Party signed its report.[193] Not one Labour MP supported an amendment to the 1944 Act which would have required all parents to send their children to a school maintained by their local authority. Although it is unlikely people would have been much moved by their aboli-

---

[193] Barker, *Education and Politics*, 112–15.

tion, public attitudes to the independent schools were probably benign or neutral. The idea of the schools which much of the population received as children through magazines like *Gem* or *Wizard* was always positive, while the enormous popularity (both as a book and a film) of James Hilton's *Goodbye Mr Chips* is a good index of opinion.

The grammar schools were never as well-entrenched as the independent schools. In the circumstances of the late 1930s, indeed, it is possible that politically non-contentious multilateral schools could have emerged out of the grammar schools. Before 1939 it was not thought necessarily party-political to support such schools and the evolution of the middle class in the thirties points as much to multilateral as it does to grammar schools. Once, however, multilateralism became associated in the 1940s with the Labour Party (even though its leadership tended to favour the grammar schools) and the trade unions it ceased to be non-political. Multilateralism did eventually come, but not consensually.

How far, then, did the educational system promote mobility? The answer is, very little. Throughout the period the dominant metaphor was 'the ladder of opportunity'; the ladder carried bright children, who earned their place on it by merit, from elementary school to university at little cost to themselves. But, as David Caradog Jones commented, the metaphor was all too apt 'for it is characteristic of a ladder that, although a number of persons may mount up it, they can do so only one or two at a time'.[194] It is better to see the system as an obstacle course which continuously eliminated working-class children except those who proved, by clambering over the obstacles, that they were fit to be co-opted. And education proved fitness, not so much by nurturing ability or teaching useful knowledge, though it could do these things incidentally, as by defining and rewarding ability in terms acceptable to the country's élites. The essence of the system was not, therefore, comprehension but selection, and selection, in turn, established a hierarchy of schools with a major boarding school at the top and a 'council school' at the bottom. Those few who did keep going then entered a university hierarchy with Oxford and Cambridge at the top and a small recently founded civic university at the bottom.

---

[194] Caradog Jones, *Merseyside*, ii. 164. More generally, see A. Little and J. Westergaard, 'The Trend of Class Differentials in Educational Opportunity in England and Wales', *British Journal of Sociology*, 15 (1964), 310–12.

TENSIONS between the 'religious' and the 'secular' in English life were profound and, throughout these years, unresolved. This chapter explores the extent to which the English practised a religion and attempts to assess how far they had religious or quasi-religious beliefs. It looks at the experience of each of the significant Christian churches over the period, how that experience differed between different churches, at the nature and meaning of 'secularization', and at the extent to which people held transcendent beliefs irrespective of church attendance or formal religious affiliation. It also considers the degree to which men and women differed in their beliefs.

1 | *The Christian religions and their membership*

The great majority of the English almost certainly thought of England as a Christian nation and most believed themselves (one way or another) to be Christian. Measuring the intensity and extent of their Christian belief, however, is not easy. Negatively, they were, if not active Christians, usually not anything else. Before Islam became a significant religion in England in the late 1950s, very few English were anything other than nominally Christian. The proportion of them who were practising Jews is not certain, but the total Jewish population was never more than about 400,000–450,000, and by no means all of these were observant. Some converted to Christianity; many practised intermittently; many simply ceased practising; exogenous marriage had its inevitable effect.[1] Although there were areas of the country with an active and numerically important Judaism—East and (increasingly) North and North-West London, Leeds, and Manchester, for example—Jews never constituted more than about 2 per cent of those who practised a religion and an even smaller proportion of the total population.

---

[1] Many Jews attended synagogue only at the New Year or the Day of Atonement—the Jewish equivalent of Christians attending church only at Easter or Christmas. Many otherwise non-practising families recognized the Passover—but that was a domestic celebration and as much a cultural as religious rite. For the Jewish population, see V. D. Lipman, *Social History of the Jews in England, 1850–1950* (London, 1954), 168–72; Geoffrey Alderman, *Modern British Jewry* (Oxford, 1992), 209–323.

In 1920, about 60 per cent of the population was nominally Anglican (or 'Church of England' as it was usually called), 15 per cent were Free Church and 5 per cent Roman Catholic. The remainder, largely in the unskilled working class, were probably nothing. But these figures, especially those for the Church of England, are misleading. Many of those who claimed a nominal Anglicanism, for instance, had no effective relationship with the Church—other than attendance at weddings and funerals (if that). The same holds true, though to a lesser extent, of those who described themselves as 'Free Church' or 'Catholic'. Thus actual membership was much smaller than the nominal.[2] For Britain as a whole the total number of 'members' of the Protestant churches and the total estimated Roman Catholic population is as follows:

	Protestant	Roman Catholic
[1910]	[5,670,000]	[2,216,000]
1920	5,654,000	2,502,000
1930	5,829,000	2,781,000
1940	5,440,000	3,023,000
1950	5,077,000	3,499,000
[1970]	[4,311,000]	[4,429,000]

In absolute numbers, the Church of England reached its apogee in the late 1930s; the Free Churches reached theirs in the late 1920s. The Roman Catholic population (and almost certainly, therefore, attendance at mass) increased steadily throughout the period. However, as a proportion of the total population which they recruited both the Anglican and Free Churches declined almost without interruption. In 1921 the Church of England could claim as members 8.766 per cent of the population over 15; in 1951 only 5.814 per cent. In 1921 2.601 per cent of the population over 15 was Methodist; in 1951 only 1.953 per cent.[3]

Perhaps the most striking figures were those for Sunday school attendance. In 1918 two million children went each week to Anglican Sunday schools; by 1953 the number had fallen to 1.3 million. In the Methodist Church the decline was even more severe. In 1933 nearly 1.3 million went to Methodist Sunday schools; in 1950 the figure was 800,000. The number of junior members of the Methodist Church was 107,626 in 1933, but only 31,843 in 1950. Parents

---

[2] The churches adopted different ways of measuring their membership. These are discussed in, and the figures drawn from, R. Currie, A. Gilbert, and L. Horsley, *Churches and Churchgoers: Patterns of Church Growth in the British Isles since 1700* (London, 1977) and R. Currie and A. Gilbert, 'Religion' in Halsey (ed.), *Trends in British Society*, 407–50. See also Caradog Jones, *Merseyside*, ii. 339, where it is pointed out that the churches tended to inflate their memberships. On Merseyside, for example, the Catholic Church claimed as adherents more manual workers than there were in the total population of Merseyside. The Protestant churches did the same for skilled workers.

[3] For the Welsh figures, which show a similar trend, see K. O. Morgan, *Wales, 1880–1980* (Oxford, 1981), 352–3.

notoriously despatched their offspring to Sunday schools for a variety of reasons, many having little to do with religion, but it was at Sunday school that most Protestant children were first exposed to formal religious practice. The falling popularity of the Sunday schools was not merely a sign of growing indifference to organized religion but also one of its causes.[4]

The two major Protestant churches and the Roman Catholic Church had in this period obviously differing histories. The Church of England and the Free Churches lost significant numbers during both world wars—despite what some contemporaries thought, there is no evidence that people in wartime turned to religion for consolation—but recouped many of them in the immediate post-war years. They did not, however, recoup them in proportion to the increase in population. In 1901 the Protestant churches could claim as members about 20 per cent of the adult population; by 1951 they could claim only about 14 per cent. The only 'Protestant' exceptions to this seemingly irreversible decline were the Seventh Day Adventists, the Jehovah's Witnesses and some of the smaller Protestant sects like the Elim Four Square Gospel Church which actually grew rapidly in the interwar years.[5] The membership of the Jehovah's Witnesses[6] rose from 6,000 in 1926 to 23,050 in 1951, a figure that continued to rise rapidly. What all these had in common, as against traditional Protestantism, was a weak or even non-existent clergy, a high degree of congregational participation, and often a strong pentecostal impulse.

The Roman Catholic Church, however, was able to resist these secular processes. Catholic Church membership rose steadily, both in absolute numbers and as a fraction of the total membership of the Christian churches. Whereas, for example, the number of marriages solemnized in the Anglican Church, as a proportion of the whole, fell from 59.7 per cent in 1919 to 49.6 per cent in 1952, the number solemnized in the Roman Catholic Church rose from 5.2 per cent to 9.4 per cent.[7] Without the success of the Catholic Church in withstanding this seemingly remorseless 'dechristianization' the proportion of the population which claimed religious affiliation would have been significantly smaller than it actually was.[8]

Within the active membership of the Christian churches itself there were several perceptible biases. Regular church attendance was much higher in the South of England than in the North, with the partial exception of Lancashire and the North-East where there were substantial Roman Catholic populations. The explanation for this is, to some extent, a class one. The middle classes were

---

[4] Currie *et al.*, *Churches and Churchgoers*, 86–7.

[5] For the Elim, see B. R. Wilson, *Sects and Society* (London, 1961), 30–60.

[6] Members of the Jehovah's Witness Society are technically called 'publishers' since they distribute the Society's publications.

[7] Currie and Gilbert, in Halsey, *Trends in British Society*, 415.

[8] J. Highet, 'Scottish Religious Adherence', *British Journal of Sociology*, 4 (1953), 151.

more likely to go to church than the working classes and the South was more 'middle class' than the North. Indeed, church membership, broadly speaking, correlated closely with social class: the higher the class the higher the church attendance.[9] Within the Anglican Church, baptized middle-class children were very much more likely to be confirmed than baptized working-class children.[10] And male unskilled workers, unless they were of Irish origin, were largely untouched by organized religion. The only Christian church whose membership roughly approximated the country's social structure was the Roman Catholic Church. But it was only a rough approximation since the comparative smallness of the Catholic middle class meant that the middle classes were as under-represented at mass as they were over-represented at holy communion.[11]

Church membership (again with the partial exception of the Catholic Church) was, furthermore, much higher in rural than in urban areas, and this was especially true for the Church of England. There were still more Anglican churches per inhabitant in the countryside than in the towns. The church also had an obvious social and cultural function in the country, which it did not in the cities. In rural England it was a focus for social activity which was often catered for in the cities by proliferating secular foci. Higher church attendance in the countryside does not, therefore, necessarily imply a greater intensity of belief; it does, however, seem to imply a greater involvement with religious practice. The BBC found that its religious broadcasts were more widely listened to in rural England than in the English towns. In London and Birmingham they were hardly listened to at all.[12]

The pattern of church attendance was also skewed by age and sex. Church attenders were younger and older than the population as a whole. The comparative youthfulness of congregations was partly the result of the lingering influence of Sunday school (which is why falling attendances were so harmful to the Protestant churches) or of compulsory attendance at public school chapels. The comparative elderliness was the result of a persistence within an older generation of habits learnt before 1914. In addition to this age-bias, all the churches, particularly the Anglican, were disproportionately female. On Merseyside, for example, where the ratio of women to men in the whole population was 111 to 100, the ratio of women to men in the Christian congregations was: 163 to 100 in the Church of England, 148 to 100 in the Free Churches, and 119 to 100 in the Roman Catholic Church. Within the Church of England the prominence of women schoolteachers and domestics was striking.[13]

---

[9] A. Hastings, *A History of English Christianity, 1920–1990* (London and Philadelphia, 1991), 39–40.
[10] In part this was due to the more or less compulsory confirmation of boys and girls at public schools.
[11] Caradog Jones, *Merseyside*, ii. 338.   [12] Highet, 'Scottish Religious Adherence', 153.
[13] Caradog Jones, *Merseyside*, ii. 330.

As with social class, the sex-ratio of the Roman Catholic Church more closely approximated that of the whole population than any other major church.

By an index of church membership the great majority of the English were Christians neither in 1918 nor in 1951. Even the Roman Catholic Church, whose increasing numbers were an essential prop to the Christianity of the whole nation, probably never recruited more than half the nominally Catholic population. By the standards of many European countries or the United States England was a 'dechristianized' country. It was, however, the Protestant churches which in this period had to cope with the obvious manifestations of the secular; the comparative introversion of the Roman Catholic community permitted the Catholic Church to escape them until the 1960s.

2 | *The established Church*

For all its status as the official church of the nation, the Church of England was losing members almost as fast as the Free Churches. Although the majority of the population professed themselves to be 'Church of England' and although it always thought of itself as the 'National Church', in no real sense was it the church of the nation: only a small and declining proportion of the whole population was actively Anglican. Yet the Church of England had certain inherited strengths denied to the Free Churches. While it might not have been a national church it was certainly an official one. It was the established Church of the kingdom of England and was thus conspicuously a part of the state and its rituals. It christened, crowned, and buried the sovereign, its 'supreme governor', and was by law, practice, and in the public mind closely associated with the royal family. Its diocesan bishops were members of the House of Lords and were, as individuals, drawn very largely from the country's élites: in 1920 over half the bench of bishops was connected with the peerage or landed gentry by birth or marriage, and almost all had been to a public school and then to Oxford or Cambridge. Virtually none had any formal theological training, but they nearly all still had immense social prestige.

The Church of England derived one other advantage from being established—it was endowed. Endowment did not make the clergy wealthy—the money value of most clergy stipends had been frozen at their 1914 levels throughout the interwar years and by conventional middle-class standards many parish clergy were actually poor[14]—but it did mean that the Anglicans escaped the full severity of the financial difficulties which faced the Free Churches after 1918. The endowment allowed it to maintain its ecclesiastical organization largely intact (at least until the 1950s), despite the shrinking congregations.

---

[14] See above, p. 52.

Being an official church, however, had the disadvantage that the Church of England's theological and institutional freedom was strictly circumscribed. It was by its constitutional status political and therefore had to endure political intervention. Nothing illustrated these constraints better than the Church's attempt to revise the 1662 Prayer Book in 1927 and 1928. The revisions to the Prayer Book, which undoubtedly would have 'Catholicized' it, particularly by allowing reservation of the sacrament, were designed partly to assimilate the Prayer Book to the usages of the Roman Catholic and Orthodox Churches and partly to recognize the preponderance of Anglo-Catholic theology amongst the clergy. The revised Book was passed by the Church Assembly in 1927 by surprisingly large majorities in all three houses.[15] Even if the Church had had an entirely free hand, however, this would still have been an intensely controversial issue, since Anglo-Catholicism was much stronger among the clergy than among the laity. And it seemed to force Anglicans to ask a question most thought it better to avoid: was the Anglican Church Protestant or not? For much of the clergy it was not so much Protestant as 'national Catholic'; for the majority of the laity it was almost certainly Protestant. Two of the most vigorous lay opponents of revision in the House of Laity were also members of the then Conservative government—William Joynson-Hicks, the home secretary who later in 1928 was to become celebrated for his part in the banning of *The Well of Loneliness*,[16] and Thomas Inskip, the solicitor- and then attorney-general. It was they who led the opposition to the revised Book in the House of Commons, whose approval, under the 1919 Enabling Act, was required for any changes to the Prayer Book of the established Church.[17] After emotional debates the measure incorporating revision was finally defeated in the Commons (June 1928) after having been passed by the Lords. The majority of practising Anglicans in the Commons (and the majority of English MPs) voted for revision; it was defeated by a Protestant coalition of evangelical Anglicans, English nonconformists, and Scots and Welsh, hardly any of whom were Anglican.[18]

---

[15] House of Bishops, 34 to 4; House of Clergy, 253 to 37; House of Laity, 230 to 92.

[16] See below, pp. 324–5.

[17] The 1919 Enabling Act established the Church Assembly and permitted it to legislate regulations for the Church, subject to the formal approval of parliament. (See R. Lloyd, *The Church of England in the Twentieth Century* (London, 1950), ii. 5–18.)

[18] The revised Prayer Book was first introduced in Dec. 1927 and defeated. (*HCD*, 5s, 211, clmns. 2531–655, 15 Dec. 1927.) The proposed revisions were then modified and the Book again presented to the House of Commons on 13 June 1928. It was defeated once more and by a larger majority— 266–220, for which it was thought at the time that the Labour vote was responsible. The archbishop of York, Cosmo Gordon Lang, believed so. The Labour Party, he wrote, had not forgiven those bishops 'who dabbled in the coal strike' (a reference to the bishop of Durham, Hensley Henson). (J. G. Lockhart, *Cosmo Gordon Lang* (London, 1949), 303.) Contemporaries were surprised by the prominence of Labour MPs in the debates: two of the most vehement opponents of revision were the Scottish Labour MPs Rosslyn Mitchell (Paisley) and James Barr (Motherwell). But Barr was a Church of Scotland minister and his opposition was not surprising. Mitchell was personally strongly Protestant, but he also had a large anti-Catholic working-class electorate. The Labour Party, in any case,

The defeat of the revised Prayer Book was often later regarded merely as yet another bizarre incident in the eccentric career of Joynson-Hicks, the famous 'Jix'. But the often heartfelt nature of the debate, the surprisingly high attendance—in 1928 (allowing for formal abstentions) more than 500 MPs were present—and its outcome suggest that it was more than that. Many MPs, particularly Labour ones, insisted that the Church of England must be Protestant and as an established Church had in itself no authority to modify a Protestant theology. Harry Snell, Labour MP for East Woolwich, argued that

the Church is not a free body; it is the Church of England, and it represents the official religion of the Nation. Its Prayer Book is of the nature of a State document and, therefore, when it comes before us Members of Parliament, we are bound to give it the same serious, and I hope unprejudiced attention, that we would give to any other Bill or Order that came before us.[19]

Rosslyn Mitchell, Labour MP for Paisley and passionately hostile to the revised Book, said that the 'Church of England is really a sort of representative Church of the whole people of England', and that as an established Church it was acceptable to this whole people only so long as it was Protestant.[20] Even the proponents of the Book agreed with this. The Conservative MP for Rusholme, Sir Boyd Merriman, who introduced the revised Book to the House of Commons in 1928, assured MPs that it preserved 'the Protestant character' of the Anglican Church and he went out of his way to disassociate the Book from 'the more lawless extravagance of certain [Anglo-Catholic] clergy'.[21]

Secular contemporaries were startled by the passions which the Prayer Book released. Some thought the debate entirely anachronistic. Yet these passions demonstrated both the residual centrality of the established Church to English public life and the strength of a kind of historic Protestantism in the English people's perception of themselves. It also demonstrated how deceived were those clergy who believed that the Church of England could claim a full theological and liturgical autonomy and yet be preserved as the national church. Many, indeed, recognized that: the defeat of the revised Prayer Book was the only occasion before the Second World War when some clergy were prepared to argue seriously the case for disestablishment.[22]

was not unanimous: though most Labour MPs who voted, voted against, both Arthur Henderson and Sidney Webb, for example, voted for, almost certainly on the disestablishmentarian principle of a free church in a free state. Henry Slesser, solicitor-general in the first Labour government, who was a member of the House of Laity, spoke and voted for the revised Book. (S. Saklatvala, the sole Communist MP, voted against.) What defeated the revised Book was not the Labour vote but the Protestant vote.

[19] *HCD*, 5.s. 218, clmns. 1082–3, 13 June 1928.   [20] Ibid., clmn. 1125.

[21] Ibid., clmns. 1179–81.

[22] In fact, disestablishment was not needed. The Church Assembly authorized the use of the revised Book by members of the parish clergy at the discretion of their diocesan bishops. This was a clear illegality which neither government nor parliament made any effort to police.

Leading the Church in these circumstances was not easy. The role of a state church in a society which combined increasingly strong secular and pluralist tendencies with a deep, if atavistic and largely unpractised Protestantism, and which also demanded that the Church make judgements on contentious politico-moral questions, was not obvious. Leadership, to the extent that the four archbishops of Canterbury in this period were able to provide it, inclined, therefore, to a cautious adjustment to political and social changes, together with a reluctance to offend the government of the day. On the whole, this was done with some skill, if only mixed success. Randall Davidson (archbishop of Canterbury 1903–28), a sensible and careful man, was able to hold the Church together, but was not able to get anything approaching liturgical agreement. He had, furthermore, his fingers badly burned during the general strike, when his attempt to broadcast the Protestant Churches' eirenic proposals on the BBC was forbidden by Sir John Reith at the instigation of the prime minister, Stanley Baldwin.[23] The defeat of the revised Prayer Book, which he promoted with little enthusiasm only two years later, was too much for Davidson and, nearly 80, he resigned the see of Canterbury the same year.

His successor, Cosmo Gordon Lang (archbishop of Canterbury 1928–42), like his predecessor a Scot and raised as a Presbyterian, was similarly inclined towards compromise. The Prayer Book fiasco (for which as archbishop of York he bore more responsibility than Davidson) induced in him an extreme caution and a fairly open Baldwinian Conservatism. As a general strategy this was not particularly controversial or unwise; but even Lang found that direct political intervention could be dangerous. It was he who had to deal with the abdication of Edward VIII, an event of peculiar sensitivity to a state church. The position adopted by Lang (which was to support the position adopted by Baldwin and the dominion prime ministers) was, from the point of view of such a church, almost certainly correct. But the manner in which he expressed that support could not have been more maladroit. Immediately after the king's abdication, on 13 December, Lang broadcast his reflections, which were intended both by himself and Baldwin to be the view of church and state. 'Strange and sad', Lang said,

it must be that for such a motive [private happiness] . . . he should have disappointed hopes so high and abandoned a trust so great. Even more strange and sad it is that he should have sought his happiness in a manner inconsistent with the Christian principles of marriage, and within a social circle whose standards and ways of life are alien to all the best instincts and traditions of the people . . . Let those who belong to this circle know that to-day they stand rebuked by the judgement of the nation which loved King Edward.[24]

---

[23] For this episode, see G. Phillips, *The General Strike: The Politics of Industrial Conflict* (London, 1976), 184–5. Baldwin's behaviour did not stop Davidson from congratulating him at the end of the strike on 'his firmness, persistent conciliatoriness, and solid practical counsel'. (Ibid. 223.)

[24] Quoted in Lockhart, *Lang*, 405. Lockhart's account of the abdication is interesting since it is effectively Lang's account.

This was an unctuous and unpleasant address, widely criticized in the upper and upper middle classes.[25] For many of them Lang was to be chiefly remembered as Gerald Bullett's famous rhyme portrayed him:

> My Lord Archbishop, what a scold you are!
> And when your man is down how bold you are!
> Of charity how oddly scant you are!
> How Lang, O Lord, how full of Cantuar![26]

Yet there is little doubt that Lang put into words what most of the English felt about the king's liaison with Mrs Simpson, as MPs of all parties discovered when they consulted constituency opinion. Several things counted against Mrs Simpson—that she was a commoner and an American were two; but that she was once and about to be twice divorced probably counted most. Some in the king's circle hoped that what was thought to be the social permissiveness of the age—in less than a year the divorce laws were to be significantly liberalized[27]—might allow for some 'arrangement' which would keep Edward on the throne with Mrs Simpson as his wife. That was never possible: a public morality which the Christian and, indeed, Jewish religions embodied and legitimated forbade it. It is hard to see how any archbishop of Canterbury could have acquiesced in the Anglican Church's supreme head behaving in the way Edward wished to.

Lang was succeeded in 1942 by the archbishop of York, William Temple (archbishop of Canterbury, 1942–4), the son, as Davidson had been the son-in-law, of a former archbishop of Canterbury. Temple was probably the most impressive churchman of his age; very different in his social thinking, though little in his theology, from his two predecessors.[28] Active in the Student Christian Movement (SCM), in 'Life and Liberty', which was instrumental in securing the 1919 Act, prime mover of the Conference on Christian Politics, Economics and Citizenship (COPEC) of 1924,[29] a member of the Labour Party (1918–21) and a leading figure in the National Council of Social Service,[30] Temple typified the strengths of 'left'

---

[25] Not least in King Edward's 'social circle'. Henry Channon, who stood in its very epicentre, wrote of the broadcast: 'Of course the most conspicuous rat of all is the Archbishop of Canterbury, Old Cosmo Cantuar, who in a monstrous broadcast last night, poured scorn on the late King, and branded his social circle as people whose ways of life were alien to all that is best in the instincts and traditions of the British people. This is a terrible indictment and an unfair one.' (14 Dec. 1936.) A few days later Channon 'wrote a dignified snorter to His Grace today. I hope the old gentleman has asphyxia' (17 Dec. 1936; Rhodes James, *Chips*, 102–4).

[26] This is the version quoted by Vera Brittain (*Testament of Experience* (London, 1957), 163), but it is only one of many.

[27] See below, pp. 302–3.   [28] For Temple, see F. A. Iremonger, *William Temple* (London, 1948).

[29] For the 'Life and Liberty' movement, see Hastings, *English Christianity*, 19, 44–5. For COPEC, E. R. Norman, *Church and Society in England, 1770–1970* (Oxford, 1976), 279–92.

[30] He resigned from the Labour Party on being appointed bishop of Manchester. For the National Council of Social Service, see Temple's introduction to the Pilgrim Trust's *Men without Work*, viii–xii.

Anglicanism, its ecumenicism and social concern, and its weaknesses, a certain intellectual woolliness and a reluctance to see things through.

Temple was in his own way as cautious as Lang. Lang's moderate Conservatism helped the Church weather a decade politically dominated by a moderate Conservatism; equally, Temple's prudent but undoubted progressivism aligned the Church to the progressivism which was ideologically predominant during the Second World War. With his death in 1944 and the appointment of Geoffrey Fisher to succeed him, the Church was once more led by a man suited to the revived moderate Conservatism which dominated the 1950s.

The very eclecticism of the Church of England, the extent to which it was becoming an arena for competing Protestant and Anglo-Catholic theologies, ensured it a religious centrality increasingly denied to the Free Churches. That it comprehended so many was, at least in its own eyes, one of the Church's strengths. But comprehension denied it intellectual or theological coherence. The Catholic and Protestant Reformed traditions were uneasy bedfellows, and any movement in one direction or the other tended to be divisive. A 'Catholic' Prayer Book was no more repugnant to some than the willingness of the Church to exploit American evangelism was to others.

In the 1930s both the archbishop of Canterbury and a number of the bishops, particularly the bishop of London, Winnington-Ingram, were prepared to work with and encourage Frank Buchman, the founder of what was originally called the 'Oxford Group' and later Moral Rearmament (MRA). To its admirers MRA was a powerful, spiritual form of contemporary personal evangelism; to its critics, a vaguely unhealthy process whereby well-born, well-mannered, and often athletic young men made unsettling disclosures at house-parties. Since it had both admirers and critics within the Church, MRA's position was always controversial.[31] Equally, Archbishop Lang's 'Back to God' campaign in 1937 and Archbishop Fisher's association with Billy Graham's famous 1954 crusade caused as much embarrassment as they did enthusiasm.[32]

While the Anglican Church was better armoured against a secular age than the Free Churches—by its endowment, its social and political status, and its openness—it lacked the single-mindedness of the smaller Protestant sects or of a still ultramontane Roman Catholicism. Its institutional decline, as measured by formal membership and practice, though not as rapid as the Free Churches, was, nevertheless, as irreversible.

3 | The Free Churches

The Free Churches coped less well with secular forces than any other major

---

[31] There is a sympathetic and informative account of MRA in the 1930s in G. Lean, *Frank Buchman: A Life* (London, 1985), 176–90.

[32] Fisher sat next to Graham at the last and most spectacular of the 1954 meetings.

religion; they were worst affected by both world wars and recovered from them with least success. Unlike the Church of England, the Free Churches had no national endowment: their structure depended upon the willingness and ability of the congregations to pay for them, and thus indirectly on the prosperity of the communities from which they drew their members. But it was these communities, the traditional strongholds of nonconformity, which were most pauperized by the unexpected depression in the old staple industries after 1920, and nowhere more severely than in coalmining (the bedrock of Primitive Methodism), and, a little later, in agriculture.[33] Throughout parts of Yorkshire, Lancashire, the North-East, the West Country, and South Wales, the actual physical survival of the Free Churches was endangered. The upkeep of chapels, the stipends of ministers, the provision of lay personnel, all became problematic as local economies decayed and as young men (and their families) moved to southern England or the Midlands, many of them never to return to the churches in which they were raised. Canon E. R. Wickham, canon residentiary of the Sheffield Industrial Mission, was so struck by the effect of this in West Yorkshire that he could speak of the 'collapse of the Churches in the inter-war years'.[34] The neglected bethels of South Wales and the crumbling chapels of Co. Durham were poignant souvenirs of these regional catastrophes.[35]

Furthermore, the severity of the interwar economic depression in the old staple industries accelerated the relative decline of those occupations from which the nonconformists had traditionally recruited—mining and quarrying, textiles, agriculture, and fishing. Between 1921 and 1951 the proportion of the total male workforce employed in them declined from 21.3 per cent to 13 per cent. In the nineteenth century they had been an abundant source of Free Church membership for which nonconformity never found an entirely adequate substitute. It would, of course, be easy to overrate the speed and depth of this change: the institutions of nonconformity never disappeared and it established itself in many areas as a suburban lower-middle-class church. But in the suburbs, unlike its old homelands, it faced the often irresistible competition of a socially superior Anglicanism or of urban indifference.[36] And eventually it ceded many members to both.

The Free Churches also lost some of their élan when the semi-political causes for which nonconformity stood, and which in many ways identified it, lost their social significance. Temperance, sabbatarianism, hostility to the established Church, secular education, all meant much less in the 1920s than in 1914. Some, like disestablishmentarianism, now counted for virtually nothing. It was on the back of these issues, however, that both nonconformity (and

[33] See above, p. 112.
[34] E. R. Wickham, *Church and People in an Industrial City* (London, 1957), 209.
[35] This is well discussed in Pilgrim Trust, *Men without Work*, pt. v (Rhondda and Crook).
[36] Currie *et al.*, *Churches and Churchgoers*, 62, 103–5.

thus the Liberal Party) had traditionally ridden and had mounted their seemingly miraculous recoveries at the turn of the century. The First World War, by significantly relaxing social attitudes and by breaking up rather inward-looking nonconformist communities, here did most harm. When before 1914 nonconformists sought from the Labour Party a commitment to legislative control of the drink trade, that was a serious business; when in 1928 Arthur Henderson, a leading lay Wesleyan and the Party's secretary, resigned from its election committee because it excluded the 'drink question' from the Party's manifesto, that simply caused irritation and derision.[37]

Given the historic significance of these issues to the ideology and membership of the Free Churches, the emergence of the Labour Party after 1918 as the principal party of the left made it even more difficult for them to reconstruct their social identity. Much of the leadership of the Labour Party in the 1920s was, of course, strongly nonconformist, as was part of its post-war electorate; but the Labour Party could never stand in relation to the Free Churches as the Liberal Party did. At a local level the Labour Party was almost wholly secular and it had few connections with the old Free Church–Friendly Society network. Its connections were with specifically working-class organizations like the trade unions and the co-ops and it was associated, both by itself and its opponents, with 'socialism'. The increasing importance to politics of 'class' and 'socialism' and the decreasing importance of education, drink, etc., undermined the self-confidence and unity of the Free Churches.[38] Whereas all nonconformists were hostile to public funding of Anglican or Roman Catholic schools, there could be no such unanimity about their attitudes to the Labour Party. Nor was it easy for them to avoid choosing between 'socialism' or 'anti-socialism'. Nonconformity became ever more divided on what was essentially a secular question. By making apparently redundant the issues upon which a once strongly partisan anti-Anglicanism, anti-Conservatism was based, the emergence of the Labour Party left middle-class nonconformity open to appropriation by an 'anti-socialist' Anglican Conservatism. The steady drift of both clerical and lay nonconformists into the Church of England in the late 1930s and 1940s was partly due to this.

A certain theological and ceremonial etiolation was probably also making the Free Churches increasingly unattractive. The plainness of the services, their deliberate austerity and non-sacramentalism, was ecclesiastically viable only as long as nonconformist moralities were generally acceptable. Once they were widely contested or ignored, however, as after 1918, Free Church liturgies tended to become rather grim injunctions against certain kinds of commonly practised behaviour. This probably did not much alienate older members but it certainly made it difficult for nonconformity to recruit newer and younger ones. The Free Churches probably had the worst of both worlds: their orders of

---

[37] McKibbin, *Ideologies of Class*, 44–5.
[38] S. Koss, *Nonconformists in Modern British Politics* (London, 1975), 145–215.

service were neither sacramental nor priestly enough to compete with the Anglicans, nor enthusiastic and participatory enough to compete with the smaller Protestant religions like the Adventists or the Witnesses.

The Free Churches were aware that they were losing ground. One response was a traditional revivalism: between 1943 and 1945, for example, the Methodists embarked upon a 'team evangelism' called Christian Commando Campaigns and in the 1950s, like the Anglicans, closely associated themselves with Billy Graham's crusades. None of these had any noticeable long- or even short-term effect.

A more obvious response was to attempt some sort of reunion. By the mid-1920s the notion that the various Free Churches should compete for the same dwindling flock seemed much less defensible than before 1914, and even less defensible for the three Methodist Churches—Wesleyans, Primitives, and United Methodists. In the economic circumstances of the 1920s, furthermore, it seemed doubtful that they could even afford to. There were also theological-political reasons for reunion. The steady growth of Roman Catholicism and the rapid spread of Anglo-Catholicism within the Anglican Church seemed to demand Protestant unity. Sir Robert Perks, long one of Methodism's dominant laymen, argued that a unified Methodism 'would help to save England from Roman Catholicism and Anglo-Catholicism'.[39] Within the Methodist churches themselves there was a powerful ecumenical movement best represented by J. Scott Lidgett, the first president of the conference of the unified Methodist Church and probably the most influential of Wesleyan ministers, and A. S. Peake. Nevertheless, the most acceptable justification for reunion among Methodists was the belief that unity meant strength. As the *Methodist Recorder* put it, 'a Revival will co-incide with the coming of Methodist Union . . . with the consummation of Union a great forward movement on quite unprecedented lines is anticipated; is indeed inevitable'.[40]

Reunion was not as easily won as many of its proponents hoped. In many ways the Wesleyan Church was like the Church of England from which it had sprung: within it the ministry was predominant and the ministry alone could dispense the sacrament. In neither the Primitive Methodist nor the United Methodist Church was this so. In rural England and in some of the more isolated towns there was often a tenacious defence of the historic Methodist plurality. It was not, therefore, until 1928 that the Wesleyans voted for reunion, and only after the other two had made large concessions on both the ministry and the sacrament,[41] and not until 1932 that it was finally achieved.[42]

[39] Quoted in Hastings, *English Christianity*, 214.
[40] Quoted in R. Currie, *Methodism Divided* (London, 1968), 299.
[41] Although the Wesleyans agreed to the lay administration of the sacrament in certain circumstances.
[42] It is worth noting that in Scotland the Church of Scotland and the United Free Church reunited at almost the same time (1929) and for almost the same reasons.

The outcome disappointed the optimists—reunion did not lead to 'a great forward movement'—although there is little evidence that the three Churches individually would have done any better. Methodism continued its demographic decline and the predominance of Wesleyans within the leadership and ministry of the unified Church worked against congregational autonomy and lay participation—traditionally the great strength of English Protestantism. That in turn made it difficult for the new Church to differentiate itself convincingly from Anglicanism, something which the Primitive Methodist Defence League had long predicted: 'The Union Church will be the high road to Anglicanism'.[43]

4 | *Roman Catholicism*

The Roman Catholic Church of the period, however, seemed impervious to the influences which were depleting the Protestant churches. The Roman Catholic population and attendance at mass rose in tandem, and there appears to have been little perceptible fall in the proportion of the Roman Catholic population which attended mass more or less regularly. There were several reasons for this. The first was the institutional expansion of the Church. In 1910 there were 3,835 priests in England and Wales; in 1925, 4,031; in 1940, 5,652; and in 1950, 6,640. There was a simultaneous church-building programme which, together with the expansion of the parish clergy, encompassed an ever larger number of Roman Catholics within the organized Church.[44]

The second reason was the working of the pastoral system and the aggressive efforts of recruiting agents like the Catholic Missionary Society. By the 1940s it was in fact difficult for members of the Catholic population to escape detection by the parish priest and much pressure, discreet but pertinacious, was exercised on non-observant Catholics to return to the flock. The ultramontane Church's utterly inflexible attitude to mixed marriages also proved to be a fruitful source of new Catholics: by the 1930s there were about 12,000 conversions a year—most of them as a result of mixed marriages.

The main reason, however, was Irish migration. The membership of the Roman Catholic Church in England was, in effect, largely dependent upon movements in the Irish and British economies. There had been a continuous migration to England before 1914 which fell away in the 1920s and remained comparatively small (though more than a trickle) throughout the interwar years. Thus the total Roman Catholic population of England rose by only about 500,000 between 1920 and 1940. In the late 1940s began a huge Irish migration—greater than any previous one—such that the whole net Irish population

---

[43] Quoted in Currie, *Methodism Divided*, 287.

[44] For a revealing example of this, see comparative figures of Easter Day mass attendance, 1931 and 1949, in the diocese of Northampton (Hastings, *English Christianity*, 276).

increase for a generation made its way to England, much of it to stay permanently. Between 1950 and 1970, consequently, England's Catholic population
increased by over two million.

Irish migration was significant not simply because it brought to England
large numbers of Catholics: it brought large numbers of working-class
Catholics whose birth-rate was higher than that of any non-Catholic English
social class, and it brought them from a society which had more successfully
resisted dechristianization than England. This cultural isolation from secular
influences was crucial to the strength of Catholicism in England throughout
the 1940s and 1950s, since there is little evidence that without it the Roman
Catholic Church would have been much more successful in recruiting and
retaining members than the Protestant churches.

In the interwar years the Church acquired one other source of new members, small in numbers but large in prestige—the writers, artists, and men of
affairs who made very public conversions to Catholicism: Maurice Baring,
Hilaire Belloc, G. K. Chesterton, Sheila Kaye-Smith, Eric Gill, Arnold Lunn,
Graham Greene, Frank Pakenham (later the earl of Longford), Ronald Knox
(the son of a fearsomely evangelical Anglican bishop), Evelyn Waugh, etc. In
the interwar years they tended to be associated with a 'snob Catholicism'
which inhabited the Brompton Oratory or the Jesuit Church in Farm Street
where Father D'Arcy encouraged the rich and famous. Ronald Knox, who
remained in Oxford as Roman Catholic chaplain after his conversion, was
notoriously at home in country houses, while Waugh never concealed a somewhat contrived snobbery. Not for nothing was he Knox's biographer. But they
were actually a rather mixed bunch. Hilaire Belloc and G. K. Chesterton
(Orwell's collective caricature 'Father Hilaire Chestnut'), both strongly influenced by the reactionary French Catholicism of Charles Maurras and the *Action
Française*, developed a Catholic neo-corporatism (called by Chesterton 'distri-
butism') quite distinct from Waugh's unsystematic disdain for modern democracy, and wholly different from the politics of Graham Greene. Equally, Greene
and Waugh were almost antithetical figures: the Catholicism of *Brighton Rock*
has little in common with that of *Brideshead Revisited*. What they shared was a
sense of the Church's historic authority, an admiration for the aesthetic of the
Roman Catholic liturgy, a common belief in sin and the imperfectibility of the
human personality, and a transcendental consciousness which they thought
inadequately represented by Protestantism.

By 1950 there were within the Catholic community a number of sub-
communities whose compatibility the triumphalist rhetoric of the period
inclined to exaggerate: a traditional recusant Catholicism, upper-class in tone if
not always upper-class in origin, High Tory or reactionary in politics, though
often culturally and socially rather isolated; a larger recusant Catholicism,
geographically concentrated, particularly in Lancashire, equally traditional but

socially more diverse and from which the relatively small Catholic middle class was still being drawn; a convert Catholicism, sometimes politically associated with upper-class recusancy, sometimes with the metropolitan intelligentsia, but usually too *sui generis* to be classified with anyone; finally, an 'Irish' Catholicism, much the biggest of the sub-communities, which comprised up to three-quarters of English Catholics,[45] and was still overwhelmingly working-class—Labour in politics and proletarian in culture. Though the Irish sub-community was largely assimilated into the liturgical forms of traditional English Catholicism, socially and politically it was a world apart. The larger Catholic community was united only when all its members felt that the Church as a Church was threatened. Nearly all Catholics, for instance, sided with the nationalists during the Spanish Civil War and many regarded Franco as providential. This caused the Labour Party and the trade unions (already becoming disproportionately Irish in their membership) some embarrassment and real personal conflicts for Catholics of Irish origin who were otherwise unhesitatingly Labour in their politics.[46] But these occasions were, perhaps fortunately, exceptional.[47]

The different worlds of English Catholicism were exemplified by the two archdioceses, Westminster and Liverpool. The English Catholic primacy was located at Westminster, surrounded by the state symbols of a Protestant establishment, subject to the influences of court and Anglican ritual—its archbishop often closeted with recusant and convert Catholics and always looking outwards, to Rome, to the British government, and to a diocese where the Catholics were still a small minority.[48] The archbishop and his suffragans were hardly ever of Irish origin.

Liverpool, on the other hand, still the most populous of the Catholic dioceses, was largely Irish and working class. It too faced symbols of a Protestant establishment, but they were the aggressive symbols of an almost areligious working-class anti-popery. Though Liverpool's Catholics were also surrounded by a Protestant majority they were there, unlike in Westminster, a large and comparatively compact minority: the Scotland parliamentary division of Liverpool, for example, returned T. P. O'Connor as an Irish Nationalist until his death in December 1929. It was an introverted diocese, in many ways unconcerned with the wider English Catholic community, to the extent that its archbishop could behave a little like a medieval palatine: Archbishop Downey told the then archbishop of Westminster, Cardinal Griffin: 'Do not forget, Your Eminence, that I rule the north.'[49]

---

[45] Currie *et al.*, *Churches and Churchgoers*, 50.

[46] For this, see T. Buchanan, *The Spanish Civil War and the British Labour Movement* (Cambridge, 1991), 167–95.

[47] Though it also occurred occasionally over educational issues. See above, pp. 213–14.

[48] Archbishop Lang secured for Cardinal Hinsley membership of the Athenaeum, traditionally the London club for Anglican bishops.

[49] Hastings, *English Christianity*, 275. For Liverpool's Catholicism, see the full account in

Furthermore, the social character of the Liverpool diocese, its huge working-class base, forced upon its clergy a certain political radicalism almost always absent at Westminster. In 1926 the archbishop of Westminster, Cardinal Bourne, attacked the general strike with a forthrightness no Anglican bishop would have dared: it was 'a direct challenge to a lawfully constituted authority . . . a sin against the obedience which we owe to God'. However, Archbishop Keating of Liverpool, who was also president of the Catholic Social Guild, said of the miners' claim: 'The poor must live; and if private enterprise cannot provide the worker with a living, it must clear out for another system which can.' These were doubtless Keating's own views but it would have been difficult for him in Liverpool to have said anything else: the only alternative was silence.

The Catholic sub-community on Merseyside was, in fact, much more like the emigrant-urban Irish Catholicism of the United States or Australia than Westminster or any other English Catholic diocese. It combined Irish devotionalism with radical-democratic politics, a simultaneous hostility to the host community and a desire to be accepted by it, and a defiant working-classness.[50] It also faced the world with a rather assertive triumphalism. In Liverpool, the most dramatic manifestation of this was to have been Lutyens's colossal and architecturally remarkable Catholic cathedral—dedicated to Christ the King and to be larger than any church in Christendom. It was to confront Giles Gilbert Scott's almost equally immense Gothic-revival Anglican cathedral which was slowly rising a few hundred metres away.[51] Lutyens's great conception never rose above its crypt and was abandoned by Archbishop Heenan in the 1950s. (The Anglican cathedral was completed in the 1970s and now stands almost empty save for astonished visitors.) The fate of Lutyens's cathedral anticipated what was to be the fate of English Catholicism. It was conceived at a moment when the Church was expanding in membership and in organization, constantly replenished by Irish migration and conversions, and apparently exempt from the secular indifference which was emptying the major Protestant churches. It was replaced by Gibberd's much more modest and very much less distinguished cathedral, which now stands on its site, at the moment when it became apparent that the Roman Catholic Church was not able for ever to withstand secular indifference. By the 1960s indifference was eating at the Catholic community as it had at the Protestant churches for the last fifty years.

P. J. Waller, *Democracy and Sectarianism* (Liverpool, 1981), 270–344. Caradog Jones found that 84% of Catholic Church attenders in Liverpool were working class (Caradog Jones, *Merseyside*, ii. 338). The Scotland seat was then inherited by Labour, as was the bulk of the Irish vote.

[50] There is a revealing account of Liverpool parish life in the 1950s in A. J. P. Kenny, *A Path from Rome* (Oxford, 1986), 151–60. Kenny's first curacy was Hall Lane, Liverpool 8, already run down but 'not as notorious for urban decay and civil disorder' as it later became. The parish priest was known as 'Patwig', the code name with which he placed his off-course bets.

[51] It seems appropriate to the slightly unbalanced religious enthusiasm which produced these two projects that Lutyens was an Anglican and Giles Gilbert Scott a Catholic.

5 | *Belief and indifference*

Sociologically, we know much about the types of people who comprised the membership of the Christian churches. We know much less about the character and intensity of their belief: how far religion determined their behaviour or was immanent in their daily lives. The conventional way of measuring belief or indifference—formal church attendance—is not an exact measure of either. Withdrawal from church attendance is, of course, an important step and has social significance; but it does not always imply a loss of belief or any sustained opposition to Christian teaching or morality. Equally, it is likely that some regular church attenders had no serious Christian beliefs at all. There was usually a grey area between active worship and active disbelief where the majority were probably to be found. Most people, for example, seem to have accepted the legitimacy of what were understood to be the tenets of Christianity. Richard Hoggart thought that middle-aged working-class men and women had certain fundamental religious beliefs. One was that life had a purpose; the other that there was an afterlife. Women thought of heaven as a place of consolation and reward—a re-creation of the happier side of working-class life.[52] In a socially mixed town like Banbury only 3 per cent of the population claimed to have no religion, and it was taboo to question the validity of Christian doctrine; to doubt anyone's Christianity caused 'embarrassment'.[53] The real distinction in Banbury was not between the religious and the unreligious but between active and passive Christians. Furthermore, a surprisingly high proportion of the English people claimed to say daily prayers (one-third) and an even higher proportion said prayers 'regularly', if not daily. While a majority did not believe in hell or the devil, as late as 1950 one-half reported that they believed in an afterlife. The vast majority, of course, said they believed in God—whatever was meant by that.[54] Nor was there outright hostility to organized religion. Although humanist bodies like the Rationalist Press Association had significant and growing memberships, they were in reality little more than articulate coteries.[55] Political anti-clericalism of the continental kind was almost wholly absent. Both the Liberal and Conservative Parties had traditional religious affiliations, while the most secular of the major political parties, the Labour Party, surprised foreign observers not simply by the absence within it of any laic spirit, but the extent to which its rhetoric was suffused with a specifically Christian vocabulary.[56]

The adherence of the majority of the English to religious rites of passage—birth, marriage, death—also suggests that the influence of organized religion

---

[52] Hoggart, *Uses of Literacy*, 116–18.   [53] Stacey, *Tradition and Change*, 57–8, 69.
[54] Gorer, *Exploring English Character*, 244–53.
[55] In 1918 the Rationalist Press Association had 2,774 members; in 1950, 4,262 (Currie *et al.*, *Churches and Churchgoers*, 194).
[56] See particularly E. Wertheimer, *Portrait of the Labour Party* (London, 1929), 193–4.

went considerably beyond its active membership. The great majority of new-born infants were baptized: in 1921 70.1 per cent of all live births were baptized as Anglicans and as late as 1950 the figure was 67.2 per cent. Indeed, the proportion of the country's newborn infants baptized reached its historic peak in the 1920s.[57] Similarly, most Englishmen and women chose to be married in church. There was, certainly, some decline in the numbers seeking religious marriage and a corresponding rise in the number married by civil ceremony. But the decline itself is comparatively small and may, in any case, be misleading. Neither the Anglicans nor Roman Catholics permitted the remarriage in church of divorced people, the number of whom was significantly increased by the 1923 and 1937 Acts.[58] It is likely that a large proportion of them would have remarried in church had they been allowed.

Virtually everybody was buried according to some sort of religious rite. In Hertford, for instance, which in the 1930s had a surprisingly low Sunday church attendance for a county town and a perceptible rise in civil marriage, no non-religious burial had been held in the previous 40 years.[59]

The popularity of baptisms, church weddings, and church burials suggests that at those moments in their lives, particularly the beginning and the end, which are thought to be peculiarly sensitive or climacteric and which conventionally involve relatives and friends, the English continued to have recourse (usually) to a Christian rite. At such moments most people relied on 'a marginal Christianity which is nonetheless strongly held'.[60] In some ways that is a more adequate description of popular attitudes to religion than one which relies on active church attendance or on belief and non-belief as the only possibilities. Most people probably half-believed; though which bits they chose to accept and which to reject were often various and unpredictable.

There is also widespread evidence that people were reluctant to deny their Christianity because they believed that religion 'taught you good behaviour', and could conceive of no alternative secular ethical system. As Mass-Observation discovered in 1947, many, 'even those who have discarded faith in the supernatural sanction behind the ethics of religion', accepted that—which is why the majority thought there should be religious instruction in the schools. There was, Mass-Observation noted,

a common code of behaviour accepted by most members of this community and they are 'shocked' when they see people deviating from it ... Though the same code of behaviour could be based on something other than religion, such as a rational ethic, in point of fact it isn't—and this fact is tacitly acknowledged by 'non-religious' people when they

---

[57] W. S. F. Pickering, 'The Persistence of Rites of Passage: towards an Explanation', *British Journal of Sociology*, 25 (1974), 64.

[58] For the acts, see below, pp. 302–3.

[59] Roper Power, 'Social Structure of an English County Town', 408.

[60] Pickering, 'Persistence of Rights of Passage', 77.

say religion 'means' what they consider good actions; and when they say that their children should be taught religion so that they will 'know right from wrong'.[61]

It made perfectly good sense, therefore, for people to say, as many did, 'I'm not religious but I'm Christian.'

Beyond the organized churches there were the quasi-religions to which many adhered with more or less credulity. Spiritualism continued to have a large number of adherents; for many, the prospect of contacting those on the other side was one of the few ways they could accept the losses of the First World War. There was also, as contemporaries noted, clear evidence of widespread popular interest in fortune-telling, prophecy, and astrology. One middle-class Land Army girl, thrown in among working-class girls for the first time, was surprised at their enthusiasm for fortune-telling and the seriousness with which they treated it.[62] Mass-Observation concluded that 'from the enormous horoscope data of the 1938 Press it is possible to construct a whole ethic of contemporary Britain'.[63] Virtually any paper or magazine with a mass sale had at least one horoscope and some had several. Many had resident fortune-tellers. About 80 per cent of the population admitted to reading more than one horoscope weekly: among working-class women 'having a look at the stars' was almost universal. Almost as common was the use of lucky charms and mascots, particularly in the 1940s, which many thought to have magical or protective effects. The use of mascots was probably a survival from the Second World War when the press gave much publicity to their use by RAF aircrew: there was a whole folklore of what had happened to airmen who flew sorties without mascots, or of men who would not fly until lost mascots had been found. Whether believed or not, the lucky charm fitted easily into the same category as the superstitious phrases with which people tried to protect their health and prolong their lives.[64]

All religions were by now predominantly female in their membership but the religion of horoscopes and charms was the most female of all. Mass-Observation found that about one-third of women believed 'in their stars', about one-third half-believed and only about one-third did not believe at all. However, only 5 per cent of men believed, while 80 per cent did not believe at all.[65] Women were not only attracted to the 'supernatural', they were widely thought to possess psychic powers unavailable to men: as one working-class woman said—almost as if she had an affliction—'I have intuition something awful.'[66]

The social anthropologist Geoffrey Gorer thought a substantial proportion of the population 'holds a view of the universe which can most properly be

---

[61] Mass-Observation, *Puzzled People* (London, 1947), 88–96.
[62] S. Joseph, *If Their Mothers Only Knew* (London, 1946), 107–8.
[63] Mass-Observation, *Puzzled People*, 20–2.   [64] Hoggart, *Uses of Literacy*, 29–30.
[65] Mass-Observation, *Puzzled People*, 20–2.   [66] Kerr, *Ship Street*, 132.

designated as magical'—a passive cosmology where there was no perceived connection between effort and outcome.[67] That so many more women than men—especially married working-class women—held to such a cosmology suggests among many of them a real social powerlessness, a feeling that they had little control over their lives. And it was this which produced such dissociation between 'effort' and 'outcome'. Horoscopes, charms, and the idea of Fate represented a transcendent analogy to the popular literature of everyday life: Fate ruled all and the most fortunate were the most lucky.[68] That women seemingly thought this much more than men is an important fact in the sexual politics of the period.

6 | *Anti-religions*

Like most other European societies England harboured 'anti-religions', themselves originally ground in religious belief systems, and still tenuously attached to them, but increasingly secular and political in character. But how religious and how political is difficult to determine. Anti-semitism, pervasive but of diminishing intensity,[69] was scarcely religious at all, at least in any theological way. To the extent that Jews were feared or disliked, it was not because they 'murdered' Christ—if only because the host community's attachment to Christianity as a formal system of belief was now so weak and the tradition of Old Testament Judaism in historic English Protestantism so strong. Anti-semitism was primarily a social and racial phenomenon, whatever had once been its roots. Jews were 'different'; they stuck together and got each other the best jobs. But the Jews were not unique in attracting this reputation. They were feared and disliked for some of the same reasons that many people (often the same people, one supposes) feared and disliked, for example, Freemasons: as a self-conscious elect who were thought to advance each other's careers. In any case, anti-semitism was significantly weaker in 1950 than in 1918. Social assimilation slowly did its work while the association of anti-semitism with the Holocaust after 1945 made overt—even covert—expressions of anti-semitism socially much less acceptable. The kinds of things people freely said even during the Second World War were more rarely heard in 1950.

Anti-Catholicism is more complicated. It did have a considerable theological and liturgical basis, and the religious practices of Roman Catholicism—or what were understood to be its practices—mattered in ways Jewish religious practice never did. Hostility to them was an essential element in English popular Protestantism, often as strongly held by those who never went to church as by those who did. Dislike of popery, Marianism, liturgical ritual, and insinu-

---

[67] Gorer, *Exploring English Character*, 266–70.   [68] For this literature, see below, pp. 493–6.
[69] See also above, pp. 55–6.

ating priests was a deeply felt emotion, which almost certainly influenced the behaviour of many MPs during the debates on the new Prayer Book. The degree to which the laity, observant and non-observant, thought the Church of England specifically Protestant was never understood by many of the Anglican clergy. Regardless of anything else, there would have been a 'theological' anti-Catholicism grounded in historic Protestantism and nourished by well-known folktales about priests and convents, the doings of the confessional, and what Catholic children were supposed to have been taught in school. And by the Catholic Church's own actions: for example, the attitude of the Church to the non-Catholic partner in a mixed marriage was widely resented, even by those who had no intention of contracting a Catholic marriage.

But the social consequences of anti-Catholicism were more profound, because it became inextricable from racial loyalties. The more the Roman Catholic Church in England became 'Irish' the more it became associated with the question of nationality. In areas of heavy Irish migration, most obviously on Merseyside, large quasi-Protestant working-class anti-Irish movements developed, whose political home was to be a popular Conservatism.[70] The more they developed, the more the Conservative Party had an interest in perpetuating English racial grievances often clothed in religious terms.[71] Consequently, Liverpool's politics, both in style and result, were closer to Belfast's than to any English city: an overwhelmingly working-class town where politics was as much determined by religious-racial allegiances as by class. And this remained so until the 1960s. Throughout this period the Conservatives failed to win a majority of Liverpool's parliamentary constituencies only once—in 1945. In 1950 it was the only major town in England where the Labour Party failed to win a majority of the parliamentary constituencies.

Furthermore, many people had the same rather conspiratorial view of Catholics as they did of Jews. The Labour Party, for instance, was convinced that Catholics were by design infiltrating the foreign office, even though an enquiry instituted by Hugh Dalton (who seems originally to have believed it) found no evidence of this.[72] Anti-Catholicism, anti-Irishism and a belief that Catholics got each other the best jobs was a powerful and familiar ideological cocktail, particularly in Lancashire. As the widow of the secretary of the St Helens Trades and Labour Council said:

[70] For this, see Waller, *Democracy and Secretarianism*, *passim*.

[71] This is not to say that the Conservative Party was itself anti-Catholic, however many of its individual members were. Recusant and convert Catholicism was often very close to the Conservative Party and cultivated it. Merseyside Conservatism was, as it were, in a different compartment. It was a genuinely working-class phenomenon: one of the few cases where working-class Conservatives took an active part in Conservative politics. It also demonstrates how successfully the Conservative Party could speak to different audiences.

[72] For an account of this, see H. Dalton, *Call Back Yesterday* (London, 1953), 220. One of the reasons for this conjecture was that the foreign office was thought by Labour to be too pro-Mussolini.

[St Helens] was a very strong Catholic town. There was a lot of bitterness. They tried to get as many Catholics on the council as they could. The Catholics used to come to their own, and my husband, who was a Catholic, used to say 'Whenever he comes, give him something'. They came round about every six weeks and I always used to say 'I'm not of your faith'. It was to keep them—I don't know how priests lived, but they seemed to do very well. I've seen Father Reilly come up with his little case to the pork butcher who used to fill it up—I've seen that with my own eyes. He was crafty, was Father Reilly. I've known children he asked all to take a potato to school—he had sacks of them at the end of it ... The priests tried to get so many of their own on the council. Then, it couldn't be proved, but jobs seemed to go to Catholics.[73]

By the usual criteria England throughout this period was becoming steadily 'dechristianized'. An increasing majority of the population took no active part in any organized religion, but the degree and speed with which they fell away was not uniform. The Roman Catholic Church and the smaller (and newer) Protestant churches were much less affected than the larger (and older) Protestant churches; though in the case of the Catholic Church that was a result of demographic good fortune which merely postponed the inevitable. In turn the Church of England was less affected than the Free Churches. A member of the middle class was significantly more likely to practise a religion than a member of the unskilled working class, and someone living in the country more likely to practise than someone living in a town. Everywhere women were more likely to practise than men. And each generation was more indifferent to religion than the generation which preceded it.

How 'secular' England had become was another matter. It had a state church, and religion was inseparable from its public life and ceremonial. Even the majority who were not observant Christians were rarely wholly indifferent and even fewer were hostile. Young working-class men—almost certainly the most secular element of the population—were sometimes vaguely contemptuous, usually on the gender-grounds that religion was 'soft' and 'women's business', and working-class communities were suspicious of those who made too much of their piety. But they always had been and it rarely went beyond suspicion. Clergymen were almost invariably treated with respect. At important moments in their lives and at their deaths the majority thought religious ritual appropriate. Many, again perhaps most, adhered to a popular Protestantism which had profound roots. Above all, most could not conceive of a secular ethics or morality: for them ethics and 'good behaviour' were grounded in religious teaching. In their mentality and habits of thought most, in fact, found it very difficult to be secular; and important areas of their lives, like sexuality,[74] became hopelessly confused with religious injunctions.

The decline in membership of the Anglican and Free Churches, however,

---

[73] Forman, *Industrial Town*, 174.   [74] See below, Chapter VIII.

and the secularization of those issues, like temperance and education, which traditionally mobilized nonconformity, undermined a political pluralism based upon warring Protestant 'families'. This, for its part, permitted an 'anti-socialist' regrouping, particularly in provincial and suburban England, whose relative beneficiaries were to be the Conservative Party and, to the extent that the churches gained at all, a conventional Anglicanism.

SEXUALITY has never been far from religion, and this chapter continues some of the themes of the previous one. It looks at the relationship between religion and sexuality and how far that affected marital sexuality, marriage guidance, and divorce. It considers the extent to which family limitation was practised, the movement for family planning, and the role of the churches in promoting or hindering it. It looks at sexual knowledge and how it was acquired (or not), homosexuality, the way sexual dissidence was policed, and the wider consequences of English attitudes to sexuality.

1 | *Sexuality and marriage*

The English, like most people, had complicated attitudes to sexuality and marriage; but theirs were complicated in a particular way. Notionally, for example, their rules about premarital and extra-marital sex were very strict. In the early 1950s half the married population claimed to have had no sexual experience with anyone other than their spouses; 52 per cent were opposed to men and 63 per cent opposed to women having any premarital sex; only a small number believed that premarital sex was 'natural', and most denied that sex had a therapeutic function. 'I very much doubt', Geoffrey Gorer wrote, 'whether the study of any other urban population would produce comparable figures of chastity and fidelity.'[1] The 'remarkable' value placed upon premarital chastity was, he suspected, 'specifically English'.[2]

Nevertheless the English often lapsed from their own high standards and many reproached themselves for failing to maintain them.[3] The social psychologists Elizabeth Slater and Mark Woodside thought their sample of wartime working-class families greatly exaggerated its virginity, and concluded that about 75 per cent of the men and about 50 per cent of the women

---

[1] Gorer, *Exploring English Character*, 87.

[2] Ibid. 97. Also S. Humphries, *A Secret World of Sex* (London, 1988), 105–7. Gorer's sample, though very large, was self-selecting and is likely to contain its own biases. In this case, however, the biases are probably no more serious than that of any survey which questions people about their sexual behaviour.

[3] Gorer, *Exploring English Character*, 94.

were not virgin at marriage.[4] This may partly be explained by the popular inclination to think that intercourse before marriage with someone you 'loved' or (more often) intended to marry did not constitute premarital sex.[5] One result of this inclination was the comparatively high rates of pregnancy at marriage. In 1938–9 30 per cent of all women conceived their first child before marriage, and no less than 42 per cent of women under 20 were pregnant at marriage. But these pregnancies were probably the occasion rather than the reason for marriage, which is why people thought them not 'really' the result of premarital intercourse.

Such figures suggest not merely that the majority of the population was not virgin at marriage, but that many more women were virgin than men. This implies that alongside the strict 'single standard of sexual morality', to which most people claimed to adhere, was a more relaxed version of a traditional double standard which rated a woman's chastity more highly than a man's. Not only did many more think a woman should be chaste at marriage than her husband, at least as many women as men thought so. And this was the case because many women, particularly working-class women, accepted prevailing views of male sexuality. It was widely thought (and repeated in the increasingly popular sex manuals) that a man needed sexual 'experience' at marriage in order to teach his wife 'techniques', without which her own pleasure in marital sexuality would be diminished.[6] They were also ready to concede that men were more sexually demanding and aggressive than women. The belief that men, especially working-class men, were sexually 'incontinent', first made popular by Margaret Leonora Eyles in the early 1920s,[7] had become a conventional wisdom of the period.

The inverse of this belief—the extreme reluctance of many women (possibly the majority) to admit their own sexual interests or to acknowledge that sexuality in marriage was important or desirable—was, in fact, the greatest obstacle to a 'single standard of morality'. Though the extent of this sexual reticence has been questioned,[8] the evidence does suggest that it was very widespread indeed. Working-class women repeatedly expressed either hostility or indifference to marital sexuality. One woman who admitted to enjoying sex assumed she was unusual in that.[9] Sex for most was a duty and there were no great expectations of pleasure: 'I'm not keen'; 'I'm not really interested'; 'I just want to get it over.' Husbands were frequently judged by the number of

---

[4] Slater and Woodside, *Patterns of Marriage*, 112.

[5] R. Davenport-Hines, *Sex, Death and Punishment* (London, 1990), 247–8.

[6] For the manuals, see below, pp. 319–21.

[7] M. Leonora Eyles, *The Woman in the Little House* (London, 1922), *passim*.

[8] W. Seccombe, 'Starting to Stop: Working-Class Fertility Decline in Britain', *Past and Present*, 126 (1990), 175–6.

[9] Shaw, 'Impressions of Family Life', 187. And in Shaw's sample, she was.

sexual demands made upon their wives; the more, the worse.[10] An undemanding husband was thus 'very good'; 'he doesn't bother me very much'; 'he's a thorough gentleman'. Many working-class women viewed sexuality 'with a barely veiled antagonism'[11] and appear to have associated it with violence and assertions of male power—as all too often it probably was. Of one working-class woman, 'Mrs Newbolt', the sociologist Elizabeth Bott wrote that 'physical sexuality was an intrusion on a peaceful domestic relationship rather than an expression of such a relationship. It was as if sexuality were felt to be basically violent and disruptive.'[12] And many men did see sex as a matter of possession and 'rights'. They rarely expected a sexual response from their wives and some thought it unnatural when it occurred.

There were, however, signs that the single standard was slowly becoming a norm. Each succeeding generation, for instance, looked more kindly upon premarital sex: 19 per cent of women born before 1904 had had premarital intercourse; but 36 per cent of those born between 1904 and 1914, 39 per cent of those born between 1914 and 1924 and 43 per cent of those between 1924 and 1934 had done so.[13] Nor were attitudes to sexuality the same throughout society as a whole. There is a clear relationship between sexual permissiveness and income levels: the higher the income the more were people ready to condone (and practise) premarital sex, to believe in an equality of sexual needs and the single standard and, perhaps most important of all, to use reliable contraception and thus eliminate that dread of pregnancy which so incapacitated working-class sexuality.

There tended in effect to be two definitions of marital sexuality: a negative one, commonly held by working-class women, which judged the success of a marriage by the absence of sexuality ('he doesn't bother me', 'he doesn't worry me'), and a positive one, increasingly found in the middle classes and (though more rarely) among the upper working class, which judged marital sex by the degree to which husband and wife established a mutually satisfactory sexual relationship. Of the two, the positive one seemed steadily to be gaining ground. Why was this so?

Change in the forms of marriage encouraged this sexual mutuality. In the 'traditional' working-class marriage husband and wife largely occupied different social and domestic spheres; in such a marriage, almost more than anything, sexual relations suffered. Husbands and wives hardly knew how to talk

[10] One woman actually told Slater and Woodside that her husband had got 'worse' after he developed a mental illness—meaning that he had become sexually more demanding. (Slater and Woodside, *Patterns of Marriage*, 172.)

[11] Ibid. 165–9. They note that of the 70 women in their sample who had never experienced orgasm, none showed surprise or disappointment. See also Gorer, *Exploring English Character*, 115; J. Chance, *The Cost of English Morals* (London, 1931), 34.

[12] Bott, *Family and Social Network*, 73.

[13] These figures are Eustace Chesser's. Quoted in Humphries, *Secret World of Sex*, 32.

about sex, let alone had anything so formal as a sexual 'relationship'. For men, therefore, sex was an indulgence and for women a duty. In those marriages based upon 'joint relationships', however, which were by 1950 more or less characteristic of middle-class marriages,[14] husband and wife were able to talk in ways which permitted a mutual sexuality. 'It was as if successful sexual relations were felt to prove that all was well with the joint relationship, whereas unsatisfactory relations were indicative of a failure in the total relationship.' Some people felt under a 'moral obligation' to enjoy sex,[15] and it can be inferred from the handbooks whose readership was still predominantly middle-class, that even if both partners did not enjoy sex, they were expected to. As more working-class marriages acquired 'joint' characteristics, so negative definitions of marital sexuality gave way to positive ones.

The slow—and difficult—'secularization' of marital relations also relaxed the force of sexual taboos. Practising Christians were 'unambiguously' those most hostile to premarital sex; and those most hostile to premarital sex were, when questioned,[16] those most likely to deny women's sexuality. Secularization thus, indirectly, 'freed' women's sexuality from certain received assumptions by partially disentangling sexuality as a whole from religious constraints.

The significance of marital sexuality, as of sexuality in general, was enormously enhanced by the growing influence in England of Freud and what people understood to be Freudian psychology. Freud had been known in England before 1914, though chiefly by coteries; but Freudian psychoanalysis became both familiar and influential in the interwar years, partly through the work of Ernest Jones, his leading English disciple and eventual biographer, partly through James Strachey's still incomplete translation of Freud's *œuvre*, partly through a greater readiness to talk about sex anyway, and partly through the notoriety which attended the interminable disputes within the English school of psychoanalysis after the formidable Melanie Klein's migration to England from Berlin in 1926. These disputes were further inflamed when Freud and his daughter Anna fled to England in 1938, a flight arranged by Ernest Jones and expedited by the British government amidst enormous publicity. Freudianism offered no easily learnt sexual lessons, but the popularizing of Freudian (or sub-Freudian) terminology in everyday speech, like 'Oedipus complex' or 'Freudian slip', made it easier for people to talk about sex with less guilt by making reference to sex almost chic and encouraging in the public mind the vague but powerful idea that sex was somehow central to existence. Nearly all the most popular sex manuals of the period were influenced by Freud, and those written by analysts or psychologists attached to the Tavistock Clinic, like Laura Hutton, were wholly Freudian. By the 1940s the

---

[14] See above, p. 90.   [15] Bott, *Family and Social Network*, 83.
[16] Gorer, *Exploring English Character*, 116, 120.

effect of these books on the sexual attitudes of the generation which grew up in the 1930s was clearly observable.[17]

This readiness to argue that sexual harmony and satisfaction was central to the ideal marriage posed problems for those who argued for a 'traditional' conception of marriage. They had been forced to concede that marital sex was not simply procreative: that marriage was, or was supposed to be, now a partnership of equals. This concession, however, conflicted with received definitions of marriage which confined both sex and wives to much narrower roles. Furthermore, the new ideal, by emphasizing sexual pleasure, threatened by implication the view that marriage was for life and that sex was for marriage. It was an attempt by the churches to escape this social and moral impasse which was primarily responsible for the rapid development of the marriage guidance movement in the 1930s and 1940s.

The National Marriage Guidance Council,[18] founded in 1948 with some home office support, was in large measure designed by the Protestant churches—or groups within them—to adjust a new sexual morality to the traditional functions of marriage. Of the three principal intellectual progenitors of marriage guidance, two, Herbert Gray and David Mace (who was, with his wife, the first co-director of the National Marriage Guidance Council), were Protestant clergyman, and the third, E. F. Griffith, though 'lay', was anxious to preserve a basically 'Christian' conception of marriage. All three had written extensively on sexuality and sexual ethics and all argued for the centrality of sex to marriage, that sex represented the perfect union of husband and wife. They also accepted, under certain conditions, the legitimacy of birth control.

In practice, it proved very difficult for them to devise a 'Christian' view of marriage based upon the centrality of sexual satisfaction, since all three had so defined sexuality that there was no logical reason why it should be peculiar to marriage. The only way out was to argue, as Maude Royden did, that sex beyond marriage was 'carnality'; that it was only the responsibility for children which gave legitimacy to sex. That suggested, however, that the function of sex in marriage was indeed procreative.

The pioneers of marriage guidance had to meet ecclesiastical pressure in two other ways. They were obliged to modify their teaching on birth control to emphasize its eugenic virtues; to agree that contraception was acceptable for the spacing of children, but unacceptable 'when it was misused to enable selfish and irresponsible people to escape the duties and disciplines of marriage and parenthood'.[19] Even this compromise was not enough for the archbishop

---

[17]   Slater and Woodside, *Patterns of Marriage*, 173–4.

[18]   This account of the marriage guidance movement is drawn largely from J. Lewis, D. Clark, and D. Morgan, *Whom God hath joined Together* (London, 1992), 44–82. See also J. Lewis, 'Public Institution and Private Relationship: Marriage and Marriage Guidance, 1920–1968', *Twentieth Century British History*, 1, 3 (1990), 233–57.

[19]   Quoted in Lewis *et al.*, *Whom God hath joined Together*, 73.

of Canterbury who declined to sit as a clerical representative on the Council. The bishop of London took his place but only on the understanding that contraception was not the only or universally accepted mode of family-limitation.

They were also obliged to emphasize the distinctive nature of women's equality in marriage. In the writings of Griffith and Mace, particularly in the late 1940s, there was much on the woman as home-maker and mother, whose role dictated different (if equal) sexual wants. For men sex meant bodily gratification; for women, home and family. This further implied that in any society which encouraged pre- or extra-marital sex the dependent woman must necessarily be the victim. Mace argued this in an increasingly tough-minded style:

So really the woman defeats her own best interests by all this demand for sexual freedom ... the true woman cheats herself out of her destiny if she is taken in by this sex equality stuff ... it's only the unnatural masculine woman who can be satisfied for very long with sex alone.[20]

The marriage guidance movement was thus in danger of alienating both its clerical and lay constituencies. In the circumstances of the 1940s, however, it was able to square the circle. Contemporary fears of family disintegration as a result of the war (including a panic about juvenile delinquency) and a renewed emphasis upon both maternal domesticity *and* a joint relationship in marriage allowed the potentially unstable ideological mix of the marriage guidance movement to survive until the 1960s.

2 | Divorce

If recourse to marriage guidance were unsuccessful, a failed marriage could end in the divorce courts, and a growing number did. Yet divorce as a social fact could no more be morally neutral than sexuality. And for the same reason. As the leading historian of English divorce law, O. R. McGregor, argued in 1957, 'until recent years Christian teaching has dominated all discussion of marriage and divorce and has determined the standard of accepted behaviour.'[21] This would itself have made divorce contentious, but was made even more complicated by the fact that the churches were not themselves agreed. The Roman Catholic position was the simplest: it was absolutely opposed. The Church of England accepted divorce in certain circumstances, though, under the influence of Anglo-Catholicism, was becoming more rather than less hostile to the remarriage of divorced people in church. The Free Churches were comparatively liberal and most accepted such changes in the divorce law as were proposed. These differences were well known and had been publicly aired during the proceedings of the 1909 Royal Commission on Divorce. The debate was not, therefore, simply one between 'Christianity' and 'secular

[20] Quoted ibid. 69.   [21] O. R. McGregor, *Divorce in England* (London, 1957), 101.

society' but also one within the Christian churches. McGregor is, however, right to the extent that both debates were essentially conducted in a Christian vocabulary.

Divorce was possible in England before 1914 but the grounds for procuring it were few and discriminatory.[22] It was also exclusive because expensive. In 1909 the majority report of the Royal Commission on Divorce recommended that the grounds on which men and women could divorce each other should be equalized, that they should be extended to include desertion, drunkenness, and cruelty, and that divorce hearings be decentralized and so made cheaper. These proposals were received with much hostility both from the Church of England and the London lawyers who had a monopoly of divorce actions. The proposals were not enacted before 1914.

The gender-discriminations in divorce law could not, however, have long survived the First World War. The 1919 Sex (Removal of Disqualifications) Act had recognized the principle of sexual equality in law and vocation—though had done little to enforce it[23]—and the existing divorce law was a notorious violation of that principle. After considerable pressure from feminist organizations like the Six Point Group, a privately sponsored Matrimonial Causes Act (1923) was introduced into the House of Commons by C. F. Entwistle, Liberal MP for South-West Hull, and in the House of Lords by the former lord chancellor, Lord Buckmaster, who had both eugenic and, through his wife, feminist interests. This bill, when enacted, equalized grounds for divorce but did not extend them: it was in the spirit of the 1919 Act, but fell well short of the recommendations of the 1909 Royal Commission.

Divorce, therefore, remained expensive, demeaning and often sordid. Increasingly, those who were determined to divorce arranged for one of the partners, usually the husband, to be caught in well-staged 'adultery' with a professional co-respondent in a hotel room.[24] This was not a practice the country could be proud of and the 1923 Act never satisfied most feminist groups, divorce law reformers, proponents of a more relaxed sexual morality, or even some churchmen. In 1937 the independent MP for Oxford University, A. P. Herbert, better known to the public as a novelist and satirical writer on the law, introduced a private member's bill which was based upon the 1909 recommendations. Herbert deliberately and skilfully framed his argument in 'Christian' terms to make the bill as inoffensive as possible to the Church of England. The 1923 legislation, he suggested, encouraged adultery and perjury, and thus immorality. The 1937 Matrimonial Causes Act, which as a result of Herbert's

---

[22] Most notoriously, while a man could divorce his wife on grounds of adultery, she could not divorce him on similar grounds.

[23] See above, pp. 48–9.

[24] Seaside resorts were favoured, particularly Brighton. Divorces procured this way came to be called 'Brighton quickies'.

tactics was comparatively uncontentious, extended grounds for divorce to desertion (after three years), cruelty, insanity, and drunkenness.

In the longer term, the Herbert Act substantially increased the number of divorces; in the short term its influence was diminished by the continuing expense of divorce actions. Until 1920 all actions had to be heard before the High Court in London. In that year, over the protests of the London lawyers, it was agreed that 'poor persons' and undefended actions could be heard in certain assize towns, which considerably reduced the costs of a divorce. It also enabled Mrs Simpson to secure that discreet divorce in Ipswich in 1936 which precipitated the abdication crisis.

Even so, the new procedure did not much alter the divorce-rates. It was the Second World War which enforced significant procedural changes. Mobilization, service overseas, and the conscription of married women without children broke many marriages. All three services recognized this and established their own 'legal-aid' schemes which arranged litigation through local solicitors or 'poor persons' procedure. This resulted in a significant rise in the divorce-rate, which was further increased by the appointment of special commissioners for divorce in 1946. The effect of the appointment of the special commissioners was to raise the number of divorces for the year 1946–7 to 60,000. It was the experience of that year which convinced parliament that without marriage guidance there would be a 'tidal wave' or 'epidemic' of divorce. That was why the National Marriage Guidance Council was given state assistance instead of the Family Planning Association as the home office wanted. In fact, 1946–7 was a freakish year, and despite the extension of legal aid to divorce in 1950, the average annual rate for the years after 1945 was much lower (though much higher than pre-war).

The major change in the rate of divorce was probably not so much due to the creation of new grounds for divorce as the widening of access made possible by legal aid after the enactment of new grounds.[25] Even with this, however, the English remained a uxorious people: at the most only 7.0 per cent of marriages ended in divorce. The grounds on which marriages were increasingly terminated, however, revealed a different side to the Englishman: those women who cited cruelty as grounds for termination rose from 2.1 per cent of all actions (the first year of the Herbert Act) to 22.7 per cent in 1954. Many of them were brought by working-class women against physically violent and often drunken husbands—the two usually went together—against whom their only protection before 1937 had been the magistrates' courts, where a working-class

---

[25] Between 1926 and 1930, when the 'poor persons' régime still operated, there were an annual average of 4,052 divorces; between 1951 and 1954 under legal aid there were 33,132. Figures from McGregor, *Divorce in England*, 36. For the details of legal aid and its development, see R. I. Morgan, 'The Introduction of Civil Legal Aid in England and Wales, 1914–1949', *Twentieth Century British History*, 5, 1 (1994), 38–76.

woman would almost never go. Even a divorce petition was usually an act of desperation, though the undoubted fact of marital cruelty served to make the 1937 Act more acceptable to the Church of England and thus had a kind of grim utility.

3 | *Conception and contraception*

In hardly any other sphere of English life did religion, sex, and class intersect with more tension than they did over birth control. Both public and private attitudes to family limitation were determined by a number of largely incompatible forces: the teachings of institutional religion, the behaviour of the medical profession, changing perceptions of individual and family self-interest, the activities of social and political pressure groups, and the growing significance of feminist arguments concerning women's sexuality and fertility. The result was that the majority of those who consciously limited their family size did so with a mixture of knowledge and ignorance, relief and guilt.

The declining fertility of *all* English social classes in this period was due to some form of birth control other than changes in the age of marriage. Furthermore, the technology of contraception was sophisticated and more or less easily obtainable for those who wanted or could afford it. And the majority of English men and women who married at any time in the interwar years deliberately practised some form of contraception.[26] Only after 1943, when the dramatic decline in national fertility was partially reversed, is it possible that a majority of newly-weds in any one class (Social Class III—the working class, broadly defined) refrained from practising family limitation.[27]

But the form of birth control people used differed from class to class. Although there was an important shift to 'non-appliance' methods in the 1920s in Social Class I and a more modest shift in Social Class II, withdrawal remained the most popular method of contraception in the unskilled working class.[28] As late as 1939 perhaps two-thirds of those families who practised family limitation did so via withdrawal.

As a technique, withdrawal had many disadvantages. It was notoriously unreliable and required the kind of continuous self-discipline many men did not possess. It frequently had deleterious effects on the sexual lives of both men and women and on their relationships with each other. Neither husband nor wife, but particularly not the wife, was likely to find much satisfaction in

---

[26] These details are from the survey conducted by Ernest Lewis-Faning for the Royal Commission on Population (1947–49): *Report on an Enquiry into Family Limitation* (HMSO, London, 1949), 52.

[27] Lewis-Faning's finding that after 1940 the majority of social class III practised no form of birth control is worrying and may be unreliable. For example, Slater and Woodside, who carried out their research between 1943 and 1946, found that only 1 in 25 of their sample of working-class families had not attempted some form of birth control. (Slater and Woodside, *Patterns of Marriage*, 195.)

[28] This, for the moment, excludes abortion as a method of family limitation.

intercourse when the merest 'slip' could end in disaster.[29] There is also evidence that husbands could employ it as an instrument of power within a marriage: the formidable threat by a jealous or suspicious husband to be 'careless' was sometimes used to enforce fidelity or obedience. Women 'blame very bitterly a husband who is inconsiderate this way, and through his carelessness or impetuosity adds so greatly to the hardship of their lives'.[30] Conversely, wives were grateful to men who practised withdrawal conscientiously, and there was a whole vocabulary of euphemisms by which gratitude was expressed: these husbands were 'thoughtful', 'considerate' or 'careful'.

The rubber sheath was the other principal form of male contraception. It became increasingly popular in the 1930s and 1940s, partly because of technical improvements in quality and reliability. The first latex condoms (called 'Dreadnoughts') were introduced in the late 1920s, and in 1932 the London Rubber Company began manufacturing them in England. By the mid-1930s it was producing two million a year; by 1945, thanks to orders from both the American and British armies, 36 million a year.[31]

The sheath was obviously much superior to withdrawal in almost every way, and in the 1930s and 1940s the form of contraception most favoured by the middle classes. Contemporary advocates of birth control were often surprised at working-class reluctance to use the sheath. Sheaths may have been thought too expensive: each packet cost 2s or 3s, a significant portion of an unskilled labourer's wage (though less than the net cost of an unwanted child). For many men, particularly those who served in the forces in either war, condoms were possibly too much associated with venereal disease and prophylaxis to be used within marriage.[32] Some men simply thought them unaesthetic. One miner's wife recalled that she 'had brought home some rubber sheaths ... and her husband had thrown them on the fire, saying that they took all the enjoyment out of sex, and were no safer than withdrawal.'[33]

The production and manufacture of condoms was also surrounded by folk myth. Some believed that manufacturers were obliged by law to make a fixed proportion of sheaths defective; some that Catholic pharmacists inserted holes in the condoms they sold. Others regarded them as infringements of their sexual autonomy. Whatever the reason, the majority of working-class families who regularly practised birth control persisted in using a method, withdrawal, which ensured that about 50 per cent of pregnancies were unwanted, or at least unplanned.

[29] Dennis *et al.*, *Coal is our Life*, 231.

[30] Slater and Woodside, *Patterns of Marriage*, 200–1.

[31] J. Peel, 'The Manufacture and Retailing of Contraceptives in England', *Population Studies* (Nov. 1963), 122.

[32] Seccombe, 'Starting to Stop: Working-Class Fertility Decline in Britain', 162.

[33] Dennis *et al.*, *Coal is our Life*, 208.

Given the apparent reluctance of many men to use 'male-appliances', proponents of family limitation increasingly encouraged women to control fertility via 'women's' techniques.[34] The Stopes and Family Planning Association clinics always recommended 'women's' appliances. Women, it was thought, had a more obvious interest in contraception than men, while the transfer of responsibility for family limitation to women meant a simultaneous redistribution of power within the family. These attempts, however, were only partly successful. In the first place, amongst women who attended clinics, those from the unskilled working class were seriously under-represented, while those from the middle classes, particularly the metropolitan middle classes, who needed little convincing anyway, were over-represented.[35] In the second, many working-class homes lacked the privacy or the bathrooms which would have allowed women to use, for example, the cap. In consequence, while the use of 'women's appliances' was becoming widespread in the middle classes, there is little evidence that (with one exception, Rendell's Pessaries)[36] they were much used in the working class.

There was also amongst working-class women a strong cultural inertia. Responsibility for contraception was traditionally the man's 'sphere', and in highly segmented marriages the invasion of the husband's sphere by his wife was risky. It involved possible ridicule by her husband—or worse—and the manipulation of the appropriate technology and social manners was often beyond her. In some working-class communities such inertia was long-lived. 'Mary' and 'Jean', for example, were told 'repeatedly of the ease of birth-control under modern clinical supervision':

Jean was at first unreceptive to the idea . . . She had a feeling there was something unnatural about it; she would feel awkward and embarrassed about going to the clinic. Secondly, and very significantly, she thought her husband would not favour the idea . . . She thought [he] would ridicule the appearance of the appliances she was shown. She had no bathroom and she would find it very awkward to use the equipment correctly . . . Her sister, Mary, however, could see clearly the advantages of family planning . . . Her husband might not take easily to the idea but she would reason it out with him . . . She soon decided she wanted to go [to the clinic] and after a few weeks persuaded Jean.

Yet neither of them went:

They never broke out of the daily routine sufficiently to fix appointments, and make the journey to nearby Bousfield. They were unused to telephones and keeping appoint-

---

[34] See Winifred Holtby's comment: 'It casts an odd reflection upon masculine tradition that though the contraceptive methods practised by men are simpler, cheaper and safer, it is for the instruction of women that clinics must be founded'. (*Women and a Changing Civilisation* (London, 1934), 68.)

[35] F. Lafitte, 'The Users of Birth Control Clinics', *Population Studies*, 16 (July 1962), 22.

[36] These were quinine-based and had been developed in the late 19th century by a London pharmacist. Sold in red boxes, they were a familiar item in pharmacist's shops until the 1960s.

ments and discussing intimacies with strangers. They hardly knew how to behave and explain themselves in front of other housewives they know . . . Mary, although she was 'potentially' more advanced than her sister, was restricted sufficiently by her social conditions to behave no differently.[37]

These were obstacles enough; even when they were apparently overcome, however, a certain fatalism could easily reassert itself. One London woman confessed that she had 'lost her cap in the raids' and had not bothered to replace it.[38] Of a group of London women questioned in the 1940s, those who used a cap did so because they were referred to clinics on gynaecological or general medical grounds. The only working-class women who used a cap, their questioners believed, were the 'most intelligent or the least healthy'.[39]

Amongst the working classes, but rarely amongst the middle classes, the woman's preferred technique of contraception was abortion. Abortion was illegal: those who sought it or executed it were liable to criminal prosecution. It was, however, known to be widely practised. It was also recognized that what many were willing to call 'miscarriages' were, in fact, abortions. The Inter-Departmental Committee on Abortion (1939) suggested that there were probably 40–66,000 abortions each year, but if to that figure the number of self-induced miscarriages is added, the total might have been between 110,000 and 150,000 a year. The 'sexologist' Eustace Chesser thought that the 'overwhelming majority' of women who had been married five years or more sought to terminate a pregnancy and that at least 20 per cent of all pregnancies ended in abortion.[40] Marie Stopes, though she strongly disapproved of it, none the less thought it the real explanation for the fall in working-class fertility. The historian Diana Gittins, on the basis of interviews with working-class women, concluded that for the unskilled working class, abortion was perhaps the most common form of birth control.[41]

There was a contemporary view that the slums of England teemed with back-street abortionists to whom working-class women regularly had recourse. There were, certainly, many abortionists and in working-class communities their identities were known. It seems more likely, however, that most women who successfully aborted a pregnancy did so by self-induced miscarriage, usually by the consumption of powerful emetics or purgatives. Within a confined working-class household these could be horrifically public events:

Not long after Joey's birth Mum found herself pregnant yet again . . . By means of gin, quinine, jumping down the stairs and similar traditional methods, she managed to abort the pregnancy . . . The foetus, raw and bloody looking, 'came away' to flop on the floor when she was in the kitchen with [Joey].[42]

---

[37] Dennis *et al.*, *Coal is our Life*, 208–9.   [38] Slater and Woodside, *Patterns of Marriage*, 205.
[39] Ibid.   [40] E. Chesser, *Love without Fear* (London, 1941), 255–6.
[41] Gittins, *Fair Sex*, 171–2; also Lewis, *Women in England*, 17.
[42] Willmott, *Growing Up in a London Village*, 60.

Provincial newspapers and many magazines advertised a wide array of potions and mixtures for 'women's problems' whose genteel names, like 'Penny Royal' or 'Bitter Apples', deceived no one.[43] Some women simply swallowed large doses of patent laxatives, like 'Jean' who achieved a succession of miscarriages 'like many another Ashton [Featherstone] wife, by means of drastic dosing with ordinary laxatives'.[44] This procedure was obviously common everywhere:

Mrs O., twenty-two ... doesn't know about birth-control and just takes a good dose of salts. Mrs M., a respectable suburban housewife ... 'doesn't believe in birth-control: it can harm your insides'. Her husband is 'careful' and she takes Beechams Pills.[45]

In August 1943, Nella Last recorded a conversation with her yet-again pregnant 'help', Tilly:

She said, 'It will not be my fault if I have it, I'll take *anything*.' I said, 'You realise that it might be worse than having a baby?' She rather took my breath away when she said largely, 'Ah, I'm going to Mr Last's [Mrs Last's brother-in-law]. He sells *hundreds* of 5 shilling bottles and is thought very highly of by the women round our way.' I know all chemists sell various kinds of 'women's medicine', but I had not realised Harry had such a good trade.[46]

The question of birth control generally and abortion particularly caused profound ideological disagreements. 'None of my things ever seems to arouse controversy,' Winifred Holtby wrote to Vera Brittain in 1934. 'My Woman book may as I've gone all out for Abortion just to give it a fillip.'[47] Nor could it ever be morally neutral, despite the efforts to treat it as an everyday 'fact' by people like Janet Chance, a pioneer of more informed and liberal sexual relationships. The Roman Catholic Church always, and the Church of England and the medical profession until the Second World War (at the least), regarded contraception as a moral issue, however much they were later obliged to accept *faits accomplis*. In 1908 the Church of England had pronounced contraception theologically, morally, and socially wrong and that remained its position until 1930. The experiences of the First World War and the clear evidence of the widespread practice of birth control compelled the Church to debate the issue at the 1920 Lambeth Conference. Despite much lobbying from birth control organizations, the bishops accepted the report of the Church's Committee on Problems of Marriage and Sexual Morality which reaffirmed its opposition to contraception.

The clergy was not, however, unanimous. The chairman of the Committee on Problems of Marriage was the bishop of London, Arthur Winnington-

---

[43] For a list of these proprietary goods, see Chesser, *Love without Fear*, 256–9; Humphries, *Secret World of Sex*, 76–8, has interesting detail.

[44] Dennis *et al.*, *Coal is our Life*, 208.   [45] Slater and Woodside, *Patterns of Marriage*, 196.

[46] Broad and Fleming, *Nella Last's War*, 256.

[47] Holtby to Brittain, 14 Apr. 1934, in V. Brittain and G. Handley-Taylor (ed.), *Selected Letters of*

Ingram, a man passionately hostile to birth control—he had once expressed a wish to dance around a lighted bonfire of condoms—and it is doubtful how representative its conclusions were. Some bishops opposed the 1920 decision because it made the Church look foolish, as did many parish clergy, particularly from working-class districts. In their view birth control should be left to the individual conscience: the position the Free Churches thought it prudent to adopt. The Lambeth resolutions were further undermined when in 1921 the king's physician, Lord Dawson of Penn, a leading Anglican layman, told a Church congress in Birmingham that the 'love envisioned by the Lambeth Conference [is] . . . an invertebrate joyless thing—not worth the having'.[48] This genuinely sensational speech (too sensational for Dawson who retired from the fray) began a steady series of ecclesiastical readjustments. In 1926, the archbishop of Canterbury, Randall Davidson, was misunderstood to have given cautious approval to voluntary birth control clinics, and he was careful not to correct the misunderstanding.[49] The opponents of the 1920 resolutions were further strengthened when in 1929 William Temple became archbishop of York. Temple confessed to Marie Stopes that he had 'long considered that the traditional attitude of the Church on this question is unwarrantable' and he discreetly lobbied a number of his episcopal colleagues. As did Stopes, less discreetly. In 1930, largely for the benefit of the Anglican bishops about to meet again in Lambeth, she published *Mother England*, a selection of letters sent to her by working-class women in 1926. The book was a moving catalogue of their worries and the humiliations they often suffered when confronted by arrogant doctors and ignorant health visitors. *Mother England* may not have converted the bishops, but they did listen respectfully to Helena Wright[50] argue the case for reducing working-class fertility, and they did (by 193 to 67) support a resolution which gave episcopal sanction to birth control in certain limited circumstances and in 'the light of . . . Christian principles'.

This resolution did not, in fact, result from any real moral or ideological conversion. The Church reiterated its view that the primary function of sex was procreative and that the best form of birth control was abstinence. The bishops did not hide their distaste for artificial contraception or any system of national birth control clinics. Their grudging approval came largely from a recognition that the Church could not indefinitely condemn an increasingly common practice without being discredited or despised. Furthermore, the Anglican clergy were among the two most infertile occupations in the country—almost

Winifred Holtby (1920–1935) (London, 1960), 275. The 'Woman' book was Holtby's *Women and a Changing Civilisation*.

[48] Quoted in R. A. Soloway, *Birth Control and the Population Question in England, 1877–1930* (Chapel Hill and London, 1982), 241.

[49] What he had actually said was that, if there were to be birth control clinics, they should be voluntary rather than state assisted or controlled.

[50] For Wright, see below, p. 320.

inevitably the medical profession was the other—and this was widely known. Many of Stopes's correspondents, for example, referred bitterly to the hypocrisy of the clergy and the doctors, as did Stopes herself, and the Church was acutely sensitive to this criticism. Like the position of the Free Churches, the 1930 resolution was prudent rather than heroic.

Heroic enough, however, to outrage the Catholic Church. The archbishop of Westminster, Cardinal Bourne, thought the Anglican bishops had 'abdicated any claim they may have been thought to possess to be authorized exponents of morality',[51] and the Catholic Church remained unwavering in its absolute opposition to birth control—an opposition reaffirmed by the encyclical *Casti Conubii* (1930). Unworried by the infertility of its own priests, the Roman Catholic Church was the most powerful opponent of either voluntary or state-assisted birth control clinics; and the leading anti-birth control organization, the League of National Life, though nominally interdenominational (it even included the chief rabbi, Joseph Hirtz) was, in fact, a Catholic front organization whose secretary, Halliday Sutherland, had been involved in a famous libel suit with Marie Stopes.

How far the teachings of the churches influenced people's behaviour is inevitably difficult to measure. The demographic history of Europe suggests that such teachings are successful only in combination with other variables—particularly the status of women. When such variables change, the church's authority becomes much weaker: indeed, the history of Catholic Europe since the Second World War is a history of its continuous decline. By the 1990s both Spain and Italy, for example, had net reproduction rates below unity. In both, rapid and profound social change encouraged people, even those who continued to think of themselves as Catholic, to practice birth control regardless of ecclesiastical injunctions.

Something of the same was true of England in the 1920s, 1930s, and 1940s. There is, for instance, little evidence that the Church of England had much direct authority over its nominal adherents—that any significant number of people decided against practising birth control *solely* because the Church either forbade or disapproved of it. Even more was this so of the Free Churches. The only church which could claim effective authority was the Roman Catholic, since it had in its mainly Irish unskilled working-class faithful a congregation peculiarly susceptible to instruction. At least this was the conventional view. Madeline Kerr, who studied a predominantly Roman Catholic working-class area of Liverpool, thought the Catholic Church's only long-term influence was in the prohibition of certain kinds of conduct—of which one was birth control.[52] Yet even here the evidence is mixed. Many Roman Catholic

---

[51] Quoted Soloway, *Birth Control and the Population Question*, 254.
[52] Kerr, *Ship Street*, 167.

women, for instance, thought self-induced miscarriage (which they would not call abortion) within the first trimester was 'all right' because it was not actually contraception.[53] Furthermore, it is not clear whether the important variable is 'Catholicness' or 'working classness'. All working-class families, Protestant and Catholic, practised birth control less frequently and less effectively than middle- or upper-class families. The lower down the social scale the more infrequent and ineffective it became—and the Catholic working class tended to be at the very bottom. When working-class attitudes changed, they changed, on the whole, irrespective of religion: they just took longer to change at the bottom. Thus in the 1940s, when the state and other social institutions became interested in the question, people were struck by the extent to which working-class opinion had become openly hostile to large families. Girls were frequently passionate on the issue, often citing their mothers' advice (not to have many children) or example (of the terrible consequences of having many children).[54] Even Roman Catholics thought family-planning 'common sense'.[55] It would, of course, be unwise to deny the Catholic Church any influence. Throughout this period Catholic families were larger than Protestant and that is probably not just a consequence of working-classness. None the less, when the 'class situation' of Catholic families began to approximate that of Protestants, so did the size of their families.

The Anglican and Catholic Churches not so much dissuaded people from practising contraception as surrounded its use with guilt and tension. Many who did not hesitate to use contraceptives nevertheless thought their use somehow 'wrong'. The Churches (though not only they) also ensured that contraception, like all aspects of sexuality, was to be a furtive and anxious business, and convinced even those who might otherwise have done well out of it: in the 1950s the country's 'largest chain of retail pharmacists' refused to stock condoms because of their association with 'promiscuity, vice and prostitution'.[56]

The position of the two other agencies most involved, the medical profession and the state, was as complicated as the Church of England's and for many of the same reasons. Before 1914 the official attitude of the doctors, as expressed by their professional organizations, was one of outright opposition to artificial contraception. It was resisted on moral, eugenic, and physical grounds. Most gynaecologists believed that contraception was physiologically harmful to women; even as late as the 1920s, one of them, F. J. McCann, claimed to have detected a new contraceptive-induced ailment, 'Malthusian

[53] Ibid. 83–4.

[54] For examples, see Jephcott, *Rising Twenty*, 42; Madge, *War-Time Pattern of Saving and Spending*, 75. Slater and Woodside, *Patterns of Marriage*, 70–1, 182.

[55] Slater and Woodside, *Patterns of Marriage*, 188.

[56] J. Peel, 'The Manufacture and Retailing of Contraceptives in England', *Population Studies* (Nov. 1963), 122.

uterus'. In fact, the attitude of most doctors depended simply on received opinions. Before 1939, and often thereafter, many doctors were almost wholly ignorant of contraceptive techniques. Until the Second World War not one medical school gave instruction in birth control, and many gave no instruction even in human reproduction. The consequence was that doctors were often as embarrassed as their patients, and embarrassment could appear as contempt or indifference. Birth control 'pioneers', like Marie Stopes or Janet Chance, were often therefore justified in their hostility to the medical profession, even if they discovered malice where there was only ignorance. Ignorance amongst general practitioners and, indeed, specialists was reinforced by the high proportion of Roman Catholics in the medical profession. In the 1940s 22 per cent of all doctors in hospital and general practice were Catholic (which makes the doctors' low fertility even more impressive) and they appear to have effectively delayed the teaching of birth control within the profession and the willingness of doctors to discuss it with their patients.[57]

Amongst women doctors, particularly gynaecologists or obstetricians, there was a quasi-feminist argument against birth control. A number of them, like the most prominent woman gynaecologist, Dame Mary Scharlieb, believed that fear of causing an unwanted pregnancy alone restrained husbands from making excessive sexual demands on their wives; a view shared by Christian feminists like Dame Maude Royden. If such a restraint disappeared, they argued, wives would have no protection against sexually aggressive or violent husbands. Some thought this a contrived argument, but it followed naturally from assumptions about male sexuality widely held in the 1920s and 1930s.

In these circumstances it is not surprising that the medical profession approached birth control as ambiguously as the Church of England did. The view which was probably predominant in the profession by the late 1920s, that contraception properly used was harmless and often legitimate, was not reached entirely by rational means. Like the Anglican Church, the doctors were divided (in part by generation); like the Church, they had their own low fertility to explain away; like many Anglican ministers, many doctors disliked contraception in principle but thought continued opposition to it made them look ridiculous. Possibly an even stronger motive, however, was a desire to gain control of a growing social practice by 'medicalizing' it, rather as childbirth had been 'medicalized'. But the only way to do this was to recognize birth control and then to declare it a medical 'problem'. In this the profession partly succeeded.

In its policies towards birth control, the state and the legal system trod the same twisted path as the Anglican Church and the doctors. The result was inconsistent and incoherent legislation and policing. Abortion remained illegal, but the many attempts to forbid the sale of contraceptives were defeated. Pharmacists could sell contraceptives but could give no advice to their customers about their purchase and use—and the Pharmaceutical Society effectively forbade any form of advertisement. In 1925 that law was modified by the crown law officers so that a chemist might give verbal but not written or printed advice to a customer. Someone could, therefore, both buy contraceptives and seek (spoken) advice about their use. He could also obtain them from barbers' and certain other shops; but he could not buy them from an outdoor slot machine. These were expelled from sight by local authorities in 1939 under a model by-law prepared by the home office, acting, probably, in response to pressure from public morality groups.

The state moved towards allowing welfare clinics to issue contraceptive advice in the same halting manner. The first legislative attempt to do this (February 1926) was defeated in the House of Commons by 167 to 81. Members of all parties voted for and against, but only one woman member (Ellen Wilkinson, Labour MP for East Middlesbrough) voted for it, and the way MPs voted was not unrelated to the religious complexion of their constituencies.[58] The House of Lords, however, which had no constituency to disturb it, shortly afterwards approved a resolution moved by Lord Buckmaster and drawn up by the largely 'middle-class' National Union of Societies of Equal Citizenship (NUSEC) which would have permitted welfare clinics to give advice on birth control.

Under heavy pressure from NUSEC, from the Workers' Birth Control Group and the National Conference of Labour Women, and from other feminist or eugenic groups, the minister of health in the second Labour government, Arthur Greenwood, agreed that medical officers of health and welfare clinics might give contraceptive instruction if (and only if) they were satisfied that a woman's *physical* health was endangered. Characteristically, the ministry declined to publish the memorandum which allowed this (153/M.C.W.) and revealed it only to local authorities which asked for a copy. It was not made public until eight months after its issue and then only because it had been leaked to the press.[59]

Local authorities generally were very reluctant to assume responsibilities under the new dispensation. For many, the issue was still too divisive. By 1939 only 280 local authorities, mostly in the greater conurbations, had agreed to give some form of birth control advice. In addition, there were nearly 70 clinics staffed by the newly formed Family Planning Association, and several more controlled by Stopes. The issue remained divisive throughout the 1940s

[58] Forty-six Labour MPs voted against. Not one Clydeside MP voted for, probably for fear of their Catholic constituents' reaction. John Wheatley, the leading Clydeside MP, who as minister of health in 1924 had refused to consider allowing welfare clinics to give advice on birth control, was himself a Catholic.

[59] There is a good account of the politics of birth control in Soloway, *Birth Control and the Population Question*, 280–318.

despite (or because of) the almost universal use of condoms in the armed forces. It was hoped that the new National Health Service would incorporate family planning within its structure, but no government was willing to do this until the Wilson Labour government grasped the nettle in the 1960s.

4 | *The Tree of Knowledge*

The argument that sexual pleasure and harmony might be the most important elements in a successful marriage often foundered, as its proponents freely admitted, upon the apparent ignorance of even the most elementary sexual knowledge amongst much of the population. In the late 1940s Mass-Observation discovered that only 11 per cent of the population were given any sexual instruction by their mothers, and only 6 per cent by their fathers. Others were astonished at the 'abysmal ignorance' of 'sexual physiology':

Ordinary men and women have not even the vocabulary with which to frame enquiries and express their puzzlement. Husbands and wives are hampered in a discussion with one another. Parents, nowadays at least, are generally well-meaning, but are themselves too ignorant and inhibited to give reliable information to their children.[60]

This reticence was due not simply to embarrassment: many people thought the possession of sexual knowledge was itself wrong—or 'rude' as it was frequently called. Nakedness, even in young children, was 'rude'; sex-play as well as sexual curiosity was 'rude'. Children were early made aware of taboos about sex and the parents who introduced them to these taboos were both helpless and unhelpful when their children reached puberty.[61] Ignorance was often identified with a quasi-Christian morality even by those who were not practising Christians. 'My mother never told me anything; I had a most true moral code,' one working-class woman said.[62] Sometimes parents nerved themselves to impart advice at the eleventh hour, but often too late. Betty Tucker, the daughter of a Stoke railwayman, received the only sexual advice her father ever disclosed as she drove with him to her wedding. 'My dear old dad told me nothing but in the taxi going to church he gave me a tin of vaseline because he said I might be a bit sore that night.' Betty had, however, already lost her virginity.[63]

It is unlikely that ignorance or reticence was confined to the working class. Janet Chance was plainly thinking of the middle classes and above when she claimed to find it 'a little surprising' to see parents and teachers

---

[60] Slater and Woodside, *Patterns of Marriage*, 173.

[61] Shaw, 'Impressions of Family Life', 191; Klein, *Samples from English Cultures*, 146–7; Hoggart, *Uses of Literacy*, 74–5.

[62] Slater and Woodside, *Patterns of Marriage*, 113.

[63] Humphries, *Secret World of Sex*, 46.

evade the subject of sex education as they do; and to watch them allow the children for whom they are responsible pick up their education from servants and school friends in a way they would consider inadequate for their spelling and their cricket.[64]

The daughter of the earl of Darnley, Lady Marguerite Tangye, remembered her mother's discomfort as she 'tried to explain the mechanics':

I looked at her and saw she was very embarrassed and I wasn't really listening. And so, I must have been thirteen, I knew what she'd said but it bore no relation whatsoever to the rest of my life. So when I grew up I knew in theory and yet I knew nothing, very difficult to explain. I think what was left out was desire, lust, the feeling that a man had when he raped someone . . . what was told you was the mechanics of it . . . The desire is what causes the trouble. She would say, 'It is either sacred or disgusting.' That was her idea of it, you either did it in a sacred way because you wanted a baby or it was disgusting and not to be mentioned . . . That's what she told me. I didn't take any notice at all.[65]

The result of parental embarrassment or prudery often meant for their daughters, the majority of whom were probably virgin at marriage, the horrors of the wedding night.

Yet people obviously acquired some sexual knowledge. Some, in fact, did get it from their parents; and of those who did, most, unsurprisingly, were daughters. But the lessons they received could be heavily negative. Girls were told what they should not do; and often then in so coded a way that they were sometimes unsure what it was they should not do. Some (both boys and girls) were taught elementary biological facts in school, but they were a minority. In 1944 only one-third of schools provided any instructions, usually by special lectures, which were, like the countess of Darnley's gauche disclosures, always confined to the 'mechanics'.[66] There were no approved texts or manuals.

To the extent that people learnt anything before marriage it was most likely from their peer group or workmates. There was much sexual play and curiosity amongst working-class children and youths. The life of the streets, with its absence of adult supervision, and the 'larking about' which went with it, always had a strong element of heterosexual experimentation.[67] In this sense, working-class children were almost certainly sexually more precocious (though not necessarily more knowledgeable) than middle-class children, and probably more experienced than middle- and upper-class children who went to public school, however pervasive the sexual atmosphere of these institutions.[68] There was also much sex-talk amongst young working-class men in

[64] Chance, *Cost of English Morals*, 30.   [65] Humphries, *Secret World of Sex*, 44.

[66] Weeks, *Sex, Politics and Society*, 211–12.

[67] S. Humphries, *Hooligans or Rebels?* (London, 1981), 136. For good examples of working-class knowingness, see Paneth, *Branch Street*, 18–22, 66–7. One of her charges, 'Don', was able to draw 'a detailed picture of the sexual organs of both sexes in the act of intercourse', an ability acquired by personal observation of parental behaviour in a one-roomed 'flat'.

[68] This was Richard Hoggart's view. Hoggart, *Uses of Literacy*, 76. For public school sexuality, see

factories and workshops, many of which, particularly in South and East London and in engineering shops generally, had specifically sexual 'initiation' rites (common well into the 1950s) for male apprentices, in which women and girls often took part. In so far as working-class boys received a sexual education it was likely to be at work.[69]

There is also strong evidence that young women and girls who worked in places where there were opportunities for the exchange of sexual confidences and humour, like factories, offices and, even more, wartime military hospitals, were more sexually *au fait* than girls who went into socially isolated occupations like domestic service. Vera Brittain, for example, pointed out how important war nursing was to the sexual education of middle- and upper-middle-class girls if only because it necessarily acquainted them with human physiology.[70] In one sample of women who grew up in this period, all who worked in non-manual work had quite explicit information about sex. Several of them admitted it was in the office where they first discovered the facts of life. One woman, having been told 'nothing' by her mother, eventually, in her early twenties, learnt them from 'one of the girls in the office'. Another recalled having some 'good times down at the office'—'There was something I said to June one day—I forget what it was—and she absolutely killed herself laughing. 'Cause I thought about once every three months or something—I didn't know you had intercourse when you wanted or anything of that, see—I thought it was once in three months! Now June, she roared!'

This contrasts with the innocence of the living-in domestic servants. One denied knowing anything before marriage:

Oh no! Sex was really out of it all, my mother was a truly old-fashioned mother ... I think that right up to the time that my first daughter was born I had an idea they cut you open to get the baby away. I had a very nice old family doctor and I remember I was terrified not because of having the baby but because I got to be chopped open, I thought, and he said, 'No, the baby will come out where it went in', you know that kind of thing, and I think that frightened me even more at the time.[71]

Of those in the sample who remained residential servants until they married,

Brian Aldiss's novel, *The Hand-Reared Boy* (London, 1970), and above, p. 247. However, the folklore about what middle- and upper-class boys learnt from the family servants is so widespread that there must be something to it.

[69] For an account of these rites, see S. Humphries, J. Mack, R. Perks, *A Century of Childhood* (London, 1988), 160; and Humphries, *Secret World of Sex*, 60–1. Humphries suggests that the 'surgical' and 'rubber goods' shops that were to be found in most large towns provided young working-class men with matter-of-fact, no-moralizing knowledge. It seems unlikely, however, that many could have resorted to these shops, given the social disapproval which surrounded them. In late 1940s London it was found that 18-year-old working-class youths were quite well informed about the physiology of sex: most information was culled from friends. (R. F. L. Logan and E. M. Goldberg, 'Rising Eighteen in a London Suburb: A Study of Some Aspects of the Life and Health of Young Men', *British Journal of Sociology*, 4 (1953), 333–4.)

[70] V. Brittain, *Testament of Youth* (London, 1978), 165–6.   [71] Gittins, *Fair Sex*, 77–9.

all claimed to have no knowledge of sex, reproduction, or birth control before then. The extreme isolation of living-in servants in the interwar years thus denied them even the elementary sexual knowledge which girls working in an office could acquire, and this partly accounts for the exceptionally high rates of illegitimate births among domestic servants.

Acquiring sexual knowledge like this, though better than nothing, had one obvious disadvantage: what was learnt was frequently garbled or plain wrong. As one woman told Marie Stopes, it was impossible to learn anything accurate from acquaintances—they simply gave 'wonderful cures'.[72] Many working-class boys and girls, for instance, held bizarre views about the transmission of venereal disease, while many men with venereal diseases still believed they could cure themselves by infecting a virgin, and repeated wildly inaccurate stories where anything beyond the most elementary facts of reproduction was involved. The knowledge acquired by middle-class children, though often second-hand and bookish, was more likely to be accurate. In the enormous correspondence which Marie Stopes received from her readers, there is a clear class distinction: working men and women were anxious to know about 'facts', how things worked, whereas middle-class correspondents wanted advice not about facts, but about the taboos which surrounded them.

The 'educational' campaigns against venereal disease apparently did little to promote knowledge. Although the Lloyd George government had introduced free and, in effect, anonymous treatment for venereal diseases in special clinics, which were important in the rapid fall in the annual rate of venereal infection during the interwar years,[73] the state itself was reluctant to participate directly in any educational programmes which might have reduced the need for treatment. The result was that such programmes were dominated by groups whose teaching was anything but objective. One of the two most important was the National Council for the Control of Venereal Disease (NCCVD), later the British Social Hygiene Council, which was closely connected to the Protestant churches, especially when Randall Davidson was archbishop of Canterbury, but which never had their wholehearted support. The other was the Society for the Prevention of Venereal Disease (SPVD), a dogmatically secular body, dominated by powerful anti-clerical doctors like Sir Bryan Donkin, whose first president was the deeply reactionary Lord Willoughby de Broke. Both organizations had markedly eugenic preoccupations and both saw the 'battle' against venereal disease as a battle for racial fitness. They differed, however, as to the weapons. The NCCVD urged chastity; the SPVD, in more secular mode, prophylaxis. Although both made some attempt to have human reproduction taught in the schools, their efforts largely

---

[72] Seccombe, 'Starting to Stop: Working-Class Fertility Decline in Britain', 168.
[73] Davenport-Hines, *Sex, Death and Punishment*, 247.

bypassed the school system; they relied rather on lectures, conferences, and (increasingly) on an unnerving array of films, like *Waste*, *The Flaw* and, most famous of all, *Damaged Goods* (an English version of a French play), all of which were shown to millions in the 1920s, and which treated sex with a terrifying frankness inconceivable in any other film of the time.[74]

These campaigns were, however, altogether too ideological to serve any balanced instructional purpose. They were too concerned to impart fear, and their vocabulary of pollution and degeneration was more likely to encourage alarm than understanding. The leaders of these bodies were also very reluctant to admit that neo-salvarsan was an effective treatment for syphilis, as they were later unwilling to acknowledge that penicillin was even better. There was, furthermore, an obvious gender-bias in the anti-venereal propaganda, a clear tendency to suggest or imply that venereal infections were something women passed on to men. This, of course, had always been implied in most attempts to suppress venereal disease, as feminists had pointed out ever since Josephine Butler led the opposition to the Contagious Diseases Act. Before (and during) the First World War it was assumed that the chief agency of venereal infection was female prostitution. In the 1920s, however, in face of the obvious decline of prostitution, and the slight relaxation of sexual mores, fear of the prostitute was overtaken by fear of the 'amateur', the easygoing girl who did it largely for fun.[75] The image of the 'amateur' was strong throughout the period and was, if anything, reinforced by a renewed panic about venereal disease during the Second World War.

The state was then obliged to intervene when the arrival of large numbers of American troops was partly responsible for sharp increases in the rate of venereal infection. The American authorities were dismayed at the absence of public educational programmes in England, and the government was compelled to set up the so-called Joint Committee of the service ministries, the home office, and the police in order to construct an 'official' policy.[76] It was not particularly successful but it did introduce a certain matter-of-factness into sexual instruction, largely because the service ministries were forced to emphasize prophylaxis and this undermined the more openly ideological precepts of the older societies.[77]

---

[74] Weeks, *Sex, Politics and Society*, 211.

[75] The novelist Winifred Holtby, combining religion and sex, drafted a short story called *The Amateur*, in which the daughter of a clergyman takes up temporary prostitution in order to earn £50. But most amateurs were thought not to demand money for favours; merely a good time.

[76] Davenport-Hines, *Sex, Death and Punishment*, 269–70.

[77] Concerned individuals were not deterred, however. Alderman Mrs Bonham Pigg, of St Pancras, argued that the way to 'dispel ignorance' was to talk incessantly about syphilis: those 'engaged in Air Raid Precaution . . . could do good conversational work on the subject'. As Davenport-Hines comments, the 'doom of spending a night firewatching on a St Pancras rooftop with someone who reiteratively and unrelentingly talked with self-conscious frankness about the perils of syphilis must have been one of the worst horrors of the blitz'. (*Sex, Death and Punishment*, 271.)

Even after the introduction of penicillin, however, the government found it difficult to exclude racial and moral metaphors from its posters and literature. Although civil servants felt 'that the moral approach does not come happily from a Government Department', and despite their wish to persuade people to seek treatment quickly, the educational programmes remained punitive—as likely to create anxiety as the urge to seek effective treatment. And this was because so many of those involved in the anti-VD campaigns, particularly in the older organizations like the NCCVD, were, in practice, more concerned to extirpate sexual promiscuity than venereal disease. For them it was sex and not its consequences which was the problem. Thus in 1939, despite all the campaigns, there was available only one book which gave full details of current prophylaxis—Marie Stopes's *Prevention of Venereal Disease*.

Yet, for all these apparent conspiracies against knowledge, people in the interwar years and the 1940s were certain they spoke about sex with an unparalleled freedom and objectivity. Both a cause and consequence of this certainty was the proliferation of sex-and-marriage manuals which had huge sales after the First World War, several of which were still in print in the 1960s. The 'sexologist' Havelock Ellis had published several articles which emphasized the pleasurable and non-procreative nature of sex, but Ellis was too unrespectable, the articles published in journals too obscure for a popular audience, and too strange in their origin[78] to be widely read. Marie Stopes first exploited what turned out to be an enormous market. *Married Love* (March 1918), which dealt specifically with sexual technique, sold over 400,000 copies by 1923; *Wise Parenthood* (November 1918) which openly taught contraception (only hinted at in the first volume), sold 300,000 copies by 1924. Stopes, whose early married life was, according to her own account, blighted by a seemingly complete sexual ignorance, was a belligerent, prickly, and publicity-avid woman whose quarrels and feuds were notorious, but who had exactly the attributes the hour demanded.[79] Her books were usually short and straightforward—which is why they were so popular—though occasionally her treatment of the climacteric moment was so mystical that it is not surprising many of her readers wondered why they had never experienced it.[80] She was also skilful in making her work acceptable to members of the medical profession by assimilating it to

---

[78] P. Grosskurth, *Havelock Ellis* (New York, 1980), 287.

[79] See the excellent account of Stopes's activities and quarrels, particularly the quarrel with the American pioneer of the birth control movement, Margaret Sanger, and of the celebrated libel suit against Halliday Sutherland in Soloway, *Birth Control and the Population Question in England*, 208–32, 246–8.

[80] See her description of woman's orgasm: 'Welling up in her are the wonderful tides, scented and enriched by the myriad experience of the human race from its ancient days of leisure and flower-wreathed love-making, urging her to transports of self-expression'. (Quoted in E. M. Holtzman, 'The Pursuit of Married Love: Women's Attitudes towards Sexuality and Marriage in Great Britain', *Journal of Social History*, 16, 2 (1982), 40.)

fashionable eugenic arguments. *Married Love* was favourably reviewed in both the *Lancet* and the *British Medical Journal*, and *Wise Parenthood* was even advertised on the front page of the *Lancet*.[81]

Stopes's main competitor in the 1930s was probably Theo Van de Velde's *Ideal Marriage* (translated by the feminist Stella Browne), described by Eustace Chesser as a 'classic',[82] but which, while good on 'the mechanics', was almost intolerably long-winded. Stopes and Van de Velde, however, were not alone. Helena Wright's *The Sex Factor in Marriage* (1930) and *More About the Sex Factor in Marriage* (1947), E. F. Griffith's *Modern Marriage* (1935), and Eustace Chesser's *Love without Fear* (1941) and *Marriage and Freedom* (1946) all sold in immense numbers. Their popularity was such that the old social purity organizations, like the very Christian White Cross League, felt obliged to enter the market on terms set by Stopes and the others. Thus the White Cross's *Threshold of Marriage* which, amongst other things, told its readers how husband and wife might achieve simultaneous orgasm, sold over 500,000 copies.[83]

These manuals had much in common. They all argued that sexual pleasure in marriage, independent of any notion of procreation, was both legitimate and necessary. Some, indeed, argued that 'healthy' sexual relations between husband and wife were essential to a marriage's survival. It followed, therefore, that the woman must have as much pleasure in sex as the man. As Chesser wrote: 'marriage means the coming together of *two equals*.'[84] They all dismissed the idea that sexual enjoyment was for men alone. They did, however, assume that a husband (being more sexually experienced or more likely to take the sexual initiative) would have to educate his wife in sexual technique—and this was the explicit purpose of the Marriage Guidance Council's very popular *How to treat a Young Wife* (later called *Sex in Marriage*). But they had no doubt that women should be sexually active, partners in love as well as in life; and this was perhaps their most subversive doctrine.

They tended, furthermore, to be comforting. While not proposing a sexual *carte blanche*, they were usually reassuring on such profound anxiety-makers as masturbation and some forms of heterosexual activity which people enjoyed but none the less thought 'wrong'. In so far as they discussed it, most were also opposed to the criminalization of consenting male homosexuality, and their brisk way with medical superstitions was a world apart from the 'advice' which readers often received from their own doctors.

Nearly all of them, however, were anxious to preserve the idea that conjugal sex was superior to all others. They might subvert received notions of women's

---

[81] Peel, 'Contraception and the Medical Profession', 138.

[82] E. Chesser and Z. Dawe, *The Practice of Sex Education* (London, 1945), 151. There is a useful bibliography of contemporary literature, 147–57.

[83] Weeks, *Sex, Politics and Society*, 207.

[84] E. Chesser, *Marriage and Freedom* (London, 1946), 115.

sexuality, they might argue that sexual union was the highest form of love, but they would not undermine the family. This was as true of 'secular' authors like Stopes and Chesser as it was of 'Christian' authors like Griffith or Wright. But this introduced a tension which in the long term was damaging to such a definition of sexuality: if sexuality were a legitimate physical pleasure dependent primarily upon technique, then it could be argued only with difficulty or by ideological sleight-of-hand that pre- or extra-marital sexuality was 'wrong'. They found themselves, therefore, in the same intellectual and social dilemma as the marriage guidance movement.

5 | *Sexual dissidence*

If heterosexual relations, however conventional, were problematical, 'deviant' sexuality, of whatever form, was doubly so. Male homosexuality was not only socially unacceptable—in the early fifties almost half the population found it 'disgusting'—it was illegal. Lesbianism was not illegal but was subject to increasingly unfavourable stereotyping and widespread dislike. Male homosexuals, unless they lived in what contemporaries thought to be 'advanced circles', like London's bohemia, or worked in professions where homosexuality was known to be common and so tacitly recognized, like the theatre, concealed their homosexuality or else revealed it at their risk. An open admission of homosexuality or, what amounted to the same thing, arrest by the police, often meant immediate dismissal from work.[85] An active homosexual, furthermore, frequently faced violence or blackmail.

The sexual life of most homosexuals, therefore, tended to be furtive and isolated. The enormous weight of legal and social disapproval tended to make homosexual activity anonymous and fast. For many that meant seeking hurried relationships in public lavatories (in London called 'cottages') or other places which provided some safety and anonymity. The blackout during the Second World War was therefore remembered by homosexual men with much affection; it was not just the general licence, which would be enjoyed by anyone, it was the particular anonymity and safety which complete darkness allowed. In London and other big towns 'cottaging' was not entirely random: certain public lavatories were known to be places where sex could be found and many of them appear to have kept their reputations and clientèle for years.[86] The West End of London, particularly, had an elaborate and extensive homosexual geography where 'cottages' were apparently socially graded:

If you wanted a piece of rough you'd look around the cottages in Covent Garden, in the

[85] Humphries, *Secret World of Sex*, 205.
[86] See Alan Hollinghurst's striking, if unsettling, novel, *The Swimming-Pool Library* (London, 1988), which is an imaginative history of West End 'cottages' and their clientèle as well as a modern genealogy of London's sexual politics.

early morning cottages, the lorry drivers' cottages. On the other hand if you wanted the
theatrical trade you'd do some of the cottages round the back of Jermyn Street or if you
did the cottage at Waterloo Station you always got a good class of trade, dear.[87]

Piccadilly was known to be a place where male prostitutes were to be found, as
were the pubs around the guards' barracks where J. R. Ackerley picked up so
many young men.

I found myself concentrating my attention more and more upon a particular society of
young men in the metropolis which I had tapped before and which, it seemed to me,
might yield, without further loss of time, what I required. His Majesty's Brigade of
Guards had a long history in homosexual prostitution. Perpetually short of cash, beer
and leisure occupations, they were easily to be found of an evening . . . in the various
pubs they frequented . . . alert to the possibility that some kind gentlemen might appear
and stand them a few pints, in return for which and the subsequent traditional tip . . .
they were perfectly agreeable to, indeed often eager for 'a bit of fun'.[88]

London, for the more adventurous, also possessed other sexual foci—pubs,
swimming-baths, 'turkish baths', and private clubs, although the clubs usually
insisted on discreet behaviour, as the extravagant Quentin Crisp found to his
cost.[89] For those who lived outside London, to the extent that there were homosexual networks, it was probably public lavatories, dangerous casual street
encounters, or nothing at all.

    Throughout this period it seems likely that metropolitan upper- and upper-
middle-class male homosexuals were able to survive more successfully than
men in other social classes. It was not simply that London provided many more
possibilities, but that money and connections made it possible to exploit
them. There was a certain class loyalty which ensured that the activities of
homosexuals in public life, like the amazingly promiscuous Tom Driberg,
though widely known to their acquaintances, were concealed from their constituents. Lord Beaverbrook, for example, succeeded in keeping out of the
press reports of a court case involving Tom Driberg (then his employee), and
Driberg himself claimed that his status as a newly elected MP saved him from
gross indecency charges during the war.[90] Well-connected persons, furthermore, were still given the opportunity to avoid prosecution by timely trips to
the Continent.

    We know much less about lesbianism than about male homosexuality, pri-
marily because it was much less obvious. Not being illegal, it was—with one
celebrated exception[91]—rarely brought to the public eye by judicial proceedings. Nor did it involve prostitution and open pursuit; nor was it organized in

---

[87] Humphries, *Secret World of Sex*, 193. The reminiscence is of the West End just after the Second
World War.
    [88] J. R. Ackerley, *My Father and Myself* (Penguin ed., Harmondsworth, 1971), 118.
    [89] Q. Crisp, *The Naked Civil Servant* (London, 1968), 84.
    [90] T. Driberg, *Ruling Passions* (London, 1978), 144–5.   [91] See below, pp. 324–5.

the same kind of networks as male homosexuality. There was a long tradition of spinsters living with each other for companionship or out of financial necessity, and it was understood that these friendships could be 'emotional': how many were sexual it is impossible to say. As with male homosexuality, discretion and well-placed connections could pass a veil over potentially embarrassing disclosures: the torrid and bizarre relationship between Vita Sackville-West and Violet Trefusis was hushed up but might, in other circumstances, have ended spectacularly in the divorce courts.[92]

Although a greater willingness to talk about sex after the First World War and an observable easing of sexual tension within society as a whole should have benefited them, there were contrary influences which tended in reality to make life more precarious for both male and female homosexuals. As Laura Hutton, a physician attached to the Tavistock Clinic, pointed out in 1937, innocence had in the past accompanied ignorance, but 'with the recent growth of freedom and of thought in regard to sexual questions, homosexual tendencies are now more often recognized as such'. As a result 'friendly couples of the same sex are now much more readily suspected of homosexual tendencies than would have been the case, say, twenty years ago'.[93] By the 1930s, the 'emotional' friendships between women, once accepted without comment, were almost impossible.[94] That also made it more difficult for spinsters to live together as companions—a hard fate indeed for those women whom the First World War had deprived of actual or potential husbands and fiancés.

The increasing tendency to treat homosexuality as an illness, which in the long term was to represent a more tolerant approach, in the short term began a new régime, often more punitive than the one it replaced. If homosexuality were a 'disease', it could be cured. Thus male homosexuals convicted of sexual offences were frequently ordered to undergo chemical or hormonal treatment—of the sort that was visited upon Alan Turing, the great mathematician and pioneer of the computer—and, in due course, aversion therapy, a 'therapy' which the psychiatric profession all too cheerfully administered.

The influence of Freudian psychology was also ambiguous. While the English Freudians were very hostile to legal constraints upon adult homosexuality, they still regarded it as, if not an illness, at least an affliction, analogous to club foot, which could produce only immature or childish relationships. To

---

[92] N. Nicolson, *Portrait of a Marriage* (London, 1973), 105–83.

[93] L. Hutton, *The Single Woman and her Emotional Problems* (London, 1937), 122–3. See also the rather defensive introduction to Vera Brittain's biography of Winifred Holtby. The 'friendships of women have usually been not merely unsung but mocked, belittled and falsely interpreted. I hope that Winifred's story may do something to destroy these tarnished interpretations, and show its readers that loyalty and affection between women is a noble relationship which, far from impoverishing, actually enhances the love of a girl for her lover, of a wife for her husband, of a mother for her children.' (*Testament of Friendship* (London, 1971), 2.)

[94] Lewis, *Women in England*, 128.

many of them, the function of the therapist, therefore, was to help homosexuals 'cope' with their affliction, though they did so more or less sympathetically.[95]

The development in the interwar years of the notion of a homosexual personality, as someone easily marked out, encouraged further legislative and
legal actions against homosexuality which now embraced lesbianism, hitherto exempt. In 1921, three Conservative MPs persuaded the House of Commons to extend the Criminal Law Amendment Act (by 148 votes to 53) to
lesbian relationships. The new clause was rejected in the House of Lords after
interventions by the lord chancellor, Lord Birkenhead, and by the former
director of public prosecutions, Lord Desart, who both argued that to make lesbianism illegal would lend publicity and glamour to an act which would otherwise remain unknown.

This curious but significant debate presaged the celebrated prosecution in
1928 of Radclyffe Hall's novel, *The Well of Loneliness*. Radclyffe Hall (always
known as 'John') was a lesbian novelist who made no attempt to conceal her
nature. Indeed, she conformed exactly to the popular idea of a lesbian; dressed
in severe masculine clothing, crop-haired and cigar-smoking, she resembled,
according to Vera Brittain, 'a handsome man in early middle age courting
depravity'.[96] She had, after some novelistic false starts, become well known
with the popular success of her novel *Adam's Breed*, one of the best-sellers of
1927. The following year Jonathan Cape published *The Well of Loneliness*, a
deeply felt, but highly charged and overwritten account of lesbian love. The
novel was riddled with class assumptions and discreet about physical sexuality; it was, in fact, a recognizable 'sensation' novel, except that the sensations
were homosexual. Shortly after its publication the editor of the *Sunday Express*,
James Douglas, attacked it in a famous editorial. 'I have seen', he wrote,

the plague stalking shamelessly through great social assemblies. I have heard it whis-
pered about by young men and young women who do not and cannot grasp its unutter-
able putrefaction . . . The contagion cannot be escaped. It pervades our social life . . . I
would rather give a healthy boy or a healthy girl a phial of prussic acid than this novel.
Poison kills the body, but moral poison kills the soul.[97]

This was a typical piece of popular journalism which Cape should probably
have ignored; but Jonathan Cape himself took fright and referred the book to
the home office for an opinion. Unsurprisingly, the home office recommended
that it be withdrawn. This Cape agreed to do, though he prudently transferred
the moulds to France where the book was printed and from where it was
imported into England. The home secretary, Joynson-Hicks, ordered its seizure

[95] Hutton, *The Single Woman*, 120–2.
[96] V. Brittain, *Radclyffe Hall: A Case of Obscenity* (London, 1968), 36.
[97] *Sunday Express*, 19 Aug. 1928.

and destruction while the director of public prosecutions took out an order against it under the 1857 Obscene Publications Act. The under-secretary at the home office hoped that a successful prosecution might 'help to stem the tide of degeneracy which is so fraught with danger'.[98] The case was heard before the chief metropolitan magistrate, Sir Chartres Biron, an elderly nonentity of strong views who apparently colluded with the home office before the hearing. Biron declined to hear 'expert' evidence submitted on the book's behalf (which was his right, since the book was prosecuted only for obscenity) and found the book obscene.[99] An appeal was lodged by Cape and the prosecution was led on this occasion by the attorney-general, Sir Thomas Inskip. The appeal failed.

The effect of the trial, which became a *cause célèbre* was, as the novelist Hugh Walpole noted, in part to achieve the opposite of the prosecution's intention.[100] But it also confirmed a lesbian 'identity' akin to the male homosexual and thus made life more difficult for lesbians. The trial began a period of sustained judicial and administrative attempts to circumscribe male and (to a lesser extent) female homosexuality. Between 1930 and 1950 prosecutions for homosexual offences increased by 850 per cent compared to 223 per cent for all other indictable offences. This was a result, not of an 'increase' in homosexuality, but of an increase of police activity, particularly in London. In most parts of the country for most of the time the police were ready to turn a blind eye to what they knew was happening.[101] But they were also quick to learn what their superiors wanted, and what was characteristic of the period was the appointment to senior positions in the home office, the police, the department of public prosecutions and the judiciary of men who strongly disliked homosexuality and who were frequently active Christians of a morally punitive kind. The campaigns against homosexuality tended to be most fierce when these men were in post: as they so often were between the 1920s and 1950s.[102]

---

[98] Weeks, *Sex, Politics and Society*, 217.

[99] A number of people were willing to testify for the book, but some declined. The refusal of John Galsworthy, the president of PEN, caused pain and surprise; that of several popular authors, like Anthony Hope, author of *The Prisoner of Zenda*, was less surprising.

[100] Lady Colefax wrote to Bernard Berenson: 'Then there is a great pother about books and poems etc seized by the police and England's (old ladies) darling Sir W. Joynson Hicks. The net result of that is an overpowering and completely new interest in "pornography" (of which they knew little) and "unnatural vice" of which they knew nothing. I am speaking of the 600,000 weekly readers of the Sunday Express.' (Colefax to Berenson [? 1929], Colefax Papers C. 3169, Bodleian Library, Oxford.)

[101] Or more than a blind eye. Homosexual folklore is full of stories of policemen corrupted or seduced in the line of duty. Paul Lanning told Humphries that his 'chief achievement' in Epping Forest was a police sergeant at Leytonstone: 'Oh that's a triumph, that's anybody's triumph to have the police sergeant' (Humphries, *Secret World of Sex*, 207). Ackerley recalled the story of 'a Hammersmith queen' who 'robbed by a guardsman of his fur coat, flew out in a rage and found a policeman, who quickly recovered the conspicuous garment and went to bed with the grateful owner himself' (Ackerley, *My Father and Myself*, 119).

[102] The principal prosecutors of *The Well of Loneliness*, Sir William Joynson-Hicks and Sir Thomas

It would be wrong, of course, to suppose that homosexuality alone was their target. In the late 1920s, Lord Byng, when commissioner of the Metropolitan Police, almost brought London's night-life to its knees by his policing of the night clubs, the destruction of which was his *idée fixe*. In the late 1930s a number of clubs both in London and in other large towns which catered for 'particular' tastes (primarily sado-masochism) were closed after well-publicized police raids.[103] Female prostitution and other forms of outdoor sex became increasingly hazardous and a number of public careers were blighted by real or imagined indiscretions in Hyde Park. The policing of Hyde Park was, indeed, the subject of ironic foreign comment:

My advice to foreign visitors has always been not to enter Hyde Park after dark unless in groups that keep carefully together, are always composed of odd numbers and contain members of both sexes. The somewhat sensational prosecutions for alleged heterosexual offences in Hyde Park . . . have not sufficed to restore full respectability to this agreeable resort.[104]

In 1926 the lord chamberlain gave the Public Morality Council 'privileged access', to the film industry's censorship system, and the president of the Board of Film Censors until 1929, T. P. O'Connor MP, a devoted Catholic, habitually consulted the bishop of London, Winnington-Ingram, the chairman of the Public Morality Council, about any doubtful film. One of his successors as chief censor, Lord Tyrrell, later became president of the National Vigilance Council. The results of these appointments were 'often absurd moral interventions in cases of obscenity',[105] as well as persistent attempts to extirpate sexual vice, however defined. And what was equally characteristic of the period was the willingness of government, civil service, MPs and the press—especially the press—to support these moral interventions, even in the face of a good deal of public scepticism.

But male homosexuality, the most apparently deviant and socially unacceptable of the sexual vices, was inevitably the most punitively policed. Throughout the interwar years the police had become much more active in their use of 'decoys'—a use which, since it constituted an incitement to commit crime, or entrapment, was probably itself unlawful—and in their readiness to give immunity to prosecution to those who would implicate others. By the early 1950s the behaviour of the police had become so irregular as to cause disquiet while at the same time 'expert' opinion was coming around to the view that homosexuality involving consent might be a sin or an illness but was not necessarily a crime. These doubts came to a head following the convictions in

Inskip, were both evangelical Anglicans who played a prominent part in the defeat of the new Prayer Book. See above, Chapter VII.

[103] Chesser, *Love without Fear*, 215–20.
[104] G. J. Renier, *The English: Are they Human?* (London, 1931), 73.
[105] Weeks, *Sex, Society and Politics*, 217.

1954 of Lord Montagu of Beaulieu and the diplomatic correspondent of the *Daily Mail*, Peter Wildeblood, for homosexual offences in which the sole evidence against the accused was provided by consenting partners who turned Queen's evidence. The only way out appeared to be that recommended by the Wolfenden Committee (appointed in 1957): the legalizing of certain forms of homosexual activity and (by implication) the return by the police to the tactic of the blind eye.

6 | The 'moral code'

Throughout the period, English attitudes to sexual morality were reinforced by what contemporaries still called 'puritanism'—a word used to describe a specifically English culture where 'Christian' and certain social injunctions were combined to restrain sexuality within highly 'ritualistic' mores. Some argued that the 'ritualistic conception' was confined to the middle classes—the working class ignored and the upper class only pretended to acknowledge it[106]—but, in so far as a 'puritan' culture did exist, everything suggests that all classes were part of it: despite what others thought, the working classes were not particularly happy in their sexuality.

Whatever we call it and whatever its origins, cultural puritanism, together with a tendency by both men and women (particularly older men and women) to deny the centrality of sex in marriage, had positive and negative consequences. The positive was to establish a comparative freedom in personal relations almost certainly favourable to women. In the early 1950s more than half the English thought it possible for people of the opposite sex to have nonsexual friendships—a proportion unlikely to be found in many other European countries. Foreign visitors to England thought relations between men and women, particularly in the middle classes, were more relaxed than elsewhere. A result of the 'puritanical attitude' to sex, one of them wrote, is that

social intercourse between the sexes has for generations been infinitely freer and less constrained in England than in the majority of countries ... It is only possible where sex has ceased to be accepted as the one and only mainspring of existence and as an uncontrollable force of nature to which it is proper and necessary to yield.[107]

Possibly also the 'puritanical attitude' not only contributed to the comparative equality in personal relationships Englishwomen were thought to enjoy with men but to the engaging character of English domesticity.

The negative consequence of puritanism was a sexual prurience and a delight in pornography famous throughout Europe. The endless battles over bathing-dress on southern beaches, the often ridiculous interventions of the

---

[106] For the 'ritualistic conception', see Renier, *The English*, 197; Balfour, *Society Racket*, 204.
[107] Cohen-Portheim, *England, the Unknown Isle*, 54–6.

lord chamberlain's office in the London theatre, the repeated prosecutions of
books thought harmless elsewhere, implied a deep and unresolved preoccupation with sexuality. The English were notorious on the Continent (as they had
been in the nineteenth century) for their tastes in diverse pornography and
erotica—Eustace Chesser thought England the 'classic land of flagellation'[108]—
and for the unending smuttiness and scatalogy of popular humour. Outsiders
marvelled at the extent to which dirty stories, limericks (like the 'two young
ladies from Twickenham') and poems (like the 'good ship Venus'), many deeply
obscene, were exchanged even in the best company, and how widely they were
known. They constituted

an unprintable literature that might well be unprintable among less squeamish
people . . . Its existence is admitted, allusions to unprintable limericks are manifold, and
the only thing not publicly proclaimed, apart from the limericks themselves, is the
names of the distinguished, learned, gallant and reverend gentlemen who love them,
compose them and transmit them.[109]

The English were themselves aware of these predilections and the more reflec-
tive were inclined to think that they represented, as they probably did, a
momentary release from the intense repressions which governed English sexuality. Even for the majority who neither had access to erotica[110] nor were
reduced to its use, religious authority, whether described as 'puritanism' or
'ritual codes', none the less determined that their attitudes to sexuality would
be ambiguous and guilty: people did not believe strongly enough to behave in
a 'Christian' way with conviction, but they did believe strongly enough to
behave in a 'non-Christian' way without much pleasure. As Janet Chance, in
the interwar years an influential proponent of a more 'rational' morality, put
it: the 'poverty, unhappiness and wretchedness' of English sexual life was 'the
price we pay for our conventional moral code'.[111]

It is hard not to conclude that these codes governed more than just sexuality; arguably, they also governed two related phenomena—personal and physical aggression. The English had once been known as a violent and unruly
people; in the mid-twentieth century they were known for their calm, orderli-
ness, and peacefulness. However exaggerated, the transformation was real. Yet
it, too, seems to have imposed severe strain. Foreigners were often surprised
and dismayed at the harshness of English justice, the retributive nature of
penal legislation, the frequent recourse to the death penalty—'the hanging
judge', Orwell thought, was as much a symbol of England as the jackboot was

---

[108] Chesser, *Love without Fear*, 219–20.   [109] Renier, *The English*, 210–11.
[110] Erotica was probably not all that hard to acquire. The 'provincial lady' records in a matter-of-
fact way the receipt of a standard letter inviting her to buy pornographic material (Delafield, *Diary
of a Provincial Lady*, 227); and for those really desperate most large towns had shops where diverse
sexuality was catered for.
[111] Chance, *Cost of English Morals*, 30.

of the Third Reich. Here also there were momentary releases: the failure to prosecute James Hadley Chase's *No Orchids for Miss Blandish* (1939)—by any standards a novel of violent male sexuality (the 'heroine' is gruesomely raped amidst a general sadistic mayhem)—when so many other more harmless books were prosecuted, was perhaps one; and if so, revealing.[112]

Geoffrey Gorer was (like outsiders) struck by the English concern with punishment, with the common view, for example, that it was better to punish than to reward children, and the bizarre way this concern was sometimes manifested.[113] Above all, he was surprised by the 'enthusiastic appreciation' people from all classes and regions had for the police. The English policeman represented for the majority of the English 'an ideal model of behaviour and character'. He was slow, clumsy, and had large feet, but was honest, kind, fair, dutiful, overworked, and utterly reliable.[114] The 'ideal model' was the preponderant cultural representation of the English policeman of the time and was typified, for instance, in the film *The Blue Lamp* (1950)—itself the model for the later television series *Dixon of Dock Green*. The 'Dixon' figure, Jack Warner, personifies the ideal, as did the other most popular representation of the policeman, PC 49 in the boys' magazine, the *Eagle*.[115] That the English police were much nicer than other people's, given what we know of other people's police, is easy to believe; and what the English admired in the police were, indeed, admirable qualities. Still, it is a remarkable fact: there are not many countries where the populace would choose the police as their role-model.

The apparently uncritical nature of this admiration for the police, the readiness to accept the 'Dixon' stereotype as the reality, is even more surprising given that the English police were known not to be perfect: the corruption in some of the forces had, for example, been widely publicized in the interwar years. Furthermore, relations between the police and the working classes were usually, at best, only an armed truce. Many young working-class men, especially, were deeply suspicious of the police, and their families and neighbours usually took their sides. In (probably) most working-class communities the police were thought to be agents of an intrusive authority—it only because they had to enforce the very unpopular off-course betting legislation, which was often responsible for the corruption.[116] The willingness of many

---

[112] It was the publication of this novel which was the occasion for George Orwell's famous essay 'Raffles and Miss Blandish' (1944), in Orwell and Angus (eds.), *George Orwell*, iii. 212–24. The novel was temporarily withdrawn but only after another of Chase's books had caused a stir and only after selling 500,000 copies.

[113] One man told Gorer that 'my eldest daughter did once tell a deliberate lie. I took off my belt let her hold it and forced her to beat me. She has never told a lie since. The moral being that if she does wrong she hurts her parents.' (Gorer, *Exploring English Character*, 197.)

[114] Gorer, *Exploring English Character*, 296–7.   [115] See below, pp. 451–2.

[116] For corruption in the police and the policing of the anti-gambling legislation, see D. Dixon, *From Prohibition to Regulation: Bookmaking, Anti-Gambling and the Law* (Oxford, 1991), 241–68.

people—though, presumably, not all—to overlook this suggests that they themselves had strongly internalized those norms for which the police were thought to stand. That was one way aggression was controlled; as puritanism controlled and partly civilized an aggressive sexuality.

Perhaps in no other area of English life did politics, religion, morality, all that we call ideology, intersect with more friction than in attitudes to sexuality. Throughout the period under consideration, religion and morality were closely related in people's minds. This was a result both of training and the repeated interventions of the churches in matters of morals at a time when the definition of 'morality' had been so narrowed that it was almost synonymous with sexuality. Increasingly the churches became known not for salvation or consolation, but as arbiters of morality. There were, of course, many who believed the churches had this authority as of right. Even if religious opinion was not always successful in establishing the constitution of morality, those like Marie Stopes or A. P. Herbert who had reason to fear church opposition, were careful to adopt arguments and vocabulary acceptable to Christian opinion.

Although many churchmen seemed content in their role as moral arbiters, they were not entirely responsible for this development. For much of the time the only area of public life where Christian teaching was thought legitimate or effective was in matters of morals. The churches had views on many subjects, including social and economic policy, but here their interventions were largely ignored. There is, for instance, a telling difference between Stanley Baldwin's reaction to Archbishop Davidson's proposed broadcast on the general strike (very unhappy) and his reaction to Archbishop Lang's broadcast on the abdication (very happy). Arguably, the churches were *permitted* to intervene only in the sphere of sexual morality, and here ministers, civil servants, and the press showed themselves noticeably sensitive to predominant church opinion, whereas (say) on unemployment the views of the churches counted for little.

'Traditional' Christian moral teachings were accorded respect and thought to be 'right'. But people frequently did not obey them; although few probably disobeyed them without some guilt. Nor was there a clear evolution of opinion. People could talk and read about sexuality with a freedom denied their parents or grandparents. That women's sexuality was legitimate was now widely accepted, if reluctantly. People could divorce more easily, though it was something most people—especially if they wanted promotion—tried to avoid. Within heterosexual relations the moral codes undoubtedly relaxed. This was, however, not true of homosexuality. If anything, stereotyping and hostility to male homosexuality intensified. Attempts were made to criminalize not merely female homosexuality, but also other forms of 'deviant' sexuality. And people continued to maintain 'self-control' by acceding to punitively authoritarian codes.

Although the 'law' relating to birth control was confused and occasionally ridiculous, it was not as severe as in many other countries. Contraceptives could be bought with perfect legality and though there were alarmist fears about the decline in the national fertility, there were few (indeed no) 'natalist' programmes (or, at any rate, no programmes whose specific purpose was 'natalist'), designed to force up fertility-rates. This, however, is not as good as it sounds. Official opinion was worried about middle-class infertility; if anything the working classes were thought to breed too prolifically. Thus there were acceptable eugenic reasons for allowing, even encouraging, the working class to practise family-limitation.

Above all, even if the 'ritual codes' were losing their moral and political force, they gave way only slowly; and not without a struggle and much personal unhappiness.

SPORT was one of the most powerful of England's civil cultures. This chapter looks at the history of both 'national' sports, those broadly representative of society as a whole, and 'sectarian' sports, those whose following was much narrower, and it considers the forces that encouraged or inhibited their popular following. The chapter also considers the relationship of women to sport, and the role of betting both in sport and society. It discusses English sport in the international sphere and what the apparent loss of international sporting competitiveness might tell us about English social codes more generally.

1 | *The national sports*

CRICKET

In so far as cricket was played and followed throughout the country by all social classes and by both men and women, it was the most 'national' of all sports. It was administered by the upper and upper middle classes, was the predominant sport in both independent and grammar schools, and was, even more than rugby, a socially useful sport which men did not hesitate to use for the advancement of their careers; but the majority of professional cricketers were of working-class origin and, although never as important to working men as football, nor played by as many, cricket was closely followed by them, particularly by skilled working men.

The number of people playing cricket in this period almost certainly rose. It is unlikely that the independent schools and the universities produced many more cricketers, but the expansion of the grammar schools in the 1930s almost certainly did, even if not all were willing recruits.[1] There was, furthermore, a steady growth in the numbers playing cricket at the elementary schools, although the degree to which it was organized probably depended upon the attitudes of individual teachers.[2] The number of works teams increased rapidly and they more than replaced the declining church-based sides. Cricket,

---

[1] See above, p. 264.
[2] J. Williams, 'Cricket' in T. Mason (ed.), *Sport in Britain: A Social History* (Cambridge, 1989), 132–3.

unlike football, appears to have been comparatively unaffected by the collapse of the local economies in the North in the 1920s. In Bolton, for example, there were 70 recreational teams in 1922, but 110 in 1939. The rate of increase in the number of clubs affiliated to the Club Cricket Conference reached its peak in the early 1930s—both in the North and the South.

Nor did public provision ever seem to meet demand. This became an important issue in the 1930s, when privately owned cricket grounds were sold for speculative building. But the distribution of public provision was very uneven. Some authorities offered none; others, like Manchester (88 public pitches in 1926) and the LCC (336 in 1926) were relatively lavish. Even so, the LCC in 1932 was only able to meet one-third of the demand for public pitches on Sundays.[3] Inequity in public provision added to the attraction of works sides, since an employer could usually be expected to provide a pitch.

There were few parts of the country—except some of the inner cities or areas where there were large Irish populations—where it was not played. Village cricket—hilariously described in A. G. Macdonnell's *England, their England* 1933)[4] and an important element in the received tradition of 'Englishness'—was a social mainstay of rural life and ideally suited to its rhythms.[5] Although cricket's demographic bias probably lay in the South, Yorkshire and Lancashire had many more clubs than any other county; and Yorkshire twice as many as Lancashire. In Yorkshire cricket was probably like rugby in Wales—a cross-class activity which united rather than divided communities, and support for which helped to define a 'Yorkshireman'.[6] The sheer size of Yorkshire and Lancashire cricket was a powerful counter to the South's administrative and social pre-eminence as well as the origin of fierce provincial loyalties.

The county championship stood at the top of organized cricket. This too was dominated by Yorkshire and Lancashire. Yorkshire won 12 of 21 interwar championships and won again in 1946 and 1949. Lancashire won five of the interwar championships. Throughout the interwar years Nottinghamshire, which had the formidable fast bowlers Larwood and Voce, were perhaps the next most successful team: they won the championship in 1929 and were in the top five for the next three seasons. Gloucestershire, with Walter Hammond

---

[3] Mason, *Sport in Britain*, 135.

[4] It is alleged that the cricket team satirized by Macdonnell was J. C. Squire's eleven. Squire was editor of the *London Mercury* and the team largely consisted of his authors.

[5] For interesting contemporary examples of the literary construction of cricket as a heightened manifestation of Englishness, see T. Moult (ed.), *Bat and Ball* (London, 1935).

[6] It also encouraged a certain complacent provincialism, typified by the doctrine that only Yorkshiremen could play for Yorkshire (a practice which eventually did much harm to Yorkshire cricket) and a belief that a man who played for Yorkshire must be as Yorkshire as Yorkshire pudding—itself an often naïve belief. How far the treatment (described below) of the county's greatest batsman, Herbert Sutcliffe, encouraged cross-class solidarity is also debatable. For Yorkshire cricket and Yorkshire 'nationality', see Dave Russell, 'Sport and Identity: The Case of the Yorkshire County Cricket Club, 1890–1939', *Twentieth Century British History*, 7, 2 (1996).

as its leading player, was the most successful of the West Country teams; Middlesex, which won in 1920 and 1921 under Pelham ('Plum') Warner, the most successful of the southern sides. Surrey, despite having Jack Hobbs, who played with them till the age of 52 and was probably the country's finest bat, failed to win at all between the wars.

The county championship, however, was not universally admired. The three-day matches were frequently tedious, played by cautious teams on over-prepared wickets. There were wide discrepancies in the quality of sides, and often a certain predictability in the outcome. Though teams frequently played at different grounds within the county (a practice which stopped after the Second World War), and so widened their potential audience, little account was taken of the working week of the average working man. Crowds thus tended to be disproportionately non-working class.[7]

The somewhat rebarbative character of the county championship partly explains the popularity in the North (particularly Lancashire) and the Midlands of league cricket.[8] This was one-day cricket between a number of adjacent sides who constituted themselves a 'league'—the 'Bolton League' for instance—and was played to fit the leisure hours of local working men and women. Although the great majority of league cricketers were amateur, most sides employed one and sometimes two professionals. Matches were highly competitive, rarely resulted (weather aside) in draws, and, given the doubtful quality of the pitches, often highly unpredictable. Increasingly the success of teams came to depend on the 'pro' and the capacity of clubs to pay them. In 1922 Nelson set a hot pace by employing the Australian fast bowler Ted McDonald (at £700 a year) and in 1929 the West Indian all-rounder Learie Constantine (reputedly at £1,000 a year).[9] The professionals, particularly Constantine, became the focus of intense community loyalty and their upkeep the clubs' principal function. Bazaars, fêtes, galas (in which women were very active) were organized to raise money and employers often subscribed significantly to club finances. The attractions of the professionals meant large gates—sometimes up to 10,000—while the return on gates meant that subscriptions could be kept low. Unlike the county associations, the league clubs, though their officers tended to be middle-class, had large working-class memberships and considerable cross-class camaraderie. The England fast-bowler Fred Root, who played both county and league cricket, wrote that league cricket 'provides *Cricket* as I understand and appreciate the game. Cricket that is scrupulously

---

[7] R. Holt, *Sport and the British* (Oxford, 1989), 179.

[8] For league cricket, see Holt, *Sport and the British*, 176; Jack Williams, 'Recreational Cricket in the Bolton Area between the Wars' in R. Holt (ed.), *Sport and the Working Class in Modern Britain* (Manchester, 1990), 102–10; Mason, *Sport in Britain*, 138–9.

[9] In August 1931 Accrington nearly made a remarkable coup, when an offer they made to Donald Bradman would have been accepted but for the strong pressure placed on him in Australia. (D. Bradman, *Farewell to Cricket* (London, 1950), 44.)

fair, never sentimental, and is just what the public thrive on'. He admired the democracy of the leagues: 'No social distinction—one common effort for one common weal.'[10]

Root was himself a professional and his praise of the leagues was not disinterested. It accompanied a bitter attack on the 'great fact' of 'first-class' English cricket: the fundamental social distinction between amateur and professional cricketers. The professionals were subjected to a number of odious social discriminations. The amateurs and professionals had separate changing rooms, and separate entrances to the ground: in 1934, a famous occasion, Patsy Hendren was the sole professional selected for the MCC against Australia and thus the sole man to enter by the professionals' gate. The professionals were obliged to call the amateurs 'Mr' and 'Sir'. They stayed at separate hotels or the less expensive rooms in the same hotel. They wore different dress: the amateurs a variety of caps and colours and the professionals county caps and blazers.[11] The professionals were picked for hard matches, and, to save money, dropped for soft ones. The professionals were obliged to go to the nets at any time with any club member who wanted to bat or bowl, and their relations with the club committees had, according to Joe Hardstaff Jnr., a 'squire and peasant character'.[12]

Above all, it was almost unknown for a professional to be given the captaincy of a county side, let alone England. Defending the appointment of the amateur A. W. Lupton as captain of Yorkshire in 1925, Lord Hawke, the chairman of the county association, said:

Pray God no professional may ever captain England ... If the time comes when we are to have no more amateurs captaining England, well I don't say England will become exactly like League Football, but it will be a thousand pities and will not be good for the game.[13]

When in 1928 the membership of the Yorkshire Cricket Association voted to give the county captaincy to Herbert Sutcliffe, a professional and Yorkshire's most distinguished cricketer, Hawke and others like-minded (it was understood) prevailed upon him to withdraw 'gracefully'. Although Hobbs once acted as captain on the field in place of an indisposed chief, not one professional captained England between the wars. But of the 47 amateurs who represented England in the same period, 16 also captained it.

The professionals reacted to this caste-system variously. Some like Harold Gimblett (Somerset and England) were 'paranoid' about amateurs; others treated them with affectionate contempt. George Brown (professional, Hampshire), when once batting with his celebrated amateur captain, Lionel,

[10] F. Root, *A Cricket Pro's Lot* (London, 1937), 185–9.
[11] According to Fred Trueman the professionals called the amateurs 'fancy caps' or 'coloured caps'. (M. Marshall, *Gentlemen and Players* (London, 1987), xii.)
[12] Quoted in Marshall, *Gentlemen and Players*, 52.   [13] Quoted in ibid. 38.

Lord Tennyson, and their appeal against the light was refused, declined a call to run with the words: 'I hear you, my Lord, but I cannot see you.' Others were much less awkward. Cyril Washbrook thought amateurs could handle county committees better than professionals; Dennis Compton simply thought amateurs thoroughly good chaps. The most revealing case was that of Hobbs. He had no criticisms of the system; he believed amateurs made the best captains, always deferred to them, and would tolerate no 'bolshieness' from the younger professionals. This certainly did him no harm. He was the first professional sportsman to be knighted and ended his days an honorary member of both the MCC and Surrey.

Most professionals would probably have lived with these discriminations had they only been social. More embittering, however, was the fact that so many 'amateurs' were anything but amateur. In 1937 Fred Root wrote that:

Many teams are 'all professional' nowadays, and I for one do not share the misgivings of a cricket bigwig when he [Lord Hawke] said 'It would be a bad day for English cricket when an England side was captained by a professional'. It is now. Our opponents are no slaves to this conventional humbug ... A title and lots of money doesn't assure the scoring of centuries. We all realize that, so why all the camouflage?[14]

Root objected particularly to the appointment of amateurs to posts such as secretary-captain of county sides often at salaries three times that of a professional. 'And so the game goes on, full of make-believe; and yet everybody intimately connected with it knows all about it'. For Harold Larwood (who had many reasons to be bitter)[15] it was amateurism as such he resented. Of a chance encounter with Bradman many years later, he wrote, 'I couldn't help thinking how Fate had treated us both ... Don was wealthy and was on the [Australian] Board of Cricket Control. I was working for a living on the assembly line of a soft drink firm. *And Don was the amateur.*'[16] To men like Root and Larwood the system was doubly vicious: not only were the amateurs being 'paid', they were being 'paid' very much more than the professionals, who were lucky to earn £300 a year net.

This hostility was not necessarily political. Larwood, who came from a Nottinghamshire mining family, perhaps always disliked the English social system. But not Root. He was an admirer of the old nobility and a member of the Dudley Conservative Association. He wrote of Lord Coventry, for example, that

---

[14] Root, *A Cricket Pro's Lot*, 178.   [15] See below, pp. 381–2.

[16] H. Larwood and K. Perkins, *The Larwood Story* (London, 1965), 222. The agreed interwar maximum wage for a professional was £440 but few received that. A professional usually had to pay his own insurance, away-match hotel bills, travel costs, and equipment. If professionals played for a big county like Yorkshire or Lancashire they might expect a generous benefit. But size of benefit was not commensurate with skill: Larwood received £2,000 from his benefit but the Yorkshire all-rounder Roy Kilmer received £4,000. (C. Martin-Jenkins, *The Wisden Book of County Cricket* (London, 1981), 56–7; Mason, *Sport in Britain*, 125.)

he 'was sport personified': 'This grand old man was honoured and revered by everybody. His tenants worshipped him. In his long innings of over ninety, he played the game of life as a pattern to every man.'[17] To Root, 'amateur' cricket was a perversion of an otherwise admirable social hierarchy based upon fairness and plain-dealing—qualities he thought preserved in league cricket.

Root claimed that *all* professionals, could they begin again, would do so as amateurs. However, the slow but continuous decline in the number of amateurs willing to turn out for first-class sides suggests that the plums were not inexhaustible. That there were plums, however, no one doubted. Certain posts were known to be open to desirable amateurs. Many accepted undemanding jobs as games masters in public schools in order to have long paid vacations. The secretaryship of a county association was a well-understood and remunerative way of concealing payment. Other amateurs could acquire generous sponsors: Walter Hammond, a professional, became an amateur when Marsham Tyres employed him at an annual salary much higher than his earnings as a cricketer. For Hammond this was a godsend. As an amateur he could captain England. Which he did.

It was also known that amateurs exploited their status to enhance their businesses. P. G. H. Fender admitted using his position as captain of Surrey to promote his wine-dealing firm. 'For example, as Surrey captain, I could have guests to lunch in the pavilion and many people with whom I did business very much liked to have that kind of opportunity to be on the inside.'[18] But Fender knew where to draw the line. His county chairman, Sir Harry Leveson Gower, was notoriously less fastidious. Fender at least assumed that amateurs should have played for their university. 'There were plenty of such people about', Fender said, but Leveson Gower,

who made his living by acting as a contact man, suggested that I should include two young cricketers who were sons of some of his business friends when they had been barely good enough to get into their college side at university. I said I wasn't willing to accommodate him.[19]

Whatever were the actual financial advantages to an amateur cricketer before 1939, the amateur–professional distinction, social discrimination and all, survived intact until the Second World War, and only a few professionals suggested it should go. But the spirit of the Second World War, democratic and generally 'progressive', was almost antithetical to this kind of discrimination. In 1943 even Hubert Preston, the editor of *Wisden*, suggested that the amateur–professional distinction should be abolished on the ground that all made money from cricket—some directly, others indirectly. Once that were admitted the demeaning discriminations would disappear.

---

[17] Root, *A Cricket Pro's Lot*, 47.
[18] Marshall, *Gentlemen and Players*, 23.   [19] Ibid.

But the distinction was not abolished; indeed, it returned with a vengeance. Ted Dexter, the future England captain, spoke frankly of his entry into cricket in the early 1950s:

But I suppose if I'm honest, when I came into the game it was still possible for a Cambridge Blue and an England amateur to mix in a social world where there were real prospects of being offered a good career because you are a well-known cricketer. So, while I was still up at Cambridge I decided that I should go all out to get Blues [that is, to represent the university] and to captain the University at cricket or golf. I reckoned that, if I did, no one would ever ask me what kind of degree I got, and that's exactly how it turned out.[20]

There was an increasing use of the secretaryship-captaincy as a way of purchasing amateurs, and a proliferation of business 'positions' made over to amateurs.[21] In 1949–50, for instance, half of the Northamptonshire county side were employed by British Timken.

Nor had the social discriminations lost their bite. In 1946 all but one county side had an amateur captain, and that county, Leicestershire, only appointed one (Les Berry) because they could find no amateur. In 1947 the selectors brought out of retirement the 45-year-old G. O. Allen to captain the England side to the West Indies rather than appoint a professional. Len Hutton, a professional, who became England captain in 1952, was only appointed after a series of humiliating defeats by the Australian post-war sides.

The post-war bolshie professionals, like Jim Laker, had as much trouble with amateurs as the pre-war bolshies. Basil Allen, the captain of Gloucestershire, was involved in an incident which would probably have been thought deplorable even in 1939:

In congratulating David Sheppard on his century for Cambridge against Gloucestershire at Bristol, Tom Graveney [a professional] called him 'David' whereupon his skipper [Allen] rounded on him with the remark 'He's Mister Sheppard to you'. He later went into the Sussex dressing-room and said to David Sheppard 'I must apologize for Graveney's impertinence. I think you'll find it won't happen again.'[22]

The eventual abolition of the distinction in the early 1960s was due not to any change of heart in cricket's authorities so much as their inability to find enough good amateurs. Despite Dexter's experience, cricket by then was not thought likely to guarantee someone an appropriate career. In the 1930s about 40 per cent of all county players were amateur; in the early 1950s less than one-quarter. This had important geographical and social consequences. Before 1939, broadly speaking, professionals dominated the North; amateurs the South. By the early 1950s this was no longer so. In 1930, four of the ten county sides employing the highest proportion of professionals were in the North. In

[20] Marshall, *Gentlemen and Players*, x.   [21] Ibid. 140–3.   [22] Ibid. 136–7.

1952, only one.[23] As southern and Midlands sides increasingly employed professionals to maintain their standards, the justifications for amateur cricket and its privileges became both unreal and embarrassing.

The system survived so long because it suited the interests of those who ran the game. Cricket—like a number of other sports—was administered, and its ethos established, by self-electing, all-male associations recruited overwhelmingly from the upper and upper middle class. At the institutional centre of English cricket was the MCC, whose 7,000 members in 1945 were as unrepresentative of the national polity as any society could be. The county associations, whose membership appears to have doubled in the interwar years, were more representative only because they were more broadly middle-class. There is no evidence of a significant working-class membership.

The structure of power within these societies gave immense authority to individuals like Lord Harris and Sir Pelham Warner in the MCC or Lord Hawke and Sir Harry Leveson Gower in the county associations. Given the comparative passivity of the memberships, their strongly held beliefs were imposed on the game with little difficulty. Furthermore, such was the power of voluntarism within the British political tradition and such the reluctance of the state to go beyond its own sphere that any countervailing governmental intervention was almost unthinkable. There is no evidence that C. R. Attlee, a cricket devotee,[24] when prime minister thought it unacceptable for one of the country's two major sports to operate in a way so at odds with the kind of society the Labour Party apparently wished to create.

Yet few players or spectators seem to have objected to the status quo. Those professionals who did rebel had little active support from their colleagues. Professional footballers were not much more adventurous but they did at least organize themselves, and eventually with some success.[25] The cricket professionals could claim nothing similar. They were, of course, on the whole better paid than footballers, but were treated almost infinitely worse. Furthermore, recreational cricketers scarcely came up against the system at all and spectators only objected to it when it seemed as if the 'divide' made their team more likely to lose. And not always then.

FOOTBALL

Football, if not as 'national' as cricket, was nevertheless the country's greatest sport. It was not played by everyone; nor was it played equally in all parts of the country, but it was played by more people more enthusiastically than any other game. Furthermore, football was *the* world sport, and that enhanced its

---

[23] J. Bale, *Sport and Place* (London, 1982), 79.

[24] It is alleged that the only reason Attlee agreed to the introduction of a telex machine in 10 Downing Street was that it gave him the cricket scores almost immediately.

[25] See below, pp. 346–7.

status, even if the English half-despised the foreigners who played it. Its primacy at home, tacitly conceded by all, was earned by the extent of its popularity among the 75 per cent of the population who were wage-earners. The English industrial working class was neither politically nor culturally homogeneous, but love of football united them almost more than anything else. Amongst them its only seasonal rival was rugby league, but that had neither the depth nor scope of football's popularity. As the sociologist J. B. Mays wrote of Liverpool adolescents, 'Above all other sports football occupies a paramount position in the estimation of these youngsters. They will play football whenever they get the opportunity . . . The urge to kick a ball is irresistible at all times and in the most unsuitable places.'[26]

One of football's advantages was its simplicity. It could be played on almost any spare piece of ground with a minimum of equipment and rules. Thus the basis of the sport was 'street football', though how many played street football in this period is unknown. In the interwar years, and even more in the 1940s, the name street football was misleading; the teams who before 1914 might have played on the street drifted on to waste ground or municipal parks. Despite the density of housing in most urban areas it was not difficult to find unused land. Slum clearance and then German bombing opened up the inner cities; even as one gap closed another appeared. While street footballers were as common then as Indian boys playing cricket on a *maidan* are today, they are now largely anonymous. The teams appear to have played regularly but had no pitches, no goals, no formal strip, and no referee. They played for about 90 minutes. J. B. Mays saw no fighting, and noted that disputes seemed to be solved by talking. The teams were usually quite well organized and democratic in structure; some even elected their secretaries by secret ballot. One team appointed a disabled boy as trainer 'so that he should have something to do and not feel unwanted'. Football was overwhelmingly important to these young men: 'Saturday afternoon, played football; evening, dances and at pubs. Sunday rose about 10.30 for breakfast then met his pals and kicked a ball on streets or on bomb sites; afternoon, played football with his street team; night, pictures.'[27] The life of such teams was probably short and dependent upon the mobility or immobility of their members: when national service was introduced some teams dissolved as soon as individual members were called up.

The 'junior clubs'—the next step from street football—were more formally organized and their continued expansion was possibly at the expense of street football. The junior clubs were usually properly kitted out and had an attachment to a permanent or semi-permanent pitch. Unlike the street sides, which were comprised of boys who knocked around together, the junior clubs were increasingly based upon institutions. Some still had their origins in blocks of

---

[26] Mays, *Growing Up in the City*, 48.   [27] Ibid. 47–8, 169–73, 198.

flats or the streets or as club 'old boy' sides, and pub football was always import-ant, but increasingly the junior clubs were works teams. Institutional ties were responsible for a large increase in the number of junior clubs: from 12,000 in 1910 to 35,000 at the end of the thirties. In Sheffield, for example, in 1936, 80 firms and 86 football teams were affiliated to the Sheffield and District Works' Sport Association. By 1946 there were 123 works sides—one-quarter of all clubs affiliated to the Sheffield Football Association.

There was a similar increase in the number of clubs affiliated to the County Football Associations and in the number of major amateur and professional sides. At the end of the thirties about 10,000 clubs were affiliated to the County Football Associations; by 1946 there were 18,000.[28] In 1914 there were 158 pro-fessional clubs; in 1951, 427. The number of major amateur clubs increased from 350 between the wars to 450 in 1950.[29]

This expansion was largely outside football's traditional heartland in the North and the industrial Midlands.[30] Professional and recreational football were beginning to occupy different territories. The North still had a dispro-portionate number of professional clubs; by the 1950s, however, the South had a disproportionate number of recreational clubs. The slide to the South was, of course, partly demographic. Many of the new southern clubs were started by men who had migrated from the North during the late twenties and thirties. None the less, the effect of the rapid growth in southern football was, *inter alia*, to modify the social composition of those who played football. Furthermore, compared with pre-1914, fewer of the professionals born in the 1920s and 1930s came from the old northern strongholds; more from the Midlands and the South.

The heart of professional football was the Football League's divisional cham-pionships. After the First World War the League, a predominantly northern body, united with the Southern League to create an organization that changed little until the 1990s. Between 1920 and 1922 a national League of three divi-sions—with a mechanism for promotion—was established: first, second, and third (Northern) and third (Southern). That structure survived until 1959 when the two third divisions were amalgamated and a fourth division created. The League championships were football's dynamo, but the Football Association Cup, for which all clubs affiliated to the Football Association could technically compete, provided an open alternative to the closed competition of the League divisions, and the Football Association Cup final (after 1923 played at Wembley) was by general agreement the climacteric of the football season: as much for the players as the supporters. In 1934, Manchester City's 19-year-old

---

[28] In 1964 the figure was 25,217. By the mid-1980s 1.6 million people were playing recreational football—20% of the male population aged between 16 and 24.

[29] N. Fishwick, *English Football and Society, 1910–1950* (Manchester, 1989), 26.

[30] Bale, *Sport and Place*, 29.

goalkeeper, Frank Swift, was so overcome by his team's victory that he fainted at the final whistle and had to be revived before he could receive his winner's medal from the king.

The football clubs were the focus of powerful personal and collective loyalties. The atmosphere in Manchester in 1958 when news was heard of the air disaster that killed almost half of United's great side was likened to that of a working-class quarter after the battle of the Somme. No one thought it mawkish that the bedroom of one of the youngest and most talented of the team, the 18-year-old Duncan Edwards, was turned by his parents into a shrine, 'shaded and spotless'.[31] Yet club loyalties could complicate even that catastrophe: one Manchester schoolboy, because he supported Manchester City, thought he could not legitimately mourn as other Mancunians did and felt isolated from what he knew to be a communal emotion.[32]

Supporters not merely supported a club or identified themselves with its fortunes, many wished actively to associate themselves with it. These urges could be so intense that clubs had difficulty in satisfying them. A frustrated desire to associate could then be transformed into a sense of exclusion. As the Leicester City supporters told the directors in the 1920s:

> Surely we supporters are entitled to some say in the government of the game we support, and surely it's not asking too much that those in authority should answer the critics?
>
> We are terribly interested in the game and its welfare in Leicester, though the City directors don't seem alive to the fact ... they veil themselves in mystery ... we grope in the darkness ...[33]

In the interwar years several clubs were saved from collapse by their supporters. The Luton supporters association, for instance, which rescued Luton Town in 1931, were able to pay for new stands and the summer wages of the team.[34] The supporters associations represented and mobilized the community, not just their own members. The successful effort to save Swindon Town 'depended on the local press, on the directors and the community as a whole, and it was the supporters' club, with its mass of social activities, that best symbolised the efforts of the community. There was thus a bond between club and community no other leisure institution enjoyed.' It would be hard 'to imagine similar efforts to save an impoverished dog track'.[35] When Stanley Matthews announced that he wished to leave Stoke City in 1938, to the dismay of the Potteries, many of those who signed the flysheet convening a public meeting to consider ways in which he might be persuaded to stay were leading figures in

---

[31] See the moving description of this in A. Hopcraft, *The Football Man* (London, 1968), 72–3.
[32] Private information to the author.
[33] R. Taylor, *Football and its Fans* (Leicester, 1992), 19.
[34] Ibid. 25–6.   [35] Fishwick, *English Football*, 44.

the pottery industry, and the several thousand who attended were widely representative of the community.[36] In turn, many clubs claimed to be peculiarly attached to their communities—like West Ham, which apparently embodied the best of East London traditions (only playing local boys, for example), even though, as with West Ham, many of these claims were overstated.[37]

A publicly asserted loyalty to the club was expected of supporters. English football crowds were known to be 'enthusiastic', perhaps the most enthusiastic in Europe ('not even excluding the Italians').[38] They were seen to be partisan, often contemptuous of the opposition and the referee's eyesight, hearing, and mental capacity. Throwing things on to a pitch was not uncommon; nor were pitch invasions. But supporters were rarely 'violent'. There was little of the 'hooliganism' or destructive vandalism that developed in the late 1960s. On the contrary, the 'mythical' Wembley final of 1923, when 250,000 people crowded into a stadium designed for 125,000 (at the most), and allowed themselves to be dispersed with good humour and without injury, was what contemporaries liked to think was the norm.[39] Whatever the reasons for this deliverance—the presence of the king or the calming influence of the legendary policeman George Scorey on his white horse—the crowd behaved with a phlegm inconceivable 50 years later. The period was not without disaster: on 9 March 1946, 33 were killed and 400 injured at Bolton Wanderers' ground, Burnden Park. But that was due to overcrowding on the terraces, not misbehaviour.

What explains this comparative tranquillity? In part, it was because the crowds were older and the comparatively few younger men who could afford to go regularly were usually kept in control by the older spectators. In part, it was because it was still comparatively rare for large numbers of supporters to go to away matches. When they did, they were more subjects of 'curiosity' than objects of territorial onslaught.[40] Most important, the 'culture' of football was still aligned to the ruling civic culture in which public violence was strongly deprecated. There was no aggrieved, young, working-class 'rump'—as there was to be—convinced that they had been excluded from a sport which, as it made itself acceptable to other social groups, became alienated from its traditional support; a sport whose original values could only be preserved by aggression and violence:

The rump has the historic task of perpetuating the traditional values of the fast disappearing football subculture and in conditions of severe restraint. For them *la lutte*

---

[36] Matthews was saved for Stoke largely by the efforts of the Potteries' directors. (Tony Mason, 'Stanley Matthews', in Holt, *Sport and the Working Class*, 163–6.)

[37] C. P. Korr, 'A Different Kind of Success: West Ham United and the Creation of Tradition and Community', in ibid. 153–4.

[38] Cohen-Portheim, *England, the Unknown Isle*, 43.

[39] For a good description of the 1923 Cup final, see J. Walvin, *The People's Game* (London, 1975), 116–17.

[40] Fishwick, *English Football*, 64.

continue at a greater intensity and a much higher cost in terms of arrest and pillory: the subculture is involved in asserting its values in the face of bourgeoisified crowds, management, players and press supported in ways very familiar to the rump, by local police and the courts.[41]

The supporters came to watch the players, and a man's skill, courage, and health was almost as important to a supporter as to the player himself. But the fame of League footballers still tended to be local and there was, until the end of the period, only a handful of players who were national figures: Tommy Lawton, Stanley Matthews, 'Dixie' Dean, Alex James, Nat Lofthouse, and perhaps one or two others. Their presence in a match could more than double a gate. Nottingham County's average attendance apparently quadrupled when Tommy Lawton (the England centre-forward) joined the club in 1948. The same happened at Blackpool when Matthews joined them in 1947. Clubs were thus reluctant to admit that one of their stars might not be playing: 'There was some suspicion locally when Sheffield Wednesday and Stoke failed to announce that Matthews would *not* be playing in a match at Hillsborough in 1945: had this been known, the gate might not have been 50 per cent above the average.'[42] There was also a category of players who acquired a national-mythic status precisely because fortune had denied them their rightful standing, like Duncan Edwards or, indeed, any of the Manchester team killed in 1958, or Derek Dooley of Sheffield Wednesday who had a leg amputated as he approached the height of his career.

Stanley Matthews stood above all. He was probably the only footballer of the period who could without exaggeration be called a household name. His modesty of demeanour and habit—he was both a non-smoker and non-drinker—and his social origins on the borderline of the working class and the lower middle class (his father was a Hanley barber) attracted a huge following.[43] Even though he played on the wing, a position becoming then almost redundant, his marvellous skill with the ball allowed him to dominate play as few others could. His career had a heroic symmetry. He played first division football until he was 50 (and for England until he was 43), but won his first Football Association Cup winner's medal (for Blackpool) in 1953, on the eve of his retirement, after a

[41] I. Taylor, ' "Football Mad": A Speculative Sociology of Football Hooliganism', in E. Dunning (ed.), *The Sociology of Sport* (London, 1971), 355. Taylor argues that there was in the late 1940s and the 1950s a 'traumatic' change in the relationship between players and the specific football subculture, as football had to compete in a rapidly fragmenting 'leisure-market'. In competing for a wider and different audience it divested itself of certain characteristics which the 'rump' thought essential to the sport. The 'rump' will typically include unemployed and unemployable young men, downwardly mobile or simply immobile who feel it their responsibility to perpetuate a 'traditional' football culture. This is a convincing account of football hooliganism, even though one of the premisses of the argument—that in the interwar years directors and managers were widely admired by supporters—was not necessarily true.

[42] Fishwick, *English Football*, 53.   [43] Hopcraft, *Football Man*, 30.

sensational final which Blackpool won 4–3, though trailing 1–3 with only 20 minutes to go. The novelist H. E. Bates wrote of that match: 'I do not think Wembley has seen anything like the miracle of Blackpool's recovery and the sheer beauty and skill of Matthews' part in it.'

The comparative paucity of nationally known footballers might seem surprising. But loyalties were still very local and only a few clubs had sides which contemporaries thought outstanding, while interest in the national team was much weaker than it was to become. Although England played many internationals, little hung on them, other than exceptional matches like that against Germany in 1938, when England's national prestige was thought to be at stake; a match made even more sensitive by Britain's failure and Germany's success in the 1936 Olympics.[44] Attitudes changed only when England entered the World Cup in 1950. Then something did matter, and thereafter much more was emotionally invested in the national side and its individual members.

The attitudes of club management and, above all, the 'maximum wage' system further bound players to one team and thus to one community. Between the wars, the maximum wage for a professional footballer was £8 a week. It was raised to £12 a week during the war and by the end of the period stood at £20 per week in winter and £17 per week in summer. The maximum wage was calculated in relation to a skilled worker's wage and no first division footballer was thought to be worth more than twice a skilled worker. But few first division footballers were actually paid twice a skilled worker's rate. In 1955–6, for example, when the average annual income for a skilled worker was £622, the average salary for a first division player was £772; for someone who played in the first team of a first division club it was £832.[45]

It was, of course, possible for a club to evade the maximum wage by hidden payments—free housing, summer jobs, help with the children's schooling, etc. A handful of leading players, but only a handful, could make some extra money on the side. In 1951 Stanley Matthews was paid £20 a week for endorsing Co-operative Wholesale Society football boots, while 'Dixie' Dean could earn up to £50 advertising a product. But few players received either perks or money on the side. In the interwar years, indeed, only 10 per cent of players received the maximum wage, although that proportion rose slowly in the 1940s. As a result professional footballers were, by the standards of a later generation, absurdly underpaid. In 1939, at the height of his career, Tommy Lawton's gross earnings were only £531.10s. Nat Lofthouse, after four years down the pits as a Bevin Boy, signed for Bolton at £1.10s per week. Stan Cullis was in Wolverhampton Wanderers' senior side at 17 1/2, captain at 19 and captain of England at 22, but did not receive the maximum wage until his third season,

44 See below, pp. 378–80   45 Mason, *Sport in Britain*, 161–2.

though he did receive a free house. 'There was a feeling of great insecurity,' he said. 'If you didn't make the grade you were on the dole.'[46]

Thus few footballers made much out of the game and most had little to sustain them on retirement. The most successful, Matthews, 'made the kind of living that could be expected by an enterprising provincial businessman with shops in two or three High streets and no time for frivolous spending'.[47] For the others, the best that could be hoped for was a job as football manager or coach, a pub licence, or a small shop. Many became miners or heavy labourers. Derek Dooley would have had nothing but for a donation of £3,000 from an anonymous pools' winner.

There were two justifications for the maximum wage. The first was that it ensured an even distribution of talent which would otherwise be monopolized by the richest clubs. The other, that it ensured a fair return to the middling professionals and encouraged a sporting egalitarianism. There was, however, a third, hidden argument: that the maximum wage kept the game as close to being amateur as a professional sport could be; this argument had much appeal to both the League and the Football Association.

Professional footballers, particularly the better ones, were rarely convinced by these arguments, and they established a players' union, the Professional Footballers' Association, to contest them.[48] The Association had 1,174 members in 1921, but it collapsed after its failure to resist pay cuts in the early 1920s. It was refounded and, by concentrating on legal work, slowly rebuilt its numbers—by 1939 it had 2,000 members, including the majority of League players. The Association was, however, hobbled by the diversity of its members' interests. The stars wanted full freedom of contract, but a system which so favoured the richer clubs had no attraction to the middling players. Nor were its members agreed on a strategy—was the Association a trade union which practised trade union techniques, or a more discreet professional body?

The conflict between the clubs and the players was increasingly one of definition. The employers still thought of the professionals as journeymen who were well paid for what they did. The best of the professionals, however, thought of themselves as star entertainers (as they obviously were) and wanted the appropriate return. Clubs insistently denied this and were happy to exploit the local press and the supporters in doing so. The argument that players were star entertainers was disliked by many supporters since it violated their own conception of the game, and it was not difficult for the clubs to work on this.[49]

It was not until the late 1940s that the directors' policy of mobilizing the middling professionals against the stars ceased to be effective. By then the

---

[46] Hopcraft, *Football Man*, 52.   [47] Ibid. 30.

[48] For the players' union, see Fishwick, *English Football*, 86–91.

[49] Even the greatest were not exempt. Matthews's testimonial at Stoke raised only £1,160 instead of the £5,000 expected.

majority of professionals were convinced that they had an interest in freedom of contract, and by the season of 1960–1 the Professional Footballers' Association led by Jimmy Hill was sufficiently united to threaten a strike of first division players unless the maximum wage were abolished. The clubs caved in, as they had to, although the 'retain-and-transfer' regulation, the other means by which players were bound to them, was not abolished until 1963.[50]

As the efforts of the supporters' associations suggest, many League clubs were in difficulties in the 1930s and it has been argued that the depression favoured the southern clubs at the expense of the northern. But there is little sign of this in the competition for the Football Association Cup. Here no single club or region dominated, either before or after the early 1930s. Between 1919 and 1931 the cup was won seven times by northern sides, twice by Midlands and twice by London and southern sides. Between 1932 and 1951 it was won nine times by northern sides, once by Midlands and four times by London and southern sides. Of the 26 cup competitions, three clubs won three times: Bolton Wanderers (all before 1931), Newcastle United (once before 1931, twice after), Arsenal (once before 1931 and twice after). Nothing in these figures, therefore, suggests that football was relatively declining in its northern heartland.

The competition for the Football Association Cup is knock-out, and its result clearly has a random element. If there were a movement to the south, the Football League championship, a more accurate measure of overall success, would have been likely to reveal it. And the southern sides do appear to have increasingly dominated the League championship. Between 1919 and 1931 the championship was won ten times by Northern sides, once by a Midlands side and once by a London side. Between 1932 and 1951, however, it was won six times by northern sides and eight times by London and southern sides. But that success is due largely to one London club, Arsenal, which won the championship five times between 1932 and 1951. Furthermore, Manchester United was the most consistently successful club in the 1940s, being runner-up in 1947, 1948, 1949, and 1951. And of the northern sides who were champions three times, only Huddersfield won all three before 1931: Liverpool won in 1947, and Everton in 1932 and 1939. Furthermore, apart from one Midlands side, Wolverhampton Wanderers in 1950, every runner-up between 1947 (the first full League year after the war) and 1951 was a Northern side.

None the less, Arsenal was the glamour team of the 1930s—the model of a successful football club; and its success and style of management did much to attract the metropolitan middle classes and, via them, the middle classes more generally to the sport, as is suggested by the increasing acceptability to a broader public of fashionable London sides like Arsenal and Chelsea, or of the great Northern sides like Liverpool, Everton, or Manchester United. Arsenal's

---

[50] Mr Justice Wilberforce ruled in 1963 that the 'retain-and-transfer' rule constituted restraint of trade. He was judging an action brought by George Eastham against Newcastle United.

success on and off the field was not accidental. Its powerful and publicity-conscious managers, Herbert Chapman and George Allison, were careful to present the club in a particular way. Chapman came to Arsenal in 1925, having been a successful manager of Huddersfield Town.[51] He practised at Arsenal the same kind of determined management, which tolerated little outside interference, with the same result. On his death in 1934, the decision of the club to appoint George Allison his successor showed how far Arsenal valued good public relations. Allison, who had been the BBC's first football commentator and who was known as 'By Jove' Allison because of his declamatory style of reporting, was a familiar figure in middle-class England, with a well-honed accent then unusual among football managers. It was under Allison that Arsenal became its most glamorous, its apotheosis coming in 1938 when the team members emerged as film stars in the popular thriller *The Arsenal Stadium Mystery*. Some dismissed Arsenal's self-publicity as 'bunkum' or 'stunts', but it seemed to work, and Chapman and Allison were followed by others like Frank Buckley at Wolverhampton and Matt Busby at Manchester United.

The club directors often did not like these masterful managers and tried to resist their appointment. They also quarrelled with players over conditions of work and with supporters, whose jealous love of 'their' game seemed to exclude the directors. Unlike the democracy of street football, the League clubs were led by a directorial stratum which can fairly be called 'middle class', since the directors, if not always born into the middle class, mostly entered it. In many ways they were characteristic of the interwar provincial middle classes:[52] often Freemasons, usually smallish successful businessmen, loyal to the club and anxious for its well-being. Although the esteem they earned doubtless helped them in business they were not in football for the money. They were not unlike Sinclair Lewis's small-town 'boosters', equally typical of the American middle classes at the same time. Directors were often attached to business and social networks which brought them together in several overlapping spheres. They were sometimes related, like the Cearns and Pratts who effectively ran West Ham for nearly fifty years.[53] The result was that directors' seats were rarely contested and men were deeply offended if they were. The clubs thus tended to be governed by the codes of those who dominated them, and who were secretive, exclusive, and resentful of outside intrusion. The epitome of such a man was J. C. (later Sir Charles) Clegg, chairman of both Sheffield Wednesday and Sheffield United, who was 'widely admired for pioneering the

---

[51] Huddersfield were first division champions in 1924, 1925, and 1926, and runners-up in 1927 and 1928.

[52] For the directors, see Fishwick, *English Football*, 11, 18, 21, 28–36, 58, 148; Taylor, *Football and its Fans*, 20–54, 180; Hopcraft, *Football Man*, 143, 154–5. The literature is, on the whole, hostile to the directors, who have yet to receive a more sympathetic scholarship.

[53] Korr, 'A Different Kind of Success', 153.

fifteen-minute AGM'.[54] The absence of a 'free market' in football and the wholly uncompetitive nature of its economics entrenched this directorial spirit. Arthur Hopcraft's description of the average director of the period, though partly a caricature, is probably not too unjust:

There is an immediate similarity in age group, worldly experience and physical look between football directors and magistrates' benches or municipal watch committees: feet-on-the-ground citizenry, local boys made good none too early in life, no fancy talk, a bit booze-stained round the edges, a high incidence of waistcoats.[55]

The reluctance of the directors to share authority is apparent in their attitude to the supporters' clubs. They were willing to turn to the clubs when in need; but not in prosperity. When the Second World War broke out, for example, and the future looked gloomy, Leicester City's directors recognized the supporters' club as a legitimate interest. After the war, however, when attendances were colossal, the directors turned cool. When approached by the supporters they pointed out that Leicester City was a 'private company' and not obliged to consult outsiders. Occasionally a representative of the supporters was co-opted as director; more usually, however, directors refused even to discuss ground facilities with their supporters. Many clubs appeared 'completely cynical in their dealings with supporters, readily benefiting from the deeply rooted affection that their football enjoyed locally'.[56]

The Football Association was no more welcoming. In 1927 a number of the supporters' clubs united to form the National Federation of Supporters' Clubs whose modest ambition was embodied in its motto: 'To Help not to Hinder'. The Football Association declined to recognize it, even though the secretary of the Association, Stanley Rous, accepted a vice-presidency of the Federation in 1935. The consequence of the Football Association's obduracy was that the majority of supporters' clubs affiliated to the Federation after the war were probably non-League or amateur.

The attitudes of the directors had material implications. Neither football clubs nor the League nor the Football Association would consider for one moment accepting money from a betting tax or any kind of levy on the pools companies since that would have meant accepting the legitimacy of betting and so infringing the quasi-amateurism to which most directors still held. The poverty of many football clubs, particularly at the worst of the depression, was widely known. Yet all schemes to alleviate it were rejected. The League would not even discuss the ingenious proposal made in 1934 by the Liverpool solicitor Watson Hartley that it should copyright its fixture list and sell it to the pools companies. Nor would it contemplate a betting levy, since such

---

[54] Fishwick, *English Football*, 18.   [55] Hopcraft, *Football Man*, 143.
[56] Taylor, *Football and its Fans*, 180.

a hypothecated tax would be 'impracticable'. Furthermore, the League's hostility to the pools was not merely passive: in a mad escapade it even tried to destroy them in 1936.[57]

Most grounds, therefore, slowly became sporting slums with wretched 'facilities'. Virtually nothing was spent on them in the interwar years, and even less in the 1940s, despite the huge gates. It is a mystery what happened to the money, though some was spent on directors' boxes and dining-rooms. The Wolfenden Report *Sport in the Community* commented severely on this protracted underfunding and pointed to damaging international comparisons. It was not until the 1980s that the first division clubs began to replace the crumbling stands and fetid terraces—and then only after a true disaster at the Hillsborough ground in Sheffield provoked a long-overdue intervention by the state.

RUGBY

Rugby's status as a national sport is unique, since its two parts, the Rugby Union and the Rugby League are by class composition and regional support almost wholly distinct. The old Rugby Union had been sundered in 1895 when 22 northern clubs seceded over the question of 'broken-time payment'[58] to found the Northern Union, which adopted the Australian name The Rugby League in 1922. By then the divisions had been institutionalized, while rule changes had introduced significance differences between the two codes. Rugby union was played by 15 men a side; rugby league by 13. The League had also attempted to make the game more exciting—to compete with football—by abolishing the 'line-out' and replacing the ruck with a 'play-the-ball' rule. The change certainly made the game tougher and more violent, but by keeping the ball with the forwards tended to close down play rather than open it up. At its worst, league became a battle of barging forward lines; at its best, union had a backline fluency league never achieved, and could produce spectacular movements like Prince Obolensky's celebrated try against New Zealand in January 1936—a legendary moment in interwar sport. But the survival of the ruck in union allowed opportunities for concealed savagery which would have been unacceptable in league.

Of the two codes, rugby union was the only one to expand after the First World War. Indeed, its expansion in the interwar years, particularly in the 1920s, was striking.[59] In that decade 231 new clubs were founded, a figure

---

[57] See below, p. 377.
[58] The issue was not payment for players, but compensation for players who lost wages by playing rugby—by 'breaking-time' in their jobs. The majority of the clubs in the English Rugby Union were opposed to any form of payment, including compensation. The northern clubs, whose sides were comprised overwhelmingly of working men, had no alternative but to secede.
[59] Details in E. Dunning and K. Sheard, *Barbarians, Gentlemen and Players* (Oxford, 1979), 236.

equalled in no previous or future decade. The 'rush to rugby' in the 1920s was an overt statement of deliberate class-differentiation and part of a much wider social phenomenon: the middle-class reaction to an apparently politicized and aggressive working class. The rush was from football, the supremely working-class game, by smaller public schools and larger grammar schools, who now did what most of the major public schools had done before 1914. Many of the new rugby clubs were founded by ex-grammar school boys and the effect of the rush was to make union socially very homogeneous: that is, overwhelmingly middle-class.[60] The number of England players who did not go to public or grammar schools was negligible; and it was not until the 1960s that the number of grammar school boys exceeded the number of public school boys. The number of ex-public school boys playing for England was at its highest when the rush was at its strongest, in the 1920s: 572 compared with 422 in 1902–11 and 262 for 1962–71.[61]

There was, however, a discernible geographical bias to rugby union. It was strongest in Cornwall, Gloucestershire, and the Bristol area.[62] This was partly due to proximity to Wales, where it was the 'national' sport; partly to its popularity in rural communities—particularly, as in the Scottish Borders, among farmers and their families. It was also in the Midlands and the South very much a game of the provincial middle classes, who often had close connections with local public and grammar schools. London, none the less, was important. There were not only well-known London suburban sides like Blackheath, but an array of institutional and émigré clubs all reflecting London's super-metropolitan character: those, for example, recruited from the great teaching hospitals, the Metropolitan Police, the London Welsh, the London Irish, and the London Scottish.

Gareth Williams has implied that there was something surprising about rugby union's expansion in the 1920s: 'as if it were actually thriving on its middle-class tennis-and-golf image of suburban sporting gentility'.[63] It was, however, precisely this 'image' which was responsible for its expansion. The clubs also became important elements in that developing network of middle-class male sociability so characteristic of interwar England. Furthermore, throughout the 1920s and 30s rugby union became central to the ethos of the smaller public schools who had 'rushed' into it after 1918 and who thereafter produced a disproportionate number of its first-class players. For them it provided the

---

[60] Ibid. 237. The rush caused problems for those boys who wished to continue playing football. When the young Bobby Charlton won a place at a grammar school, he was allocated to Morpeth, which was, according to his primary school headmaster, 'one of those snooty schools where they play rugby. We got him transferred to the grammar school at Bedlington.' (Hopcraft, *Football Man*, 88.)

[61] Gareth Williams, 'Rugby Union' in Mason, *Sport in Britain*, 325; Dunning and Sheard, *Barbarians, Gentlemen and Players*, 239.

[62] Bale, *Sport and Place*, 65.   [63] Mason, *Sport in Britain*, 325.

opportunity to attain a new standing. In a comparative small public school, for example, like Trent in Derbyshire, rugby was much more important than cricket, and for a few years in the 1930s the school could field a peerless side of almost international quality. Not altogether surprisingly, since its wing three-quarter was Prince Obolensky, and Trent was where he acquired his nickname of 'Obo'. For such schools, which had to work hard to achieve fame, rugby union was a boon. Rugby also restored a balance to middle-class winter sport when it became obvious that 'middle-class' teams could no longer win at football.

As a sport it had the further advantage of being international. It was played as the major rugby code in the three other home countries—Wales, Scotland, and Ireland—in France, New Zealand, and South Africa, and in Australia as an important minor code. In New Zealand and South Africa it was, as in Wales, the 'national' game and the standard of play formidable. The internationals became immensely popular in the 1930s with regular attendances at Twickenham of 70,000: Obolensky's try in 1936 was remembered not only because of its brilliance but because England beat New Zealand 13–0 before such a crowd.

The social and regional structure of rugby league was almost the inverse of rugby union's. It was as 'working-class' as union was 'middle-class'; and the most geographically concentrated of the major English sports, confined to a comparatively narrow strip of northern England with Liverpool at one end and Hull at the other.[64] But this narrow strip embraced the heartland of much of the historic industrial working class: Burnley, Widnes, St Helens, Wigan, Warrington, Leigh, Oldham, Castleford, Huddersfield, Halifax, Dewsbury, Bradford, Leeds, Featherstone, Kingston-upon-Hull. The problem for the Rugby League was that this was an economically and demographically declining part of the country, and all attempts to break out of the heartland in these years failed. In Wales competition from rugby union, the 'national' code, was too strong; in London and the South-East the League could never detach any of the Union's middle-class support nor any of football's entrenched working-class support. The decision in 1929, made after much heart-searching, to play the annual Challenge Cup final at Wembley—'the annual hopeless trip to Wembley'[65]—was a defiant gesture of frustrated missionary purpose. Rugby league was unusual in that the broadcasting (1927) and then the televising (1952) of the Challenge Cup final appear to have done it little immediate good. Nor was rugby league part of a real international circuit. It was not played at all in South Africa and struggled for life in France (whose federation was established only in 1934) and New Zealand, where it was played as an amateur game.[66] In Australia alone was it a major code; and even there confined to two of the six states.

---

[64] Bale, *Sport and Place*, 59.   [65] Jackson and Marsden, *Working Class Community*, 116.

[66] Most English league players were amateurs and the professionals usually only semi-professional. None then made a living from the game.

The result was an inward-looking sport which despite, or because of, its introversion earned the passionate loyalty of its followers. League was admired for its physicality and toughness, players for their strength and size; both frequently contrasted with 'soft' rugby union and its effete retinues. It stood for the higher morale of the working class and the superiority of the North over the South. Where the League was strong it was very strong: a comparatively small mining town like Featherstone could maintain 13 supporters' clubs.

Loyalty to the game was intensely local. Thus one day in 1953, when a League international between France and England was televised live at the same time as Featherstone was playing at home, only a handful of men watched the international while 3,400 went to watch Featherstone Rovers.[67] Wherever rugby league was played, Richard Hoggart wrote,

the home team . . . is an important element in the group life of the district. They are spoken of with genuine pride as 'our lads' and many of them may well be local boys— huge ex-miners or heavy steelworkers. I remember Hunslett [in Leeds] Rugby team bringing the Cup home from Wembley years ago, coming down from the City station into the heart of the district on top of a charabanc. They went from pub to pub in all the neighbourhood's main streets, with free drinks at every point, followed by crowds of lads prepared to risk staying out all hours after their bedtime for the excitement of seeing their local champions.[68]

This was a world away from the Rugby Union.

HORSE-RACING

Like rugby, horse-racing was a national sport only by a somewhat skewed definition of 'national'. What made it 'national' was popular betting which linked a mass of working-class betters to a sport which was, in fact, aristocratic-plutocratic. Without betting it would have been no more national than 12-metre yachting or deer-hunting. Furthermore, though punters were often extremely knowledgeable about betting, many had little interest in horses or horse-racing as such. The middle classes as a whole and the sober, serious working class were even more indifferent; indeed, were often hostile. Yet, whatever the cause, racing's status within the national culture as a sport which successfully and consciously bridged England's rural past and its urban-industrial present is undeniable.

At the top of flat racing was the Jockey Club, a self-recruiting association charged with overall supervision of the sport. The Jockey Club was probably the last genuinely aristocratic body in England. At one moment in the inter-war years it had only two non-titled members, and the first self-made man to be elected was Lord Glanely (W. J. Tatem, a Welsh ship-owner, who was

---

[67] Dennis et al., *Coal is our Life*, 156–8.   [68] Hoggart, *Uses of Literacy*, 109–10.

ennobled by Lloyd George) in 1929. The Jockey Club's authority was based not on statute but on convention, though its authority was real enough.

The leading owners were socially more mixed. The only one from the traditional racing aristocracy was Lord Derby, but he did very well indeed. His stud included the finest mare of the period, Sansovino, with which he won the Derby in 1924, and the finest stallion, Hyperion, which won him both the St Leger and the Derby in 1933. Many of the most successful owners—as always in the history of racing—were 'new money' or otherwise outside the old magic circle: Lord Woolavington (James Buchanan), the whisky distiller; Tom Walls, the comedian and veteran of a thousand Ben Travers farces, who was trainer and part-owner of the 1932 Derby winner, April 5, and leader of a theatrical syndicate rumoured to have won large sums betting on his horses; J. B. Joel of the Transvaal South African Goldfields and partner in Barnato Brothers, who married the daughter of the aircraft manufacturer Thomas Sopwith, bought the stud of the 'furniture king' Sir Blundell Maple, and who described his recreations as 'all kinds of sports; shooting; fishing; keeps a large breeding and racing stud'; Edgar Wallace, the crime writer, whose frantic production was required partly to keep his racing (and betting) interests afloat; an Indian prince, the Maharajah of Rajpipla, who won the Derby in 1934 with his first runner, Windsor Lad; the Hon. Dorothy Paget, daughter of Lord Queenborough, who owned the 1943 Derby winner, Straight Deal, and who was 'invariably accompanied by a platoon of female aides-de-camp';[69] the bookmaker William Hill, who owned the 1949 Derby winner, Nimbus. All these were widely representative of English and imperial wealth.

But the most successful owner-breeder of the time, in both England and France, was the Aga Khan. His Irish and French studs permitted him to race on a matchless scale. He won the Derby five times—1930, 1935, 1936, 1948, and 1952. He was leading owner 13 times, leading breeder eight, and won 741 flat races with prize money of over £1 million. He was, however, not just in racing for the sport and his commercial-mindedness did not always earn him friends. In 1940, of all years, he exported two of his finest horses, Barham and Mahmoud—an act which outraged racing and patriotic opinion.

In 1920 there were 317 licensed jockeys, but only a few earned much from riding. In 1929 47 per cent and in 1938 50 per cent of all races were won by the 12 leading jockeys. Of this élite, two, Steve Donoghue and Gordon Richards, were outstanding. Donoghue was the most successful jockey of the early and mid-twenties, winning the Derby in 1921, 1922, 1923 and 1925. Donoghue, who had a colourful early life and career, rode with great style, was immensely popular with crowds and punters—'Come on Steve' was a common catchphrase in the 1920s—but much less popular with owners. Richards was almost

---

[69] R. Mortimer, *The History of the Derby Stakes* (London, 1973), 541.

the opposite; reliable and reserved. He was first champion jockey in 1925 and by his retirement in 1954 had been champion 26 times. His career ended on a high note; he became the first jockey to be knighted and at the age of 49 won his first Derby (on Pinza) in the coronation year, 1953.

Most jockeys, however, ended their sporting lives much less fortunately. Their careers, like those of the majority of all English professional sportsmen, even if they gave them an adequate living, left them ill-equipped on retirement. Of 317 licensed jockeys in 1920, only 7 per cent later took a trainer's licence: most returned as stable lads or worked as labourers around the racecourses. If anything, that was even worse than the fate of most professional cricketers or footballers.

The poverty of English racing was one of the reasons so many jockeys ended as they did. Despite the huge number who directly or indirectly followed it the sport was financially decrepit, and stakes never came close to covering costs. During the interwar years each horse needed about £650 even to get it to the starting gates; yet prize money met less than one-third of this. Virtually no one, with the possible exception of the Aga Khan, made money out of racing. Most raced for other reasons: because they had inherited a stud; because it purchased social prestige and status; because they liked racing. Almost nothing was spent on those courses that remained open, and the Ilchester Committee (set up in 1943) was very critical of the shabby facilities and general disrepair of England's race-courses. A combination of low stakes and low investment made English racing uncompetitive with the better-funded French racing.

The Jockey Club was not unaware of this, but neither by inclination nor training were its members able to do much about it. The Club had, for instance, been very slow to police the courses against the criminal gangs who preyed upon the bookmakers after 1918; indeed had done nothing, until the bookies were driven to defend themselves. Above all, the Club's passivity disabled it from seeking state assistance either directly or via betting levies. As Lord Ilchester's report ruefully noted, the English were punters rather than race-goers. And the future of racing could only be guaranteed if the huge sums spent on betting were taxed. In this the Jockey Club's position was analogous to that of football's administrators. It did not react as blockheadedly to the prospect of betting levies as they did, but was unready to take the initiative, possibly for fear that a full-scale betting duty could presage a wider state intervention. Attempts to levy betting in the 1920s had been disappointing and were abandoned. Returns on a betting duty, however, could never be significant until off-course cash betting were legalized—something the Jockey Club understood but did not press for. In the meantime English racing continued its decline until the 1960s, when legalization of off-course betting (1961) and the creation of the Horserace Betting Levy Board resuscitated it via large tranches of public money.

ANGLING

The fifth of the major national sports was fishing; but, as with rugby, different kinds of people did it in different ways in different places. There was a fundamental social distinction between those who fished for 'game' (salmon or trout) and those who fished for 'coarse fish' (roach, rudd, dace, chub, pike, perch etc.). Game fishing—unless a fisherman owned his own runs—was very expensive. The cost of renting game fishing rights was throughout this period such as to exclude all but the wealthiest. Men and women who fished for game did not have to be upper class, but they did have to be rich. Few anglers could hope to fish for trout (let alone for salmon) until the late 1950s, when the farming of rainbow trout made it possible to stock them in rivers, reservoirs, or rehabilitated gravel pits, where once only coarse fish could be found.[70]

There developed during the interwar years in places like the Norfolk Broads a 'middle-class' angling, based upon small hotels or guest houses located near good fishing, usually coarse or sea fishing but, if the hotel could afford the rent, occasionally for trout. Such fishing was either an adjunct to the family holiday and done for pleasure or a more serious masculine affair, when the family was left behind and the competitiveness, though tacit, was real. It was for these fishermen that the purpose-built 'fishing estates' originally began to be built in the late 1940s and which thereafter grew rapidly in number.

Working-class angling was likewise both recreational and competitive. Typically, however, the competition was more overt and formally organized, usually around angling clubs attached to pubs, workingmen's clubs and (increasingly) larger factories and workshops. In Featherstone, the angling clubs, which were attached to the workingmen's clubs, held about 20 club matches a year.[71] Many of these clubs had substantial memberships: in 1930 Birmingham had about 14,250 organized anglers. Even a town as depressed as Wigan had 1,900. Matches became important for the clubs in the 1920s. Two men would fish for one to one-and-a-half hours with a prize of £10 to £20. There was much betting on the side. Matches could reach extraordinary proportions: in 1926, 3,800 Birmingham anglers competed in a single match along 40 miles of river bank—18 miles on one side and 22 on the other.

The Second World War broke up many of the angling clubs but post-war prosperity hugely increased the number of fishermen. Fishing had always been comparatively expensive and before 1939 confined to the best-paid working men. After the war many more men could afford tackle, and middle- and working-class angling began to converge. Fishing in restored and landscaped gravel pits became popular as men could increasingly afford membership of those clubs which purchased their fishing rights. As a sport, the future lay with

---

[70] J. Lowerson, 'Angling' in Mason, *Sport in Britain*, 35–6.
[71] Dennis *et al.*, *Coal is our Life*, 150–1.

fishing. By the 1970s there were nearly 3.5 million anglers drawn broadly from all social classes, making it by far the most popular participatory sport. Unlike other post-war recreations, however, such as motoring, fishing did not bring the family together. It remained, apart perhaps from game fishing, overwhelmingly masculine; like the allotment, it permitted men to escape the family, and that was one of its unconcealed attractions. Many wives, therefore, hated it as much as they had hated football or rugby before the Second World War.

2 | *Sectarian sports*

HUNTING AND ROWING

There were a number of sports—not necessarily minor—whose following was socially and/or geographically limited. And in most the tendency to limitation increased throughout this period. The most exclusive sports, with one partial exception, were exclusive by convention or cost rather than by fiat. Hunting, perhaps the most exclusive, is a good example. It was an expensive sport, traditionally associated by outsiders with the aristocracy and gentry. Though that was still true, it is best understood (for these years) as the most superior of the rural sports. By the end of the nineteenth century farmers had largely made their peace with the hunts and most hunts were careful to give larger farmers equal rights to hunt with landowners, subscribers, and covert owners, and to elect them to hunt committees.[72] Indeed, the hunts began to defend themselves against the growing number of their critics on the ground that hunting was a rural not a class sport, legitimated by rural communities and traditions.

The one exception, the sport which formally prescribed social exclusion, was that part of rowing represented by the Amateur Rowing Association (ARA). English rowing had split in 1890, seven years after the ARA had adopted a set of rules which excluded professional oarsmen and effectively all working men. In September 1890 the National Amateur Rowing Association was established. Though amateur, it made no attempt—rather the reverse—to bar working men *qua* working men. A number of the leading clubs affiliated to it, and it had the patronage of grandees like the duke of Fife and Lord Iveagh who were dismayed at the ARA's narrowness.[73] The Henley Regatta, the smartest and best-known of the English regattas was, however, run by the ARA; and there, until 1936, it practised what it preached. In that year it nearly untethered an international incident by refusing to allow the Australian Eight, *en route* to the Berlin Olympics, to compete on the grounds that the crew were all Sydney policemen. The matter was raised in parliament and the ARA were obliged to

---

[72] D. C. Itzkowitz, *Peculiar Privilege: A Social History of English Foxhunting, 1753–1885* (Hassocks, Sussex), 173–5.

[73] C. Dodd, 'Rowing' in Mason, *Sport in Britain*, 285–87.

drop the offending rule and begin a prolonged amalgamation with the NARA, not completed until 1956.

It is doubtful if this made much difference to the social composition of rowing. The fall in working-class participation was not due to exclusion from Henley. Working-class rowing was a professional sport dependent on prize money and betting. The insistence on amateurism by both governing bodies and the greater convenience of betting on horses killed it, and with it an important tradition of working-class sport. Furthermore, the dock and riverside occupations which produced so many working-class rowers, powerful watermen and bargees whose job was their best training, were declining rapidly. The result was that oarsmen were increasingly drawn from the public schools and the universities where the tradition still flourished. The social base of rowing was thus probably narrower in 1950 than in 1850.

ATHLETICS

By 1918 athletics had become a sport very much of the older universities, the public schools, and the South-East of the country. Throughout the interwar years the bulk of the running tracks and the majority of the 1,000 clubs affiliated to the Amateur Athletic Association (AAA) were concentrated in the South. The administration of the sport was also overwhelmingly 'Southern'. It had thus become a sport biased very much by class and region. This had not always been the case. Professional running ('pedestrianism'), often of a high standard, had been very important in working-class communities in the late nineteenth century, particularly in the North. As a sport, however, it had no organization and, above all, depended on betting. When people found it more convenient or exciting to bet on horses, dogs, or football pedestrianism, like working-class rowing, withered away. Furthermore, as athletics became organized on an amateur basis, professional running became excluded competitively: performances in professional events, no matter how good, were never recognized by the amateur authorities. With the passing of pedestrianism went the tradition of competitive running, amateur or professional, amongst much of the industrial working class. By the outbreak of the First World War working-class males had almost completely withdrawn from athletics.

None the less, the clubs were numerous and there were many amateur athletes. In the 1920s they also had considerable international success. Of the twelve gold medals won by Britain in the Olympics between 1920 and 1952, nine were won in the 1920s. Nine of those twelve were in middle-distance events and there were some outstanding individuals: A. G. Hill, Eric Liddell (a Scot, who also won seven rugby caps for Scotland), and D. G. A. Lowe and Lord Burghley in the hurdles. The 4 × 400 metres relay was won twice. The other three gold medals were in the 100m in 1924 (Harold Abrahams) and two in the 50 kilometre walk. After almost vanishing, the middle-distance tradition revived in the 1950s with a brilliant generation of Oxford and Cambridge athletes, including Roger Bannister, the first man to break four minutes for the mile.

The continuing competitiveness of the middle-distance runners was probably due to the popularity of middle-distance running at the public schools and the older universities, as well as at the polytechnics and the athletic clubs which still inclined to follow their lead. Overall, however, it was rather a grim record, as contemporaries reluctantly concluded. In 1934 the AAA launched its first summer school at Loughborough, and in 1936 the School of Athletics, Games and Physical Education was opened there, the beginning of a process by which Oxford and Cambridge were to be marginalized in university sport (largely by the products of Loughborough). The brilliant Oxford and Cambridge generation of the 1950s was also to be the last. In addition, after Britain's comparatively feeble performance in the 1936 Olympics—though it was the best since 1924—the state made the first halting signs of intervention.

While the men of the 1920s remained in control of athletics, however, state intervention was not necessarily welcome. In the 1920s itself, athletics was dominated by the Achilles Club, as association founded by Oxford and Cambridge graduates to encourage 'university men' to continue running after graduation. The Club was in turn dominated by Harold Abrahams, Lord Burghley, and D. G. A. Lowe—all of whom strongly held to an amateur and voluntarist code which had served them well. Abrahams became secretary of the AAA in 1931 and his rather brusque way alienated many. Although the spirit of the Achilles Club weakened over time the tensions between it and a less gentlemanly approach dogged English athletics in general and the national team in particular. A. G. Hill, for example, double gold medallist in 1920, who came from Gainsford AC and Polytechnic Harriers, felt ill-treated by the AAA and in 1939 migrated to Canada. The choice of a team captain was a peculiarly delicate matter—with social class at its heart.[74]

GOLF AND TENNIS

Like hunting and rowing, golf and tennis had clear social demarcations, though these may not have been as rigid as many people thought. Of the two, golf was the socially superior—if only because it was the more expensive. The cost of equipment and club subscriptions would have eliminated many who played tennis. The widespread assumption that golf was, on the whole, a 'business' middle-class game was, therefore, probably correct. Furthermore, unlike tennis, the heroic age of golf's expansion was in the late nineteenth and early twentieth centuries, and it was specifically intended to meet the requirements of the substantial middle class. Five hundred and twelve clubs were

---

[74] J. Crump, 'Athletics' in ibid. 53–4.

founded before 1914; only 239 in the interwar years. But golf had a particular importance in the sociability of the interwar business class. Proximity to a golf course was always thought desirable in one of the better housing developments; clubhouses became increasingly opulent, with 'many more facilities than lockers and washrooms';[75] and the nineteenth hole, where, as Henry Longhurst said, 'conversation turns on motor-cars, his day's play, income tax, his day's play, the Minister of Transport and his day's play',[76] became an essential part of middle-class business and social networks. Like amateur cricket or rugby union, golf was a networking sport. The interwar golf clubs became associated with a certain laboured and easily satirized masculine style—the clubhouse bore, a hearty and ill-concealed snobbery which had anti-semitic overtones, a heavy emphasis on the notion of the 'good chap', an aggressive hostility to trade unions. P. G. Wodehouse, A. G. Macdonnell, even Agatha Christie in The Murder on the Links, found easy literary pickings in the golf clubhouse.

Although the rate of golf's expansion diminished after 1918, that was not true of its technical and social development. The dominating technical change was the invention of the tubular steel shaft—recognized by the Royal and Ancient in 1929—and the standardization and cheapening of the golf ball. The steel shaft greatly improved on the drive and flexibility of the old hickory sticks and its comparative cheapness made it possible for the average player to buy a complete set of clubs—expensive though they were by non-golfing standards. The predictable effect of the new shafts was to raise significantly the general level of play.

Golf was a British sport; one of its characteristics, therefore, was a tense relationship between amateur and professional. At bottom, as so often, it was a matter of class. Both its social environment and cost alienated working men. In an attempt to overcome this Lord Riddell and J. H. Taylor founded the Artisan Golfers' Association in 1921, and by 1927 the Association had 15,000 members. There, however, the figure stuck. The idea of 'dependent clubs' patronized by the existing institutions—as the artisans' clubs were—was not popular. Nor was the social exclusion practised by the founder-clubs. And the name 'artisan' was anachronistic even when it was adopted. The result of the comparative failure of artisans' golf was that the professionals were often working in an environment which was hostile to them and to professional sport. In the eyes of his employers the function of the professional was to coach and to run a small golfing shop attached to the club. He was a servant of the club and usually denied entry to the clubhouse. Some were treated not much better than caddies. Even the best of the professionals were subject to the system. But the best could go elsewhere. Tommy Armour, who won the Open in

---

[75] John Lowerson, 'Golf' in ibid. 193.   [76] Quoted in ibid. 204.

1924, went to the United States in 1920 as professional at the Westchester Club, never to return. Henry Cotton, who won the Open in 1934, migrated to Belgium in 1928 as professional at the Royal Waterloo Club; though he did return. There were also the usual embarrassing international complications: Walter Hagen, the greatest of the American professionals in the 1920s, competing for the Open in 1920, hired a chauffeur-driven Rolls Royce as a changing room on not being admitted to the clubhouse at Deal. In 1923 (when he was runner-up) he refused to attend the prize ceremony because the clubhouse had been closed to the professionals for the whole period of the competition. The ordinary jobbing professional could not escape so easily. The formation of the London and County Professional Golfers' Association helped, but their position was much inferior to the American professionals. Only well after the Second World War—and then partly as a result of Cotton's efforts—did it significantly improve.

The best professionals had another escape route—the competitive golfing circuit which, having begun before 1914, developed rapidly in the interwar years. Unlike cricket, where amateurs could still compete with professionals, few amateur golfers could compete with the professionals: Bobby Jones's astonishing victory in both the 1930 United States and British Open and Amateur titles was quite exceptional. The leading professionals increasingly had little connection with amateur golf and often only a notional one with any golf club. This competitive circuit was dominated by Americans. Although Great Britain won the Ryder Cup in 1929 and 1933, Cotton was the only British golfer who could compete with Hagen, Jones, Barnes, Sarazen, Hogan, etc. The American domination was, however, probably inevitable: there were many more American clubs; their resources were greater; college sport was beginning to produce large numbers of high-calibre players; and British golf suffered heavily in the Second World War, when many of the courses were ploughed up and their professionals conscripted. Even so, it seems unlikely that the relentless amateurism and petty snobberies of English golf played no part in the Americans' superiority.

Although 'tennis-and-golf' were linked in the popular mind and thought to be played by the same kind of people, tennis was actually a more broadly based middle-class sport. Its costs (unlike golf) were small enough to be accommodated in most middle-class incomes but large enough to exclude most working-class incomes. It was an ideal sport for the newish middle class. It could be played enjoyably by those only moderately competent; there was a high degree of gender-equality which made it attractive to both women and younger men; and courts were comparatively cheap to purchase and establish. Builders of moderately priced housing estates offered proximity to tennis courts as an inducement. Tennis thus expanded at the same rate as new middle-class housing. In 1925 1,620 clubs were affiliated to the Lawn Tennis Association; 2,500 in

1930 and 3,220 in 1938.[77] The centrality of tennis to middle-class sociability in the suburbs was well understood; 'Bridge parties and dances, picnics and smoking concerts, even elocution lessons were part of the social life of the tennis club and its suburban constituency.'[78] The enthusiasm for tennis anticipated the enthusiasm for other racquet sports, particularly squash—an Indian sport, introduced by former officers of the Indian Army. The first public squash court was opened in Ealing in 1931; by 1947 there were 150 clubs and 260 courts. The geography of these racquet sports suggested to one scholar that they were part of a life-style which defined 'a kind of outer-metropolitan popular culture'.[79]

DOG-RACING, SPEEDWAY, BOXING

At the bottom of the social scale were a clutch of sports which, though working-class, were not working-class in the way (say) football was. That had a status which earned it full recognition by society. This was not true of dog-racing, speedway racing, or boxing. Although their inclusive nature was always emphasized by their supporters—King Alfonso of Spain and Prince Bernhard of the Netherlands were allegedly enthusiasts for the dogs and the future King George VI for speedway racing—they were not, in fact, socially inclusive sports. The handful of high-born persons who occasionally attended dog races were slumming it, participating in a sporting bohemianism which harmlessly satisfied democratic impulses. Despite their sometimes huge following, they were outsiders' sports, genuinely proletarian, dissidents in the English sporting tradition, and inconceivable without betting. They were increasingly catered for by a specialist press. In the 1920s anyone wishing to know the result of a first division football match could find it in any half-serious newspaper. He would rarely find the result of a dog race, however important. A significant part of English sporting life was simply unknown to most members of the middle class and to much of the working class as well. Despite his making a film with Flanagan and Allen (*The Wild Boy*, 1934), the greatest dog of the period, the remarkable greyhound 'Mick the Miller', was not a household name.[80]

Dog-racing had its origins in working-class husbandry.[81] The breeding of dogs, usually whippets, and of birds, usually pigeons and canaries, had become an important activity amongst the upper working class in the later nineteenth century. The miners were particularly attached to whippet and pigeon breed-

---

[77] Figures in H. Walker, 'Lawn Tennis' in Mason, *Sport in Britain*, 250. They differ somewhat from Bale, *Sport and Place*, 94. In the early 1930s it was calculated that there were about 25,000 tennis players in Liverpool, and it was the fastest-growing sport, the only one whose facilities significantly improved after 1921. (Caradog Jones, *Merseyside*, ii. 291–2.)

[78] Holt, *Sport and the British*, 127.   [79] Bale, *Sport and Place*, 106.

[80] For Mick the Miller, see L. Thompson, *The Dogs* (London, 1994), 91–2.

[81] For dog-racing, see Zweig, *Labour, Life and Poverty*, 31–7 and *British Worker*, 154–5; S. G. Jones, 'Working Class Sport in Manchester between the Wars' in Holt, *Sport and the Working Class*, 71; Holt, *Sport and the British*, 186–7. There is an affectionate and informative account in Thompson, *The Dogs*.

ing. The whippets were usually raced. Sometimes there was 'live coursing', when the dogs would chase and often kill a hare. This was not, however, a satisfactory coursing. It was socially frowned upon and as a race rarely led to an agreed result. Since there was much betting this was an obvious disadvantage. More frequently, the dogs would be released in the direction of a man flapping a cloth. This was better than live coursing, but not much. The obvious solution—mechanical hare-coursing around an established track—was introduced in the United States in 1925. The first British stadium was opened at Belle Vue in Manchester in July 1926, constructed by Alfred Critchley and Sir William Gentle with American support. Belle Vue, White City in West London, and Walthamstow in East London became the three palaces of greyhound racing. The sport spread with extraordinary speed. By 1927 there were 5.5 million attendances at registered tracks; 13.5 million in 1928; 50 million at its peak in 1945–6, when there were 77 registered tracks. London alone had 17. Not all courses were alike. There was a first-class tier licensed by the National Greyhound Racing Club (founded in 1928 to license stadia and regulate the rules and organization of the sport) with reasonably good facilities and usually honest racing. But there was a lower tier of unlicensed tracks, the so-called 'flapper tracks', where honest racing, or honest anything, could not be guaranteed.[82]

The dogs themselves, who were increasingly bred in and imported from Ireland, thus further distancing the English sport from its origins, ran in either 'graded' or 'open' races. The great majority of dogs were 'graders' and ran in races graded to suit their capacities. Only the best dogs ran in 'open' races. It was not an adventurous sport: unlike Australia, there were few handicaps and, unlike the United States or Australia, prize money was very low, so that owners had to place bets on their own dogs. The sport consciously adopted the nomenclature and vocabulary of English horse-racing. Many of dog-racing's ten 'classics' therefore had familiar names: the Cesarewitch, the Derby, the Grand National, the Oaks, the St Leger. The English Derby, run at Wimbledon, was the high point of the racing year, and by the late 1930s about 50,000 attended it, most of whom bet on the result. Even more than horse-racing, dog-racing was unimaginable without betting.

Until the outbreak of the Second World War dog-racing was at night, and it only survived the war by moving to the afternoon. Like all sports it had a glorious year in 1946. More came and more bet more money than in any previous year. The winter of 1947–8 was, however, a disaster. Most tracks had to be closed for several months, and when they reopened the sport began to decline in popularity. By 1960 there were only 16 million attendances; in 1993 only 4 million attendances at 37 tracks, while a mere 8,000 went to the Greyhound

[82] The origin of the name 'flapper track' is uncertain. It probably came from the rag men used as a 'hare' in whippet-coursing. It may have been a derogatory reference to contemporary 'flappers'— as in the 'flappers' franchise', the 1928 legislation which enfranchised women under 30.

Derby. No sport was exempt from this decline, but dog-racing had problems peculiar to itself. It became—much more than horse-racing—associated with dishonesty and 1940s' spivery, an association emphasized both by the literature and films of the period—particularly by the so-called 'spiv films'.[83] Any sport whose *raison d'être* was betting was almost inevitably open to this criticism. Dog-racing also paid for its proletarian character and outsider status. Had the National Greyhound Racing Club the social cachet of the Jockey Club (for instance) its repute would have suffered less. The general sense of seediness was also a result of the apparent meanness of dog track life. Even the best of the courses were shabby by 1945; the 'flapper' tracks looked irreparably run-down, inhabited (it seemed) by shady bookies who presided over races of dubious probity, on whose results men and women[84] bet frantically in order to win money there was little way of spending anyway. This was a caricature, of course, but not so far from the truth as to be absurd.

Outsiders, in so far as they knew about it, often coupled speedway racing (or 'dirt-track' racing as it was sometimes called) with dog-racing, largely because the two most famous speedway tracks—Manchester Belle Vue and White City— were also two of the most famous dog tracks, and in a number of provincial towns the same tracks served both sports. There was also considerable betting on speedway, though never as much as on the dogs. In the late 1940s speedway acquired somewhat the same off-colour reputation as dog-racing—partly via Jack Lee's film *Once a Jolly Swagman* (1948), which, Raymond Durgnat wrote, did for speedway racing what *This Sporting Life* did for rugby league 20 years later.[85] In fact, speedway and the dogs had little in common. Speedway racing, particularly, had many more participants and spectators—though its popularity was subject to almost inexplicable crazes and falls. It was introduced to England from Australia in 1927 and thence exported to Scandinavia, where it was to be very popular. The first two leagues were established in 1929, with 13 clubs in the North and 12 in the South. In the 1930s it was mainly confined to the larger towns, particularly London, Birmingham, and Manchester, but expanded rapidly after 1945. In 1946, 6 million attended speedway meetings—making it second only to football as a spectator sport. By 1951 most towns had at least one track.[86] There was also a rapid increase in the number of clubs, particularly on the newer working-class estates: on the Barton estate in Oxford most new clubs were formed between 1949 and 1951.[87]

---

[83] For the 'spiv films', see below, Chapter XI.

[84] Zweig estimated that about 15% of spectators at a stadium in 1946 were women and that larger numbers of women, for whom actual attendance would not be 'respectable', bet off course. (Zweig, *Labour, Life and Poverty*, 31.)

[85] For this film, see Durgnat, *A Mirror for England*, 51–2.

[86] Bale, *Sport and Place*, 135–6; D. Robins, 'Sport and Youth Culture', in Hargreaves, *Sport, Culture and Ideology*, 138–42.

[87] Mogey, *Family and Neighbourhood*, 114–15.

The attraction of speedway was indeed its speed, and the 'thrills' that went with speed on dirt-tracks. There was also the attraction of the motor bike itself. In this period the motor bike was to the better-off working-class male as the motor car was to the better-off middle classes. To young men, especially those who lived in towns like Birmingham and Coventry, where the BSA, Norton, and Triumph machines were made, the power of the bikes was almost irresistible—though the speedway bikes themselves were stripped-down affairs designed largely for acceleration. As a sport it was highly participatory; such was its popularity that young men who did not own motor bikes would race pedal bikes in lieu.[88]

Unlike most other predominantly working-class sports, speedway attracted many women and children as spectators to the tracks. This was probably due to speedway's closeness to the family. The clubs were neighbourhood-based and their members usually well known. Furthermore, because so many young men participated, at whatever standard, families were intimately involved with the races and their results. Women came to see husbands, brothers, or sons; children to see fathers or brothers. It is also possible that many women simply found it more exciting to watch than football or rugby league and less encumbered with masculine traditions and rituals.

Boxing had an amateur and professional game and, although good amateurs often became professionals, there was little institutional association between the two.[89] Organized amateur boxing was a missionary sport brought to working-class England from the public schools via settlements, church groups and the boy scouts. The Amateur Boxing Association (ABA) had from its foundation in the 1880s held its own championships, and by the 1920s also supervised the Business Houses', Boy Scouts' and Federation of Social Clubs championships. These involved tough but carefully controlled bouts of three rounds each; the boxers often having much family and neighbourly support. The ABA's rules were adopted internationally and the Association was itself largely instrumental in having boxing established as an international and Olympic sport.

Although the participants, and even more the winners, were nearly all working-class boys or young men, the administrators of amateur boxing were nearly all middle-class or above: the prince of Wales became patron in the 1920s. Local businessmen often acted as benefactors, and club officials 'labour[ed] hard for the love of the sport'[90] since no profits were to be made, though some business goodwill might have been earned. The result was a sport

[88] Ibid.
[89] For boxing, see S. Shipley, 'Boxing' in Mason, *Sport in Britain*, 78–115; Holt, *Sport and the British*, 301–3; Jones, 'Working Class Sport in Manchester between the Wars' in Holt, *Sport and the Working Class*, 69–71.
[90] Mason, *Sport in Britain*, 86.

which consistently had a large number of enthusiastic participants, but was also under-funded and thus under-equipped. None the less, amateur boxing, because of its popularity in state schools and clubs, showed little sign of giving ground—unlike professional boxing.

Professional boxing in some form long predated amateur boxing; like horse-racing it was a sport designed for gentlemanly betting. Until 1929, when the British Boxing Board of Control was established, the sport was administered and supervised (to the extent it was) by the National Sporting Club, a body in its origins and social composition rather like the Jockey Club. Professional matches were often brutal and prolonged: it was not until the late 1920s that the American 15-round match was adopted in place of the old British 20-round contest, and not until after the Second World War that the over-boxing of professionals was relieved. There was much public and competitor opposition to the use of headguards or anything that would make the sport less dangerous and so less 'exciting'. The bloodlust of the spectators was heightened by the way most matches were fought. Before 1939 there was professional boxing every night in London and on most nights in other large towns. A majority of the bouts were held in so-called 'small halls'—cramped arenas with over-full audiences composed largely of young working-class men, where both the temperature and the temper were easily inflamed in an atmosphere made even more feverish by betting and (often) racial tension. Those who boxed in small halls were badly paid—£1.10s for a win and £1 for a loss in a six-round bout; underpayment, plus betting, made many boxers willing to 'stage' or 'throw' a match. Few made much from boxing but those who did could make a great deal: C. B. Cochran, prince of promoters, paid Tommy Milligan £3,000 to fight the American Mickey Walker at Olympia in 1927. Professional boxing was perhaps the most 'outsider' sport of all. Not only were its followers disproportionately young proletarians, it was a sport of ethnic minorities—in this period principally Jews and Irish.

Its strength among East End Jewry was due largely to the refusal of observant Jews to play football on the sabbath. Certain East End halls became known as Jewish halls and it was they who turned out that large proportion of interwar boxers who were Jewish, including two world champions: 'Kid' Lewis, who was several times world welterweight champion between 1915 and 1917 and 'Kid' Berg, who was world light welterweight champion in 1930 and 1931. The Irish community in Manchester and Liverpool also produced a disproportionate number of boxers, and their significance increased as the Jewish community gradually withdrew from boxing in the 1940s and 1950s.

English boxing reached its peak in the late 1940s and early 1950s; the precise moment probably being when Randolph Turpin, amidst great excitement, won the world middleweight title from Sugar Ray Robinson. Thereafter all was decline; at least for a generation. A large number of the best English boxers traditionally boxed in the lighter divisions—flyweight, light-welter, welter. They were small: hence the ubiquity of nicknames like 'Kid', 'Titch' or 'Nipper'. But improvements to working-class diet 'decimated' the flyweights[91] and other lighter divisions. The slow decline in the number of unskilled workers diminished the stock of heavy labouring occupations from which boxers had traditionally been drawn, while economic prosperity in the 1950s destroyed the culture of the small halls where most of the registered professional boxers had once fought. Finally, the emigration of much of the Jewish community from the inner cities to the suburbs, which had begun in the 1930s and rapidly accelerated after 1945, further reduced the number of potential professional boxers. That was to some extent also true of the English-Irish community. Increasingly, successful Irish boxers came not from England but from Ireland itself.

There was, of course, a new ethnic community developing which was increasingly to dominate both amateur and professional boxing, and to revive the fortunes of both. But until 1948 the National Sporting Club and then the Board of Control had forbidden black boxers to represent Great Britain or to hold British titles. As a result, several black boxers, were never able to fulfil their talents. By the 1960s and 1970s, however, English boxing was as dependent upon blacks as it had previously been on Jews and Irishmen.

3 | A woman's place

The history of modern English sport is largely part of the history of the modern English male, but the degree to which women were absent from it or absented themselves varied. Working-class women, both as girls and adults, were much more disfavoured than middle-class women and disfavour began at the beginning. Almost as soon as they could answer the question working-class girls declared themselves not only non-participants but actually uninterested in the country's major sports.[92] They were not, however, equally hostile to physical activity. Cycling was popular with working-class girls—and it had done as much to emancipate them physically as it had for middle-class girls. So was swimming, which the majority of town-dwelling girls considered one of their favourite summer pastimes.[93] Netball, where possible, was also liked and was the only team sport played by significant numbers of working-class girls. But working-class girls in practice had little opportunity to play 'girls' sports' like netball or tennis, because council schools rarely provided the facilities. School provision slowly improved but municipal provision was patchy. Girls clubs did their best, but that was frequently not enough and too few girls belonged to

---

[91] Ibid. 107.
[92] K. E. McCrone, *Sport and the Physical Emancipation of Women* (London, 1988), 239.
[93] Ward, *Children Out of School*, 41.

them. Absence of provision was not, however, the only problem: all 'girls' sports', regardless of social class, were thought inferior unless, like tennis or golf, they were played by men as well. The difference was that the hostility to girls playing sport of any kind was much stronger in the working class than in the middle. The Football Association, for example, banned women's football in 1921—ostensibly to prevent the commercial exploitation of women; in fact to stop women playing a 'man's game' whose social prestige depended upon its remaining a man's game.[94] The three most powerful figures in a working-class girl's life—her Gran, her Mum and her husband—all disliked women playing sport and often did their best to stop it.[95]

The sporting experience of non-working-class women was more complicated. They were much more likely, for instance, to play organized sport at school. The tendency of both girls' independent and grammar schools to base their curricula on that of similar boys' schools extended to sport. Sport did not dominate them as it did the boys. But it almost did. Girls were expected to play netball, hockey, lacrosse, increasingly athletics, and perhaps tennis or cricket, and the heartily masculine tone adopted by many sportsmistresses was an educational and gender cliché:

Nor shall we easily forget [Roy Lewis and Angus Maude wrote in the 1940s] the experience of hearing from beyond the wall of a girls' school, amid the scuffle of a basket-ball game, the cool, brisk voice of feminine authority: 'Now, Cynthia, they are pressing the attack. If I were you, I should be cunning. I should put my men *here* and throw the ball *there*...[96]

The girls' grammar schools, furthermore, were much influenced by the tradition of Swedish gymnastics popularized in England by Per Henrik Ling and Mme Bergman-Osterberg. The colleges of physical education where Swedish gymnastics was taught, and later the German variants introduced by Rudolf Laban when he migrated to England in 1938, had no male equivalent. The graduates of the colleges were very influential in the girls' grammar schools but much less so in the elementary or secondary modern schools.[97] The popularity of girls' gymnastics in turn encouraged in the 1930s those movements, like the Women's League of Health and Beauty or the Keep Fit Movement, which promoted the ideal of women's athletic fitness and were an important element in middle-class culture.

Few upper- or middle-class women maintained much of an interest in hockey or lacrosse after they left school but there were a number of sports which it was entirely acceptable for them to play. Women could hunt (both on

[94] Fishwick, *English Football*, 17.

[95] C. Griffin *et al.*, 'Women and Leisure' in Hargreaves, *Sport, Culture and Ideology*, 95.

[96] Lewis and Maude, *The English Middle Classes*, 241.

[97] S. Fletcher, 'The Making and Breaking of a Female Tradition: Women's Physical Education in England, 1880–1980', in J. A. Mangan and R. J. Park (eds.), *From 'Fair Sex' to Feminism* (London, 1987).

horse and foot) and participate fully in equestrianism; they could game-fish—the duchess of York (later Queen Elizabeth) became one of the country's best-known game fishermen; they could sail, and two women, Frances Revell-Carnac (1906) and Dorothy Wright (1920) won Olympic gold medals in 7-metre yachting—both crewing with their husbands. The social acceptability of women as pioneer aviators, like Jean Batten or Amy Johnson, or even as motor racers (both aviation and motor racing being essentially upper-class-plutocratic sports) was probably the same phenomenon.

Women could play cricket, tennis, or golf and, of course, much middle-class sociability depended upon their doing so. It is here that the sporting life of working-class women differed most: there was no working-class equivalent of social tennis or social golf—sports where the participation of women was not only permissible but necessary. But in none of these sports were women admitted as equals, and in some they were thought no better than working men or professionals. Of them all, tennis most approached gender equality. Tennis was so central to middle-class sociability that a rough equality was inevitable. The competitive acceptability of women's tennis had been established in the nineteenth century and the All-England mixed doubles championship hooked competitive women's tennis on to men's. This really was important since it allowed the Frenchwoman Suzanne Lenglen to appear at and win the Wimbledon women's singles title in 1919 and 1920.

Lenglen was probably the most influential sportswoman of the interwar years, largely because she violated nearly all the contemporary stereotypes of the sportswoman. She appeared at Wimbledon in 1919 in a calf-length pleated skirt, which gave her a freedom of movement hitherto denied women tennis players. She was also dramatic; ebullient at a time when reticence was the prevailing female sporting mode. From the famous chiffon *bandeau* and the bobbed hair she wore at Wimbledon in 1920 to the restorative flasks of cognac her father hurled on to the court during play, Lenglen presented a carefully constructed persona which effaced that of her male contemporaries. The All-England courts, indeed, were moved to Church Road partly because the old stands could not cope with the numbers who wanted to see her. She was doubly important for women's sports: she created a style of dress which, besides being enormously fashionable, was emancipatory, and she established the precedent of a powerful and successful female sporting personality. Both were made possible by the comparative gender-equality of tennis. But it was only comparative. They could take virtually no part in the administration of the sport, and in competition women played only the best of three sets (as they do still) instead of the best of five; and that carried with it, in the guise of physical frailty, the clear implication of inferiority.

Yet tennis did not practise the outright exclusions common in other women's sports. Of these, golf was most like tennis. The development of handicapping made possible the 'mixed foursomes' which became increasingly popular in social golf. Some men's clubs began to admit women as 'associates', though often with no more standing than the club professional. The match organized by Prince's in 1938—Prince's Ladies (of whom one was Lady Astor) against Prince's 'Artisans'—was a revealing allocation of women in the social hierarchy of golf.[98] Nearly all the first rank of clubs in England and Scotland remained closed to women; including Muirfield, where Britain first won the Curtis Cup (the women's equivalent of the Ryder Cup), which neither admitted women as members nor allowed either of the two Curtis Cup teams any use of the club's facilities. Otherwise women's golf remained segregated. The Ladies Golf Union, founded in 1893, organized the women's clubs quite independently of men's golf.

The two other major women's sports, athletics and cricket, had no institutional attachment to the men's sports and both, particularly athletics, existed despite open hostility from the men's organizations. There was hardly any women's athletics in England before 1914. The first competitive events were organized by the services in 1918 and 1919, and the first Women's Amateur Athletic Association championship held in 1923. The popularity of women's athletics is probably related to the popularity of women's gymnastics and female athleticism more generally, to a reluctant admission by doctors that women's athleticism was not necessarily medically harmful, and to a post-war emphasis upon slimness, boyishness, and physical energy as desirable female attributes. Like gymnastics, women's athletics had close connections with certain colleges and universities, particularly Kensington Borough Polytechnic, Regent Street Polytechnic, Woolwich Polytechnic, and Manchester University, and their graduates promoted athletics as they did gymnastics.

The AAA had not concealed its opposition to women's athletics. It had voted against the introduction of women's events at the 1928 Olympics and opposed any kind of institutional integration with women's athletics in England. The WAAA was itself understandably nervous about integration. Mrs V. Searle, formerly the WAAA 440-yards champion, said in 1928 that

We strongly object to the mixing up of men and women in the Olympic Games or at any other meeting. If this actually happened it would kill our movement, and we should be absorbed by the men as in other countries. In England we have nothing to do with the AAA; we are entirely a separate body.[99]

Although English women did participate in the 1932 Olympics they unsuccessfully opposed the amalgamation of the *Fédération sportive féminine internationale* and the International Amateur Athletic Association in 1936. Given the widely known views of the AAA, anything else would have been surprising.

The WAAA thereby secured a certain freedom for women's athletics which

[98] Lowerson in Mason, *Sport in Britain*, 207.   [99] Ibid. 63.

an integrated male-dominated body would probably have denied it. It spread rapidly in the schools (including some of the elementary schools). The first schools' championship was held in 1925, and the popular press, detecting newsworthiness, supported inter-club competition. By the mid-1920s the WAAA had 23,000 members. No other woman's sport could claim such growth.

Many fewer played women's cricket. Some women had played cricket before 1914 but, like athletics, it was essentially a product of the 1920s, popularized by women who wanted a summer alternative to hockey and lacrosse, which were usually winter games. It had grown enough for the Women's Cricket Association to be founded in 1926. Its geography was much the same as men's cricket, but there was little development after its early expansion.[100] Although it was viable as a game, it was always a minor sport. It received little press support—even internationals were not much reported. In fact, women's place in cricket was more usually ancillary or social—making afternoon tea or organizing fêtes. Perhaps 20 per cent of cricket club members were women but they had the same status as 'associates' in golf; and they had to face many of the same taboos.

4 | Betting

Betting was absolutely central to English sport and the place sport had in the national culture is inexplicable unless we accept that. For millions of Englishmen and (increasingly) women sport was not only an occasion to admire physical skill or athletic competitiveness, it was an occasion to bet. And for many the bet was more important than the sport.[101]

Not everyone, however, bet; nor did gamblers bet on every sport. Who bet and on what depended on several things: social class, religious adherence, the nature of the sport, the facilities available for betting. There were some sports, like greyhound-racing, which existed for and by betting. But greyhound-racing was overwhelmingly a proletarian sport, and that is suggestive. Broadly speaking, any sport which provided good opportunities for betting and was popular with the working class would be the subject of betting. Thus people would bet on crown bowls (but almost certainly not on lawn bowls), angling, football, horse- greyhound- and pigeon-racing, boxing and rugby league. There was little betting on rugby union, tennis and other racquet sports and comparatively little on cricket. Rugby union and tennis were almost wholly middle-class, and the middle classes rarely betted on sport. Cricket's status is more complicated. It had a great working-class following, but also a great upper- and

[100] Bale, *Sport and Place*, 89.
[101] There is now a substantial scholarly literature on modern betting. See particularly, C. Chinn, *Better Betting with a Decent Feller* (London, 1991); M. Clapson, *A Bit of a Flutter: Popular Gambling and English Society, c.1823–1961* (Manchester, 1992); Dixon, *From Prohibition to Regulation* (cited Chapter VIII).

middle-class following. And amateurs set the tone: there was a certain cultural exclusivity about cricket which may have deterred betting. Yet licensed book-makers would certainly offer odds on first-class cricket, and particularly on tests. The tone perhaps deterred working-class punters, but clearly there was at least some betting on cricket.

The 'tone', however, was not the only deterrent to betting on cricket. Like all sports involving just two competitors the better was unlikely to get good odds. Thus while there was heavy betting on boxing or wrestling around the ring, it was highly localized, a product of the intense but narrow sporting culture of the 'small halls'. What the average punter demanded was good odds—or its equivalent—and ease of betting. It was these which made horse-race betting and the football pools so attractive.

Mass betting on horses was well established by the end of the nineteenth century. Horse-racing was not unlike greyhound-racing: although some owners bred for the honour of winning and the competitive pleasure of the race, horse-racing could not have survived without betting. Even when the race was a 'match'—one gentleman betting his horse against another's—betting was the rationale. The introduction of handicapping made betting on horses even more interesting and potentially remunerative, since the return on outlay if the bet were successful was greatly magnified. The handicap, indeed, was ideally suited to a small bet.

A large and sophisticated industry was constructed to meet the demands of the small better. A press with a huge circulation told him (more rarely her) what he needed to know to make an informed bet; an army of tipsters was at hand to assist him further; and, above all, in most pubs and clubs, in nearly every factory or workshop and on the streets of every working-class com-munity there was a bookmaker with whom he could make that bet. There was only one problem: it was illegal.

The law on betting was not a sound edifice, constructed as it was on the shaky foundation of statute law, judge-made law and municipal by-law. Nev-ertheless, by this period the legal conventions governing betting were fairly clear and generally accepted. Credit-betting off-course with licensed book-makers was legal; ready-money betting on course was legal—which is why greyhound-racing was so popular; cash betting off-course was illegal. Since the vast majority of bets were for cash off-course the vast majority of bets were illegal. Though illegal, however, there was nothing secret about street betting: it was one of the most distinctive features of English town-life, observable to anyone. The street bookies did make some attempt at concealment, employing 'watchers' either as decoys or alarms; but the police had little difficulty in making arrests if they wanted to. The ubiquity and illegality of the bookie made social life for the police difficult. To maintain any kind of social relations, for example, a policeman-member of a workingman's club had to ignore the criminality which pullulated all around him. Which is why the police tended to have their own clubs or simply socialize together.

The other principal instrument of mass betting was the football pool. Although there had been some betting on football by coupon before 1914, the modern football pool was a product of the interwar years. A number of companies operated pools but it was largely the genius of John Moores, the founder of Littlewood's, which established the football pool as a fact of English social life. Moores first saw the possibilities of mail-order betting when employed as a telegraphist at the Commercial Cable Company, which he joined as a 16-year-old. He introduced his first pool in 1923, using boys to distribute forms at football matches. The subsequent police prosecution, which was quashed in the appeal court, gave him the necessary publicity to found the Littlewood's pool company[102]—though the main responsibility for running the organization fell to his brother, Cecil, when John became chairman of Everton Football Club.

Like the handicap, the pool offered betters (or 'investors' as the pools' operators preferred to call them) good odds with considerable variety. The legal status of the pools was uncertain. Moores had originally been prosecuted under the Ready Money Betting Act; but that action failed. Throughout the 1920s several more legal attempts were made on the pools which the operators ingeniously fended off. The result was that the pools were not so much legal as not illegal; and there they remained. The greatest threat, in fact, was not the law but the Football League.[103]

Who bet on sports? And in what numbers? Before the Second World War no reliable figures were available, except for the pools.[104] Although many people offered numbers they were usually only guesses, more or less uninformed. In the light of survey evidence from the late 1940s, together with anecdotally informed hunches, it seems reasonable to conclude that about 4 million people bet regularly on horses and perhaps double that number—those who liked a 'flutter'—less frequently.

How many bet on greyhounds is also difficult to discover. Given the ease of access to the tracks it is unlikely that there was much off-course betting on dogs: the number of attendances, therefore, was probably close to the number of betters. But dog-racing was for serious betters; and they went regularly.[105] The total number of attendances enormously inflates in the total of those who actually bet on dogs. After the war, for example, while 44 per cent of adult men were found to bet on horses, only 4.1 per cent bet on dogs. The number of *individuals* attending dog-races was probably no more than about half a million. Many of them presumably also bet on horses.

---

[102] Littlewood was the middle name of one of his early partners.
[103] See below, p. 377.
[104] I have attempted to calculate overall numbers in *Ideologies of Class*, 109–10.
[105] For a grim picture of dog-track betting in the late 1940s, see Zweig, *Labour, Life and Poverty*, 32–7.

We have more accurate figures for the pools. By the late 1930s about
10 million people were on the operators' books and about one-third of the
whole population at some time returned coupons. By 1950 that figure was
probably closer to half. In the mining town of Featherstone, a place where gambling 'dominates almost every form of leisure activity', 6,000 to 7,000 coupons
were delivered weekly in a town of 14,000 people—that is, on average, at
least one per household.[106] Featherstone was not representative of the entire
country, but these figures do suggest why the broadcaster John Hilton called
the pools 'one of the most momentous happenings of our time'.[107] Furthermore, many of the coupons were completed by women and often *en famille*.
Wednesday night was frequently the one 'family night' since that was the
night the pools were done. The pools, therefore, represented many working
women's only access to sport.

The total number of betters cannot be computed by the simple addition of
pools betters plus horse-race betters plus dog-race betters, since many bet on
more than one sport and the numbers who bet on sports like crown bowls or
angling are unknown, but it is safe to conclude that the number of regular
betters was between 10 and 15 million.

The large majority of those who bet on sport were almost certainly working
class. In the nineteenth century there was much upper-class betting on horses,
particularly by owners for whom horse-racing was not otherwise profitable. By
the turn of the century it was assumed by the upper classes themselves that
this had largely stopped. Indeed, betting by owners was tacitly discouraged by
the Jockey Club. In the interwar years this probably remained true, although
there is evidence of 'plunging' (and of large winnings) by syndicates of
owners—usually not top-drawer. But even if, which is unlikely, most owners
did bet, the number of upper-class betters as a proportion of the whole can only
have been small, particularly as racing became increasingly marginal to their
interests. Credit betting (that is, legal betting) did, it is true, sustain the liveli-
hoods of a considerable number of licensed bookmakers, and anecdotal evidence suggests that in clubland many had recourse to them. But there appears
to have been no significant betting on 'middle-class' sports; the more 'middle-
class' a community, the fewer were the pools coupons delivered, and street
betting did not take place in leafy avenues. The 1949 Royal Commission found
a clear negative relationship between middle- and upper-class incomes and the
propensity of their earners to bet. Above all, the opportunities for cultural and
intellectual expression were so much wider for the middle classes than for the
working classes that betting either as an economic and intellectual activity
was for them a very low-order attraction.

How much did people bet on sport? This was always worried about in the

---

[106] Dennis *et al.*, *Coal is Our Life*, 159.   [107] Hilton, *Rich Man, Poor Man*, 122–3.

non-betting classes. But, although doubtless some working men did bet 'to the point of ruin', there was little evidence that many working men or women bet beyond small sums. Police witnesses, who repeatedly, if reluctantly, agreed that sums expended on betting were normally only small, were often not believed by outsiders, as this exchange between the chairman of the 1932 Royal Commission on Betting and the chief constable of Manchester suggests:

[Chairman] When you say 6d or 1s you do not surely mean only 6d a week?

[Chief Constable] It will depend on the programmes that are being run. If there is any local or popular race during the week, it may happen two or three times during the week perhaps.

[Chairman] It seems to me unlikely that a man will have only 6d bet?

[Chief Constable] Yes, during the season they probably bet more heavily than at ordinary times; but during the winter time the football betting is once a week . . .

[Chairman] Do you put it as 6d or 1s a week for the average better?

[Chief Constable] Yes, I should think it would be about that; 6d up to 2s a week.

[Chairman] It seems an extremely low figure, and totally against anything I have ever heard of?

[Chief Constable] Wages are so low.[108]

Throughout the interwar years the average bet was probably between 6d and 2s a week; bookies were surprised if it reached half-a-crown. The poorest were thought to bet least, the skilled working class most. This was true even after the Second World War when money wages were significantly higher and unemployment almost non-existent. The survey undertaken for the 1949 Royal Commission on Betting and Gambling strongly implied that most working-class betting was a regular but a small item in the weekly expenditure;[109] one that households could 'afford'.[110]

Why did people bet on sport? In part, they bet for the reasons people have always betted—for the physical and psychological excitement a bet inevitably generates. This was important, but is itself an insufficient explanation. Many bet, particularly women, in the hope of modest financial gain. John Martin, who wrote the section on gambling in the *New Survey of London*, thought many bet 'because they want a specific object, to buy a gramophone, or to buy a wireless set, or to go for a holiday'.[111] When the broadcaster John Hilton invited his listeners to tell him why they did the pools, he was struck by how many wanted household acquisitions: 'If I won bigger money, I should go in for a new house, which would be built to our own idea, so that we could get a better scullery.'[112] People seem rarely to have envisaged winnings going on anything unfamiliar

[108] Royal Commission on Lotteries and Betting, 1932–3, *Minutes of Evidence*, QQ 801–9, at p. 16.

[109] Source: W. F. F. Kemsley and D. Ginsburg, *Betting in Britain* (Central Office of Information, NS 710/4, London, 1951), 11.

[110] During the depression, however, these customary small bets might have been too big.

[111] Royal Commission on Lotteries and Betting, *Minutes of Evidence*, 1932–3 Q 2092, at p. 144.

[112] J. Hilton, *Why I go in for the Pools* (London, 1936), 26.

or spectacular. What distinguished English betting, however, was its markedly intellectual character. Betting, particularly regular betting by men, was designed to eliminate luck from the bet.[113] The enormous apparatus of English betting was based upon 'systems' and knowledge. If a man were adequately informed he could make an informed bet; if he were informed he was—it was thought—more likely to win. The urge to systematize betting and to acquire the appropriate knowledge explains the endless discussion of form both at work and during leisure hours. This also explains the appeal of tipsters and all those who claimed to know the latest from the horse's mouth: they possessed the secrets and, for a consideration, would impart them. The belief that there was in betting a rationality which could be apprehended was perhaps characteristic of Anglo-Saxon betting as a whole. As one American scholar wrote of a group of American working men: they all assumed that in betting there was 'an underlying order, a principle that can be figured out and mastered by a skilled observer'.[114]

The assumption of the 'underlying order' was also applied to the pools. How far skill and knowledge can in fact determine winnings on the pools, or even minimize losses, is conjectural. Nevertheless, the amount of time people in the 1930s and 1940s spent poring over form and guides suggests they brought to the pools the same intellectual and systematizing techniques brought to horse-race betting. It was a system of knowledge potentially open to all working men.

Those who bet on sport were not necessarily interested in sport as such. Hilton found that many of his respondents were only 'interested in *results*, because the results may mean that they are one of the 67 who have won £124 each.'[115] The Pilgrim Trust concluded of the unemployed that betting did not necessarily involve a 'direct interest in sport, but it derives from that and gives glamour to everything and everybody that has to do with sport'.[116] But for a working man in this period it would have been difficult to have bet on anything other than sport, while the centrality of sport within working-class culture encouraged an intellectualized betting, because it was one of the few areas of working-class life where an overt intellectualism was socially permitted. Furthermore, the intellectual satisfactions of 'rational' betting, far from being antithetical to the physical and psychological excitements of gambling, were an essential part of them.

Almost as sensitive an issue as sexual morality, people found it as difficult to hold coherent views on betting as they did on sex. Class was a powerful

---

[113] I have discussed this in more detail elsewhere. See *The Ideologies of Class*, 119–24.

[114] I. K. Zola, 'Observations on Gambling in a Lower-Class Setting', in R. D. Herman (ed.), *Gambling* (New York, 1967), 26.

[115] Hilton, *Why I go in for the Pools*, 12.

[116] Pilgrim Trust, *Men without Work*, 99–100.

determinant of what they did and believed, but Protestantism was probably even more powerful. Of the population generally, a nonconformist of whatever class was most likely to oppose gambling; a 'secularist' of whatever class was least likely to oppose it. But a 'secular' working man was much more likely to bet than a 'secular' member of the middle classes. In turn, this meant that the state's official view of betting, that it was destructive of the moral and financial welfare of the working class, was strong enough to obstruct the legalization of off-course betting throughout this period, but, since there was no ideological consensus about betting, too weak to do much else—particularly, to suppress street betting, or even seriously to try. In the meantime, the police continued their fitful efforts to eliminate off-course betting, knowing that they were futile, made them hated by many working men and were the result of class-biased legislation, while the post office did its best to frustrate these efforts so that the huge revenues it earned from both legal and illegal betting should not be interrupted.

With the exception of horse and dog-racing, where the authorities could scarcely object to it, most of those who administered the country's major sports intensely disliked betting. They took their stand not just on the 'official' view, but also on something closely related to it, the amateur code. In most sports this mattered little; in football, however, it mattered a great deal. So hostile to betting were football administrators that in February 1936 the League attempted to destroy the pools by suppressing advanced publication of its fixture lists, so making preparation of the coupons impossible. Thus began the 'pools' war' on 22 February 1936. The League's action was a mistake: in face of a 'popular revolt' and a threatened boycott of matches the League gave in ('Result: League 0–Pools 1', wrote the *Oxford Times*), taking refuge in what was to be yet another failed parliamentary attempt on the pools.[117] It was a foolish and mean-minded episode, but demonstrated yet again how isolated from its popular following were so many of the administrators of English sport.

5 | *England and the wider world*

Throughout this period one of the striking features of English sport was the decline in its international competitiveness. Since every major international sport, with the exception of basketball, was English (or, in the case of golf, British) in origin; since, therefore, England had enormous advantages in experience and tradition, such decline was for the English surprising and depressing. Furthermore, the decline was obvious in all sports, though most marked in those played in the Olympic Games. In 1920 Britain won 13 gold medals in the Olympics; in 1948 and 1952 one. The 13 gold medals won in 1920 were in a

---

[117] Fishwick, *English Football*, 130.

broad range of sports, including the (last) tug-of-war. Thereafter most of the few gold medals were in athletics, topped up by oddities like the victory in 1936 of the ice-hockey team—most of whom were Canadians. But given the centrality of athletics and swimming in the Games and the extent to which both sports were popular in England/Britain, the comparative failure even in these is striking. In 1920 four gold medals were won in athletics; in 1948 and 1952 none. Apart from Lucy Morton's victory in the 200-metre breaststroke in 1924, Britain was wholly uncompetitive in swimming. All the athletics gold medals were won by men. Despite the large number of British girls who competed in organized athletics none won a gold medal in the three Olympics in which they competed. Areas of traditional strength, middle-distance running particularly, prospered intermittently; elsewhere, however, the decline seemed irreversible. In most other Olympic sports, with individual exceptions like the outstanding sculler Jack Beresford Jr, Britain was scarcely in the competition. Astonishingly, given the popularity of riding in its army and the landed classes, it failed to win a gold medal in any Olympic equestrian event until Colonel Harry Llewellyn saved the nation's honour in 1952.

Even sports like tennis and football, in which England had considerable success in the interwar years, suddenly collapsed. The Davis Cup was won in 1933, 1934, 1935, and 1936; Fred Perry won Wimbledon in 1934, 1935, and 1936 and 'Bunny' Austin was runner-up in 1932 and 1936. English women players won the Weightman Cup (the competition between Britain and the United States) in 1924, 1925, 1928, and 1930; Kitty Godfree won Wimbledon in 1924 and 1926 and Dorothy Round in 1934 and 1937; Betty Nuthall was runner-up in the United States in 1930 and France in 1931. But these successes depended on a small number of outstanding individuals. England was never again to win the Davis Cup and Fred Perry was the last Englishman to win Wimbledon. Indeed, he and Austin were the last to reach a final.

In football England had some international success in the interwar years, including winning the crucial match against Germany in 1938. Since, however, it was for much of the time not a member of FIFA (*Fédération internationale des Football-Associations*) and declined to play in the World Cup it is uncertain how competitive it really was. Scotland won a majority of the home internationals in the interwar years and it is perhaps as well for the prestige of English football that it did not face the formidable Latin American sides. How routinized English football was became clear after 1945: a series of shaming defeats (including one by the United States in the 1950 World Cup) which culminated in the famous lost match against Hungary in 1953.

In sports where the movement was more cyclical, the balance lay against England: on balance the New Zealanders and South Africans were better at rugby; on balance the Australians were better at cricket. In golf, despite Henry Cotton, the balance had tipped irrecoverably to the United States.

Why did this happen? Why was the country which more or less invented modern sport so soon surpassed by its pupils? Strict purists argued the question was not worth asking: sport was for the playing not the winning. That was, however, in practice not the view the English took. These defeats caused much anguish at all levels, and contemporaries themselves freely offered explanations and excuses. Furthermore, answers to the question tell us much about English society, its social behaviour and its predominant social codes.

It was always argued that the United States and the white dominions were particularly favoured by wealth, climate, and general living standards as against England. This is obviously true of the United States; given its size and resources England could not hope to compete with it on equal terms in sport or anything else. The white dominions probably were favoured by climate and standard of living; but their populations were much smaller and the resources they brought to sport certainly no greater. More pointedly, England was increasingly unable to compete with countries favoured neither by climate nor wealth and in whose national culture sport had traditionally been much less important.

It was also argued that a move from formal sport to more informal and socially casual activities, particularly in the 1930s, weakened competitive sport in England. Both the middle and working classes, for example, took up cycling and hiking enthusiastically. By the mid-1930s 1.5 million cycles were being sold annually, and one of the great sights of the English weekend were the fleets of cyclists riding countrywards along the arterial roads of the major towns. Some belonged to clubs; others were simply groups of friends. There were as many young women as men: another of its undoubted attractions.

The popularity of hiking was closely related to this new informality. By the late 1930s there were about 500,000 regular walkers and nearly 300 youth hostels. Membership of the Youth Hostel Association had risen from 6,000 in 1934 to 83,000 in 1939. The growth of hiking was the result of several influences: an increasingly pervasive urban view of rurality—that of the countryside as a recreational resource; keep-fit movements and the fashion for sunbathing; the craze for 'naturism'; institutions like the Women's League of Health and Beauty and the Co-op's version of the scouts and guides, the Woodcraft Folk; to some degree the scouting movement itself.[118]

The huge numbers of cyclists and hikers were of the age groups from which sportsmen and women were normally drawn and who, in other circumstances, might have played cricket or football, run, or swum. There is thus probably some truth to the argument that what cycling or hiking gained competitive sport lost. How much it lost is, however, questionable. The popularity of cycling and hiking was international, partly owing its inspiration in

[118] J. Hargreaves, *Sport, Power and Culture* (London and Cambridge, 1986), 87.

England to the example of Germany and Scandinavia, where cycling and hiking accompanied the development of organized sport rather than constituting alternatives.

More convincing explanations for the competitiveness weakness of English sport are essentially 'political': its excessive voluntarism and the social codes of those who governed it. The voluntarism of English sport was once the pride of the English and reflected its nineteenth-century origins. But it was a decaying ideology and throughout this period its proponents consistently exaggerated its efficacy.[119] The state was not uninterested in sport, especially in the late 1930s when the sporting success of Germany and Italy was embarrassing. The English football team which beat Germany in 1938 was very much put together and trained under foreign office pressure. The National Fitness Council was established in 1937 with power to make financial grants to voluntary organizations. But it was small beer and presaged little. The Attlee government, for instance, gave no assistance to the British team for the 1948 Olympics even though the Games were held in London.

Against the passivity of the state contemporaries set the increasing strength of works-based sport. From the 1920s on many of the larger and newer English firms began to provide sporting facilities for their employees. Individual firms had long been associated with sporting teams, but these were usually only casual ties which rarely involved much active assistance. Business welfare sport—formally known as Business House Sport—was very different. The facilities provided by employers were often lavish: the Merseyside firm of J. Bilby and Sons provided 75 acres of grounds, including five football, two hockey and two cricket pitches, four tennis courts, and a bowling green. This provision, though generous, was not exceptional. Many of the motor car and engineering plants in the South were similarly equipped. By the early 1950s much of the country's recreational sport, particularly football and cricket, was unquestionably works-based and without a works-based 'infrastructure' several of the country's major sports, as popular activities, would probably have disintegrated.

There were, however, two difficulties with business welfare sport. First, it was not 'neutral', not designed just for the pleasure of the workforce. The works clubs were rarely, if ever, independent and it was no secret that their main function was to encourage loyalty to firms. Employees were, therefore, often uneasy about works sports: they were suspicious of the firm's motives and feared their mates' disapproval. Yet it was often works sports or none at all, but with all the disadvantages of the *faute de mieux*. Second, though the firms provided 'facilities' they provided little else, and could hardly be expected to. Works teams were still heavily dependent on their members

---

[119] See Fishwick's comments on voluntarism in football, *English Football*, 11.

financially and on their willingness to give up time and energy. Even with the support of business British sport remained under-funded and under-supported.

As a result of the unwillingness of the state, or any other external authority, to intervene as an agent of social change, most sports continued to be administered by male self-recruiting corporations. What had once been customary, *ad hoc* rights—like those of the MCC or the Jockey Club—had by the twentieth century become an institutionalized authority used, and quite deliberately, in an almost wholly undemocratic manner. The MCC, the Jockey Club, the Football Association, the Lawn Tennis Association, the AAA, etc. were all governed by men with little sympathy for the democratic impulses of English life. In administering their sports they practised a social exclusion and social inhibition whose legitimating ideology was the amateur code.

We have seen how universal was social exclusion within English sport. In cricket and golf distinctions between amateur and professional were rigidly enforced; in football the players were at the bottom of the heap and the supporters, if possible, even lower; tennis was riddled with snobbery; athletics and rowing solved their social problems simply by excluding the working class altogether. Everything was done by sporting élites to promote social harmony by the exclusion of those whose background was not 'quite right' and who might not 'fit in'. In cricket, golf, and even football, those who might not fit in were simply decanted into a different area of the sport altogether. Social exclusion ineradicably marked sport at home; but it also had international consequences. Fred Perry, for instance, felt excluded and did not conceal it. As the son of Sam Perry, the Labour MP for Kettering, for whom the young Fred actively campaigned, his background was certainly not quite right. 'A young man', he wrote, 'was bound to feel that snobbery very keenly and I still get very angry about the shabby way I was treated when I won Wimbledon in 1934.'[120] Perry then excluded himself by migrating to America and taking American citizenship. It was utterly characteristic of English cricket that a highly competitive (if unethical) and successful strategy like 'bodyline' bowling should have ended as a demeaning episode in the history of the English caste system which did more damage to English cricket than anyone else's.[121]

---

[120] F. Perry, *An Autobiography* (London, 1984), 10–11.

[121] 'Bodyline' bowling (or 'fast leg theory' as it was euphemistically known), was devised by the England captain, Douglas Jardine, for the 1932–3 Ashes against Australia in order to curb the prodigious genius of Don Bradman; and he had in Harold Larwood, probably the fastest bowler of the era, just the man to do it. 'Bodyline' was, broadly speaking, a way of bowling such that the batsman was either bowled out while trying to avoid the ball or caught out if he used his bat to defend himself against it. The latter was rendered likely by new ways of placing the fielders. England won the Ashes and 'bodyline' was probably decisive; though since Larwood was always ferocious on Australian pitches, England might have won anyway. The practice caused tremendous ill-will, though the MCC was reluctant to acknowledge that. In the long term, of course, leg theory was intolerable since it would, if persisted in, have literally brought cricket to its knees. The MCC recognized this and, both

The social comfort purchased by exclusion was furthered by inhibition. Competitive play was discouraged in favour of social compatibility; anything which disrupted sociability, like over-competitiveness, was deprecated. This was an extension into sport of the apolitical sociability which, as we have noted,[122] was increasingly governing middle-class social relationships: a sociability whose primary characteristic was inhibition. The working-class idea of sport was, however, socially competitive. In working-class sport '[competition] goes on full blast . . . it restores the atrophied parts of the [the worker's] body and his mind.'[123] Mutuality was not absent; much working-class sociability occurred within sporting associations. But the wish to win was strong, the emphasis upon social harmony weaker, the adherence to the rules of the game less enthusiastic, and the spectators more frankly partisan. Even the word 'sport', always the working-class usage, implied differences: middle-class 'boys' played 'games'; working-class 'lads' played 'sport'. 'Games' suggested a certain carelessness; 'sport' a seriousness of purpose.

The amateur code justified both exclusion and inhibition. Since those who might not fit in were more likely to be professionals, amateurism justified their partial or complete exclusion. Since they were also more likely to be competitive, and hence disruptive of a social harmony based upon inhibition, amateurism again justified their partial exclusion. The imposition, as rules for sporting behaviour, of exclusion and inhibition undermined the creativity and spontaneity of English sport: it too became exclusive and inhibited. Perry believed that one of the reasons he was unpopular was because the Wimbledon crowds 'had never really seen an Englishman of this era who didn't like to lose'.[124]

Cultural insularity was not unrelated to inhibition, and the principal victim of this was probably the competitiveness of English football. Throughout the period English football regarded the rest of the world at best ambiguously: its fretful relations with FIFA; the constant resignations and rows; the contemptuous refusal to participate in the first World Cup in 1930;[125] the reluctance to

---

publicly and via a rule-change, repudiated it. Jardine flounced out of the game, though pretty much on his own terms. Larwood, however, was asked to sign a statement apologizing for what he had done in Australia. This he refused to do. He was never picked for England again. Larwood, a professional from a Nottinghamshire mining family, had no doubt that he was a victim of the English social system. And indeed it is hard to believe that had he been, as was Jardine, an amateur and a Wykehamist, he would have been treated like that. It was this sense of betrayal that finally brought him (with the assistance of two Australian prime ministers, J. B. Chifley and R. G. Menzies), *mirabile dictu*, to migrate to Australia in April 1950. (For Larwood's views, see Larwood and Perkins, *Larwood Story*; for 'bodyline' see L. Le Quesne, *The Bodyline Controversy* (London, 1983) and P. Derriman, *Bodyline* (Melbourne, 1984).)

[122] See above, pp. 95–8.   [123] Zweig, *British Worker*, 125–6.
[124] Perry, *An Autobiography*, 10–11.
[125] The letter of refusal from the secretary of the FA, Sir Frederick Wall, read:
　　　Dear Sir,
　　　　The letter of the 10th ultimo from the Asociacion Uruguaya De Football inviting a Representative Team of the Football Association to visit Uruguay in July and August next to play

accept rule changes which it did not initiate; even the baggy bloomers worn by the English players—all these were part of an introverted sporting culture which could not compete with the rest of the world when England did enter it seriously after 1945. That the glory of English football lay in the clubs and not the national sides was a defence frequently offered by football's authorities when pressed to explain the failure of an English team. It is true that English football was very club-centred, but it was a defence which was tested when the Europeans, in part to expose it, established the European Cup in 1955—and it was 12 years before an English side won that Cup. Football, however, as an English sport was not alone in its plight.

The reason for the comparative failure of English women's sport is probably more complicated. It has been argued that the 'femininity' of successful sporting women could be questioned; that women were, therefore, reluctant to be over-competitive. This probably has some truth; and the comparative failure of white American women in sports, particularly in 'un-feminine' ones like athletics, lends more support to this argument. But it was not the case in Australia or New Zealand, where, if true, the argument should be equally true. Furthermore, there were different ideals of femininity: the 'athletic woman', slim of build and vigorous of step, is an English invention, largely a product of the girls' public schools. Likelier is that English women suffered even more from exclusion and inhibition than men: working-class girls were almost completely excluded from sport by cultural pressure and were themselves often hostile to it. Middle- and upper-class girls, though encouraged to play sport, in playing it were subject to tighter constrictions than men. It was then in the nature of things that sociability and harmony were thought more desirable for women even than for men; and competition less. The outcome was comparatively uncompetitive sport.

Throughout this period the popularity of the great spectator sports, like cricket or football, moved in rhythm. They were very popular in the twenties, less so in the early thirties, but recovered in the mid-thirties. The flattening of attendances in the late thirties suggests that with increasing real income people were beginning to disperse their interests—to cycling, fishing, hiking, motoring, longer holidays—at the expense of the older spectator sports. This trend was halted by the Second World War. Throughout the forties there were huge attendances at all major sports—as at the cinema and the dance hall. It scarcely mattered what it was, people would attend. The peculiar circumstances of 1940s England were responsible for this. Throughout the

in the World's Championship in Montevideo has been considered by our International Committee.

I am instructed to express regret at our inability to accept the invitation. (Quoted in Mason, *Sport in Britain*, 176–7.)

decade, except for the winter of 1947–8, unemployment was negligible; but rationing and controls were severe. People accumulated wages which they could not spend. They thus fell back on what was there—the existing sporting infrastructure, or sports like speedway racing which could be developed easily via the existing infrastructure. 'Working-class' sports were the main beneficiaries of these conditions: for the first time in a generation they catered for a class in full employment. 'Middle-class' spectator sports, like rugby union, though hugely attended, made fewer relative gains because they had less slack to take up.

The period was not equally kind to all sports. As a rule, 'middle-class' sports did well, especially in the interwar years, by exploiting the physical and numerical expansion of the middle classes. Those primarily dependent on the industrial working class did not. Many football clubs, almost irrespective of region, suffered during the depression. Yet the great professional sides of the north, with more behind them, were much less affected; they remained fully competitive throughout. As a sport, something people played rather than watched, however, football's centre of gravity moved south. But that was less true of recreational cricket. The northern clubs were more resilient, probably because a higher proportion of their players were middle-class, and less likely to be unemployed or migrate.

A common love of play, which the English were thought to possess, did not imply a common right to play. Boys and girls who went to 'good' schools played much more sport with far more lavish resources than those who went to state schools. The growth of grammar schools and the sporting opportunities they provided some working-class children modified this inequality, but often by making them play sports they disliked. Except in genuinely working-class sports like speedway, class distinctions operated everywhere, even in sports like football or cricket whose following was significantly or predominantly working-class. The administration and ownership of Football League sides was almost always middle-class, while in cricket class and status distinctions were overt and at its upper reaches usually crushing. In such mixed-class sports this caused immense strain since the assumptions and codes of those at the top were often antithetical to those at the bottom; and it was in these sports that amateurism was most tenacious. Here a discreet class war was conducted in the guise of a code of honourable practice.

'Sport' was largely a masculine activity from which many women were deeply alienated. The degree of their alienation principally depended on their class. Women were subordinated in all sports, but only in working-class sports were they almost wholly excluded, except for sports like swimming or netball which they normally abandoned on leaving school anyway. Working-class men discouraged women from playing sport, partly because the standing of sport depended upon its masculinity. After 1918 women did not play football or rugby league; they did not play crown bowls; they neither bred nor raced dogs or pigeons. They hardly ever watched a football match. They did, however, play cricket, lacrosse, or hockey if they went to the appropriate schools, as they did tennis or golf when they left school. Furthermore, the conventions of middle-class sociability encouraged mixed-sports, and in certain circumstances almost demanded them.

It should be apparent that the government and spirit of most British sports in this period was almost wholly at variance with anything approaching democracy, even in the 1940s when a radical definition of democracy was politically preponderant. That so few contested this in something so central to the national culture as sport suggests how comparatively limited was the scope of English democracy. Contemporaries argued that the Englishman's common love of sport was civilizing; that it introduced into political life a discourse of restraint. The notions of 'fair play' and being a 'good sport' became conventional injunctions of politics: in effect, constitutional principles. This was an undeniable consequence of such a discourse; and the comparative absence of political extremism in England during this period is partly a tribute to its ideological power. But its power also trapped the English within an essentially Edwardian political rhetoric which frustrated as much as encouraged democracy.

The English thought of themselves, and were then thought by others, to be unique in their love of sport and the place of sport in their lives. In fact, the English were not unique; merely first on the path on which most others were destined to go. But as they were first it was their sports that others played. Sport, therefore, became an instrument of anglicization. By the 1950s, when the authority of England and its empire was almost at one with Nineveh and Tyre, English sport and its vocabulary were helping shape the modern world. A fact the English were slow to realize.

x   Music For the People

THE great majority of the English were attached to two forms of music—middlebrow and popular—and for many, their attachment to one or the other was not exclusive. This chapter examines the historical development of a middlebrow 'canon' of music and of popular music and dancing after the First World War. The middlebrow canon, aside from its native origins, was drawn largely from European influences, but outside influences on popular music were almost entirely American. The chapter assesses how far English popular music succumbed to or withstood America and looks more generally at the part dancing played in people's lives, at the way popular music became divorced from dancing and at the evolution of the hit song and the hit parade.

1 | *Popular classics and the middlebrow market*

Just before the end of the Second World War, Lady Colefax wrote to Bernard Berenson:

The war has proved my pet thesis—! In spite of our dear Kenneth [Clark], Eddy Sackville West, the intelligentzia—the enthusiasm of the English for music has been proved up to the hilt—hitherto the music was too expensive and either by day when the workers could not go or by night when they were too tired or it was too dear—All through the war there have been concerts in the lunch hours in factories people like Thibaut (who can't get over the audience he has had in the circumstances) Myra Hess—in fact first rate music—has all been received with touching enthusiasm.[1]

Lady Colefax's 'pet thesis' was not as original as she thought. It was the working hypothesis of the interwar BBC and of the Council for the Encouragement of Music and the Arts, which was founded at the outbreak of the Second World War, that, in the right circumstances, the democratic public could be brought to an understanding of 'serious' music. There is, however, no evidence that this happened, any more than the apparent enthusiasm during the war for 'good' literature denoted any significant change in what people wished to

---

[1] Lady Colefax to Bernard Berenson, [undated] 1945, Colefax Papers C. 3169, Bodleian Library, Oxford.

read. A poignant example of the BBC Symphony Orchestra's experience in Bedford is probably a better indicator of democratic taste. Evacuated to Bedford during the war, it regularly filled the Corn Exchange when its broadcast concerts were open to the public. In the early 1960s, however, when the Orchestra under Rudolf Schwarz went to Bedford for a visiting concert, the Exchange was half-empty.[2] It was more likely that there developed throughout the period not a big demand for 'serious' music, but a canon of 'middlebrow' music which was established before the First World War. This had its origin in both religious and secular music, was enormously reinforced and extended by the cinema and the radio, and further reinforced by certain wartime varieties of 'serious' music.

Before sound, music was an essential element in films for the setting of an appropriate 'mood'. Initially, what was played tended to be random, often depending on the inclinations of the conductor or the pianist. Pianists had a 'distinctive repertory' which ranged from the 'Maiden's Prayer' and the 'Robin's Return' to Beethoven's 'Moonlight' or 'Pathétique' sonatas.[3] The music publishers like Paxton, Novello, and Boosey and Hawkes soon began to issue 'photo-play' compositions—formulaic arrangements designed to 'fit' any particular film.[4] Publishers' catalogues listed titles by mood: 'agitatos, church, sad, sinister, happy, chase, furious, majestic'. A Bach cantata could be listed as 'adagio lamentoso for sad scenes'. A tremolo 'Hearts and Flowers' became 'inextricably associated' with pathos and an 'urgent "Hall of the Mountain King" with menace'.[5] The demand for cinema sheet music was immense: by the mid-1920s the proceeds from the sale of sheet music to the cinemas was five times that from the music halls.[6]

Even after the wiring of the halls for sound it remained customary in the larger and more pretentious cinemas to have 'musical interludes'—quasi-concerts—which complemented the films. Most cinema orchestras usually consisted of 12 or so players, but some could be much larger. In 1922—a celebrated example—Eugene Goossens conducted the music (his own) to United Artists' *The Three Musketeers* at Covent Garden with 65 players. These interludes, sometimes advertised as 'the supreme pages of musical literature', might include, for instance, the overture to *The Magic Flute* and Schubert's B Minor Symphony or a Rossini overture (without the repeats), and a shorter Beethoven symphony. But they might also include, if the pianist felt up to it, Litolff's 'Scherzo' (later to become a standby in the radio programme 'Housewife's Choice'), or even as a 'lollipop' Albert W. Ketelbey's 'In a Monastery Garden'

[2] E. D. Mackerness, *A Social History of English Music* (London, 1964), 269.
[3] C. Ehrlich, *The Music Profession in Britain since the Eighteenth Century* (Oxford, 1985), 197–8.
[4] Mackerness, *Social History of English Music*, 244.
[5] Ehrlich, *Music Profession in Britain*, 197–8.
[6] C. Ehrlich, *Harmonious Alliance: A History of the Performing Rights Society* (Oxford, 1989), 66.

(1915), 'In a Persian Market' (1920), or 'Bells across the Meadows' (1921). Ketelbey, whose nephew was the pianist Clifford Curzon, wrote enormously popular music which occupied that wide grey area between 'serious' and 'not serious'. 'In a Persian Market' was the most frequently played piece in the history of British music and it was calculated in 1924 that one or another of Ketelbey's compositions was played three or four times a day in most cinemas and restaurants.[7] The radio tended to continue the practices of the cinemas. The BBC's very popular 'Fred Hartley's Novelty Quintet', which began in 1931, would thus play sentimental songs of the day like 'Little Man You've had a Busy Day', 'well-loved' ballads like 'The Rosary', but also the 'ripened fruits of Chopin's works, the brilliant gems of Liszt and the superb arrangements of Fritz Kreisler', together with fantasies on hornpipes, country dances, etc.[8] This kind of music came to be what most people understood as 'classical' music and was what the wartime orchestras usually played: a well-known overture, a well-known symphony, and 'lollipops'.

The huge popularity in the 1940s of Richard Addinsell's 'Warsaw Concerto' is also a good guide to taste. The 'lovely' 'Warsaw Concerto',[9] was written as music for the film *Dangerous Moonlight* (1941). (Rachmaninov himself had originally been invited to write the music, but had declined on the ground that he would need two years.) It was a pastiche of a late-romantic piano concerto (indeed *à la* Rachmaninov) and colossally successful—far exceeding in popularity anything written by contemporary 'serious' composers, and repeatedly recorded. The taste for the 'highlights' of romantic opera was confirmed by the enormous success of Joan Hammond's recordings of late romantic operatic arias—which in September 1941 made 'O My Beloved Father' from Puccini's *Gianni Schicchi* perhaps the first classical 'hit'. Almost certainly it was the first to sell more than one million copies.

The brass bands and the great Northern choirs were also responsible for establishing a canon of acceptable classical music. By the interwar years the repertoire of the choirs was anchored in an over-used repertoire of choral warhorses: Handel, Haydn, Mendelssohn, Elgar. The same was true of the brass bands, still a significant factor in the social and cultural life of upper-working-class men, and still usually attached to factories and pits, as the names of many of the leading bands suggest (Black Dyke Mills, Foden's Motor Works, Grimethorpe Colliery, St Hilda's Colliery, Creswell Colliery, Brighouse and Rastrick, Munn and Felton's, Fairy Aviation, CWS Manchester, etc.). They were the closest many working men came to 'serious' music and many 'serious' musi-

---

[7] For Ketelbey, see ibid. 37–8.

[8] P. Scannell and D. Cardiff, *A Social History of British Broadcasting*, vol. i: *1922–1939* (Oxford, 1991), 212–13.

[9] Quoted in J. P. Mayer, *British Cinemas and their Audiences* (London, 1948), 24. See also Vaughan, *Something in Linoleum*, 181.

cians composed for them, including Elgar, Holst, Vaughan Williams, Ireland, Bliss, and Bantock. Despite this, their repertoires, too, were limited, heavily dependent upon a familar array of names and tunes: Handel, Haydn, some Beethoven, Mendelssohn; suites from popular nineteenth-century operas like *Aida* or *Carmen*; and arrangements of hymns or sentimental songs. The growing importance to the bands of 'contesting'—which culminated in the British Open championship at Manchester Belle Vue and the National in London—tended to narrow repertoires further by encouraging the performance of well-known, well-liked, and well-rehearsed pieces.

The popularity of this canon, or of the 'Warsaw Concerto', demonstrated the size of the 'large and relatively unadventurous "middlebrow" musical audience of catholic rather than discriminating taste'.[10] Not for nothing was Eric Coates, mellifluous composer of 'light' and 'semi-light' orchestral music, then Britain's highest-paid composer.[11] People were aware of themselves as musical 'middlebrows' and often had a well-considered notion of what was 'middle-brow' taste, as in the case of one man, who described himself as 'lower mid-dlebrow' and who listed in precise order his 'Six Great Melodies': 1. 'Ave Maria', Schubert; 2. 'Liebestraum', Liszt; 3. 'Blue Danube', Strauss; 4. 'Salut d'Amour', Elgar; 5. 'Elégie', Massenet; 6. 'Black Eyes', Ferraris.[12] It was argued that this audience acted as a 'bridge' between the audiences for classical and popular music. Its taste, however, was probably 'middlebrow' in both. Thus two observers of 'new' middle-class families in the 1950s noted the portable gramophone 'with bright record covers from *Oklahoma!*, *Beethoven's Eroica*, *Bing Sings* and *Tchaikovsky's Fifth*'.[13]

By the early 1950s the middlebrow classical canon was fixed and probably will remain fixed. As in literature, the predominance of modernism in musical high culture largely excluded the middlebrow audience from contemporary music. Except for pastiches or oddities it is unlikely, therefore, that the middlebrow canon can be expanded, particularly as a 'classical' notion of melody remains at its heart. Thus in 1996 one of the better-known British music clubs was able to issue a classical music anthology, *Your Hundred Best Tunes*, which would have been completely recognizable to the middlebrow audience in 1950. Amongst its '100 favourite tracks' it advertises Pachelbel's 'Canon'; 'Arrival of the Queen of Sheba'; 'Jesu Joy of Man's Desiring'; 'Pomp and Circumstance No 1'; Vaughan Williams's 'Fantasia on Greensleeves'; the duet 'Au Fond du Temple Saint' from the 'Pearl Fishers'; 'The Marriage of Figaro' Overture; Brahms's 'Lullaby'; 'Abide with Me'; 'Jerusalem'; 'Für Elise'; 'Take a Pair of

[10] Mackerness, *Social History of English Music*, 270.

[11] Ehrlich, *Harmonious Alliance*, 99–100. Coates was a very English figure, but he earned some international fame when the American trumpeter and bandleader Harry James turned one of Coates's 'valses dansantes' into the song 'Sleepy Lagoon'.

[12] Scannell and Cardiff, *Social History of British Broadcasting*, 207.

[13] Jackson and Marsden, *Education and the Working Class*, 157.

Sparkling Eyes'; the first movement of Tchaikovsky's piano concerto no 1; the second movement of Mozart's piano concerto no 21; the first movement of Beethoven's 'Moonlight Sonata'; Massenet's 'Meditation'; 'Nessun Dorma', etc. This list contains nothing unfamiliar to an audience even in the interwar years, and the construction of such a canon, both timeless yet strictly finite, is one of the most striking cultural acts of that period.

2 | Palais de danse *and hit parade*

In this era popular music, which meant popular commercial music, was genuinely popular. Whereas there was no common literary culture in England there was a common musical culture, even if some were reluctant members of it. It was difficult for anyone to escape popular music and dance. It was possible, furthermore, for someone to like both classical and popular music, to be a member of both publics (whereas it was very unusual to find someone who liked both James Joyce and Mills and Boon). The fashions and crazes which characterized popular music and dance were known and followed in all social classes: virtually everyone knew of the Charleston even if only some had danced it. Probably most could hum the tune of 'Pennies from Heaven' even if they had not consciously learnt it. The author Richmal Crompton, a student of middle-class rather than popular culture, begins one story with William, to the despair of family and neighbours, 'singing' Vincent Youmans's 'I Want to be Happy' (1925), one of the hit songs of the decade. And it became increasingly common to couple particular events—to fix them in the memory—with whatever were the popular songs of the moment. Thus the 'phoney war' was inexpungeably associated in people's minds with 'Run, Rabbit, Run' and 'South of the Border'—two of the hit songs of the time. Not everyone, it is true, liked exactly the same thing: the music and dancing of the West End was not identical to that of the Hammersmith Palais. But the differences were in nuance and style rather than in kind.

Like the cinemas, English popular music was subject to relentless American influence. The English had always bought and listened to American ballads, novelty and nonsense songs—whether or not they were that year's craze. But there were three particular moments when American influence was so strong as to change the way the English thought of music and dance: in the First World War and the years immediately after, when 'ragtime' and 'jazz' profoundly modified popular musical culture; the late 1930s and 1940s when 'swing' and 'bop' did something similar; and the late 1940s and early 1950s when 'country and western' and 'rhythm and blues' were introduced to England with unexpected long-term consequences.

Even before 1914 there were detectable American influences on what was still a largely self-sufficient popular musical culture. Victor Herbert's operettas were popular in England, but they were a recognizable genre, as much English as American, as were the vaudeville songs which were popularized in the English music halls. The minstrel shows had also been anglicized— in part because many of the famous 'zip coon' songs like 'Jim crack Corn' and 'Turkey in the Straw' were possibly of British or Irish origin anyway. In the 1890s genuine 'coon music'—a term of art as well as a racial epithet—was popular, as were accompanying dances like the 'cakewalk'. Minstrelsy and coon music, however, tended to be fashions: the Americanization which began with imported rag music was irreversible. Irving Berlin's 'Alexander's Ragtime Band' (1911) was enormously popular in England as elsewhere, and his revue *Everybody's Doin' It Now* (1912 in London) entrenched ragtime, or what Berlin thought was ragtime, in England, both as music and dance. The tango, which was also introduced to England in 1912, was the last popular dance to come from Paris; thereafter, most came from New York. Even Latin American dances which had hitherto, like the tango, come to England via Paris or the Riviera, were, like the popular Cuban dances of the interwar years, the rumba, the pasa doble and the conga, filtered through New York, though not always in the American version. The tango, which remained important as an exhibition dance and had, as the 'new tango', considerable popularity in the 1920s, soon gave way to ragtime dances—the one-step, the turkeytrot and, above all, the foxtrot. The immense success of the foxtrot was the 'real revolution' in popular music and dance: it not only confirmed the status of rag and then jazz, it began the huge boom in public dancing which lasted until the mid-fifties.[14]

The foxtrot's conquest of the night clubs and the dance halls was due partly to the expulsion of the 'brilliant' German and Austrian bands in 1914, creating a gap which was slowly filled by visiting American bands.[15] Their audience was in turn much augmented by the large number of American troops who were based in or found their way to England towards the end of the war. The effect of American soldiers on popular culture generally was profound: they were to 'democratize' it everywhere by creating a music and dance which was not only thought democratic but associated in the popular mind with the immense material success of American democracy. The foxtrot and other rag dances, unlike the waltzes formerly played in the better hotels and restaurants by the vanished Germans, were designed for and adopted by democracy: popular amongst all social classes but danced with a spontaneity and physical vigour which made them particularly attractive to younger working men and women.

During the war itself people found it difficult to distinguish rag from jazz. Jazz, first heard in England in 1917, was initially thought to be a dance and as

---

[14] F. Rust, *Dance in Society* (London, 1968), 82–3.
[15] P. J. S. Richardson, *A History of English Ballroom Dancing, 1910–1945* (London, 1947), 32.

a word was familiar to comparatively few.[16] It was the triumphant appearance in England of Nick La Rocca's Original Dixieland Jazz Band in 1919 which introduced jazz to the national culture. This was a white band from New Orleans and La Rocca, its cornettist and leader, made exaggerated claims for its originality. It did not, as he suggested, 'invent' jazz, nor did he write the band's most famous song, 'Tiger Rag'—both were unquestionably black ('coloured') in origin. But it did bring jazz to Chicago and New York and was the first band to make an acknowledged jazz recording.[17] Unlike most later white bands, moreover, the Original Dixieland Jazz Band played from memory and with a free use of black techniques of ragging and syncopation. It was also still in the tradition of the black 'novelty' bands—where bandsmen clowned and where whistles, saucepans, bells, zinc baths, etc. were blown, rung, or beaten, as well as conventional instruments played. By the end of the war it was the best-known jazz band in the United States.

It was invited to England by the Savoy Hotel to play at its victory ball—so beginning a long association between the Savoy and jazz—and was simultaneously booked to appear in the revue *Joy Bells* at the London Hippodrome—with the 'prime minister of fun', George Robey, topping the bill. They played there one night (7 April 1919) with such amazing effect that Robey, never one to share the limelight, insisted they not appear again. The band then went to the Palladium and on 28 November 1919 began a nine-month engagement at the new Hammersmith Palais de Danse. That they created a sensation was admitted by all. How influential they were in the long term is less certain; but they popularized in England a form of syncopated music in which the saxophone predominated—whether the jazz was 'white' or 'coloured'. The pre-war string orchestras, though still up to the demands of the palm court or the *thés dansants* where the 'new tango' was danced in the mid-1920s, lacked the volume which the new kind of dancing demanded. That was provided by the saxophone. Jack Hylton, perhaps the most popular of the 1930s bandleaders, wrote in 1926 that the typical dance band now

consists of three saxophones, three brass instruments, and four rhythmic instruments, the latter acting as a background for all other effects. Thanks to the saxophones, the volume created by a small dance band of this type can equal that of a full 'straight' orchestra comprising three or four times the number of players.

As W. W. Seabrook said in 1924, 'Every legitimate night-club proprietor . . . knows that he might as well be out of business as to be without a saxophone

---

[16] For the early history of the word 'jazz' in England, see M. Hustwitt, ' "Caught in a whirlpool of aching sound": the production of dance music in Britain in the 1920s', *Popular Music*, 3 (1983), 10.

[17] On 26 Feb. 1917, for the Victor Talking Machine Co. The sides included 'Livery Stable Blues' and 'Original Dixieland One-Step'.

performer.'[18] The Original Dixieland Jazz Band demonstrated just what a colossal and aggressive volume of sound could be produced by a 'saxophone performer' while its exceptional success at Hammersmith confirmed that the wartime popularity of public dancing was no mere fad. The rapidity with which jazz and its derivations penetrated and in part conquered English popular music was not due just to its novelty. Jazz attained its power precisely because it packed an explosive rhythm within a recognizable musical idiom. Its 'predominant components', in Marshall Stearns's well-known formulation, were 'European harmony, Euro-African melody and African rhythm'.[19]

It was immediately realized that the existing dance halls, like the old string orchestras, could not cope with the mass of new dancers, being either too small or too expensive. In 1919 the first and most famous of the great '*palais de danses*'—a name which acknowledged French hegemony over English dancing at the moment of its passing—was built by Messrs Booker and Mitchell at Hammersmith. For the next eight years or so, and particularly in 1925, the year of the Locarno Treaties, large palais were built in all major towns. Some, like the Locarno at Streatham or the Astoria in Central London, were of great size and splendour. Their success owed much to C. L. Heimann who had been employed by Mecca Cafés to cater for the dances that Bertram Mills, the circus owner, held at Covent Garden in 1925. As a result of his experience there Heimann became convinced that the palais, if better organized, could become central to working-class life. He persuaded Mecca to buy Sherry's in Brighton in 1927 with himself as manager. Impelled by his success there, and under Heimann as managing director, Mecca throughout the late twenties and thirties bought some of the best-known halls in the country, including the Locarnos at Streatham, Glasgow, and Leeds, the Ritz and the Plaza in Manchester, and the Paramount, Tottenham Court Road. During the Second World War, Heimann took over Covent Garden, converting it into a kind of super-palais. By then Mecca Dancing was one of the best-known national institutions and no one disputed its claim that ten million people a year took to its floors. The large palais, especially those owned by Mecca, provided good bands and facilities and spacious and excellently sprung floors—unlike the smart hotels and restaurants of the West End which usually had good and often outstanding bands, but wretched and overcrowded floors. Most of the larger palais had 'learner-nights'—evenings when part of the floor was roped off for beginners—and trained teachers, some, like Adele England at the Streatham Locarno, became

---

[18] Seabrook quoted in Mackerness, *Social History of English Music*, 247. For the Original Dixieland Jazz Band in England, see A. McCarthy, *The Dance Band Era* (London, 1971), 38; J. Godbolt, *A History of Jazz in Britain, 1919–1950* (London, 1986), 8–13. It has been said that Lord Donegal organized a visit by the band to Buckingham Palace where they played 'Tiger Rag' for the king and queen. I have, alas, found no confirmation of this.

[19] Quoted in S. Frith, *Sociology of Rock* (London, 1978), 177.

celebrities. The result was that dancing skill tended to vary inversely with social class. In this sense, the palais were like the super-cinemas being built at the same time: they allowed working men and women collectively a luxury denied them as individuals.[20]

Who danced in these democratic palaces? Except on special evenings when there was formal ballroom dancing, or during the war when older servicemen and women would dance, there were few 'adults'—i.e. those over 24 or so.[21] There were invariably more girls than boys and the girls were slightly younger. In smaller towns dancing could be more important even than the cinema as the focus of teenage life. In Featherstone, for example, in the early 1950s, the Miners' Welfare Institute held dances every Saturday night. Four to five hundred attended, most between 17 and 20—the majority of the town's teenagers. In the early 1950s Mark Abrams estimated that about three million people weekly went to the halls licensed exclusively for dancing; the numbers who went to halls not used exclusively for dancing is unknown.[22]

Halls varied in 'tone'. The grander palais, particularly Meccas's, were strictly policed. No alcohol was served and young men trying to come in at pub-closing time were usually excluded. Even the presence of professional partners, though 'quite harmless', was abandoned since it 'on the whole proved repugnant to those who usually use palais-de danse'.[23] What was true, however, of a Mecca palais was not necessarily true of a small all-purpose hall. In Featherstone, for example, the dances were organized by an ex-overman of the Ashton Colliery under the slogans 'Saturday Night is Riot Night'. 'Come and Have a Riot of Fun with George and his Boys'. Nor was the word 'riot' used carelessly: many of the revelling dancers ended up in the magistrates' courts.[24] For boys, the main function of the dances, whether at a palais or miners' institute, was primarily social. They allowed couples to meet and, usually, part amicably while doing away with the need to make 'polite conversation' beforehand. Dancing was a way of testing the sexual water.

Boys liked dancing and some became expert, but as an interest or physical activity it mattered less to them than sport.[25] For girls dancing was much more

---

[20] For the palais, see Richardson, *English Ballroom Dancing*, 143; Rust, *Dance in Society*, 86.

[21] It is possible that the domination of the palais by younger dancers declined after the Second World War. At the Coventry Locarno, a super-luxury hall opened in 1960 and one of the last Mecca palais to be built, 'palais' dancing was confined to Saturday night. The other six nights were allocated to different ages and styles: one night was for teenagers, one for over-21s, one for old-time dancing etc. In a reversal of all current trends, the Coventry Locarno is now the city's public library. (H. Ichihashi, 'Working-Class Leisure in English Towns, 1945–1960, with special reference to Coventry and Bolton', unpublished Ph.D. thesis, Univ. of Warwick (1994), 330–1.) Old-time dancing was very popular in Coventry: in 1947 the GEC Old Time Dance Club, for example, had more than 1,000 members. (Ibid. 270.)

[22] Dennis *et al.*, *Coal is our Life*, 126; B. S. Rowntree and G. R. Lavers, *English Life and Leisure* (London, 1951), 279–85.

[23] Rowntree and Lavers, *English Life and Leisure*, 281.

[24] Dennis *et al.*, *Coal is our Life*, 126–7.   [25] Frith, *Sociology of Rock*, 67.

important. In its physical and creative aspects, it was to most working-class girls as sport was to boys. Dancing—particularly for working-class girls—*was* their sport. Even by the 1950s when public dancing had begun to decline as an adolescent activity, girls were significantly more attached to it than boys. In 1950 20 per cent of boys but 39 per cent of girls said that dancing was their 'favourite' way of spending a Saturday evening, and more 'interesting' than the cinema. For boys sports and the cinema were always greater 'interests' than dancing.[26] During the 1940s when alternative social activities were either rationed or non-existent dancing was hugely popular with teenage girls. Many appear to have danced two or three times a week: between them a sample of working-class girls in London, who were asked how they spent their leisure during one week in Autumn 1941, went four times to an evening class, four times cycling or hiking, nine times to church, 52 times to the cinema, and 54 times dancing.[27]

Dancing, of course, was an acceptable way of meeting boys. When one girl said 'Even now at 18, I can't dance, which I consider is one of my downfalls' it was understood what she meant. After the First World War, except for débutantes, who continued to be chaperoned during the season, dancing in hotels and restaurants (for girls technically adult) and in the palais (for girls of any age) was an activity beyond parental control. This was important for both sexes but doubly so for girls. A dance was one of the few social occasions where convention permitted them to take the sexual initiative. During the so-called 'excuse me' or 'buzz-off' dances ('ladies' choice' higher up the social scale) girls could choose partners, an opportunity many took, with mixed success.

But for girls dancing was clearly more than just a sexual or social encounter. For many, dancing itself provided a powerful intrinsic satisfaction. Younger girls would practice steps with their older sisters and would first go to dances in their company.[28] Many attended learners' nights and would willingly dance with each other—often to a high standard. They were quicker than boys to adopt new dance crazes and were much more knowledgeable about dance bands and their personnel. For many girls, dancing was to some degree creative and expressive, particularly if a girl were lucky enough to have a good partner. 'On occasion', the social worker Pearl Jephcott wrote during the Second World War, 'the couple will come together with a skill, abandon and unselfconscious enjoyment which suggests that this, for a few moments, is a genuinely creative activity and on a different plane from jiving under certain other conditions.'[29] That was one of the reasons why American soldiers could be so popular: they were not merely 'overpaid, oversexed and over here'—they were also better dancers. The excellence of black GIs as dancers, especially in

---

[26] Wilkins, *Adolescent in Britain*, 87–9.   [27] Jephcott, *Girls Growing Up*, 117.
[28] Kerr, *Ship Street*, 32.   [29] Jephcott, *Rising Twenty*, 150.

basically black dances like the jitterbug, partly explains why English girls were so ready to violate the US army codes which attempted to proscribe black–white social relationships in England.

The renewed craze for dancing during the Second World War was, therefore, in part, and can only be understood as, a phenomenon of the American occupation after 1942; an aspect of the sexual and social relationships between English girls and American servicemen. In those areas where Americans were stationed the dance halls became one of the principal sites of 'Yank-hunting'. The attractions of the Yanks were all too familiar: the material abundance, often much greater than GIs knew in civilian life, their uniforms, their physical size and vaguely Hollywood looks and deportment, the conventions of 'dating'—the chocolates and flowers—with which English girls were familiar from American films. As one Land Army girl who had met a US soldier at a dance in Evesham said:

It took quite a lot of persuading from the other girls to keep that date. I guess they were thinking of the gifts the Americans were said to give. Nylons, chocs, cigarettes, gum and fruit juice that we could only dream of. I wasn't happy about their reputation but I went and had such a lovely time.[30]

There is little doubt that girls sought out 'Yanks' and were not too squeamish about showing it. 'In Bridgwater', one young member of the Fleet Air Arm, recalled,

there was a dance hall called the Blake Hall; it was a scruffy looking place that held the weekly hop . . . once on leave, I went inside and saw scores of girls lined up along one wall, three deep. There were some GIs who would walk up and down this line surveying the girls and then select one, who would gladly go and dance with him. I was pretty horrified by this slave market attitude. Then a smart-looking British soldier walked along the line asking girls to dance with him, but none would. I have never forgotten it.[31]

Nor were the Americans themselves particularly subtle. In Greenock (Scotland), where there was a big American transit base, girls called one of the GIs' sexual strategies the 'Y dance': 'they got one leg between yours . . . it was like in the centre of the floor . . . they didn't move. You got up there [the dance floor] and in went this leg.'[32] Such behaviour, and the extent to which some girls went in hunting Yanks (like the girl who brought home for the night 13 Canadian airmen—who counted as Yanks—she had met in a pub)[33] caused real angst

---

[30] J. Gardiner, *'Over Here': the GIs in Wartime Britain* (London, 1992), 114. See also D. Reynolds, *Rich Relations: the American Occupation of Britain, 1942–1945* (London, 1995), 264–5.

[31] Gardiner, *'Over Here'*, 114.

[32] R. A. Thomson, 'Dance Bands and Dance Halls in Greenock, 1945–55', *Popular Music*, 8 (2), May 1989, 149.

[33] Jephcott, *Rising Twenty*, 66.

among British servicemen and often turned dances into occasions of Anglo-American hostility in which the advantages seemed to lie almost wholly with the enemy.

Dancing meant so much to girls that the ban newly-wed working-class husbands often placed upon it impoverished women's married lives. For middle-class girls—particularly middle-middle-class girls, who rarely had recourse either to a palais or a night club, dancing was probably less rewarding. It was too dominated by the dance schools and formal sociability (often with a parental presence) to have the comparative freedom of the dance hall. The outcome was frequently a rather starchy inhibited style, anything but expressive.[34] Furthermore, middle-class girls, as we have seen, were much more likely to be actively sporting since they were more likely than working-class girls to go to schools which both encouraged sport and had the facilities to play them. Theirs was more the culture of the playing field than the culture of the dance hall.[35]

The dynamic of English popular music and dancing after 1918 was undoubtedly American, but both were anglicized in ways which distanced them from their American origins. In dance music this produced a suave, mellifluous, and technically polished version of New York 'white' jazz; in dancing a smooth style based on 'natural movement' which became the internationally predominant form of ballroom dancing.

The development of a distinctly English style of jazz was, however, neither rapid nor continuous. Throughout the twenties there was a mixture of styles whose adoption partly depended on the few institutions which could afford first-class bands. Of these, the most important was the Savoy Hotel. The Savoy had not only brought the Original Dixieland to England in 1919 but in the Savoy Orpheans and Savoy Havana Band it had the first two nationally known dance bands. They were the highest-paid British bands contracted to EMI in the 1920s and made over 300 records between 1922 and 1927. In 1925 the Hotel Cecil employed Jack Payne's band, one of the first broadcast, until 1928 when Payne became the BBC's director of music. The most successful of the 1920s bands was Bert Ambrose's. Ambrose had emigrated to the United States after the war but in 1920 was induced by the owner of the Embassy, the most fashionable of the West End clubs, to lead its band, which he did, with one short break, until 1927. In that year he took the band to the Savoy—at a reported £10,000 a year, then a fabulous sum—and remained its leader until 1934. Ambrose was enormously popular and established a reputation which spread to Europe and the United States. The members of his band were of remarkable quality: Ted Heath, Lew Stone, Stanley Black, George Melachrino, and George Shearing all at one time played in it. Vera Lynn was one of its vocalists.

[34] For her reminiscences of middle-class dancing I am grateful to Dr Enid Fox.
[35] See above, pp. 368–9.

One of the striking features of British dance bands in the 1920s was the number of first-rate Americans who played in them. Rudy Vallee, later famous as the first of the crooners, played saxophone in the Savoy Havana Band and Carroll Gibbons later directed the Savoy Orpheans. Ambrose, who was often criticized for English over-smoothness, employed several Americans and developed an Ellington-style rhythm. Indeed, in 1929 he made the first recording (for Decca) of Johnny Green's classic, 'Body and Soul'. Throughout the twenties there were regular visits by American bands, of both colours. Paul Whiteman came twice, 1923 and 1926, and in the longer term had probably more influence on British dance music than any other individual. Paul Specht came in 1923 and 1925; Ted Lewis in 1926. Sidney Bechet, the clarinettist and soprano saxophonist, toured with the Southern Syncopators in 1920.[36] Moreover, black Americans liked coming to England, as to France. There was usually no problem, or fewer problems, with hotels and not many of the thousand petty humiliations of black life in the United States. Armstrong in 1932 and 1934, and even more, Ellington in 1933, were fêted wherever they went, not least by the king's sons, one of whom, the prince of Wales, joined Ellington in a celebrated jam-session.

'Fred' Elizalde's career shows how 'open' English jazz was in the earlier 1920s; how 'closed' by the later. Elizalde, a Filipino of wealthy parents who had been educated in Spain, the United States, and (like so many jazz musicians and enthusiasts) Cambridge, was much influenced by American hot jazz. The band he organized for the Cambridge Footlights gained a reputation for adventurous jazz and did much to make Armstrong's and Ellington's music known in England. His music was 'so advanced', the dance band historian Albert McCarthy wrote, that it was astonishing he ever got an engagement,[37] and even more surprising, though much to its credit, that the Savoy should have asked him to form a hot band for their dance floor. The group Elizalde assembled had three Americans, including Adrian Rollini, the outstanding bass saxophonist of the time. Despite its quality, however, the band was, not surprisingly, a failure. The Savoy's patrons found they could not dance to hot music, nor was it popular with the BBC's listeners. The Savoy ended Elizalde's contract in July 1929 whereupon the band went on a disastrous tour of the Northern halls whose audiences were even more uncomprehending. Elizalde's real influence probably rested upon the recordings he made between 1928 and 1930, but their distinction could not conceal the fact that he had lost his wider audience.

By the early 1930s English 'dance-band jazz' had been largely closed to newer American influences. The decade was to be dominated by a technically sophisticated and well-drilled dance music which did indeed owe much to an

---

[36] It was in London that Bechet discovered the soprano saxophone—the instrument in which he excelled.

[37] McCarthy, *Dance Band Era*, 47.

American, Paul Whiteman, but little to anyone else. Whiteman's visits in the twenties had greatly impressed English bandleaders. In 1925 he staged a much publicized, though bizarre, concert in the Aeolian Hall in New York (for which George Gershwin wrote 'Rhapsody in Blue'), which did much to establish the canon of 'white' jazz.[38] Whiteman, though called the 'King of Jazz', was no innovator, but he employed a large band and outstanding players. He created a technically faultless style which was much admired in England. But admiration for Whiteman tended to foreclose admiration for much else.

There were two reasons for this. The first lay in the structure of the musical profession itself. The wiring of most cinemas for sound had devastated the profession. By 1932 the talkies had cost perhaps 12 to 15,000 musicians their jobs, and this established a decline which it took a generation to reverse. Between 1931 and 1951 the number of professional musicians declined from 21,000 to 15,000; the number of music teachers from 21,000 to 11,000.[39] The depression itself was also responsible for a fall (if short-lived) in the demand for musicians. When demand recovered there was still a huge surplus of musicians seeking work, even though most were not of the quality that a good band would expect. In these circumstances (August 1930) about 500 of the leading dance band players met to found a separate dance band section of the Musicians' Union whose purpose was to obtain the exclusion of all 'aliens'—that is, Americans. The ministry of labour was happy to co-operate and routinely denied work permits to any but the most illustrious of popular musicians. Armstrong and Ellington were sufficiently stellar to be admitted; though, had Ellington's visit not been arranged by Jack Hylton, even he might have been refused entry.[40] Exclusion was maintained until 1954 when a reciprocal agreement with the Americans was reached, and led to some grotesque episodes. In 1949, Humphrey Lyttleton, having failed to obtain a work permit for Sidney Bechet, who had returned to live in France and who still had no peer in England, invited him to England for a 'holiday', arranged for him to attend a concert equipped by chance with his saxophone and, when he was introduced to the audience, arranged for it to demand 'spontaneously' that Bechet play. This rather obvious ruse was unsuccessful: Lyttleton was prosecuted by the Musicians' Union and fined. The result of the bans was not so much to exclude American influence altogether—which would have been impossible—as to filter it and to confine knowledge, particularly of black music, to enthusiastic coteries.

---

[38] For this concert see D. Clarke, *The Rise and Fall of Popular Music* (London, 1995), 107–8. Amongst other curiosities, the concert ended with one of Elgar's 'Pomp and Circumstance' marches.

[39] Ehrlich, *Music Profession in Britain*, 210.

[40] Hylton was also successful in gaining a work permit for the saxophonist Coleman Hawkins who played with Hylton in 1934–5 and 1939. Britain was not alone in practising exclusion. The pit orchestras in New York struck rather than play under Jack Hylton, while Harry Roy was denied an American work permit in 1948.

The second reason was the musical culture of the dance and variety halls. Elizalde's experience suggested that bands had to play within well-understood and fairly narrow boundaries. Anything which went much beyond ragtime or 'white' jazz—the tradition in which most British bands played—was usually unacceptable. The great popularity in the late thirties of Victor Silvester's 'strict tempo' makes the point.[41] The result was the highly polished and skilful but rather unadventurous British dance bands of the 1930s—Harry Roy, Roy Fox (who was an American), Ray Noble, Henry Hall, Jack Hylton, Bert Ambrose, even Lew Stone. With the exception of Ray Noble, who was director of the EMI house band before he went to the USA in 1934, all had at some time been based in West End hotels or restaurants: Roy at the Café de Paris, Café Anglais and the Hotel Mayfair, Fox at the Café de Paris and the Monseigneur restaurant, Stone at the Café de Paris, the Monseigneur, and the Dorchester Hotel; Henry Hall at the Gleneagles Hotel, Hylton at the Piccadilly Hotel, Ambrose at the Embassy and the Mayfair Hotels. Most of their live performances, therefore, were given to more or less fashionable, upper-middle-class London audiences whose tastes were largely conventional.[42]

The most interesting of these men was probably Ray Noble. As director of the EMI house band, the New Mayfair, he made records with a distinctly American flavour and his partnership with the South African vocalist Al Bowlly (who joined the band in 1930) was artistically very productive, if not altogether appreciated at the time. He and Bowlly went to America in 1934. In 1936, Bowlly returned and was to be killed in the blitz, leaving the field to more orthodox practitioners of 'white' jazz, of whom in the thirties, aside from Bert Ambrose, the most popular were Jack Hylton and Henry Hall. Hylton was a marvellous exponent of 'sweet' jazz. His style was 'straight in flavour, playing smooth dance music and featuring light orchestral pieces'.[43] He toured widely in Europe to great success which, had his band not been barred, he would probably have repeated in the United States. The historian Eric Hobsbawm remembers him 'as the accepted last word in jazz in Central European secondary schools, 1928–1933'.[44] In 1929, for example, the band gave 700 performances, travelled over 63,000 miles and sold 3.2 million records. By the end of the 1930s his was probably the best non-swing dance band in Europe. The BBC broadcaster Christopher Stone wrote of him in 1933 as 'still the most important unofficial ambassador of England on the Continent'.[45] He consciously attempted to be the English Paul Whiteman, and he succeeded. Hylton, whose father had managed a socialist club in Lancashire, was, despite the compara-

---

[41] For Silvester, see below, pp. 405–6.

[42] Though not always. Stone (with the rising Mantovani) was chosen to open Butlin's new holiday camp at Clacton and had played a week at the Skegness camp.

[43] P. Gammond, *Oxford Companion to Popular Music* (London and NY, 1991), 281.

[44] F. Newton, *The Jazz Scene* (London, 1959), 62.

[45] C. Stone, *Christopher Stone Speaking* (London, 1933), 107.

tive conservatism of his style, none the less broad in outlook. He had, of course, brought Ellington to England in 1933 and he tried unsuccessfully to take his band to the Soviet Union in the same year. Despite Nazi disapproval, he made a highly successful tour of Germany in 1935.

Henry Hall was in every respect more orthodox than Hylton but equally suc-cessful. He had, like Eric Ball, a background in the Salvation Army, where he learnt the trumpet, though he made his name as a jazz pianist. He became con-ductor at the Gleneagles Hotel, and in 1929 musical director of the LMS hotels. In 1932 he was asked to succeed Jack Payne at the BBC and to form a regular BBC house band. The BBC Dance Orchestra first broadcast on 15 March 1932 to huge success. Hall knew his audience: the *Radio Magazine* praised him for not being infected 'with the virus of West Endism'. He thought the music of Schoenberg and hot jazz appealed mainly to Jews and he blotted his copybook by taking the band to Germany in 1938 on the understanding he would not play Jewish music; which presumably meant not playing, amongst others, Irv-ing Berlin and George Gershwin—a real sacrifice to a man of his musical tastes.

The technical quality of the English non-swing bands is indisputable, and it was widely assumed that they were, if anything, superior to their American counterparts. They were not, however, universally admired in England. *Melody Maker*, which first appeared in January 1926 as an exponent of hot jazz, particu-larly of Armstrong and Ellington, rather despised English white jazz, and Hall's most of all. It objected to the prettification of jazz largely for the reasons that Constant Lambert criticized George Gershwin—that he exploited 'only the non-barbaric, non-violent elements of jazz', leaving, as with 'Rhapsody in Blue', just the 'sophisticated trappings'.[46] Thus to one jazz historian sympa-thetic to *Melody Maker*, Hylton's bringing Ellington to England 'unwittingly helped to clarify the wide difference between ordinary dance music [Hylton] and the vitally alive and creative music called jazz [Ellington]'.[47] In fact, jazz was now going the way of classical music, with a decreasing audience for 'pure' jazz and an increasing audience for an eclectic jazz which was liked sim-ply as an element in the much larger category of commercial popular music.

The dance bands had two functions: one was to play music for dancing; the other was to promote sales of popular music. They reached a comparatively large audience through the halls and by dint of repetition could 'plug' a song, but the crowd in a dance hall was at any one time only a small fraction of the potential market. In the early twenties when sheet-music sales were still important, the large department stores or music shops employed vocalists to sing and make familiar, and so to encourage demand for the latest songs. But

---

[46] Quoted in A. Hutchings, 'Music in Britain: 1918–1960', in M. Cooper (ed.), *The New Oxford History of Music*, x (London, 1974), 523–7.

[47] Godbolt, *Jazz in Britain*, 147.

that was a dying art and the gramophone and the record killed it off.[48] Even before the First World War there were thought to be songs which had sold more than one million records. Furthermore, the standard 3-minute, 78rpm record, a major constraint upon the satisfactory recording of classical music, was ideally suited to the popular song, particularly when electrical recording replaced the inferior acoustic technique in 1925. By 1939 both 10-inch and the cheaper 8-inch records were being sold not only in music shops but in chain stores like Woolworth's and Currys. And both encouraged sales by the constant playing of their stock. E. M. Delafield noted in her 'diary': 'Go to Woolworth's to buy paper handerkerchiefs . . . and hear sixpenny record, entitled "Around the Corner and Under the Tree", which I buy. Tune completely engaging, and words definitely vulgar but not without cheap appeal.'[49] By the early 1950s the significance of the record was enhanced by the introduction into England of the juke-box whose appearance in the United States in 1936 had had such profound effects on popular music.

The most powerful instrument, however, for the promotion of popular music was the radio—in effect, the BBC—and its influence increased proportionately to the number of licence-holders. From 1925 on, between 10.30 and midnight every day except Sunday (when Radio Luxembourg and Radio Normandie filled the gap) the BBC played dance music. Moreover, it tended, unlike the commercial stations, to give dance bands a good run—even if it gave Louis Armstrong only 20 minutes in 1932. The national reputation of a band could be made and unmade by the BBC. Ambrose's Saturday night broadcasts and Harry Roy's on Friday did much to establish their bands' status, as did the broadcasts of Hylton, Fox, and Stone and, of course, Henry Hall. Furthermore, the propensity of the corporation to broadcast live gave the English bands an enormous advantage over American bands in the English market. Although there was always a school which regarded anything English as second rate, a listener had to be remarkably well informed to make such a judgement since the BBC scarcely gave them the opportunity for comparison. It was, indeed, doubly advantageous because the BBC broadcast a great deal of dance music—possibly more than any other broadcasting organization in Europe. As one historian has pointed out, someone like Victor Silvester was a product of the BBC monopoly.[50]

Despite this intimacy, relations between the bands and the corporation were often strained, notably over the issue of 'song plugging'. In the 1920s the BBC took the view that it could not assist the promotion of individual songs. The bands, however, together with the sheet-music and recording industry, argued that plugging was an intrinsic part of popular music—that songs were

---

[48] For the decline in sales of sheet-music, see Ehrlich, *Harmonious Alliance*, 66.

[49] Delafield, *Diary of a Provincial Lady*, 190–1.

[50] D. Harker, *One for the Money: Politics and the Popular Song* (London, 1980), 67–8.

popular in themselves, not something simply to be danced to. They had, more-over, every interest in plugging records they themselves had recorded. In 1929 the BBC attempted to ban vocals, and then tried to deny bandleaders access to the announcing microphone. These were deeply unpopular measures, both with listeners and bands, and the corporation was obliged to withdraw them. Wrangles over plugging went on for years before the BBC abandoned as futile attempts to stop it.

The corporation was put under more pressure by Radio Luxembourg and Radio Normandie, who were happy to promote individual songs and were by the late thirties playing something like hit parades on the American model. Nor was the BBC consistent. It could almost claim in Christopher Stone, who was given a programme to play his own favourites in 1927, the world's first disc-jockey, though he eventually found the atmosphere at the corporation too stultifying and joined Radio Luxembourg.[51] In the later thirties it conceded a daytime novelty feature which was in practice a hit parade, though it was to be many years before the corporation formally instituted one—long after Radio Luxembourg introduced a formal Top Twenty in 1948. Given the over-whelming importance of radio to the sheet-music and recording companies—who now together comprised a formidable industry—and their determination to use the radio for self-advertisement the battle over plugging was one the BBC could not win, whatever it did.

By the late 1930s the dance bands had become as much agents for the pro-motion of individual songs as anything else, but for most of the interwar years their primary role was to play dance music. The history of music was, there-fore, almost indistinguishable from the history of dancing. In the twenties dancing was, like popular music, vigorous, experimental, and subject to crazes. Wartime enthusiasm for the foxtrot and the turkeytrot survived into the early years of that decade, stoked-up by the 'fast foxtrot' brought to Eng-land by Paul Whiteman in 1923. The fast foxtrot was related to several black dances (including the 'jive') which had led fugitive existences among the black communities long before 1914 and were introduced, with explosive effect, into white music and dance in the mid-1920s. The most popular was the Charleston, a traditional black dance of furious kicking steps possibly derived from the 'shimmy'. The shimmy, originally a women's dance, had been modi-fied sufficiently to be danced by a couple which it was, widely and wildly, in 1919 and 1920, encouraged by the popularity of Clarence Williams's and Louis Armstrong's 1919 song 'I wish I could shimmy like my sister Kate'. The Charleston was danced in black musicals in 1922 and 1923 and then to white audiences in the Ziegfeld Follies of 1923. It first appeared in England in 1925 in

---

[51] For Stone, see S. Frith, 'The Making of the British Record Industry, 1920–1964', in J. Curran, A. Smith, and P. Wingate (eds.), *Impacts and Influences* (London and New York, 1987), 284.

a revue at the Hotel Metropole and became an immediate craze which reached its peak in December 1926, when C. B. Cochran staged a competitive Charleston extravaganza in the Albert Hall with Fred Astaire as one of the judges.

The Charleston was succeeded as a craze by two related and even more furious dances—the 'black bottom' and the 'varsity drag'. Like the Charleston, the black bottom had been danced by blacks long before it was known to whites. It appeared publicly in the black musical *Dinah* in 1924, and made familiar to a white audience in *George White's Scandals* of 1926 with a new song 'Black Bottom' by the white composers Ray Henderson, Buddy DeSylva, and Lew Brown. This memorable ragtime song established the popularity of the dance in both America and England. The varsity drag, another high-voltage dance, was popu-larized, like the black bottom, by a song of the same name, also by Henderson, DeSylva, and Brown.

For all their extraordinary popularity these were rather anti-social dances—particularly the black bottom with its alarming side-kicks. According to P. J. S. Richardson, editor of the *Dancing News*, the Charleston threatened to turn 'the ballroom into a bear garden'.[52] Some halls banned it and its two successors; in others, the notice P.C.Q.—Please Charleston Quietly—was seen. By 1928 the craze for them had largely abated and, like dance music, dancing 'stabilized' at the level of foxtrots, tangos, one-steps and older dances like the waltz until a new craze for social dancing and the jitterbug developed in the late 1930s.

This 'stability' was partly due to the professional exhibition dancers and teachers of ballroom dancing. Throughout the 1920s they had had two ambitions: to determine what was danced in the ballroom and to gain control of the burgeoning number of dance competitions. The second was achieved more easily than the first. The popularity of dancing after 1918 was reflected in the many dancing competitions held under various auspices, most of them judged by amateurs. In February 1922, however, the *Daily Sketch* promoted with much publicity a national amateur foxtrot and waltz competition and the professionals succeeded in convincing the *Sketch* that the significance of the event demanded professional juries. Thereafter, all major competitions were judged by professionals and, almost uniquely among English competitive sports, the professionals were able to attain a status superior to that of amateurs.

The attempt to dominate dancing itself was more protracted and less successful. In May 1920 dancing teachers met informally in London to devise ways of regularizing ballroom dancing and ending 'freakish dancing'. The tone of the meeting was set by M. Maurice. Simplicity, he said,

is the essence of good form in the ballroom. He protested against the admission of jazz music and dubious steps into decent places, emphatically insisting that they originated

---

[52] Richardson, *English Ballroom Dancing*, 62–5.

in low negro haunts and had *au fond* a prurient significance. In America the jazz music was confined to third and fourth rate places and he thought that the lack of melody and rhythm in many of our bands was responsible for much of our bad dancing.

The teachers agreed. They unanimously resolved 'to do their best to stamp out freak steps, particularly dips and steps in which the feet are raised high off the ground and also side steps and pauses which impede the progress of those who may be following.'[53]

The following year Richardson, perhaps the most important 'political' figure within dancing, reminded the teachers that dancing had acquired a 'bad name', was being attacked by the churches for its immorality and 'stressed the importance of making our dancing above suspicion'. To that end they agreed that in modern dancing 'the knees must be kept together in passing and the feet parallel', and repeated their view that 'all eccentric steps must be abolished'. In 1924 the professionals succeeded in establishing a separate ballroom section of dancing's governing body, the Imperial Society, and it was a committee of this section which was responsible for the standardizing of ballroom dancing. Its dominating member was the 24-year-old Victor Silvester who, two years previously, had become the first Englishman to win the world ballroom-dancing championship. Silvester was a proponent of the 'natural style'—a fluid and unfussy type of dancing—and an enemy of fancy or balletic steps. It was this style which the 'Great Conference' of teachers accepted in 1929. Four regular dances—waltz, foxtrot, quickstep (a modified form of fast foxtrot) and tango were prescribed and each dance was standardized.

Within two years the geography and style of British ballroom dancing was largely fixed. In 1931, to celebrate the redecoration of the Winter Gardens in Blackpool, the first British amateur and professional championships were held in the huge Empress Ballroom and there they remained. There was more northern influence than mere location. In 1932 'pattern dancing'—later to be known as 'formation dancing'—was introduced by Olive Ripman. It soon became competitive in the North, particularly between school sides, and spread South, becoming a familiar element in organized ballroom dancing.

The 'English style' was rapidly adopted abroad. Its elegance and decorum was widely admired and became the predominant form of ballroom dancing in Britain, the dominions, Germany and Scandinavia, the east coast of the United States, Japan, and China (Chou en-Lai was an enthusiastic practitioner), and influential in France and Italy. Much of this success was due to Victor Silvester himself. As a result of his work in the 1920s he published *Modern Ballroom Dancing* which had sold one million copies by 1945 and like all bibles had the force of holy writ. Silvester also popularized an appropriate musical rhythm. He became convinced that contemporary dance music, because it lacked 'strict

[53] Ibid. 43.

tempo', was in practice unsuited to dancing. In 1935 he formed a small strict-tempo orchestra which produced four records a month for EMI, with much success. In 1937 the band made its first BBC broadcast with equal success; in 1941 the broadcasts became the BBC Dancing Club and in 1948 the Television Dancing Club.

The 'English style' was defended exactly as Henry Hall defended his music— that it was 'democratic' and untainted by 'West Endism'. Commending the influence of Silvester, P. J. S. Richardson wrote:

> It will be seen that the development of the 'English Style' was in the hands of the frequenter of the Palais and the public dance hall and not in those of the smart West Enders. These latter maintained what we might call a cosmopolitan style whose spiritual home was New York City.[54]

There is an obvious truth in this. Ballroom dancing was socially eclectic; although its locus was probably middle-class, its reach embraced all classes— unlike the West End restaurants and hotels. But a price was paid. The freedom and spontaneity equally characteristic of dance in the palais and hall was actively discouraged. The Official Board—the ruling authority of ballroom dancing after 1929—was constantly on the hunt for heterodox steps. In the mid-1930s, for example, the tango, in the Board's view, became subject to 'exaggerated movements' while the quickstep was in no better way: its deformations were 'largely caused by the desire of competitors to win approval from the crowd. On spacious floors the amount of travel became abnormal and many stunts, even including a modified "splits" were introduced by some dancers'. Fortunately 'good taste' prevailed. The result, however, was that by the outbreak of the Second World War, as even Richardson conceded, the 'style', for all its elegance, had become rigid and formulaic. Furthermore, the surviving Frenchifications (as in the names of many of the teachers), as well as the dread of innovation, exposed ballroom dancing to easy satire.[55] The effect of the American invasion in 1942 and after was, therefore, almost wholly beneficial; its effect was to subvert 'good taste' and open ballroom dancing to reform, even if reform were defensive and designed largely to pre-empt something worse.

By the late 1930s, popular music and dance had an established structure and technology: a large music-writing and recording industry operating within a small number of established genres, unprecedently powerful instruments of promotion in the radio and gramophone, and lavishly provided palais and dance halls, to which was attached a highly organized system of ballroom

---

[54] Richardson, *English Ballroom Dancing*, 90. See Lee's comments on Silvester: 'The world-acclaimed "strict tempo", stripped of its brain-washing publicity, reveals itself as no more than the regularity which has been required in social dancing in Europe since the earliest times'. (E. Lee, *Music of the People* (London, 1970), 155.)

[55] And still does, as anyone who has seen the Australian film *Strictly Ballroom* (1992) will know.

dancing. How effective these were as elements in the national culture was demonstrated by the remarkable craze for the Lambeth Walk in 1938–9. As a song, the 'Lambeth Walk'—named not after the dance but a well-known promenade in Lambeth—sold more records, and faster, even than 'Yes, We Have No Bananas'. As a dance, it was the only English one of the period to have been adopted internationally and was probably exceeded in immediate popularity only by the Charleston.

The 'Lambeth Walk', with music by Noel Gay and words by Douglas Furber, first appeared in a revue *Me and My Girl* at the Victoria Palace at Christmas 1937. The song was conceived by Noel Gay to be specifically English: he was sure that working people were 'sick of American heaven in your arms and moon on silent waters'. He deliberately went, he said, for 'everyday homely symbols, with simple repetitions, or otherwise new angles on old situations'. The comedian Lupino Lane played Bill Snibson, a cockney who inherits an earldom but remains a cockney. Bill decides to give a grand party and invites his old Lambeth pals as well as the toffs. The toffs are shocked by the behaviour of Bill's pals but when he starts to sing his song and do his walk 'there is a terrific effect of social breakdown, everyone joins in and shouts "Oi!" and the Duchess finally goes into dinner on Bill's arm, wearing his bowler on her head.'[56] Bill's walk was a sort of 'drunken, syncopated' step supposed to be suggestive of a cockney swagger.

C. L. Heimann, by now managing director of Mecca Dancing and thus, as Mass-Observation noted, one of the 'cultural directors' of English life,[57] was attracted by Lupino's walk and asked the resident instructor at the Locarno, Streatham, Adele England, to transform it into a novelty dance. She devised a highly rhythmic foot-to-heel walk accompanied by knee and forehead slapping. The jaunty 'Oi!' at the end of each round was Heimann's idea. Miss England then danced it in exhibition at many of the Mecca palais:

I started in the Locarno [Streatham Hill] then I went round to the Ritz, Manchester; the Grand Casino, Birmingham; Sherries [sic], Brighton; the Locarno, Glasgow and the Piccadilly Club, Glasgow; the Palais, Edinburgh and the Royal, Tottenham. I did it all in a month.[58]

She designed the dance for a couple, but it was almost instantly turned into a serial dance like the Conga, the Chestnut Tree, or the Hokey-Cokey, which were very popular in the late thirties. It was this simplicity and flexibility which doubtless partly accounted for its success. As popular in the West End as in the palais, it swept its predecessor, the Big Apple, off the boards. Despite the self-conscious Englishness of both song and dance it did the same in the United States (where it was introduced by Prince Serge Obolensky). There it was more

[56] C. Madge and T. Harrisson, *Britain by Mass-Observation* (Harmondsworth, 1939), 157.
[57] Ibid. 141.   [58] Ibid. 160–2.

usually danced to Duke Ellington's arrangement which was, *Time* magazine sniffily noted, 'doubtless played more interestingly than it ever was at its point of origin, London'.

The radio was crucial for the transmission of both song and dance. Of a sample interviewed by Mass-Observation half had first heard of it on the radio, nearly one-fifth had seen it danced, the remainder heard of it through friends, the papers, or other sources. The catchiness of the song, the comparative ease of the dance, and the power of the radio and Mecca Dancing almost guaranteed its success.

The Englishness or cockneyness of the dance is, however, questionable. When interviewed at the time neither Lupino Lane nor Adele England were aware of any formative influences.[59] Some nevertheless thought the steps were derived, however unconsciously, from older dances typical of London's coster-mongers (fruit and vegetable sellers), particularly as practised by the cockney comedian, Alec Hurley. He popularized a 'coster walk' which was widely enough known for Major Cecil Taylor, prominent in ballroom dancing, to organize a coster walk competition. The existence of older, indigenous cockney dances is not in doubt. During the First World War cockney soldiers often danced 'knees-up's and were, outside certain Scottish regiments, the only soldiers who customarily danced with each other. These knees-ups often involved elaborate 'walks' with much self-display. The tradition was obviously maintained, as this account of a private party in Lambeth in the 1930s suggests:

> The striking feature of the dancing was the rolling tempo, less nerve-taut than American swing and hot rhythm, somewhat less martial than the tune Noel Gay wrote for the 'Lambeth Walk' . . . [But] it was most obvious when they did their own dances, with improvised steps . . . They did jigging steps with their feet, plus some high kicking, then the two lines crossed over, turned over and reformed. As they crossed they walked in the half-lilting, half swaggering way that Lupino Lane used in his Lambeth Walk. For the men it is a swagger, arms out from the sides, like a boxer playing for position; for the women it is more of a lilt with the hips swaying.[60]

What was the origin of this curious strut? We can probably discount the sociologically implausible explanations proffered at the time—that, for instance, the shoulder swagger came from bare-knuckle boxing or that the crooked thumb was a sign of aggressive intent. It may be impossible to discover any 'origins', but (as some noted) the Lambeth and coster walks were strikingly like those 'coon dances', the cakewalk and ballin' the jack, which were very popular in the music-halls of East and South London in the 1890s. Both were swaggering walks dependent upon a rolling motion of heel and foot: the cakewalk was, the *Daily Telegraph* said in 1898, 'a graceful motion, conducted upon the toes and the ball of the foot'. It survived in London, though ballin' the jack,

---

[59] Madge and Harrisson, *Britain by Mass-Observation*, 159–62.   [60] Ibid. 146.

as a recognizable song or dance, disappeared in England until, as a song, it was unexpectedly revived by Danny Kaye in *On the Riviera* (1951). It is, therefore, at least arguable that both the coster and Lambeth walks were derived from these 'coon dances' and absorbed within an existing tradition. (That cockneys also danced in the 1930s something suspiciously black-sounding called 'the twist' might be pure coincidence.) In its anglicized form, the Lambeth Walk, a dance many thought to be peculiarly English, was then re-exported to the United States where its similarity to the cakewalk may account for its surprising success there. If so, then the cultural relationships between the United States and England in the interwar years appear not so one-sided but more complicated, with movements in both directions.

Beginning fitfully in the late 1930s, the second wave of American popular music broke over the whole of English musical culture in 1942 with the arrival of American soldiers, bands, and radio programmes. To most people this wave meant 'swing'. Swing probably originated in Kansas City in the mid-thirties as a style of big-band jazz which aimed at generating maximum excitement 'by use of loud, hard-hitting effects, a steady pushing four-in-a-bar rhythm and the constant repetition of simple melodic phrases'.[61] The best known of the early swing bands was Count Basie's, but it soon became associated with white bands—Tommy Dorsey, Artie Shaw and, above all, Benny Goodman, the 'King of Swing'. Swing was intended to be dance music and its pounding rhythms encouraged violent, acrobatic high-voltage dances like the lindy hop and the jitterbug.

The Americans also carried in their baggage 'bebop'—a deliberate reaction to the harmonies of white jazz by younger black musicians like Charlie Parker, Dizzy Gillespie, and Thelonious Monk. Its aim, amongst others, was to exclude white musicians, who were getting all the best and most lucrative contracts, by designing a more complicated and 'difficult' jazz—bebop was to jazz as was twelve tone to classical music. The result of exclusion, however, was a smaller audience. Although bop was itself vulgarized and made accessible, the early admirers of Charlie Parker *et al.* in England were jazz purists, not the denizens of the palais.

Swing was known in England before the war but not to many. This was partly the doing of the BBC which regarded it as connoisseurs' music and gave it little radio time.[62] The lindy hop and the jitterbug were also known but danced with more enthusiasm than skill. The war changed all this. Dancing, like the cinema, having lost a little ground in the late 1930s, became hugely popular once more and the palais began employing 'named' bands—Joe Loss, Lew Stone, and Geraldo (Gerald Bright) packed the dance halls. The arrival of the Americans, furthermore, changed both standards and styles. The American

---

[61] Lee, *Music of the People*, 141–2.
[62] Scannell and Cardiff, *Social History of British Broadcasting*, 189–92.

bands, including the most popular, Glenn Miller's United States Army Air Force Band, all played swing, and the British bands were compelled to follow. Nor did the best of the British bands lose much by comparison. The three services each had their own bands, the most famous of which, the Squadronaires, was largely Bert Ambrose's band in RAF uniform. It played hot swing; hotter than Glenn Miller whose music, though distinctive and attractive, was decidedly conventional and sweet. Nothing, as one historian has pointed out, could have been 'sweeter', than 'Moonlight Serenade', Miller's signature tune.[63] The difference was, of course, that however skilled the English swing bands were, they were playing somebody else's music derivatively. Swing, furthermore, was American in a patriotic sense. Whereas the music with which the English officially identified during the war were sentimental and optimistic ballads of the Vera Lynn–Anne Shelton kind, America's wartime music *was* swing and the popular songs that emerged from it. The Americans, in a sense, did not need a specially crafted wartime music: it developed naturally from their own musical culture but served the same purpose as George M. Cohan's noisily nationalistic songs had done in the First World War.

The verve and skill of American dancing had its inevitable effect in the dance halls. Jitterbugging, though physically antisocial, was danced everywhere, almost as big a craze as the Charleston and the Lambeth Walk, though more difficult than both. Even ballroom dancing had to give way in the end. Its first reaction to jitterbugging had been unremittingly hostile. One of its officials wrote:

An All England Jitterbug Championship, not recognized by the Official Board, has just been held in London, and I must confess that it was about the most disgusting and degrading sight I have ever seen in a ballroom. Leap-frog, double somersaults, 'kicking the ceiling' and 'peckin'' were but a few of the 'steps' used by the competitors in their efforts to gain applause.

'In spite of this', he added cautiously, 'I still think that there is room for a mild jitterbug dance on our ballrooms at the present time.'[64] The Official Board agreed. The jive was to become a domesticated jitterbug and an acceptable part of the ballroom repertoire.

The war represented the high point of the dance bands and perhaps prolonged their lives. In England several of them, Geraldo, Ted Heath, Billy Cotton, continued in being well into the fifties, though usually heavily dependent on television. For the rest, the circumstances which undermined the bands in the United States within a few years did so in England as well.

The speed with which dance band culture, seemingly so strong during the war, collapsed in the United States surprised many. In a single month in 1946

---

[63] Lee, *Music of the People*, 141–2.
[64] S. Nelson, 'Dance Bands', in Richardson, *English Ballroom Dancing*, 141–2.

Benny Goodman, Woody Herman, Tommy Dorsey, Benny Carter, Harry James, and Les Brown all dissolved their bands, most of them permanently. Technological and social changes, to some extent frozen by the war, moved with great speed to marginalize the bands as soon as it ended. As a way of selling records the radio and the disc-jockey were much more effective: by the late 1940s, for instance, no American bandleader had the influence of the disc-jockey Alan Freed.

Furthermore, the increasing popularity of romantic and novelty songs raised the status of the vocalist at the expense of the band. Throughout the 1920s and most of the 1930s the vocalist was usually a kind of additional instrument. By the late thirties, however, some outstanding vocalists like Bing Crosby, who had sung with Paul Whiteman and Gus Arnheim, had come to regard the band as only an accompaniment—indeed, Crosby recorded his signature tune, 'In the Blue of the Night', in which the vocalist is clearly dominant, as early as 1931. Frank Sinatra's apprenticeship was even shorter: he sang for three years (1939–42) as vocalist with Harry James and Tommy Dorsey, but by 1942 was clearly a soloist whose accompanying bands were there to provide a smooth backing for a dominant vocalist. Even Peggy Lee, who sang with Goodman and married his guitarist, Dave Barbour, had gone solo by 1942. Between 1940 and 1955 a ranking of the top ten recording artists in the United States includes only three bands.[65] To some extent the same happened in England. Both Vera Lynn, who had been vocalist with Joe Loss and Ambrose (and married one of Ambrose's clarinettists, Harry Lewis), and Anne Shelton, who also had sung with Ambrose, became hugely successful soloists during the war.

The growing predominance of the vocalist was a result of the increasing popularity of the song *qua* song. For much of the interwar years the song was an adjunct to dancing with the dance bands as the primary medium. By the 1940s most songs had been divorced from dancing, the music itself becoming intensely absorbing even to those without any other discernible intellectual interests—'a new kind of emotional and sensual self-expression'.[66] Many songs, of course, could be danced to but that was not necessarily why they were written. This divorce was accelerated by the invention of the juke-box in 1936. The nickleodeon, a sort of coin-in-the-slot pianola, had been a proto-juke-box, but technically crude. The juke-box, however, was easy to play and worked in tandem with the radio hit parades which had been first broadcast in the United States in 1935—though not in England until some time later. The juke-box was even longer in coming to England: not until the early 1950s and closely associated with the fashion for coffee-bars. But the effect was the same: to make the dance band almost redundant.

---

[65] C. Hamms, *Yesterdays: Popular Song in America* (New York and London, 1979), 387–8.
[66] Logan and Goldberg, 'Rising Eighteen in a London Suburb', 331.

The juke-box as apparatus for promotion had one other consequence whose significance for both American and English popular music can scarcely be overrated. It allowed blacks and whites in the Southern states to play their own music and encouraged record companies to set up recording facilities in the South, particularly in Nashville and Memphis. As a result 'country and western', 'rockabilly', and what was originally called 'race music' but after 1949–50 'rhythm and blues', was introduced to an American and then an international audience. This was the third wave, which reached England in the early 1950s, though with consequences for English and, indirectly, American popular music which could not have been predicted then.

The developing significance of the vocalist and an eclectic popular music—this 'hybrid and polluted jazz'[67]—was due not only to changes in the technology of popular music, but also to changes in its market. From the early 1950s the market for commercial popular music was increasingly a teenage one. Until then popular music had not been written consciously for the young: if consciously written for anyone it was the family. Thereafter, as the discretionary income of teenagers rose steadily they became the preferred market simply because they listened more—in 1954 90 per cent of London teenagers spent some time listening to popular-music records[68]—and because they listened more they now bought more. Musical taste was becoming determined by age; each generation remembering the popular music of its youth as the best of music—after which all was decline. The growing preponderance of teenagers in the market was, for example, represented by the changing relative fortunes of *Melody Maker* and the *New Musical Express*. *Melody Maker* was a trade paper which also promoted 'pure' jazz; *New Musical Express* (founded in 1952) was a popular music paper which almost immediately sought a teenage readership. In 1955 the circulation of *Melody Maker* was 107,308, *New Musical Express* 93,127. By 1958 *Melody Maker*'s was 99,104 and that of *New Musical Express* 122,267.

In 1947, the music historian Stanley Nelson wrote that

our dance music is coloured more and more by the negro jazz palette, but it is vital and compelling. Indeed so compelling that I see an entirely new lease of life for this American jazz music, the modern dance music which has almost become the folk music of the world.[69]

In general Nelson's comment was true of England. American jazz had been the most powerful single influence on English popular musical idiom since the First World War. Even as that influence petered out in the late 1940s and early 1950s the dynamic remained American: the vocalists who were following in Bing Crosby's steps—Frank Sinatra, Frankie Laine, Guy Mitchell, Eddie Fisher,

[67] Newton, *Jazz Scene*, 31.   [68] Frith, *Sociology of Rock*, 37–8.
[69] Nelson, 'Dance Bands' in Richardson, *English Ballroom Dancing*, 141–2.

Perry Como, Rosemary Clooney, Dinah Shore, Doris Day, Kay Starr, Jo Stafford—were as popular in England as in the United States. And they earned the sincerest form of flattery: imitation. English vocalists tended to adopt a mid-Atlantic singing accent; some, even American clothes and hairstyles. The epitome of this cultural deference was probably the Cliff Richard of *The Young Ones* and *Summer Holiday*. Furthermore, the recording of cover versions made it possible for English vocalists to ride the success of American songs and vocalists. Jimmy Young, for example, cut his teeth at No. 1 with that teenage heart-trembler of them all, 'Unchained Melody'—displacing Al Hibbler's original recording. Lita Roza's version excluded from No. 1 the Patti Page original of Bob Merrill's famous novelty song, 'How Much is that Doggie in the Window?'.

In a narrower sense, however, it is easy to exaggerate the influence of American music and, particularly, of American jazz. English music was very adept at assimilating and modifying American popular music. There was, it is true, nothing like the Stéphane Grapelli–Django Reinhardt combination, which produced a 'European' jazz owing little to American sources, but (as we have seen) the quality of English dance bands was very high, being internationally admired, like English ballroom dancing, for suppleness of style and ensemble. Furthermore, a number of the most popular songs of the period were English: Ray Noble's 'Goodnight Sweetheart', 'Love is the sweetest Thing', and 'The very Thought of You', and Jack Strachey's 'These foolish Things' are among the best sweet jazz songs of the era. As Alec Wilder said of Noble, his songs were 'so American in style and so loved by Americans that he is musically American by adoption. I doubt, in fact, if most of those who like his songs know that they were written by an Englishman.'[70] In 1932 Reg Connelly, having written 'Show me the Way to go Home' in 1925, produced 'Underneath the Arches', immemorially associated with Flanagan and Allen, and 'Try a little Tenderness', two of the most popular songs of the decade. Gracie Fields made enormously popular both 'Sally' and the song Harry Parr-Davies wrote for her, 'Wish me Luck as you wave me Goodbye' (1939). One of the most treacly, but popular, of the Christmas novelty songs, Tommie Connor's 'I saw Mommy kissing Santa Claus', written for the American market, was—alas—also of English make.[71] Noel Gay's 'Lambeth Walk', of course, outsold nearly everything else.

There was, furthermore, an 'alternative' Anglo-American musical tradition which owed as much to English popular music as American: the tradition of variety and the musical. The English music hall and American vaudeville were closely related both as social and musical institutions. Before the First World War they shared artists and songs and were primarily responsible for the

[70] A. Wilder, *American Popular Song* (New York, 1972), 424.

[71] It was a huge best-seller in the American market as, of course, were all Christmas songs. Connor was not a despicable lyricist. He wrote the English words to 'Lili Marlene', the song which made Anne Shelton a star.

existence of a largely common Anglo-American musical culture. Even by 1900 it was clear that vaudeville was the more fertile of the two but the music hall still had much cultural power. Thus genuine Edwardian Anglo-American 'hits' like 'Bicycle built for Two' and the famous novelty song 'Ta-ra-ra-boom-de-ay' were unpublishable in the United States until they had become enormously popular in London. And American musicals, which were especially popular in the 1940s and 1950s, were, broadly speaking, derived from both Viennese operetta and English musical comedy. Thus Jerome Kern was sent to London in 1905 in order to complete his musical education and many of his earlier songs were written either for the London stage or for English revues shown in America. Before 1914 nearly all half-successful West End musical comedies went to New York, and some clearly influenced the development of the American musical. The most influential was probably Leslie Stuart's *Florodora* (1899)—itself a good example of the complicated nature of Anglo-American cultural relations.[72] Stuart, who is now best remembered as the composer of 'Lily of Laguna', was himself much influenced by the 'coon music' and cakewalk rhythms of the 1890s, which he incorporated into *Florodora*. Though its sextet 'Tell me pretty Maiden' was popular everywhere, *Florodora* was more admired in New York than in London and acknowledged as influential by Jerome Kern and even Richard Rodgers, who was not born until 1902. No English musical of the period was anywhere near as brilliant as Rodgers's own *Oklahoma!* (New York, 1943; London, 1947) or even *South Pacific* (New York, 1947; London, 1951), but the style was very familiar to the English public and the tradition remained strong in England—in the long run, perhaps stronger than in the United States.

Nor did the tradition of the music hall and the musical revue die in England. C. B. Cochran's and Noel Coward's revues in the 1920s and 1930s produced much witty music popular in both England and the United States—though Coward's earlier music was itself much influenced by 1920s New York—but neither, and hardly any American, approached the success of Jimmy Kennedy, who demonstrated how lively and lucrative the English music hall still was. Kennedy, who had begun his career as teacher and then member of the colonial service, was a phenomenon who, sometimes in collaboration, wrote at least seven of the most popular songs of the era: 'The Teddy Bear's Picnic' (1933); 'The Isle of Capri' (1934); 'Red Sails in the Sunset' (1934); 'Roll along covered Wagon' (1935); 'South of the Border' (1939); 'My Prayer' (1939), and 'We're gonna hang out the Washing on the Siegfried Line' (1939). 'South of the Border', as sung by the most popular of the singing cowboys, Gene Autry, was No. 1 in America, as was 'My Prayer'. That these songs drew on many sources—novelty, the Western, Latin America, the pseudo-religious and the cheery-patriotic—was entirely characteristic of the music hall, a tribute to its vigour.

[72] For Stuart, see T. Staveacre, *The Songwriters* (London, 1979), 11–29.

The large public for this alternative tradition was older. Although there was as yet no 'teenage market' in England for popular music there was already a noticeable generational dimension to popular musical taste. A survey of radio-listening in the late 1930s, for example, found that while the majority of young women and the great majority of children could immediately identify their favourite bandleader, older women were 'completely indifferent'.[73] It was the completely indifferent who largely determined the repertoire of the clubs, institutes, and army barracks—the places where good singers were described as 'vocalists', less good as 'versatile', and the worst as 'popular vocalists',[74] where all tried to sound like Peter Dawson and where 'Come Back to Sorrento' was always a 'classical' favourite.[75] It was this public for whom Rodgers and Hammerstein and, even more, Jimmy Kennedy wrote, or for whom the brassbands played 'Abide with Me' or 'Bless this House', a public deeply attached to musical genres strongly influenced by the United States, but native to England and anything but dead.

Equally vigorous was the tradition of the sentimental ballad and the novelty song, the public for which was almost certainly larger than that for jazz or jazz-inspired music. Aside from being vaguely syncopated, most of the popular ballads of the period owed little to jazz and more to musical comedy, operetta or popular religious music. Furthermore, these songs were as popular in the United States as they were in England. Numbers 1 and 2 in America's first published hit parade (April 1935) were Jerome Kern's 'Lovely to look at' and 'I won't dance'; the songs most frequently heard in the pre-pop parades were Irving Berlin's 'White Christmas', as sung by Bing Crosby and probably the most popular record ever made, and Richard Rodgers's 'People will say we're in Love'. The Second World War emphasized the popularity of ballads and novelties. In England Vera Lynn's 'White Cliffs of Dover' and 'We'll meet again' and Anne Shelton's 'I'll be seeing you', 'Lay down your Arms' and, of course, the English version of 'Lili Marlene', were hugely popular—as in both countries were novelty songs like 'Mairzy Doats-and Doazy Doats' (1943), 'Open the Door Richard' (1947), 'Woody Woodpecker' (1947), 'Come-on-a-my House' (1951); vaguely Latin American songs like 'Rum and Coca-Cola' (1944) or 'Mañana' (1948); and even more vaguely 'Western' songs like 'Ghost Riders in the Sky' (1949), 'Mule Train' (1949) or the astonishingly popular 'Don't Fence Me In' (1944), which Cole Porter wrote as a deliberate parody of the genre.[76]

The tendency of vocalists to sing them reflected and accentuated ballads' intrinsic appeal. Bing Crosby's own career exemplifies this. Although he had a background in white jazz, was an admirer of Bix Beiderbecke, made records

[73] H. Jennings and W. Gill, *Broadcasting in Everyday Life* (London, 1939), 14.
[74] Jackson, *Working-Class Community*, 56. For a good description of a club concert, see Dennis *et al.*, *Coal is Our Life*, 147.
[75] Vaughan, *Something in Linoleum*, 223.   [76] Hamms, *Yesterdays*, 388–9.

with Duke Ellington and Louis Armstrong and had a certain jazz-singer's style and rhythm, his reputation (and fortune) were increasingly made by ballads or covers of already popular songs. His three best-selling songs were 'White Christmas', 'Adeste Fidelis' ('Oh Come all ye Faithful') and 'Jingle Bells', while many of his other best sellers, like 'The Bells of St Mary's' or 'Sweet Leilani', were as lushly sentimental as anything written—as were most of his 22 million-sale recordings.

The popularity of ballad and novelty in England continued well into the 1950s: they were 'the order of the day' the *New Musical Express* commented.[77] In 1952, the year when the *New Musical Express* began to publish the English hit parades, Vera Lynn's 'Auf Wiedersehen' was long No. 1 in both England and America, while Al Martino's 'Here in my Heart' topped the *New Musical Express*'s first official singles' chart (15 November 1952). Before the mid-1950s much the most popular songs in England were Frankie Laine's 'I believe' (1953), which was usually called 'inspirational' and was No. 1 for 18 weeks, a figure exceeded neither before nor since; David Whitfield's 'Cara mia' (1954, composed with Mantovani); Eddie Calvert's 'Oh mein Papa' (1954), which came from a German-language Swiss musical; and Slim Whitman's 'Rose Marie' (1955). The first 'rock' song to appear in the charts was Bill Haley's 'Shake, Rattle and Roll' (December 1954), but it was not No. 1. 'Rock around the Clock', buoyed by the success of the film *The Blackboard Jungle*, first become No. 1 in January 1956, but only as a re-entry, having got nowhere a year earlier. Presley entered the charts for the first time in May 1956 ('Hearbreak Hotel') but did not reach No. 1 until 1957, with 'All Shook Up'.

Throughout this period there were three musical publics, though the relationship between them was always fluid. There was a very small public for 'serious' music; a considerably larger one for 'middlebrow' music, and a much larger one for 'popular' music. But some middlebrow music, like *Beethoven's Eroica*, was also popular with the serious musical public, while popular music, though based very largely on those who were only interested in it, had an audience everywhere. Furthermore, popular music itself had fragmented. Although jazz had enormously influenced popular dance and music, it was by the 1950s almost completely divorced from the public which was listening to the hit parade. There was also an established middlebrow canon of very eclectic origins, and that canon was what most people understood by classical music. By the 1950s it was largely fixed since serious music was now being written in styles which could never be assimililated by middlebrow music. But the public for middlebrow music was so large that it must be considered, unlike serious music, one branch of popular music: it, like popular commercial music, was the music of democracy.

<hr>

[77] D. Ross, Barry Lazell, and Roger Osborne (eds.), *Forty Years of NME Charts* (London, 1992), 5.

The middlebrow canon was the product of many influences, none predominant. But English popular commercial music was subject to very powerful influences from one source—American popular music—and more open to them than any other musical culture outside North America. The jazz-historian Francis Newton attributes this to the fact that American folk-music was 'never swamped by the cultural standards of the upper classes':

English musical working-class culture in the nineteenth century consisted of a patently dying rural and pre-industrial folk-music, a musically extremely shoddy music-hall song, and the twin pillars of organised working-class music, the classical oratorio and the brass band. But however admirable the *Messiah* or the test pieces at the brass band festivals, they are working-class conquests of orthodox culture, not independent folk-music . . . and [America's] persistent supremacy over Britain derives largely from this.[78]

This is an interesting argument, but only partly true. It implicitly exaggerates the influence in the United States of black music and under-rates that of Tin Pan Alley. But the American market for popular music was highly segmented, as was indicated by its three hit parades: conventional popular music, black music, and country music. Though some songs 'crossed over', this was still comparatively unusual. And much the largest of the three segments was dominated by Tin Pan Alley—a pluralistic tradition which certainly drew upon jazz and country and western, but even more heavily upon vaudeville and operetta, which in turn drew heavily upon English music hall and musical comedy. Furthermore, Tin Pan Alley predominated throughout this period: as Charles Hamms pointed out, the vocalists selling most records between 1940 and 1955—long after black music had become familiar to a white audience— were singing second or third generation Tin Pan Alley songs.[79]

Newton also exaggerates the attachment of the working class to the oratorio—the singing of which was almost certainly more a lower-middle-class than a working-class activity—and underestimates the continuing energy and 'folkness' of the English music hall tradition. Indeed, its folkness could be too much for the Americans. One reason why vaudeville management was nervous of employing English music hall artists was that they were often too earthy for American taste. There was, of course, constant pressure to raise the tone of the English music hall by eliminating its more specific working-class and demotic features—but only with partial success. What did more to prettify the music hall tradition was the ease with which the two media which continued it—the cinema and radio—were pre-censored. Even here, however, censorship was never complete: George Formby's film songs, like 'When I'm Cleaning Windows' (banned by the BBC) or 'With My Little Stick of Blackpool Rock', were notorious for their *doubles entendres*, and were given general release largely, one presumes, because the members of the British Board of Film

<hr/>

[78] Newton, *Jazz Scene*, 43.   [79] Hamms, *Yesterdays*, 405.

Censors did not understand them. Nor did the music hall tradition, at least as memory, ever really disappear. Paul McCartney's 'When I'm Sixty-Four' (1967), for instance, enormously popular in both England and the United States, was pure music hall.

Thus the relationship between imported American music and English popular musical culture is more complicated than Newton suggests. Music for English dance—with the significant exception of serial dances like the 'Lambeth Walk' and the 'hokey-cokey'—was almost entirely imported, either directly, like jazz, or indirectly, like Latin American music, from the United States. But imported American songs were usually in some way Tin Pan Alley and by no means crowded out English popular song. But Britain was so open to Tin Pan Alley, its composers and lyricists so adept at 'copying' it, because the genre was entirely familiar and partly of English origin, just as the notion of the 'hit' song, so characteristic of Anglo-American music, was of English origin.

The relationship was further complicated by the direct commercial interest England had in American popular music: the two largest producers of popular music, EMI and Decca, were largely English in ownership. Both Edward Lewis's Decca and, even more, Louis Stirling's EMI had by the late 1930s developed into colossal combines which dominated the international distribution of popular music. The creation of EMI in 1932 brought together in one firm HMV, Columbia, Parlophone, Regal Zonophone, and MGM. Decca owned the London label and bought Brunswick in the United States. In buying Brunswick it bought Bing Crosby.[80] And the fortunes of these companies depended largely upon the sales of songs written within the tradition not of jazz but of Tin Pan Alley.

---

[80] Frith, 'British Record Industry', in Curran, Smith, and Wingate, *Impacts and Influences*, 281–3. In 1955 EMI and Decca together produced 77.5% of the top 10 singles in Britain (Frith, *Sociology of Rock*, 98).

THE cinema was the most important medium of popular culture in the period, and the English went to the cinema more than any other people. Indeed, they made up one-tenth of the world market. It was also a very powerful force for Americanization, something which alarmed many in the country's élites. This chapter discusses what films people preferred and why; how far the cinema did Americanize English culture and how far, other things being equal, the English actually did prefer American films. The chapter also looks at the way the state tried to limit American influence and how effective it was. It considers the different genres of English films and their social and cultural significance.

'Going to the pictures' was not simply the most important leisure activity of the English, at least outside the home, it was more important to them than to any other nationality. In 1950 the average Englishman and woman went to the pictures 28 times per year, more than 10 per cent of *total* world cinema attendance, a per capita figure not even exceeded in the United States.[1] Throughout the 1930s there were 18–19 million weekly attendances, a number hugely increased during the Second World War. By 1945 it was 30 million. In 1946, the year when cinema attendance was at its highest, one-third of the whole population went to the pictures at least once a week, and there were a total of 1,635 million attendances.[2] That number declined slowly throughout the rest of the decade; yet in 1950 it was still 40 per cent higher than in 1939. Excluding radio-listening, which was largely a household activity and available to the majority of the population only from the mid-1930s,[3] but not excluding sport, no other cultural activity of the period approached cinema-going in its general popularity.

Yet the English did not love the cinema equally: attendance was much influenced by age, class, gender, and place of residence. Adolescents, for example, went most; the elderly least. In 1946, 69 per cent of 16–19-year-olds but only

---

[1] J. Stacey, *Star Gazing* (London and New York, 1994), 83. In 1950 the United States and Britain together made up more than half of total world cinema attendance.

[2] K. Box, *The Cinema and the Public*, Social Survey, NS 106 (1946), 3.

[3] See below, Chapter XII.

11 per cent of those over 60 went to the cinema at least once a week. Twenty-two per cent of those over 45 never went.[4] Even in 1950, when attendances had declined, 60 per cent of adolescent boys who had left school admitted going to the cinema at least twice a week.[5] And even they could not get enough. Adolescents drew a sharp distinction between their 'favourite' and 'main' activity— and the cinema ranked higher as 'favourite' than as 'main'.[6]

The extent to which adolescents, adolescent boys particularly, went to the cinema was associated, both in fact and in people's minds, with a battery of other characteristics. Boys who were restless at work or who were constantly job-changing were most prone to picture-going. They were least likely to read books or belong to clubs. They went to secondary modern schools and were not very happy there. They came from crowded households with fathers in low-paid occupations.[7] Contemporaries, alarmed at the 'problem' of post-war juvenile delinquency, were not slow to note the apparent relationship between frequent cinema attendance and delinquency.[8]

Adolescent cinema-going, even among those who went comparatively little, should be seen as the peak of cinema-going which rose in childhood and declined in adulthood. 'Going to the pictures'—nearly always on Saturday morning regardless of whenever else they went—was a very important part of children's lives. It was not just the pictures; it was the camaraderie, the tacitly permitted 'boisterousness', and the exchange-and-mart atmosphere where comics and magazines were swapped. In encouraging this, cinema management knew what it was attempting—to socialize children into a lifetime of cinema-going. Thus the ubiquity of the cinema clubs which were more popular with children, until they were about 13, than any other club or society. The clubs were not, in fact, altogether unlike the cubs or brownies. The Odeon clubs, for instance, even had a club hymn:

> 'To the Odeon we have come
> Now we can have some fun
> . . .
> We are a hundred thousand strong,
> So how can we all be wrong.'

—and a club promise: to obey one's parents, to be kind to animals, and to make the country 'a better place to live in'.[9] The clubs, which organized competitions, projects, and expeditions, were very effective at assimilating children into a cinematic sub-culture, if not necessarily for life.

---

[4] Box, *Cinema and the Public*, 3.   [5] Wilkins, *Adolescent in Britain*, 97.

[6] Ibid. 85–6. It should be noted even of this figure that adolescents were reluctant to admit how frequently they did go to the pictures.

[7] Ibid. 63, 97.   [8] T. Ferguson, *The Young Delinquent in His Social Setting* (London, 1952), 38–9.

[9] J. Ward, *Children Out of School*, Social Survey, NS 110 (1948), 28–9. For the cinema clubs, see J. P. Mayer, *Sociology of Film* (London, 1946), 51–7.

Social class was the second major determinant of cinema attendance. Among children in the late 1940s cinema attendance fell as socio-economic status rose. Thus three times as many secondary modern as grammar school pupils went to the cinema more than once a week,[10] while a much higher proportion of secondary modern pupils belonged to cinema clubs.[11] These differences reflected not simply individual propensities, but different domestic cultures. A significantly higher proportion of 'middle-class' than 'working-class' mothers knew what films their children saw[12] and this suggests much closer parental supervision (i.e. restriction) of their offspring's cinema-going. Among adults, all levels of the working class went more often than the middle or upper classes. But skilled workers and clerical and distributive workers went 'significantly' more often than unskilled workers, who as adolescents were likely to go most but who in adulthood could afford it least. Though the non-working classes went less frequently they bought more expensive seats and so spent per capita almost as much as anyone else.[13]

Cinema attendance was biased by gender as well as class: except during adolescence, when boys were likely to go at least as often as girls, women always went to the cinema more than men. By the 1930s, film-makers, those in Hollywood particularly, assumed they were making movies largely for women. One product of this assumption was 'women's films'—romantic-sexual 'problem' movies made specifically for women and from what was understood to be the woman's view.[14] The cinema was ideally suited to women at a moment when their own cultural lives were necessarily passive, their routines largely determined by the demands of husband and children. And for much of this period the cinema was very cheap—half the seats cost less than 6d[15]—and to housewives always worried about domestic budgets (and who spent less on themselves in the cinema than anyone else)[16] this was an exceptionally economical form of entertainment. Furthermore, the matinée, which had always been the 'women's programme', fitted well into domestic routines. The matinée was also important, especially for middle-class women, as an occasion for sociability. Shopping, meeting for lunch, and going to a matinée (or the reverse) was a regular arrangement for women throughout the country.

Cinema attendance was also skewed by place of residence. Country people, not surprisingly, went to the cinema much less often than town and city dwellers. While, for example, in 1946 48 per cent of urban children went to the cinema at least once a week, only 29 per cent of rural children did so.[17] For children evacuated during the war, the scarcity of cinemas was one of the

---

[10] Ward, *Children Out of School*, 42.   [11] Ibid. 31.

[12] Box, *Cinema and the Public*, 9. The principal reason for this was, of course, homework: grammar school pupils had too much and secondary modern pupils too little.

[13] Ibid. 4, 12.   [14] Stacey, *Star Gazing*, 85–6.

[15] P. Miles and M. Smith, *Cinema, Literature and Society* (London, 1987), 164.

[16] Box, *Cinema and the Public*, 12.   [17] Ibid. 5.

The Cinema and the English

main drawbacks of country life and one of the main reasons for their initial hostility to local children—they had so little in common to talk about.

There were equally striking regional differences in levels of attendances. People in the North were almost twice as likely to go to the cinema as those in the South; the only place in the South which approached northern levels was London. There were even marked differences between the North and the industrial Midlands. In 1950–1 in north-western towns of over 100,000 the average person went to the cinema 45 times a year, whereas in an equivalent Midlands or North Midlands town the figure was only 35. At the extreme, differences were so wide—in Coventry the figure was 27 and in Preston 53[18]—as to be puzzling. Preston and Coventry were of similar social composition and in 1950 there was full employment in both. Differentials in personal wealth may be partly responsible. Coventry was a rich town, drawing its wealth from a motor industry then at the height of its prosperity, and had, unlike Preston, been rich for a generation. People of all classes could, therefore, afford alternatives to the pictures. The variety of Coventry's associational life is indeed impressive, but not that much more various than (say) Mass-Observation's 'Worktown' (Bolton), particularly after 1945. Even if per capita income were higher in Coventry than in the North it seems unlikely that this alone would explain such differences in leisure preference.

It may be that northern working-class culture was simply more inactive. People in the North tended to 'watch' while those in the South tended to 'do'. Participatory sport, for instance, was much stronger in the South than in the North. Such differences were, again, partly due to income: watching was cheaper than playing, and the North was poorer than the South. Yet this is not a wholly convincing explanation. We have seen that with adolescents high cinema attendance apparently correlated with low reading habits, but in Bolton, where cinema attendance was comparatively high, one in three residents was registered with the public library, whereas in Coventry, where cinema attendance was comparatively low, only one in five were registered.[19] Whatever the explanation for such variations in cinema-going, however, does not invalidate the fact that going to the pictures was the country's principal extra-domestic leisure activity, and in the degree to which it was practised England had no peer.

The social centrality of the cinema to English life was measured by the increasing size and opulence of the cinemas themselves. Before the First World War cinemas were usually small—not unlike boxing's 'small halls'—and many local cinemas remained small and unpretentious. But in the 1920s cinemas of deliberate sumptuousness and fantastic style were built in the centres of the larger towns or in densely populated suburbs. Egyptian, Graeco-Roman, Byzan-

---

[18] Ichihashi, 'Working-Class Leisure in English Towns', 325.   [19] Ibid. 483.

tine, Inca, rococo, baroque or a bit of everything—these were the so-called 'atmosphere' cinemas, appropriate for the decade's 'atmospheric' films: vamps, sheiks, Latin lovers, romantic adventures in faraway places. The 'super-cinemas' of the 1930s, in their turn, reflected the greater matter-of-factness of 1930s movies: as the vamps and Latin lovers departed the cinema, so did the architectural ebullience. The 'Odeon' chain, founded by the Birmingham busi-nessman Oscar Deutsch, exploited the suburbanization of England in the 1930s and became for ever identified with it. The Odeons themselves, many designed by George Coles, had bold, clear lines with the plainness broken by discreet art-deco flourishes, and emphasized comfort rather than luxury. In that, and their other facilities, unlike the architectural extravaganzas of the 1920s, they implied a style of life—an American style—which cinema-goers, or their children, might reasonably aspire to.[20] The Bolton Odeon, for example, opened in 1937, housed 2,534 people, with seat charges ranging from 6d to 1s 6d. It changed programmes weekly, and there were continuous showings from Monday to Friday with three separate houses on Saturday. It employed 41 people, including page boys, usherettes, chocolate girls, doormen, and those who served in the cinema café.[21] People remembered the comfort and warmth of the cinemas with real pleasure, particularly during the 1940s when it might be the only comfort and warmth there was.[22] Many of the larger cinemas had their own cafés, restaurants, and bars, sometimes a crèche, sometimes even tennis courts: when people bought tickets to the cinema they were not merely buying the right to see a film. The cinemas, like the 'super-palais', the newer chain-stores, or, as J. B. Priestley observed when he began his English journey, the new long-distance motor-coaches, represented an important stage in the development of people's expectations as to comfort.

The country's élites were convinced that the extreme attachment of the Eng-lish people to the cinema was such that it could not be allowed to operate unshackled. In this period it was shackled in two ways: by direct censorship and by interventionary legislation designed to ensure that a significant pro-portion of what people saw was made in Britain. The legal basis for censorship was the Cinematograph Act (1909) which gave local authorities the power to licence the showing of films in public places of a certain size.[23] The Act was originally fire and safety legislation but its remit was extended so that author-ities could licence (or not licence) the exhibition of any film. There was no statutory body of censors; nor did the home secretary have the power to censor

---

[20] For the cinemas see particularly M. O'Brien and A. Eyles (eds.), *Enter the Dream-House* (London, 1993), which has beautiful illustrations and an evocative text. Also R. Low, *Film Making in 1930s Britain* (London, 1985), 13–16.

[21] J. Richards and D. Sheridan (eds.), *Mass-Observation at the Movies* (London, 1987), 32.

[22] Stacey, *Star Gazing*, 94–5.

[23] For the details of the Act, see Commission on Educational and Cultural Films, *The Film in National Life* (London, 1932), 28–32.

films. All he could do was to issue guidelines to local councils of which the
most important was Para. I:

No film shall be shown which is likely to be injurious to morality or to encourage or to
incite to crime, or to lead to disorder, or to be offensive to public feeling, or which contains any offensive representations of living persons.[24]

In practice, there was a central body, the British Board of Film Censors
(BBFC), whose judgements acquired a quasi-statutory force. The board was
established by the trade itself in order to pre-empt formal state censorship—
part of the trade's long tradition of getting in first.[25] Its membership was nominally independent, but in fact its chairman had to be approved by the home
secretary and there was clearly an identity of view between the board and the
home office. Although its first president, T. P. O'Connor MP, described himself
as 'a passionate advocate of the freedom of art', there is little of that in the
board's reports. They are, on the contrary, 'noteworthy for their clear and complete lack of interest in the cinema as such, for their absorption in those
nuances of language and gesture which might suggest the merest hint of
moral and political depravity'.[26] The '43 rules' which O'Connor devised in 1917
governed the board's actions throughout the interwar years. At his death in
1929 he was succeeded (at age 68) by the former Conservative home secretary,
Edward Shortt, who was in turn succeeded (at age 69) by the former diplomat
Lord Tyrrell, active proponent of moral purity, who died in office at age 81.

Aside from the president, the board consisted of a secretary and four examiners. The secretary, J. Brooke Wilkinson, was, like O'Connor, a known 'tough
disciplinarian' of rigid moral views. The examiners were anonymous but
Shortt disclosed that at one point they were two ex-army officers, an ex-
politician and a woman 'with many years social work at the L.C.C.'[27] There is no
sign that any had either technical or cultural qualifications for the job. This
mattered, because the decisions of the board, although meant to be advisory,
took on the force of law for most local authorities: without a BBFC classification films could not be shown.

The sexual prudery of the board was notorious and intense; but it was not
sex alone which agitated it. Anything which undermined respect for authority
or which appeared politically partisan was unacceptable: thus Vigo's *Zéro de*

---

[24] Reprinted in ibid. 175.
[25] The industry was itself responsible for the first enquiry into the moral consequences of film
and it asked the National Council of Public Morals to undertake it. The report and evidence was published as *The Cinema* (London, 1917).
[26] Miles and Smith, *Cinema, Literature and Society*, 169. For the personnel of the BBFC see Low, *Film
Making in 1930s Britain*, 56–70; J. Richards, 'The British Board of Film Censors and Central Control in
the 1930s: Images of Britain', *Historical Journal of Film, Radio and Television* (1981), 111; J. C. Robertson,
The Hidden Cinema (London, 1989).
[27] Low, *Film Making in 1930s Britain*, 67.

Conduite was banned and *Love on the Dole* was not made at all until the outbreak of the Second World War when its themes could be treated in a homiletic way.[28] No one in authority or who claimed authority—like doctors, lawyers, clergymen, civil servants, even dentists—could be openly criticized, though it was possible to get around that. Anything that showed 'white women' in an unfavourable light (like the *Relief of Lucknow*) was 'suspect'. In the later 1930s, films critical of Nazi Germany or the National Government's foreign policy were impermissible. Under no circumstances were people's religious views to be 'offended' or was the body of Christ to be depicted.[29] Any language even mildly strong was deprecated: during the Second World War there was an absurd dispute between the board and the ministry of information over the word 'bloody',[30] and it was thought some sort of triumph when Robertson Hare was allowed to say 'bugger the neighbours' in one of the ministry's morale-boosting films.[31] Anything which might even have the potential to cause offence was unacceptable. The surrealist film *La Coquille et le Clergyman* (1928) was 'banned on grounds which became famous': 'So cryptic as to be almost meaningless. If there is a meaning it is doubtless objectionable.'[32]

Part of the problem was the limited utility of the board's system of classification. Until 1937, when the category 'H' was introduced for horror films, there were only two categories—'U', suitable for universal exhibition and 'A', suitable for adults only. But children were allowed into 'A'-category films if accompanied by an adult. Children hanging around cinemas in the hope of persuading an adult to 'accompany' them was a common sight; there was the celebrated case of a cinema being fined for admitting a woman 'accompanied' by 45 children to an 'A'-category film. The consequence of the system was that all films were thought of as, in effect, children's films and treated as such.

Between 1928 and the outbreak of the Second World War the board banned outright (that is, refused to classify) 140 films, including, controversially, *Battleship Potemkin*, *Strike*, and *October* (which were shown in cinema clubs or miners' halls); alterations were required of several thousand more; many scenarios were discussed with the board in advance and judiciously altered or, like *Love on the Dole*, simply abandoned. Lord Tyrrell thus had reason to be pleased with his work. 'We may take pride in observing', he said in 1937, 'that there is not a single film showing in London today which deals with any of the burning questions of the day.'[33]

---

[28] The film itself ends with a statement from the Labour MP and first lord of the admiralty A. V. Alexander, who said that the film was about conditions which had now passed and would not be allowed to return—which was why we were fighting the war.

[29] Ibid. 68. [30] A. Aldgate and J. Richards, *Britain Can Take It* (Oxford, 1986), 266–7.

[31] Durgnat, *A Mirror for England*, 49–50.

[32] Low, *Film Making in 1930s Britain*, 70.

[33] Quoted in M. Dickinson and S. Street, *Cinema and State: The Film Industry and the British Government* (London, 1985), 8.

The board censored films for the usual reasons: sexual prudery, fear for the political and religious status quo, a determination to protect the *amour propre* of the ruling classes. But the board was also driven by an almost obsessive fear of causing 'offence'—by an assumption that cultural representations of politics or religion (let alone sex) were inherently divisive, that any proposition about them must necessarily offend. This was the principle around which English sociability was increasingly organized; as an organizing principle, however, it was originally designed to 'depoliticize' individual social relationships in the private sphere.[34] It was, however, all too easy to impose this principle on collective cultural life, particularly in a society which had always been reluctant to distinguish between the private and the public spheres.

Although, according to J. P. Mayer, the effect of censorship was to make the British cinema 'sterile' and 'empty',[35] there is little evidence that producers much objected to it. As Michael Balcon said in 1951 of Ealing films: 'None of us would ever suggest any subject, whatever its box office potential, if it were socially objectionable or doubtful.'[36] Nor was there anything party-political in this. While Alexander Korda and Michael Balcon were (at one time) close to the Conservative Party, the Del Giudice brothers, founders of the company Two Cities and refugees from Italian Fascism, made little effort—at least in the 1930s—to undermine or by-pass the board. Nor did the Ostrer brothers, owners of the great cinema-chain Gaumont-British, and themselves sympathetic to the Labour Party. The only part of the industry, however, where there was a politically *conscious* self-censorship was in the production of newsreels—particularly in the 1930s when the newsreels were deliberately framed to support the National Government.

This was the more significant in that film censorship was harsher even than the Lord Chamberlain's censorship of the London stage. His office frequently behaved preposterously, but its intervention was erratic and susceptible to discreet pressure from authors and producers. Thus it licensed Miles Malleson's *The Fanatics* (1927), whose theme was trial marriage, and Jon van Druten's celebrated *Young Woodley* (1928–9, 425 performances), which concerned the love of a 17-year-old schoolboy for his housemaster's wife.[37] Almost certainly neither would have been licensed by the BBFC because it was assumed that film audiences were predominantly female and working class, and therefore more 'vulnerable' to corrupting or unsettling influences than the middle-class audiences of the West End theatre.

The cinema audiences themselves do not appear to have objected to censorship. The Commission on Educational and Cultural Films described the critics of the BBFC as 'numerically negligible but culturally important'.[38] Indeed, the

---

[34] See above, pp. 95–6.   [35] Mayer, *Sociology of Film*, 281.
[36] C. Barr, *Ealing Studios* (London, 1980), 58.   [37] Jackson, *Middle Classes*, 258.
[38] Commission on Educational and Cultural Films, *The Film in National Life* (London, 1932), 34–5.

kind of film produced by censorship (both in Britain and the United States) was the kind people usually wanted. As Sklar has noted of the American production code, which was quite as severe (though in somewhat different ways) as the BBFC, it forced Hollywood to produce 'glamorous and mythical films', which is what the public actually liked.[39] The informal relaxation of the British code during the Second World War, though not unpopular with audiences, was not a result of their efforts.

The effect of censorship was the deliberate exclusion of much of human experience from films shown in England. But censorship was not the only way the British cinema was regulated. From 1927 on the distribution of films was partly determined by legislation: in that year parliament passed the first of several acts whose purpose was to increase the proportion of home-made films exhibited in Britain. Their explicit purpose was to reduce the number of American films shown. Before 1914 about 25 per cent of films shown in Britain were British, but the First World War almost destroyed the local industry. By 1925 that figure was only 5 per cent and the overwhelming majority of films exhibited were American.[40] The American hegemony was enhanced by the system of 'block' or 'blind' booking whereby distributors bought 'blocks' of American films unseen—a practice encouraged by the developing combines, like Gaumont-British or Associated British Picture Corporation, on grounds of administrative simplicity. American domination of the cinema, however much film-goers liked it, was unwelcome to many. 'We have', the *Daily Express* wrote in 1927, 'several million people, mostly women, who, to all intents and purposes, are temporary American citizens.'[41] This also was the view of much of the country's political and cultural élite. In 1927 parliament, therefore, enacted a quota system under which, by 1936, 20 per cent of all films released in Britain were to be British-made. The legislation, however, made no specification as to the quality or content of such films.

The result of the Act was the so-called 'quota quickies', cheap, undemanding, rapidly produced films which satisfied its requirements while allowing exhibitors to get on with the real business of showing superior American movies. The consequence of the quickies is disputed. Rachel Low thought the Act 'had a profound and damaging effect on the structure of the British film industry'.[42] Quickies became notorious for shoddiness (some were 'desperate cases') and were one reason why so many film-goers said they disliked British films. Many actors found them demeaning—like the young Irish-Australian Errol Flynn, who made one quickie and then decamped permanently to

[39] R. Sklar, *Movie-Made America* (London, 1975), 173–4.
[40] In 1926, 625 feature films were released in Britain, 25 from continental Europe and 23 from Britain itself. The remaining 577 were all American.
[41] *Daily Express*, 18 March 1927, quoted in Dickinson and Street, *Cinema and State*, 30.
[42] Low, *Film Making in 1930s Britain*, 33.

Hollywood. The quota did, however, maintain the infrastructure of a British film industry which made possible the production of very much better films in the late 1930s and 1940s.[43] The Americans believed that the genres in which the quickies specialized—detective thrillers and light romances—were actually popular in Britain and well-suited to the wired cinemas which quickly became the norm after 1930. This belief was given some support by those who argued before the Moyne Committee (established in 1936 to examine the workings of the 1927 Act) that the unpopularity of the home-product was exaggerated. There were even those who argued that the American renters themselves were primarily responsible for the more disreputable quickies.

The 1927 Act was superseded by legislation in 1938 which made significant concessions to the Americans. The Moyne Committee had recommended an eventual quota of 50 per cent, a continued ban on 'blind' booking, a 'quality test', and a separate quota for shorts. Few of these recommendations found their way into the 1938 Act. The agreed quota for exhibitors and renters was much smaller, the Act was overseen by a weak advisory committee and the American distributors ignored the ban on 'block' and 'blind' booking. Furthermore, the Act, together with the 'crisis of production' within the domestic industry in 1936–7, left many unemployed and much capacity unused. Nor could it prescribe any way whereby the British industry, with a comparatively small home market—relative to the American—and irregular access to the American, could consistently make films able to compete with Hollywood in either quality or profitability other than by large-scale state subsidies or much greater protection, which would never have been forthcoming.

If, however, it could not guarantee that, it did establish a régime under which the quality of home-made films improved markedly, and its financial provisions encouraged American companies, particularly MGM, to make good films in Britain. The first, *A Yank at Oxford* (1938), starred Robert Taylor, already an international heart-throb, and made a star of Vivien Leigh. It was highly successful in both Britain and the United States, as were its two successors, *The Citadel* (1938) (based on A. J. Cronin's best-seller)[44], which starred Rosalind Russell and Robert Donat and was directed by King Vidor, one of MGM's most powerful directors, and *Goodbye Mr Chips* (1939), which also starred Donat and for which he got an Oscar. Simultaneously MGM financed Carol Reed's *The Stars Look Down* (1939), another film based on a Cronin novel, and set in a mining village in County Durham (though filmed in Cumbria). Starring Emlyn Williams, the young Margaret Lockwood, and Michael Redgrave, it too was very successful.

These films were important—especially the Cronins. Although their polit-ical implications were fudged and the scripts purged of any taint of 'socialism'

[43] Dickinson and Street, *Cinema and State*, 40–2.   [44] For *The Citadel*, see below, pp. 484–6.

or sympathy for trade unions (for the American market), their success did suggest that both British censors and British audiences could, by the late 1930s at
least, be induced to accept 'social-issue' movies so long as they were well-
directed and technically superior. Furthermore, they encouraged British producers to make similar films. It is unlikely, for example, that Ealing's *The Proud
Valley* (1940), another mining disaster film, would have been made otherwise.
The Proud Valley, indeed, went beyond MGM: the political implications were not
ducked and the hero, inconceivable in Hollywood, was a black, Paul Robeson.

They also introduced English audiences to a new genre: the Hollywood-idea-
of-England film. Such films, though about England (or Scotland or Wales) and
usually starring British actors, developed from and catered to American
stereotypes of England. Oxford colleges or English public schools, for instance,
could easily be made to conform to these stereotypes. *A Yank at Oxford* and *Goodbye Mr Chips* began a long tradition of 'American' British movies of which the
most famous was probably *Mrs Miniver* (1942), which starred the Irish-born
actress Greer Garson (whose first film had been *Goodbye Mr Chips*) and was based
loosely on the doings of a fictional upper-middle-class Englishwoman created
by Jan Struther.[45] These films all departed significantly from their sources—
often for the worse—in order not to undermine the stereotypes; but their conventions were quickly understood by English audiences who learnt to
discount their more rebarbative aspects. None the less, the cinematic American version of England itself attained a kind of reality—as the rest of the
world's idea of America did in the United States—and became a part of the
complicated picture the English had of themselves.

The régime established by the 1938 Act was anything but stable. It was overtaken by war and circumstances which, though favouring the quality and
popularity of British films, made it almost impossible for the British industry
to fulfil its quota. Although by the end of the war the British industry was the
only serious competition the Americans faced anywhere, in 1946 it could
release for British exhibition only 83 films as against 342 American. The result
was, for all the brave talk, particularly by the biggest of the British producers,
J. Arthur Rank, that when the moment came in 1947 British film-makers could
not exploit it. After 1945 films were one of Britain's most expensive imports
from the United States and by 1947 the government had concluded that their
dollar-costs were unacceptable. In mid-1947, therefore, it imposed a 75 per
cent duty on the receipts of American films: only 25 per cent of their profits
could be repatriated in dollars. In reply, the American producers and distributors, as they threatened they would, boycotted the British market. The outcome of this 'crisis' was important for both parties. For Britain 'success' would
mean the saving of many vital dollars and monopolistic access to the world's

---

[45] For Mrs Miniver, see A. Light, *Forever England: Femininity, Literature and Conservatism between the
Wars* (London, 1991), 113–55.

second-largest market. For the Americans 'failure' would mean exclusion from a market that guaranteed profit to large numbers of American films, many of which only broke even (or worse) in the American market.[46]

As was perhaps inevitable, victory went to the Americans. The board of trade bungled the whole affair. It had not believed the Americans would carry out their threat and had made no plans in case of a boycott. It did not consider importing films from Europe and rejected an approach from the Italians on the grounds that the English did not like dubbed films—an assertion for which there was no historical support. Nor did it seek to reduce the screen-time occupied by American movies, to eliminate or cut the number of double features or twice-weekly programme changes. This was, no doubt, in part simply incompetence, but almost certainly also a result of sheer ignorance. These decisions were made—or not made—by upper-middle-class males for whom the world of the cinema, predominantly working-class and female, was unimportant and not, therefore, to be treated seriously.

It became obvious, furthermore, that the British industry, which in effect meant Rank, was incapable of filling the gap left by the Americans, although J. Arthur Rank had assured himself and others that he could. Rank was a film producer of international standing; individually as important as most of the American producers. But he was really an Anglo-American producer: his American affiliations were essential to him. Without them he was not a major producer, as the boycott demonstrated. Furthermore, the English audiences made it plain that, however ambiguous their attitude to America, they wanted their regular diet of American films.

In March 1948 the government reached a settlement with the Americans which gave Hollywood pretty much what it wanted, including the withdrawal of the duty. The quota was, however, restored and was again set at 30 per cent. In 1949 the government set up the National Film Finance Corporation to give direct assistance to the industry and in 1950 introduced the 'Eady Levy' (named after Sir Wilfred Eady, the civil servant who devised it) by which the distributors agreed to subsidize British producers by a levy on admissions charges.

These attempts to protect the British film industry were by no means unsuccessful, and without such protection it is doubtful whether it could have continued to exist in any significant way. The episode of the boycott, however, did suggest that there were real limitations both to the independence of the British industry and the extent to which the government could guarantee it. The agreement in 1948 with the Americans

pointed to the essentially colonial nature of American control of the British film indus-

[46] For details of the boycott, see Dickinson and Street, *Cinema and State*, 180–98; P. Stead, *Film and the Working Class* (London, 1991), 156–7; P. Swann, *The Hollywood Feature Film in Postwar Britain* (London, 1987), 101, 133.

try and the British film audience—both had conspired against the dictates of their own government. National economic policy might require that precious dollars go to pay for necessities, but ultimately it was found that so far as the rank and file of the British audience were concerned, American films were a necessity.[47]

Censorship was implicitly, and the quota system explicitly, anti-American. Censorship existed not only to eliminate sex, violence, and politics from the cinema, but to eliminate American sex, violence, and politics. As for the quota, its aim was never concealed: to minimize the influence of American films by regulating the number which could be exhibited. Within their own terms, both measures failed: there is little evidence that they significantly excluded American influence, halted the process of Americanization, or diminished people's desire to see American movies. From the early and mid-1930s onwards, English picture-goers, when asked, almost invariably said they preferred American films to British. For this they gave both positive and negative reasons.

To almost everyone, American films had dynamism and toughness; they were slick, polished, fast-moving, and technically first-rate. Their actors were 'natural' and 'life-like'.[48] There was no reticence; American movies were, on the contrary, 'vehement to the point of hysteria'.[49] Simple issues were strongly handled; individual dilemmas always had solutions. This dynamic simplicity was one of the reasons why American films were more popular in England with the working class than with any other. Furthermore, the Hollywood 'star system', promoted in England by huge-selling magazines like *The Picturegoer* and newspapers which had to compete with movie-magazines, created marked identifications between viewers and actors ('I think in those eras, we were more inclined to put stars on a pedestal. They were so far removed from everyday life they were magical . . . These days stars are so ordinary—the magic has gone. Hollywood will never be the same again').[50] The star system was important since English film-goers, when pushed, admitted to liking American actors more than American films. For the English, the stars, by force of personality and reputation, added lustre to what were often not very good films.

Although men and women gave largely the same reasons for preferring American films, there were important differences in nuance. For many women, almost independently of class, American movies were associated with 'glamour'—that key word of the time—and the more austere life became in the 1940s the stronger was the association. 'Glamour' implied a whole world— physical surroundings, clothes, cosmetics, luxury—and 'glamour' was almost always the word used to describe it:

[47] Swann, *Hollywood Feature Film*, 101.
[48] Richards and Sheridan, *Mass-Observation at the Movies*, 34–9.
[49] Durgnat, *A Mirror for England*, 6.   [50] Stacey, *Star Gazing*, 91.

'I preferred Hollywood stars in the forties. It had mostly to do with glamour. No matter what our girls did they just couldn't hold a candle to the American girls. I remember I went to see a British musical called *London Town* the attempt at glamour was so awful it just made us giggle.'[51]

The contrast between Hollywood and English life in the 1940s was so obvious that women made no attempt to conceal their day-dreams—even women who otherwise might have despised them, like the librarian who confessed, 'I would just add that I do sit and sigh for the kind of clothes Ginger Rogers and Lana Turner wear and would also be influenced by the Hollywood home with the pretty curtains and marvellous kitchens if Mr Dalton [the chancellor of the exchequer] would let me be.'[52]

At a time when a woman's identity depended so much upon looks, clothes, and style Hollywood was immensely influential in setting the standards. 'One begins to realise', Pearl Jephcott wrote, 'when talking to these girls the amazing extent to which the minutiae of the clothes and hair arrangements of an American actress may affect the spending habits of a child in a mining village in Durham or a girl in a tenement in central London.'[53] Women's attitudes, especially when given in retrospect, were perhaps more complicated than we allow; in acknowledging Hollywood's primacy many probably reacted as they felt was expected of them—women were supposed to put stars on pedestals, so they put stars on pedestals. Yet there seems little reason to doubt the reality of such influence, particularly on hairstyles (witness the speed with which Veronica Lake's 'peek-a-boo' hair-do spread in the 1940s) and on cosmetics and the detail of the sophisticated life: like the 17-year-old who wished to smoke just as Katharine Hepburn did in *The Philadelphia Story*.

It is also possible that what English women identified with was the power of certain American stars. While Lana Turner, Ginger Rogers, and Veronica Lake were admired for their glamour, they were usually socially passive; they acted out in luxurious surroundings women's conventional roles. But the stars of the great Hollywood melodramas, especially Joan Crawford, Bette Davis, and Barbara Stanwyck, represented aggression and independence. In many cases—most spectacularly Joan Crawford in *Mildred Pierce* (1945)—they portrayed women who forsook conventional 'happiness' for domination. Although such women often came to sticky ends, the American melodrama, like the British melodramas of the 1940s, gave women the opportunity to portray 'masculine' cinematic attributes—strong intelligence, ambition, ruthlessness.[54] Many women film-goers clearly felt an affinity with these attributes and the women who possessed them.

---

[51] Stacey, *Star Gazing*, 113.   [52] Mayer, *Sociology of Film*, 190.
[53] Jephcott, *Rising Twenty*, 62–3.
[54] M. Landy, *British Genres: Cinema and Society, 1930–1960* (Princeton, NJ, 1991), 189.

Hollywood's celebration of competitive individual achievement also attracted young men. Whereas British films, including the best, tended to emphasize a non-competitive collective or community ethos, particularly during the 1940s when such an ethos was arguably in the national interest, American films stressed a dynamic competitiveness.[55] Within English working-class culture there were powerful competitive impulses, the stronger for being largely repressed, and American movies, like sport, unquestionably exploited them.[56]

This explains the popularity of anti-heroes like James Cagney or Edward G. Robinson with cinema audiences.[57] Such men were arch-individualists willing to risk much in the pursuit of success. In American films crime was problematic. It was 'wrong' and condemned, but condemnation was often trite, while the criminals were potent and interesting figures. During the 1940s many young English working-class males lived, as did Humphrey Bogart even when playing the hero, within or close by a criminal sub-culture; and they were familiar with its ambiguities, as implied in most American but not most British films.[58]

The American movie, as it appeared in the 1930s, was thought vigorous, materialist, and democratic. Those who disliked British films disliked them because they were none of these. Most widely disliked was the accent of the actors and, even more, the actresses. The talkie had cruelly exposed the British film. There were almost immediately complaints about the 'prissiness' and 'stageyness' of the diction, of 'by joves' and 'I says', 'Oxford accents' and 'BBC voices'.[59] Many British actors and actresses had indeed trained for the stage and this was all too apparent when they appeared before cameras. C. B. Cochran, who as one of the greatest theatrical entrepreneurs of the age had reason to know, contrasted the naturalness of American actors with the 'obvious acting' of British actors 'on a scale and a tempo' that might be acceptable in the theatre but not in the cinema.[60]

English film-goers complained of the lifelessness of British films, the restricted and 'poverty-stricken' settings, the lack of 'action.' In other words, they disliked the attempt to transfer the direction and *mise en scène* of the theatre to the movies. The working-class part of the audience was also unsympathetic to the extreme emotional restraint of many British films—even the most widely admired, like *Brief Encounter* (1945), which was by almost universal consent a 'classic' British movie, yet not really popular in England outside the suburbs. People were offended by Celia Johnson's 'prissiness' and found her

---

[55] Swann, *Hollywood Feature Film*, 63–4.   [56] McKibbin, *Ideologies of Class*, 162–4.
[57] Miles and Smith, *Cinema, Literature and Society*, 174–5.
[58] Durgnat, *A Mirror for England*, 52.
[59] Richards and Sheridan, *Mass-Observation at the Movies*, 88.
[60] Barr, *Ealing Studios*, 26.

moral dilemma incomprehensible.[61] Of British films of the 1930s, it is difficult to disagree with George Perry:

The British cinema had become a middle-class institution; it was the 'cultured' West End accent that was heard and it was the *mores* of the county drawing room that were being observed. In Middlesbrough and Smethwick they opted for the classless accents of America, just as they preferred the slicker pace and the glossier technique . . . Most British films failed absolutely to sense the mood of the audience and equated it with the same people who paid fifteen shillings for a stalls seat in Shaftesbury Avenue.[62]

The cultural hegemony of the American film in the interwar years had several predictable consequences. The first was the rapid Americanization of vocabulary and idiom. The Americanization of English had, of course, a long history; but in the interwar years American idiom entered the language, and left it, with a speed contemporaries actually noticed.[63]

The second was that women became more Americanized than men. This was so in part because they were more exposed to American popular culture as a whole than men. They liked American music and dancing more than men did, and were more expert in both.[64] Because they watched more films than men they *ipso facto* watched more American films. And the American films they watched were increasingly made for female audiences. They were also more likely to have idealized images of America. Men had a general idea of America; of power, equality, and excess—which they either liked or disliked. Women's views were both general and specific: a surprising number, for example, wished England had 'colleges' and 'drugstores' as in America. They could, therefore, couple a generalized view of America as metropolitan and sophisticated with a much more domestic view of (say) the small-town America associated with the Andy Hardy movies.

The third consequence was that the English had fully-fashioned stereotypes of America before American troops arrived in large numbers in 1942. The way they reacted to the American 'occupation' was, therefore, significantly determined by the images of America already drawn from American movies.

The widespread admiration for American life as presented in American films was, however, accompanied by an equally widespread anti-Americanism. But this is less paradoxical than it seems. While most people might have been 'anti-American' they were anti-American in different ways. Some did not like American films or the American way of life at all and they were well represented in the country's censoring and quota-setting classes. For them, American democracy was dangerous to both England's political and social hierarchy. But there was also a 'democratic' rejection or half-rejection of American films.

[61] Jephcott, *Rising Twenty*, 155.   [62] Quoted Barr, *Ealing Studios*, 26.
[63] See below, pp. 511–13.   [64] See above, pp. 394–6.

The membership of the Commission on Educational and Cultural Films was, for example, almost wholly comprised of consciously democratic 'educated' opinion: their objection to American films, whose technical distinction they conceded, was that to function democracy had to be informed and no informed democracy could be based upon a genre, the American film, whose essence was escapism.[65]

Nor was the mass audience ever entirely uncritical. People did not necessarily believe, particularly during the Second World War, that the Americans deserved their abundance and good fortune and they had a more realistic view of life's chances than the Americans: this was the other side of the widely observed fatalism. However much they admired the optimism and self-confidence of American films and however much they might have wished otherwise, they understood that the world was not really like that and tended to discount a good deal of what they saw in American films. Moreover, the English could be clearly aware that the fantasy world of American wealth, the feeling that it could be on another planet, was as much to do with *them* and their emotional and physical needs as with a transatlantic cornucopia, which might or might not exist. Nor were they unaware that American movies, even the most popular in England, were designed to present the United States in particular ways. When one 18-year-old fan of American movies told Pearl Jephcott that she realized American films were all 'more or less lies', Jephcott took this opinion as a sign of maturity.[66]

Throughout the interwar years American films were numerically and intellectually predominant in England; and, as we have seen, people almost invariably said they preferred them to British films. In practice, however, film-goers' attitudes were more complicated. Even in the 1930s not all British films were thought wholly contemptible: a number, indeed, were very popular. Several of these were made by a Hungarian émigré, Alexander Korda, who arrived in England in 1932 (after working in films in both Germany and France) and in that year established London Films with the Conservative MP, A. C. N. Dixey. Korda was to become one of the dominating figures in the British film industry in this period—immensely ambitious, often imprudent and driven by a determination to out-do Hollywood. Korda's first big success, a formula he had tried before and was to try again, was *The Private Life of Henry VIII* (1933), which was hugely popular in both Britain and the United States, making the careers of both Charles Laughton and Korda's future wife, Merle Oberon. He never quite matched this before the war, but several other films were very successful: *Catherine the Great* (1934) and *The Scarlet Pimpernel* (1934), which established Leslie Howard, *Sanders of the River* (1935), which

[65] Commission on Educational and Cultural Films, *The Film in National Life*, 11.
[66] Jephcott, *Rising Twenty*, 155–7.

starred Paul Robeson, and two large-scale 'imperial' films, *The Drum* (1934) and *The Four Feathers* (1939).[67]

Michael Balcon at Gainsborough (which was owned by the Ostrer brothers) was one of the first to realize the importance of the star-system as a form of bond between viewer and film, and he created the first British 'star', Jessie Matthews. More unusually, he kept her from Hollywood. Matthews was a graceful dancer and singer with a winning manner and had great hits with Balcon's musical version of J. B. Priestley's exceptionally popular novel, *The Good Companions* (1933), and three other musicals, *Evergreen* (1934), *It's Love Again* and *Head Over Heels* (both 1936). Balcon also 'rescued' Hitchcock whose career had floundered after the success of *Blackmail* (1929).[68] It was for Balcon that Hitchcock directed the 1930s thrillers which made his name: *The Man Who Knew Too Much* (1934), *The Thirty-Nine Steps* (1935), *Sabotage* (1936), and *The Lady Vanishes* (1938). *The Lady Vanishes* was a very mature film, possessing all Hitchcock's characteristic mannerisms before they became predictable, well acted by two rising stars as hero and heroine, Michael Redgrave and Margaret Lockwood, humorous (especially the hilarious turn by Basil Radford and Naunton Wayne as a pair of silly-ass Englishmen), and skilfully directed. Though it was his last British film before Hitchcock went to Hollywood, it was as good as anything he did there.[69]

Korda and, to a lesser extent, Balcon thought of themselves as making 'international' films and thus competing with Hollywood. Even the best of these, however, struggled against this competition; but there were two genres, not made for the international market, which were very popular with the English. The first comprised the 'national-celebratory' films Herbert Wilcox made with his wife Anna Neagle. Wilcox had been best known for his film versions of the Aldwych farces with Tom Walls, but in 1934 he made *Nell Gwynn* and in 1935 *Peg of Old Drury* which were successful enough for him to go into production as an independent. The result was two enormously popular films, *Victoria the Great* (1937) and *Sixty Glorious Years* (1938). These were uncritical pieces of English myth-making (though *Victoria the Great* was very popular in America) happily accepted by the public—despite Anna Neagle's accent and the socially conservative nature of both films. Their success anticipated the popularity of the 'Mayfair' films Wilcox made with Anna Neagle and Michael Wilding in the 1940s.

The second, and more popular genre, consisted largely of films made by Gracie Fields and George Formby in the 1930s. Both were Lancastrians, juvenile performers, spoke with (modified) Lancastrian accents and practised a form of

---

[67] For Korda in the 1930s, see Low, *Film Making in 1930s Britain*, 166–9; M. Stockham, *The Korda Collection* (London, 1992), 6–99.

[68] Low, *Film Making in 1930s Britain*, 139. In the early thirties Hitchcock was even reduced to directing a musical, *Waltzes from Vienna* (1933).

[69] For Balcon in the thirties, see Low, *Film Making in 1930s Britain*, 134–9; Barr, *Ealing Studios*, 4–5.

good-natured apolitical 'democratic' comedy. Gracie Fields was well known on the stage as singer and dancer before Basil Dean persuaded her to take the title role in Ealing's *Sally in Our Alley* (1931), in which she sang what became her signature-tune, 'Sally'. This and *Sing as We Go* (1934), based upon a story by J. B. Priestley, were two of the most popular films of the interwar years, as were several of the other films she made for Ealing. They were technically competent, had some memorable songs and in Fields an ingratiating performer. The emphasis of her films was on cheerfulness and personal courage. Although they were, in effect, social-problem films, and the problems, like unemployment, were important, there is no suggestion that such problems might have social or political solutions. Gracie, as in *Shipyard Sally* (1939, released in 1940), just sings her way to London and sings her way back—having *en route* somehow solved the depression. Fields's style was very English: attempts by MGM and Twentieth-Century Fox to repeat her English successes in America never succeeded.

Fields's popularity in England encouraged Dean to employ another well-known artist, George Formby. Formby, at one time a professional jockey, was the son of an equally well known Edwardian music hall performer, George Formby Sr. (Formby was a stage-name adopted by George Sr. as a tribute to the Lancashire town where he had his first success). George Jr. took the name Formby when he married a dancer, Beryl Ingham, a powerful and apparently unlikeable woman who dominated him until her death. By the time he made his first film he had developed a well-honed persona: as a small, rather gormless, bashful, ukelele-playing representative of the ordinary man who, despite overwhelming odds, always wins his girl because, however beautiful, she prefers a heart of gold to the oily sophisticates who surround her. Like Fields', his songs were good; and, unlike hers, several were off-colour, which made them better. Dean, who wanted to make cheap profitable films to finance his more 'serious' efforts, brought Formby to Ealing where he made his first film, *Boots, Boots* in 1934. For the rest of the decade and into the early forties Formby made a series of social-satirical films which were, outside London, immensely popular and utterly formulaic: 'George is goomph; George meets girl; George plays "uke"; George beats villain; George gets girl.'[70] Between 1938 and 1944 he was the most popular male film star in England: not even the Hollywood heart-throbs were his equal.

Formby's appeal is probably now almost irrecoverable. In part, it is the appeal of the oldest of romantic plots—virtue and true love triumphing; the victory of the small man over those who have all the advantages, money and good looks especially. The humour is largely slapstick: falling ladders, car chases, high windows, absurd mix-ups, comic policemen, from all of which the

[70] A 25-year-old engineering draughtsman, quoted in Mayer, *British Cinemas and their Audiences*, 222. The description, though accurate, was not meant to be complimentary.

small man somehow emerges unscathed. It was a form of humour particularly popular in England; practised, for example, and very much better, by Charlie Chaplin and Stan Laurel, who made it international. Formby's is the humour of a working class whose life chances are slight, but not hopeless. In *No Limit* (1935), for instance, George ends up winning the Isle of Man TT race. That, of course, was ridiculous; but the possession of a motor-bike was not. *No Limit* was a success precisely because there was a point of identification, the motor-bike and its liberating speed, between audience and star.

Despite the received view of British films in the interwar years, there were types of British film that people did like, even if they were small-scale, like the Fields–Formby ones, and rather despised by the admirers (who included most critics) of the American feature films. From the late 1930s the tendency for people to go to British movies and even to prefer them became much stronger; a result largely of the marked improvement in the quality of British films which, *pro rata*, at least in England, more than held their own against Hollywood.

The first reason for this was the size and nature of the British market. Though small compared to the American, it was none the less the second largest in the world. This meant that comparatively small-scale films could be made and exhibited profitably in Britain, even though British costs were much higher than American. What Britain could not make competitively were large-scale 'Hollywood' films: the type, in fact, that Korda and Rank always wanted to make.

The British market was also culturally integrated. People generally liked the same kind of film everywhere: musical romances, drama and tragedy, history and crime, nature and reality.[71] There was little regional or gender bias in those preferences, though men tended to like crime films more than women. Nor was there in that most sensitive measure of regional difference, humour. Max Miller was more popular in the South and Duggie Wakefield in the North, and Frank Randle, whose cheap Manchester-made films were very popular in some northern towns, was hardly known in the South. But Formby, Fields, Will Hay, Arthur Askey, and Will Fyffe were popular almost everywhere, as was the gruesome catalogue of English humour: ill-health, deformity, sexual abnormality and potential death ('including war').[72] And film audiences always insisted that they could never get enough of 'humour' in the cinema. Although not particularly unsophisticated by international standards, English film-goers were easy to please and easily pleased by the same kind of thing. There were thus few cultural (or financial) obstacles to making films for the national market—if companies were prepared to make them.

The second reason for the improvement was the influx of foreign-born pro-

---

[71] These categories are Mass-Observation's. (Richards and Sheridan, *Mass-Observation at the Movies*, 34.)

[72] Ibid. 214.

ducers, directors, cameramen, and technicians throughout the 1930s. Many, like the Kordas (Alexander and his brothers Vincent and Zoltan), were Hungarian-Jewish and Korda, Balcon, and the Ostrers were well known for employing them. The unions, of course, did their best to exclude them, particularly after the 'production crisis' of 1937 when unemployment in the industry was high. Their presence and success had its inevitable consequence in an industry where Jews like Oscar Deutsch and the Ostrer brothers were already prominent. In 1939 *Kine Weekly*'s 'Screencomber' distributed his 'annual awards' with jack-booted humour as follows:[73]

Best Director of a British Film: Leopold Kryshic Stockolevitch
Best Script of a British Film: Hiram Z. Wimplepole
Best Photography of a British Film: Zchshwwsky Owyowschekkow
Best Bit of Carpeting in a British Film: Bill Smithers Esq.

Not all émigrés were Jewish. Alberto Cavalcanti was a Brazilian who came to England in 1933. He made his name in John Grierson's GPO Film Unit (later the Crown Film Unit), directing two of its best-known documentaries, *Coal Face* and *Night Mail* (both 1936), before becoming an independent director during the war.[74] Filippo Del Giudice was a wealthy refugee from Italian Fascism who in 1938 effectively took control of Two Cities (i.e. London and Rome), a company originally promoted to make Anglo-Italian films, which made a star of Ray Milland in *French without Tears* (1939), one of the most popular British films of the 1930s. Del Giudice was to produce many of the most successful wartime British movies. The effect of the émigrés, as in so many other spheres of English life, was to infuse talent, vigour, and a wider view into the highly introverted cinematic culture they found.

The third reason was the growing abundance of first-rate actors and actresses. The 'stagey' older generation was giving way to one which, though also trained in and for the theatre, made the transition to films comparatively easily. Increasingly, the problem was not the finding of actors, but the keeping of them. Indeed, one of the reasons why British films improved so markedly during the war was the patriotic return of much of Hollywood's English colony—including major figures like Laurence Olivier, Vivien Leigh, David Niven, and Leslie Howard. This abundance of talent is well illustrated by *Gone with the Wind* (MGM, 1939), much the most successful film of the period: of the four principals, three were English, or English-born—Vivien Leigh, Olivia De

---

[73] Quoted in Durgnat, *A Mirror for England*, 5.
[74] For the GPO Film Unit, Grierson and Cavalcanti, see P. Swann, *The British Documentary Film Unit* (Cambridge, 1989). Grierson and Cavalcanti eventually fell out over the nature of the documentary. Grierson, who was much influenced by Paul Rotha's anti-American, anti-commercial *The Film Till Now* (1930), saw the documentary as having a democratic educational function; Cavalcanti always favoured the techniques of the commercial cinema and his move to commercial films in the early 1940s was not surprising.

Havilland, and Leslie Howard. To a lesser extent, the same is true of directors: Hitchcock was not the last to go to Hollywood, though much the most successful of those who did. Even allowing for such migration, from the late thirties Britain was never short of first-rate directors.

Finally, the British industry had in J. Arthur Rank and in a form of state protection a source of direct or indirect funding that guaranteed it at least a minimal existence. Rank had acquired his film holdings almost, as the British allegedly did their empire, in a fit of absence of mind. He was not particularly interested in films as such, but as an evangelical Christian he saw in them an effective way of spreading the gospel; though he actually made no attempt to use his holdings for that purpose. In one way alone did he have an active cinematic purpose—he wanted to make more successful films than the Americans. By 1943, after a series of skilful financial manœuvres, he found himself almost a monopolist: he owned two of the three major cinema circuits, the most important British film distributor, General Film Distributors (which he later renamed JARFID—J. Arthur Rank Film Distributors), two of the biggest modern studios, Denham and Pinewood, and four smaller ones. He controlled Gaumont-British and Gainsborough, was chairman of Independent Producers Ltd and he financed Del Giudice's Two Cities. He also had substantial interests in two American companies, Universal and Twentieth Century-Fox. In the knowledge that Rank was the only reliable source of funding, even independent producers like Balcon, once his strongest critic, took shelter in the Rank Organization. In 1947, three years after he had negotiated Rank's support for Ealing, Balcon wrote: 'Unquestionably the appearance on the film scene of Mr J. Arthur Rank has contributed in no small measure to the present healthy state of the industry.'[75] In the long term, of course, Rank's lack of interest in films *qua* films and his determination to match Hollywood led him to throw away much of the stability he gave the industry in the 1940s: too much was spent on films Britain could not make and not enough on those it could.

The quota system provided another form of shelter. Although the state, until the very end of the period, always refused to fund directly British films the quota did at least ensure access to the British market and hold off what could otherwise have been complete American domination. If, in the end, the British film industry could not fully exploit this, that was only in part the state's fault.

It was generally believed at the time that there was a marked improvement in the quality of British films after the outbreak of the Second World War, and that belief is supported by what we know of cinema attendances. Of the 12 top box-office films for the years 1939 to 1950, six were American and six British:

---

[75] Quoted in Dickinson and Street, *Cinema and State*, 173.

1939	The Citadel (US)	1945	The Seventh Veil (GB)
1940	Gone With the Wind (US)	1946	The Wicked Lady (GB)
1941	49th Parallel (GB)	1947	Courtneys of Curzon Street (GB)
1942	Mrs Miniver (US)	1948	The Best Years of Our Lives (US)
1943	Random Harvest (US)	1949	The Third Man (GB)
1944	For Whom the Bell Tolls (US)	1950	The Blue Lamp (GB)[76]

Furthermore, of the six American films, three had British locales: *The Citadel*, *Mrs Miniver*, and *Random Harvest*. *The Citadel* was an MGM-Britain film with British actors. Two were 'Hollywood British' films. Only *Gone With the Wind*— whose stars gave it a marked British interest anyway—and *The Best Years of Our Lives* had American settings.

The *Daily Mail* reader survey, which measured not receipts but film-goers' preferences, produced results which were even more favourable to British films. According to it, the four most popular films of the war were all British: first, the war film *The Way to the Stars* and (in order) three Gainsborough melodramas, *The Man in Grey*, *Madonna of the Seven Moons*, and *They were Sisters*. The popularity of the Gainsboroughs was matched by that of their stars. Margaret Lockwood was the most popular actress in 1943, 1944, 1945 and 1946, and James Mason the most popular actor in 1944 (when he succeeded George Formby), 1945, 1946, and 1947. The second most popular actor was the other principal male in the Gainsborough melodramas, Stewart Granger.

Aside from *Gone with the Wind*, the most popular American films in wartime England were *Rebecca* (1940), *The Great Dictator* (1941), *Mrs Miniver* (1943) and *For Whom the Bell Tolls* (1944). But *Rebecca* was based upon Daphne du Maurier's novel, had British direction (it was Hitchcock's first American film), and British (or half-British) stars, Laurence Olivier, Joan Fontaine, and Judith Anderson. It is unlikely that many film-goers thought of it as American.

What these figures conceal, however, is 'depth': the proportion of the commercially successful films in any one year which were British. Here the record is patchier. Thus in 1942 the only really successful British film was Leslie Howard's *The First of the Few*; in 1944, of the 12 most successful films only two were British: *This Happy Breed* and *Fanny by Gaslight*, a Gainsborough starring Stewart Granger. In 1945, while *The Seventh Veil* was the most popular film, only four of the 22 runners-up were British, although one was the extremely popular Gainsborough *Madonna of the Seven Moons*. In 1949 and 1950, while the top films were British, very few of the runners-up were, though they included

[76] Due to changes in the way information was gathered these ratings may not be entirely accurate; but they would certainly not be seriously in error. There seems little doubt that *No Orchids for Miss Blandish* (GB) would have been the top box-office film of 1948 had it not been banned in much of the country. In those areas where it was shown it broke all records.

Ealing's *Passport to Pimlico* and 'Hollywood British' films like *Treasure Island* and *The Mudlark*. On the other hand, in 1948 when William Wyler's *The Best Years of Our Lives* was the most popular film, nine runners-up were British, including Powell and Pressburger's famous technicolor film, *The Red Shoes*.

The British industry, 1948 notwithstanding, simply could not compete in terms of numbers. Even under the quota the great majority of widely exhibited films were American. Unless he or she made a point of it, it was statistically not possible for the average picture-goer to see more British films than American. The film-going diary of a London shopgirl for one week in each of May, July and August 1945 confirms this.[77] Of the 16 films she saw only two were British. This girl may have been untypically enthusiastic, but the mix of romance, comedy, thriller, and musical she saw was not untypical.

After 1939, it was the sheer number rather than the quality of American films that mattered, since, film for film, British movies were thought by British audiences to be then as good as and probably better than American. In Sidney Bernstein's 1946 survey of the cinema, 96 per cent of those polled thought British films had improved since 1939, while only 26 per cent thought American films had improved.[78] Film-goers willingly agreed to say why they thought British films were now much 'better':

Although I used to avoid British films, it is now my aim to see everyone I can that comes to the local cinemas. It is very seldom that one finds faked scenes obviously filmed and the stories are extremely good, also the best point the acting is magnificent and nothing Hollywood can produce will convince me that we have not the finest actors and actresses in the world. Some of the recent British films I have enjoyed were *This Happy Breed*, *The Way Ahead*, *Waterloo Road* . . . and others too numerous to mention. . . . . . . Now I come to British films, which have improved so much in the last few years. Such films as *First of the Few*—the *Way Ahead* [sic]—*49th Parallel* (what a loss to our films is Leslie Howard—a magnificent actor) *Dangerous Moonlight* (lovely Warsaw Concerto), our own stars in our own films proving that these at least can hold their own with the American standard . . . *The Man in Grey* one of the best British—and some brilliant acting from James Mason, the perfect screen villain—and our own Shakespeare adopted for the screen—*Henry V*—the beginning, I hope of a series of Shakespeare plays brought to the screen. What a pleasure to hear our language spoken correctly and in such beautiful tones. Lastly the two BEST British films ever made—*In which we Serve* and *This Happy Breed*, such realism, such tradegy [sic] and humanity . . .[79]

Attempting to explain this new popularity, the film critic Roger Manvell wrote:

The qualities which are uppermost in our cinema are humanity of characterisation . . . and a growing ability to create a cinematic poetry peculiar to British films. This poetry is a sign of a nation's artistic maturity . . . It is to be found in *In Which We Serve*, *The First*

[77] Jephcott, *Rising Twenty*, 154.   [78] Richards and Aldgate, *Best of British*, 40–1.
[79] Quoted in Mayer, *British Cinemas and Their Audiences*, 92, 214. The spelling and punctuation are uncorrected by Mayer.

of the Few, The Gentle Sex, Millions Like Us, San Demetrio-London, The Way Ahead and especially *The Way to the Stars*. These are war films; it is also present in films like *The Stars Look Down, The Proud Valley, Love on the Dole, This Happy Breed, I Know Where I'm Going* and especially *Brief Encounter*.[80]

'Cinematic poetry', however, is hard to define, as is 'humanity of characterisation'. Manvell is presumably arguing that these films are all united by a governing moral code of personal and collective decency—or something like that. But in fact they have little ideological or artistic unity—nor is there much cinematic poetry in the conspicuously unmentioned (but hugely popular) Gainsborough melodramas or in the murderous 'spiv' films. There were in the 1940s a number of cinematic genres; but there was no necessary unity either between or within them.

During the war there was a definite category of 'war' films: movies either about combat or preparation for combat. All of them were 'patriotic' and in some sense propagandist. Beyond that they had little in common. As measured by popularity there were four war films which stood above the rest: *49th Parallel, In Which We Serve, The Way Ahead*, and *The Way to the Stars*.[81] The first, *49th Parallel*, was the most overtly propagandist. A German submarine is wrecked off the coast of Canada and its crew try to make their way to safety across Canada. In passage, they meet a selection of Allied 'types', each representing a 'reason' why Britain and her dominions are fighting the war. The Germans, though unpleasant, are not caricatured. But it was not just as a propaganda piece that the film was popular: it was a thriller and its powerful cast was dominated by Laurence Olivier and Leslie Howard. Ever since *Wuthering Heights* (1939) and *Rebecca* (1940), it was obvious that Olivier could make a film by his presence. Even more could Leslie Howard. His performance in *Gone with the Wind* had confirmed him as international heart-throb, while his return to England and his highly publicized war work confirmed him as national treasure. And his death in 1943—when the plane on which he was returning from Lisbon was shot down—confirmed him as national martyr. He 'became a sort of icon, a popular hero representing everything that was best about the British character—gentleness, humour, unassuming courage—an incarnation of British traditions, but at the same time a standard-bearer of a new sort of British society.'[82] Regardless of their merits, the *49th Parallel* and Howard's other two war films, *Pimpernel Smith* and *The First of the Few* appealed to audiences because he was in them. That popularity might depend on stars was a lesson not all 'war' film producers learnt.

Noel Coward's *In Which We Serve* (1942) was a different sort of film. Coward

---

[80] Cited in Richards and Sheridan, *Mass-Observation at the Movies*, 13.

[81] For the war films, see Aldgate and Richards, *Britain Can Take It*, passim; R. Murphy, *Realism and Tinsel* (London, 1989), 15–72; Stead, *Film and the Working Class*, 122–36; Landy, *British Genres*, 140–88.

[82] For the cult of Howard, see Aldgate and Richards, *Britain Can Take It*, 51–73.

had been rather at a loose end since the outbreak of war and was the subject of more or less malicious press criticism. But he was anxious to help out and was sentimentally patriotic. He had written *Cavalcade* in 1931 to cheer everyone up and in 1939 *This Happy Breed*, a study of a lower-middle-class family in interwar London. Both were deeply complacent and politically conservative. Coward had been excited and moved by the loss of *HMS Kelly* during the Crete campaign, partly because *Kelly* had been commanded by his friend Lord Louis Mountbatten. He decided to make a film about it and won the support of Mountbatten (not surprisingly), the admiralty, the ministry of information and the film producer Filippo Del Giudice of Two Cities. Coward had originally envisaged a film in which Mountbatten's identity would be only lightly disguised. This alarmed Mountbatten, who insisted that the ship's captain should not be a member of the aristocracy. He thus became 'Captain Kinross', member of a 'typically upper-middle-class' family. Most of its action, however, drew upon the saga of the ship. *In Which We Serve* had a strong cast which, apart from Coward himself as Captain Kinross, included John Mills, Celia Johnson, Michael Wilding, Bernard Miles, Richard Attenborough, and Kathleen Harrison. The support of the Royal Navy gave the film some striking verisimilitude. David Lean co-directed; given Coward's directorial inexperience, in practice he did the hard work.

In Which We Serve was not a forward-looking film. It was a paean to the social status quo in general and the upper middle class in particular, in the tradition of *Cavalcade* and *This Happy Breed*—(itself filmed in 1944). But it was not a reactionary film, only conventionally patriotic. England will survive so long as all classes and conditions respect each other and stand together. The ship stands for England and, although it goes down, enough of the crew survive to man new ships. In them, England is renewed. Coward did not miss a trick: the film begins and ends with statements as to its and the Royal Navy's purpose read by Leslie Howard. It was an immensely successful film and in England received uncritically: an exciting film, well-made with a fine cast.

The ministry of information, impressed by the success of *In Which We Serve* and RAF films like *The First of the Few*, commissioned David Niven, Peter Ustinov, Eric Ambler, and Carol Reed, all of whom were in the army, to devise an equivalent for the army. Ambler and Ustinov, who wrote the script, deliberately chose not to follow *In Which We Serve* and set the film in the infantry, the least glamorous part of the army. They were influenced, revealingly, by the documentary technique of an army instructional film, *The New Lot*. The film, *The Way Ahead*, became a 'plain tale of typical Britons of this generation who were called from the plough, the bench, the office: the man with the white collar, the man without a collar'.[83] The film showed the new lot training, learning

---

[83] Quoted in Stead, *Film and the Working Class*, 135.

discipline, how to get on with each other and a martinet sergeant, then going into action. Combat gives meaning to what they have learnt and justifies it. The film is both 'democratic' and socially accurate. The one officer (David Niven) is of working-class background; he owns a small garage and began life as a motor-mechanic. The industrial working class is under-represented; rightly, since so many of the working class were in reserved occupations. Carol Reed directed and Filippo del Giudice, who as a man of the left, was much more sympathetic to *The Way Ahead* than to *In Which We Serve*, produced. A strong cast was led by Niven, Stanley Holloway, and William Hartnell.

The Way Ahead was, technically and intellectually, probably the best of the war films, and the only one which consciously aligned itself with wartime democracy. It was not, however, the most popular. That was *The Way to the Stars*, an RAF film released just after the war in Europe ended, and voted in the *Daily Mail* poll the most popular film exhibited in England during the war. It had two themes: the effect of combat on personal relations, and its effect on Anglo-American relations. The script was by Terence Rattigan, an officer in the RAF, and its first theme suggested by his successful play *The Flare Path* (1942), whose locale is a hotel near an RAF base and whose protagonists are service wives. The play is written around their reaction to their husbands' night flights. The second theme Rattigan had already touched upon when he drafted the script of an 'Anglo-American' airforce film. The proposed film was to be directed by William Wyler and produced by Twentieth Century-Fox. Wyler shot considerable footage but decided that the material was better suited to a documentary. The result was one of the most famous wartime documentaries, *Memphis Belle*. But the film itself was never made. With the support of the ministry of information and the White Russian émigré Anatole de Grunwald, Rattigan combined the two themes and his new script became *The Way to the Stars*. It was directed by Anthony Asquith, who had worked successfully with Rattigan before, particularly on *French without Tears* (1939); and co-produced by de Grunwald and Two Cities. The cast was exceptionally good: Michael Redgrave, John Mills, Rosamund John, Trevor Howard, Basil Radford, Renée Asherson, Bill Owen, and the very young Jean Simmons. The leading American part was played by the Canadian Douglass Montgomery.

The film was popular not because it was a war movie but because it was a powerful sentimental drama whose power was (for once in a British film) increased by the restraint with which it was played. And there was much to be restrained about: three of the four principals were killed. The film's emotional level was heightened by the poem John Pudney wrote for the American principal (Johnny), 'Johnny-in-the-Clouds', which was enormously admired and did for *The Way to the Stars* what the 'Warsaw Concerto' did for *Dangerous Moonlight*.[84]

---

[84] *Johnny-in-the-Clouds* was the American title of the film.

Although *The Way Ahead* was implicitly democratic, none of these films was socially subversive; which was true of all the major commercial war films, with the possible exception of Alberto Cavalcanti's *Went the Day Well?* (1942). Cavalcanti's film, which also had ministry of information support, was distantly related to a Graham Greene short story, *The Lieutenant Died Last* (1940). It (and the film) is concerned with two of the preoccupations of the early war years: the danger of invasion and the activities of the fifth column. By the time *Went the Day Well?* was released both of these had lost their edge, as the producers (Ealing, with Michael Balcon in charge of production) recognized. The film takes the form of a flashback, a story recounted after victory.

The film's location is an English village (which sits amidst much idyllic rurality) on Whitsun weekend in 1942. A unit of 'Royal Engineers' arrives, is accepted, billeted by the villagers and settles in. The 'Engineers' are in fact Germans, whose aim is to set up a machine that will disable the country's radar system at the moment of invasion. Their contact-man turns out to be the village squire, much respected by the villagers. The German cover is penetrated, and the villagers rounded up and imprisoned. Help is sought by the local poacher and a high-spirited cockney evacuee; and the villagers resist and do battle with the Germans until it arrives. *Went the Day Well?* can be interpreted in various ways. By English standards it was very violent, and Cavalcanti was not squeamish about showing it. Women are axed and bayoneted, something then shocking to an English audience. Conventional social hierarchies are reversed. The traitor is the squire, and the village is saved by those at the bottom of the social heap—the poacher and the evacuee. It is easy to see a social critique in this—and some do.[85] *Went the Day Well?* arguably falls into a wartime tradition of socially radical cinema. As Aldgate and Richards point out, however, the squire is shot by the vicar's daughter[86]—and not by any socially marginal figure. Nor do the villagers appear to draw wider conclusions from the squire's behaviour. But the film does show the villagers, not as simply stoical in the face of catastrophe—a well-known English response—but as active and inventive and capable of strong collective action. On balance, the film is democratic. Although the superior persons are capable of great courage, like the lady of the manor, it is the inferior ones who react first, and most effectively— partly because they are less impressed by social convention and polite manners.

All these films see something unique in the history and traditions of England (more rarely Britain). All stress the national community and social solidarity. But none do more than imply that England will be a better place after the war and only *The Way Ahead* argues that this is a war of the ordinary

---

[85] See, for example, Durgnat, *A Mirror for England*, 15–16; Murphy, *Realism and Tinsel*, 38–9. Murphy argues that 'stock British types' behave with a savagery never before seen; Barr, *Ealing Studios*, 30–3.
[86] Aldgate and Richards, *Britain Can Take It*, 131.

man, let alone the ordinary woman. Furthermore, the rhetoric of 'Englishness' is often very conservative, most obviously in the right-wing appropriation of Shakespeare. Three wartime films borrow from John of Gaunt's famous speech in *Richard II*: *This England*, *This Happy Breed*, and *Demi-Paradise*. All of them ooze self-satisfaction. They are patriotic, but represent only one of several possible patriotisms.

Films which, like *The Way Ahead*, were influenced by the documentary movement of the 1930s stand for an alternative patriotism. They portray England at war as the apotheosis of democracy. Even more, some of the best known, like Frank Launder and Sidney Gilliat's *Millions Like Us* are about women: 'the conscripted woman, the mobile woman'. *Millions Like Us* emphasizes the disruptive nature of the war; the tensions war establishes between the old life and the new; the problems of conscription and mobility; the difficulties in learning new tasks; the development of a specifically feminine solidarity. It also poses directly the question of how far pre-war Britain and its relationships should be restored. Hardly at all, seems to be the answer. *Millions Like Us* was the best of a mere handful of 'women's' war films: much better than the patronizing *The Gentle Sex* (1943), with its toe-curling final voice-over from Leslie Howard,[87] and more interesting, because more ambitious than Launder and Gilliat's *Two Thousand Women* (1944).

The Crown Film Unit also produced two famous feature films which were documentary in form and, to a considerable degree, in fact: Humphrey Jennings's *Fires Were Started* (1943), a loving tribute to the Auxiliary Fire Service and Pat Jackson's *Western Approaches* (1944), a similar tribute to the Merchant Navy. These are fine films which both place the ordinary Englishman at their centre. Yet neither, nor *Millions Like Us*, had anything like the popularity of the commercial features. Typically, the teenage girls with whom Pearl Jephcott worked found *Western Approaches* 'boring'.[88] War films were popular if they were exciting and/or sentimental, featured well-known and preferably star casts, were not too political, but not necessarily without some sort of 'message' about the future. Not, therefore, very different from a popular pre-war film. Which is why *The Way to the Stars* and, alas, *Mrs Miniver* were so successful.[89]

Taken as a whole, however, the most popular films of the 1940s were not, with the exception of *The Way to the Stars*, war films, but the famous

---

[87] For an excellent discussion of *The Gentle Sex* and *Millions Like Us*, see Landy, *British Genres*, 206–7. Howard concluded *The Gentle Sex* by saying: 'Let's give in at least and admit we really are proud of you, you strange, wonderful, incalculable creatures. The world we shape is going to be a better world because you are helping to shape it. Silence, gentlemen, I give you a toast. The gentle sex.'

[88] Jephcott, *Rising Twenty*, 155.

[89] See Durgnat's comment on *Mrs Miniver*: 'Seeing that dreadful film now, it is hard to believe that at the time Mrs Miniver was accepted as a national heroine whose glycerine tears and saccharine trials seemed of Boadicean proportions.' (*A Mirror for England*, 31.) Much of the film's popularity was due to the personal popularity of Greer Garson. For that, see Mayer, *Sociology of Film*, 112–13.

Gainsborough melodramas: especially *The Man in Grey* (1943), *Fanny by Gaslight* (1944), *Madonna of the Seven Moons* (1944), *They Were Sisters* (1945), *The Seventh Veil* (1945), and, most famous of all, *The Wicked Lady* (1945). Gainsborough, needing quick profits, decided to make a series of films not unlike (and therefore as successful as), the semi-gothic 'romances' which sold in colossal numbers. The first of the Gainsboroughs, *The Man in Grey*, was based upon Lady Eleanor Smith's 'gothic' novel of the same name. Smith specialized in romances more in the tradition of Eleanor Glyn than Ruby M. Ayres. They have something in common with Barbara Cartland or Mills and Boon romances, but are much more violent and allow women more heterodox roles.[90] The films are, in many ways, conventional 'bodice-rippers' and have many of their standard props, like gypsies with second sight.

The *Man in Grey* and *The Wicked Lady* were specifically historical but all were vague as to period. 'Historical' settings, however dubious, allowed the luxurious and dramatic *mise-en-scène* and dress in which the films specialized. They were heavily 'gothic' in style as well as plot and owed more to the UFA films of the 1920s than to Hollywood. And the heroines displayed a *décolletage* Hollywood would never have permitted. The Gainsborough melodramas were 'women's films'. The action of the plot revolves around women: however helpless the heroine or anti-heroine, she is at its centre. The women represent marked polarities of which 'chasteness' and 'unchasteness' is the most important. In most of the films different actresses stand for different polarities, but in *Madonna of the Seven Moons* Phyllis Calvert stands for both: Maddalena, a virginal, nun-like mother, who has another life as Rosanna, a passionate free spirit in love with a gypsy thief, Nino (Stewart Granger). Maddalena's double life is apparently the result of her having being raped as a convent girl: the most dramatic of the female traumas common to all the Gainsborough melodramas.[91]

Their argument is simple. 'Goodness' and 'badness' are stark oppositions. The bad girls are very bad, partly because they are hedonistic and boldly sexual. They are not unlike Carmen and often come to a similar end. Like Carmen, however, they are more interesting than the good girls. The principal anti-heroine was Margaret Lockwood, who had been a bad girl even in earlier films like *The Stars Look Down*. Although nearly all the Gainsborough women seek adventure or freedom, they are obliged, even the bad girls, to mediate their roles via men, who also represent sharply opposed polarities. Men were either sensitive and responsible or brutal and uncaring. James Mason, who was usually the villain, was either a rapist or murderer. Gainsborough was, by contemporary standards, open about violence and sex. In *Madonna of the Seven Moons*, Maddalena is raped as a schoolgirl and it seems clear, for those good at

---

[90] For romance novels, see Chapter XIII below.   [91] Landy, *British Genres*, 216–26.

mental arithmetic, that her daughter Angela (Patricia Roc) is the offspring of that rape and not of Maddalena's marriage to a gentlemanly banker. It is a comment both on the films and their audience that the popularity of Lockwood and Mason was due almost entirely to the badness of the people they portrayed.

Women, young women particularly, said they 'sympathized' with the Gainsborough women whose sexual and social dilemmas seemed in some sense 'real' to them.[92] The melodramas made stars of Calvert, Lockwood, Roc, and Jean Kent, whose standing was comparable with Googie Withers, who at Ealing rather languished until 1945 when she became a spectacularly bad girl in *Pink String and Sealing Wax*.

Despite their popularity, the critics and male stars rather despised the Gainsborough melodramas. Stewart Granger thought them 'junk' and James Mason denounced them and the British cinema before he left for Hollywood— only to discover that Hollywood was no better. Studio politics undermined them and the attempt by Rank to raise their tone, as in *The Bad Lord Byron* (1949), failed badly. After 1947 no more 'classic' Gainsborough melodramas were made. This meant that there were few strong roles for women in British cinema; Calvert, Lockwood, Roc, and Kent never found really satisfactory alternatives. They were uncomfortable in the reticent mode *à la* Celia Johnson, too mature as actresses for the Rank charm school and not suited to the kind of light comedy popularized by Kay Kendall. This in turn hastened the flight to Hollywood. Jean Simmons and Deborah Kerr, though definitely not Gainsborough girls, thought prospects for women in the British cinema too limited.[93] Audrey Hepburn was lent to Paramount because there was nothing for her to do in England.

The passing of the Gainsborough melodramas left the way open to Anna Neagle, Michael Wilding, and the 'upper-class' films they made with Herbert Wilcox in the late 1940s. *The Courtneys of Curzon Street* was the most popular film of 1947 and though not conventionally upper-class—Neagle plays a working-class girl, Cathy, who marries into the aristocratic Courtneys and 'saves' them by doing so—it is an implicit affirmation of an upper-class *raison d'être*. Their 'Mayfair' films, like *Spring in Park Lane* (1948) and *Maytime in Mayfair* (1949) were, as Swann points out, the 'white telephone' movies of the period.[94] They involved much singing and dancing in super-comfortable surroundings which were foreign even to Mayfair in 1948–9. As such, they were very popular, and

---

[92] Jephcott, *Rising Twenty*, 155.

[93] Deborah Kerr as an actress in many ways personified reticence and repression—as her role in *Black Narcissus* (1947) demonstrated—and most of the films she made were in the reticent manner. But in John Baxter's *Love on the Dole* (1941) she goes off to be the mistress of the odious bookie, something few actresses did in 1941. And her love scene on the beach with Burt Lancaster in *From Here to Eternity* (1953) was one of the great moments in the history of cinematic sexuality.

[94] Swann, *Hollywood Feature Film*, 76.

might have done better than the melodramas anyway. Those, for all their unreality, had had a toughness and a certain democracy appropriate to a heroic moment in British history. The late 1940s, however, were not heroic; they were grim. The 'Mayfair' movies, set very much in the present, but a present stripped of rationing and austerity, were also, like the Hollywood glamour films, 'women's films'; but of women as consumers and home-builders, proponents of the long-delayed good life, rather than as gypsies, highwaymen (as Lockwood was in *The Wicked Lady*), or vengeful lovers.

Akin to the Gainsborough melodramas as a genre were the so-called 'spiv' films: a group of films made between 1945 and 1950 whose locale was criminal and often the black market. Like the Gainsboroughs they could be violent, occasionally extremely violent. And, as in the Gainsboroughs, this was comparatively new to the British cinema. There had been crime films before the war, often influenced by contemporary American gangster movies and some, like Arthur Wood's *They Drove by Night* (1938), were commercially successful. But pre-war British censorship made the treatment of crime difficult. It became easier in the 1940s, partly because censorship was relaxed, partly because violence (in some form) was no longer exceptional in people's lives, partly because the black market, the closest Britain had to American prohibition, had made the opportunities for crime innumerable, and partly because the political culture of the 1940s encouraged the making of 'social problem' films.

The first acknowledged 'spiv' film was Sidney Gilliat's *Waterloo Road* (1945). This was intended as an 'all-in-it-together' movie in which the consensual values of the nation-at-war were emphasized. The plot, however, broached the tricky subject of wartime marriage and adultery. The hero, John Mills, goes AWOL to save his marriage after his wife takes up with a racketeer, Ted (Stewart Granger). Although the hero thrashes him and indeed saves his marriage, the film's dominating figure turns out to be Ted. This was a consequence of Granger's looks and personality, but also of the characteristics that went with the role: flashiness, fast money, toughness, a certain malevolence, and a disregard of all those things Britain was supposed to be defending. Ted established the cinema's definition of the spiv.

The origin of the word 'spiv' is obscure.[95] The flamboyant dress owes something to 1930s American gangster movies, something to the dress of American blacks (the zoot-suit particularly, popularized by Cab Calloway), but as much to the peacock tradition of the young British working-class male—the

---

[95] For the spiv and his origins, see D. Hughes, 'The Spivs' in M. Sissons and P. French (eds.), *Age of Austerity, 1945–51* (2nd ed., Oxford, 1986), 71–88; D. Hebdige, 'The Meaning of Mod' in S. Hall and T. Jefferson (eds.), *Resistance through Ritual* (London, 1989), 89; G. Pearson, *Hooligan: A History of Respectable Fears* (New York, 1984), 21–2; S. Cosgrove, 'The Zoot Suit and Style Warfare', *History Workshop*, 18 (Autumn 1984), 77–91.

bell-bottomed trousers, the colourful waistcoats, the high-heeled shoes, all common in the late Victorian and Edwardian period, a style which went to ground in the interwar years.

Until the early 1950s, however, the cinema's portrayal of the spiv was consistently hostile. In cinematic usage, 'spiv' was an inclusive rather than technical term: all dangerous young males tended to be thought spivs. The first film whose central character was a spiv was Cavalcanti's *They Made Me a Fugitive* (1947). Here the spiv, Narcy, is exceptionally unpleasant and the setting irredeemably severe. It was none the less very popular, as were its two successors *It Always Rains on Sunday* (1948) and *Brighton Rock* (1948). *Brighton Rock* is honest to Graham Greene's novel. The film makes it clear that its location is pre-war Brighton. But it looks like 1948; and in Pinkie (Richard Attenborough) it had a young psychopath who was a model of the dangerous young male. *No Orchids for Miss Blandish* was also released in 1948, and though distant from James Hadley Chase's novel it had a whole gang of dangerous young males.

The last and best of the spiv films was *The Third Man* (1949). This is a genuinely sinister film. Even off-screen, as he is for much of the time, Harry Lime (Orson Welles) dominates the film, and is an overwhelmingly malign presence when he does appear. With its skilful use of *film-noir* techniques, a dangerous setting (occupied Vienna), a distinguished cast, a theme song for zither by Anton Karas which itself became an international hit, the film was hugely successful both in Britain and America. But it was in a way a farewell to the spiv film. The conditions in which spivvery flourished, the black market, were disappearing as the Western European economy became de-rationed: 1949–50 was about the last time a serious spiv film could be made. Furthermore, the locale of *The Third Man* was too exotic, Harry Lime as super spiv—he traded in diluted penicillin— too improbable, the plot too tied to a particular moment for the tradition to continue.[96]

As the spiv tradition was worked out the theme of the dangerous young male became more prominent. He was increasingly detached from the black market to become part of the 'problem' of post-war juvenile delinquency. Like the spiv the delinquent was thought to be created by the war: by absent fathers and divided families, by a confusion of norms and values, by universal violence. At his worst the young delinquent became wholly alienated from family and society—from morality as such.

This was the theme of the *The Blue Lamp* (1950), an important film and very popular, whose direct antecedent, even in the cast, was *The Boys in Brown* (1949). *The Boys in Brown* is set in a borstal whose governor (Jack Warner), an enlightened figure, has to sort out three young criminals, played by Richard

[96] Marcia Landy sees *The Third Man* as a 'cold war' film, and there is something in that, though the division of the city is a comparatively minor theme. (Landy, *British Genres*, 182–3.)

Attenborough (who had just made *Brighton Rock*), Dirk Bogarde, and Jimmy Hanley. Of the three, it is the Bogarde character, Alfie, who is most dangerous and morally irreparable. He is irreparable because, unlike the other two, he has no social or familial ties: he embodies the anomic young male.

In *The Blue Lamp*, an Ealing film written by T. E. B. Clarke (himself an ex-policeman) and directed by Alexander Mackendrick, Warner, Bogarde, and Hanley were reunited. The locale is Paddington Green, which became Dock Green in the famous TV series. Warner plays Dixon, an older, good-tempered, and shrewd copper who takes under his wing the young PC Mitchell (Hanley), who eventually lodges with Dixon and his wife. The police are depicted as a kind of extended family, but also a community deeply attached to the wider community of Paddington Green. The relation of Dixon to Mitchell is paternal; as is the relationship of the police to the wider community. Bogarde is Tom Riley, a loner, whose only relationship (with Diana) is profoundly flawed. He is a victim of war, and dangerous for it. Riley kills Dixon. He is then hunted by the whole community (including its older criminal element) and run to earth in a greyhound track.

The Blue Lamp is significant. It stands for a socially integrative value-system which concedes much to the working class but in which the community—conceived essentially in non-class terms—is predominant. The values of *The Blue Lamp* are, then, acceptable to more or less everybody. In asserting them against Riley, who could claim to have been one outcome of the war, the film also suggests that these were the values for which the war was fought and won. As Dixon's values and those of the community that unites against his killer, they are unambiguously affirmed by the destruction of Riley.

Equally significantly, the police are given central place as both upholders and representatives of the victorious value-system. This was something new in the cinema. As Raymond Durgnat points out, in pre-war films the attitude to the police was much less enthusiastic.[97] In them the police are more likely to be treated as boobies than bobbies. After the war, however, the police (particularly as Dixon-figures) stand for the nation-as-family; and for the virtues of the nation. *The Blue Lamp* promoted this view; but it also symbolizes it. By 1950, there were large numbers of people, as we have noted,[98] willing to assert that the nation's virtues were summed up by its policemen. A view the police themselves understandably did not discourage.

Alongside the melodramas and the spiv films the British cinema produced some notable comedies in the 1940s and early 1950s. The comedians who had been successful in the 1930s, other than Gracie Fields, continued to make films—though not always with the same success. In George Formby's *Let George Do It* (1941), George, in a famous dream sequence, takes on Hitler personally.

[97] Durgnat, *A Mirror for England*, 136.   [98] See above, pp. 329–30.

But he went to Columbia from Ealing in 1941 and the formula never quite worked again. *George in Civvy Street* (1946) was a failure and Formby made no films after 1947. Will Hay made his last film in 1944 (*My Learned Friend*, a black comedy), and the 'provincial' comedians, Frank Randle, Arthur Lucan, and Kitty McShane all made popular movies in the war. Arthur Askey, unlike Tommy Handley and ITMA,[99] successfully made the transition from radio to film and was one of the most popular actors of the 1940s. They were all in a tradition of non-metropolitan humour which (just) survived the late 1940s, to be carried on by Norman Wisdom and, above all, the innumerable *Carry On* films, in which every cliché of English humour is triumphantly exploited.

The dominant comic genre of the post-war years, however, was not the basically working-class humour of the 'provincial' comedians but the 'middle-class' humour of Launder and Gilliat and what came to be called the Ealing comedies. The success of the Launder and Gilliat films was due (like the Ealing comedies) to an ensemble of brilliant comic actors—Margaret Rutherford, Alastair Sim, George Cole, Terry-Thomas, Joyce Grenfell and (in *The Rake's Progress*) Rex Harrison—and in the atmosphere of misrule which prevailed in nearly all the films. The relentless satire of stock English types and institutions, particularly public schools and the civil service, and the almost unbalanced eccentricity of some of the characters guaranteed their success.

More important were the comedies of the Ealing Studios, since they were better and more overtly 'social' films. Ealing had made the Fields–Formby movies under Basil Dean, but there was a clear change of direction after Balcon made his peace with Rank in 1944. Balcon was hostile to the predominant style of interwar British films and was also influenced by wartime democracy:

> By and large we were a group of liberal-minded, like-minded people … We were middle-class people brought up with middle-class backgrounds and rather conventional educations … We voted Labour for the first time after the war: this was our mild revolution.[100]

The 'mild revolution' infuses the Ealing comedies. They are democratic (but not working-class) and consensual. The community, not the individual, dominates the action, and the community always masters dissident individualism. They are hostile to authority and bureaucracy; but in nearly all cases, with the possible exception of *Kind Hearts and Coronets*, the revolt of the small man is either momentary or unsuccessful. Unlike most British and American films of the time the Ealing comedies are not studio-bound. As a result, a number, like *Hue and Cry* or *The Lavender Hill Mob*, give the viewer a rather good picture of what London was like after the war. Ealing was served with outstanding casts (who were often the same as Launder and Gilliat's), and in *Kind Hearts and Coronets* and *The Lavender Hill Mob* Alec Guinness gave bravura performances. Just how good these casts were can be seen by comparing any Ealing comedy with

---

[99] For ITMA, see below, Chapter XII.   [100] Quoted in Barr, *Ealing Studios*, 9.

its nearest American equivalent, the highly regarded *Arsenic and Old Lace* (1944), where Cary Grant's over-acting only embarrasses.

The first of the comedies was T. E. B. Clarke's charming *Hue and Cry* (1947), in which a group of London boys uncover a criminal gang whose unknown chief establishes contact with his gang and announces its *modus operandi* via the magazines the boys read. In *Hue and Cry* the community is represented by the boys and their peers. At its end the small gang-busting group is rescued by a mobilization of the whole juvenile population of the area.

Passport to Pimlico (1949), the most popular of the Ealing comedies, is a more ambiguous film. The small community of Pimlico, London, discovers a medieval charter which suggests that Pimlico is actually part of the Grand Duchy of Burgundy. This being a straitened time in England, Pimlico decides to exercise its sovereignty and secedes. For a time there is a carnivalesque atmosphere; but independent Pimlico is invaded by spivs, crooks, and wide-boys of various kinds, while the British state puts it under siege. Eventually it abandons its independence and its inhabitants accept that they cannot turn their backs on the wider community or escape their responsibilities. The film ends with a message almost explicitly supporting the policies of the Attlee government. This dénouement, however, is strained and the film is at least half-sympathetic to independent Pimlico in its struggle against a bullying British bureaucracy.

The anti-bureaucratic theme is more obvious in Alexander Mackendrick's *Whisky Galore* (1948), based on a novel by Compton Mackenzie. The film was shot on the Isle of Barra and is set in the war. A ship containing thousands of cases of whisky founders off the island and the islanders determine to save the whisky for themselves. This pits the community against a narrow and author-itarian English customs officer (Basil Radford). Radford understands nothing: neither the islanders, their habits and the effect of wartime privation, nor the life-enhancing properties of whisky. He stands for the worst of bureaucracy and the community restores itself in its battle against him.

The Lavender Hill Mob (1951), written by T. E. B. Clarke and directed by Charles Crichton, is a film about the futility of hoping for too much. Alec Guinness, a bank clerk, who has followed a blameless and deadening routine all his work-ing life, has secret fantasies of kicking over the traces in the high life of South America. He decides to steal the gold it is one of his duties to guard and com-bines with Stanley Holloway and two small-time crooks, Sid James and Alfie Bass, to do it. After a series of very funny escapades, including madcap chases, Guinness makes it to South America. But then we learn that the person to whom Guinness narrates his story is the policeman who has come to arrest him. The bank clerk's revolt against life has failed. The best he can hope for is what he refuses to accept: the regular routine and small satisfactions of the bank. *The Lavender Hill Mob* has affinities with *The Blue Lamp* which, of course,

Clarke also wrote. Both concern revolt and its suppression; both elevate the community and the consensual norms by which it operates. Riley, violently, and the bank clerk, pointlessly, seek to overcome them. Neither succeeds. But the tension between reality and aspiration was necessary for the Ealing films. Once the tension is eliminated, Ealing comedies, like *The Titfield Thunderbolt* (1953), became apolitical and backward-looking.

Robert Hamer's *Kind Hearts and Coronets* (1949) fits awkwardly into the Ealing comic genre, though it has since become the most famous of the comedies. Louis Mazzini (Dennis Price), whose mother is of noble birth but disowned by her family after she marries an Italian street-singer (Price's father), decides to avenge her by wiping out all those who stand between him and the family dukedom. This he does but, in the end, is brought down by the malice of Sibella (Joan Greenwood) after he chooses Edith (Valerie Hobson), the widow of one of his victims. The film is flawlessly acted, wittily written and tightly directed. But it is dark and unsettling. The D'Ascoyne family, as played by Guinness (all of them, including the suffragette Lady Agatha, who fell to earth in Berkeley Square), are absurd. As a representative of the upper class, they are the subject of sustained satire. Nor is the dénouement Ealing-like. Louis is ruined not by the mobilization of the community, nor even by the fact that he leaves his 'confession' in his cell, but because Sibella is even more heartless than he.

It is this darkness which perhaps accounts for its immediate reception in England. It was nowhere near as popular as *Passport to Pimlico*, or *The Chiltern Hundreds*, which is reactionary at all levels. Initially, it was more popular abroad, and its reputation as the 'classic' Ealing developed only slowly. Certainly Ealing never tried to repeat it, and, though it made Guinness's international reputation, Hamer, Price, and Greenwood never got such a good film again. And the British industry made few films of similar bite until the 1960s, and then under very different conditions and often with émigré American directors.

Throughout these years the cinema was profoundly important in English cultural life. The way they saw their own society and the wider world was significantly mediated by the cinema. Furthermore, love of the cinema was common to the whole country. Although women and children went more than adult men and although picture-going was more popular in the North than the South, such variations were not large. On the whole, what people liked they liked together.

Contemporaries thought the cinema was a uniquely powerful medium. The country's élites were persistently worried about its potentially subversive effects on England's politics and morality. They particularly feared the influence of the United States and its 'democracy' on what was thought to be the structured and stable social hierarchy of England. To limit this influence the state imposed both informal and formal constraints on American movies: an informal but strict system of censorship and formal legislative quotas which specified what proportion of the home market American films could have.

Before the Second World War British films were rather disliked. People were offended by the mannered style, the accents and the emotional restraint of films and actors. American films were preferred because they were energetic, unrestrained, sentimental and full-blooded. Furthermore, their glamour was more glamorous than English glamour.

From the late 1930s, however, British films became much more popular. They were technically better (partly as a consequence of the Jewish emigration from Central Europe), and they employed actors and actresses who were more familiar with the demands of the film and less in thrall to the stage. Although a number of successful British films out-Hollywooded Hollywood most of the successful ones were those which appealed to a more specific English taste. Throughout the 1940s, therefore, the English showed no particular preference for American films, and the most popular actors and actresses of the decade were nearly always English. Where the British industry could not compete was in numbers: the great majority of films shown throughout the period as a whole were American. Furthermore, the advantages the British industry had—a comparatively uniform market and a form of state protection—were often thrown away, as in the case of Korda or Rank, by a determination to beat the Americans at their own game and by a reluctance to continue making the kind of films the English clearly liked.

By the 1950s the English had become very familiar with the United States as it appeared in American films. But they were not completely taken in, and there is little sign of the wholesale Americanization that people so feared before and during the war. Nor is there much to suggest that American movies were socially subversive in practice. They were energetic etc, but theirs was a democracy of manner rather than content. In the end, their result was probably to increase the demand for a notionally apolitical glamour whose implication was, if anything, conservative rather than democratic.

THE increase in ownership of radios in England was very rapid from the late 1920s; within 10 years a majority of English households owned one. The radio was a unique medium in England: domestic transmission was a monopoly of a state-chartered body—the BBC. But the BBC had competition from commercial English-language stations which transmitted from the Continent. The commercial stations themselves broadcast American radio programmes and the BBC was forced to compete with them as well. This chapter is concerned with the BBC's relations with its listening audience and the way in which the corporation reacted to the commercial stations. It considers the role of John Reith and the extent to which Reith's hopes for broadcasting and its educational function were met. It suggests that the outcome was a fair compromise. Much of what Reith wanted was achieved; at the same time, however, the BBC was always sensitive to the wishes of its audience, even without the competition of the commercial stations. The chapter also looks at the part the radio played in domestic life.

Throughout the interwar years, the number of households possessing radios increased every year without exception. The most rapid growth was in the years 1930–2, the bottom of the depression, when the consumption of all other household goods fell sharply: an important index of how valued the radio had become, especially as an instrument of consolation. Between 1922 and 1939 the number of radio licences per 100 households increased from 1 per cent to 71 per cent—from a total of 36,000 to 8.9 million.[1] Ownership was densest in London and the South-East and the Midlands; slightly lower in the North. Density was lowest in predominantly rural areas like the north of Scotland. Although about two-thirds of radio licences were held by those earning between £2 10s and £4 per week, about one-third, or a little more, of working-class households were without radios. That was so until the last years of the war when the cheap 'utility' set was introduced. By 1945 there were 10.8 million licences—which represents a large majority of households in all social classes.

[1] M. Pegg, *Broadcasting and Society, 1918–1939* (London, 1983), 7.

The consequence of the radio was, of course, to keep people at home, particularly when alternative activities, like seeing the family or going to the pub, required time and effort. It was ideal for the new suburban estates, whether private or local authority.[2] That it was socially isolating people realized, and there was an attempt in the 1930s, partly by the BBC and organizations like the Left Book Club, to make 'listening in' the focus for sociability (or for political consciousness-raising). This had some success when the radio was still a novelty, but little thereafter.

Families differed in the way they listened. There was a tendency in working-class households to turn the set on and leave it on. Middle-class households were more discriminating: the set was turned on for particular programmes and turned off when they ended. In households where children were under pressure from school and parents to do homework, the radio was even more strictly policed. In some households, when conversation drowned the broadcast, the radio was simply turned up, while in others silence was insisted upon. Whether the radio promoted domestic harmony, however, people were undecided:

'In the old days one would start chipping and then another, and it would end in a quarrel. Now they sit and listen instead of quarrelling'. But others thought the programmes themselves caused disharmony. One young woman said, she avoided discussing them as it 'wasn't worth it'.[3]

Most children and adolescents 'listened' to the radio differently from adults: it was not an 'activity' in itself. For them, the radio was like a piece of furniture—and increasingly *was* a piece of furniture[4]—especially if it were on all the time. It was simply there; an accompaniment rather than alternative to something else. It was precisely the radio's centrality to domestic life as a kind of constant noise, to which one listened or not as one pleased, that distinguished it from other activities. Adolescents, therefore, described listening in as one of their *least* favourite ways of spending an evening; and only 5.5 per cent said it was the way they had actually spent the previous evening[5]—a figure which can be right only if listening in is defined as a conscious act. The radio was much less favoured than sport, the cinema, or dancing since it was, at one level, all the things they were not: at home, unsociable, and unexciting. Yet we know the radio was central to the lives of children and adolescents—if only for music, sport, and, in the 1940s, serials. But because the radio was so often a continuous noise, listening was effortless. It involved no preparation and (frequently) no anticipation, which is why, when asked, children and adolescents rated it a

---

[2] For radio in its domestic setting, see above, p. 197.
[3] Jennings and Gill, *Broadcasting in Everyday Life*, 23.
[4] For the radio-as-furniture, see Pegg, *Broadcasting and Society*, 56–7.
[5] Wilkins, *Adolescent in Britain*, 85–91.

least favoured activity. A different question, however, would have got a different answer.

The régime under which people listened in was almost unique to Britain. For virtually the whole period the British Broadcasting Company, as it was until 1927, when it became by charter the British Broadcasting Corporation (the BBC), had a statutory monopoly of all broadcasting within Britain. It was financed not by advertising revenue but a licence fee which every person who owned a radio had to pay. This monopoly was acceptable to most of the country's vested interests: to the political parties because it kept the BBC broadly neutral and, if necessary, quiescent; and to the press because it eliminated a competitor for advertising revenue. The dominating figure in the organization, first as general manager (1922–7), then as director-general (1927–38), was John Reith, a Scot trained as an engineer.[6] Reith, who had never heard of broadcasting until October 1922, came to the BBC as a formidable administrator with strong views. It was not, in fact, as much under his thumb as outsiders thought or as he would have liked, but he unquestionably set the tone. The BBC, in his view, was to be authoritative, impartial, and to embody the best in the values of the educated classes. Commenting on a report that the Manchester children's programme had been 'reformed in the direction of greater dignity and less informality', Reith wrote:

In some stations I see periodically men down to speak whose status, either professionally or socially, and whose qualifications to speak seem doubtful. It should be an honour in every sense of the word for a man to speak from any broadcasting station, and only those who have a claim to be heard above their fellows on any particular subject in the locality should be put on the programme.[7]

This was a not unworthy object, but in practice it put a high premium on polish and manner. According to Peter Eckersley, the chief engineer of outside broadcasts, before any appointment was made, the question was put: 'Is he a gentleman?' Reith, furthermore, was a snob. 'I sized him up at once', he said of a Glasgow scholarship boy who had applied for a minor post, 'as a type of young Scottish nobody.'[8] The result was that boys from public schools and the ancient universities held a near monopoly of the corporation's important posts.

Authority, which is what Reith wanted of the BBC, came armed with propriety. In November 1924 it was decided that all announcers, many of whom had been hitherto well known, were to be anonymous, and the following year, that they were to wear dinner-jackets when actually broadcasting. Announcers

---

[6] For the details of Reith's appointment, see A. Briggs, *The Birth of Broadcasting* (London, 1961), 133–42.

[7] Quoted in Scannell and Cardiff, *Social History of British Broadcasting*, 316.

[8] D. L. LeMahieu, *A Culture for Democracy* (Oxford, 1988), 183.

were to think of themselves as 'men of culture, experience and knowledge', and anonymity and dinner-jackets were marks of culture, experience and knowledge. The BBC thus deliberately rejected the 'American' or 'commercial' model whereby listeners were encouraged to identify programmes with personalities and individual style. Anonymity and dinner-jackets, not surprisingly, exposed the BBC to some derision. *Punch*, killing two birds with one stone—anonymous announcers and unremittingly serious music—depicted Stuart Hibberd, already well known, saying: 'Good Evening, Everybody. XXX calling. We will now have a Fugue.' Anonymity also encouraged a blandness which Collie Knox, a *Daily Mail* columnist and professional critic of the BBC, thought sounded like the 'bored, listless manner of a dying duck'.

Reith's attitudes were easily derided but they none the less formed a coherent theory of broadcasting. For Reith, the BBC had a clear pedagogic function: 'Give the public slightly better than it now thinks it likes.'[9] This was a defensible policy and in the long run served both the BBC and the country well. In the short run, however, it caused problems. The major one was the working class. The corporation found it immensely difficult to approach working men and women without condescension or to devise ways in which working-class accents and styles of conversation could be assimiliated to the Reithian tone. The producer of the programme *Men Talking* (1937), a series meant for the unemployed, conceded that 'this question of the working classes is very difficult indeed. We know very few broadcasters who would fulfil the role without sounding like *In Town Tonight* or the *Punch* idea of a working man.'[10] Thus in *Men Talking* there were objections that 'all the speakers appeared to belong to the same minority group and did not have children in state schools.'[11] The BBC recognized this and agreed that it was unacceptable for men with 'thousand-a-year' voices to discuss 'details of the family budget', but before the outbreak of war, and even after, the BBC was rarely able to give the working class an authentic voice.

The only way out, other than by excluding working men and women altogether, was to 'embellish' what they said. There were several notorious examples of this. In a series devoted to people's daily work-routines, 'Bill', a docker, ended 'his' talk as follows:

Arriving at Higham Bight in the early grey of the morning I have looked at the Hulks and across the Essex shore . . . and fancied in the rising mists the faces of hunted convicts and Joe Gargery and Pip and remembered that it was somewhere in their search of the river that David Copperfield said adieu to Mrs Peggotty and Mrs Gummidge where little Em'ly waved her last farewell.

The producers must have been conscious of the falsity of all of this since they

[9] A. Briggs, *The Golden Age of Wireless* (London, 1965), 55.
[10] Scannell and Cardiff, *Social History of British Broadcasting*, i. 171.   [11] Ibid.

wrote a spoof talk from a 'burglar' who, after a hard night's work, retired to bed with Spinoza.[12]

The other consequence of Reith's attitude was an extreme diffidence in the presentation of news and an often embarrassing prudery. The notion of anonymity and authority effectively meant that the BBC was not to have any views of its own since partisanship was neither authoritative nor anonymous. Producers and journalists were, therefore, under constant pressure to efface, if not themselves (since some had to be identified), then their views. In practice that was a conservative doctrine and implied that in moments of crisis the BBC would support the governing party. Even when it was dependent for news on Reuters, the organization was on the hunt for any incorrect thoughts, however trivial. It objected, for example, to a news item, 'Princess Mary's [King George V's daughter, the Princess Royal] Babes Come to Town':

> We feel for instance that it was unnecessary to use two particular phrases in last night's bulletin—(1) that the babes were in a reserved carriage with two nurses and (2) that the younger one, nine weeks old, was carried on a white silk cushion. This sort of information, we believe, only helps to stimulate feelings akin to Bolshevism.

Reuters promised to avoid in future 'anything that might stimulate feelings akin to Bolshevism'.[13]

At a higher level, particularly at moments when the BBC's position was thought peculiarly sensitive, the general strike (1926), for instance, or the Munich crisis (1938), the BBC simply took the government's side. Although Reith objected to the government's proscribing broadcasts by the archbishop of Canterbury and Ramsay MacDonald during the general strike, he knuckled under. Indeed it was Reith who wrote the end of Baldwin's broadcast on 8 May 1926 and he congratulated him on his handling of the strike. During the Munich crisis the corporation's news and reporting was strongly biased towards the government and its stance compared unfavourably to the more open reporting of the American networks.[14]

The BBC's difficulties here were partly due to Reith's literal-mindedness and his determination not to go the way of the press. News, to him, was news: not sensation, gossip, crime, or human interest. This led inevitably to the famous news bulletin on Good Friday 1930 when the announcer simply said 'there is no news tonight'.

The reticence which accompanied anonymity made the BBC even more fearful of giving 'offence' than most other English institutions of the time. There was the usual fuss about 'suggestive' songs. Before the war the corporation made itself look foolish by banning George Formby's popular song 'When I'm

---

[12] Ibid. [13] Ibid. 106–7.

[14] For the BBC during the general strike, see Briggs, *Birth of Broadcasting*, 360–84; for the Munich crisis, Scannell and Cardiff, *Social History of British Broadcasting*, i. 129–31.

Cleaning Windows'. But it learned no lessons. In 1947 it issued the bizarre instruction that the 'hit' novelty song of that year, 'Open the Door, Richard' was not to be sung in a 'drunken manner', and in 1948 (perhaps with more reason) it banned 'Get Up Those Stairs, Mademoiselle' and 'Two Old Maids in a Folding Bed'. The talks and drama departments were subject to similar censorship, though they showed some skill in evading it.

The tone was reinforced by the morality which governed the organization itself and by Reith's commitment to a specifically Christian interpretation of the BBC's purpose. Its employees were expected to lead irreproachable private lives, the moral equivalent of the dinner-jacket, and could be forced out if they did not—as was the chief engineer of outside broadcasts, Peter Eckersley, when he was cited as co-respondent in a divorce case. Reith and the director of the religious department, F. A. Iremonger, imposed the funereal Sunday on the corporation, one of its heaviest burdens, when only religious services and religious or 'serious' music was played. And both were very obdurate about modifying Sunday's programmes.

As alarming to the BBC as sex, since as liable to offend, was humour. From the beginning it had employed comedians, some of national repute, but was perpetually anxious that they should not cross the line. New artists were handed a card which said boldly: 'No gags on Scotsmen, Welshmen, Clergymen, Drink or Medical Matters. Do not sneeze at the microphone.'[15] It also forbade jokes about politics, politicians, prohibition in the USA, or advertisements. Since these bans excluded about 95 per cent of English humour, it was, as the BBC conceded, all too easy for comedians brought up in a music hall tradition to cross that line. As a result the corporation found itself policing the pettiest transgressions. On 31 January 1935 it apologized to listeners

'for the inclusion in the *Music Hall* programme . . . of certain highly objectionable remarks'. The remarks were an exchange between popular comic duo Clapham and Dwyer: 'What is the difference between a champagne cork and a baby?' Answer: 'A champagne cork has the maker's name on the bottom'.[16]

In such circumstances there was not much else for comedians to do but satirize the BBC itself. In 1931 a vaudeville programme ended:

Next week we 'ope to present a startling series of attractions—including Sir Walford Davies and Mr Thomas Handley in that rollicking knockabout act 'Laying the Foundations of Music'—the six genuine Greenwich Pips in Stravinsky's opera 'Time Gentlemen Please' and twelve talks on 'glue'.[17]

The drear Sunday and the rigid attitude to humour gave the off-shore commercial stations their opportunity. The BBC had a monopoly of broadcasting

---

[15] Briggs, *Birth of Broadcasting*, 289.
[16] Quoted in Scannell and Cardiff, *Social History of British Broadcasting*, 226–7.   [17] Ibid. 253.

within Great Britain but could not stop continental stations, providing they had powerful enough transmitters, from broadcasting to England. The *Daily Mail* had made a feeble attempt in 1928 to establish an illegal transmitter on its broadcasting yacht, *Cato*. This, however, represented no challenge to the BBC. That came in 1931 with Radio Normandie, which had, through Stephen Williams, links with the *Sunday Referee*, and with Radio Luxembourg which Williams established in 1933.[18] The offshore stations financed themselves by advertising and adopted 'American' broadcasting techniques: personalized programmes, hit parades, and popular music (introduced, the BBC claimed, in a 'blatantly American manner') and American comedy, recorded in the USA and re-broadcast, which introduced listeners to Jack Benny, George Burns, and Gracie Allen. The humour, British and American, was more knowing and relaxed than BBC humour. The patter-exchanges between Ted Ray and Billy Cotton on the *Kraft Show* were full of *doubles entendres* and 'vulgarities' forbidden by the BBC. Like the Odeon cinema chain, the commercial stations, particularly Radio Luxembourg (usually known as the 'Lux'), set about capturing a young audience. Under the aegis of the child impersonator, Harry Helmsley, it organized the 'League of Ovaltineys' which, the Lux claimed, had 1.2 million members by 1939.

The commercial stations adopted the policy of 'short programming': many items and none very long, rarely more than 15 minutes. The schedule for 18 June 1939 gives a good idea of their programming:

Programmes of Radio Normandie, 18 June 1939

7.10	Radio Reveille	15.30	Theatre Organ
8.00	Sacred Music	16.00	Variety
8.15	Sing Song	16.45	'Personalities'
8.30	(French News)	17.00	Sing Song
8.40	Astrology	17.15	'Discoveries'
8.45	Musical Adventure for	17.30	Variety
	Children	17.40	Dance Music
9.00	Cabaret	18.00	Songs
9.15	'Hit' Songs	18.30	Variety
9.30	Dance Music	19.00	Crime Serial
9.45	Sports Review	19.15	Light Music
10.00	Dance Music	19.30	(French Programmes)
10.30	Variety	22.00	Motor Magazine
11.00	Soloist	22.30	Cinema Organ
11.15	Variety	22.45	'Hit' Songs
11.45	(French Programmes)	23.00	'Musical Comedy Memories'
13.30	Singing, Fun and Music	23.15	Variety
14.00	Sponsored Show	23.45	Light Music

[18] For Williams, see C. Welch, 'Stephen Williams' in the *Independent*, 26 Nov. 1994.

14.30	'Teaser Time'		24.00	Melody at Midnight
14.45	Light Music		24.30	Dance Music
15.00	Dance Music		1.00	Goodnight Music—Close[19]

Amongst British artists who appeared on that day were George Formby, Tommy Handley, Jack Warner, Vic Oliver, Bebe Daniels, Leonard Henry, Olive Groves, Donald Peers, Anne Ziegler and Webster Booth, Phyllis Robins, and Reginald Foort. The commercial stations usually broadcast after the BBC closed, except on Sunday (as above) when they broadcast almost all day. What proportion of the listening audience they had is uncertain, but they probably had a majority, at least of working-class listeners, on Sunday. Radio Luxembourg's Littlewoods Pools Programme, which was broadcast every Sunday at 1.30 p.m., was probably as popular as any BBC programme. The apparent success of the commercial stations, as Briggs notes, shows what could be done 'if conceptions of balance were thrown to the winds'.[20] The BBC and most of the press moved heaven and earth to suppress the commercial stations. The press, of course, wanted to remove them as competitors for advertising revenue. When the *Sunday Referee* began to print Radio Normandie's programmes it was expelled from the Newspaper Proprietors' Association. When it returned and gave up printing the commercial programmes, the *Radio Pictorial* was published: a sort of commercial *Radio Times* which sold about 200,000 copies a week.[21] The BBC tried to have the commercial stations put out of business by the International Broadcasting Union and put heavy pressure on those of its employees who worked for them—like Christopher Stone, who lost his regular BBC programme.

The commercial stations were serious competitors, which is why they were feared by the corporation; yet, Sunday apart, they were not as serious as they might have been. They could never match the corporation's formidable resources, which were perhaps more profuse than any other radio network in the world. This was manifested weekly to the English by the BBC's outside live sports broadcasts—from 1927 onwards the BBC broadcast all major sporting events and had regular weekend sports broadcasts—and manifested to the world by its broadcast of George VI's coronation in 1937. Furthermore, unlike the commercial stations, it had a large and growing guaranteed income, independent of advertisers and their whims. The income came not only from the licence fee but from the sales of the *Radio Times*: in 1939 already 2.6 million. It was the sheer size of these resources that allowed the BBC, for example, to pioneer the regular transmission of television, well ahead of any American network.

Furthermore, if listeners wearied of the National Programme there were the

---

[19] Programme in Briggs, *Golden Age of Wireless*, 54–5.   [20] Ibid.

[21] LeMahieu, *Culture for Democracy*, 278.

regional programmes which were usually free of the Reithisms which could blight the 'National'. They were readier, particularly the Northern Region (housed in Manchester), to discuss social and political questions openly, and several of their documentaries, like the Northern Region's celebrated 'Coal', on which the young Joan Littlewood worked, could never have been made in London. The regional stations were thought very much second-best by those wedded to the metropolitan culture of the National Programme, but because they had a duty to 'express' local concerns, they were more 'working-class' than London and less fussed by the 'problem' of the working class. They were also more adventurous; another reason why Reith regarded them with a rather cold eye.[22]

In any case, the view that the BBC under Reith was insensitive to listener opinion is untrue. Nor did Reith invariably appoint stuffed-shirts. The first editor of the *Radio Times* was Leonard Crocombe, the former editor of *Tit-Bits*, who edited it rather as though it were *Tit-Bits*. This eventually proved too much for Reith who had Crocombe dismissed. But it was clear that Crocombe's formula was (more or less) what people wanted; hence in 1927 Eric Maschwitz was appointed editor, and he edited it in distinctly 'popular' style. What Reith would not have was an institution *dominated* by listener preference—as he believed the press was by reader preference. But he accepted the view that in the formulation of programmes the corporation had to take into account listener preference. In fact, there had never been much doubt about what people wanted. The *Daily Mail* poll of 1927 suggested that much the most popular programmes were variety and concert parties, light orchestral music, military bands, dance music, topical shorts and news—though the support for 'serious' music and opera was 'not despicable'.[23] In 1935 Seebohm Rowntree, using the records of the Relay Company (the majority of whose listeners were almost certainly working-class), found that in York the programme order of popularity was 'roughly as follows':[24]

1 Littlewood's Pool Programme (Radio Luxembourg)—100% load.
2 Variety
3 Sport—especially racing which had a 100% load.
4 Religious services—especially Roman Catholic—50%–60% load.
5 Over the period it was found that dance music was declining and giving away in popularity to light music. Cinema organs very popular.
6 Talks—but response varied. John Hilton's talks to the unemployed took 'heavy load'. Most household talks fairly popular.
7 Plays increasing in popularity, especially short ones. Shakespeare not popular.

[22] For a good discussion of the regional stations, see Scannell and Cardiff, *Social History of British Broadcasting*, i. 330–44.
[23] Pegg, *Broadcasting and Society*, 108.
[24] B. S. Rowntree, *Poverty and Progress: A Second Social Survey of York* (London, 1941), 409–10.

8 Children's Hour could not compete with light music.
9 Increasing number listening to classical music, particularly 'standards'.

These surveys were supported by anecdotal evidence as well as common sense. In 1935 the corporation put listener surveys on a formal basis when Sir Stephen Tallents, who had almost a genius for publicity,[25] was appointed controller (public relations). Tallents was responsible for the establishment in October 1936 of the Listener Research Committee under Robert Silvery. Silvery was influenced by American market survey techniques, and employed the same US-based firms—Gallup and Crossley—as did the commercial stations. Their surveys largely confirmed the results of the *Daily Mail* poll. People preferred in order: variety, theatre and cinema organs, military bands, musical comedy, brass bands, talks, discussions, cricket commentaries, serial plays, light opera, vocal recitals, tennis commentaries, piano recitals, grand opera, violin recitals, serial readings, chamber music.[26]

The BBC responded to this. There was a huge increase in the size of the Variety Department after Eric Maschwitz was appointed director: in 1930 there were two variety producers; in 1936, 29. Maschwitz was a pro. He knew the world of variety and popular music—he had *inter alia* written the lyrics to 'These Foolish Things' and 'A Nightingale Sang in Berkeley Square'. The real obstacle, however, to more 'popular' programming was the existence of only one national programme. The BBC's pluralism, its belief that all cultural interests should be represented, and Reith's insistence on 'mixed' programmes, that is, effectively compelling people to listen to things they might not otherwise listen to, tended to make programming inflexible. They could only have been made flexible by breaking up the National Programme—which Reith would never have accepted.

Although its critics were reluctant to admit it, the corporation had devised a number of very popular programmes by the late thirties. While the departure of Reith to Imperial Airways in 1938 doubtless assisted (the corporation began the first Reith-free Sunday with 'Who's Afraid of the Big Bad Wolf?'), most of these programmes had either begun or been planned while Reith was director-general. *In Town Tonight* and *Monday at Seven* were both immensely popular variety programmes, combining comedy, music, and 'human interest'. Both, despite Reith's hostility to the press, had a newspaper feel about them. *Band Wagon*, perhaps the most popular of all BBC programmes, was also a variety programme but soon came to be identified with its two regular comedians, Arthur Askey and Richard Murdoch, who supposedly lived in a flat at the top of Broadcasting House. *Band Wagon* made Askey a national figure, and his catch-

---

[25] For an excellent discussion of Tallents at the Empire Marketing Board and the post office, where he made his name, see M. Grant, *Propaganda and the Role of the State in Inter-War Britain* (Oxford, 1994), 50–2, 111–19.

[26] Pegg, *Broadcasting and Society*, 139.

phrase 'Aythangyou' ('I thank you')—borrowed from London bus conductors—entered the language.[27] His success in *Band Wagon* propelled him into an equally successful film career.

Some of the more popular programmes were surprises. C. H. Middleton's gardening talks turned into one of the corporation's greatest successes ('When Mr Middleton's on you mustn't breathe'), tapping the interests of those millions in the interwar years who had become first-time gardeners. Moreover, two of the most popular programmes of the 1940s had pre-war origins. *It's That Man Again*, the celebrated *ITMA*, was designed in June 1939. The corporation wanted a comedy on the American model, like the Burns and Allen show, which the experience of both *Band Wagon* and the commercial stations had shown to be very popular.[28] In the same year, the corporation broadcast the first of its Francis Durbridge thrillers, *Send for Paul Temple*, whose immediate success anticipated the enormous success of Paul Temple and Dick Barton in the 1940s.[29]

Finally, it must be said that for all Reith's snobbery and self-importance his policy as director-general was largely successful. The majority of those who had an opinion actually preferred the BBC as a whole to the commercial stations, for all their Americanization.[30] Jennings and Gill, when they surveyed opinion in 1938–9, found that on the score of entertainment the BBC received 'universal praise'. It 'cheered', 'comforted', 'brightened', 'abolished loneliness' and steadied the nerves—things not to be despised in 1938–9.[31] They also concluded that the corporation had, at least partly, succeeded in its educational purpose; if only as a corrective to the unreality of the cinema. The Continent of Europe was thus

more real to [listeners] than the neighbouring county was to their grandfathers . . .

America becomes increasingly concrete, losing something of the fantastic quality it owed to popular conceptions of Hollywood and Chicago. This has been due largely to Raymond Gram Swing's weekly talks, President Roosevelt's intrusion into European politics, and the occasional feature items relayed from the States or Canada.[32]

And the BBC did acquire authority. While it often tailored its news, largely by omission, Reith's doctrine that you should not knowingly lie gave it a weight no other medium had. The dignity with which the news was delivered, the

---

[27] According to Paul Vaughan a boy at his school (Raynes Park) was caned for 'Saying "I thank you" in tones of Arthur Askey at end of Lord's Prayer yesterday' (Vaughan, *Something in Linoleum*, 137).

[28] For the origins of *ITMA*, see Briggs, *Golden Age of Wireless*, 118.

[29] Scannell and Cardiff, *Social History of Broadcasting*, i. 378.

[30] In Dec. 1937 Gallup asked those who listened to commercial radio whether they preferred it to the BBC. Seventeen per cent preferred the commercial stations, 46 per cent the BBC. Thirty-seven per cent had no opinion.

[31] Gill and Jennings, *Broadcasting in Everyday Life*, 13; See also Rowntree, *Poverty and Progress*, 411.

[32] Ibid. 12.

distancing of presentation from the events themselves, added further weight. In consequence, the overwhelming majority of listeners thought the radio news more reliable than the press.[33]

The BBC had a good war, though not without a false start. The television service closed without warning or explanation on 1 September—in the midst of a Mickey Mouse cartoon—and remained closed for the next seven years. The National and Regional Programmes were abruptly suspended, to be replaced by continuous organ music broken by the odd government announcement. This was the behaviour of what was now literally a monopoly. The offshore stations closed at the outbreak of war, and it is an interesting question how the corporation would have coped had the commercial stations remained in operation; or whether the BBC would have become so closely identified with the nation-in-arms. It was also the behaviour of a cultural élite used to deferring to government at moments of crisis; hence the corporation only regained its nerve when the government did the same and rescinded the bans on cinemas and theatre performances which it had imposed when war was declared.

Although the BBC acquired enormous international authority during the war, it never had the freedom some outsiders believed. Its reporting was strictly censored and it was under constant political pressure of one sort or another. Its comparative freedom—as compared with most other national broadcasting networks—was due largely to the British government's unwillingness to go too far and a recognition (only slowly learnt) that something approximating the truth was in the long run less damaging than outright lies. Furthermore, the Overseas Service was not so subject to direct political pressure because its programmes were thought not so politically sensitive. The Overseas Service, for example, treated the Beveridge Report much more openly than the Home Service. Abroad the Beveridge Report was one of the things we were fighting for; at home it was by no means what we were all fighting for and the corporation knew better than to take sides.[34]

The BBC, if not as independent as its admirers thought, was not, however, as susceptible as its domestic critics supposed. Patrick Ryan, a civil servant who had been placed by the ministry of information in the corporation as a watchdog, to some extent went native—conciliating critics rather than chastising the BBC. And what was thought the most notorious example of corporation weakness, the Priestley affair, was much more complicated. Between June and October 1940, J. B. Priestley gave a series of talks as a 'Postscript' to the Sunday evening news. Such talks had been given since the outbreak of war, but with mixed success. The ministry of information hoped that Priestley, already a national figure as novelist and playwright, would fit the role. His

[33] Gill and Jennings, *Broadcasting in Everyday Life*, 14–15.
[34] For this, see A. Briggs, *The War of Words* (London, 1970), 604–10.

'Postscripts', beginning with Dunkirk, were an amazing success. At his best 44 per cent of the adult population listened to them: 'He might be Stalin himself—the fuss that is being made'.[35] Priestley specialized in a comforting and democratic Englishness, delivered in a pleasing Yorkshire accent. He also (increasingly) specialized in a diffuse, non-party-political radicalism which alarmed some in both the corporation and the Conservative Party. In October 1940 he gave the last of his eight (originally six) 'Postscripts'. Priestley claimed to have been dismissed for political reasons and worked up considerable press support. But the BBC had never intended that he should be a fixture: partly because of its traditions of anonymity, partly because it genuinely believed radio to be a device for demagogues or a device which turned people into demagogues. Moreover, Priestley's own egotistical and petulant behaviour (not unconnected with his fee) alienated even his admirers at the corporation. In any case, he was to broadcast repeatedly throughout the war; and much as he had always done.[36]

The BBC responded to rather than promoted the changes in the country's wartime political mood. The appointment of a Yorkshireman, Wilfred Pickles, as an announcer in 1942 followed sustained criticism of the corporation on grounds that the accents of its announcers inadequately represented the accents of democracy—though the fuss his accent caused suggested how incomplete that democracy was: 'On the wireless tonight the new announcer "William Pickles" (gorgeous name!) read excellently, though his accent is a combination of Lancashire, Yorkshire, Oxford and I know not what.'[37]

The corporation's tendency to 'adjust' is well illustrated by the evolution of one of its most popular programmes, *The Brains Trust*, which had had its origins in an American programme *Information Please*. It was first broadcast on 1 January 1941 as *Any Questions*, with Donald McCullough as 'questionmaster' and C. E. M. Joad, Julian Huxley, and Commander A. B. Campbell as the team. The first question put to it, 'What were the seven wonders of the world?', no member of the team could answer. The questions soon became less factual and more 'political' and 'philosophical'; the programme was renamed *The Brains Trust* and the regular team were joined by guests chosen to ensure that opinion was balanced. The programme's success was quite unexpected: at its peak in December 1943 almost 30 per cent of the adult population was listening to it. Its progress is well described in Vere Hodgson's diaries:

2 July, 1941: Listened last week to the Brains Trust on Forces Programme. Really very good. Lady Oxford [Margot Asquith], Professor Joad and Julian Huxley ... I must listen again—it is one of the best things I have heard.... 19 April, 1942: Back in time for Brains

[35] V. Hodgson, *Few Eggs and No Oranges* (London, 1976), 135.

[36] For a full account of this, see S. Nicholas, ' "Sly Demagogues" and Wartime Radio: J. B. Priestley and the BBC, 1939–1945', *Twentieth Century British History*, 6, 3 (1995).

[37] Donnelly, *Mrs Milburn's Diaries*, 6 Dec. 1942.

Trust ... Miss M. and Auntie Nell are aroused to frenzy by this programme. But surely it is an education to the British public to listen to entirely opposite views expressed with politeness and good humour.[38]

Vere Hodgson herself came from a family of teachers and what would now be called social workers, and the success of *The Brains Trust* was a product of the 'politicization' of much of the professional and technical middle class—even to the point of 'frenzy'—which began in the late 1930s and accelerated during the war. Although some of the corporation's right-wing critics saw *The Brains Trust* as part of a BBC project to deliver the country to socialism, it is clear that both the form and success of *The Brains Trust* was unplanned by the BBC, several of whose leading officers were actually worried by its popularity.

But the corporation's real triumph was the Forces' Programme. Once the BBC had recovered from the shock of war, it decided to create a service for the armed forces and, in order 'to give the Forces' public what it wanted', based it upon extensive listener research. It was, in fact, as the historian of the BBC has noted, a 'light' programme, not unlike Radio Luxembourg: something Reith would never had permitted.[39] Almost immediately the Forces' Programme became more popular with civilians than the Home Service, the domestic successor to the old National Programme. Moreover, the Forces' Programme was left largely to itself, unlike the Home Service, which was under constant ministry of information pressure to produce more or less overt propaganda—and this partly accounted for its popularity.

The Forces' service devised a string of exceptionally successful programmes, some of which, like *Desert Island Discs*, which began in January 1942 with Vic Oliver as the first guest, long outlived their epoch. John Dickson Carr's weekly thriller *Appointment with Fear* was immensely popular: foreigners were bemused by parents, who unhesitatingly raised their offspring during the blitz, wondering whether *Appointment with Fear* might not be too frightening for the children. The Forces' service also became intimately involved with civilian morale, particularly via *Music While You Work* and *Workers' Playtime*. Both were based upon the piped factory music which became very popular in the 1930s as an aid to production. Both were very cheerful and in the case of *Workers' Playtime*, filled out with variety and comedy. The popular programme *par excellence*, and broadcast on the Home and the Forces', was *It's That Man Again, ITMA. ITMA* had been planned in 1939 but Tommy Handley's career as its star had been intermittent. In 1941 the BBC had begun to broadcast *Broadway Calling*—on the model of the now defunct commercial stations—which, by playing the Jack Benny and Bob Hope shows, raised listeners' expectations of comedy. In September 1941, therefore, Handley was induced to return to *ITMA*

---

[38] Hodgson, *Few Eggs and No Oranges*, 164, 228.
[39] A. Briggs, *The BBC: The First Fifty Years* (London, 1985), 186.

and British wartime comedy never looked back. To the extent that the war had a representative programme, something which seemed peculiarly appropriate to the way the British experienced the war, it was *ITMA*. It owed its spectacular success to its harmonious combination of traditional English comic genres and satirical contemporary comment. *ITMA* was filled with stock types, formulae and catchphrases which out of context could scarcely raise a smile. In context, however, and by dint of repetition and comic association, like Mrs Mopp's standard cue, 'Can I do you now, sir?', they reduced half the nation to tears. The constant lampooning of the country's bureaucratic élite (though much less its political and military élite) also, and inevitably in the circumstances, chimed with the popular mood. In 1942–3, especially, *ITMA* was a national institution, but, unlike *Desert Island Discs*, tied to its moment. After the war, it rather lost its way, unable to adjust its style to post-war conditions. The characters were reshuffled—'Mona Lott' replaced 'Mrs Mopp'—but with diminishing effect, and the BBC, which had for some time thought it needed 'a long rest', willingly dropped it when Handley died in 1949.

The structural changes which the BBC introduced during the war continued into the peace. No attempt was made to restore the old National Programme. In its place were three separate services: the Light Programme, which began on 29 July 1945, was the direct successor to the Forces' service; the Home Service; and the Third Programme, which went on the air on 29 September 1946. The Regional Programmes (which had been scooped up by the Home Service in 1939) were restored in July 1945. Television transmissions resumed on 7 June 1946. On that day the interrupted Mickey Mouse cartoon was completed.

Although television was predictably the wave of the future—and there were 126,700 licences by 1949—the BBC had little interest in it. The choice of programmes was narrow and few of the corporation's intellectual or financial resources went into it. The BBC and particularly its director-general, Sir William Haley, not unreasonably in the circumstances, were determined to exploit the radio fully. The Light Programme was the corporation's great success. It regularly had about two-thirds of listeners, and most of the BBC's better-known radio productions were on the Light: *Housewives' Choice* (1946), *Woman's Hour* (1946), *Mrs Dale's Diary* (1948), and, for younger children, the hugely popular *Dick Barton, Special Agent*.[40] In 1948 the Midland Region began to broadcast *The Archers*, a deathless programme, designed, rather oddly, to be a 'farming *Dick Barton*'.

With the partial exception of *The Archers*, these programmes marked an important shift in the BBC's assumptions: whereas the tendency of wartime programmes had been social or collaborative, the tendency of post-war productions was domestic and individual. They were designed not for women at

---

[40] For children's preferences, see Ward, *Children Out Of School*, 48.

war, but women at home. Indeed, the whole of the Light Programme was 'feminized'—one sign of which was the unimportance of sports broadcasting. In 1948, despite the record attendances at all sporting events, only 3 per cent of the Light's air-time was given to sport. The general 'atmosphere' of the Light was middle-classish, feminine, and domestic. There is little evidence that a majority of listeners objected to that, as the wide popularity of *Mrs Dale's Diary*, utterly middle-class, feminine, and domestic in every respect, suggests.

These programmes were well crafted and shrewdly produced but not especially innovative. More remarkable were the brilliant comedy programmes which the corporation broadcast in the later 1940s and early 1950s. *Much Binding in the Marsh*, which confirmed Richard Murdoch as a comic master, sustained *ITMA* in its dying days, but was not alone sufficient to compete with the memory of the American comedies broadcast on *Broadway Calling*. The competition, when it did come, was not *Much Binding in the Marsh* but *Take It From Here*, written by Frank Muir and Denis Norden, two exceptionally gifted writers of comic scripts, which was first broadcast in March 1948. *Take It From Here* in fact took a little time to find its feet: it was not until the variety format was modified and the 'Glum' family introduced that it achieved its colossal success. It was a 30-minute programme, the first half variety, the second a kind of serial involving the 'Glum' family—'Mr Glum' (Jimmy Edwards), his son, the hopeless 'Ron' (Dick Bentley), and Ron's long-suffering fiancée, 'Eth' (Joy Nichols, then June Whitfield). Although undoubtedly innovative, *Take It From Here*, like *ITMA*, conformed closely to the rules of English humour. The programme was formulaic, the audience knew exactly what to expect, and the characters were associated with the same endlessly repeated cues, the most memorable of which were June Whitfield's 'Oh Ron' delivered in an elongated manner as 'Ohhh Ronnn', and Dick Bentley's response, 'Yes Eth', uttered in a muted Australian drawl, to great effect.

The 'Glums' were a marvellous comic creation; despite this, however, the corporation remained unhappy at the apparent lack of depth in its variety programmes, and this led to an 'unremitting' search for new comic styles.[41] The upshot was *The Goon Show*, first broadcast in May 1951 with Harry Secombe, Spike Milligan, and Peter Sellers as the Goons. This was a memorable programme which, as Briggs notes, could not have been produced by any other radio network in the world.[42] Although the overall 'sense' of *The Goon Show* was surreal, the humour was perfectly recognizable to anyone acquainted with English cultural traditions:[43] the schoolboy jokes, the wonderful silly voices

---

[41] A. Briggs, *Sound and Vision* (Oxford, 1979), 545.   [42] Ibid.

[43] *The Goons*, for example, though it later developed a cult following there, was not and could never have been popular in North America. It was, however, inexhaustibly popular with Australian middle-class schoolboys of the 1950s (who were familiar with the tradition), largely determining their daily mode of speech.

(mostly Sellers), the endless puns on names, like the Chinese Nationalist leader General Cash My Cheque (to whom the Goons were required to deliver a second-hand rosewood piano) or Neddy Seagoon (Harry Secombe) himself, the stock comic types, like Major Bloodnok, the repeated catchphrases ('He's fallen in the water' had the same effect as 'Can I do you now, sir?' did ten years before), the nonsense songs and patter. Some of the humour, however, was wildly outside the traditional genre and one or two of the characters, like Blue-bottle, were bizarre, half-mad. It was this combination of tradition and lunacy that made *The Goon Show* so popular with boys and young men, though less, one suspects, with girls and young women.

Take It From Here and *The Goon Show* were the most successful of the comedy programmes but not the only successful ones. *Educating Archie* (1950), for example, was very popular and at various stages included amongst the cast Max Bygraves, Hattie Jacques, Tony Hancock (perhaps the most talented of the radio comedians), Beryl Reid, and Harry Secombe.[44] The BBC's worry about lack of depth is puzzling, since these programmes rested upon an outstanding and possibly unequalled generation of comedians.

Probably only a monopoly could have produced *The Goons*. Certainly only a monopoly could have produced the Third Programme. The Third Programme was the outcome of the corporation's conviction that one of its main responsibilities was the encouragement of classical music, particularly the broadening of its 'appreciation' by the general population. In 1927, for example, it took responsibility for the Promenade Concerts when the music publisher Chappells withdrew its sponsorship. This was largely Reith's doing but it was enthusiastically supported by Sir Henry Wood, the founder of the Proms, in very Reithian language: 'With the whole-hearted support of the wonderful medium of broadcasting, I feel I am at least on the threshold of truly democratising the message of music and making its beneficial effect universal'.[45] The corporation's educative purpose was furthered not simply by financing institutions like the Proms, whose educational function was implicit, but by exploiting the wonderful medium directly. Percy Scholes and Walford Davies, both organists, scholars and active in the 'music appreciation' movement, regularly used the radio as a way of proselytizing 'serious music'.

The corporation, however, sharply distinguished between popularizing and vulgarizing classical music, a distinction which inevitably caused tensions. The 'Foundations of Music' (begun in the late 1920s) which the BBC intended to be the prime vehicle for its music-education programmes, made no concessions: heavily weighted towards Gothic, Pre-Renaissance, Renaissance and Baroque music, it used a musical vocabulary then unfamiliar even to the

[44] Briggs, *Sound and Vision*, 714.
[45] Scannell and Cardiff, *Social History of British Broadcasting*, i. 198.

musically literate—as the Third Programme was to do. Although many conscientiously followed the 'Foundations of Music' most listeners found it hard going, while the level of musical competence it required was repeatedly satirized. One typical cartoon shows two working men sitting by the fire listening to the radio. One says to the other: 'The *pizzicato* for the double basses in the coda seems to me to want body, Alf.' Yet, although Reith and the music department often differed, they were agreed that the corporation's role was missionary. Since the department increasingly believed that the conventional symphonic repertoire was 'middlebrow', though admittedly popular, it demanded ever more stringent refinements to public musical taste, which, it thought, should embrace chamber music and modern composers like Schoenberg, Stravinsky, and Bartok.

Disputes between the 'high' and 'middlebrow' within the corporation and between the BBC and its critics in the popular press could not be resolved within the old National Programme. The breaking up of the National Programme during the war into the Home and Forces' Programmes (Light Programme) and the establishment of the Third Programme in 1946 meant that the 'low', 'middle' and 'highbrow' did not have to compete for the same airtime. How far the BBC achieved that uplift of taste sought both by the corporation and Reith is uncertain. The musical public was introduced to unfamiliar composers, like Schütz and Monteverdi, who were soon to be introduced into the classical repertoire. Something was done to open the English musical imagination to the music of France and Eastern Europe.

The Third Programme of the late 1940s was remorselessly intellectual, even by the standards of most of the country's cultural élite, and was heavily biased to continental European 'high culture'. Unlike almost all other British cultural media, the Third Programme virtually escaped the influence of the United States. It was however much influenced, either directly or indirectly, by European émigrés, and their influence, as in the universities, was irreversible. But the Third Programme did not have the self-confidence of the other services, partly because there was little agreement about what its function should be, how 'high' was to be the 'high' culture it broadcast, and if too 'high', how justifiable was the service in a democratic society. In practice, by associating in the public mind 'difficult' composers like Bartok or Schoenberg with 'serious' music, the corporation risked alienating people from classical music altogether. The result was probably to strengthen the middlebrow canon rather than weakening it.

The BBC effectively preserved its monopoly until 1948. Radio Luxembourg, whose station had been used though not destroyed by the Germans, began broadcasting again in January 1946. But exchange controls almost prohibited British advertisers from buying its air-time, and the station only just survived— partly with the assistance of the BBC which lent it programmes via a landline until 1947, when it concluded that the 'Lux' had no future. It held on, however, and after 1948, as it became easier for British advertisers to procure foreign exchange, it began to prosper. Its strategy did not change: it broadcast popular programmes that the BBC would not do. And that in practice meant popular music. Its hit parade was restored in 1948, and increasing amounts of its air-time became devoted to popular music, particularly in the 1950s when Radio Luxembourg became the principal medium for the broadcasting of rock-and-roll in England. The BBC introduced a hit parade in the 1950s but remained adamantly opposed—in the face of all social developments—to the large-scale broadcasting of popular music, since that would have probably required the dissolution of the Light Programme, and it also remained adamantly opposed—as ever—to anything that seemed like song 'plugging'.[46] In this sphere, the assumptions of a monopolist encouraged the behaviour of a bully: throughout the 1950s and 1960s it harassed the 'Lux' and even more the so-called pirate radios, like Radio Caroline (named after President Kennedy's daughter), moored off the Thames Estuary, which were exclusively popular music stations. It continued this behaviour until the late 1960s when the Marine Offences Act (1967) made it illegal to advertise on the pirate radios and the BBC did indeed break up its networks. Radio 1 became a pop-rock station, which rather shamelessly employed the best of the pirate disc-jockeys. This was a concession to reality, but not as big as it appeared: by then the importance of the Light Programme had been much reduced by the primacy of television, which fatally weakened the case for preserving it.

The structure of broadcasting in England (and Britain) was unique. Many other countries had state broadcasting systems, but few had the relative autonomy of the BBC. The corporation from time to time (notoriously) kept its head down and was extremely sensitive to anything that would appear partisan, but it was never the government's agent. Nor was it at the whim of advertisers as were the American networks. The BBC had a cultural freedom of manœuvre almost unknown elsewhere.

The ambitions of the organization were élitist, but not the way some of its critics suggested. The BBC, including Reith, assumed that England was now a democracy, however imperfect; the function of the BBC was, therefore, to educate a democratic society, in order that it should function better as a democracy. Reith was a snob and often patronizing. He was not, however, an anti-democrat; even less so were most of those who worked with him.

The corporation was a monopoly and occasionally acted like one. It could behave foolishly, as with 'song plugging' or the anonymity of news broadcasters. It could also behave insensitively as it did with its attempts to

---

[46] For 'plugging', see above, pp. 402–3.

impose a particular conception of 'serious' music on its listeners. But the BBC was always pluralist: partly because it did face the competition of the commercial stations, partly because it was always aware that there were different audiences. Reith held so doggedly to the National Programme not because he wished to force an élitist culture upon the English, but because he wanted one audience to be aware of the tastes of another. Perhaps predictably this did not work. Even under Reith, however, the National and Regional Programmes catered to diverse tastes.

The BBC was also aware of America and the attraction of certain kinds of American broadcasting. Under Reith, particularly, it was slow to react; but faster when he left the corporation. Nevertheless, it reacted effectively. The audience, though not uncritical of the BBC, consistently preferred it to the highly Americanized commercial stations. Radio Luxembourg and Radio Normandie were successful by filling niches, like the hit parade, which the BBC did not fill, or filled without enthusiasm.

The BBC was consistently more successful than the British film industry, not simply in holding off the Americans, but in providing the market with pretty much what it wanted. The main reason for that is the degree to which the state gave the BBC privileged access to the market. The corporation was a monopolist; it was, furthermore, financed by a compulsory levy on its listeners which gave it the resources few other broadcasting systems had. It was, therefore, *more* successful in meeting the varied demands of the home audience than was the British film industry which, though given a guaranteed access to the market, was anything but a monopoly and constantly starved of resources.

THERE is hardly anything more culturally sensitive than language and its media. What people read and how they spoke is the subject of this final chapter. It looks at the development of a middlebrow literary culture and examines its social and political significance. It also considers the genre of the popular romance—Ruby M. Ayres or Mills and Boon, for example—and a more overtly working-class literature: 'erotic bloods', 'Yank mags', sporting and crime 'novels'. It notes how important gender was, as well as class, in determining what kinds of fiction people read. It discusses children's literature and the development of the press and mass-circulation periodicals. Finally, the chapter looks at the spoken language, the extent of Americanization of vocabulary and idiom, working-class attitudes to language, the attempts to establish a 'correct' speech, and the reasons why that failed.

The 'literacy' of the English people, what they read and how they expressed themselves in writing, was largely determined by five variables—class, sex, age, geography, and America. None of these variables was independent, even class. Within the working-class, for example, there were important gender-determined differences in what people read. But of the variables class was, none the less, the most powerful.

All English literary genres were class-bound, with the partial exception of high culture—the one contemporaries increasingly called (as with music) 'highbrow'. Highbrow culture was the culture of an élite, which was, in class terms, probably upper-middle-class; but many of its members were not upper-middle-class in their social origins. Furthermore, to the extent that highbrow literature was upper-middle-class, only a small minority of that class adopted it. And the tendency of highbrow culture to be institutionalized within an expanding university system increasingly made it the preserve of a cultural élite whose vocation was the definition of a canonic literary tradition often sharply distinguished from the literary tradition of the ordinary 'educated' reader. The classic type of this élite was almost certainly F. R. Leavis. Whether Leavis was right in his view that ordinary 'educated' readers had been deliberately excluded from the canon, had been convinced that they would never 'understand' *The Waste Land, Hugh Selwyn Mauberly, Ulysses,* or *To the Lighthouse,* it is true that Eliot, Pound, Joyce, or Woolf were not read by the larger 'educated' readership until they became part of the canon by being taught in universities and secondary schools.

The partial triumph of 'modernism' in post-1918 literature also had the effect of hardening the demarcation between highbrow and middlebrow literature. Indeed modernism made the demarcation possible. That moment 'in or about' December 1910 when, according to Virginia Woolf, human character changed, also changed the character of the reading audience. Until then, more or less, literature had been written within a recognizable tradition; modernist literature, however, largely left the readership behind. Much, though certainly not all, of the middlebrow literature of the interwar period was in the pre-modernist, neo-realist tradition familiar to the readership. Arnold Bennett, therefore, continued to be very popular in the 1920s for the same reasons that Dickens would have been considered middlebrow had he written in the 1920s or 1930s. Or else people wrote in the pre-war tradition of the novel of manners: Hugh Walpole, for example, wrote, or believed he wrote, in the style of Henry James.

There was, of course, as in music, a grey area. There continued to be the literary equivalent of the classical 'standards' listened to by large numbers on the radio: literature acceptable to the cultural élite and the ordinary 'educated' reader. Scott and Dickens among the dead; Evelyn Waugh and (perhaps) Aldous Huxley among the living. And, also among the living, writers of detective novels—though more likely Dorothy Sayers or Edmund Crispin than Agatha Christie. None the less, it seems unlikely that even Waugh or Huxley were much read by the large audience for interwar middlebrow literature. Furthermore, the development of a specifically middlebrow literature, something that can confidently be called middlebrow, as Sheila Hodges described A. J. Cronin, 'a middlebrow writer *par excellence*',[1] was institutionalized, as the universities institutionalized highbrow literature, by the development of the Book Society and the Book Guild. The Book Society (like the term middlebrow) came from the United States, and was modelled upon the American Book of the Month Clubs. Hugh Walpole became chairman of its selection committee in 1929, and its advisers tended to be those who wrote in the same style.[2] The Book Society's choices were widely publicized and loathed by those who loathed the selectors. F. R. Leavis wrote of Arnold Bennett, who had willy-nilly become the doyen of middlebrow writers: 'To compute how many bad books a year, on the average, Mr Bennett has turned into literature would hardly be

[1] Sheila Hodges, 'A. J. Cronin' in *Dictionary of National Biography, 1981–1985* (Oxford, 1990), 103.
[2] There is an interesting account of the Book Society in Q. D. Leavis, *Fiction and the Reading Public* (London, 1939), 22–4. For its foundation, see R. Hart-Davis, *Hugh Walpole* (London, 1952), 298–9.

worth the labour.'[3] The Book Society, wrote Q. D. Leavis, recommended 'novels of such competent journalists as G. B. Stern, A. P. Herbert, Rebecca West, Denis Mackail . . . Sapless "literary" novels, or the smartly fashionable (Hemingway, Osbert Sitwell)'. It established 'a middlebrow standard of values'.[4] As for these authors, they were now 'the staple reading of the middlebrow; they will be observed on the shelves of dons, the superior sort of schoolmaster . . . and in the average well-to-do home'.[5] Although her husband, F. R. Leavis, was absurdly intemperate in his attacks upon the Book Society and middlebrow authors, there was probably something to his view that the insistent pejorative use of the word 'highbrow' in Book Society propaganda did convince readers that they would not 'understand' Eliot or Woolf, let alone Joyce.

There were three predominant types of middlebrow literature in the period; all of which sold especially well in the interwar years: a 'literature of conflict', a 'literature of modernity', and a 'literature of sexual romance'. The literature of conflict was anchored firmly in the early 1920s and the angst with which much of the middle class experienced those years. Class conflict was, directly or indirectly, central to this genre. Such conflict is usually seen by the reader through the eyes of an ex-officer and it is around his status in post-war Britain that the plot flows. The protagonist is often only a 'temporary gentleman' and that heightens status-tension.[6] Aside from the two great sensation novels of the period, *The Sheik* and *Beau Geste*,[7] the three best-selling middlebrow novels of the 1920s were novels of conflict. In two, A. S. M. Hutchinson's *If Winter Comes* (1921), which had 19 impressions in its first six months of publication, and Robert Keable's *Simon Called Peter* (1921), which had 16 impressions even before the 'popular edition' was published in 1923, the conflict is effectively unresolved since the protagonists persist in seeing both sides of the question. In the third, Warwick Deeping's *Sorrell and Son* (1925), it is faced squarely and sides taken. All three are about class, problematic sexual relationships, and what the First World War did to both. Two, *Simon Called Peter* and *If Winter Comes*, are also about religion and its redeeming power. Their ideological and rhetorical locus, like the politics of their time, is recognizably Edwardian, both in manner and theme. Their preoccupations are Edwardian preoccupations which the pre-1914 political and social system managed to contain, but which the war liberated.[8]

---

[3] F. R. Leavis, *Mass Civilisation and Minority Culture* (Cambridge, 1930), 13–16. This is unfair. Bennett no doubt puffed second-rate authors, but it was his enthusiastic review of *Decline and Fall* (1928) in the *Evening Standard* which established Evelyn Waugh's reputation.

[4] Q. D. Leavis, *Fiction and the Reading Public*, 22–4.   [5] Ibid. 37.

[6] M. Petter, ' "Temporary Gentlemen" in the Aftermath of the Great War: Rank, Status and the Ex-Officer Problem', *Historical Journal*, 37, 1 (1994), 129–32; more generally, S. Hynes, *A War Imagined: The First World War and English Culture* (London, 1992 ed.), 269–423.

[7] See below, pp. 486–7.

[8] For the post-war novels, see H. Cecil, *The Flower of Battle: British Fiction Writers of the First World*

Simon Called Peter is about loss of vocation and religious crisis, and is partly autobiographical. Its hero, Peter Graham, is an Anglican clergyman from a polite West London parish who becomes a military chaplain in France. He rapidly discovers the unimportance of official religion to the men in the trenches:

[The British tommy] doesn't care a damn if a chap drinks and swears and commits what the Statute-Book and the Prayer-Book call fornication. And certainly doesn't think there is an ascending scale of sins, or at any rate that you parsons have got the scale right.

This discovery provokes in Graham a sense of the futility of his vocation. At the same time he becomes strongly tempted by the flesh. He meets Julie, a nurse, who is a free spirit unlike anything he has previously met. Her moral standards are so different from his that he is 'absolutely floored'. His path goes steadily downward. He takes up with a French prostitute, Louise, first as friend, then as sexual partner. It is in her company, at a mass for Corpus Christi, that he has the first of two religious experiences—the second is in Westminster Cathedral—which restore his vocation, for the sake of which Julie gives him up.

Simon Called Peter is not without merit. Its account of the Western Front and of soldiers' attitudes is unadorned and sensible. But it is a book about Sin, and its eroticism is highly charged. 'I've a body, like other men,' Peter says to Louise on the night of their first sexual encounter. 'Let me plunge down deep tonight, Louise.' And the description of the nights of passion with Julie is not reticent: 'Undress me, will you? I want you to. Play with me, own me, Peter. See, I am yours, yours, Peter, all yours.' Furthermore, the notion that faith can be rekindled via extra-marital sexual delights was clearly what its huge readership wanted to read. Indeed, its 'obscenity' was obviously a major element in its success.

The rediscovery of faith was described in terms common to the Edwardian sensation novel. All else is secondary to 'the great thing, the only good thing . . . God . . . Almighty God: Jesus, if you will . . .'. The 'idea' is 'colossal. It's a thing to which one might dedicate one's life. It's a thing to live and die gladly for. It fills one.' Thus the 'solution' to the social crisis of the post-war years, the clashing of classes, is the return to a mystical Christianity—to which Keable himself was always drawn.

A. S. M. Hutchinson's *If Winter Comes* is much more overwrought, and to that degree, even more in the tradition of the sensation novel. Its hero, Mark Sabre, works in a firm which provides books and materials for churches and private schools. He handles the text-books and is himself writing a school history of England whose first sentence runs:

They made the flame of England bright and ever brighter; and you, stepping into all

War (London, 1995); also C. Cockburn, *Bestseller: The Books that Everyone Read, 1900–1939* (London, 1972).

they have made for you, will make it bright and brighter yet. They passed and are gone; and you will pass and go. But England will continue. Your England. *Yours.*

In 1915, partly to escape a loveless and failed marriage, though medically unfit and in his late thirties, Sabre joins up, is badly wounded, and invalided out. He is deeply alarmed about England:

Shaking her head whereon had fallen stunning and unexpected blows, as it might be a lion enormously smashed across the face; roaring her defiance; baring her fangs; tearing up the ground before her; dreadful and undaunted and tremendous; but stricken; in sore agony; in heavy amazement; her pride thrust through with swords; her glory answered by another's glory; her dominion challenged; shaken, bleeding.

'England'.

He sees the class struggle at hand. 'We've been nearly four years on the crest, Hapgood—on the crest of the war—and it's been all classes as one class for the common good. I tell you, Hapgood, the trough's ahead; we're steering for it; and it's rapid and perilous sundering of the classes.' His remedy, not unlike Keable's, is the 'old remedy. The Old God. But it's more than that. It's Light: more Light.' Sabre, who was known at school as 'old Puzzlehead' and who *always* sees both sides of the question, finds 'the key to the riddle that's been puzzling me all my life. I've got the revelation in terms good enough for me to understand. Light, more light. Here it is: God is—*love* . . . I can reduce all the mysteries to terms of that.' The key, it appears, is a form of English Christianity which resolves the struggle of classes. In fact, the novel is irresolute even on that. After a wildly melodramatic dénouement, Sabre abandons 'all that', is divorced by his snobbish wife, and marries his childhood love, the widowed Lady Tybar. None the less, in so far as the novel has a resolution, this is, as in *Simon Called Peter*, the reChristianization of England.

This sort of resolution is, of course, no resolution at all—particularly as both protagonists (unlike the readership) wish to remain neutral in the conflict of labour and capital. The great success of these novels, their political contemporaneity apart, was probably due to style—the overwrought manner of the sensation novel, which still sold well. *Sorrell and Son* was overwrought but not neutral. It was an astonishing best-seller: 41 editions and innumerable impressions, read and re-read long out of its time. Warwick Deeping was trained as a doctor, though he practised for only a year before beginning to write somewhat low brow novels. *Sorrell and Son*, however, was a much more serious effort of clear political intent.[9] Although it is characteristically unpleasant about the *nouveaux riches*, what is striking about *Sorrell and Son* is its unvarnished hostility to the working class.

---

[9] Q. D. Leavis thought *Sorrell and Son* lowbrow ('a common bestseller') rather than middlebrow, but that the reader of *A Passage to India* could not tell the difference anyway. (*Fiction and the Reading Public*, 251.)

Its hero, Stephen Sorrell, an ex-officer (with the Military Cross), has fallen on hard times. He and his son Kit have been abandoned by his wife. Kit is obliged to go to a council school: 'He had hated it . . . He had all the fastidious nausea of a boy who has learnt to wash and use a handkerchief.' The working classes are full of malevolence towards Kit, whose father 'had seen that these sons of working men hated the son of an ex-officer. They hated his face, his voice, his pride, his very good temper. They hated him for his differences, his innocent superiorities.' Thus, despite his vicissitudes, Sorrell was unattracted by socialism:

He had seen too much of human nature. Labour, becoming sectionalised, would split into groups, and group would grab from group, massing for the struggle instead of fighting a lone fight. Only the indispensable and individual few would be able to rise above this scramble of the industrial masses.

Sorrell and Son had everything; there was scarcely an English prejudice to which it did not appeal:

As for the so-called 'Oedipus Complex', it did not appear to exist in Kit . . . Nor had it existed in Sorrell. And yet it did not seem to him that either he or his son were abnormal. He rather thought the abnormality could be looked for on the Continent and in the mental make-up of a certain sort of Continental youth who grew up to be a professor.

The book is also profoundly misogynist. Women are dangerous, untrustworthy, a burden to a man on life's journey; though the misogyny did not seem to worry Deeping's huge female readership—even if they noticed it. *Sorrell and Son* had a simple lesson: the middle classes were morally and intellectually better than the working classes, and that is why they would win.

Despite *Sorrell and Son's* enduring popularity, the almost talismanic significance it apparently had for some, it had no ideological successor before the Second World War. Although the notion of the 'damaged man', the ex-officer as a permanent social casualty of war, did not disappear,[10] it was mostly uncoupled from class conflict. It assumed the character of individual tragedy rather than tragedy representative of the fate of a whole social class. This was largely a result of the disappearance of the ex-soldier as an issue in British politics. Remarkably quickly, perhaps faster than in any other country, the existing social system absorbed and politically neutered ex-soldiers as ex-soldiers.[11] From the mid-1920s onwards their fate was bound up with civil society: working-class ex-soldiers with the working class as a whole; middle-class ex-soldiers with the middle class as a whole. Thereafter, if an ex-officer of the middle class were hostile (or well disposed) to the working class, he was hostile

[10] See Petter, ' "Temporary Gentlemen" ' and Hynes, *A War Imagined* for the continuation of the theme.

[11] For a discussion of this, see A. P. Latcham, 'Journey's End: Ex-servicemen and the State in England, *c*.1914–1925', unpublished Oxford D.Phil. thesis, 1996.

(or well disposed) as a member of the middle class, not as an ex-officer who happened also to be middle-class. But after the mid-1920s overt middle-class hostility to the working class had much diminished anyway because the middle class, as a whole, had won.

The disappearance of the novel of conflict was also partly due to changes in the composition of the middle class. The middle class which had suffered and survived the early 1920s was still largely Edwardian; the middle class of the 1930s, however, was, as we have seen, larger, more technical in occupation and education, more diverse in its social origins, more 'modern'.[12] Not only was it more distant from the conflicts of the early 1920s, more of its members identified themselves with social change and saw themselves as its promoters. In these circumstances the ordinary 'educated' reader turned from a literature of conflict to one of modernity—a literature in which a self-confident middle class stood, as a modernizing class, against both the working class and even, though less confidently, against the upper class.

Alison Light has argued that the readers of Agatha Christie's detective novels, whose popularity in the interwar years no one could miss,

> were invited to identify with a more inward-looking notion of the English as a nice, decent, essentially private people. This was an idiom more about self-effacement and retreat than bombast and expansion, one which could lie both at the heart of a class-formation and reach across the classes; it allowed for new forms of enjoyment and pleasure. It takes us further toward understanding the meaning of what used to be a middlebrow culture of the period.[13]

What is striking about Christie's interwar writing is not its snobbishness 'but its comparative freedom from much of the rancour and discontent about an expanding middle class which motivates her fellow [detective] writers.' Christie's middle class, while it does include colonels and vicars' wives, also includes secretaries, commercial salesmen, shopkeepers, receptionists, shop-girls, nurses, solicitors, housewives, doctors, and dentists. Her stories suggest 'an interwar imagination in which the middle classes are the modern class, less sentimental, more unbuttoned than their pre-1914 versions.' Neither of her principal detectives is from Oxford which may have come 'as a welcome relief'.[14] The dominant interwar female idiom 'could "feminise" the idea of the nation as a whole, giving us a retiring and private people, pipe-smoking "little men" with their quietly competent partners, a nation of gardeners and house-wives'.[15] It is an idiom and a class indifferent to power and politics at large.

Light's is a brilliant description of a class possessing inward poise and

---

[12] See above, pp. 46–7.   [13] Light, *Forever England*, 11.

[14] Ibid. 79–86. Dorothy Sayers's detective, Lord Peter Wimsey, was Oxford; Margery Allingham's, Albert Campion, was Cambridge. Both were aristocrats. Christie's detectives were neither Varsity nor aristocrats. One was a woman and one Belgian.

[15] Ibid. 211.

confidence; it presents an England self-absorbed and, whatever family rows there might be, at one: the sort of England which made for the immense popularity of J. B. Priestley's *The Good Companions*. But it exaggerates middle-class retreat from politics by under-rating the degree to which the literature of modernity was also a literature of public life. Equally representative, for example, of the 1930s middle class were Winifred Holtby and A. J. Cronin, who wrote two of the best-sellers of the decade: Holtby's *South Riding* (published posthumously in 1936) and Cronin's *The Citadel* (1937). *The Citadel* had the biggest (and fastest) sales of any book of the 1930s and was made by MGM into a highly successful film.[16] But *South Riding*, as novel and film, was not far behind. Both books had real personal and dramatic interest. *South Riding*, is in many ways, as one would expect, a feminist novel; the heroine, a headmistress, is a 'career' woman who nevertheless has a testing love-life. In *The Citadel*, the hero, a young doctor, also has an intense and difficult personal life, which includes the loss of his wife. But the structure of both books is public and political. *South Riding*, which was partly based on Holtby's mother's experience as the first woman alderman on the East Riding (Yorkshire) County Council (and was, perhaps prudently, dedicated to her), is arranged around the functions of local government—education, housing, etc. Holtby argues that there can be no real distinction between public and private life: personal and social evolution both occur within the political sphere.

   The Citadel is more explicitly political; it has a point and makes it without much subtlety. Cronin, like Deeping, was a doctor, but, unlike Deeping, practised extensively, as a medical inspector of mines and as a general practitioner in London. Both these experiences figure prominently in his heavily autobiographical novels. In 1931, after the great success of his first novel, *Hatter's Castle*, he retired from medicine. His second novel, *Three Loves* (1932), was not a success, but his third, a mining novel, *The Stars Look Down* (1935), whose dénouement was a Zolaesque mining disaster, was very successful (as novel and film) and prepared the public for his next, *The Citadel*. This follows the life of its hero, Manson, a young Scottish doctor, as a doctor in a mining town in South Wales and then in London, first as home office medical inspector and then as general practitioner. Despite its significant personal and sexual theme, it is essentially a novel of public life, a critique of Britain's medical hierarchies and (in part) of private medicine itself. Published by Gollancz and launched by Gollancz himself in his Left Book Club stage, *The Citadel* sold as well as *The Good Companions* had done in 1929.

   It is undoubtedly a 'progressive' novel; but not 'socialist'. Nor does it give the working class any particular, let alone unique, place in the march of mind:

---

[16] *The Citadel* sold 40,083 copies in nine days—a bookselling record (J. McAleer, *Popular Reading and Publishing in Britain, 1914–1950* (Oxford, 1992), 56). Dr McAleer's book is indispensable for the study of popular reading in this period.

There ought to be some better scheme, a chance for everybody—oh, say state control. Then he groaned . . . No, damn it, that's hopeless—bureaucracy, chokes individual effort—it would suffocate me [Manson].

It was a wonderful ideal, the group of working men [miners] controlling the medical services of the community for the benefit of their fellow workers. But it was only an ideal. They were too biased, too unintelligent ever to administer such a scheme progressively.

The Citadel, unlike *Sorrell and Son*, is not anti-working class; on the contrary, it is sympathetic. It merely argues that the working class, at its present cultural level, cannot be progressive. In *The Citadel* social progress is represented by professional, technically innovative, and socially conscious young doctors who despise their snobbish and incompetent elders. The novel can be interpreted as a wider attack upon the traditional upper middle class: *The Citadel* ends with Manson and two of his peers leaving London for a provincial town uncorrupted by medical chicanery, there to establish a kind of advanced polyclinic.

In February 1938 Gallup asked its sample which book of all had impressed them most. Only a minority felt able to answer; but of that minority two books alone (other than the bible) had any significant number of votes: *Sorrell and Son* and *The Citadel*. Although these two books are not polar opposites—both believe in the predominance of an individualist middle class—the enormous popularity of *Sorrell and Son* in the 1920s and *The Citadel* in the 1930s is suggestive of the altered mood of the 'broad' middle class. In the 1920s the mood is resentful, defensive, and primarily anti-working class. In the 1930s it is self-confident and, if anything, primarily anti-traditional upper middle class. Above all, the working class is no longer seen as menacing. In Cronin the middle-class hero is now not a warrior or man of destiny, nor a retiring gardener or crossword-puzzler, but a socially and technically progressive proponent of modernity. The idiom is not 'feminine' and reticent but 'masculine' and public.

The extraordinary success in the later 1930s and the war years of Penguin and the Left Book Club can only be explained by the existence of such a class. Allen Lane had originally established Penguin Books (1935) as a cheap middlebrow publishing house, largely reprinting Jonathan Cape's distinctly middlebrow list of the 1920s.[17] His ambition was for Penguin eventually to bridge the gap between middlebrow and 'serious' literature. Its list thus combined 'artistic and serious novels, previously available only to a small audience, with the sort of middlebrow titles found alongside feminine romance in the circulating libraries run by Mudie's (until 1937), Boots and W. H. Smith.'[18] Penguin, and its ornithological derivatives Pelican and Puffin, were, of course to diversify almost, it seemed, exponentially, but its real successes before 1945 were the

---

[17] For Penguin, see N. Joicey, 'A Paperback Guide to Progress: Penguin Books, 1935–c.1951', *Twentieth Century British History*, 4, 1 (1993), 25–56.
[18] Ibid. 29.

Penguin Specials, political tracts for the day, which began in November 1937 with Edgar Mowrer's *Germany Puts the Clock Back*. The Specials had extraordinary success, particularly after the outbreak of the Second World War, and several sold over 100,000 copies.

Victor Gollancz, in establishing the Left Book Club, had wider ambitions than Lane, if a somewhat similar success. Founded in 1936, the Left Book Club was conceived as a partisan anti-fascist alliance (which sometimes meant pro-Communist)—a literary Popular Front—based upon an active politically interventionist readership. But that readership was (so far as we can tell) not very different, if at all, from the readership of *The Citadel*. Although 'left-wing', unlike *The Citadel*, Penguin–Left Book Club politics were modern-minded and depended upon members of the modern-minded middle-class—many, one suspects, employed by the central state or local government. This type of politicization, which is unique in the recent history of England, reached its apogee in the war; and then, almost abruptly, died. By the late 1940s it was inconceivable that novels based upon local government or a critique of private medicine could be among the best-sellers of the decade.

Although there was a middle-class 'woman's novel' in the period—novels about the 'condition' of the middle-class woman, sometimes written from a feminist perspective, notably by E. M. Delafield and Winifred Holtby—none of them, with the exception of *South Riding* (which was half a feminist novel), were best-sellers of the middlebrow genre. Furthermore, none of the 'political' middlebrow novels were written specifically for women, even if a majority of their readers were women. Certainly a majority of Deeping's were. As John Osborne wrote of his grandmother, 'The truth was that she thought her husband incapable of even choosing a book for her whereas at the tuppenny library they knew, of course: Ethel M. Dell, Netta Muskett and that pre-war Dickens of them all, read and reread again, Warwick Deeping.[19] But there were best-selling middlebrow 'women's novels' in the interwar period—novels *intended* primarily for women drawing upon several traditions—and they constitute a literature of sexual romance. The most characteristic of these, and certainly the best-selling, were E. M. Hull's *The Sheik* (1919), P. C. Wren's *Beau Geste* (1924), and Hugh Walpole's *Rogue Herries* (1930). *The Sheik* was a 'sensation' novel which was a sensation, and E. M. Hull, a Derbyshire pig-farmer's wife, its very unlikely author.[20] In some ways it was descended from Elinor Glyn's immensely popular erotic novel *Three Weeks* (1907): the heroine, Diana Mayo, an English rose, is captured by a sheik, a man of great strength and good looks;

---

[19] Osborne, *A Better Class of Person*, 46. See also Betjeman's poem, 'Station Siren': 'She sat with a Warwick Deeping, / Her legs curled round in a ring, / Like a beautiful panther sleeping, / Yet always ready to spring . . .

[20] For Hull, see N. Beauman, *A Very Great Profession: The Woman's Novel, 1914–1939* (London, 1983), 88–9; Cockburn, *Bestseller*, 129–38. It was, of course, the film version of *The Sheik* that made Rudolph Valentino's career.

Diana, since she never consents, is raped every night while she remains his prisoner. At the end of the novel she is rescued but, shockingly, chooses to stay with the sheik. Her choice is not quite so shocking as it appears, since the sheik (typically) turns out to be half-English and of noble birth. But the novel departs from Elinor Glyn in its sexual implications. Not only is Diana repeatedly raped but her love for the sheik grows the more she is violated. *The Sheik*, Alison Light suggests, was 'part of a new popular culture of female eroticism which played with the idea of sexual violence'.[21] But its plot is darker than that, and relies less on an idea of sexual violence, more on an 'unhibited sado-masochism'.[22]

Nothing quite like the *The Sheik*, not even Ethel M. Dell's *Charles Rex* (1922), was openly published in England before *No Orchids for Miss Blandish*, but P. C. Wren adopted many of the conventions of the North African fantasy in *Beau Geste*, immensely popular as novel and film—it was filmed twice in the 1920s and again in 1966. Wren, a former teacher, member of the Indian Educational Service and officer in the Indian Army Reserve, had an imperial imagination—though the imagined empire is French rather than British. He wrote the first of his Foreign Legion novels, *The Wages of Virtue*, in 1916, and he was to write two more after *Beau Geste*—*Beau Sabreur* and *Beau Ideal*. Both were also filmed. The plot of *Beau Geste* would be thought comic were it not plainly meant to be serious. For the purposes of gallantry, which involves a fabulously expensive jewel, a woman of virtue, and a brutal husband, three aristocratic brothers independently join the Foreign Legion with the inevitable melodramatic consequences. Although the sexual violence is absent, the overall geography, physical and human, is clearly *Sheik* territory. Wren, to judge by his own utterances, was hugely philistine, and either deceived by or unready to admit the nature of his market. 'The bulk of my readers', he told Q. D. Leavis,

are the cleanly-minded virile outdoor sort of people of both sexes, and the books are widely read in the Army, the Navy, the Universities, the Public Schools and the Clubs ... Although I now make a good many thousands per annum, I still am not a 'professional novelist', nor, as I have said, a long-haired literary cove, but I prefer the short-haired executive type.[23]

Whatever the market for his other books, the market for *Beau Geste* was not in the clubs or the universities; or, at any rate, only a small part of it.

The greater part was, almost certainly, also the market for Hugh Walpole's *Rogue Herries*, the best-seller of 1930, and the first of four Herries volumes. Walpole was already a famous middlebrow writer by 1930. He had made a reputation before 1914 with *Mr Perrin and Mr Traill*, a book set in a boys' school which suggested he might have something significant to say; and he had written powerfully, if gushingly, about his service with the Russian army during the First World War. But, despite his emulation of Henry James, his literary

---

[21] Light, *Forever England*, 175.   [22] Beauman, *A Very Great Profession*, 88–9.
[23] Q. D. Leavis, *Fiction and the Reading Public*, 52.

trajectory was downwards, accelerated by an almost fatally fluent pen. *Rogue Herries* was set in Regency England, mostly in the Lake District where Walpole lived, and involved all too many of the stock types of the Regency Novel, including masterful men (Herries) and high-spirited women. The 'Regency', not too closely defined, was a well-understood device by which novelists could obtain a certain licence (the same applies to the North Africa fantasy). Mary Webb used the same device in *Precious Bane*, thanks to Stanley Baldwin one of the best-sellers of the 1920s.[24] *Rogue Herries* thus had more than a touch of Georgette Heyer, though written with more dash and style. But its sales, like that of *Beau Geste*, suggest how successfully the old formulae could be exploited, even among a modern-minded middle class.

These novels were 'erotic', either overtly or by suggestion, as well as romantic. They depended heavily on individual sales: which is why, taste aside, they were largely confined to middle-class readers. There was, however, a genre of 'romantic' fiction, very rarely erotic, written exclusively for women almost exclusively by women, of which almost countless examples were read by lower-middle-class and upper-working-class women. While contemporaries knew of this literature, there was a curious reluctance to admit its centrality to the reading public. When people spoke of best-sellers they rarely meant romantic fiction, though only the best of best-selling middlebrow novels could exceed in sales even a moderately popular romantic novel. This point was made by an outsider, Mary Ellen Chase, when describing the reading matter of the third-class railway carriage:

Although one frequently sees *The Argosy*, *True Romances*, and *The Happy Magazine*, one forever sees those sixpenny and ninepenny volumes common to English news-stands and immensely popular in third-class carriages . . . Zane Grey, Edgar Wallace and Ethel M. Dell are popular associates in third-class carriages. So is Tarzan in his various portrayals . . . [Dell's] stories and those of Mr. Grey and Mr. Wallace are not, however, at least according to my researches in third-class carriages, the most beloved. This distinction I would unhesitatingly assign to Ruby M. Ayres . . . She is the author of numerous books with stirring titles such as *A Gamble with Love*, *The Second Honeymoon*, *Brown Sugar*, and *The Remembered Kiss*.[25]

Ayres (1883–1955) was 'Queen of Fiction' though she faced strong competition from Barbara Cartland and several writers from the Mills and Boon stable. Ayres perfected a formula very different from the erotic or sensation novels. A young, good-hearted, virtuous girl of modest birth meets, and after the usual misunderstandings, marries her love. Her love, however, is rarely glamorous or aristocratic, though often strong and silent. The *mise en scène* is frequently

---

[24] Baldwin was induced to declare publicly that *Precious Bane* was one of his favourite books. To him therefore we indirectly owe Stella Gibbons's *Cold Comfort Farm* (1932), a marvellous satire on Webb and her followers.

[25] Chase, *In England Now*, 192.

more than comfortable, but rarely luxurious: usually a businessman's comfort in the modern style. There is no sex—other than chaste kissing and holding of hands. Ayres always adhered to the advice given her by Lord Riddell: she should 'take her heroines as far as the bedroom door and then leave them'. While her heroines were usually 'old-fashioned', Ayres did recognize social change. Mary, for example, without an independent income, is forced to take in a paying guest. As a 'lady' she is rather dismayed at this. But her friend tells her, 'Ladies do all sorts of things nowadays, Mary—keep shops and make beauty creams and drive motor-cars, and it doesn't hurt them, or lower their dignity in the least' (*The Big Fellah*, 1931). Ayres's heroines are definitely not 'modern girls'; and modern girls are often no better than they should be.[26] But the supposed attitudes of the modern girl are understood to be legitimate:

Did other men speak to their wives in such a manner? If so it was no wonder that the modern girls so often refused to give up their independence. Christine knew several who took the attitude:

'If marriage is always like my mother's—*no thank you*.'

And yet if a girl had no money, what was there for her but marriage? It must be either that or a lonely middle age on an insufficient income. (*And Still They Dream*, 1939)

Ayres's style was straightforward and sufficiently cliché-ridden to be familiar to her readers:

'He's a damned young fool!' the older man spluttered. 'A damned young fool! Taken with the first pretty face he sees. I won't hear of it—I refuse to hear of it. I'll cut him off with a penny! I've my own idea as to the sort of wife he's to marry. A farmer's daughter, indeed! Three acres and a cow sort of business. (*The Marriage of Barry Wicklow*, 1920)

One 'very popular woman novelist', anonymous, but who could well have been Ayres by the tone of the comment, told Q. D. Leavis: 'I imagine the bulk of my readers to be fairly simple people (mostly women) who want to read of romance in a form not incompatible with their own opportunities. People usually give as their kind [of] reasons for liking my work (a) That I am "human", (b) Seem to "understand".'[27]

This is a sensible and accurate analysis both of Ayres's formula and her readership—whoever wrote it. The principal beneficiary of the formula, other than Ayres herself, was the publisher Mills and Boon.[28] Mills and Boon had been founded in 1908 by two former employees of Methuen's and had had originally a decidedly mixed list, which included not only school texts but socialist

---

[26] Mary 'was ashamed for the modern girl with her too short skirts and her bobbed hair, and the vulgar slang and her impudent disrespect for old age' (*The Big Fellah*).

[27] Q. D. Leavis, *Fiction and the Reading Public*, 58.

[28] For Mills and Boon, see J. McAleer, *Popular Reading and Publishing in Britain*, 100–32; and J. McAleer, 'Scenes from Love and Marriage: Mills and Boon and the Popular Publishing Industry in Britain, 1908–1950', *Twentieth Century British History*, 1, 3 (1990), 264–88.

'classics' and 'labour' autobiographies as well as fiction. But romantic novels had always been an important part of the list: Georgette Heyer's first novel had been published by Mills and Boon in 1923 and several of the great names of the later Mills and Boon lists, like Sophie Cole, Joan Sutherland, Louise Gerard, and Dolf Wyllarde, appeared in the 1920s. It was the rapid growth of the 'tuppenny libraries' in the interwar years which transformed Mills and Boon into a firm which exclusively published romantic fiction.

Mills and Boon became *the* 'library house'. It did not publish in paperback until the 1960s, most of its books being sold not to individuals but to the commercial libraries. These represented huge sales: some of the big library chains, like Boots and W. H. Smith, would buy up to 500 copies per title. Mills and Boon distinguished itself by publicizing its list rather than its authors, by convincing readers that they could 'trust' a Mills and Boon publication, regardless of who wrote it, simply because it was Mills and Boon. This was an explicit element in its otherwise thin advertising:

The Fiction market of to-day is overburdened with new novels, and the ordinary reader finds it most difficult to choose the right kind of story either to buy or to borrow. There are always the big names, which, by the way, do not always give satisfaction, but here at any rate in the main there should be no difficulty in making a choice. Best sellers are not published often enough to keep the ordinary reader going, and the average person has to pick and choose between hundreds of titles, many of which would have been better never to have seen the light of publication. Really the only way to choose is to limit your reading to those publishers whose lists are carefully selected, and whose Fiction imprint is a sure guarantee of good reading.

The reason, therefore, why you should choose a Mills and Boon novel is because, without exception, only the best type of Fiction is accepted by them, whether it is by a known or an unknown author. (Mills and Boon publicity)

The firm spent very little on publicity, but relied on word of mouth, a catalogue which told readers of forthcoming titles, a huge 'live' publication list—in 1939 it had over 450 titles in print—and the familiar brown covers.

The obvious consequence of this style was to diminish the significance of the author. Though a number of Mills and Boon authors did become well known, and some, like Denise Robins, Annie Swan, Mary Burchell and Jean Macleod, very well known, it was not a 'star system'. Those who did not want to become just library house authors kept away from Mills and Boon. 'The authors rated not at all,' Barbara Cartland's agent said. 'It was just another romance. And we never classed Barbara in that sort of writing. She was always above that.'[29]

Mills and Boon's exact sales for the 1930s and 1940s are now hard to find, but the firm revealed in 1949 that Mary Burchell's novels had sold over 400,000 copies—and Burchell was not the most successful of the firm's authors. But its

---

[29] McAleer, 'Scenes from Love and Marriage', 279.

importance as a 'library house' is suggested by a 1935 analysis of the stock of 'one of the largest and newest' of the commercial libraries. Among the firms' authors listed as best-sellers were Denise Robins (36 titles), Joan Sutherland and Sophie Cole (26 to 30 titles each), Louise Gerard (21 to 25 titles each), Elizabeth Carfrae (16 to 20), and Deidre O'Brien and Marjorie M. Price (10 to 15 each).[30]

The firm kept a tight control of plots. The story was always told from the heroine's view and the hero was always immensely attractive (an 'Alpha man'), though not necessarily handsome or rich. Morality was always conventional. The heroine was (or should be) virgin until marriage; love-making, as in Ayres, was chaste, confined usually to delicate kisses; women who became pregnant, while treated sympathetically, found that life was overwhelmingly against them. The Mills and Boon editors would probably have permitted no other morality anyway, but the censorious and super-cautious editors of the women magazines, which published many of the novels as serials, put the issue beyond question. There were, of course, more or less acceptable ways around this which some authors exploited. Mills and Boon heroines were always fainting or falling unconscious, to be revived by the anguished, not-so-delicate kisses of the beloved. More dangerous themes could be implied without breaking the rules: in *The Net Love Spread* (1935), Dicky Bannister falls in love with his step-sister; in *Lady By Marriage* (1935), Joan (unhappily) marries her adoptive father. Occasionally authors got away with something 'stronger', as Mary Burchell did with *Wife to Christopher* (1936), but these were known to be exceptional.

Sexual morality was not the only conventional component of a Mills and Boon novel. The *avant-garde* was always treated as unsound and its practitioners as poseurs:

> Mara Temple [a modern girl], who talked incessantly about giving birth to drawings, was at first inclined to be friendly, but when Elizabeth [the heroine] had been taken one evening by a ribald band of her friends to look upon 'Rima' [Epstein's then controversial sculpture] and Paddy had publicly proclaimed next day that Elizabeth, like themselves, thought the sculpture an absolute mess, Mara's interest withered and died.
>
> (Constance M. Evans, *The Pattern of a Star*, 1932)

Elizabeth, a 'healthy-minded' girl did not 'always feel comfortable' when listening to her artist-friends' conversation.

As with Ruby M. Ayres, the heroine was an ordinary, sensible girl who was ready to work hard and often had to keep herself on meagre earnings. A common theme is the provincial girl who goes to London to better herself and finds life there a constant struggle. In *The Pattern of a Star*, Elizabeth Warren is forced to live in kitchenless digs in Earls Court:

[30] Ibid. 272.

She dined upon sausages and mashed potatoes, with fruit and coffee, at Lyons'; she ate beefsteak pie, apple turnover and an ice, at the A.B.C.; she was served with a heaped plateful of good solid fare at Blanchard's. She manipulated macaroni at an Italian delicatessen shop in the Vauxhall Road ... She sampled fish and chips at a saloon kept by a gentleman in a red waistcoat and curled quiff, who styled himself the 'Fried Fish King'.

The charmless digs or the austere hostel for working girls, differing little from the 'May of Teck' where Muriel Spark's *Girls of Slender Means* battled to make ends meet in the mid-1940s, are common terrain in a Mills and Boon novel.

Furthermore, the overall geography of a Mill and Boon romance is usually neither exotic nor luxurious. There are no North African sheikdoms or Balkan principalities. There are bright young things and 'petting parties', and occasionally the *vie de bohème*—but all rather suburban. The hero is hardly ever of noble birth, and if he is wealthy he is either a businessman or vaguely connected to the City. Increasingly, he was becoming a doctor. As George Orwell noted, the heroines of such romances were more likely to marry bank managers than earls. What the hero offers is love, honesty, and a companionate marriage, in which he will not only be her lover, but helpmeet and best friend. The relationship between hero and heroine before marriage is equally restrained. It might be tossed about by misunderstanding or disappointment, even by the malicious intervention of others, but it is basically grounded in reality. During the late 1920s, Nicola Beauman suggests, writers like Ayres and Robins 'began to make millinery shops, advertising agencies or tennis courts almost as torrid as any hill-station or bazaar'.[31] But the millinery shop or advertising agency was the site of love, rarely of passion. The Mills and Boon novel of the 1930s and 1940s was a romance of everyday life, and in its very matter-of-factness, its eschewing of the unreal or exotic, it represented the matter-of-factness of the contemporary English middle classes. But because of that its conventional moralities were not unbending. Mills and Boon was a didactic firm, but was also aware that the views of the readership did move on. It kept a close eye on what its readers thought conventional at any particular moment. The conventions governing its morality thus did change, if at glacier-speed rate: unlike Barbara Cartland, who takes her stand on the morality of eternal chastity.

The romantic fiction of Ayres and Mills and Boon largely departed from the tradition of the Victorian and Edwardian sensation novel. That tradition, however, survived in the 'erotic bloods' read in vast numbers by teenage girls and young women from the working classes.[32] Ayres and Mills and Boon novels were semi-realistic; the erotic bloods, except for Ayres's commonsensical

---

[31] Beauman, *A Very Great Profession*, 195.
[32] 'Bloods' were, originally, the low-grade, rather lurid popular magazines of the 19th century. By the 20th century, all magazines for children and young adults were known in the trade as 'bloods', though usually by their readers as 'comics', 'magazines', 'books', or 'novels'. For use of the word

advice column in the *Oracle*, made no such claim. They represented escapist literature in its purest form. Their readers nearly always referred to these magazines as 'books', partly because so many of their stories were called 'novels', partly because some, like the fourpenny 'pocket novels', referred to themselves as 'books', and for many working-class girls they were as close to books as anything they would read. The names of the magazines suggest the tone: *Oracle, Miracle, Red Star Weekly, Red Letter, Silver Star, Glamour, Lucky Star.* Only *Peg's Paper* and *Family Chat* seem out of place here. Many girls read several of them, by purchase, borrowing, or exchange. Pearl Jephcott cited the not utterly untypical case of one of 'her' girls who obtained in a single week: *Oracle, Miracle, Weekly Welcome, Red Letter, Red Star, Family Star, Picture Show,* and *Glamour*, together with three non-blood women's magazines. She borrowed from her particular friend *Lucky Star, Silver Star* and (somewhat surprisingly) *Melody Maker.* In the same week she read a 4d romance, *Love Tangle,* and a 1s 3d book, *Unsuspected Witness.* The latter was bought on exchange, but the girl still spent 5s a week.[33] The magazines could be bought at any newspaper shop. The 'novels' could be bought or borrowed from back-street general shops 'with a couple of shelves of books among the soap and the hair curlers', or small commercial libraries, the larger stationer's shops, or even big chains like Boots. The erotic bloods and novels were remarkably long-lived genres; unlike other magazines they lost little of their circulation in the late thirties. Even as late as 1947, *Red Letter* alone still had a readership of one million.

The erotic bloods dealt only in strong emotions starkly conceived. There is always love, but when love comes 'it comes in a sea of jealousy, scandal, revenge, lying, guilty secrets, murder, bigamy and seduction'.[34] There is much violence, and women are surprisingly often murderesses. Nor is murder casual:

Grace Calvert, lying on her side, moaned and put out a hand along the carpet as if seeking support.

A moment later, Robina Dawson had the dagger, sharp and deadly in her hand. With clenched teeth and eyes that blazed like burning coals, she crouched and plunged it into the back of the defenceless girl. (*Red Letter*, 16 Sept. 1933)[35]

As a result, the police and the courts are regular props—'Sarah will swing for this'—as are all the devices of melodrama. ' "I don't know you", Tessa said. "How strange!" His voice was menacing. "I'm the man you named the Father of your child" ' (*Oracle*, September 1941).

'blood' see A. J. Jenkinson, *What Do Boys and Girls Read?* (1st ed., London, 1940), 64. The Hulton-Deutsch *Readership Survey, 1950,* suggested that the readership for these magazines was overwhelmingly in the age-group 16–24.

[33] Jephcott, *Rising Twenty*, 113. [34] Jephcott, *Girls Growing Up*, 109–10.
[35] Quoted in McAleer, *Popular Reading*, 195.

The plot of *Fires Unseen*, a 'Romance Pocket Novel' has a heroine who is a star of musical comedy, a complicated will, a lost and orphaned baby, an unknown wife, blackmail, and a jealous lover who tries to stab the heroine.[36]

The publishers, particularly D. C. Thomson, which owned a considerable number of the bloods, did worry about their 'morality'. The reasons for this were as much commercial as ideological. Editors were afraid of offending readers, or more plausibly, readers' parents. *Red Letter* and *Red Star Weekly*, for example, were prudently subtitled 'For the Family Circle'. The emphasis on morality led, paradoxically, to endless bigamy. Heroines frequently found themselves married to ogres. But since morality forbade divorce, separation, or even flight the plots were compelled to introduce unknown or vanished first wives who render the heroine's marriage to the ogre bigamous and so invalid.[37]

Characters, like plots, are strongly stereotyped. The desirable heroine was beautiful, passionate, brave, childlike, delicate and shy, yielding and submissive to men. The ideal hero was masterful, stern, passionate, hard, and wealthy. Undesirable female traits were ambition, jealousy, cruelty, and bitterness; in males, dependency, indecisiveness, submission, helplessness, and frailty. The undesirable male, in other words, had all the traits of the desirable female. These stereotypes softened somewhat after the Second World War: heroines became less childlike and prone to fainting away; heroes more boyish and shy. But gender-roles remained as heavily typed as ever.

There was nothing suburban about the erotic novels. They were not set in advertising agencies or milliner's shops. When at home, everything was de luxe; when abroad, exotic or adventurous:

[The heroine] is transported to the Grand Hotel, to an expensive furnished flat in London, to a lido beneath the snow-capped Mountains of Switzerland or to a spot where desert stars look down . . . People in this world still [1942] go abroad for their holidays. They drive round Europe in 'luxurious and speedy cars'; they have smart maidservants . . . Expensive clothes occupy a very important place in the picture and we hear much of silk brocade pyjamas, fox furs, 'faultlessly cut lounge suits of pale grey' and simple fragments of satiny material that pass for swim suits.[38]

In 1936, *Peg's Paper* had four serials with a foreign location. One, 'When a Man Sins', set in Canada, began, 'Lawless love, unfettered hate, primitive passion, all awaited June when she went to the Backwoods of Canada to become a bride . . . She preferred the hero to most of the others—he was white.'[39]

This literature is almost wholly asocial, apolitical, and atemporal. Compare

[36] Jephcott, *Girls Growing Up*, 101–2.

[37] 'Presumed-dead first spouses return in droves in the Thomson papers' (McAleer, *Popular Reading*, 194).

[38] Jephcott, *Girls Growing Up*, 108–9.

[39] Quoted in G. Murphy, 'Media Influence on the Socialisation of Teenage Girls', in Curran, Smith, and Wingate, *Impacts and Influences*, 215.

the reader of a Mills and Boon, for example, who was clearly expected to know about 'Rima': that there was such a sculpture and that it had caused much controversy. There was no similar expectation of the reader of *Oracle* or *Glamour*. In the interwar years, for example, there is scarcely mention of unemployment or poverty; if there is unemployment or poverty, however, they are usually the result of moral failing or bad luck. During the Second World War, Canadian airmen, ATS workers, or the blitz occasionally appear, but non-contextually. The war is simply part, a small part, of the scenery. Only personal relations matter.[40] Plots centre on misunderstandings, the malign intervention of a villain or villainess (often a failed rival of the heroine), or, increasingly, the mysterious or supernatural—where rational explanation can be abandoned entirely.

Inequalities of wealth are not absent. How could they be when the heroine was so often low-born? The implied explanations of inequality and status-changes are hardly ever in social terms.[41] The rich and successful are rich and successful because they work hard—yet it is not hard work, but the inheritance of wealth, that provides the main route upwards. There is much casual upward and downward social mobility; and this, like unemployment, is usually attributed to good or bad fortune. The rich are just like the reader, and wealth purchases only material goods, not status or power. The only vice the rich might have is snobbery; and if the rich are not snobbish, they are open to no criticism whatsoever. This is complicated by the fact that the stories themselves are often snobbish. Heroes and heroines all too easily hurdle the obstacles in life's path by discovering that they are the lost offspring of dukes. Even in the rare case when the distribution of wealth is questioned, the problem is solved by a rich philanthropist and his 'magic goodwill'.[42]

The erotic bloods had not always been so asocial. Before 1914 they had had a much harder edge and their plots were frequently set in the workplace. By the 1940s this was no longer true.[43] Work now played little part in the bloods. The change is also to be seen in the kind of copy that editors sought. In 1923 *My Weekly* asked for 'strong love stories of the novelette type, and all subjects of

[40] See also Jephcott, *Rising Twenty*, 41.

[41] See B. Fowler's excellent account, ' "True to me always": an analysis of women's magazine fiction', *British Journal of Sociology*, 30 (1979), 110–15.

[42] Ibid. 114.

[43] See McAleer, *Popular Reading*, 191, for two revealing comparisons. From *My Weekly*, Jan. 1911:

Our Great Drama of Factory Life:
'A Daughter of the Mill', by Stuart Martin
The Characters.
Emily Kay, the heroine, a weaver at Palm Mill, who is pursued by the evil intentions of Frank Booth, manager at the Mill.
John Hall, a young operative at Palm Mill, who rescues Emily from Booth's hands . . . His plans for a new and improved loom, deposited with Mr Livesey, late manager of the Mill, have been stolen by *Frank Booth* . . .

feminine interest . . . stories of the adventuress "above her station" type . . . All contributions should make their appeal to the working classes.' In 1939 the last sentence read: 'All contributions should make their appeal to the modern woman.'[44] The disappearance of 'The Great Drama of Factory Life' certainly owed something to the influence of the cinema: to the plot and locales of the popular women's films of the interwar years. But it was also in part due to the self-conscious modernity of the 1920s and 1930s: the implication that the modern woman was of no particular social class because she fulfilled herself in the sphere of leisure and consumption rather than the sphere of work. In this case, modernity did not mean progress.

There was no real male equivalent to the women's erotic bloods; that is, magazines for men whose stories were primarily concerned with sexual and personal relationships. Nor, other than *Detective Stories* or *Thriller*, both doubtful cases anyway, were any adult male bloods published by English or Scottish houses. The closest English equivalents were probably 'sporting novels' like Aldine's Boxing Novels, but the nearest equivalents were the so-called 'Yank mags'—imported, often it was alleged, as ballast in merchant ships, very second-hand American crime, gangster, Western and boxing magazines—*Fight Stories*, *Action Stories*, *Crime Stories*, *Western Short Stories*, etc. They were sold at 2d or 3d each and could be bought almost anywhere. Orwell thought they were a product of the back-street newsagency, but Q. D. Leavis noted the brisk sales of 'Yank Magazines: Interesting Reading' in Woolworth's.[45] In the Yank mags the violence was usually more violent than in the English versions, and the sex, which often accompanied the violence, more overtly pornographic.

Young working-class males, when left to themselves, read crime and gangster fiction, or science fiction with a marked crime or horror element. Crime writers, like Edgar Wallace, or Western-crime writers like Zane Grey, were enormously popular, and English crime writers were much influenced by the style of American crime fiction. Richard Hoggart was inclined to believe that James M. Cain's *The Postman Always Rings Twice* (1934) set the tone.[46] Whether true or not, an Englishman, René Raymond, whose *nom-de-plume* was James Hadley Chase, took it even further with *No Orchids For Miss Blandish*. This gruesome piece lost nothing to American competition, in either violence or sales,

From *My Weekly*, 18 Nov. 1944:

'It Happened That Way', by Dorothy Black.
Barbara Tetley was peculiarly alone in the world. Four years before, not long after she had left school and started work in a Government office, her father and mother were killed in an air raid . . .
One thing she had no financial worries. Her people had left her amply provided for, and she had a pleasant home in a pretty, modern flat.
And she was in love. In love with Derek Lancing, a squadron leader in the RAF . . .

[44] McAleer, *Popular Reading*, 191.   [45] Q. D. Leavis, *Fiction and the Reading Public*, 14.
[46] Hoggart, *Uses of Literacy*, 258.

but Chase was probably exceptional among English writers. There were a number of more 'conventional' English thriller writers whose plots were much influenced by the dime novels and who wrote a not bad imitation of American crime-speak *à la* Mickey Spillane.

It was, Hoggart suggests, National Service which, by encouraging men to read such literature, habituated them to reading in a scrappy, disconnected way. But men had always done so. Though they were read almost universally by 'other ranks' during the war itself, the popularity of the Yank mags and their English derivatives long predated the war. And the 'crime-mag' was only one of several genres read by young men. Of the others, the two most important were the popular newspapers, themselves scrappy and disconnected, which had always been read by men,[47] and the rapidly increasing number of sport, hobby, and technical magazines—widely read throughout the period—of which there were by the early 1950s about 250.

The habit of reading magazines and calling them 'books' was acquired at school, even by a large proportion of grammar school boys.[48] And the 'books' they overwhelmingly read were the boys' and girls' tuppenny magazines or comics. The majority of these were founded after the First World War, including the most popular, D. C. Thomson's 'big five': *Adventure* (1921), *The Rover* (1922), *The Wizard* (1922), *The Skipper* (1930) and *The Hotspur* (1933). Of the major magazines, the two least popular, the Amalgamated Press's *Gem* and *Magnet*, were both founded before 1914. The most popular of the girls' magazines (all owned by the Amalgamated Press), *School Friend*, *Schoolgirl's Own*, *Schoolgirl's Weekly* and *Crystal*, were also all founded after 1918. A majority of boys of all ages and in all kinds of state school read comics. *Wizard* alone was read by half of grammar school boys and two-thirds of senior school boys.[49] Moreover, a quarter of the time girls spent reading magazines was devoted to the boys' comics; a remarkable fact, given that they made no concessions to female readers.[50] Many children read more than one. Of 1,850 girls and boys surveyed in London in the 1930s, over 50 per cent read three or more magazines a week (mostly comics), and of that number 30 per cent read six or more. This multiple reading was made possible by the elaborate swapping arrangements in which boys especially participated. The boys' magazines were as close to a universal literature as England had: they were read by a majority of boys from all social classes and by a substantial number of girls from all social classes.

Their circulation, however, was not uniform over the period. Between the early 1920s and 1930 there was a slow decline—partly due to competition from the radio—which slightly accelerated during the 1930s. Sales recovered strongly during the war, as they did with all forms of literature, and rose

[47] For the papers, see below, pp. 503–7.
[48] Jenkinson, *What Do Boys and Girls Read?* (2nd ed., London, 1946), 66.
[49] Ibid. 68–71.   [50] Ibid. 217.

steadily throughout the 1940s. In the 1950s, however, all the traditional magazines suffered, first from the success of the Hulton Press's *Eagle*, an all-comic magazine on the American model whose sales were over a million from the beginning (1950), and second, more insidiously, from television.[51]

The 'big five' were more popular than the older magazines because their content was more diverse. *Gem* and *Magnet*, which brought to the world Billy Bunter and Tom Merry, were exclusively school stories. *The Wizard* and its stable-mates each had six or seven different kinds of story (at least one of which was a school story), a joke page, and a competition (with prizes) page. Each had a 'bumper' Christmas annual of about 130 pages. All of them attempted to bind the reader to the magazine by featuring as a regular a particular character, like the detective-adventurer, 'Dixon Hawke' in *Adventure* or the 'Wolf of Kabul' in *The Wizard*. To their readership, the editors adopted an intimate and confiding, rather creepy approach. *The Wizard* featured a page called 'Step Right Up and Have a Chat with Your Editor':

My dear chums,
See the heading? That's the spirit. No hanky-panky, get right down to bedrock and have a chat, you and I, like two pals . . .[52]

In 1940 George Orwell wrote a celebrated attack on the boys' magazines.[53] 'In reality', he wrote, 'their basic political assumptions are two: nothing ever changes, and foreigners are funny.' Their mental world was stuck at 1914: no slump, unemployment, trade unions, strikes, or Fascism. The working classes are absent except as comic figures or semi-villains. 'The outlook inculcated by all these papers', he suggested, 'is that of a rather exceptionally stupid member of the Navy League in the year 1910.' Was Orwell right? The philistine and self-satisfied reply of Frank Richards, creator of Billy Bunter, suggests he was, as does a casual reading of these magazines. Particularly powerful were the racial stereotypes. Most whites were good, except (unsurprisingly) Germans, who were often not good. There was a pervasive pan-Anglo-Saxondom, as in much children's literature of the time, which incorporated as honorary Anglo-Saxons Afrikaners; so South Africans, Americans, Australians, etc. were particularly good. Blacks and Chinese were the subject of intense ridicule. The 'Coalblacks' tribe were inherently risible, as were Sing Small and his Chinese pals. The evil Chao-Feng was fond of saying 'The white race will learn one day the power of the Yellow Peril.' 'Ju', the 'Black Giant' of Nigeria, goes berserk and terrorizes Bedford and Leighton Buzzard. Cannibals proliferate and many white adventurers meet (or almost meet) unhappy ends.

Even if Orwell were right, however, did it matter? We do not know how

---

[51] For figures, see McAleer, *Popular Reading*, 172.   [52] Quoted in ibid. 177.

[53] In *Horizon*, 1940; reprinted, together with Frank Richards's reply, in Orwell and Angus, *Collected Essays . . . of George Orwell*, i. 460–93.

much ideological baggage children carry with them into adulthood, especially from things like these magazines, which appealed at different levels. A large number of those who voted for the first time in 1945 and who voted Labour had been drenched in their ideology. To vote Labour, however, by no means implies a serious departure from received ideas, or a wider critique of the English social system. The lack of resentment by the bulk of the electorate, for example, of the public school and its product, might be explained by the public school fantasies which clearly gave the readership of the magazines so much satisfaction. They might also, via insistent racial stereotyping, have contributed to the widespread failure to apprehend the change in Britain's international position after 1945. Whatever their effect, given that so many boys read only them or sport magazines, they had the field to themselves.

A large number of working-class boys and girls gave up reading books altogether when they left school. At school, however, there was considerable pressure on them to read real books. This meant, in practice, the reading of adventure, mystery, and detective novels. As boys got older adventure and mystery declined (as did school stories) while the popularity of detective novels rose continuously. The rise of the detective novel was no doubt part of the young English male's fascination with criminal literature, but the detective novel in the Agatha Christie sense was more a middle- than a working-class genre. Middle-class boys read them much more than working-class boys who remained attached to the crime-thriller, which they classified as 'adventure'. More revealing of the infantilization of the working-class boy's imaginative life is that at 14 plus twice as many boys at senior schools continued to read school stories as did boys at grammar schools.

What surprised observers was the popularity of Dickens amongst all schoolboys and all age groups:[54]

Popularity of 'Adult' Fiction Among Secondary and Senior School Boys

Age	Secondary
12+	1 R. L. Stevenson [*Treasure Island*], 2 Dickens, 3 Defoe [*Robinson Crusoe*]
13+	1 Dickens, 2 Stevenson, 3 H. G. Wells, 4 C. Kingsley
14+	1 Dickens, 2 P. G. Wodehouse, 3 Stevenson
15+	1 Dickens, 2 Wodehouse, 3 (aeq.) Wells, Rider Haggard and G. K. Chesterton
	Senior
12+	1 Dickens, 2 Stevenson, 3 Defoe, 4 T. Hughes [*Tom Brown's Schooldays*]
13+	1 Dickens, 2 Stevenson, 3 Defoe, 4 Hughes
14+	1 Dickens [by far], 2 Stevenson, 3 Defoe

The general configuration of these lists, the similarity between the two particularly, suggests strong school influence, or is a tribute to Dickens's capacity to devise plots and characters always attractive to schoolboys. Notably absent

[54] Jenkinson, *What Do Boys and Girls Read?* (2nd ed., London, 1946), 16.

are the old Victorian imperial novelists like G. A. Henty or Captain Marryat, though they were still fodder for school prizes. The appearance of Hughes in the senior school list seems to confirm the persistent appeal of 'school stories' to working-class boys.

Schoolgirls' orders of preference differed markedly from the boys':[55]

Popularity of 'Adult' Fiction among Secondary and Senior Schoolgirls

Age	Secondary
12+	1 Dickens, 2 Baroness Orczy
13+	1 Orczy, 2 Dickens
14+	1 Orczy [by far], 2 Dickens, 3 Buchan, 4 (aeq.) E. Brontë, A. Dumas, Rider Haggard, Stevenson.
15+	1 Orczy, 2 Dickens, 3 (aeq.) Wodehouse, G. S. Porter, Wells, Chesterton, Buchan, A. Conan Doyle, 9 Buchan
	Senior
12+	1 Dickens, 2 Kingsley, 3 Lewis Carroll
13+	1 Dickens, 2 (aeq.) J. Swift, the Bible and Kingsley, 5 (aeq.) H. B. Stowe [*Uncle Tom's Cabin*], Stevenson
14+	1 Dickens, 2 Stowe

The prominence of Orczy in the secondary list and her complete absence from the senior is surprising. That Orczy was popular with girls is not surprising: her stories, both *Pimpernel* and the romances, fall desirably half-way between a boys' blood, like the *Hotspur* and an erotic blood, like *Red Letter*. But the market for such stories was always significantly larger among girls at senior schools than those at grammar schools. As Margaret Phillips said in 1922: 'It would appear . . . that the demand of the girl wage-earner is primarily for personal romance—of the type so liberally supplied by Baroness Orczy and others.'[56] We should, therefore, approach the 'senior list' with some scepticism, or else assume that teachers in senior schools were much more effective in supervising their students' reading. The popularity of Harriet Beecher Stowe, however, is less surprising. *Uncle Tom's Cabin* was still quite popular with working-class girls and was probably vaguely associated by them with *Little Women*, perhaps the most popular single novel among senior school girls. Indeed, the absence of Louisa M. Alcott from this list is as puzzling as the presence of Orczy in the other.

English has a remarkably rich children's literature and this period was no exception. While older novelists like P. F. Westaway (boys' adventure) and Angela Brazil (girls' school stories) were still popular and Arthur Ransome widely read, the 'public library market' (broadly speaking, middle-class) was dominated by three enormously popular authors: Enid Blyton, W. E. Johns, and

---

[55] Jenkinson, *What Do Boys and Girls Read?*, 186–200.
[56] Phillips, *Young Industrial Worker*, 107–8.

Richmal Crompton. Blyton, the most popular, was a world phenomenon: by 1977 200 million of her books had been printed in almost all the known languages. She wrote with staggering fluency (10,000 words a day was her cruising speed), which permitted her not only to write books without number but to edit her own magazine and deal personally—she had no agent—with her 40 publishers. She was tough and quick to take offence. In 1952 she mounted a legal action against the BBC for a humorous reference to her in *Take It From Here*.

Her first children's book was a collection of poems, *Child Whispers*, and she wrote a large number of children's stories from the late 1930s on. Her real success, however, came in the 1940s with the *Famous Five* and *Secret Seven* stories. These were well-crafted children's adventure stories, carefully designed to appeal to both boys and girls, and in 'George' in the *Famous Five* she created an exceptionally determined tomboy—so determined as to hint at sexual transgression—who enabled Blyton to disrupt the traditional sexual stereotyping of the children's story in an acceptable way. But there was no other subtlety to her adventures: vaguely upper-middle-class children were nice and good, while the villains were vaguely working-class and definitely bad. But they had, as contemporaries said, 'pace' and moments of seemingly genuine danger. The contrasts Blyton continuously drew between the effectiveness of the children and the ineffectiveness of adults generally added to the stories' attraction.[57] Their popularity amongst middle-class children should not surprise.

Blyton's apotheosis was her invention in 1949 of 'Little Noddy'. Noddy and the other characters of 'Toyland', based upon drawings of puppet figures by the Dutch artist, Harmsen van der Beek, rapidly became part of the nation's cultural repertoire—not least PC Plod who gave his name (pejoratively) to the country's police. Toyland was a fantasy of English village life, and thus falls into a well-established tradition, but it had charm and an appeal universal enough to make Toyland popular throughout much of the world.

W. E. Johns is best known as creator of 'Biggles' (a diminutive for 'Bigglesworth'). Biggles was a classic Royal Flying Corps pilot, as Johns had been: daring, chivalrous, patriotic. He was successively a First World War 'ace', an adventurer, a squadron-leader in the Second World War and an 'air-detective' at Scotland Yard. He first appeared as a story in the magazine *Popular Flying*, of which Johns was founder-editor, and as a book in 1932 (the first of 104), *The Camels are Coming*. They were enormously successful in England and much of the 'white' empire: so successful in recruiting for the RAF that in 1941 the Air Ministry persuaded Johns to create a female Biggles, 'Worrals', to assist in recruiting for the Women's RAF. In addition to Biggles, Johns wrote 11 Worrals books and 10 'Gimlet' books—'Gimlet' was a commando, but less popular than Biggles or Worrals.

---

[57] M. Hilton, 'Manufacturing Make Believe: notes on the toy and media industry for children', in M. Hilton (ed.), *Potent Fictions* (London and New York, 1996), 41–2.

Johns is probably best understood as a Henty of the modern empire. He appealed to a powerful theme of the 1930s: that modern technology could be exploited for imperial purposes. Aviation, as the acme of that technology, could reintegrate the empire by overcoming the vast distances which seemed to be driving it apart. Furthermore, against those who did not wish to be reintegrated, aircraft suggested a new policing weapon. A high proportion of Biggles stories are set in the Middle East—John's had served at Gallipoli and Salonika—where there were, indeed, vast distances, which the RAF had been controversially active in policing in the 1930s. The Johns stories are white man's stories from the officer class; good yarns tied to a modern imperial technology. An attractive combination in the 1930s and 1940s, but one which lost appeal when the empire decayed.

As a writer, in general intelligence and style, Richmal Crompton is in a class by herself, even though her 'William' books sold only in millions. Crompton, the daughter of a clergyman, was a classics teacher who wrote her first 'William' story in the *Home Magazine* in 1919, and several were published there and in the *Happy Mag*. In 1922 George Newnes published a selection of the stories in two volumes, *Just William* and *More William*. Thereafter, all the stories were published as chapters in books whose popularity was enhanced by Thomas Henry's wonderful drawings. William was so successful because he appealed to two markets—10–12 year olds for whom the stories were 'adventures', and 12–15 year olds for whom they were 'humour'—and were exceptionally deft satires of southern English middle-class life. Crompton's classical training shows: the language is Latinate and not necessarily easy going for younger readers.

William's social origins are carefully kept indistinct. It is never quite certain what sort of middle class William's family is; they are 'comfortable' and Mr Brown is a 'businessman'; but they are not grand, and easily intimidated by those who are. They have domestics and a gardener but are very nervous in establishments with a butler. Their own house begins as a 'modern' semi-detached but at some point detaches itself. Nor is it quite certain what kind of school William attends. His parents acquire a car in the 1930s. But judging from the significance of the tennis club to his siblings, particularly Ethel, herself a suburban goddess, they appear to be pretty much suburban.

Theirs is also an inward-looking middle class. Though the empire occasionally appears in the guise of missionaries or uncles from the colonies , it is not, as in Biggles, an imperial middle class with a heroic destiny. Crompton's middle class is more like Agatha Christie's: comfortable, reticent, domesticated, garden-loving. It is also generously defined and without bile. Although William's village houses a classic *nouveau riche* family, the Botts, who made their millions from Bott's Digestive Sauces, they are depicted affectionately, including their daughter, the famous Violet Elizabeth, who could 'thcream

and thcream till she was thick', one of the great emasculating females of English literature. But the stories were recognized to be middle-class: whereas
many grammar school girls read William, scarcely any senior school girls
did.[58]

Though the stories are full of contemporary political reference, 'anti-
socialism' or hostility to the working class are wholly absent. When the working class appears it is usually as tough, courageous, devil-may-care youths or
likeable tramps, both of whom are admired by William because of their
contempt for the respectable life which William himself finds so tedious. The
humour is provided by the havoc William and his gang wreak on institutions
which Crompton took very seriously: the Church of England, the Conservative
Party, spiritualism, sales-of-work, Latin masters and, not least, spinster
females who earned their living writing about 11-year-old boys. The William
stories are almost perfect examples of their kind, but Crompton was not able
to repeat that success with the serious literature which meant most to her. Her
39 adult novels were then, as now, largely unreadable.

The English were a people of the book. Even more were they a people of the
press. In 1934, before newspaper reading reached its peak, every 100 families
in Britain bought 95 daily and 130 Sunday newspapers. In the larger non-
metropolitan towns a majority of households also bought a local paper—usually an afternoon one. During the war, when patterns of newspaper reading
were often disrupted, 77 per cent of the population saw a morning newspaper
'every day or most days'; 87 per cent saw a Sunday paper 'last Sunday'.[59] In
1950, five papers had readerships of 10 million or more; another four had
readerships of 5 million or more. The *Radio Times* was almost stratospheric,
with a readership of over 20 million.

Readership in Millions of Ten Most Popular Newspapers in 1950[60]

[Radio Times	20.470]	Daily Mirror	10.140
News of the World	17.630	Sunday Express	9.530
People	13.020	Picture Post (weekly)	8.680
Sunday Pictorial	12.180	Daily Mail	6.200
Daily Express	11.630	John Bull (weekly)	5.060

Newspaper reading was increasingly dominated by the London press, invariably called the 'national' press. The number of provincial dailies declined from
41 in 1921 to 25 in 1937, while the circulation of the London press more than
doubled in the same period. Over the period as a whole there were some
important changes in the comparative popularity of the London dailies.

---

[58] Jenkinson, *What Do Boys and Girls Read?* (2nd ed., London, 1946), 178.

[59] L. Moss and K. Box, 'An Enquiry into Newspaper Reading Amongst the Civilian Population
(June–July 1943)', Wartime Social Survey, NS No. 37a, ii (London, n.d.).

[60] Hulton-Deutsch, *Readership Survey, 1950* (London, 1950), 5.

Percentage of Total Readership held by National Dailies[61]

	1931–2	1950
Daily Express	18.67	31.4
Daily Herald	11.82	12.2
Daily Mail	26.64	16.7
News Chronicle	13.05	9.3
Daily Mirror	8.97	27.4
Daily Sketch	8.15	n/a
Daily Telegraph	3.84	6.9
Morning Post	1.98	n/a
Times	3.11	1.9

The two most obvious changes over the period were the steady decline in the relative readership of the *Daily Mail* and the big rise in that of the *Daily Express* and, even more impressive, of the *Daily Mirror*. The position of the Sundays is different: what distinguishes them is the huge increase in multiple readership.

Percentage of Total Readership Held by Sunday Newspapers[62]

	1931–2	1950
News of the World	24.32	47.6
People	22.55	35.2
Sunday Pictorial	18.87	32.9
Sunday Express	12.49	25.8
Sunday Chronicle	10.87	6.3
Sunday Dispatch	12.22	16.8
Empire News	10.17	10.3
Sunday Graphic	8.55	6.7
Sunday Times	3.55	4.5
Observer	2.86	4.3

The *News of the World* and the *Sunday Express* were the most spectacular beneficiaries of this, but only the *Sunday Chronicle* and *Sunday Graphic* failed to benefit at all.

There were few significant regional variations in the readership of the national dailies explicable only by regional loyalties or traditions. One 'national' paper alone had a manifest regional bias: the Manchester-based *Empire News*, a Sunday, the bulk of whose readership was in Lancashire. Yet even its position was being eroded. In the early 1930s it outsold by a fair margin the *News of the World* and the *People* in Lancashire. But by 1950, even there,

---

[61] This table is derived from the *Investigated Press Circulations* (London, 1932), and the Hulton-Deutsch, *Readership Survey, 1950*. See also the results of Mark Abrams' 1934 survey in Jeffrey and McClelland, 'A World Fit to Live In', in Curran, Smith, and Wingate, *Impacts and Influences*, 38.

[62] Ibid.

it had fallen behind both. The *Daily Express* historically had a metropolitan bias and the *Daily Mail* a provincial one. By 1950 this too had almost disappeared. Although the *Daily Mail* retained a slight provincial bias, the *Daily Express* easily outsold it in all parts of the country. The *Daily Mirror*, even at its most popular, was primarily a southern paper. Such bias as there was in the reading of the national press was in fact largely determined by relative prosperity. The North-West of England, its least prosperous region, bought and read fewer papers of every category than the rest of the country.

What did survive in the larger provincial towns, particularly in the larger provincial towns, was localism. An extraordinarily high proportion of households in such towns took a local paper:

Percentage of Households Taking Local Papers in Selected Towns[63]

Town	Paper	
Newcastle	Newcastle Evening Chronicle	69.59
Bristol	Evening Times and Echo	68.05
Manchester	Manchester Evening News	64.98
Liverpool	Liverpool Echo	82.44
Leeds	Yorkshire Evening Post	78.38
Birmingham	Birmingham Mail	66.29
Plymouth	Western Evening Herald	68.24

Most of these papers were evening and did not, therefore, compete with the national dailies. Nevertheless, their readership is striking. More than twice as many households in these towns took a local paper as took any one national daily, including the Sundays. Sport was one reason for this. All these towns, including Plymouth, had, for example, at least one football team of national repute, and Manchester, Liverpool, and Birmingham (just) had two. The sporting news, particularly football, was of real significance to local males. They also had an exchange-and-mart element as guides to the sale of second-hand goods. More generally, for their residents the larger provincial towns still had an importance as a focus for daily life which the national dailies could not represent.

Furthermore, the provincial dailies were much more socially inclusive than the national press. Unlike them, the readership of the national dailies, with the partial exception of the *Daily Express*, had distinct social characteristics. The Wartime Social Survey found in 1943 that only the *Daily Express* had a substantial readership among all social groups, though it was little read by those with higher incomes or university degrees. The *Daily Herald* had a relatively high proportion of male readers, but was especially popular with those with an elementary education, workers in heavy manufacturing, miners, and transport and building workers. It was very much the paper of the Labour-voting

[63] These figures are from the *Investigated Press Circulations* and are for 1932.

male working class. The *Daily Mail*, as we know, was more popular in the provinces, but also with older readers. The *Daily Mirror*'s readership was comparatively young and poor. Amongst civilians it was more popular with women than with men. It became, however, a forces' paper, read widely by young soldiers and sailors, and that redressed the balance. The *Daily Telegraph* was increasingly the paper of the 'established' middle class, particularly at the expense of the *Daily Mail*. The *Times* remained the paper of the country's élite.[64]

Although there was a fairly high degree of stability among readerships, papers were in active competition for new readers. These could be acquired either from other papers or from the non-reading part of the population. In competing for readers papers tended to adopt both strategies. The famous 'circulation war' of the early 1930s between the *Daily Herald*, the *Daily Mail*, and the *Daily Express* was largely the result of an attempt by the *Daily Herald* to steal the readership of the other two—but not entirely. The policy of the *Daily Mirror* after 1935 was largely to recruit new readers—but again not entirely.

Who did well or badly, and why? Over the whole period two kinds of papers suffered. The first were the excessively political. The *Daily Mail* (as we have seen)[65] over-committed itself to a rather crude anti-socialism. It lost readers to the *Daily Express* which, particularly under Arthur Christiansen, emphasized sport, women's interests, novelties, and the good life, without ceasing to be an anti-Labour paper. In the same way the *Morning Post*, almost a caricature of a Tory middle-class paper, lost ground to, and was eventually absorbed by, the *Daily Telegraph* which, while equally Conservative, was less openly partisan and possessed a wider 'non-political' sphere. The second kind of newspaper was the over-restrained. The 'circulation war' had begun when J. B. Elias sought to popularize the *Daily Herald* by reducing the size of its pages, putting illustrations on every page, increasing the emphasis upon sport and racing and confining politics (pro-Labour) to the editorial page. The *Daily Express*, in its successful efforts to compete, followed the same strategy. The *Daily Mirror*, partly on the advice of the American advertising agency J. Walter Thompson, took this a step further after Rothermere sold it in 1935 to H. G. Bartholomew and Hugh Cudlipp. Under them, the headlines got bigger, the stories shorter and the illustrations more profuse. During the war it skilfully presented itself as the spokesman for other ranks everywhere and for everyone with a grievance. It was brassy, but had room for an acerbic columnist 'Cassandra' (William Connor) as well as the voluptuous comic-strip heroine Jane, whose clothes kept falling off.

All papers which wished to survive were forced to accept the trend towards greater informality. Much of what happened, particularly in sports reporting, was thought 'American'. A number of papers, like *People*, *The News of the World*,

---

[64] Moss and Box, 'An Enquiry into Newspaper Reading', 2–3.
[65] See above, p. 68.

and the *Daily Express*, began to write their sports reports in an aggressive mid-Atlantic style. Butler of *The News of the World* and Wignall of the *Daily Express* were particularly influenced by the manner of American sports reporting and the example of America's highly commercialized sport. The result was a formulaic, violent, pseudo-American demotic style very similar to and perhaps based on the dialogue of the pseudo-American crime novels: 'Put another nickel in', 'I've a hunch Chelsea are gonna kick history right in the pants', etc.[66]

How readers reacted to this is hard to tell. They were presented with strong images, as they were in most American popular literature, and many obviously liked them. But people reacted against American overstatement—distaste for American 'bullshit' united nearly all serving men and women during the Second World War—in part because its permanent hyperbole eliminated nuance. No one, for instance, knew whether a goal really was as stupefying or a manager as utterly incompetent as the papers described them. Its real effect was probably political. The newspapers which published this highly charged 'democratic' anti-sports' élite commentary—the *People*, for instance, strongly supported the football players' union against 'corrupt' administrators— were themselves strongly Conservative. Furthermore, the mid-Atlantic style adopted by Hoby *et al.* was not, in fact, very different from the *People*'s or the *News of the World*'s plain-man, no-nonsense political rhetoric. By associating a Conservative political rhetoric with a 'democratic' style of reporting, these papers were able to give a 'democratic' face to modern Conservatism.

The *Daily Express* and, for a time, the *Daily Herald* were popular because they associated themselves with changes to the market. In doing so their direction was generally downwards. But the market's movements were not universally downwards. The best example of a journal exploiting its upwards direction was the British edition of an American import, the *Reader's Digest*. By 1950 this had a British readership of 4.6 million and had excited some British imitation. The *Reader's Digest* was well-produced but it was quite within the tradition of British papers like *Tit-Bits*. It combined humour, human interest, popular science, truth-stranger-than-fiction, and 'current affairs' in a lively manner. Readers could also buy, and did, *Reader's Digest* novels: well-known novels of the day abbreviated for a market which was interested but would not have read them full-length. Much more sophisticated than *Tit-Bits* and other variety magazines, it was read by men more than women and counted on an evolving literacy. The *Reader's Digest* came closer to representing a mass middlebrow market than anything else in the period, precisely because it was accessible to those whose reading had hitherto been only lowbrow.

Women read fewer papers than men largely because the newspapers were written primarily for men, despite the increasing attention to 'women's

---

[66] Fishwick, *English Football*, 101–5.

interests'. Both the national and provincial press continued to be dominated by 'masculine' themes, sport, crime, politics, and sex, all reported in an aggressively off-putting way. A sense that this was not their world drove women to magazines tailored exclusively for them.

There had always been a large number of women's papers and magazines. In 1932 there were 25 women's weekly magazines with significant sales, one fortnightly (*Vogue*), and 14 monthly. The most popular magazine by some margin was *Woman's Weekly* with a readership of nearly 1.1 million, followed by *Home Notes* (684,000) and *Home Chat* (601,000). The fourth largest was a woman's blood, *Red Letter* (595,000).[67] By 1951, *Woman's Weekly* had been displaced by *Woman* and *Woman's Own*, which had huge readerships: nearly one-quarter of all women read at least one of them. *Woman's Weekly* was read by less than half that number. *Red Letter* was now only 16th in order of popularity. *Woman and Home*, *Vogue*, and *Good Housekeeping* were now 5th, 6th, and 7th. There was some class bias in that order. *Vogue* was very much an upper-middle-class magazine, though it had a considerable circulation among the middle class as a whole. *Good Housekeeping* and *Ideal Home* were also very middle-class. *Woman and Home*, *Picturegoer*, *Woman's Illustrated* and *Home Chat* were disproportionately working-class. But the two great mass circulation magazines, *Woman* and *Woman's Own*, though having a slight bias towards working-class women, were read almost equally amongst all social classes. The dethroned *Woman's Weekly*, however, clearly had a disproportionately working-class readership.

Woman and *Woman's Own* were both introduced in the late 1930s and were markedly superior in production to their competitors. Gravure-printed and in colour, they were modelled on the better American women's magazines. With the partial exception of *Vogue*, in which there was much *haute couture*, the more successful women's journals, unlike the chatty and bitty women's papers of the past, now emphasized consumption, 'modern' housekeeping, and femininity. The typical reader of *Woman* and *Woman's Own* was conceived as a well-informed and professional home-maker, who would, somehow, be able to employ the new technology of housekeeping as both a pleasure and a full-time job. Many women, particularly those influenced by American styles, obviously found this approach acceptable, partly because it effectively excluded men from any role in the domestic sphere—despite the injunctions of the companionate marriage which all were simultaneously urged to follow. For other women, however, they established domestic standards as the norm which could not possibly be reached, short of an exhausting routine.

Throughout this period the means by which speech and style of writing might be made uniform were transformed. The nineteenth century had exposed the English to something like a popular press and a standard written

---

[67] For *Red Letter*'s circulation, see above, p. 493.

language. In the interwar years, however, the popular press became a mass press and was joined by two even more powerful agencies, film and radio. By the mid-1950s a significant and rapidly increasing number of people possessed in television a yet more powerful agent. The immediacy and universality of press, cinema, and radio had implications for language as a whole—accent, syntax, and idiom; and an idiom (so powerful were these agencies) which might be as much American as English. Some did not worry about this. Others, however, did. How English was spoken, and whose English was spoken, became, therefore, serious political and social issues.

The issue of accent and syntax, always a cause for anxiety in England, became even more fraught when the BBC attempted to impose a form of 'educated' English on the nation via the accents and linguistic manners of its announcers. In 1926 the corporation appointed an Advisory Committee on Spoken English under the chairmanship of Robert Bridges, a founder member of the Society for Pure English, to rule on matters of linguistic good form. The committee also included another founder member of that society, the phonetician Arthur Lloyd James, another professor of phonetics, Daniel Jones, and Jonathan Forbes Robertson, 'renowned as the finest speaker of Shakespeare'.[68] Lloyd James wished to identify a form of 'educated' English which would fall within a 'narrow band' of southern English whose practitioners would be 'recognized as educated speakers throughout the country. They may broadcast without fear of adverse intelligent criticism.'[69] The corporation wanted to avoid 'extreme variants'. The BBC, the announcements editor said,

can only be thought of by the listener as individual. It has many voices but one mouth. It can speak in many styles, but the variety is due to the differences in subject matter and must not betray any inconsistency of treatment. It was a commonplace that 'announcers sound alike'. That is a tribute to their training.[70]

The BBC had originally embarked upon this enterprise, characteristically for the time, in order to avoid giving 'offence'. It sought an accent that would be acceptable to all listeners and concluded that 'educated English' was the one. Unwisely, however, the corporation began to think it was determining the English of the future. The more overt became its intention the more controversial was the policy. The correspondence columns of the *Listener* published endless comment; the press was full of cartoons of BBC announcers speaking with hot potatoes in their mouths; and papers with large working-class readerships, like the *People*, continuously attacked 'BBC English'.[71] George Orwell spoke of a BBC 'dialect' which working men and women 'instinctively

---

[68] P. J. Waller, 'Democracy and Dialect, Speech and Class', in P. J. Waller (ed.), *Politics and Social Change in Modern Britain* (Brighton, 1987), 7.

[69] Ibid. 8.   [70] Scannell and Cardiff, *Social Survey of British Broadcasting*, i. 176.

[71] Pegg, *Broadcasting and Society*, 160–1.

dislike and cannot easily master'. In any case, he thought the 'educated' English accent 'undoubtedly very bad and ... likely to be abandoned'.[72] Compton Mackenzie dismissed it as 'finicking, suburban, synthetic, plus-fours gentility'.[73]

As a policy it did not have much immediate effect. Jennings and Gill wrote of the BBC's influence that

with few exceptions, syntax remains unaffected, and in ordinary conversation in the home, especially among the older people, the local colloquial mode of speech with its native raciness holds its own. In some instances, whether as a result mainly of broadcasting or of education in the schools, there appears to be a conscious use of two distinct modes of speech in the homes and at business or for social purposes.[74]

The encouragement of two 'languages' was, of course, the policy of the board of education, which made plain its hostility to any attempt to impose a bloodless 'official' language on children in state schools at the expense of the demotic. Although individual teachers were certainly sympathetic to the BBC, the corporation received no support from the board as a whole.[75]

The BBC overrated the power of radio and the susceptibility of its listeners— partly because changes to language are usually very slow rather than abrupt. In 1920 H. C. Wyld argued that English was moving in two directions:

The first is the gradual decay of ceremoniousness and formality which has overtaken the speech and modes of address, no less than the manners of good society. The second is the effort ... after 'correctness' or correctitude which, on the one hand, has almost eliminated the use of oaths and has softened away many coarsenesses or crudities of expression ... while on the other it has, by a rigid appeal to spelling—the very worst and most unreliable court for the purpose—definitely ruled out as 'incorrect' or 'slipshod' or 'vulgar', many pronunciations and grammatical constructions which had arisen in the natural course of the development of English, and were formerly universal among the best speakers.[76]

The decline of 'incorrect' upper-class English and the decay of formality were, he argued, the result of 'bringing different classes of the population into positions of prominence and power' and the proportionate decline in the authority 'of the older governing classes'. Linguistic changes were a result of natural social interactions rather than a form of social coercion.

Many people, particularly mothers ambitious for their children, did worry about accent, and a sizeable part of the country's educational system was devoted to inculcating a 'correct' one. The fear for accent and syntax was not confined to an upwardly mobile middle class. Working-class mothers who

[72] Orwell, 'The English People', in Orwell and Angus, *Collected Essays ... of George Orwell*, iii. 27–9.
[73] Scannell and Cardiff, *Social History of British Broadcasting*, i. 298–9.
[74] Jennings and Gill, *Broadcasting in Everyday Life*, 19.   [75] See above, p. 265.
[76] H. C. Wyld, *A History of Modern Colloquial English* (London, 1920), 18.

wanted 'the best' were equally sensitive. 'Mrs Cook', the wife of Walter Brier-ley's miner-hero, 'Jack',

insisted that her husband should not use the dialect when speaking to their son; she quite realised that in the streets and at school it must inevitably beat into his nature, but at home, at least, he must know that there was another language. Later she would tell him that unless he could use this other language, there would be small chance of his escaping from the poverty and dullness which even now he was beginning to see was limiting him. His mother, in her youth, had had lessons in elocution, and it was her speech and manner which had made her such a success as maid to the local doctor.[77]

Everywhere, however, local accents (if not dialects) and usages remained common. Anyone who served in the forces during the Second World War learnt how far from a single speech community England was. The development of a common colloquial language, Wyld argued, was the result of participation (men more than women) in different 'speech communities'. Colloquial English emerged as a 'compromise' between the different idiom of such communities. The existence of several distinct speech communities was well understood by those, like 'Mrs Cook', who were ambitious for themselves or their children. The extent to which regional/local accents survived suggests that much of the English working class and a smaller part of the middle class still inhabited single rather than several speech communities. Social and occupational relationships remained so localized that the linguistic 'compromises' which constitute language-change rarely had to or could be made. The radio itself, of course, like the cinema or television, was a speech community, but membership of it was passive rather than active. Though powerful, it was never as powerful as the BBC, for example, thought, because as a community it involved no linguistic exchange. People could (and did) copy it but they could never 'compromise' with it.

The Americanization of the language was almost as fraught a question as accent. The English had long been aware that their English was being permeated by American usage. Some regretted it, but most accepted it as a fact of life. In this period, however, the issue acquired a much sharper political and ideological edge, due largely to the fact that Britain's status *vis à vis* the United States was much more problematical than it had been in 1914, and that the technology of American influence—the cinema, radio, record player, magazines, and pulp fiction—had become exceptionally authoritative in a short period of time. Moreover, during the Second World War itself, there were real linguistic exchanges with real Americans, so encouraging those 'compromises' which Wyld suggested determine the colloquial. Contemporaries probably exaggerated the relative speed with which the language would be Americanized, for the reasons they exaggerated the speed with which

---

[77] Brierley, *Means Test Man*, 21.

'educated' English would come to predominate. None the less, defence of the purity of English English at the time could and did take on an openly anti-American turn. The BBC explicitly associated its attempt to promote 'educated' English with attacks upon American usage. In 1929 the supervisor of outside broadcasts argued that 'the national outlook and with it, character, is gradually becoming Americanized'. In 1931, Basil Maine in the *Radio Times* concluded that Americanization was responsible for 'new manners of thinking, for higher pressure of living, for discontent among normally contented people, for big ideas and for "Oh yeah".' The controller of programmes even criticized locutions like 'We bring to you', 'We offer you', used by some of the corporation's announcers. All remained a persistent preoccupation of the Programmes Board.[78]

The reality of Americanization is hard to assess. The cinema almost certainly hastened it since its linguistic styles, like the closely related style of the American crime novels, were all too imitable. A young English farmer wrote of the movie *To Have and Have Not* (1944), which made Lauren Bacall instantly famous, as follows:

Another new film that gave me pleasure was *To Have and Have Not*—and I must admit that my pleasure was derived from the presence of Miss Lauren Bacall, she's terrific, she's disturbing and she can act. She is seductive but not voluptuous, alluring but not flashy, sophisticated but not haughty and I think she's the most startling thing to flit across the screen in years—if she had not been in the film I would not have been impressed—her personality literally radiates virility and a sort of slithery fascinating glamour.[79]

This, of course, is a caricature of what Bogart himself might have said in *To Have and Have Not*, or any gumshoe in a Mickey Spillane novel—a testimony to the peculiar power of the genre and its attractiveness to the English.

There was also a self-conscious borrowing of American idiom in perhaps an unprecedented way. E. M. Delafield records that as she (the 'provincial lady') left on her first trip to the United States, she had an urgent request from her son for any '*new*' American slang: 'Not, he explicitly states, words like Jake and Oke, which everybody knows already.'[80] The introduction of American slang into the conversation was often prefaced by a half-apologetic 'as our American cousins would say'. But, half-apologetic or not, people still used it.

Orwell thought there were three reasons for the large-scale importation of American usage into English English: because it was vivid; because it was often time-saving; and because (most important) the English could adopt Americanisms 'without crossing a class barrier'. A 'snobbish' Englishman would call a policeman a 'cop', but not a 'copper'. For the working classes use of American-

[78] Scannell and Cardiff, *Social History of British Broadcasting*, i. 292.
[79] Mayer, *British Cinemas and their Audiences*, 225.
[80] Delafield, *Diary of a Provincial Lady*, 295.

isms was a means of escaping from 'Cockney' (*sic*) without adopting BBC English. Especially in big towns, he suggested, working-class children used Americanisms from the moment they learnt to talk—even when perfectly good English expressions already existed. American influence, he thought, would be irresistible until 'new life' could be put into English:

And it is difficult to do this while words and idioms are prevented from circulating freely among all sections of the population. English people of all classes now find it natural to express incredulity by the American slang phrase 'sez you'. Many would even tell you in good faith that 'sez you' has no English equivalent.

He cited several equivalents, such as 'garn' or 'come off it'.[81]

Orwell wrote this in 1943–4 when both the presence and influence of Americans were at their height, and when the self-conscious borrowings of Americanisms were at their height. In fact, the tendency was for self-conscious borrowings to have a comparatively short life. 'Sez you', for example, has long been dead in English usage (and American), while 'come off it' is very much alive. Indeed, the whole of the 'sez who–sez you' business of the 1940s was more a fad than anything. There is, however, some plausibility to his argument that American expressions were class-neutral. North Americans and antipodeans traditionally had a certain licence not open to the English working class precisely because they were outside the class system, and, therefore, could not be expected to know better. The same was perhaps true of their accent and idiom. But this argument goes only so far. It is in reality highly unlikely that a 'snobbish' Englishman would then have called a policeman a 'cop' and working-class children were more likely to use American vocabulary primarily because they were more exposed to American popular culture—films, popular music, comic strips, and cheap magazines. As E. M. Delafield's experience suggests, children and teenagers generally were more prone to Americanisms because American popular culture was more familiar to them than to adults.

The influence of American usage was persistent and irreversible. But not all idiom had a long life. Many of the borrowings did not survive the American occupation during the war, and of those that did, a number, like the verbal nouns 'finalize', 'hospitalize', etc., were plainly useful.

The comparative propensity of the English to read benefited many. The middlebrow novels, though much despised by high culture, were nearly all reasonably well written and usually (though certainly not always) about non-trivial subjects; they—and the book clubs which promoted them—introduced many to the idea that 'serious' literature was at least approachable. Penguins were, via middlebrow literature, eventually to make available the 'classics' of European literature to many who would never have otherwise read

[81] Orwell, 'The English People', 27–8.

them. The middle class on the whole exploited its literacy in culturally positive ways. Whether the working class did, however, has been questioned. In 1957 Richard Hoggart published *The Uses of Literacy*, a largely pessimistic analysis of the ways the working class had used, or been permitted to use, their literacy. His criticism of working-class culture—the excess of 'homeliness', the personalization of social and political issues, the inability to pursue an abstract argument, the non-existence of the 'future', the difficulty many working men and women had in combining their roles as individual members of a family and as citizens, the ease with which they were 'duped' when approached in a 'homely' way—were not new and within a year elevated into a sociological law by Basil Bernstein.[82] What distinguished Hoggart's argument is the emphasis he placed upon 'literacy', upon what people read, and upon socio-linguistic and, therefore, conceptual incapacity. So, for example, the magazines designed for the working class

must be capable of being read in a very easy gear, or more, in a free-wheeling sort of way. There must be no connected sequences of any length; everything is interesting, as interesting as the next thing, if only it is short, unconnected, and pepped-up. The rain of undifferentiated anecdotes pours down: a hen is born at Bolton (Lancs.) with two heads, a politician commits suicide, a mother in Edmonton (Alberta, Can.), has her third set of triplets, what odd habits lemmings have, a cyclist in Sunderland is lifted clean off the road by a freak wind. One doesn't read such papers; one 'looks at' them.[83]

One consequence of this was that 'a very large number of people are being held down at an appallingly low level in their reading.'[84] Working people were being 'culturally robbed';[85] and literature not so much used as abused.

Hoggart's argument is not easily proved or disproved. One of its major premisses, that papers and magazines read by the working class 'have become a good deal worse during the last fifteen or twenty years than they were during the fifty years before',[86] is probably false. Furthermore, an argument which depends upon the view that *Police News* and 'old broad sheets' on executions represented a superior literacy to the twentieth-century press is not convincing.[87] In any case, a good deal of the popular middle-class press of the time was not much better. Yet Hoggart is right that much of what the working class read was characterized by bittiness and equivalence—everything was equivalent to everything else—which undeniably had political consequences.

As typical, however, of working-class literacy as bittiness was what Hoggart himself has called the 'baroque'. What was admired was the grand manner, the florid style, convoluted evocations of passion: the most obvious qualities of the erotic bloods, romances, and over-written crime thrillers and Westerns

    [82] B. J. Bernstein, 'The Sociological Determinants of Perception', *British Journal of Sociology*, 9 (1958), 160–5; reprinted in Bernstein, *Class, Codes and Control*, i (London, 1971), 23–38.
    [83] Hoggart, *Uses of Literacy*, 202–3.   [84] Ibid. 234.   [85] Ibid. 243.   [86] Ibid. 211.
    [87] Ibid. 232.

read in their tons by working people. The grand manner much influenced the writing style of young working-class women particularly, either in prose exercises or in the torrential letters they wrote each other.[88] Working people could thus acquire rather ornate vocabularies. Jackson and Marsden, for instance, were careful to note that the working-class men and women they interviewed 'had larger vocabularies than they could pronounce, and larger too than they would easily find in their daily paper'.[89] The baroque, however, might simply be something which left outsiders perplexed. E. M. Delafield described as an 'extraordinary legend' an evacuee version of *Under the Spreading Chestnut Tree*:

> Under a spreading chestnut-tree
> Stands the bloody A.R.P.
> So says the ——ing B.B.C.[90]

Marie Paneth, working with children who were by conventional standards more or less illiterate, was repeatedly amazed by their grim humour and literary adventurousness. Asked to write a Christmas play they chose to set it (and Christmas Day) in a mortuary, and to make the mortuary keeper its hero: ('Then in came the mortuary keeper, his belly full of beer, / Get down you silly bath-buns you can't do that here'). She also recorded a legend even more extraordinary than E. M. Delafield's: a letter written during the war by a North Paddington child to American children thanking them for Christmas presents. Dr Paneth, without exaggeration, called it 'an astonishing piece'.[91]

Dear——
  I hope you are all right
  or half left
  how are you getting you old cock sparrow
  how do you like it ~~were you are~~ in americar
  I have no more to say so good night my pretty cock sparrow
          Amen Amen
          xxxxxxxxxxxxx
          Good day

Whatever is said about the grammar or spelling it cannot be denied that the child had flair, as did those who wrote Christmas Day in the Mortuary. This, in reality, was perhaps the worst abuse of working-class literacy: that the linguistic ebullition and confidence working-class children could display came to so little in adulthood. For many working men and women there was nothing between an almost inarticulate fragmentation of speech and an overcharged grand manner.

---

[88] For their prose style, see Phillips, *Young Industrial Worker*, 104–12; Jephcott, *Rising Twenty*, 182–200, where she reprints a novella, *Greater Love*, by one of her club girls.
[89] Jackson and Marsden, *Education and the Working Class*, 50.
[90] Delafield, *Diary of a Provincial Lady*, 383.　　　[91] Paneth, *Branch Street*, 29.

At the beginning of the chapter it was suggested that what people read depended upon a number of variables. 'Being English' was not one of them. There was no common literature and the reading public was markedly segmented by class, age, sex and, to some extent, region. The closest England came to a common literature was probably the boys' magazines, which, though not much read by adults, were at least read by boys *and* girls from all social classes and all regions. Furthermore, apart from the success of some of the women's magazines in crossing class boundaries, there were few signs of convergence. A common reading public was almost as non-existent in 1951 as in 1918.

The preponderant literature of the period, culturally and politically, was middlebrow. This was so because the middlebrow literary canon included not merely sensation novels or romances or a good read, like J. B. Priestley's novels, but also 'political' novels, novels of conflict, like Deeping's, or novels of social engagement, like those of A. J. Cronin or Winifred Holtby. The latter were 'democratic' novels of social progress, a genre which was, like the Left Book Club or the Penguin Special, virtually killed stone dead by the Labour victory in 1945.

'Popular literature', lowbrow literature, was itself strongly segregated: there was no mass literature as such. Men's fiction, particularly young men's, was almost exclusively sport, sex (in so far as there was a popular sexual literature), crime, and violence. Women's literature was divided between a 'realistic' romantic fiction, like Ruby M. Ayres or Mills and Boon, and the erotic bloods, in which romance was anything but realistic. The Second World War made very little difference to the content of such literature. Stereotypes were somewhat modified and plots more down-to-earth, but they all remained largely asocial and apolitical. The reader of a Mills and Boon, it is true, might have got an inkling of what happened in the 1940s, but not a reader of the erotic bloods. There is, however, little to the view that there was a 'decline' in what the working classes read, as Richard Hoggart implicitly argues. There was nothing to decline from. Indeed, given the big growth in the working-class readership of hobby, technical, and scientific magazines, there may actually have been intellectual development.

English popular literature was throughout the period, particularly during the Second World War, subject to continuous and pervasive American influence. This was both direct and indirect: directly via imported American books and magazines; indirectly via borrowings—of sports reporting or the style of thrillers, for instance. As with American films, many worried about the 'democratic' implications of this. In practice, American style bolstered the status quo: the borrowed literature was usually apolitical anyway, while the English press was able to use a 'democratic' rhetoric, as in the reporting of sport, to legitimate 'anti-socialist' politics.

The English read more newspapers than any other people in the world. The 'national' (i.e. the London) press steadily encroached upon the regions, and the number of regional papers declined throughout the period. In the larger towns, however, there was still great loyalty to local papers, certainly the evening ones, and a large majority of households in the bigger provincial cities still took one. The papers which did well were those, like the *Daily Express*, which were not overtly political, but emphasized leisure and the possibilities of the good life. The success of the *Daily Mirror* in combining a no-nonsense radicalism with a relentlessly 'popular' style was unique and had much to do with the circumstances of the Second World War.

The attempt to promote or impose a common accent and idiom failed. In fact, a form of upper-middle-class speech probably was becoming the 'correct' one, and there was much pressure on people everywhere not to use dialect or a 'bad' accent. But this was very slow to work itself out (and may never do so). 'BBC' English was rather despised by everyone and even the BBC recognized its limitations. The persistence of regional and class accents and idiom was evidence of how still comparatively isolated from each other England's speech communities were. As they were in a wider cultural sense.

Conclusion

Classes and Cultures has sought to analyse English society and its civil cultures at a peculiarly heightened and potentially transformative moment in England's history. The book has several concurrent arguments and we should now bring them together.

1 | *Men and women*

At a public level England remained an almost exclusively single-sex society. State and economy were dominated by men, and this changed little over the period. At all levels, the most important variable which determined membership of formal associations—in effect, participation in public life—was neither class nor region but gender.[1] Thus most women's relationships with the world were mediated in some way by their relationships with their husbands, fathers, or brothers. These relationships were not, however, socially uniform. In most working-class families role-segregation, even at the end of the period, was still severe. Men inhabited the public sphere, their lives centred, if not upon work as such (to which many were indifferent), then upon the workplace and its sociability. For some men, like miners, this sociability could be so intense as almost to exclude their families entirely. It was usually agreed that the family's 'public opinion', on politics for example, was left to the husband—'who knows about these things'. Even when a wife thought he did not know about these things, which was probably quite often, she thought it prudent not to intervene. The working-class family, therefore, was often 'politically' fractured: role-segregation encouraged in husbands and wives different views of the world. One probable result was the greater inclination of women to vote Conservative.

Husbands and wives rarely had friends in common—had, in fact, different definitions of friendship. The more 'traditional' the family, the more the wife's 'friends' were her family; while her closest 'friend'—often the dominating influence of her life—was her mother. But in those same households the wife's hegemony in the private sphere, the home, could be as complete as her hus-

---

[1] T. Cauter and J. S. Downham, *The Communication of Ideas: A Study of Contemporary Influences on Urban Life* (London, 1954), 64.

band's in the public. In them the husband might be a shadowy figure, whose presence was expressed only by alternating bouts of violence and generosity. In retrospect, offspring of those interwar households thought women pecu- liarly disadvantaged: 'the thirties', Phyllis Willmott wrote of her working-class mother, 'were not a good time to be a wife and mother.'[2] But they were no worse than any previous decade, and in the sexual politics of the period there was at least one ground, the domestic, where a woman might hope to approach a man at least as his equal.

Rehousing, either enforced or voluntary, slowly changed the pattern, as did the tendency at the end of the period for women to have their (ever-) smaller number of children in the early years of marriage, which freed them to rejoin the labour force. The matrilocality of working-class households was necessar- ily then weakened, and with it the authority of 'Mum', who in any case was likely also to have joined the labour force. Higher real wages and the thinning- out of an exclusively masculine work-based sociability kept the husband more at home, and blurred sexual roles: men became on the whole readier to share in household tasks and the raising of children, and were encouraged to culti- vate that love of home and family they shared with most other Englishmen, but which the sheer nastiness of older housing usually frustrated. Patterns of sociability did not, however, 'converge' with middle-class sociability. Men saw less of workmates, wives less of family, but neither necessarily saw more of neighbours, who remained as they always had been—acquaintances rather than friends. Families tended to become more isolated rather than members of new social networks—at least when their children were young.

In middle-class households gender relations were probably more compli- cated. Though middle-class women accepted that their role was primarily domestic, role-segregation was hardly ever as remorseless. Husbands were expected to be—and many plainly wanted to be—domestically active. In the 'companionate marriage', the ideal which middle-class spouses were increas- ingly being urged to practise, they were assumed to have interests and friends in common. And most middle-class families seem at any rate to have approxi- mated this norm. Social relations based upon shared friendships with non-kin continued to distinguish middle- from working-class sociability. There is also evidence that where job-satisfaction was intrinsically low middle-class men found the home genuinely a place of recreation, where social energy could be expended. Furthermore, a middle-class man's occupational status—particu- larly in business or the free professions—was increasingly coming to depend (as to some extent it always had) on his wife's social skills.[3]

But the companionate marriage was itself problematical. The absent

---

[2] Willmott, *Growing Up in a London Village*, 134.
[3] Lewis and Maude, *English Middle Classes*, 15.

husband was not only a working-class phenomenon; an inescapable fact of the time was the development of a predominantly masculine and almost coercive middle-class sociability. Although, for example, the Freemasons denied that the lodges had become agencies for job-promotion, it was widely assumed they had, and in many private and public sector occupations (including the armed forces) it was thought that membership of a Masonic lodge (or something similar) was necessary for advance. While women could have a subordinate, very subordinate, adjunct role in all this they were, unlike working-class women whose social exclusion by their menfolk was mainly informal, formally excluded from lodge sociability, except for the annual dance. Women had alternative social networks, like the Women's Institutes or Townswomen's Guilds, and middle-class men spent less time at pub or club; nevertheless there was an important area of a man's life where the wife had little or no place; and this was true of a growing number of middle-class families.

Nor could role-sharing do much to ease the frustrations of 'over-educated' middle-class women. The school system did not, on the whole, train middle-class girls to be middle-class wives: many of the girls' secondary schools were very reluctant to teach 'domestic' subjects at all. By the mid-1950s, when a significant proportion of middle-class girls was going to university, the phenomenon of the non-working wife with the same and sometimes better educational qualifications as her husband was not unknown. A public role via the Women's Institutes or Townswomen's Guilds was not a satisfactory substitute for a professional career; nor was it easy to turn domesticity into one. Nor, indeed, was there a single ideal of domesticity. There were those women in particular who, influenced by American models, were enthusiastic home-builders for whom a modern, 'labour-saving', and increasingly servantless domesticity was a vocation and to whom the middle-class women's journals appealed; there was an aggressive, rather politicized domesticity; and there were those who simply made the best of things with a less than total commitment.

It had been generally accepted since the late nineteenth century that women could have a public role—even if few did—and they were more prominent in public life in 1950 than before the war. There were, for example, 21 women MPs in 1950 compared with 9 in 1935—though there was no significant rise in their number for another thirty years. But this role allowed them only a kind of public domesticity. There were certain understood 'women's interests'—health, education, housing—and women were normally confined to them. With the possible exception of Margaret Bondfield (minister of labour, 1929–31), all the women who held political office (including the two other women cabinet ministers, Ellen Wilkinson and Florence Horsburgh)[4] served in 'domestic' departments.

---

[4] Both were ministers of education—*the* 'domestic' portfolio for women.

At no point in this period were feminist organizations really able to weaken such stereotyping. The enfranchisement of women in 1918 and 1928, which seemed to complete one episode in feminist history, together with the strong assertion of domesticity in the interwar years, left feminism in an impasse. The times seemed not to favour radical political feminism, yet the case for an active feminism was as strong as ever. In the event, most feminist organizations adjusted to circumstances and politicized domesticity. The campaigns for family allowances, birth control, the health of mothers, and the conditions of urban life were, in effect, highly political, but political in the private rather than the public sphere. And here they had some success.

They were less successful in the sphere of work. The 1919 legislation was never enforced and in several professions (notably teaching) the restriction on women's entry were even tightened in the interwar years. After the Second World War the marriage bar was dropped in a number of professions and some, like the diplomatic service, opened to women for the first time. The campaign for equal pay, despite the setback of the 1944 Education Act,[5] became serious. Yet the net effect of these advances was minimal: the proportion of women in the higher professions in the early 1950s was no higher than in 1914. The willingness of married women after 1945 to return to work significantly modified the age-specificity of the female workforce, but that was neither the product of nor did it produce new social attitudes. It was mainly the result of changes in the labour market: particularly the creation of large numbers of unskilled and part-time jobs in light industry and the service sector. Where women worked they continued to work for inferior pay; and jobs which were not already inferior became inferior as soon as women entered them. Furthermore, the culture of women's work was relatively poor; though many married women enjoyed the social relationships of the workplace, such relationships were, unlike men's, marginal to their lives. Only older, single women seem to have invested much social or emotional energy into their jobs.

This was partly due to the fact that the Second World War had comparatively little influence on the way women perceived their public lives, even if its effect was not negligible. For a woman like Nella Last it represented apparent liberation from her own fears and her husband's 'moods'.[6] For others whose husbands were in the forces it provided a period of freedom from men and thus led to mixed feelings about demobilization. Many single women and childless married women enjoyed war work and its sociability, and some had a sense of participating in a world-historical event—though few put it that way. But most recognized, often with pleasure, that their post-war role would be domestic and what they wanted from the war was, therefore, also domestic: better housing, better clothing and education, jobs for their husbands. And that they got.

---

[5] When women teachers failed to get equal pay.
[6] For Nella Last, see above, pp. 56–7 n, 308.

2 | *Religion and morality*

England was by formal criteria—meaning, usually, church attendance—one of the most secular societies in the world. Only a comparatively small and declining proportion of its population attended worship regularly; of that proportion fewer working men and women went to church than those of other classes, while working-class social networks were increasingly likely to be secular. Women, regardless of class, made up a growing majority of church attenders—part of that long evolution by which Europe's Christian denominations were becoming 'feminized'—and the relationship between gender and church attendance is probably stronger than any other.

How far people's mentality was secularized is, however, much less certain. There is abundant evidence that various kinds of religious and quasi-religious belief tenaciously survived. The assumption that morality could only be found in religion—'Sunday school teaches you good behaviour'—and not in any secular ethical system was widely held among all social classes. It was this which partly explains why there was so little opposition to the religious prescriptions of the 1944 Education Act. And the belief that 'good behaviour' could be taught only by religion was very resistant to secular changes, as was the belief in semi-religions, vaguely transcendental doctrines, spiritualism and various superstitions; all remained very strong, particularly among women. The presence of astrologers in nearly every popular newspaper and magazine, the eagerness with which they were read and the willingness—the wish—to half-accept their findings was well known, as was the popularity of the charms and good lucks commonly believed (especially during the war) to have protective power.

Attitudes to sexuality and sexual and marital relations were also inextricably tied to popular religion and religious admonitions—particularly to that native Protestantism which destroyed the new Prayer Book. And sexuality was one of the few remaining subjects on which churchmen could pronounce and expect to be heard. Throughout the period, although there was some liberalization of sexual mores (which contemporaries rather exaggerated), fear of sex and sexual knowledge remained very powerful, and for this the churches, and a readiness of state and people to defer to a highly conventional religious definition of sexuality, must bear some of the responsibility.

Whether English 'puritanism' was or was not grounded in English religion, the fear of sexuality, the harshness of discipline, the authority of the 'ritual codes', suggest intense socialization and self-repression: not for nothing were two of the best-known films of the 1940s, *Brief Encounter* and *Black Narcissus*, about sexual frustration. Beyond that the historian is struck by the fear of spontaneity and loss of control in personal and collective behaviour—of which the national agreement to admire the police might be one example. The extraordinary range of taboo subjects implied by the country's censorship of films, theatre, books, and public behaviour was the result both of a fear of disorder in public life and of causing 'offence' or embarrassment in personal relations, and thus disrupting the ideal of depoliticized sociability.

Although these taboos were frequently the subject of ribald humour few were prepared to contest them openly, and there is little evidence that one class was markedly more 'liberal' than another. The thousands who read *No Orchids for Miss Blandish* (if they could lay their hands on it) or who rushed to see it (highly sanitized) as a film (if their local authority had not banned it) rarely disputed the right of the police to seize or the local authorities to ban it. Nor did the millions who bet off-course ever seriously deny the premises of anti-betting legislation or clerics' alarmist prophesies. This was partly a result of the helplessness ordinary people felt before authority; but also of the ideological power of received moralities which persuaded people that certain things they enjoyed and would do whenever they could—like reading salacious novels or betting off-course—were, nevertheless, in some way 'wrong'.

3 | *England, America, and democracy*

The history of England in this period is also the history of the English idea of America. After the First World War when, as Sellar and Yeatman concluded *1066 and All That,* America became 'clearly top nation and history came to a . [full stop]', the United States was a seemingly overwhelming presence at all levels of English life. Even in élite or 'high' culture its influence was strong, if often indirect. As a mass culture, however, 'America' had no rivals: it constituted a number of very powerful and easily perceived images. Its films depicted wealth, glamour, violence, but also sentimentality, domesticity, the good life. Its music was even more 'democratic' than its films, so dynamic and expressive that hardly anyone, however culturally isolated, could escape it. America's literary and spoken idiom, always easily assimilated by English English, was absorbed after 1918 with unprecedented speed—the result of film, radio, pulp literature, and the occupation of England during the Second World War by 1.5 million American servicemen. It was not, in fact, so much its content which made American culture seem 'democratic' as its ebullience, enthusiastic appropriation of new technology, the social possibilities it suggested, the disregard for restraint. It was, Claud Cockburn wrote, the democracy and equality of American culture which 'led British statesmen, thinkers and leaders of the upper sort in general to observe it with alarm and utter their warnings against it'.[7]

However, the 'democratic' nature of American culture was both exaggerated and, to the extent that it was democratic, not easily exported. In England, those who feared American democracy feared most its films. But American films were

---

[7] Quoted in Scannell and Cardiff, *Social History of British Broadcasting,* 298–9.

more democratic in appearance than in fact. Especially after the introduction of the Hayes Code, American film-makers became as nervous of politics as of sex. The films of the 1930s had energy and style but, with one or two notable exceptions, few suggested that the status quo was seriously imperfect. Indeed, like the doings of Society in England, they made inequality acceptable by making it glamorous. Nor were several of their other 'democratic' attributes, like accent or speech, subversive out of context. In any case, though English film-goers repeatedly said they preferred American films to English, in practice they showed no stronger preference for them, and consistently preferred several genres, like the George Formby comedies, which could hardly be less American.

Americanization of the press, in so far as the English press needed Americanizing, positively reinforced the status quo. The 'practical' radicalism of the press, particularly (but not only) its sports reporting, the 'democratic' anti-bureaucratic style, the personalization of issues, the emphasis upon human interest and daily wonders, presented its readership, especially its working-class readership, with a certain form of reality which much favoured a social and political conservatism in general and the Conservative Party in particular.

Attitudes to the United States amongst all social classes were too ambiguous to permit an uncritical assimilation of American culture. All too many were aware of America's economic and military power and their implications for England's international standing to be able to observe American culture other than with mixed feelings. Nearly everyone in the 1940s, however much they admired and envied American power and wealth, thought it in some way unearned. The Americans had entered the war late, had let their allies do the fighting and had then pauperized them: these widely shared feelings were the obverse of the extraordinary popularity of Russia during the Second World War and early post-war. And it meant that English gratitude for Lend-Lease and Marshall Aid was never unalloyed. This accounts not just for the comparative unpopularity of the United States in the two years after the war, but its increasing unpopularity. It was thus difficult, even in the late 1940s and early 1950s, for the élites to co-opt 'America'—as they did a generation later—in an 'anti-socialist' crusade, since that almost certainly would have alienated as many as it attracted.

Acquaintance with real Americans during the Second World War further complicated English responses. American and English soldiers, for example, on the whole worked amicably together *qua* soldiers. The English genuinely admired American ingenuity and easygoing manners. As men *qua* men, however, relations between them were usually hostile or non-existent. And the reason was usually, though not always, sexual jealousy and distrust. The fear of losing girlfriends or (worse) wives to Americans was intense and corrosive.

What was bad for English males should have been good for English females. One-sided competition between British and North American soldiers could only benefit them. In practice, most women's attitudes were also mixed. Though many did it, obvious 'Yank-hunting' was rather frowned on, and over-conscientious Yank-hunters often faced hostility from their workmates. For some women it was a matter of loyalty: you stuck to your own, regardless. Others, who liked the occasional—or even the frequent—fling with GIs, none the less thought, like so many of their countrymen, that the Americans did not deserve their good fortune. Women, less fond of sport and more fond of films and music, were culturally more Americanized than men, more attracted to American styles of life, and almost certainly more sympathetic to Americans—but they were not as sympathetic as they might have been.

The racism of white Americans also caused ill-feeling, which both government and Americans attempted to conceal. English attitudes to black GIs were themselves not straightforward. The government would have preferred no blacks at all, and many worried about the sexual consequences of their presence.[8] When it was clear that Britain would have to accept black servicemen, the home office and the police, in a shaming episode, did all they could to extend US Army segregation into English civilian life—for the most part unsuccessfully.[9] Black GIs, whose numbers were comparatively small anyway, were usually popular; often, indeed, more popular than white Americans. There were several well-publicized cases, some violent, where English civilians took the side of black GIs against white American servicemen. Both the British government and the American authorities were compelled to recognize indigenous attitudes: on arrival white Americans were warned that segregation did not operate in Britain and urged them to accept that. The issue of segregation was not marginal to Anglo-American relations: it was widely discussed, widely disliked and, outside official circles, did not enhance the appearance of America in English eyes.

The English idea of America, of course, often had more to do with England than America. Many English, for example, 'read' American films according to their own circumstances and not as the Americans themselves might have 'read' them. In the 1940s the imagined glamour and wealth of the United States was almost in direct proportion to the perceived austerity and deprivation of English life. Many of the 50,000 British GI war brides discovered to their dismay that the United States was not always as it seemed (or as they wished it to seem) in the pictures; and was also often without the minimum social support they would have received in England.[10]

[8] See, for instance, J. L. Hodson, *Home Front* (London, 1944), 182.
[9] For details, see Reynolds, *Rich Relations*, 216–37. On civilian attitudes, C. Thorne, 'Britain and the Black GIs: Racial Issues and Anglo-American Relations in 1942', *New Community*, 3 (1972); G. A. Smith, 'Jim Crow on the Home Front, 1942–45', *New Community*, 8 (1980).
[10] J. Virden, 'South Atlantic Alliances', *Times Higher Education Supplement*, 29 Oct. 1993; Gardiner, *'Over Here'*, 204–8.

No Englishman or woman could escape America, but how they chose to envisage it was unpredictable and subject to contrary circumstances. To some, that their little country was the heart of a great empire-commonwealth did much to shut out America. To others, that within their own lifetimes such a God-given imperial system should give way to the United States was a cause for anguish. Most, however, were probably torn between both emotions. Furthermore, and not unrelated to this empire-commonwealth, the enormous strength of English sporting traditions—England was to popular sport as America was to popular culture—almost wholly isolated huge areas of English life from American influence. Borrowings, when they did occur, tended to be technological (like the electric hare), and little different from the kinds of things people expected from America anyway.

Moreover, English culture tended to 'smooth out' overt Americanization either, as LeMahieu notes, by domesticating it,[11] or by assimilating it to a familiar, common Anglo-American culture. That most internationally known symbol of 'American' culture, Charlie Chaplin, is a good example.

Nor should we underestimate the effectiveness of the state in protecting indigenous culture. Aside from the press, the principal media of England's popular culture—the cinema, the radio and, at the end of the period, television—all operated within state-delimitated boundaries. The more tightly drawn the boundaries the more successful the medium. By the early 1950s, the one least protected, the film industry, was the one most obviously failing. British television, which in effect became the national cinema, became the national cinema because the state, as it did with the radio, rigged the market against the Americans.

The idea of America was not, therefore, as centrally problematic in England as, for instance, Detlev Peukert has argued it was in Germany: 'The public debate about "America" was really a debate about German society and the challenge that modernity posed to it.'[12] This was not so in England. Furthermore, while it is conventional to speak of England's cultural insularity, no other major state was culturally so open. America, except at the highest levels, was culturally self-sufficient, while France, Germany, Italy, and Russia for much of the time were under régimes which attempted to close them to outside cultural influences. However, whole areas of English life, the cinema, the arts, the sciences, the universities, the press, came under strong continental influences, particularly via Jewish emigration, and in many cases were subject to a long-overdue Germanization.

American democracy could have presented an alternative to English democracy, more open, less inhibited, more energetic, and more self-confident; had it done so those of the English élite who feared it would have been right to fear

---

[11] LeMahieu, *Culture for Democracy*, 82.
[12] D. J. K. Peukert, *The Weimar Republic* (London, 1991), 178.

it. As it turned out, however, they had nothing to fear: partly because of the inherent limitations of American democracy itself; partly because it is very difficult to export a whole social system; partly because the state had some success in keeping America out; partly because the English were always ambiguous about America; and partly because of the resilience of England's own popular culture. In the end the influence of American culture on England was aesthetic and not political. Energy was admired for its energy; toughness for its toughness; glamour for its glamour. In fact, if any other political system was influential at all in the period it was wartime Russia rather than the United States.

4 | *A common culture?*

England had no common culture, rather a set of overlapping cultures. Professor LeMahieu is probably right to argue that in so far as there was a 'democratic' culture in interwar England it was the culture of the new middle class of London, its suburbs and their equivalent elsewhere.[13] This was a class more Americanized, more mobile, less attached to older class cultures. It is also reasonable to argue, as he does, that J. B. Priestley was the representative 'democratic' writer of the period.[14] But 'democratic' culture was as much bound by class, region, and sex as any other. Priestley, for example, was indeed a best-seller, but the majority of the population probably never read him. That people knew and enjoyed certain things in common is true: much popular music, some films and some radio programmes were widely liked and probably even more widely known about. But this does not constitute a common culture.

On the whole, people's cultural preferences were self-enclosed and largely determined by class and sex. 'Books', for instance, to most working men and women did not mean J. B. Priestley but the magazines, newspapers, and paperbacked short stories read by a huge audience, few of whom were middle class. There was, furthermore, within each class a marked gender-bias: throughout the period, for instance, working-class women and girls read in undiminished numbers romance magazines and 'sensation' novels. The closest this readership came to a common culture were Mills and Boon or Ruby M. Ayres's novels, where extravagances of plot and style were moderated by a certain realism. Equally, working men and boys continued to read sports magazines, thrillers and crime novels, various penny dreadfuls, and mass-circulation newspapers. The closest many of them came to a common culture was probably the 1940s *Daily Mirror* where up-to-the-minute techniques of modern journalism were combined with punchy radical politics. The content of mass literature actually changed little: it was melodramatic and largely asocial and apolitical, as were

---

[13] LeMahieu, *Culture for Democracy*, 230–1.   [14] Ibid. 232.

the Gainsborough melodramas—consistently the most popular films of the war years. Military service in the Second World War revealed even to those from the modest middle class, perhaps especially to them, how different the cultural world of the working class was from their own.

The same distinctions operated in sport, another paradigm of the national culture. The English were a sports-loving people, and that was one of their characteristics which outsiders immediately identified. But they loved different sports; only cricket is a possible exception. At the extremes some sports were so socially specific as to be undefinable except by those who played them. And at all levels the sport people played or followed was, like what they read, determined by class, modified, though not by much, by place of birth or residence.

But such obvious cultural distinctions do not appear to have caused significant political resentment except in those spheres, like industrial relations, where there were power structures which institutionalized it. Otherwise resentment was depoliticized by its being confined to the personal. Thus the notoriously bad relations in this period between domestic servants and their employers do not appear to have had wider consequences for class relations. 'Bad' employers were just that: bad employers. Nor did speech and accent—otherwise a social minefield—appear to have caused a specific *political* resentment. One of the things people said they disliked most about British films—at least in the 1930s—was the 'affected' accents of the actors and especially the actresses. Yet basically, for all the apparent unattractiveness of tone and diction, they spoke as the ruling classes spoke. And superior speech, connoting a superior education and social skill, was what many working-class men and women expected of their leaders—as working-class Tories repeatedly admitted. This suggests that hostility to those with affected accents was contextual. In the public sphere a genteel accent was a sign of fitness to govern; in the private, the sphere of personal relations, as in the cinema, it was thought socially aggressive, particularly if the genteel persons were, as English film stars were often believed to be, *arrivistes*. The effect of the distinction between public and private, as of the continuing popularity of an almost wholly apolitical and personalized mass literature, was thus to depoliticize socio-cultural expressions of class difference other than in exceptional periods of social tension.

5 | *Class, democracy, and war*

The First World War seriously disturbed the pattern of English class relations and for the first few years after its end they were very unsettled. By the mid-1920s a social peace was achieved which enthroned the middle class but which did not unseat the upper class, and effectively subordinated the working class. The Second World War, almost inevitably, overthrew that settlement and established a new status quo—though one less favourable to the working class than it might have been.

Contemporaries thought these changes occurred with tranquillity. In fact, they occurred non-violently, which is rather different. Because England's experience in the interwar years *was* so tranquil compared with that of the other major European powers, it is easy to underestimate the degree of social antagonism which underlay it. But the restabilization of English society in the early and mid-1920s did not come easily. We tend to overlook just how intense class-consciousness was, especially among the middle class, in the years after the First World War. It was middle-class bitterness that brought down the Lloyd George coalition in 1922 and it was largely their interests which the interwar political economy was designed to serve. This development was not politically illogical. Although they comprised not much more than one-quarter of the population, the middle class as a whole was the fastest-growing class. The huge expansion of the 'black-coated' middle class, much of it recruited from the upper working class, was one of the most striking social facts of the time. It was also a class changing in composition. The old Edwardian upper middle class gave way as its children declined to enter the church or govern the empire but became businessmen instead. Those who did choose the church or the empire, or free professions like the law, found that their relative emoluments, if not their standing, had perceptibly declined. The middle-middle and lower-middle classes in turn became decreasingly clerkly. By the late 1930s the typical middle-class male was as likely to be a draughtsman as a clerk—a process hastened by the prestige of science and technology in the 1930s and, even more, the 1940s. He (or she) was also less likely to be self-employed; at all levels of the middle class, men and women were becoming employees of others. The new composition of the middle class has historical significance: it meant that the English middle class was at least as attuned to the rhythms of the twentieth century as the German or French. Furthermore, the English ideal of suburban rurality was a very particular form of *rus in urbe*; a pastoralism entirely in harmony with twentieth-century technology, as the increasingly rustic behaviour of the middle classes throughout Europe and North America was to confirm.

The interwar political economy revolved around the 'modern' middle class. So much so that there was a real possibility of conflict within the middle classes between an essentially Edwardian middle class and the newer middle class that grew so rapidly in the 1930s. This conflict was not realized because the Conservative Party was open enough to incorporate both. The Conservative Party, indeed, anxious both to assimilate and represent the newer middle class, was even ready to connive at the weakening of the old. Relatively, the 'modern' middle class was the principal beneficiary of the social and educational systems put into place in the 1930s. Not for nothing did they look on those years as a golden age. Although differences of religion continued to

divide the middle classes—it was still possible, just, to speak of the nonconformist middle class in the late thirties—the decay of these differences, accelerated by the common fear of 'socialism' which united all the middle class,
Edwardian and post-Edwardian, made possible a secular associationalism
which both encouraged an 'apolitical' sociability and a strong sense of middle-
class self-confidence; a belief that English democracy would be defined in its
terms.

Such a democracy, however, did not eliminate the 'upper class'. On the contrary, in some ways it invented the upper class. Although, as we would expect,
the formal 'decline' of the aristocracy continued—though that can be exaggerated—an upper class embodying wealth, power, glamour, and a good part of
the aristocracy flourished in its place. The constant recruitment of wealth,
glamorous persons and avocations, an ever-growing peerage, an honorific system topped by a judiciously popularized monarchy and social élites who could
still be integrated—partly by hostesses who saw to it that they were—preserved
an articulated social hierarchy which combined the dignity of the old aristocracy with the democracy of the modern middle classes.

The 'treaty' negotiated by the middle and upper classes largely, though not
entirely, excluded the working classes. Despite the gains made by working-
class families in the First World War, the fortunes of the working class *as a
whole* throughout the interwar years were mixed at best. Much of the 'traditional' working class did not recover from the disaster of 1920–1 and of those
who did many went under again ten years later. The effect of these disasters,
on the economies of the North particularly, was to fragment the working class
and its historical experience, by comparison with which the experience of the
middle class *as a whole* was more uniform and benign. What sort of a life
working-class families could make depended on whether the husband (or in
some cases the mother) were unemployed or not, where they lived, what sort
of housing they occupied, whether the husband/father had migrated to
another part of the country, and how many children they had. There were thus
real differences in working-class living standards: the families of skilled working men in the South or the Midlands were by the late 1930s beginning to taste
the 'affluence' thought to typify them in the late 1950s, while the families of
the long-term unemployed in the North were usually wretchedly poor.

The working classes were also divided by political allegiance. Throughout
the interwar years about half the working class voted Conservative; about half
Labour.[15] This had a major political consequence: it almost guaranteed the stability of the British political system relative to most continental states, since in
no other country did such a large proportion of the industrial working class

---

[15] Some, of course, voted Liberal and continued to do so, but the numbers of working-class voters
who did was proportionately very small by the late thirties.

vote for a right-of-centre party instead of, as people in the 1920s expected, voting for one committed to the destruction of the status quo.

By the end of the 1930s the Conservative Party had created a huge, heterogeneous, but stable coalition. There was nothing to suggest it was provisional; everything to suggest that it was a natural historical outcome. The only obvious threats to it were external. In this sense the Second World War threw British history, and, even more, English history, off course. It led to a new political settlement which could not have been predicted in the 1930s and whose origins are only partially to be found in the 1930s. What then did the war do? The first and most important thing was to renew the 'traditional' working class. The war restored the old staple industries to full employment and thus restored the integrity of those great working-class communities which had half-collapsed during the interwar years. It also partially corrected regional imbalances. The relentless flow of men and wealth to the Midlands and the South was temporarily reversed or at least slowed. Further, the revivifying of the North and its political culture at the expense of the South and its political culture necessarily strengthened the Labour Party at the expense of the Conservatives. But it also universalized a working-class political culture: it allowed the Labour Party to recruit large numbers of working men and women—Birmingham is a good instance—who in the 1930s had conspicuously stood outside that culture. The degree to which this happened in some parts of the country was so spectacular that *only* the war can account for it.

Both wartime policy and rhetoric, by emphasizing equality of sacrifice and provision as ideologically good in themselves, and not simply as instrumental to winning the war, further redistributed social esteem. Such redistribution was accepted by the losers as almost inevitable, though not always with good grace.

The second consequence of the war was the widely noted 'rudeness' of working men and women, and particularly of working-class servicemen, an abandonment of traditional courtesy (or deference); what the journalist J. L. Hodson called a 'mild revolt against society'.[16] Accompanying the mild revolt was a probably unprecedented politicization of the population—especially among the middle classes—and an obvious lurch to the left in working-class opinion. Politicization did not necessarily mean conversion—often quite the opposite. For many it was simply a willingness to talk about politics; a readiness to concede, something many would not have conceded before, that it was a socially legitimate discourse. The remarkable reaction to the publication of the Beveridge Report (December 1942) is probably the best-known example of this. For some members of the middle class it did, of course, mean conversion, if only momentarily, and in so far as the movement to the left was given voice

---

[16] J. L. Hodson, *The Sea and the Land* (London, 1945), 302–3.

it was usually by them.[17] Many members of the Left Book Club probably belonged to the 'public' middle class, those employed by the government, locally or nationally. They were a growing, but still comparatively small part of the middle class. Many did not yet think of themselves as a 'public' middle class—and in the late 1940s, very much not. But there were signs, as yet only incipient, of a conflict between public and non-public middle class which Harold Perkin has suggested was to become a fundamental fissure in English 'professional society'.[18]

The movement to the left among the working classes was less well articulated but more permanent; and among young working men, particularly, more strongly felt. We should not underestimate how radical this movement was and how widely and unexpectedly it could be seen. Thus the social psychologists Elizabeth Slater and Mark Woodside, who were actually studying working-class attitudes to marriage in 1943, were soon made aware 'of the signs of that swing towards Socialism that subsequently surprised the country at the general election of 1945'.[19] The expression of grievance could be so intense as to be apparently contemptuous of conventional politics as such—even for famous forums of wartime radicalism like the 'Cairo parliament'.[20] Furthermore, this expression was not always easy to categorize so that observers often overlooked or misunderstood what was developing: 'a strong but unformed and not always coherent radicalism', as the military censors described it.[21]

A more coherent element in wartime radicalism was the popular admiration for Russia—as the Soviet Union was almost always called. Admiration for Russia was not, of course, confined to the working class; it was also very much part of the world of the Left Book Club and the Penguin Special—and indeed was encouraged by the government and the king himself.[22] But in the working class the admiration was more widespread and less cautious. No one who spoke to working-class audiences could miss it. As Harold Nicolson noted, references to America and China received merely perfunctory acknowledgement; one had only to mention Russia, however, and the 'whole meeting flames'.[23] This sentiment produced the notable Gallup poll finding of April

---

[17] For the Beveridge Report and popular interest see, for instance, Hodgson, *Few Eggs and No Oranges*, 274, 298. For amusing confirmation of the Beveridge Report's effect, see Donnelly, *Mrs Milburn's Diaries*, 198 (17 Jan. 1944).

[18] H. Perkin, *The Rise of Professional Society: England since 1880* (London, 1989), 472–519.

[19] Slater and Woodside, *Patterns of Marriage*, 82–3.

[20] For the 'Cairo parliament', see Bill Davidson, 'The Cairo Forces Parliament', *Labour History Review*, 55, 3 (1990), 20–6. For more general hostility to conventional politics, see S. Fielding, 'The Second World War and popular Radicalism: The Significance of the "Movement away from Party" ', *History*, 80 (June 1995), 259.

[21] Quoted in Hodson, *Sea and the Land*, 216–19.

[22] The government made much of Red Army Day and the Sword of Stalingrad was presented by the king to the people of Stalingrad after the victory over the Germans in 1943.

[23] Quoted in Hodson, *Home Front*, 44; see also Nicolson, *Diaries and Letters, 1939–1945*, 250, 308.

1943. When asked which 'United Nations' country had so far done most to win the war, 42 per cent of the sample replied Britain, 50 per cent Russia, 5 per cent China, and 3 per cent America. In relation to the United States the judgement of this poll is entirely rational. What is surprising is the comparison with *Britain*: rarely do people depreciate the efforts of their own country like this— even to the extent that they did for Gallup.

The result of this radicalization, primarily of working-class voters, was to redefine 'democracy' at the expense of the 'democratic' middle class. More or less everyone in the interwar years agreed that England was a democracy. The question was—whose democracy? Before the outbreak of war the question seemed to have been answered thus: English democracy was defined by the 'modern' middle-class of the 1930s. It was a democracy up-to-date, individualist, but also socially engaged. That was so because the politicized working class had seemed definitely marginalized in the 1930s, and there was nothing then to suggest that it would recover; nor that the self-confidence of the 'democratic' middle class would within a few years be so reduced. This class was much weakened once progressive politics became inextricably associated with the organized working class; and for that the Second World War was responsible. In the 1930s the ruling definition of democracy was individualist and its proponents chiefly a modernized middle class; in the 1940s the ruling definition was social-democratic and its proponents chiefly the organized working class. The class, therefore, which in the 1930s was the class of progress became in the 1940s the class of resistance.

Yet the social-democratic definition of democracy, at least as it was manifested in the 1940s, was incomplete. Given how deep were the grievances released by the war and how ready people were to express them, there could well have been a more radical reconstruction at its end than there was. But throughout the 1940s there were strong counterweights to the social radicalism of that decade. A powerful rhetorical device of both the war and the Attlee government emphasized social harmony and 'fair shares'—and fairness meant fairness. Plainly the working class did better from this than anyone else, but 'fair shares' went in both directions and suggested a line beyond which radicalism could not go. That, in turn, diminished the chances of a radical reaction by those who were comparative losers. Though increasingly disliked by everyone, rationing, for instance, together with food subsidies, prevented that explosion of food prices which so angered the middle classes after the First World War. Shopkeepers were certainly not popular in 1945; but they were not the hated profiteers of 1918. Although the spiv was an unappealing figure, and in films like *Waterloo Road*, a sinister one, he could metamorphose into George Cole's 'Flash Harry' in the 'St Trinian's' films. But there was nothing comic about even a metamorphosed profiteer.

Victory in war, furthermore, inevitably legitimated at least some existing institutions, quite apart from the police who were such unexpected beneficiaries. Thus, for example, while the pre-war social hierarchy had certainly lost esteem by 1945, the exceptional popularity of the monarchy throughout the war—a lucky escape, given George VI's commitment to Chamberlainite Conservatism—did much to shield the old élites. That, and the fact that members of the ruling class, however defeatist some of them may have been privately in 1940, plainly did their bit and sometimes more than their bit, allowed them to emerge from the war more unscathed than they possibly deserved. The partial disintegration of the élites after 1945 was indeed largely due to the war, to the diffusion of power and status for which it was responsible, but not primarily to discredit or popular hostility.

Above all, the decision of the victorious Labour Party not to enter the sphere of civil society, except in the most modest way, meant that the potential of wartime radicalism was never fully exploited. We should, of course, not take the achievements of the Attlee government for granted. The enactment of that government's legislative programme—the combination of large-scale nationalization and major reforms of the social security system—was inconceivable in 'normal' political circumstances. Before the outbreak of war, when asked, the majority of people said they 'wanted' much of what became that programme, but there is no evidence that they would have voted for it then if that meant voting Labour at a general election. And the programme was both coherent and completed: by 1950 the government had done virtually all that it had said it would do in 1945. In addition, it was doubtless aware that working-class cultural preferences had been much less modified by the war than their party-political allegiances. In both the content and style of sport, cinema, music, literature, indeed, nearly everything which might be defined as 'cultural', working-class taste clearly preferred, and continued to prefer, the products of commercial capitalism to any known 'socialist' alternative. Such a preference obviously suggested constraints upon government action.

The Attlee government operated deeply, but on a narrow front. As an instance, it abolished the voluntary hospitals but left intact an independent education sector which guaranteed those who attended it a privileged access to both public and private labour markets without equal in any comparable country, and which enormously reinforced social stratification; and it encouraged the development of a system of secondary education in which Labour's working-class supporters were definitely not favoured. Nor, as another instance we have seen here, did the Attlee government reform or, more to the point, cause others to reform, powerful quasi-political organizations like those that controlled sport throughout the country. Such organizations continued to be ruled by social oligarchies nearly always deeply hostile to the Labour Party and what it represented.

Why was the operational front of the Attlee government so circumscribed?

One answer is that the expressed wishes of Labour voters were not much less circumscribed. They, to the extent that such things are ever certain, wanted an end to the voluntary hospitals, but did not seem to care too much about the public schools. They wanted a decent life, decent housing, and a decent environment in which to raise their children. All these could be achieved within the boundaries the Attlee government set itself. And few refused to vote Labour in 1950 because the government had not been left-wing enough.

A second answer is that Labour in practice left untouched those institutions of the state and of civil society which were strongly defended. No one, for instance, was ready to go to the stake for privately owned coal mines or railways, but they were prepared to go to the stake for the cavalry regiments, the public schools, or even the grammar schools. The grammar schools, indeed, are an exemplary case: the eleven-plus was very unpopular with working-class parents, and was known to be so, but to have abolished it implied the abolition of the grammar schools, and that the Labour Party of the 1940s was not willing to do. Broadly speaking, the institutions of civil society which had *ideological* value to their members were left alone. Furthermore, once a decision had been made to exclude from the Labour government's programme those areas of society which would be strongly defended at the only moment when their defences might have been overcome with popular support, the Labour Party let slip an opportunity which was unlikely ever to recur. England thus settled for an awkward compromise: an individualist but 'progressive' middle-class democracy was abandoned in the 1940s to be replaced by an all-too-limited social democracy which had worked itself out even before the Attlee government left office in 1951.

The festival of Britain (1951) and the coronation of Queen Elizabeth II (1953) were celebrations of what contemporaries thought was a uniquely harmonious society. Of that coronation the sociologists Edward Shils and Michael Young wrote:

Over the past century, British society, despite distinctions of nationality and social status, has achieved a degree of moral unity equalled by no other large national state. The assimilation of the working class into the moral consensus of British society, though certainly far from complete, has gone further in Great Britain than anywhere else, and its transformation from one of the most unruly and violent into one of the most orderly and law-abiding is one of the great collective achievements of modern times.[24]

It would be wrong to deny the extent of this social integration, or that it seemed most complete in the 1940s and early 1950s: but it was not the product of the long evolution suggested by Shils and Young. The degree to which the working class was assimilated into the 'moral consensus' was the result of the Second World War; it was not something that anyone would confidently have

---

[24] Shils and Young, 'The Meaning of the Coronation'.

predicted in 1939. When in the 1950s or 1960s people spoke of the 'traditional' working class, they were speaking of a class which was re-created in the 1940s, just as the 'traditional' matrilocal working-class household was in part created in the 1940s. It was this reconstructed working class which largely accounted for the almost transformed relative positions of the Labour and Conservative Parties in 1950 as compared with 1939.

Anyone who visited in England in 1939 and then in 1950 would have been astonished at the political transformation. The extraordinary hegemony of the Conservative Party had been overthrown quite unexpectedly and in its stead a Labour government had carried through a programme of social welfare and nationalization which would have seemed impossible in 1939. But the visitor would have found the institutions of civil society almost wholly recognizable and the old 'ideological apparatus of the state' largely intact. Outside the realm of social services or nationalized industries the visitor would not have observed a social democracy. This had a major political implication. Because a social democratic definition of democracy had not entrenched itself in civil society or civil cultures, the political settlement on 1945 depended for its existence on the physical survival of the industrial working class as a class; that is, upon a series of historically specific social and political relationships—predominantly male and predominantly located in the highly unionized reaches of the economy—which in the nature of things could not survive indefinitely. It was not supported by the diffusion within civil society of social democracy as an ideology independent of such historic relationships—something which alone could have given it longer life.

Select Bibliography

I have largely excluded from the bibliography sources which were used in the chapters on betting and unemployment in my previous book, *The Ideologies of Class*; but where used here they have been fully cited in the footnotes. I have also excluded reports of government enquiries or material drawn from private papers. These are also fully cited in the footnotes.

ALBERTI, J., 'The Turn of the Tide: Sexuality and Politics, 1928–1931', *Women's History Review*, 3, 2 (1994).

ALDERMAN, G., *Modern British Jewry* (Oxford, 1992).

ALDGATE, A. and RICHARDS, J., *Britain Can Take It* (Oxford, 1986).

ALLEN, J. E., 'Some Changes in the Distribution of the National Income During the War', *Journal of the Royal Statistical Society*, lxxxiii, pt. i (Jan. 1920).

ALLEN, R. G. D. and BOWLEY, A. L., *Family Expenditure* (London, 1935).

ANDERSON, M., 'The Emergence of the Modern Life Cycle in Britain', *Social History*, 10 (1985).

—— 'The Social Implications of Demographic Change', in F. M. L. Thompson (ed.), *The Cambridge Social History of Britain, 1750–1950*, ii (pb. ed. Cambridge, 1993).

ANDERSON, M., *The Missing Stratum: Technical School Education in England, 1900–1990s* (London, 1994).

ARMYTAGE, W. H. G., *Civic Universities and the State* (London, 1955).

BAKKE, E. W., *The Unemployed Man* (London, 1933).

BALE, J., *Sport and Place* (London, 1982).

BALFOUR, P., *The Society Racket* (London, 1933).

BAMFORD, T. W., *The Rise of the Public Schools* (London, 1967).

BANKS, O., *Parity and Prestige in English Secondary Education* (London, 1955).

—— *The Attitudes of Steelworkers to Technical Change* (Liverpool, 1960).

BARKER, R., *Education and Politics, 1900–1951* (Oxford, 1972).

BARR, C., *Ealing Studios* (London, 1980).

BATES, J. W. B., 'The Conservative Party in the Constituencies, 1918–1939', unpublished Oxford D.Phil. thesis (1994).

BEAUMAN, N., *A Very Great Profession: The Woman's Novel 1914–1939* (London, 1983).

BERDAHL, R. O., *British Universities and the State* (London, 1959).

BERNBAUM, G., *Social Change and the Schools* (London, 1967).

BERNSTEIN, B. J., *Class, Codes and Control*, i (London, 1977).

BIRNBAUM, N., 'Monarchs and Sociologists', *Sociological Review* NS, 1, 3 (1955).

BOCOCK, B., *Ritual in Industrial Society* (London, 1974).

BOND, B., *British Military Policy between the Two World Wars* (Oxford, 1980).

BONHAM, J., *The Middle Class Vote* (London, 1954).

BOTT, E., *Family and Social Network* (London, 1957).

BOWKER, D., 'Parks and Baths: Recreation and Municipal Government in Manchester between the Wars', in Holt, R. (ed.), *Sport and the Working Class* (Manchester, 1990).

BOWLEY, A. L., 'Occupational Changes in Great Britain, 1911 and 1921', in *London and Cambridge Economic Service* (May, 1926).

—— *Some Economic Consequences of the Great War* (London, 1930).

BOX, K., *The Cinema and the Public*, Social Survey, NS 106 (1946).

—— *Recruitment to the Civil Service*, Social Survey, NS 80 (1946).

BRIERLEY, W., *Means Test Man* (London, 1935).

BRIGGS, A., *The Birth of Broadcasting* (London, 1961).

BRIGGS, A., *The Golden Age of Wireless* (London, 1965).
— *The War of Words* (London, 1970).
— *Sound and Vision* (London, 1979).
— *The BBC: The First Fifty Years* (London, 1985).
BRITTAIN, V., *Radclyffe Hall: A Case of Obscenity* (London, 1968).
— *Testament of Youth* (London, 1978).
— and TAYLOR, G. HANDLEY (eds.), *Selected Letters of Winifred Holtby, 1920–1935* (London, 1960).
BROAD, R., and FLEMING, S. (eds.), *Nella Last's War, 1939–1945* (London, 1981).
BROADBERRY, S. N., *The British Economy between the Wars* (London, 1986).
BURNETT, J., *A Social History of Housing, 1815–1970* (London, 1978).
BURT, C., *The Young Delinquent* (London, 1925).
CAMPBELL, F., *Eleven Plus and All That* (London, 1956).
CANNADINE, D., 'The Context, Performance and Meaning of Ritual: The British Monarchy and the "Invention of Tradition", *c*.1820–1977' in Hobsbawm, E. and Ranger, T. (eds.), *The Invention of Tradition* (Cambridge, 1983).
— *The Decline and Fall of the British Aristocracy* (New Haven, 1992).
CANNON, C., 'The Influence of Religion on Educational Policy, 1902–1944', *British Journal of Educational Studies*, xii (2 May 1964).
CARADOG JONES, D., 'The Cost of Living of a Sample of Middle-Class Families', *Journal of the Royal Statistical Society*, xci, pt. iv (1928).
— *The Social Survey of Merseyside*, 3 vols. (London, 1934).
CARR-SAUNDERS, A. M., and CARADOG JONES, D., *A Survey of the Social Structure of England and Wales* (2nd ed., London, 1937).
—— and MOSER, C. A., *A Survey of Social Conditions in England and Wales* (Oxford, 1958).
CAUTER, T., and DOWNHAM, J. S., *The Communication of Ideas: A Study of Contemporary Influences on Urban Life* (London, 1954).
CECIL, H., *The Flower of Britain: British Fiction Writers of the First World War* (London, 1995).
CHANCE, J., *The Cost of English Morals* (London, 1931).
CHAPMAN, D., *A Social Survey of Middlesbrough*, Social Survey, NS 50 (1945), pt. i, pts. iv–viii.
— *The Home and Social Status* (London, 1955).
CHAPMAN, G., *Culture and Survival* (London, 1940).
CHASE, M. E., *In England Now* (London, 1937).
CHESSER, E., and DAWE, Z., *The Practice of Sex Education* (London, 1945).
CLARK, C., *National Income and Outlay* (London, 1938).
— *Conditions of Economic Progress* (London, 1951).
CLEMENTS, R. V., *Managers: A Study of Their Careers in Industry* (London, 1958).
COCKBURN, C., *Bestseller: The Books That Everyone Read, 1900–1939* (London, 1972).
COHEN-PORTHEIM, P., *England, the Unknown Isle* (London, 1930).
COLE, G. D. H., *Studies in Class Structure* (London, 1955).
Commission on Educational and Cultural Films, *The Film in National Life* (London, 1932).
CURRAN, J., SMITH, A., and WINGATE, P. (eds.), *Impacts and Influences* (London and New York, 1987).
CURRIE, R., *Methodism Divided* (London, 1968).
— GILBERT, A., and HORSLEY, L., *Churches and Churchgoers* (London, 1978).
DAHRENDORF, R., *LSE: A History of the London School of Economics and Political Science, 1895–1995* (Oxford, 1995).
DALE, H. E., *The Higher Civil Service of Great Britain* (Oxford, 1942).
DAVENPORT-HINES, R., *Sex, Death and Punishment* (London, 1990).
DEACON, A., *In Search of the Scrounger* (London, 1976).
DEAN, D. W., 'Difficulties of a Labour Educational Policy: The Failure of the Trevelyan Bill, 1929–1931', *British Journal of Educational Studies*, 17 (1969).
DELAFIELD, E. M., *The Diary of a Provincial Lady* (Virago ed., London, 1984).
DENNIS, N., HENRIQUES, F., and SLAUGHTER, C., *Coal is our Life* (London, 1956).

DENT, H. C., *Education in Transition* (London, 1944).
—— *Growth in English Education, 1946–1952* (London, 1954).
DICKINSON, M., and STREET, S., *Cinema and State: The Film Industry and the British Government* (London, 1985).
DONNELLY, P. (ed.), *Mrs Milburn's Diaries* (London, 1979).
DUNNING, E. (ed.), *The Sociology of Sport* (London, 1971).
—— and SHEARD, K., *Barbarians, Gentlemen and Players* (Oxford, 1979).
DURANT, H., *The Problem of Leisure* (London, 1938).
DURANT, R., *Watling: A Social Survey* (London, 1939).
DURGNAT, R., *A Mirror for England* (London, 1970).
EHRLICH, C., *The Music Profession in Britain since the Eighteenth Century* (Oxford, 1985).
—— *Harmonious Alliance: A History of the Performing Rights Society* (Oxford, 1989).
ELBAUM, B., and LAZONICK, W. (eds.), *The Decline of the British Economy* (Oxford, 1987).
EYLES, M. L., *The Woman in the Little House* (London, 1922).
FEINSTEIN, C. H., *Statistical Tables of National Income, Expenditure and Output of the United Kingdom* (Cambridge, 1972).
FIDLER, J., *The British Business Elite* (London, 1981).
FISHMAN, N., 'Reflections on the Command Structure and Strategy of the Trade Union Movement in the Ford's War at Dagenham, 1931–1946', Paper for the Eighth British–Dutch Conference on Labour History (September, 1992).
FISHWICK, N., *English Football and Society, 1910–1950* (Manchester, 1989).
FLEXNER, A., *Universities* (New York, 1968 ed.).
FLOUD, J. E., HALSEY, A. H., and MARTIN, F. M., *Social Class and Educational Opportunity* (London, 1956).
FORMAN, C., *Industrial Town: Self-Portrait of St Helens in the 1920s* (London, 1978).
FOWLER, B., ' "True to me always": An analysis of women's magazine fiction', *British Journal of Sociology*, 30 (1979).
FRITH, S., *The Sociology of Rock* (London, 1978).
—— 'The Making of the British Record Industry, 1920–1964', in Curran, J., Smith, A., and Wingate, P., *Impacts and Influences* (London and New York, 1987).
GARDINER, J., *'Over Here': The GIs in Wartime Britain* (London, 1992).
GARSIDE, W. R., *British Unemployment, 1919–1939* (Cambridge, 1990).
GATHORNE-HARDY, J., *The Public School Phenomenon* (London, 1977).
GINSBERG, M., *Studies in Sociology* (London, 1932).
GITTINS, D., *Fair Sex: Family Size and Structure, 1900–1939* (London, 1983).
GLASS, D. V., and GRAY, J. L., 'Opportunity and the Older Universities: A Study of the Oxford and Cambridge Scholarship System', in Hogben, L. (ed.), *Political Arithmetic: A Symposium of Population Studies* (London, 1938).
—— (ed.), *Social Mobility in Britain* (London, 1954).
GLUCKSMANN, M., *Women Assemble: Women Workers and the New Industries in InterWar Britain* (London, 1990).
GLYNN, S., and OXBORROW, J., *Interwar Britain: A Social and Economic History* (London, 1976).
GODBOLT, J., *A History of Jazz in Britain* (London, 1986).
GOLDTHORPE, J. H. (with Llewellyn, C. and Payne, C.), *Social Mobility and Class Structure in Modern Britain* (Oxford, 1980).
—— LOCKWOOD, D., BECHHOFER, F., and PLATT, J., *The Affluent Worker: Industrial Attitudes and Behaviour* (Cambridge, 1968).
——— *The Affluent Worker in the Class Structure* (Cambridge, 1969).
GORER, G., *Exploring English Character* (London, 1955).
GOSDEN, P. H. J. H., *Education in the Second World War: A Study in Policy and Administration* (London, 1976).
GRAY, J. L., and MOSHINSKY, P., 'Ability and Opportunity in English Education' and 'Ability and Educational Opportunity in relation to Parental Occupation', both in Hogben, L., *Political Arithmetic: A Symposium of Population Studies* (London, 1938).
GUTTSMAN, W. L., *The British Political Elite* (London, 1965).

HALL, L. A., *Hidden Anxieties* (London, 1991).

HALL, J., and CARADOG JONES, D., 'The Social Grading of Occupations', in *British Journal of Sociology*, 1 (1950).

HALSEY, A. H. (ed.), *Trends in British Society Since 1900* (London, 1972).

— and GARDNER, L., 'Selection for Secondary Education and Achievement in Four Grammar Schools', *British Journal of Sociology*, 4 (1953).

— and TROW, M. A., *The British Academics* (London, 1971).

— HEATH, A. F., and RIDGE, J. M., *Origins and Destinations: Family, Class and Education in Modern Britain* (Oxford, 1980).

HAMMS, C., *Yesterdays: Popular Song in America* (London and New York, 1979).

HANNAH, L., *Inventing Retirement: The Development of Occupational Pensions in Britain* (Cambridge, 1986).

HARGREAVES, J., *Sport, Power and Culture* (Oxford and Cambridge, 1986).

— (ed.), *Sport, Culture and Ideology* (London, 1982).

HARKER, D., *One for the Money: Politics and the Popular Song* (London, 1980).

HASTINGS, A., *A History of English Christianity, 1920–1990* (London and Philadelphia, 1991).

HAXEY, S., *Tory MP* (London, 1939).

HEARNSHAW, L. S., *Cyril Burt: Psychologist* (London, 1979).

HEBDIGE, D., 'The Meaning of Mod', in Hall, S., and Jefferson, T., *Resistance Through Ritual* (London, 1989).

HILTON, J., *Rich Man, Poor Man* (London, 1944).

— MALLON, J. J., MAVOR, S., ROWNTREE, B. S., SALTER, A., and STUART, F. D., *Are Trade Unions Obstructive?* (London, 1935).

HILTON, M. (ed.), *Potent Fictions* (London and New York, 1996).

HODGSON, V., *Few Eggs and No Oranges* (London, 1976).

HODSON, J. L., *Home Front* (London, 1944).

— *The Sea and the Land* (London, 1945).

HOGBEN, L. (ed.), *Political Arithmetic: A Symposium of Population Studies* (London, 1938).

HOGGART, R., *The Uses of Literacy* (Pelican ed., Harmondsworth, 1966).

HOLT, R., *Sport and the British* (Oxford, 1989).

— *Sport and the Working Class in Modern Britain* (Manchester, 1990).

HOLTBY W., *Women and a Changing Civilisation* (London, 1934).

HOLTZMAN, E. M., 'The Pursuit of Married Love: Women's Attitudes towards Sexuality and Marriage in Great Britain, 1918–1939', *Journal of Social History*, 16, 2 (1982).

HOPCRAFT, A., *The Football Man* (London, 1968).

HOWARTH, J., and CURTHOYS, M., 'The Political Economy of Women's Higher Education in Late Nineteenth and Early Twentieth Century Britain', *Historical Research*, 60, 142 (1987).

HUGHES, D., 'The Spivs', in Sissons, M., and French, P., *Age of Austerity, 1945–51* (Oxford, 1986).

HUGHES, M. V., *A London Family between the Wars* (London, 1940).

HULTON DEUTSCH, *Readership Survey* (London, 1950).

HUMPHRIES, S., *Hooligans or Rebels? An Oral History of Working-Class Childhood and Youth, 1889–1939* (Oxford, 1981).

— *A Secret World of Sex* (London, 1988).

HUNT, F. (ed.), *Lessons for Life: The Schooling of Girls and Women, 1850–1950* (Oxford, 1987).

HUSTWITT, M., ' "Caught in a whirlpool of aching sound", the production of dance music in Britain in the 1920s', *Popular Music*, 3 (1983).

HUTCHINGS, A., 'Music in Britain, 1918–1960', in Cooper, M. (ed.), *The New Oxford History of Music*, x (Oxford, 1974).

HUTCHINSON, B., *Willesden and the New Towns*, Social Survey, NS (Dec. 1947).

HUTTON, L., *The Single Woman and her Emotional Problems* (London, 1937).

HYNES, S., *A War Imagined: The First World War and English Culture* (London, 1992).

ICHIHASHI, H., 'Working Class Leisure in English Towns, 1945–60, with special reference to Coventry and Bolton', unpublished University of Warwick Ph.D. thesis (1994).

Investigated Press Circulations (London, 1932).

ISAACS, S. (ed.), *The Cambridge Evacuation Survey* (London, 1940).

JACKSON, A. A., *Semi-Detached London* (London, 1973).

—— *The Middle Classes, 1900–1950* (Nairn, 1991).

JACKSON, B., *Working Class Community* (Pelican ed., Harmondsworth, 1972).

—— and Marsden, D., *Education and the Working Class* (London, 1962).

JARVIS, D., 'Mrs Maggs and Betty: The Conservative Appeal to Women Voters in the 1920s', *Twentieth Century British History*, v. 2 (1994).

JEFFEREYS, K., 'R. A. Butler, the Board of Education and the 1944 Education Act', *History*, 69 (1984).

JEFFERSON, T., 'Cultural Responses of the Teds', in Hall, S., and Jefferson, T., *Resistance through Ritual* (London, 1989).

JEFFERY, T., and MCCLELLAND, K., 'A World fit to live in: the *Daily Mail* and the middle classes', in Curran, J., Smith, A., and Wingate, P., *Impacts and Influences* (London and New York, 1987).

JENKINSON, A. J., *What Do Boys and Girls Read?* (2nd ed., London, 1946).

JENNINGS, H., and GILL, W., *Broadcasting in Everyday Life* (London, 1939).

JEPHCOTT, A. P., *Girls Growing Up* (London, 1942).

—— *Rising Twenty* (London, 1953).

JEVONS, R., and MADGE, J., *Housing Estates* (Bristol, 1946).

JONES, E., 'The Psychology of Constitutional Monarchy', *New Statesman*, 1 Feb., 1936.

JONES, S. G., 'Working-Class Sport in Manchester between the Wars', in Holt, R. (ed.), *Sport and the Working Class in Modern Britain* (Manchester, 1990).

JOSEPH, S., *If Their Mothers Only Knew* (London, 1946).

KALTON, G., *The Public Schools: A Factual Survey* (London, 1966).

KAMIN, L. J., *The Science and Politics of IQ* (Harmondsworth, 1974).

KERR, M., *The People of Ship Street* (London, 1958).

KLEIN, J., *Samples from English Cultures*, 2 vols. (London, 1965).

KNELLER, G. F., *Higher Learning in Great Britain* (Berkeley and Los Angeles, 1955).

KNOWLES, K. G. J. C., *Strikes* (Oxford, 1954).

KORR, C. P., 'A Different Kind of Success: West Ham United and the Creation of Tradition and Community', in Holt, R. (ed.), *Sport and the Working Class in Modern Britain* (Manchester, 1990).

Labour Research Department, *Studies in Labour and Capital*, iii, 'Labour and Capital in Parliament' (London, 1923).

LAFITTE, F., 'The Users of Birth Control Clinics', *Population Studies*, 16 (1962).

LANDY, M., *British Genres: Cinema and Society, 1930–1960* (Princeton, 1991).

LARWOOD, H., *Body-Line?* (London, 1933).

—— and PERKINS, K., *The Larwood Story* (London, 1965).

LEAVIS, F. R., *Mass Civilisation and Minority Culture* (Cambridge, 1930).

LEAVIS, Q. D., *Fiction and the Reading Public* (London, 1939).

LEE, E., *Music of the People* (London, 1970).

LEES-MILNE, J., *Caves of Ice* (London, 1984).

LeMAHIEU, D. L., *A Culture for Democracy* (Oxford, 1988).

LEWIS, J., *Women in England: Sexual Divisions and Social Change, 1870–1950* (Brighton, 1984).

—— CLARK, D., and MORGAN, D., *Whom God Hath Joined Together* (London, 1992).

LEWIS, R., and MAUDE, A., *The English Middle Classes* (2nd ed., Bath, 1973).

LEYBOURNE, G. G., and WHITE, K., *Education and the Birth-Rate* (London, 1940).

LIEPMANN, K., *The Journey to Work* (London, 1944).

LIGHT, A., *Forever England: Femininity, Literature and Conservatism between the Wars* (London, 1991).

LIPMAN, V. D., *A Social History of the Jews in England, 1850–1950* (London, 1954).

LITTLE, A., and WESTERGAARD, J., 'The Trend of Class Differentials in Educational Opportunity in England and Wales', in *British Journal of Sociology*, 15 (1964).

LLEWELLYN SMITH, H., *The New Survey of London Life and Labour*, 9 vols. (London, 1930–1935).

LLOYD, R., *The Church of England in the Twentieth Century*, 2 vols. (London, 1950).

LOCKHART, J. G., *Cosmo Gordon Lang* (London, 1949).

LOCKWOOD, D., *The Black-Coated Worker* (London, 1958).

LOEWE, A., *The Universities in Transition* (London, 1940).

LOGAN, R. F. L., and GOLDBERG, E. M., 'Rising Eighteen in a London Suburb: A Study of the Life and Health of Young Men', *British Journal of Sociology*, 4 (1953).

LORENZ, E., and WILKINSON, F., 'The Shipbuilding Industry, 1860–1965', in Elbaum, B., and Lazonick, W. (eds.), *The Decline of the British Economy* (Oxford, 1987).

LOW, R., *Film Making in 1930s Britain* (London, 1985).

LOWNDES, G. A. N., *The Silent Social Revolution* (London, 1937).

McALEER, J., *Popular Reading and Publishing in Britain, 1914–1950* (Oxford, 1992).

McCARTHY, A., *The Dance Band Era* (London, 1971).

McCARTY, E. A., 'Attitudes to Women and Domesticity in England, ca. 1939–1955', unpublished Oxford D.Phil. thesis (1994).

McCRONE, K. E., *Sport and the Physical Emancipation of Women* (London, 1988).

McGREGOR, O. R., *Divorce in England* (London, 1957).

MACK, E. C., *Public Schools and British Opinion* (New York, 1973 ed.).

MACKERNESS, E. D., *A Social History of English Music* (London, 1964).

McKIBBIN, R., *The Ideologies of Class* (Oxford, 1990).

MACKINTOSH, N. J. (ed.), *Cyril Burt: Fraud or Framed?* (Oxford, 1995).

MADGE, C., *War-Time Pattern of Saving and Spending* (National Institute of Economic and Social Research, Cambridge, 1943).

—— and HARRISON, T., *Britain by Mass-Observation* (Harmondsworth, 1939).

MAILLAUD, P., *The English Way* (London, 1945).

MAKOWER, H., MARSCHAK, J., and ROBINSON, H., 'Studies in Mobility of Labour: Analysis for Great Britain', pt. i, *Oxford Economic Papers*, 2 (1939).

MANGAN, J. A., and PARK, J., *From 'Fair Sex' to Feminism* (London, 1987).

MARSHALL, M., *Gentlemen and Players* (London, 1987).

MARTIN, K., *The Magic of Monarchy* (London, 1937).

MASON, T. (ed.), *Sport in Britain: A Social History* (Cambridge, 1989).

—— 'Stanley Matthews', in Holt, R. (ed.), *Sport and the Working Class in Modern Britain* (Manchester, 1990).

Mass-Observation, *The Pub and the People* (2nd ed., London, 1970).

—— *War Factory: A Report* (London, 1943).

MASSEY, P., 'The Expenditure of 1,360 British Middle-Class Households in 1938–39', *Journal of the Royal Statistical Society*, cv, pt. iii (1942).

MASTERMAN, C. F. G., *England After War* (London, 1922).

MASTERS, B., *Great Hostesses* (London, 1982).

MAYER, J. P., *The Sociology of Film* (London, 1946).

—— *British Cinemas and their Audiences* (London, 1948).

MAYS, J. B., *Growing up in the City* (Liverpool, 1956).

MILES, P., and SMITH, M., *Cinema, Literature and Society* (London, 1987).

MOGEY, J. M., *Family and Neighbourhood: Two Studies of Oxford* (London, 1956).

MORGAN, K. O., *Consensus and Disunity* (London, 1979).

MORTIMER, R., *The History of the Derby Stakes* (London, 1973).

MOSS, L., and BOX, K., 'An Enquiry into Newspaper Reading Amongst the Civilian Population' (June–July 1943), Wartime Social Survey, NS 37a, ii (London, n.d.) 1943.

MOSSE, W. E., *Second Chance* (Tübingen, 1991).

MURPHY, G., 'Media Influence on the Socialisation of Teenage Girls', in Curran, J., Smith, A., and Wingate, P. (eds.), *Impacts and Influences* (London and New York, 1987).

MURPHY, R., *Realism and Tinsel* (London, 1989).

NEWTON, F., *The Jazz Scene* (London, 1959).

NICOLSON, N. (ed.), *Harold Nicolson: Diaries and Letters*, 3 vols. (London, 1966–8).

NORDLINGER, E. A., *The Working Class Tories* (London, 1967).

NORMAN, E. R., *Church and Society in England, 1770–1970* (Oxford, 1976).

NORWOOD, C., *The English Tradition of Education* (London, 1929).

OLECHNOWICZ, A., 'The Economic and Social Development of Inter-War Out-County Municipal Housing Estates, with Special Reference to the London County Council's Becontree and Dagenham Estates', Oxford D.Phil. thesis (1991).

OSBORNE, J., *A Better Class of Person* (London, 1981).

OTLEY, C. B., 'The Educational Background of British Army Officers', *Sociology*, 7 (1973).

—— 'Militarism and Militarization in the Public Schools', *British Journal of Sociology*, 29 (1978).

OWEN, A. D. K., *A Survey of Juvenile Unemployment and Welfare in Sheffield*, Sheffield Social Survey Pamphlet No. 6, April 1933.

PADLEY, R., and Cole, M., *Evacuation Survey* (London, 1940).

PANETH, M., *Branch Street* (London, 1944).

PEAR, T. H., *English Social Differences* (London, 1955).

PEEL, J., 'Contraception and the Medical Profession', *Population Studies*, 18 (1964).

PEGG, M., *Broadcasting and Society* (London, 1983).

PERKIN, H., *The Rise of Professional Society: England Since 1880* (London, 1989).

PETTER, M., ' "Temporary Gentlemen" in the Aftermath of the Great War: Rank, Status and the Ex-Officer Problem', *Historical Journal*, 37 (1994).

PHILLIPS, G., *The General Strike: The Politics of Industrial Conflict* (London, 1976).

PHILLIPS, M., *The Young Industrial Worker* (London, 1922).

PICKERING, W. S. F., 'The Persistence of Rites of Passage: towards an explanation', *British Journal of Sociology*, 25 (1974).

PILGRIM TRUST, *Men without Work* (Cambridge, 1938).

PRAIS, S. J., and HOUTHAKKER, H., *The Analysis of Family Budgets* (Cambridge, 1955).

PRIESTLEY, J. B., *English Journey* (London, 1934).

RAMSDEN, J., *The Age of Balfour and Baldwin* (London, 1978).

RENIER, G. J., *The English: Are They Human?* (London, 1931).

REYNOLDS, D., *Rich Relations: The American Occupation of Britain, 1942–1945* (London, 1995).

RHODES JAMES, R. (ed.), *Chips: The Diaries of Sir Henry Channon* (London, 1967).

RHONDDA, MARGARET, VISCOUNTESS, *Leisured Women* (London, 1928).

—— *Notes on the Way* (London, 1937).

RICHARDS, J., and ALDGATE, A., *Best of British: Cinema and Society, 1930–1970* (Oxford, 1983).

—— and SHERIDAN, D. (eds.), *Mass-Observation at the Movies* (London, 1987).

RICHARDSON, P. J. S., *A History of British Ballroom Dancing, 1910–1945* (London, 1947).

ROOT, F., *A Cricket Pro's Lot* (London, 1937).

ROPER POWER, E. R., 'The Social Structure of an English County Town', *Sociological Review*, 29 (1937).

ROSE, K., *King George V* (London, 1983).

ROUTH, G., *Occupation and Pay in Great Britain, 1906–1979* (2nd ed., London, 1980).

ROWNTREE, B. S., *Poverty and Progress: A Second Social Survey of York* (London, 1941).

—— and LAVERS, G. R., *English Life and Leisure* (London, 1951).

RUBINSTEIN, D., and SIMON, B., *The Evolution of the Comprehensive School, 1926–1972* (London, 1973).

RUBINSTEIN, W. D., 'Wealth, Elites and the Class Structure of Modern Britain', *Past and Present* (August, 1974).

—— *Men of Property* (London, 1981).

RUNCIMAN, W. G., *Relative Deprivation and Social Justice* (Harmondsworth, 1972).

RUSSELL, D., 'Sport and Identity: The Case of the Yorkshire County Cricket Club, 1880–1939', *Twentieth Century British History*, 7, 2 (1996).

RUST, F., *Dance in Society* (London, 1968).

SAMUEL, R., 'The Middle Class between the Wars', *New Socialist*, Jan./Feb., 1983, March/April, 1983.

SAVAGE, GAIL, L., 'Social Class and Social Policy: The Civil Service and Secondary Education in England during the Interwar Period', *Journal of Contemporary History*, 18, 2 (1983).

SAVILLE, J., *Rural Depopulation in England and Wales, 1851–1951* (London, 1957).

SCANNELL, P., and CARDIFF, D., *A Social History of British Broadcasting*, i. *1922–1939* (Oxford, 1991).

SECCOMBE, W., 'Starting to Stop: Working-Class Fertility Decline in Britain', *Past and Present*, 126 (1990).

SHAW, L. A., 'Impressions of Family Life in a London Suburb', *Sociological Review*, (1954).

SHILS, E., and YOUNG, M., 'The Meaning of the Coronation', *Sociological Review*, 1 (1953).

SKLAR, R., *Movie-Made America* (London, 1975).

SLATER, E., and WOODSIDE, M., *Patterns of Marriage: A Study of Marriage Relationships in the Urban Working Classes* (London, 1951).

SMITH, G. A., 'Jim Crow on the Home Front, 1942–45,' *New Community*, 8 (1980).

SMITH, H. L., 'British Feminism and the Equal Pay Issue in the 1930s', *Women's History Review*, forthcoming.

—— 'Gender and the Welfare State: the 1940 Old Age and Widows Pensions Act', *History*, forthcoming.

—— (ed.), *War and Social Change* (Manchester, 1986).

SOLOWAY, R. A., *Birth Control and the Population Question in England, 1877–1930* (Chapel Hill and London, 1982).

STACEY, J., *Star Gazing* (London and New York, 1994).

STACEY, M., *Tradition and Change: A Study of Banbury* (Oxford, 1960).

STAVEACRE, T., *The Songwriters* (London, 1979).

STEAD, P., *Film and the Working Class* (London, 1991).

STONE, C., *Christopher Stone Speaking* (1933).

STOPES, M. (ed.), *Mother England* (London, 1929).

SUMMERFIELD, P., *Women Workers in the Second World War* (London, 1984).

SUTHERLAND, G., *Ability, Merit and Measurement* (Oxford, 1984).

SWANN, P., *The Hollywood Feature Film in Postwar Britain* (London, 1987).

SWENARTON, M., *Homes Fit for Heroes* (London, 1981).

—— and TAYLOR, S., 'The Scale and Nature of the Growth of Owner-Occupation in Britain between the Wars', *Economic History Review*, 38 (1985).

TAYLOR, I., ' "Football Mad": A Speculative Sociology of Football Hooliganism' in Dunning, E. (ed.), *The Sociology of Sport* (London, 1971).

TAYLOR, R., *Football and its Fans* (Leicester, 1992).

THOMAS, G., *Population and Housing in England and Wales*, Social Survey, NS 60 (1947).

—— *Women and Industry*, Social Survey, NS 104 (1949).

—— *Labour Mobility in Great Britain, 1945–1949*, Social Survey, SS 134 (1951).

THOMPSON, L., *The Dogs* (London, 1994).

THOMPSON, F. M. L., 'English Landed Society in the Twentieth Century: I, Property: Collapse and Survival', *Transactions of the Royal Historical Society*, 5 series, 40 (1990); 'II: New Poor and New Rich', 6 series, I (1991); 'III: Self-Help and Outdoor Relief'; 6 series II (1992); 'IV: Prestige without Power', 6 series, III (1993).

THOMPSON, F. M. L., *The University of London and the World of Learning, 1836–1986* (London, 1990).

THORNE, C., 'Britain and the Black GIs: Racial Issues and Anglo-American Relations in 1942,' *New Community*, 3 (1972).

TRUSCOT, B., *Red Brick University* (Pelican ed., Harmondsworth, 1951).

VAMPLEW, W., *The Turf* (London, 1976).

VAUGHAN, P., *Something in Linoleum: A Thirties Education* (London, 1994).

VIRDEN, J., 'South Atlantic Alliances,' *Times Higher Education Supplement*, 29 Oct., 1993.

WAKEFORD, J., *The Cloistered Elite* (London, 1969).

WALLER, P. J., *Democracy and Sectarianism* (Liverpool, 1981).

—— 'Democracy and Dialect, Speech and Class' in Waller, P. J. (ed.), *Politics and Social Change in Modern Britain* (Brighton, 1987).

WALVIN, J., *The People's Game* (London, 1975).

WARD, J., *Children out of School*, Social Survey, NS 110 (1948).

Wartime Social Survey, *Credit Buying*, NS 23 (1942).

WEEKS, J., *Sex, Politics and Society* (London, 1981).

WEINBERG, I., *The English Public Schools* (New York, 1967).

WERTHEIMER, E., *Portrait of the Labour Party* (London, 1929).

WHITING, R. C., *The View from Cowley* (Oxford, 1983).

WILDER, A., *American Popular Song* (New York, 1972).

WILKINS, L. T., *The Adolescent in Britain*, Social Survey, SS 148(P) (1955).

WILLIAMS, R., 'Minority and Popular Culture', in Smith, M. A., Parker, S., and Smith, C. S. (eds.), *Leisure and Society in Britain* (London, 1973).

WILLIAMS, W., *Full Up and Fed Up* (London, 1921).

WILLMOTT, P., *Growing Up in a London Village* (London, 1979).

WILLMOTT, P., and YOUNG, M., *Family and Class in a London Suburb* (London, 1960).

WILSON, B. R., *Sects and Society* (London, 1961).

WYLD, H. C., *A History of Modern Colloquial English* (London, 1920).

YOUNG, M., and WILLMOTT, P., *Family and Kinship in East London* (Pelican ed., Harmondsworth, 1970).

YOUNG, T., *Becontree and Dagenham* (London, 1934).

ZWEIG, F., *The British Worker* (Pelican ed., Harmondsworth, 1952).

— *Labour, Life and Poverty* (London, 1948).

— *Women's Life and Labour* (London, 1952).

ZWEINIGER-BARGIELOWSKA, I.-M., 'Rationing, Austerity and the Conservative Party Recovery After 1945', *Historical Journal*, 37 (1994).

Index